Uneasy Asylum

Stanford Studies in Jewish History and Culture
Edited by Aron Rodrigue and Steven J. Zipperstein

Uneasy Asylum

*France and the Jewish
Refugee Crisis, 1933–1942*

Vicki Caron

Stanford University Press
Stanford, California 1999

Stanford University Press
Stanford, California
© 1999 by the Board of Trustees of the
Leland Stanford Junior University
Printed in the United States of America

CIP data appear at the end of the book

To Bob

Acknowledgments

This book, which I began working on in the early 1980's, and which has expanded in ways I had never imagined, would not have been possible without the generous support of numerous individuals and institutions. First and foremost, I would like to express my deepest appreciation to those foundations that provided the financial support that enabled me to carry out the travel, research, and writing involved in this project: the Memorial Foundation for Jewish Culture; the National Endowment for the Humanities; and the Institute for Advanced Study, in Princeton, New Jersey. Given the difficulties involved in gaining access to archival material pertaining to the period covered in this book, not to mention the restrictive hours at several of the archives, this project could never have gotten off the ground had I not been able to spend extended periods of time in France in 1985–86 and again in 1987–88. Moreover, the fellowship I had at the Institute for Advanced Study in 1990–91 provided me with the ideal environment, both stimulating and peaceful, in which to begin writing this book. In particular, I would like to thank Professor Peter Paret, director of the School of Historical Studies, for his support and warm hospitality during that time.

With respect to the intellectual origins of this project, I am indebted to Professors Michael R. Marrus and Robert O. Paxton for having invited me to serve as research assistant during the writing of their book *Vichy, France, and the Jews* in 1977–78, when I was a graduate student at Columbia University. As I assisted in their research on the roots of Vichy antisemitism, I became intrigued with the subject of France and the Jewish refugee crisis in the 1930's and realized that this topic in itself would provide a fascinating subject for a book, particularly because scarcely anything had been written about it to date. Fortuitously, it was around this time that the French archives on this period were beginning to open up, and so I am grateful to Michael and Bob for having involved me in their project.

The research for the present volume could not have been completed without the patient and generous assistance of the staffs of a great many libraries and archives in France, the United States, and Great Britain. I would like to express my appreciation to the staffs of the following institutions in France: the Archives Nationales, Paris; the Archives de Paris; the Archives of the Paris Prefect of Police; the Archives of the Foreign Ministry, Paris; the Library and Archives of the Alliance Israélite Universelle, Paris; the Bibliothèque Nationale, Paris; the Departmental Archives of the Bas-Rhin, Strasbourg; the Archives of the Jewish Consistory of the Bas-Rhin, Strasbourg; the Bibliothèque de Documentation Internationale Contemporaine at the Université de Paris-X, Nanterre; and the Archives of the Service Historique de l'Armée de Terre, Vincennes. I would also like to thank the staffs of the following institutions in the United States: the Jewish Theological Seminary, New York; the Rockefeller Library of Brown University; the Columbia University Library; the New York City Public Library; the Herbert H. Lehman Collection at the School of International Affairs, Columbia University; the Leo Baeck Institute, New York; the American Jewish Joint Distribution Committee, New York; the Franklin Delano Roosevelt Library, Hyde Park, New York; and the National Archives, Washington, D.C. I am grateful as well to the staff of the Public Records Office, in London, which graciously permitted me to view a huge amount of material over a period of three days, a courtesy that obviated the need for a return visit. Finally, I would like to offer special thanks to Chantal Bonazzi and Mademoiselle Vayassaire of the Archives Nationales; to Yvonne Levyne, former head librarian at the Alliance Israélite Universelle; to Philippe Landau, Conservateur-en-Chef at the archives of the Central Consistory and the Consistory of Paris; to Brigitte Lainé, Conservateur-en-Chef of the Ile-de-France region at the Archives de Paris; to Jacques d'Orléans, Conservateur-en-Chef of the Departmental Archives of the Bas-Rhin, in Strasbourg; to Denise Gluck, former director of archives and records at the American Jewish Joint Distribution Committee, and her assistant, Regina Chimberg, for their personal attention in helping me track down pertinent information; and to Jean Favier, who formerly headed the Direction des Archives at the French Ministry of Culture, for granting me numerous "dérogations," or special permissions to consult materials normally closed to researchers.

Many friends and colleagues have contributed to this project over the years. Joel Blatt, Michael Miller, Simon Epstein, and Harriet Jackson provided me with invaluable leads to archival materials that I never would have located on my own. Juliette Nunez, whom I befriended in the archives of the Quai d'Orsay and who subsequently became an archivist at the Outremer section of the Archives Nationales in Aix-en-Provence, also kindly provided me with a copy of Christophe Delabroye's essay *Enquête sur un projet de colonisation juive à Madagascar, 1936–1942*. I have also benefited greatly from the comments, criticisms, and suggestions of many friends and colleagues who gave their time unselfishly and read chapters of the manuscript or, in some cases, the entire text. Here I would like to thank Joel Blatt, Richard I. Cohen, Alice Conklin, Calvin Goldscheider, Alice Goldstein, Nancy Green, Bill Hagen, Paula Hyman, Harriet Jackson, Dan Moran, Bob Paxton, Bob Stoll, and Alan Zuckerman. I would also like to thank the two readers for Stanford University Press, Carol Fink and an anonymous reader, for their extremely helpful comments and criticisms, which improved this book and spared me several embarrassing errors. Joel Blatt has my special appreciation for his insights, which greatly enriched this project, into problems concerning Italian émigrés in France during the interwar period.

I would also like to thank the journal editors and book publishers, among them Marion Berghahn of Berghahn Books, who graciously allowed me to republish material that originally appeared in the pages of the *Journal of Contemporary History*, the *Journal of Modern History*, the *Leo Baeck Institute Year Book*, *Historical Reflections/Réflexions Historiques*. I also thank the Faculty Development Fund of Brown University, as well as the Program in Judaic Studies at Brown for its research subsidies over the years.

I would like to thank Norris Pope, director of Stanford University Press, for taking this project under his wing and shepherding it through the various stages of the review process. My production editors, Xavier Callahan and Stacey Lynn, also did a fine job, and I am particularly grateful to my copy editor, Jennifer Harris, for her careful attention to detail and her willingness to edit my footnotes, a task I realize was rather daunting.

Finally, I would like to thank my friend and companion Bob Stoll for his extraordinary patience and encouragement during the many years I have worked on this project. His willingness to read and reread the manuscript has, I believe, made this book accessible to an audience beyond the scholarly community, and I have benefited immensely from his wisdom, insight, and plain good sense. It is with warm affection that I dedicate this book to him.

V.C.

Contents

Uneasy Asylum

CHAPTER ONE

Introduction

In recent years, a huge amount of scholarly attention has been paid to the anti-Jewish policies of the Vichy regime, and especially to Vichy's complicity in the Final Solution, which involved the French bureaucracy and police in the deportations of Jews to the death camps in Eastern Europe beginning in 1942.[1] Far less attention, however, has been devoted to the French government's policies toward German and Central European refugees in the 1930's, despite the fact that these policies played a critical role in paving the way for Vichy's anti-Jewish policies.

After Hitler's seizure of power in 1933, France emerged as the major haven for German and Central European refugees, the overwhelming majority of whom were Jews. France's role in this respect was conditioned by several factors. Politically, the French government felt vindicated for the hard-line stance it had taken toward Germany since the Treaty of Versailles, and to many government officials it seemed only proper that France now assist those individuals victimized by Hitler's reign of terror. On a more mundane level, France, in sharp contrast to Great Britain and the United States, had never imposed an anti-immigration statute; indeed throughout the 1920's, France had actively recruited foreigners, including thousands of East European Jews, in an effort to supplement its labor force, which had been decimated by the loss of 1.4 million men during the First World War.[2]

Finally, the simple fact that France shared a long border with Germany made it an attractive haven.

As a result, by the summer of 1933, at the height of the first wave of the refugee crisis, France had absorbed some 25,000 refugees from Germany, placing it first among refugee-receiving countries. And while this number ebbed in subsequent years, it swelled to over 30,000 in early 1939 following the Anschluss, the Munich crisis, and Kristallnacht. Although France fell behind Great Britain in 1939 with respect to the number of Jewish refugees on its soil, the presence of another 15,000 to 20,000 illegal East European Jewish refugees—either from Germany or from Poland, Romania, or Hungary, where antisemitic regimes had come to power—as well as France's reception of approximately one-half million Spanish republicans in early 1939, permitted France to retain its ranking as foremost nation of asylum in the world.[3]

Despite France's role as a principal haven for Central European refugees in the 1930's, only in recent years has French refugee policy begun to receive significant scholarly attention. This is true despite the fact that the refugee policies of the other Western powers—Great Britain, the United States, Canada, and the Netherlands—have been the subject of major scholarly studies and despite the fact that the refugee crisis of the 1930's has increasingly been recognized as an essential ingredient in understanding the Holocaust.[4] Why then has comparatively so little attention been paid to France? First and most obviously, a great deal of the archival record from this period has only recently become available, and indeed much of it, especially the records of the Ministry of the Interior's security services, the Sûreté Nationale, remains classified even today and can be seen only after obtaining special permission from the Ministry of Culture. Second, as Gérard Noiriel has argued in his important study, *Le Creuset français: Histoire de l'immigration XIXᵉ–XXᵉ siècles* (Paris, 1988), France has had enormous difficulty coming to terms with her immigrant past. Despite the fact that France has always been a nation of immigration—according to a 1985 national demographic survey, one out of every four French inhabitants is either foreign or has a foreign parent or grandparent—the dominant ideology of assimilation has steered scholars away from questions regarding immigration and ethnicity.[5]

To be sure, these attitudes have undergone a sea change in the past two decades, and there is now a burgeoning literature dealing with immigration in general, as well as various aspects of the Central European and Spanish refugee crises of the 1930's. Nevertheless, there is still no comprehensive survey of France's reception of German and Central European Jewish refugees in the 1930's, and it is my hope that this study will fill this lacuna. An examination of the Jewish refugee question during this period will reveal not only a great deal about the official policies and popular attitudes that paved the way for Vichy's anti-Jewish policies in the 1940's, but it will also shed considerable light on the larger political, economic, and cultural forces at work during the last decade of the Third Republic. As we shall see, the Jewish refugee crisis was never simply a marginal issue, as Eric Conan and Henry Rousso have recently contended.[6] Rather, the Jewish refugee question was always inextricably linked to a wide array of issues, and indeed I would suggest that the general contours of French political and cultural history during this period cannot be fully understood without an in-depth examination of this subject.

In this study, we will examine the evolution of French policy toward Jewish refugees in the 1930's from three interrelated vantage points: government policy, public opinion, and the role of the native Jewish community. Insofar as government policy was concerned, the various strategies the government devised to deal with the refugee crisis were by no means as straightforward as historians in the past have portrayed them to be. Rather, as we shall see, official policy toward the Central European refugees followed more of a "twisted road" than a straight line, to borrow a term coined by Karl Schleunes to describe a different set of historical circumstances.[7] Historians who have hitherto dealt with France's Central European refugee policy have generally noted a progressive hardening of policy after a brief liberal period in 1933, culminating in the extremely harsh anti-immigrant decree laws* in 1938, which sharply curtailed immigration at the border and made it extremely difficult for refugees already in the country to stay. According to this view, by late 1938 the stage was set for the mass internments of Central European refugees following the declaration of war in September 1939, and these internments in turn paved the way for the internment of foreign Jews by the Vichy administration.[8]

This picture is by no means entirely incorrect, and indeed a major focus of this study will be to examine those forces that encouraged a hardening of refugee policy after 1933. Nevertheless, this view is vastly oversimplified, and it ignores the multiplicity of factors that fueled refugee policy, as well as the fact that this policy did not evolve in a linear fashion. As we shall see, there were actually two major periods in the anti-refugee crackdown of the 1930's, which were motivated by somewhat different concerns. The first phase of the anti-refugee crackdown came in 1934 and 1935, after the conservative Bloc National governments of Pierre-Etienne Flandin and Pierre

---

*During the interwar years, the parliament voted full powers to the administration to enact legislation that was considered necessary but was too unpopular to win a parliamentary mandate. The use of decree laws became especially common under the premierships of Pierre-Etienne Flandin and Pierre Laval in 1934 and 1935 and during Edouard Daladier's ministries in 1938–40.

Laval came to power. This offensive was fueled almost exclusively by economic factors linked to the Depression, and it reflected the administration's decision to rely heavily on the anti-immigrant campaign as a weapon in its anti-Depression arsenal. This campaign was by no means aimed exclusively at refugees; rather, it was targeted at France's sizable immigrant population in general, which according to the 1931 census numbered 2.7 million, or about 7 percent of the total population.[9]

This crackdown nevertheless had a particularly severe impact on the refugees. As the most recent immigrants, they were also the most vulnerable, particularly since the majority of them had never acquired the right to work, which would have afforded them some modicum of protection. Moreover, the popular campaigns to oust foreigners from the middle-class professions—commerce, artisanry, and the liberal professions, especially medicine and law—were indeed aimed primarily at the refugees, together with East European Jewish immigrants, who had come to France in large numbers during the previous decade. These campaigns assumed a markedly antisemitic tone and ultimately played a critical role in paving the way for Vichy's antisemitic legislation.

The second major period in the anti-refugee crackdown came in 1938, during the premiership of Edouard Daladier, the head of the major center-left party—the Radicals. Now, in addition to economic factors linked to the Depression, political factors, and especially the government's growing commitment to appeasement—the desire to prevent war at any price—contributed to the shaping of refugee policy. In 1938, as the refugee crisis reached new heights in the aftermath of the Anschluss, the Munich crisis, and Kristallnacht, a number of high-level government officials, and most notably Daladier's powerful foreign minister, Georges Bonnet, came to believe that the refugees, together with their alleged communist allies, were seeking to drag France into a war against Hitler merely to satisfy their personal lust for revenge. These fears of Jewish warmongering, which received popular expression in the anti-Jewish riots that broke out in towns and cities throughout France at the time of the Munich crisis, were ultimately mirrored in the policies of the Foreign Ministry as well, particularly after Kristallnacht, which seriously threatened to unravel Bonnet's dream of Franco-German rapprochement.

In addition to delineating the various stages in French refugee policy in the 1930's, this book will also challenge the prevailing view that refugee policy became progressively harsher as the decade progressed. First, as I will show, the coming to power of the Popular Front made a considerable difference. Not only did the Popular Front introduce a more humane tone into the debate over refugee policy, but it also implemented a number of policies aimed at overturning the harsh measures implemented in 1934 and

1935 by Flandin and Laval. Moreover, the Popular Front displayed a willingness to consider several radical solutions to the refugee problem that would have included even East European Jews, who continued to stream into the country illegally throughout the 1930's. These solutions included the establishment of agricultural settlements for the refugees either in French colonies or in the increasingly underpopulated regions of southwestern France. To be sure, these strategies did not go much beyond the planning stage in 1936 and 1937. Yet this failure must be attributed primarily to lack of time rather than to any absence of will. Moreover, some version of these plans was ultimately implemented, albeit on a small scale, in 1938 and 1939, and in that sense they were not without consequence. Thus, although several historians have recently dismissed the Popular Front's contribution to Central European refugee policy as relatively insignificant, it will be argued here that the Popular Front's policy represented a sincere attempt to implement a more humane refugee policy, which marked a radical break from the harsh policies of the previous Bloc National governments.

The other important factor almost entirely ignored by scholars who have dealt with France's refugee policy in the past is that strong countervailing forces were at work throughout the 1930's that tended to mitigate the severity of many of the anti-refugee initiatives. On the humanitarian front was the fact that France had always had a strong tradition of refugee asylum. As Gérard Noiriel has recently shown, this tradition extended back not only to the French Revolution (it was even incorporated into the Constitution of 1793), but even to the ancien régime. To be sure, the various governments in power in the nineteenth and twentieth centuries frequently found ways to circumvent this commitment. In the mid-nineteenth century, legal provisions were introduced that allowed the government to expel foreigners considered subversive, whether or not they were refugees. And indeed this provision was invoked with some regularity in the twentieth century, and especially in the late 1920's, when the government began to expel large numbers of foreigners, mostly Italian antifascists, who were deemed undesirable for political reasons.[10] Nevertheless, the existence of a strong tradition of asylum, and the link of this tradition to the larger republican creed, provided pro-refugee advocates with a bludgeon to remind the government whenever it strayed from its republican commitments.

Practical considerations also worked to preclude the implementation of an overly harsh refugee policy. First, although the Depression encouraged the government to adopt a policy of repatriating large numbers of immigrant workers, the fact is that France continued to import foreign workers throughout the 1930's due to persistent labor shortages in certain industrial and agricultural sectors. Moreover, the introduction of the 40-hour work week in 1936 further exacerbated these labor shortages and increased the nation's dependence on foreign labor.[11] To be sure, Jewish refugees were generally not deemed suitable for jobs in these sectors. Nevertheless, pro-refugee activists as well as Jewish organizations persistently argued that Jewish refugees were capable of being retrained for these jobs, and indeed this notion became an integral element of the schemes to create agricultural and colonial settlements for Jewish refugees in 1938 and 1939.

At the same time, military needs also tended to militate against an over-zealous anti-immigrant policy. In the mid-1930's, France embarked on the *années creuses*, or lean years, in which the small military classes born during the First World War began to be called up for conscription. As a result of this shortfall in recruits, which coincided with mounting international tensions, the army chief of staff determined that immigrants could not be excluded altogether from military service. In 1937, provisions were made to incorporate the 400,000 Nansen refugees who had found asylum in France after the First World War into the armed forces.[12] These were refugees who had become stateless after the First World War—Russians and various groups from the former Ottoman Empire, including Armenians and Kurds, who in the early 1920's had come under the protection of a League of Nations High Commissioner for Refugees, headed by the Norwegian explorer and scientist, Fridtjof Nansen.[13] To be sure, refugees from Germany were not included in this category, and whether they too would ultimately be considered eligible for military service in France was not initially clear. Still, the military's desire to increase recruitment by means of a growing reliance on foreign troops continued to serve as an important impetus in encouraging a more liberal refugee policy. As we shall see, in the spring and summer of 1939, measures were implemented that allowed many Central and East European refugees to enlist for certain types of military service, and during the "phony war" these same military exigencies paved the way for the eventual release of the vast majority of "enemy aliens" from the internment camps.

Two other aspects of government policy need to be elucidated as well. Although some scholars, most notably Barbara Vormeier and Gérard Noiriel, have argued that all refugees in the 1930's—Germans, Austrians, Czechs, East Europeans, Spaniards, and Nansen refugees—were treated in the same fashion, this is simply not the case.[14] First, the Nansen refugees who arrived in the 1920's had their own international status and their own League of Nations High Commissioner for Refugees. Their rights and privileges were completely separate from those of refugees from Germany who came to France following the Nazi seizure of power in 1933. This latter group came under the jurisdiction of a new office—the High Commission for Refugees, Jewish and Other, Coming from Germany (HCR)—which was created in the fall of 1933 and was, at least initially, autonomous from the League.[15]

Second, it is also important to note that even among the refugees who came to France in the 1930's, there was never a single legal statute covering them all. Rather, each group was treated separately depending on its nationality of origin. This policy was due largely to the fact that refugee issues were regarded in part as foreign policy matters to be negotiated with the respective governments involved. It was also related to the fact that there were different international mechanisms set up to handle different groups of refugees. Not only was the Nansen Office separate from the High Commission for Refugees from Germany, but also even the jurisdiction of the High Commission for Refugees from Germany was defined very narrowly. East European Jews, including those who came from Germany, were never included in the High Commissioner's mandate, and it was only after international deliberation in 1938 that Austrian Jews came under the High Commissioner's protection. Moreover, the French government in 1936, in conjunction with a League of Nations accord dealing specifically with German refugees, granted an amnesty to German refugees who had come to France between 1933 and 1936, regularizing their legal status so that they would no longer have to face the constant threat of expulsion. This provision did not extend to East European Jewish refugees, however, even those who came from Germany; nor did it automatically extend to German refugees arriving after August 1936.

It is only by recognizing that there were distinct groups of refugees, even among the Central and East Europeans, that we can begin to understand why the influx of the refugees from Germany was considered so significant a threat. The fact is that the number of German refugees, especially in the early 1930's, was relatively small, and there is little reason to believe, as historians Andrew Sharf and Rita Thalmann have noted, that this influx could not have been absorbed by the Western democracies with little difficulty.[16] Nevertheless, as Michael Marrus has observed, the great fear regarding the influx of Jewish refugees from Germany and Central Europe was that they would be followed by a deluge of East European Jews, who would have numbered not in the tens or even hundreds of thousands, but in the millions.[17] These East European Jewish refugees were generally held in far lower esteem than the Germans, and their continued illegal entry into France throughout the 1930's was considered a serious threat by government authorities. Finally, it must be stressed that the Spanish refugee problem and the Central and East European refugee problems were rarely treated as a single phenomenon. While the influx of the Spanish refugees in late 1938 and early 1939 certainly did much to highlight France's general refugee problem, the official strategies devised to deal with these two crises were not related.

A second major focus of this study will be the role of popular opinion in the shaping of refugee policy. Here we will examine two specific aspects of this problem. First, we will look at the way in which popular opinion actually drove government refugee policy, especially through the lobbying efforts of the various middle-class professions. These groups, particularly in the two major areas of refugee settlement—Paris and the provinces of Alsace and Lorraine—exploited the opportunity opened up by the Depression to press for increased government restrictions against immigrant competition, and even against competition from recently naturalized foreigners, many of whom were foreign Jews. Moreover, these groups proved immensely successful in blocking efforts to allow Jewish refugees to work, even when there were economic inducements encouraging the use of immigrant labor. The medical profession, for example, made it impossible for refugee doctors to work anywhere, even in rural areas in southern France or in the colonies, notwithstanding severe shortages of medical practitioners in these regions. And local chambers of commerce blocked the introduction of all foreign-owned firms, despite the fact that by 1939 the army, as well as the minister of commerce, favored the establishment of these firms as a means of preparing France for the possibility of war.

The role of this middle-class lobby in fueling anti-refugee, and ultimately antisemitic, attitudes has been severely underestimated in the historiography of French antisemitism during this period. This historiography has tended to focus primarily on the political determinants of antisemitism: the role of the extreme right-wing leagues, the influence of Nazi propaganda, and the hate campaign targeted at Léon Blum, which, as Pierre Birnbaum has pointed out, became the principal vehicle for the expression of anti-republican sentiments.[18] Yet, while these political factors were by no means unimportant, socioeconomic concerns, which had played a major role in nineteenth-century antisemitic movements, continued to have an impact as well.[19]

Our other major focus with respect to public opinion will be to examine the extent to which anti-refugee and antisemitic sentiment permeated beyond the ranks of the radical right. In the early 1930's, while the extreme right adopted a fiercely anti-refugee stand from the start, the bulk of moderate opinion was nevertheless strongly sympathetic to the refugees. Yet, as the decade progressed, this moderate bloc became increasingly prone to anti-refugee sentiment. Why did this shift occur? In part, because of the Depression and the desire of many moderates, including the Radical Party leader in the early 1930's, Edouard Herriot, to embrace the anti-immigrant campaign as a means of remedying the country's economic woes. But political factors played a role as well. There is little doubt that the election of the Jewish socialist Léon Blum as head of the Popular Front in May 1936 provided the occasion for a massive outpouring of anti-Jewish and anti-leftist hatred, which now coalesced as never before.

Moreover, the fierce anti-war sentiment that gripped much of the country in late 1938 and 1939 also exacerbated anti-refugee sentiment, since the refugees, together with their alleged communist allies, were blamed for seeking to drag France into a war for their own selfish ends. This animosity, which erupted in anti-Jewish riots at the time of the Munich crisis, had widespread popular support, even among many moderates, who in the aftermath of the Popular Front victory feared that a war against Germany would lead to civil war at home, and ultimately a Bolshevik victory. Hence, despite the focus of previous historiography on the anti-refugee and anti-Jewish views of extreme right-wing groups, it is also imperative to examine the degree to which these attitudes filtered down to more moderate circles, including a wide swath of Radical opinion. Such an investigation will reveal not only the ways in which anti-refugee sentiment became embroiled in the larger anticommunist crusade, but it can also illuminate the extent to which a major theme of Vichy's anti-Jewish propaganda—the notion that Jews and communists were responsible for the outbreak of war and especially for the humiliating defeat—had a deep resonance for much of the French public.

Another important point about popular opinion vis-à-vis the refugee question that has hitherto been largely ignored is that there was a significant body of opinion sympathetic to the refugee cause.[20] Although the size of this pro-refugee lobby shrank considerably as the decade progressed, a substantial sector of opinion—including the Communist and especially the Socialist Parties, the League for the Rights of Man and Citizen, the Catholic left, and a few isolated conservatives—nevertheless remained staunchly pro-refugee until the end of the decade and lobbied incessantly for a more liberal policy of asylum.

Not only did these groups play an influential role in the formulation of the Popular Front's refugee policy, but they also exercised a strong countervailing influence on the refugee policies of less sympathetic administrations. As we shall see, these groups, together with Jewish refugee organizations, launched a vigorous battle to overturn the harsh anti-immigrant decree laws of 1938, and they even impelled the Daladier administration to consider granting an amnesty to refugees from Germany and Central Europe in the summer of 1939. This pro-refugee lobby would almost certainly have been less successful had its efforts not dovetailed with the advent of military and economic exigencies that also encouraged a more rational use of the refugees to prepare for war. Nevertheless, this fact does nothing to diminish the extraordinary efforts of many groups and individuals to secure a more humane and liberal refugee statute, one that would clearly define who constituted a refugee and that would set forth in precise terms the rights such an individual could expect. Although these groups have frequently been blamed for not having defended the refugees vigorously enough—and indeed they often reproached themselves for this failure as well[21]—a careful assessment of this question will reveal this judgment to be unduly harsh. Whatever failures the pro-refugee lobby ultimately experienced were due more to the general political climate, and ultimately to Vichy's coming to power, than to any lack of will on their part.

The third and final focus of our attention will be on the role played by the native Jewish community. This issue has inspired considerable debate in recent years, especially since several historians and publicists, some of whom are themselves the children of East European Jews deported from France during the Second World War, have charged the native Jewish community with having betrayed them. Not only did the principal Jewish refugee committee fail to provide adequate philanthropic assistance to refugees in the 1930's, but these critics claim it also collaborated with the government to secure restrictive immigration policies, since native Jews feared that an overly liberal refugee policy would ultimately inspire an anti-semitic backlash. This view, as we will see, is vastly oversimplified, and it ignores the complexity of native Jewish responses to the refugee crisis, as well as the fact that the native response changed over time.

During the early years of the refugee crisis, prior to 1936, the harsh assessment of these critics is not unjustified. While native Jewish opinion regarding the refugees was divided, a group of native leaders we have called the "hard-liners" ultimately came to dominate refugee policy. These individuals discouraged the distribution of refugee relief, fearing that an overly generous assistance program would only attract more refugees to France, and they did in fact lobby the government to close the border. After the Popular Front came to power, however, more moderate spokesmen came to the fore. These Jewish leaders favored a more activist refugee policy, not only with respect to providing refugee relief, but even in terms of lobbying the government for more liberal refugee policies. Indeed, in 1938 and 1939, these Jewish leaders joined other pro-refugee groups in launching a vigorous campaign to overturn the decree laws altogether. While it is understandable that the refugees and immigrants tended to blame their misfortunes on the Jewish refugee committee, with whom they had extensive day-to-day contact, the fact is that the policies causing their misfortunes were overwhelmingly the work of the government, and not the native Jewish leadership. Native Jews may have exercised some control over those policies in the early years of the refugee crisis, but their leverage was severely diminished by 1938–39, and by the time Vichy came to power, it was reduced to almost nil.

While the roots of Vichy's antisemitic policies clearly lay in the 1930's and were, to a great degree, bound up with the refugee policies of those years, there was nothing inexorable about the advent of a blatantly antisemitic regime in 1940. Although Gérard Noiriel has recently argued that the adoption of discriminatory antiforeign and anti-Jewish legislation by Vichy in 1940 was linked to structural factors—the rise of modern bureaucracies, with their tendencies to identify and keep track of people—such explanations do little to enhance our understanding of either the refugee policies of the 1930's or the antisemitic policies of Vichy. Noiriel is undoubtedly correct to point out that the state's desire to define the rights of citizens as opposed to those of foreigners is a distinctly modern phenomenon, linked to the rise of the modern welfare state, but there is no reason to believe that bureaucracies in and of themselves ineluctably give rise to antisemitic and antiforeign legislation, although they undoubtedly facilitate such legislation when discriminatory regimes come to power.[22]

Rather, the development of anti-refugee policies and attitudes in the 1930's needs to be understood within the context of that decade's historical developments: the Depression and the government's attempt to resolve it by protecting the middle classes in particular from all immigrant competition; the political polarization of the 1930's, which became especially acute after the Popular Front victory of 1936; and last, the politics of appeasement. At the same time as these factors were encouraging a hardening of refugee policy, however, strong countervailing forces—military and economic needs that encouraged a more liberal refugee policy, in addition to the persistent lobbying efforts of pro-refugee groups and increasingly the native Jewish community—were also at work to overturn the harsh anti-refugee measures of 1934 and 1935, and especially those of 1938 and 1939. These countervailing pressures continued to operate up until June 1940, and even afterward they did not cease to function altogether. As a result, the refugee question in the 1930's remained in a state of considerable flux, and it was only after Vichy came to power in 1940 that refugee policy took a decidedly hard-line turn. Yet even under Vichy, as we shall see in Chapter 15, some room for maneuvering remained, but the range of available options had become significantly more narrow, due to the antisemitic ideology of the Vichy leadership, the influence exerted by the Germans, and the suppression of all voices that in earlier years had pressed for a more liberal refugee policy.

Thus, this study, in contradistinction to Noiriel's, will give greater emphasis to historical contingency—the influence of individuals and groups in the determination of refugee policy—as well as to the impact of unfolding political events. It is the fluidity of refugee policy that will be stressed here, a fluidity that in many respects mirrored the larger political, cultural, and economic context of the time, and especially the constantly shifting balance of power between republican and antirepublican forces. In the 1930's, as had been the case ever since the emancipation of the Jews in 1791, the Jewish question remained an integral element of the larger republican agenda. It is therefore not surprising that the republic's collapse in 1940 had profound implications for Jews, native as well as foreign. Only in 1945, after 20 percent of the Jewish population of France had perished in the Holocaust, would those countervailing forces that had sustained the republic throughout the 1930's become operative again.

CHAPTER TWO

Refugee Policy and Middle-Class Protest During the Great Depression, 1933–36

On January 30, 1933, Hitler became chancellor of the German republic, and he at once set to work to implement two of his long-standing aims: to purge the nation of all "unhealthy" political elements and to eliminate the Jews from the nation's economic, cultural, and political life. Invoking the emergency measures of Article 48 of the Weimar Constitution, Hitler persuaded President Paul von Hindenburg on February 4 to ban all public meetings by groups or political parties opposed to the regime and to crush all dissenting voices in the press. At the same time, the Parliament was dissolved, and new elections were scheduled for early March. These elections, Hitler hoped, would provide the regime with a clear-cut electoral majority, a goal that had hitherto eluded the Nazis, but one they continued to seek to bestow upon their actions the veneer of legitimacy.

After the burning of the Reichstag on February 27, a crime the Nazis blamed on the communists although they themselves were almost certainly responsible, the government unleashed a reign of terror against its political opponents: liberals, socialists, communists, and trade unionists. On March 23, after the Nazis failed to achieve an electoral majority, the Parliament, cowed into submission through outright terror, passed the Enabling Act, which granted the chancellor the right to govern by emergency decree. Street beatings and summary arrests became common, and anti-Nazi activists who had not yet fled the country began to disappear into the regime's newly created concentration camp network. By the summer of 1933, Hitler had completed the process of *Gleichschaltung*, or coordination, having eliminated or brought into line every independent political party, organization, and organ of the press. The single-party dictatorship was thus firmly established.[1]

As Hitler moved to eliminate his political opponents, he also moved to eliminate the group he believed most threatened the nation's racial integrity: the Jews. On April 7, the Nazis passed the Law for the Reconstruction of the Professional Civil Service, which barred from the civil service all "non-Aryans," who at this point were defined as persons with at least one grandparent of the Jewish faith. Despite exemptions for Jews who had served in the civil service prior to 1914 or who had fought in the First World War, thousands of Jewish lawyers, judges, teachers, and state-employed doctors lost their jobs. German educational institutions were similarly purged: on April 25, 5 percent quotas were imposed on all non-Aryan students currently enrolled in secondary schools and institutions of higher learning and a 1.5 percent quota was imposed on incoming students. Parallel measures were taken to expel Jews from positions in Germany's artistic and cultural life. On July 14, another law was passed that stripped Jews naturalized since November 9, 1918, of their citizenship, transforming them into a mass of stateless refugees.[2] At the same time, the Nazis embarked on an economic drive to oust Jews from the German economy, calling for a nationwide anti-Jewish boycott on April 1. Although this initiative lasted only one day, it nevertheless marked the beginning of a long crusade to strip Jews of their property and wealth and to deny them any means of earning a livelihood in Germany. This drive was further sustained by the process of "aryanization," which transferred Jewish property and businesses into the hands of non-Jews. This process too was not completed until the end of the decade, but some 75,000 Jewish firms were liquidated during the first two years of the regime.[3]

This wave of oppression sent thousands of people fleeing across the borders in search of asylum, and in 1933 France received by far the largest contingent of refugees—some 25,000 out of a total of 60,000 to 65,000. Of these, about 85 percent were Jews.[4] Why France emerged as the premier nation of asylum in the world during this first phase of the refugee crisis was due to several factors. Geographical proximity obviously played a role. Political refugees hoping to coordinate an anti-Nazi resistance movement had no desire to go far afield, and France provided a convenient watch post from which to monitor developments back home.[5] Nonpolitical refugees too generally preferred to remain close by so that they could return in the event of an anti-Hitler coup. Moreover, many Germans had friends and relatives, and sometimes even business interests, across the border, especially in

Alsace and Lorraine, which had been annexed to Germany between 1871 and 1918, and the widespread use of the German language here constituted yet a further inducement.

Most important, however, was the fact that France had not yet implemented immigration restrictions, in sharp contrast to Great Britain or the United States, the former having allocated visas on a highly selective case-by-case basis aimed at weeding out refugees without substantial financial means, whereas the latter adhered rigidly to the quota system implemented in the 1920's.[6] Rather, as we have seen, France continued to recruit thousands of foreign workers up through the early 1930's to compensate for the labor shortages after the First World War.[7] And finally, France had diplomatic reasons to welcome the refugees. The Nazi seizure of power was widely perceived as a vindication of France's hard-line stance toward Germany, a stance that had been severely criticized by the United States and Britain throughout the 1920's. For many French statesmen, a generous reception of the victims of Nazi terror offered the prospect of restoring the anti-German coalition hammered out so painstakingly at Versailles.

This generosity proved short-lived, however. By the end of 1933, France served notice that she would no longer serve as the world's "dumping ground."[8] To the extent that asylum would still be granted, Senator Henry Bérenger, France's representative to the newly created League of Nations High Commission for Refugees (HCR), announced in December that France would henceforth serve solely as a "way station" for refugees en route to final destinations elsewhere.[9] By the time of the Nuremberg Laws of September 1935, which stripped German Jews of their citizenship and ostracized them as an alien race, it had become official policy to bar the entry of further refugees and seek the reemigration of those still remaining in France. Indeed, according to the HCR, the French government considered none of the 14,000 German refugees still living in France in the spring of 1935 as having been definitively settled; instead, it expected the League of Nations to redistribute them all in the near future.[10] Thus, although it has been commonly asserted that France officially ceased serving as country of refuge at the time of the Evian Conference in 1938,[11] this goal had in fact been embraced already by the end of 1933.

In this chapter, we will examine two aspects of this first phase of the refugee crisis: the liberal reception accorded refugees in the spring of 1933 and the subsequent collapse of that policy. While several factors clearly played a role in this reversal, including long-standing antipathy toward Germans, fear that the refugees might constitute a fifth column of German spies, and the ambivalence, and at times even hostility, of certain sectors of the French Jewish community, there can be little doubt that the principal factor in this turnaround was the Depression. Although the Depression hit France late, with the first signs of economic downswing appearing only at the end of 1930, it nevertheless hit hard, and by 1935 close to one million people were out of work.[12] One consequence of this deteriorating economic climate was a sharp rise in popular animosity toward France's immigrant population, which numbered 2.7 million in 1931, or about 7 percent of the total. Voices ranging from the extreme right to the moderate left of the political spectrum began to demand the repatriation of the immigrants in order to free up jobs for the nation's unemployed.[13]

But while the anti-refugee campaign has frequently been linked to this broad-based anti-immigrant backlash, it was in reality motivated by somewhat different concerns. Unlike most other immigrants in France, who were concentrated primarily in industrial and agricultural occupations, Jewish refugees were disproportionately represented in middle-class professions, especially commerce and the liberal professions.[14] The principal charge against them was not that they were stealing jobs from French workers, but rather that they were engaging in "unfair" competition with their middle-class counterparts. Although several politicians, well-known publicists, and organizations (such as the League for the Rights of Man and Citizen) consistently argued that an influx of refugees, particularly those with capital, would constitute an economic boon, creating new jobs and lowering consumer prices, the administrations that governed between 1933 and the spring of 1936, when the Popular Front came to power, refused to countenance this view. Instead, they caved in almost entirely to protectionist demands. Ultimately, it was the success of this middle-class lobby in eliciting a protectionist, or Malthusian, response from the government that served as the principal determinant of refugee policy during this period. Indeed, this middle-class campaign against the refugees, which increasingly developed into a campaign against all Jewish immigrants, constituted a critical stepping stone in paving the way for Vichy's anti-Jewish legislation.

It is nevertheless imperative to remember that when the refugees first began to arrive in the spring of 1933, there were few signs of the conflicts soon to emerge. In March, consular officials began to report that they were being deluged by requests for visas, particularly from well-to-do Jews, and they asked for instructions from Paris.[15] Several weeks later, French Jewish leaders, through the Alliance Israélite Universelle (AIU), the organization that represented Jewish interests abroad, appealed to the administration to receive the refugees as liberally as possible, promising that the Jewish community would accept full financial responsibility for the refugee relief effort.[16]

With this guarantee, the Cabinet met in early April and decided that France "loyal to its generous traditions of hospitality with regard to political refugees without distinction of opinion is obliged to welcome the German refugees in the same manner as it has previously received . . . Italian,

Spanish or Russian immigrants."[17] The foreign minister, Joseph Paul-Boncour, advised French consulates in Germany "to welcome in the most generous manner and the most liberal spirit requests for visas presented by Jews," and he instructed them to grant visas to Nansen refugees—Russians, Greeks, Armenians, and others who had become stateless after the First World War and had come under the protection of the League of Nation's Nansen Office, which granted them travel documents and identity papers. As he explained, the situation of these stateless refugees, most of whom were Russian Jews, "is even more precarious than that of the German Jews themselves."[18]

Paul-Boncour's counterpart at the Ministry of the Interior, Camille Chautemps, similarly issued a circular on April 20 calling on French border police to grant residence permits and identity cards* to refugees "without difficulties," and he ordered police to enlarge their staffs and even provide translators to welcome the refugees "with the greatest possible benevolence."[19] Indeed, Chautemps went so far as to waive the normal visa regime altogether, mandating that refugees could enter France without visas as long as they reported to the police within 20 days. Indigent refugees were to be granted identity cards free of charge, and refugees who desired to transfer their movable property to France were to be exempted from the usual customs duties.[20] The sole condition of these liberal provisions was that the refugees obey French law and abstain from political activity on French soil.

In early April, Chautemps reiterated these policies during an exchange on the floor of the Chamber of Deputies, when the socialist deputy, Jules Moch, inquired into the measures taken to date to assist the refugees. Without hesitation, Chautemps declared that "the sufferings of tens or hundreds of thousands of people, who find themselves pariahs in their own countries, have had a profoundly painful impact on the national soul," and he informed Moch that the government was determined to provide the most liberal terms of asylum. It was, Chautemps noted, "an honor for our nation to remain loyal to the generous traditions of hospitality on which it has always prided itself."[21]

Pro-refugee sentiment ran high in other ministries as well. Just days after Moch's interpellation, the minister of education, Anatole de Monzie,

---

*In addition to a passport and visa, all foreigners over fifteen years of age who intended to stay in France longer than two months but did not intend to hold a salaried job were required to apply for a *carte d'identité des étrangers sans profession* (identity card for foreigners without profession) at their local police department within eight days of their arrival. This card, which cost a fixed fee and was granted only after an investigation, was generally valid for three years and constituted a *permis de séjour*, or residence permit. Immigrant workers were required to show valid work contracts from the Ministry of Labor prior to receiving a special *carte d'identité*, which indicated their right to work. See Livian, *Le Régime juridique*, pp. 67–89; Leven, p. 17; Feblowicz and Lamour, pp. 38–46.

one of the most vocal supporters of the refugee cause, submitted a bill to Parliament calling for the creation of a chair for Albert Einstein at the Collège de France. This bill, which was cosponsored by two of the nation's most prominent deputies—Louis Marin, leader of the Republican Federation, the leading conservative party, and Emile Borel, a prominent Radical-Socialist—passed in both houses of Parliament with overwhelming support, despite a vitriolic campaign in the extreme right-wing press that accused Einstein of being a Bolshevik agent.[22] De Monzie also declared that refugee students would be granted "the greatest possible opportunities to pursue their studies in France," and he worked assiduously to ensure that they would receive equivalency credits for course work completed in Germany.[23] Indeed, in early 1934 he submitted another bill to Parliament that would have permitted refugee students to practice medicine once they had completed their studies in France, without having to undergo naturalization, contrary to the terms of the recently passed Armbruster Law of April 21, 1933, whose impact we will examine shortly.[24]

This warm reception did much to boost French prestige in the eyes of the international community. According to the *Manchester Guardian*, the liberal British daily, French generosity offered a stark contrast to the restrictive policies of its own government. "No Frenchman," the *Guardian* declared, "no matter how nationalist, reactionary, or even anti-Semitic, would consider it decent to refer to the German refugees—as a certain Tory gentleman in the House of Commons did the other day—as 'undesirable aliens.'"[25] Jewish leaders were no less effusive in their praise. In May 1933, a representative of the American Jewish Joint Distribution Committee (JDC), the premier international Jewish relief organization, headquartered in New York City, proclaimed that "the attitude of the French government and people has been . . . 100 percent sympathetic."[26] In a further sign of gratitude, Jewish newspaper editors in the fall of 1933 listed Chautemps as one of the 12 greatest Christian friends of the Jews.[27]

The French diplomatic corps too took note of the gains to be reaped from this upsurge of pro-French and anti-German sentiment. According to the French ambassador to Brazil, Hitler's anti-Jewish movement "has provoked . . . throughout South America, where Jewish finance possesses numerous means of action, an emotion that has yet to calm down, and [it] will reconcile to us that sector of public opinion that had previously become estranged due to the success of German propaganda." In Brussels, the French ambassador reported that the persecution of the Jews and the emigration of prominent German Jewish intellectuals like Einstein had similarly turned Belgian public opinion strongly against Germany, and he predicted "an improved international atmosphere for the ideas our country defends."[28]

But nowhere was this shift more apparent than in Britain, where throughout the 1920's the political establishment had never ceased to castigate France for its unyielding position vis-à-vis the Germans. Now, however, the French ambassador in London noted that the persecution of the Jews had awakened "sentiments of mistrust toward Germany." To illustrate this shift, he reported that when he had remarked at a recent dinner at the home of Sir Austen Chamberlain "'that France had abandoned the occupation of the Rhineland only at the request of Great Britain; otherwise, she still would have had the legal right to be there, and if our troops were still there at this moment, German Jews would not now be being harassed and mistreated.' All the English agreed."[29] At home too, politically influential figures, such as the right-wing French steel magnate François de Wendel, believed that France stood to benefit from Germany's foolhardy embrace of antisemitism. "France," de Wendel commented in a private exchange, "which yesterday was still isolated and considered the spoilsport, is today witnessing the rapprochement, if not of [Ramsay] MacDonald and Roosevelt, then at least of that sector of opinion they represent."[30]

But at the lower levels of the administrative hierarchy, some officials were already counseling a more cautious approach. Among consular officials in Germany, a few began to recommend a selective refugee policy, one that would weed out individuals who did not possess substantial financial means or who were not of German nationality, categories that frequently overlapped. Writing in early April, Pierre Arnal, the French chargé d'affaires in Berlin, reported that although many Jews who had left in February and March had been quite wealthy, the majority of those requesting visas now were of "inferior status" and many had "come to Germany only very recently." Since these individuals were likely to become public charges, he recommended the implementation of a "serious screening process" to ensure their exclusion. But even insofar as better-off refugees were concerned, Arnal warned of potential problems down the road. In particular, he noted that the arrival of so many liberal professionals would ultimately pose "delicate questions with respect to the domain of professional competition."[31]

Jean Dobler, the French consul in Cologne, expressed similar concerns. He too argued in favor of a more selective policy, one that would allow entry to only the intellectual elite, as well as wealthy businessmen and industrialists "who would bring us commerce, industry and capital and would truly increase the strength of the asylum granting nation." As for the others, concentrated overwhelmingly in small-scale commerce, Dobler considered them thoroughly "undesirable." They would either compete with French merchants and artisans or become public charges, and he therefore recommended that their visa applications be "mercilessly rejected." He further counseled, together with the extreme-right-wing Paris municipal councilor Robert Bos, that France adopt a policy like Britain's whereby only Jews with substantial financial means be granted entry visas.[32]

Still other officials began to express concern that the refugees might con-

stitute a security risk, either because of their left-wing orientation or because they were Germans—the traditional enemy—and could therefore
never be trusted. To be sure, this concern did not prevail at the highest levels of the administration—in the spring of 1933, both the Foreign Ministry and the Ministry of the Interior concurred that the reception of Germany's top-ranking socialist and communist émigrés, including Rudolf
Breitscheid, Rudolf Hilferding, and Willy Münzenberg, posed no security
threat whatsoever.[33] But among lower-level officials, greater caution seemed
advisable. According to a police report of November 1933, although Jewish
refugees were believed to pose a minimal security risk, since there seemed
little incentive for them to spy for the Nazis, the same could not be said of
the tiny minority of non-Jewish political refugees, about 10 percent of the
total. Unlike the Jews, these people "are, for the most part, 100 percent true
Germans," and most of them "have not left their country without the hope
of returning." This report therefore suggested that these refugees be placed
under heightened surveillance.[34]

Other security agents were dubious even with regard to the Jews. According to the chief of the Sûreté Nationale in Alsace, the large contingent
of East European Jews among the refugees, whom police estimated as constituting 40 to 50 percent of the total, were not political refugees at all, but
were "swindlers and agitators" who deserved to be hunted down by the
Nazis.[35] Yet another police agent, writing in November 1933, predicted in a
somewhat antisemitic vein that these largely bourgeois Jews would invariably turn to communism, since they would "not find here their erstwhile
easy life, of which in Germany they had been almost the exclusive beneficiaries (which also helps explain a bit better the resentment of the Prussians toward them)." As a result, he continued, they "will soon constitute groups
of discontented and violent exiles: veritable ghettos from the moral point
of view, as well as the point of view of hygiene! Foreign colonies whose
members will not be disciplined by any consulate nor made to respect the
flag, a milieu altogether ripe for communist propaganda."[36]

But for many French officials, the greatest political danger inherent in an
overly generous refugee policy was that these refugees were German, and it
was difficult to believe they had turned so completely against their mother-
land, despite their rift with the current regime. In response to an appeal
from the French consul in Frankfurt requesting that a group of German
Protestant clergymen of Jewish origin be granted permission to settle
in Alsace or Lorraine, the French ambassador in Berlin, André François-
Poncet, advised against this move, claiming that these Protestant clergymen
had always been among the most fervent German patriots and would constitute "centers of resistance to assimilation and perhaps even to the national idea."[37]

Similarly, the prefect of the Haut-Rhin rejected the application for asylum of a German Jew because he had once served as an officer in the German army. "The presence of this former German officer is undesirable in France," he declared, since as a "former officer of the enemy army, he is, without doubt, disposed to render his country the highest services." Moreover, he added, "the avalanche of Jews of this category in [the border town] of Saint-Louis constitutes a great danger from the national point of view."[38] Jacques Fouques-Duparc, assistant director to the French delegation at the League of Nations, similarly worried that the refugees would remain agents of Germanic culture and civilization, thus threatening French interests at home and abroad. No matter where they settled, "these Jews chased out of Germany risk, by means of an almost fatal reflex, becoming German minorities, transmission and preservation agents of the German culture and, incidentally, the German influence." Such a tendency constituted a serious danger that "we must ward off through a vigilant surveillance effort."[39]

But while these security considerations played a role in dampening French enthusiasm for the refugees and inspired a shrill anti-refugee campaign in the far-right-wing press,[40] there is little doubt that the principal factor behind the reversal of refugee policy was the Depression. In the spring of 1933, the minister of labor had signaled to Jewish leaders and the League for the Rights of Man and Citizen that although he could not exempt the refugees from the provisions of the Law of August 10, 1932, which had imposed quotas—generally 10 percent—on the numbers of foreigners allowed to be hired as wage laborers,[41] he would nevertheless attempt to grant refugees work permits* as liberally as possible.[42] Within weeks, however, the Ministry realized that in response to popular opposition, these efforts would have to be scrapped.[43]

Although the leadership cadres of the Confédération Générale du Travail (CGT) and the communist-affiliated Confédération Générale du Travail Unitaire (CGTU), as well as the Socialist and Communist Parties, consistently upheld the right of asylum, a right they maintained was inseparable from the right to work,[44] the rank and file of the labor movement had no desire to see yet another group of immigrants stealing jobs, which they be-

---

*In order for immigrants to hold a salaried job, they needed to obtain a special identity card, the *carte d'identité des étrangers exerçant une profession* (identity card for foreigners exercising a profession), also known as a work permit. To obtain this card, immigrants had to secure in advance of coming to France a contract from an employer that had been approved by the Services de la Main d'Oeuvre Etrangère (MOE) of the Ministry of Labor. Work permits were valid only for specified professions and departments, and they were allocated on the basis of need in various regions or sectors of the economy. See Leven, pp. 12–13; Vormeier, "La République," pp. 17–21; Feblowicz and Lamour, pp. 61–71.

lieved rightfully belonged to French workers. Thus, the Comité d'Aide et d'Accueil, the principal Jewish relief committee in the spring of 1933, which soon became the Comité National Français de Secours aux Réfugiés Allemands, Victimes de l'Antisémitisme, noted as early as May that "a certain opposition is manifesting itself among the ranks of organized labor against the granting of work authorizations to our refugees because certain émigrés would accept work at sub-standard wages and for more than an eight-hour-day."[45] Similarly, Socialist and Communist Party militants continually felt compelled to remind their followers to demonstrate greater solidarity toward their German comrades.[46] Seeking to diffuse this hostility, Léon Jouhaux, head of the CGT, appealed to the International Labor Organization to effect a more equitable geographical distribution of refugees so that France would not have to bear so great a burden, and he furthermore proposed to settle refugees in agricultural areas in southern France so that they would not compete with French workers.[47]

Faced with this backlash, the minister of labor swiftly retreated from his initial promises. In October, the *Univers israélite*, the chief periodical of the Jewish community, reported that no more than 200 work permits had been granted to date, despite intense lobbying by the Comité National as well as the League for the Rights of Man, and police reports of November set this figure even lower.[48] So sensitive had the Ministry become that when a leading member of the Comité National, Jacques Helbronner, suggested in November that the government might use the refugees as an unpaid labor force on public works projects, the minister refused. "Unemployed Frenchmen," he declared, "would never understand our employing foreign refugees even without pay, and such a measure could therefore stir up difficulties."[49] A police report from the same time similarly noted that although many French Jews, and even a few celebrities, such as Josephine Baker, were eager to hire refugees, the Ministry had decided that work permits would be granted only in exceptional circumstances so as not "to disquiet public opinion."[50]

Such working-class hostility was not, however, the chief source of the anti-refugee backlash. Rather, the anti-refugee campaign was led primarily by a coalition of middle-class groups (merchants, artisans, and liberal professionals, especially lawyers and doctors—in other words, those professions in which the vast majority of refugees were concentrated). These groups had a single concern during the Depression: to protect their existing socioeconomic status against any competitive threat. According to their Malthusian world view, they perceived the economy to be a fixed entity incapable of further growth, and they believed that the introduction of new producers, no matter how few their number, would automatically ensure that they would be left with a smaller share of the pie.[51]

To be sure, not everyone adhered to this view. Pro-refugee advocates, as well as a number of journalists and government officials, insisted that the refugees need not be considered an economic threat, especially since many of them had been able to get a portion of their wealth out of Germany through a variety of subterfuges.[52] According to these spokesmen, not only would the refugees constitute a new group of consumers, but most importantly, they would create new businesses and industries, which in turn would generate jobs for thousands of French workers.[53] As one Sûreté Nationale report from the spring of 1933 noted, "the creation of new enterprises in France, the influx of new capital, the use of this capital in our country, the establishment of merchants and industrialists with clienteles abroad could represent definite advantages for the national economy, the repercussions of which could be long-lasting."[54] And indeed, wherever refugee firms were created, such predictions proved correct. In the Alsatian district of Haguenau, for example, a newly created refugee-owned shoe manufacturing firm had, according to the subprefect there, created hundreds of new jobs and had "thoroughly eliminated all fear of unemployment in this important locale."[55] Other influential personalities, such as Senator André Honnorat, who served as president of the Comité des Savants, which supervised the placement of refugee scholars in France, lobbied the government to grant tax exemptions and other incentives to prominent refugee merchants, such as the Leipzig furriers and the Nuremberg toy manufacturers, claiming that their formidable export trade would significantly enhance the national wealth.[56]

French businessmen were far from pleased, however. Within weeks after the refugees began to arrive, the principal organizations representing French business interests—the Confédération Générale de la Production (CGPF), as well as local Chambers of Commerce—began to appeal to the government to protect them against an "invasion" of German Jewish competitors. Referring specifically to the influx of German Jews into Alsace and Lorraine, the CGPF requested that the government "exercise a strict control over the refugees and ensure that the establishment of numerous businesses and industries . . . not cause harm to those enterprises currently functioning."[57] Over the summer, the Chambers of Commerce of Metz, Strasbourg, and Colmar staged mass public protests against the commercial activities of the refugees who "frequently dispose of important sums of capital," and they petitioned the government to ban all further refugee settlement in the region and revoke the 1927 Franco-German commercial treaty, which accorded German businesses in France most favored nation status. As the Metz Chamber of Commerce declared, "These undesirable elements will become a veritable plague for honest French merchants," and it warned the government that allowing the refugees to remain "will inevitably lead to the ruin of the merchants, small-scale industrialists and artisans of this region."[58] Several weeks later, street demonstrations erupted anew in both Paris and Alsace when it was announced that German refugees were planning to open new chains of *prix uniques*, or discount stores, long considered the bane of French merchants' existence.[59]

Artisans too expressed deep disgruntlement. Fernand Peter, the president of the Alsatian Chamber of Artisan Trades, condemned as "revolting," the "insouciance with which a large number of foreigners have engaged in a competitive struggle, without mercy and often without loyalty, against their French competitors." It was up to the government, he proclaimed, to prevent the devastation of French artisanry "by an army of foreigners who have come to France with business concepts and commercial values incompatible with the traditions of French artisanry."[60] Although Peter did not refer specifically to refugees in this particular petition, his backers in Parliament, led by a contingent of deputies from Alsace and Lorraine, stated explicitly that the status of French artisanry had deteriorated sharply "since the most recent invasion of political refugees." In late 1934, these deputies submitted a bill that echoed Peter's grievances almost verbatim and called on the government to impose quotas on foreign artisans, similar to those already in place for wage laborers. And, while claiming to have no desire whatsoever to overturn France's long-standing tradition of asylum, it was, they noted, "precisely because of its hospitality that France has been cruelly struck and duped. . . . French artisanry, too, has a right to that minimum of guarantees with respect to competition from foreigners."[61]

Beneath this veil of patriotic rhetoric lay several very real economic complaints that reflect the corporatist, anticapitalist, and antimodern outlook of these commercial and artisanal groups. On the economic front, it was alleged that the refugees sold goods below price; produced shoddy merchandise by using mass production techniques, which these middle-class groups referred to as "un-French," "disloyal," and even "communistic"; engaged in "unfair"—that is, innovative—marketing practices; and paid higher wages to attract skilled workers away from French firms, exacerbating an alleged labor shortage in the region.[62] This last claim, as one might imagine, was dismissed as laughable by several government officials in view of the severe unemployment crisis. According to Jean Morize, the French representative to the Saar Governmental Commission, if such labor shortages indeed existed, "it would be an excellent policy to bring to Lorraine the 36,000 unemployed Saarlanders to ward off this embarrassment, so rare in Europe today."[63] But essentially, what these corporate groups argued was that despite their apparent economic benefits, the long-term impact of these firms would be disastrous. Once their competitors had been ruthlessly driven out of business, they would be free to depress wages and jack up prices to their heart's content.[64]

To buttress their case, these associations, which on occasion included even Jewish business interests, imbued their grievances with political significance as well. The owners of one shoe manufacturing firm in Alsace, who happened to be Jewish, charged their refugee competitors with "systematically denigrating everything that is French." While acknowledging the circumstances that had compelled these refugees to leave Germany, they nevertheless insisted that they *"are and remain German from every point of view."* [65] The extremely protectionist Shoe Manufacturers Association of Alsace and Lorraine similarly charged that the refugee firms were *"foreign saboteurs,"* bent on "introducing among us the German conception of business that has led that country to ruin," by which they meant mass production techniques that had led to overproduction, which many French believed had caused the Depression. [66] Others went so far as to accuse these refugee firms of spying. According to one Haguenau shoe manufacturer, who was himself an East European Jew who had previously worked for one of these firms in Germany, these companies were in reality "camouflaged Nazi cells." Not only were they seeking to "derail the French market" by underselling their competitors, but they were engaged in more insidious activities as well, such as military espionage and pro-Nazi propaganda. [67]

Not surprisingly, such arguments found a sympathetic hearing among some intelligence agents. As one of them noted, the vast majority of German firms in Alsace "have at their service a large number of German employees, all of whom are spies in the pay of their government." [68] The chief of the Sûreté Nationale in Alsace similarly claimed that extreme caution had to be exercised since many of these firms "seek to confer upon their personnel the mentality of the Third Reich." [69] Fully aware of the impact this security theme would have in Paris, the local Chambers of Commerce played it to the hilt. According to the petition of the Metz Chamber of Commerce, "the presence of thousands of Germans in this border region, the battlefield of yesterday and tomorrow, is contrary to the national interest." The Strasbourg Chamber of Commerce similarly warned that these refugees would surely return to Germany one day, only "to commit treason against that country that had so generously offered them hospitality." [70]

Despite the involvement of several Jews in this campaign, these protests quickly assumed a strong antisemitic hue. In response to the street demonstrations of the summer of 1933, the prefect of the Bas-Rhin, Pierre Roland-Marcel, noted, "It's indisputable that a certain antisemitism has awakened here against which we must take guard," and he even met with the chief rabbi of France to ensure that "this exodus not . . . bring about an antisemitic movement in Alsace." [71] The American press too signaled the emergence of an antisemitic backlash in Alsace and Lorraine. Reporting on the protests of the local Chambers of Commerce, the *New York Herald Tribune* ran the headline "German Jews as Competitors Harass French," and the

New York Times announced, "French Hit Jewish Shops: Price Cutting in Alsace and Lorraine is Denounced."[72]

In Lorraine, Jewish communal leaders also complained that this anti-refugee campaign was in reality an extension of a long-standing drive sponsored by the Metz Chamber of Commerce to rid the region of recently arrived East European Jews, whom the prefect of Moselle had once described as the least desirable of all immigrants since they "swarm toward the towns and industrial centers, where they engage in sometimes disloyal competition with local commerce."[73] And indeed, in 1933 both the Metz and Colmar Chambers of Commerce had petitioned the government to outlaw peddling, an activity generally associated with East European Jews, which they described as "a veritable abscess on our national economy."[74] The anti-semitic aspect of these grievances surfaced even in Parliament. In November 1934, Lionel de Tastes, deputy of the Seine, recommended that the police and prefects be granted enhanced surveillance powers so they could monitor more closely "the numerous foreigners established in France as merchants, and especially German Jews, several of whom seem more inclined to be swindlers than merchants."[75]

Local officials, whose municipalities had much to lose from the ouster of the refugee firms, did not stand idly by. Instead, they launched a vigorous counterattack to persuade the government to allow these firms to remain in operation. The subprefect as well as the mayor of Haguenau, for example, repeatedly pointed out that these refugee firms had promised to hire nearly all French workers and had even agreed to take French partners in an effort to placate local business interests. They furthermore claimed that they had no choice but to create new jobs since their municipal coffers were being depleted by the high costs of unemployment benefits. Relations between these officials and the professional associations at times became acrimonious. When the honorary president of the Shoe Manufacturing Syndicate accused the mayor of Haguenau of furthering the interest of his municipality at the expense of the greater national interest, the mayor fired back an angry response to the prefect. Although ready to "bow respectfully before this personality's high competence in the matter of manufacturing shoes," the mayor insisted that he was not prepared to take a course in political economy from him. Moreover, he declared, when faced with the problem of having to:

arbitrate between a municipality, which was seeking to create work and requested nothing for itself, and the industrialist, who profits from the situation to defend his personal interests, seeking to transform the national economy into a closed field solely for the profit of the first occupant, it should not be difficult for the administration to decide which of the two parties is the true defender of what we call the "country's general interests."[76]

Such arguments were ultimately to no avail. The prefects, and ultimately the central government in Paris, fearful of alienating their middle-class constituencies, eventually caved in to these protectionist pressures. Insofar as artisans were concerned, although the protectionist legislation proposed in November 1934 was not passed by Parliament, the conservative government of Pierre Laval, which came to power the following June, issued a decree law on August 8, 1935, that conceded nearly all the artisan associations' demands. From now on, these associations were granted the right to impose quotas on foreign workers, similar to those in effect for industrial wage laborers. Moreover, any foreigner wanting to work as an artisan would now have to get special permission from the Ministry of Labor, and this permission was to be granted only after consultation with the local artisan associations. To be sure, this law did not explicitly single out any particular ethnic group. Nevertheless, it did mention homeworkers in the garment trades—"pieceworkers for the most part"—as the most persistent abusers of French labor legislation. Many of these workers, particularly in the Paris metropolitan region, would have been recently arrived East European Jews.[77]

Still, these artisan associations remained dissatisfied because what they wanted was an absolute veto with respect to the distribution of artisan permits. To achieve this end, the Alsatian Chamber of Artisan Trades in early 1936 vetoed every one of the 346 dossiers of foreign artisans forwarded to them by the prefect of the Bas-Rhin. As Fernand Peter explained, the association's goal was to ensure that "the proportion of foreigners authorized to settle in the department of the Bas-Rhin as artisans be fixed at 0 percent— that is, that not a single artisan card be delivered to them."[78] A new prefect had now been appointed, however, who was less sympathetic to the artisan's demands than his predecessor, and he returned these dossiers to the Chamber of Artisan Trades, insisting that they be reviewed on a case-by-case basis.[79]

Although similar rights were not accorded to the Chambers of Commerce on a nationwide basis until 1938,[80] merchants nevertheless won important concessions as well. Already by the summer of 1933, Chautemps decided to restrict refugee settlement in Alsace and Lorraine, in response to complaints from local business interests. As early as May, he informed the Senate that although the government had a "duty to welcome them and to permit them [the refugees] to lead a decent life," it also had a duty to "protect our merchants and industrialists against competition."[81] On May 27, at the First Interministerial Meeting on German Refugees—a body convened by the prime minister to coordinate the refugee policies of diverse ministries—Undersecretary of State Guy La Chambre furthermore urged the administration to curb the "German infiltration" into Alsace and Lorraine, claiming that the antisemitic backlash developing there threatened to play into the hands of the pro-German autonomist movement.[82]

In July, Chautemps moved to end refugee settlement in the border provinces altogether, citing the "complex political and material problem" posed by "the influx of a large number of German refugees, nearly all Jews, into the recovered departments." From now on, only refugees with French relatives would be allowed to remain, together with a few deemed non-competitive by the prefect, who henceforth was ordered to consult with the Chambers of Commerce before making this determination.[83] As for the approximately 2,000 refugees already settled in the border provinces, they were to be evacuated to the interior, especially Paris, notwithstanding the protests of the prefect of the Seine, who demanded that his department too be closed to refugee settlement and that a nationwide ban be imposed on refugees working in commercial professions.[84]

In yet a further concession to merchants, the Parliament, once again in response to the lobbying efforts of representatives from Alsace and Lorraine, passed a law in October 1935 restricting the right of foreigners to engage in peddling. From now on, only foreigners who had resided in the country continuously for at least five years could apply for peddling permits. The impact of this law was even harsher than it appeared, since the previous July, the Ministry of the Interior had barred the distribution of peddling permits altogether to foreigners, irrespective of how long they had been in the country.[85]

The liberal professions, especially law and medicine, were no less immune to these protectionist demands, particularly since the arrival of the refugees merely reinvigorated long-standing campaigns to oust foreigners, and especially East European Jews, from their ranks. In 1934, the association representing law students, "having observed that 300 young German refugees were about to complete their juridical studies," persuaded their parliamentary spokesmen to sponsor a bill mandating that naturalized foreigners be made to wait ten years before being allowed to hold public office, including inscription in the bar.[86] This law, passed on July 19, for the first time in the history of the Republic created a two-tiered system of citizenship with regard to professional rights, granting fewer rights to recently naturalized citizens while requiring them to fulfill all the obligations of citizenship, including military service.[87] Moreover, although this law was formulated as a general measure aimed at foreigners in the civil service, there is no question, as Ralph Schor remarks, that it was "a law made by lawyers, for lawyers, against foreigners who were generally Jewish."[88] Although some aspects of this law were deemed unconstitutional in 1936 — its retroactive character and failure to exempt foreigners who had performed military service in France[89] — it otherwise remained on the books and served as the model for every other middle-class professional association.

The most virulent of all professional campaigns waged against foreign Jews was, however, that led by the Confédération des Syndicats Médicaux, the association of French doctors, together with its student affiliates. From the late 1920's on, this association never ceased to complain of what it called "the medical plethora," a supposed surplus of doctors caused overwhelmingly by foreigners. Although foreigners constituted a mere 3 percent of practicing doctors in France in 1930, and only 11 percent of those in the Paris region,[90] the Medical Association argued that the real danger lay with the high proportion of foreign students enrolled in French medical faculties. By mid-1934, foreigners constituted 21 percent of all medical students in France.[91] At some faculties, including Paris, Montpellier, and Strasbourg, they comprised over one-third of the student body, while at Nancy, they constituted over 50 percent.[92]

Although these statistics in and of themselves reveal no specific anti-semitic animus, a closer look at the rhetoric of these groups shows that their wrath was directed very specifically against Jews. According to a 1931 report, Romanians alone constituted a full one-third of the foreign student body at the Faculty of Medicine in Paris,[93] and of these students it was estimated that 85 percent were Jews.[94] Two factors account for this trend. First, Romanian students were able to take advantage of an 1857 Franco-Romanian treaty that allowed their Romanian secondary school diplomas to be counted as the equivalent of the French baccalauréat, thus permitting them to enroll in French medical faculties on the basis of a simple entrance exam.[95] But the principal reason for their immigration to France was that Romanian universities had imposed a strict *numerus clausus*, or quota, on Jewish university students in the 1920's.[96] From the perspective of French doctors, these East European Jews were the least "desirable" of all foreigners because they, unlike the majority of other immigrants, had no intention of returning home.[97] Indeed, this impression was borne out by statistical evidence as well. For the 1933–34 academic year, the Medical Faculty of Paris awarded 125 *diplômes d'Etat*, a degree required of foreign medical students only if they intended to stay in France. Ninety-seven of these, or 78 percent, went to Romanians, another six went to Poles, and five went to Russians. These recipients too were almost certainly Jews.[98]

In response to this situation, the medical associations, even before the arrival of the refugees, had initiated a fierce battle to exclude these recently arrived Jews from their professional ranks. In 1931, in the midst of a parliamentary debate over whether to limit the access of foreigners to the medical profession, Professor Balthazard, president of the Confédération des

Syndicats Médicaux and former dean of the Paris Medical Faculty, declared war against the "veritable Romanian invasion." The French government, he insisted, had never intended for the 1857 treaty privileges to be used by "this legion of Jews,"[99] and he even suggested that the government allow only Christians to study in France.[100] Moreover, to ensure that these Romanian Jews never be granted refugee status, Balthazard denied the existence of antisemitism in Romania, declaring: "Do specific measures to throw the Jews out of higher education really exist in Romania? Are the Jews threatened with anything like a pogrom. Not in the least."[101] But for Balthazard there was a moral aspect to this problem as well. As he proclaimed in a 1929 speech: "The Romanians are not always the best elements among us; there are a few excellent ones among them, . . . but I myself much prefer the ones that return to Romania. Those who remain here are not always brimming over with scruples."[102]

Balthazard's views were far from unique. According to Jean Regaud, president of the Professional Association of Parisian Hospital Interns, the Romanian Jews who came to France "are generally not the best" since they had already been selected out by the Romanian *numerus clausus*.[103] Others charged that due to their low moral caliber, East European Jewish doctors were especially prone to illegal practices—quackery, abusive use of drugs, and above all abortion.[104] Still others, such as Georges Lafitte, president of the National Student Union, insisted that their lower living standards gave them an unfair competitive edge. "Accustomed for generations to living in misery, they will completely overtake us in the struggle for existence, since we are weighted down by the exigencies of an old civilization."[105] More significantly, it was alleged that these foreign students benefited from a host of privileges. They supposedly received preferential treatment on their exams and were exempted from the first year of medical studies, known as the PCN (Physics, Chemistry, and Natural Sciences). Above all, it was charged that because they tended to postpone their naturalization until after the age of 28, they were able to evade military service, giving them a two-year advantage over their French counterparts.[106]

As in the case of merchants and artisans, a sector of public opinion found these arguments unconvincing. The majority of liberals and leftists, as well as left-wing Catholics, insisted that the "medical plethora" was a complete myth. The real problem, they claimed, was a bad distribution of physicians, and as proof they cited statistics indicating that France had one of the lowest ratios of doctors to the population as a whole of any European country, even in urban areas. Many commentators also noted that there were severe shortages of doctors in rural areas as well as in the French colonies.[107] According to these critics, the medical profession's campaign against foreign Jews was fueled more by greed than any real threat to the profession, a claim substantiated by contemporary scholarship as well since, as Alfred Sauvy and Serge Berstein have shown, the liberal professions emerged from the Depression almost unscathed.[108]

Nevertheless, doctors were anxious to defend their existing status against any competitive threat, and they succeeded in mobilizing parliamentary support for this demand. On April 21, 1933, after two years of heated debate, the Parliament, spurred to action by the recent arrival of the refugees from Germany, enacted the Armbruster Law, which restricted the practice of medicine to French citizens, subjects, and residents of French protectorates, and required all students to obtain the *diplôme d'Etat*.[109] Now in order for even the most eminent foreign doctors to practice, they were required to redo not only their entire university education, but even their last year of high school, in order to acquire the *baccalauréat*.[110] Still, the profession remained dissatisfied because the Armbruster Law exempted foreigners who had already commenced their medical studies from the naturalization requirement and permitted them to practice merely by acquiring the *diplôme d'Etat*. Moreover, native doctors continued to complain of the ease by which naturalized doctors evaded military service. What they therefore wanted was a law just like that pertaining to the legal profession—a ten-year waiting period from the date of naturalization until the time a naturalized citizen could begin to practice legally.[111]

These preoccupations, heightened by rumors that the Ministry of Education was on the verge of exempting all refugee doctors and medical students from the Armbruster Law,[112] stimulated a new spate of legislative initiatives in 1933 and 1934 aimed at closing loopholes in the Armbruster Law and at securing the desired waiting period for recently naturalized foreigners.[113] In the meantime, however, the student unions, impatient with the slow pace of the legislative process, declared a one-day nationwide strike in January 1935, which they promised to renew the following month if their demands were not met. This strike enjoyed enormous support, not only from students, who were eventually joined by their peers in dentistry and law, but even from school administrators, who in some cases closed down their campuses in a show of sympathy.[114]

Although generally depicted as xenophobic rather than antisemitic, there is little doubt that these strikes were aimed specifically at Jews. In one instance, a female Jewish student, who happened not to be foreign, was nearly lynched after she allegedly threw a vial of acid at the head of one student demonstrator.[115] On another occasion, a Russian Jewish student was badly beaten and the student perpetrator was arrested.[116] According to the Radical paper *L'Oeuvre*, a "pogrom-like atmosphere" prevailed, and another Radical paper, *L'Ere nouvelle*, similarly reported that "doctors and [medical] students of Jewish origin have been cruelly beaten and molested."[117]

Moreover, the strike organizers, while abjuring antisemitism, nevertheless declared that they had no objection to foreigners in general, but only to those who remained in France, and these, they noted, stemmed almost exclusively from the "ghettos of the Orient."[118] Finally, although nearly all liberal and left-wing papers condemned the strike, the conservative press gave it nearly unanimous support. Even Emile Buré, editor of the prominent conservative paper *L'Ordre*, who later would become one of the most outspoken pro-refugee advocates, denounced the "intolerable competition" posed by immigrant doctors. Their repatriation, he noted, would have the added benefit of sharply reducing the number of "foreign doctors [who] preach revolution among us."[119]

In the wake of this strike, doctors as well as dentists scored a major legislative victory with the passage of the Nast Law in the summer of 1935. Although this law stipulated that naturalized foreigners who had completed their military service could begin practicing immediately, it followed the civil service law of the previous year by imposing a waiting period on recently naturalized doctors who had not completed their military service. The medical profession had initially demanded a ten-year waiting period, like that in place for the civil service, but the Nast Law stipulated a four-year waiting period—that is, double the length of military service—for naturalized foreigners entering private practice and a five-year waiting period for those embarking on careers in public service. The effect of this law was profound: not only did it prevent the majority of recently naturalized doctors from practicing altogether, which frequently spelled the end of their careers, but it also banned them from serving as medical replacements and even from filling prescriptions.[120] As for non-naturalized foreign doctors, including the refugees, any hope of establishing a practice in France was dashed forever. Despite de Monzie's initial promises to refugee students, the Nast Law stipulated that study abroad could not, under any circumstances, be counted toward a diploma in France, and it eliminated the special exemptions Romanian students had enjoyed.[121]

Once again, however, the Nast Law's most significant innovation lay in the realm of naturalization. Not only did the law create yet another group of second-class citizens, but it also ceded to the doctors' associations the right to be consulted in every case involving the naturalization of a foreign doctor.[122] To be sure, this provision did not give the medical profession an absolute veto over naturalizations. Yet by bringing doctors into the naturalization process, even in an advisory capacity, the central government had taken a huge step toward handing over one of its most important prerogatives to these protectionist and blatantly antisemitic corporations.

This tidal wave of middle-class protectionism, even more than the aforementioned security considerations, impelled the Daladier administration and its successors to retreat from the liberal asylum regime of April of 1933, and not merely in Alsace and Lorraine. Ironically, this decision was made precisely at a moment when French diplomats in Germany, as well as Jewish organizations, were reporting a sharp deterioration in the situation of German Jewry.[123] According to an internal Foreign Ministry note of July 1933:

Several hundreds of thousands of Jews still live in Germany despite their precarious conditions of life, and it seems that the National Socialist authorities will not be content to allow them to remain. Reports from our consuls as well as from the British press coincide to signal a renewal of the boycott, more discreet, but also more systematic, and therefore, more effective. If this situation persists, the Jews will almost certainly seek to expatriate en masse.[124]

But whereas the Foreign Ministry, in response to similar reports in the spring, had concluded that a liberal asylum policy was in order, it now maintained, "No matter how desirous we are of offering refuge to these Jews, it is certain that we could not absorb them into the French labor market without provoking serious reactions in our own country."[125]

Although the goal of reversing the liberal regime had been embraced by the summer of 1933, the means of achieving this end were not yet clear. For the moment, radical solutions, such as mass expulsion, were ruled out. As Chautemps conceded at the Second Interministerial Meeting on Refugees on October 16, "It would be deplorable from the international point of view to proceed with massive expulsions after having opened our borders so liberally to the German emigration."[126] Nor did France ever announce a complete closure of its border, in contrast to the more restrictive refugee policies of its allies, Great Britain and the United States. Nevertheless, by the fall of 1933 the government had embraced three strategies that went far toward closing off France as a nation of asylum: a revocation of the liberal visa regime, a narrowing of the eligibility criteria for refugee status, and an attempt to "internationalize" the refugee problem, either by pressuring Britain to open Palestine to refugees already in France or, more significantly, by persuading the League of Nations to take over the refugee problem so as to ensure a more equitable distribution of refugees in the future.[127]

The process of revoking the liberal visa regime began in July 1933, just as the Foreign Ministry was announcing that the refugees could no longer be received "en masse in our country."[128] On July 18, the Foreign Ministry decided that refugees seeking to enter France through a third country would no longer be granted refugee status, and instructions to this effect were sent out to consulates on August 14.[129] This policy was designed to head off an increasingly common practice whereby France's neighbors literally shoved hundreds and sometimes even thousands of refugees across the border into France.[130]

At the same time, the administration began to beef up police surveillance at the German border. On August 2, the Ministry of the Interior issued a circular instructing border police to bar entry to all refugees not possessing consular visas unless they could prove that their lives were in danger. Claiming that these refugees were likely to be "suspect elements," this circular declared that "the admission of Jews expelled from Germany into France must be continued with extreme circumspection."[131] Several days later, the Foreign Ministry also ordered its consulates in Germany and elsewhere in Europe to curb the issuance of visas since France was no longer able to support "the growing charge that has fallen upon us as a result of the influx of refugees from Germany."[132]

Then, in what constituted the major policy statement of this period, the Foreign Ministry informed the Ministry of the Interior on October 19 that the liberal visa regime of April had been abrogated. To prevent the settlement of foreigners on French territory, two measures were to be adopted: first, the liberal visa policy was to be discontinued and the previous visa regime restored; second, a more restrictive visa policy was to be put into place. Since France had already accepted between 17,000 and 20,000 refugees, the Foreign Ministry declared, "we are no longer able to continue our effort until the new organization envisioned by the League of Nations endeavors to undertake a more equitable reclassification and redistribution of the refugees among the different countries likely to receive them and grant them work." Moreover, the Foreign Ministry noted that the liberal visa regime was no longer necessary anyway since "German Jews no longer seem to be at immediate risk," a statement that flew in the face of a mountain of diplomatic evidence but provided a convenient excuse whenever civil rights groups, such as the League for the Rights of Man, protested the reversal of policy.[133] Although the Foreign Ministry claimed that the new policy represented a return to the status quo ante, it in fact inaugurated a far harsher regime since it singled out Jews for special scrutiny, less because they were Jews than because as Jews they were most likely to stay.[134]

Besides abrogating the liberal visa regime, the administration took steps to narrow the eligibility criteria for refugee status. Over the summer, the Ministry of the Interior and the Foreign Ministry agreed that only two groups of refugees—those possessing German citizenship and stateless persons (that is, bearers of Nansen passports)—were to be granted refugee status. All others, who constituted at least 35 percent of the total, were to be excluded.[135] These refugees, primarily Jews of East European origin, largely Poles, had been living in Germany for varying lengths of time. Many had even been born there, but had never acquired German citizenship because of restrictive naturalization procedures.[136]

While aware of mounting antisemitism in Poland and elsewhere in Eastern Europe, French officials nevertheless decided to consider these refugees economic rather than political refugees, and as such, they were to be denied visas or, if they were already in France, they were to be repatriated to Eastern Europe. While motivated in part by practical considerations, and especially by the fact that repatriation to a country other than Germany was possible,[137] there is little doubt that this decision was inspired in part by a certain brand of antisemitism, one directed specifically against East European Jews. At the Second Interministerial Meeting on German Refugees, the director of the Foreign Ministry's Immigration Bureau proclaimed that he had already taken steps to "unmask the false political refugees"—that is, the East European Jews—and indeed, two years earlier, this same official had railed against East European Jews as a particularly undesirable element. While describing Slavic Poles as highly assimilable—"a physically robust element, healthy and hard working," Polish Jews, he insisted, were economically useless since they "seek out commerce more than productive activities." Culturally too they were resistant to assimilation: they remained "isolated from the rest of the population and indifferent to the life of the nation as a whole, its mentality, its habits and its customs."[138]

Regardless of the motive, by the summer of 1933 the policy of forced repatriation was in full swing, notwithstanding the protests of the Polish ambassador, who opposed the return of these Jews to Poland, as well as the League for the Rights of Man, the Comité National, and the HCR.[139] To defend themselves, these refugees even created their own organization, the Committee for Polish Jewish Refugees from Germany, which had the support of the Polish ambassador in Paris. These lobbying efforts proved futile, however. As many commentators noted, these East European Jewish victims of Nazism perhaps suffered most in France.[140] Those who refused to return to their countries of origin were forced to join the burgeoning ranks of illegal aliens, and as such, they became vulnerable to the periodic waves of expulsions that began to strike the immigrant community in late 1934 and early 1935.

Aside from weeding out refugees of East European origin, a second method of *filtrage*, or selection, was to limit visas to refugees with substantial financial means. Jean Dobler, the French consul in Cologne, was especially insistent in pressing this view since he believed that less well-to-do Jews would eventually steal jobs from French artisans, liberal professionals, merchants, and commercial employees. In April, Dobler, on his own initiative, implemented a procedure requesting Jewish visa applicants alone to fill out detailed questionnaires regarding their financial circumstances. He then proceeded to weed out "those who possessed no financial resources or only insignificant ones."[141] At that time, he received a harsh reprimand from the Quai d'Orsay, claiming that discrimination against refugees on the basis of wealth constituted a breach of international law.[142] Nevertheless, by the winter Dobler's views prevailed. In December, a Foreign Ministry official recommended that a questionnaire similar to Dobler's be introduced at all French consulates, and consular officials were instructed to reject visa applications from Jews unable to prove independent financial means.[143]

Finally, French authorities narrowed the category of those eligible for asylum by making it increasingly difficult to authenticate one's status as a political refugee. By early 1934, despite numerous diplomatic reports chronicling the deteriorating situation of German Jewry,[144] consulates in Germany as well as border police were instructed to grant visas or identity cards only to individuals able to prove that they had been physically molested and that their lives were in imminent danger. Being a Jew in and of itself no longer sufficed to guarantee refugee status.[145] Indeed, many French officials even began to claim that Jews in particular, whom they increasingly referred to as "self-proclaimed refugees from Germany," were not political refugees at all, but had come to France merely to enhance their economic well-being.[146] As one security report noted, Jews who had remained in Germany seemed to be prospering, and many of those who had fled,

had already returned home without difficulty; some, it is true, supposedly returned to retrieve their property, but others did so to supervise the management of their commercial enterprises, after having profited by their stay abroad to establish a subsidiary or branch firm. . . . One cannot but suppose that certain businessmen, who had nothing to fear by remaining in Germany—except perhaps to see their commercial operations slow down a bit—have taken advantage of the Hitlerian tempest to seek their fortunes upon new shores.

This agent then proceeded to dismiss the anti-Jewish persecutions as acts "committed by overly zealous Nazis who have certainly exceeded their orders," but added, "strictly speaking there have not been pogroms."[147]

The third and most important government strategy to reverse the liberal asylum policy of the spring was the effort to "internationalize" the refugee problem—that is, to persuade other nations to accept a greater share of the refugee burden. Although the obvious forum for such a policy was the League of Nations, it was in fact several months before France approached the League on this issue. Instead, France's initial strategy was to press for an "internal" solution to the problem, one that would stanch the flow of refugees at the source—that is, inside Germany itself. To achieve this end,

France waged a vigorous battle from May through the fall of 1933 to force Germany to submit to the minority rights treaties that had been imposed on other Central and East European nations by the Treaty of Versailles, a battle indicating that at least at this point, France and the League were prepared to intervene in Germany's domestic affairs.

To be sure, Germany had never signed these treaties, nor had German Jews ever been considered a national minority. Nevertheless, an incident occurred in the spring of 1933 that provided an opportunity to extend these treaty provisions to Germany as well. This was the so-called Bernheim Affair, in which a Jewish delegation from Upper Silesia, then under German rule, protested to the League regarding the dismissal of a Jewish civil servant, Franz Bernheim, as a result of the introduction of Nazi antisemitic legislation, despite the fact that Germany had signed a minority rights treaty for Upper Silesia when it had secured that territory from Poland in 1922.[148] France, together with the other West European democracies, hoped to use this case not only to protect the Jews of Upper Silesia, which they succeeded in doing until 1937, but to extend these treaty obligations to Germany as a whole, thereby ending the persecution of the Jews and stanching any further exodus of refugees.[149] On October 3, the French delegation, led by Henry Bérenger, who was also president of the Senate Foreign Relations Committee, scored a major victory when it convinced the entire membership of the League, with the sole exception of Germany, to support a 1922 proposal calling on member states to adhere voluntarily to the minority rights treaties, whether or not they had signed them.[150] This victory proved short-lived, however, because Germany pulled out of the League on October 14.[151]

Once it became clear that Germany would never submit to an "internal" solution to the refugee problem, France began to consider some sort of "international" solution, which entailed getting other nations to bear a greater share of the refugee burden. Already in the spring of 1933 the Foreign Ministry had instructed its consulates to sound out settlement possibilities abroad.[152] After every one of these inquiries came back negative, the Foreign Ministry considered the next best option as trying to persuade Great Britain to open the gates of Palestine to at least some refugees already settled in France. Indeed, in late August, the Cabinet, increasingly concerned with the domestic consequences of the refugee question, adopted a resolution calling on the Foreign Ministry "to bring before the League of Nations the question of German refugees in France and to study ways to encourage their settlement in Palestine."[153]

Although a resolution to this effect was brought to the floor of the League in September, the Foreign Ministry ultimately decided not to press too hard on the Palestine issue since it had no desire to raise the broader issue of Middle East mandates in light of its own ongoing negotiations with the Arabs over Syria.[154] The Foreign Ministry therefore opted for a bilateral approach. In early September, the French embassy in London approached the British Foreign Office to see whether 300 to 400 Palestine certificates* might be set aside for refugees already in France since, as the embassy reminded the British, France had borne a disproportionate share of the refugee burden.[155] While refusing to answer the French definitively, the British nevertheless stated that from their point of view, refugees already in France did not constitute prime immigration material for Palestine, and that in the long term the refugee crisis could best be solved by all nations absorbing refugees already on their soil—an answer that obviously suited the British, who had so far received only about 2,500 refugees, but one that did little to appease the French.[156]

Still, this idea was not dropped altogether. At the Third Interministerial Meeting on Refugees in late October, Jacques Helbronner, representing the Comité National, mentioned that the Foreign Ministry had recently approached the British with a scheme whereby Palestinian Arabs were to be transported to Syria in exchange for an equivalent number of German Jews being allowed to settle in Palestine. Yet, as Helbronner acknowledged, there was scant chance that the British would ever agree to such a population transfer "for fear of the disorders such a measure would certainly provoke."[157]

By October, in the wake of these rebuffs, the French seized upon what would become their principal strategy for the next two years: the attempt to force the League to take over the refugee problem, not only with respect to refugees who might depart from Germany in the future, but also with respect to those refugees already in France. Initially, Foreign Ministry officials had expressed concern that the internationalization of the refugee problem involved "inconveniences and serious risks." According to these officials, the creation of a special refugee body within the League might actually encourage Hitler to expel more Jews by conveying the impression that no one objected to their mass expulsion. Concern was also expressed that such a body might interfere with French sovereignty, either by limiting the government's right to expel foreigners or by broadening the definition of refugees to include Jews of East European origin, thus forcing France to accept

*In the 1930's, there were two major types of Palestine certificates. *Category A* certificates were granted without restrictions to anyone with at least £1,000. They were also allocated to liberal professionals who possessed at least £500 or skilled craftsmen who possessed at least £250, as well as to some other individuals if they had at least £500 and were considered economically useful by the Department of Migration. *Category C* certificates, or Labor certificates, were allocated without regard to the prospective immigrant's financial resources. Rather, they were granted to individuals who had definite job prospects in Palestine. See Tartakower and Grossmann, pp. 57–58.

refugees it was currently repatriating.[158] Even as late as October 3, when the Dutch submitted a proposal to create a special body within the League to deal with the refugees, the French delegation had not yet made up its mind how to respond.[159] When it became clear, however, that the new organization, ultimately named the High Commission for Refugees, Jewish and Other (HCR), would have extremely limited powers—to appease the Germans, it was headquartered in Lausanne instead of Geneva, and its funding was to be derived entirely through private donations—the French dropped their objections and endorsed the idea.[160]

Once the HCR came into existence and was placed under the directorship of an American international relations expert, James G. McDonald,[161] the French position began to emerge more sharply. With respect to the HCR, France had two goals that were in reality contradictory. On the one hand, France wanted a weak high commissioner precisely because it feared an infringement of French sovereignty on issues such as visas and expulsion.[162] On the other hand, France wanted a high commissioner strong enough to compel other nations, especially in North and South America, to accept a greater share of the refugee burden, including a significant portion of those already in France. As Bérenger, France's chief delegate to the HCR, declared at that body's first meeting on December 7–8, France had already done more than its share to help solve the refugee crisis. It had absorbed nearly 30,000 refugees, more than any other nation; it had raised nearly eight million French francs (about $2 million); and it had placed 40 scholars in academic posts and placed another 4,000 refugees in jobs in small-scale commerce and domestic service.[163]

While France took great pride in these contributions, there were, Bérenger insisted, no jobs for these primarily middle-class refugees. Indeed, the government as well as the private relief organizations were rapidly running out of funds, and France could not support these refugees indefinitely. Thus, according to Bérenger, France would henceforth "serve as a way station for refugees, but not as a permanent dumping ground." It was time for the HCR to carry out that task for which it had been created: "to proceed as quickly as possible with the reclassification and redistribution of refugees to other parts of the world," especially in North and South America.[164] Although Bérenger delivered two other speeches to domestic audiences at this same time in which he blasted Germany for its antisemitic policies and defended the right to asylum as being "at the heart of our civilization," he never again resorted to such combative language.[165] Instead, the plaintive tone of his statements to the HCR in December became standard French rhetoric on the refugees from this point on.

By the end of 1933, the situation for the refugees did not appear bright. Not only was there little hope of their obtaining the right to work, but even

their right to asylum was being challenged. In October, the German socialist leader, Rudolph Breitscheid, warned his compatriots to steer clear of
France, citing difficulties in obtaining identity visas and identity cards.[166]
At the same time, the Paris police were reporting that growing numbers
of refugees were working illegally, engendering the very situation labor
unions had hoped to avoid.[167] The inability of the refugees to find work had
also imposed an enormous strain on the resources of the private relief committees, and especially the Comité National, which warned the administration as early as the fall of 1933 that it was on the brink of bankruptcy and began to press for government assistance, despite its previous pledge not to allow the refugees to become wards of the state.[168] To alleviate this burden,
the government donated several military barracks and an abandoned hospital in the Paris region, equipped with bedding and kitchen facilities, to serve
as temporary shelters.[169] With no job prospects, however, the refugees
parked in these camps grew restless and demoralized, and as we will see in
Chapter 5, disturbances and, in one instance, a full-scale riot broke out. Describing the refugee situation in France at the end of 1933, the American
journalist Emil Lengyel painted a grim picture: "Many are looking wan,
and the suicide rate is high. Pauperization is progressing rapidly in their
ranks and the coming winter may see many of them without overcoats and
in rags. . . . What most of them find is misery and, perhaps, burial in a pau-
pers' grave. Their story is one of the darkest chapters of Europe's post-war
history."[170]

To conclude, it is clear that the abrupt turnaround in refugee policy in
1933 had little to do with political or foreign policy considerations. Rather,
it was due above all to domestic factors, especially the government's desire
to placate middle-class grievances, which had reached fever pitch with the
onset of the Depression. By 1934 and 1935, both the medical and legal professions had succeeded in excluding from their ranks not only foreigners,
but also recently naturalized citizens, and their protectionist battle had by
no means come to an end. After 1935, these groups would continue to call
for even more restrictive measures, including rollbacks in naturalizations
already granted, a concession the republican administrations in the 1930's
refused to make, but one agreed to readily by the Vichy regime.

Merchants and artisans won similar gains. By the end of 1933, they had
succeeded in closing Alsace and Lorraine to further refugee settlement, and
they had persuaded the prefect of the Seine to call for similar measures for
his department as well. Although such a ban was not implemented at the
time, it did become law under the Daladier administration in 1938. Moreover, by 1935 artisans had secured strict quotas on the employment of foreigners in their professions, and although merchants would have to wait an-

other three years to win this concession, they had nevertheless secured a ban on peddling by this time.

Perhaps most important, by 1935 both these groups had won the right to be consulted over the naturalization of foreigners in their professions, and although this right did not give them an absolute veto over naturalizations, it did bring them into the decision-making process on a matter of vital national importance. Furthermore, although these middle-class grievances have generally been described as xenophobic, there is no doubt that they were aimed almost exclusively at foreign Jews, since Jews, unlike the majority of other foreigners in France, were overwhelmingly middle class. It is also clear that these anti-refugee campaigns grew out of earlier middle-class campaigns aimed at curbing the economic influence of East European Jews, who had come to France in large numbers after 1919 and constituted approximately one-half of the approximately 260,000 Jews in France in 1933. While native Jews were generally exempted from these attacks in the early 1930's, except among the most extreme-right-wing circles, it is not difficult to envision how easily such attacks could escalate into a more generalized antisemitic campaign.

In light of their fiercely protectionist aims, it is not surprising that these middle-class associations embarked on these xenophobic and antisemitic crusades. What seems more puzzling, however, is why the government caved in so quickly to their demands. As we have seen, many government officials, as well as prominent intellectuals and journalists, had argued in favor of a more generous refugee policy, or at least one that would attract refugees with capital or with technical expertise. From their point of view, the new businesses and industries created by the refugees would expand French export markets and create thousands of new jobs, enhancing France's economic position. Nevertheless, the various administrations in power between 1933 and 1935, regardless of whether they were dominated by Radicals or conservatives, refused to challenge these middle-class pressure groups, since they were all heavily dependent on middle-class electoral support.

The government's susceptibility to middle-class lobbying was further heightened by the chronic political instability of the Third Republic, especially during the 1930's. Between January 31, 1933, and May 1936, the government changed hands no fewer than seven times, and this pattern would continue for the rest of the decade. Under these circumstances, few politicians, no matter how sympathetic to the refugees, were willing to risk alienating so important a sector of electoral support.[171] As we will see, even the socialists, who consistently demanded not only the right to asylum, but also the right to work, would shy away from direct confrontation with these protectionist middle-class groups once they came into power in 1936–37. Instead, they would seek to circumvent these groups altogether, focusing on the creation of agricultural or colonial settlements for refugees, so as to prevent them from being perceived as a competitive threat.[172]

This middle-class opposition thus sharply circumscribed the range of available options for dealing with the refugee problem. Moreover, as we will see in Chapter 3, the parameters defining these options became even more narrow in 1934 and 1935, when conservative administrations came to power and implemented even tougher anti-immigrant and anti-refugee policies as part of their strategies to alleviate the Depression. Moreover, during these years the refugee question would become bound up with a broader right-wing agenda, which lambasted the refugees not only as an economic threat, but also as a political one, identifying them with the forces of social revolution. At the same time, this anti-refugee backlash impelled pro-refugee groups to consolidate their forces and articulate a liberal refugee program that insisted on the right to work as well as the right to asylum. Although these groups had little success in 1934 and 1935, the Popular Front victory would afford them a long-awaited opportunity to put their program into action. In the next chapter, we will examine how the debate over the refugees became engulfed in the larger political currents of 1934 to 1935 and especially in what Robert Paxton has called the "French civil war," whose opening battle was fought in the streets of Paris in the spring of 1934.[173]

CHAPTER THREE

The Conservative Crackdown of 1934–35

With the mounting tensions that characterized French political life in 1934 and 1935, the refugee issue became increasingly politicized, adding yet another dimension to the debate. By 1935, two principal camps had emerged. On the conservative right, which included not only the two major conservative parties, the Republican Federation and the Democratic Alliance, but also the right wing of the Radical Party, an increasingly hard-line stance emerged, which held immigrants and refugees responsible for the Depression and increasingly identified them with the parties of social revolution. In response, liberals and leftists began to articulate a pro-refugee platform, which differentiated refugees from economic immigrants and called for the implementation of a special refugee statute that would provide not only the right to asylum, but also the right to work. Although the hard-liners appeared fully in control by late 1934 and 1935, when a series of harsh anti-immigrant measures were implemented, the pendulum would swing back to the camp of the left in 1936, with the election of the Popular Front.

The refugee issue was by no means at the top of the agenda of any of the major political parties; nevertheless, because the drive to eliminate foreigners emerged as a principal strategy for dealing with the Depression, and because the refugee issue became entangled with the broader political battle between left and right, it was by no means a peripheral issue either. Thus, while the refugee situation appeared dire at the end of 1933, the situation in

1934–35 would deteriorate further, especially under the conservative administrations of Pierre-Etienne Flandin and Pierre Laval. Although France would absorb the German refugees from the Saar in the wake of the pro-German plebiscite of January 1935, it would thereafter close its borders altogether to German refugees. At the same time, the government would embark on a conscious policy to drive out refugees already in France, forcing many of them to leave. By September 1935, when the Nazis proclaimed the Nuremberg Laws, which stripped German Jews of their citizenship and defined them according to racial lines, the right to asylum in France existed in name only.

The first sign of this tougher attitude emerged at the time of the Stavisky Affair, the opening salvo of what Robert Paxton has called the "French civil war," which began in early 1934 and continued until the end of the Second World War. In late 1933, the press revealed that a well-known swindler, Serge Stavisky, had been floating fraudulent Bayonne municipal bonds with the knowledge and backing of prominent members of Parliament and the administration. In January, Stavisky committed suicide to avoid capture, though there were rumors that he might have been murdered by those politicians whose reputations had been sullied by the affair. At the end of January, confronted by this and other scandals, Chautemps's government resigned, and a new cabinet, led by the Radical politician Edouard Daladier, came to power. On February 6, following Daladier's dismissal of the Paris prefect of police, Jean Chiappe, a hero of the political right, the right-wing leagues decided the moment was ripe to stage a massive demonstration against the detested republic. Thousands of their supporters gathered at the Place de la Concorde, and when the order was given to march against the Chamber of Deputies, bitter street fighting ensued. The police resorted to gunfire in defense of the government, killing 15 people and wounding another 200 so seriously that they required hospitalization. In an effort to quell these tensions, the Daladier cabinet resigned, and a new national unity government was created under the premiership of the centrist politician Gaston Doumergue.[1]

The Stavisky Affair did much to enhance the climate of xenophobia and antisemitism in France, in part because Stavisky himself was of Russian Jewish origin, but also because many immigrants and refugees participated in the left-wing counterdemonstrations of February 9 and 12. In the wake of these events, Norman Bentwich, a British Jewish member of the High Commission for Refugees (HCR), reported that French public opinion toward the refugees had become "very excited," and he warned that "there is a dangerous 'psychose' in France at the moment about German and other refugees, which makes it most urgent to cope with the immediate . . . problem."[2] Felix Warburg, the New York banker and former chairman of the

JDC, similarly informed the HCR in late February that "antisemitism is growing in France by leaps and bounds."[3]

Moreover, according to Emile Kahn, secretary general of the League for the Rights of Man, the Doumergue government "was immediately distinguished by a renewed outbreak of severity with regard to foreigners, and especially those not observing the most strict political neutrality." Whereas *refoulements** had rarely been enforced in 1933, they were now executed in an increasingly harsh manner, and even refugees previously promised asylum "now find themselves refused an identity card and are induced to leave the territory."[4] Work permits too became increasingly difficult to procure, and any hopes Jewish leaders may have held that some portion of the refugees might be settled in France were dampened considerably. In mid-February, Jewish leaders even decided to drop a program designed to retrain 250 to 300 refugees as artisans, citing the Ministry of Labor's refusal to grant them work permits.[5] According to Raymond-Raoul Lambert, secretary-general of the Comité National: "The Ministry of Labor, which was at first very willing to help, has stated that in view of the critical political situation, it must now be more reserved."[6]

The most severe crackdown, however, followed the assassination in Marseilles on October 9, 1934, of the Yugoslavian king and the French foreign minister, Louis Barthou, by a Macedonian terrorist working for the extreme-right-wing organization known as the Ustache. This incident, followed in November by the collapse of the government and the formation of a more conservative cabinet under Pierre-Etienne Flandin, unleashed a veritable reign of terror against the foreign population in general, and refugees who had previously been promised asylum were increasingly treated no differently from other immigrants. According to Bernhard Kahn, the European director of the JDC, "the events in Marseilles have made matters

---

*The French term *refoulement* will be used here since there is no precise English equivalent and this term is still used today by international refugee agencies. *Refoulement* implied an administrative decision by the prefect to refuse an immigrant the legal right to remain in France either by refusing to grant that immigrant an identity card or by refusing to renew an identity card already granted. An immigrant who received a *refoulement* order was asked to leave the country within a fixed period of time, although it was generally possible to obtain an extension. By contrast, an expulsion order, as mandated by the law of Dec. 3, 1849, entailed the forcible deportation of a foreigner. Expulsions had to be issued directly by the minister of the interior, rather than the prefects or the police, and police or military escorts could be used to transport foreigners to the border. According to the law of Dec. 3, 1849, failure to comply with an expulsion order was punishable by a prison sentence of one to six months, without any right to appeal. See J.-Ch. Bonnet, p. 107; Cross, pp. 180–81; Fabian and Coulmas, pp. 32–33; Feblowicz and Lamour, pp. 408–27; Leven, pp. 7, 19; Livian, *Le Régime juridique*, pp. 206–17; Peterson, p. 74; Schor, *L'Opinion française et les étrangers*, p. 281; Schramm and Vormeier, pp. 217–18; Tartakower and Grossmann, p. 137.

more difficult. . . . There is now such a strong hatred against foreigners and refugees that it is very difficult to undertake any measures which have for their goal the settling of any number of refugees in France."[7] Morris Troper, also of the JDC, similarly noted that "since the Marseilles affair . . . there is a more defined sensitiveness."[8]

On October 26, the new minister of the interior, Paul Marchandeau, issued a circular warning all immigrants, regardless of whether they were refugees, that they would be ruthlessly expelled if they did not abstain from all criminal and political activity in France,[9] and on November 6, police were ordered to expel all foreigners who had overstayed their visas or whose papers were not in order.[10] Beginning on the evening of November 24, the Paris police launched a series of roundups in the immigrant districts of Paris that continued for four nights. According to the *New York Times*, raids of this magnitude had not been conducted in France for years, and café owners in the Montmartre district of Paris claimed that their immigrant clients had been dragged away by the police "with blows and kicks."[11] By the end of these raids, the press reported that over 400 immigrants had been arrested, generally on charges that their papers were not in order, and after the Marseilles incident expulsions of foreigners increased dramatically.[12]

Police raids were not the sole means of cracking down on foreigners, however. Although Marchandeau, in the aftermath of the Marseilles incident, criticized the émigré community for having transported their civil wars to France, the Flandin administration used the Marseilles incident primarily as a pretext to crack down further on the approximately 800,000 immigrant workers in France as part of its anti-Depression campaign. As his minister of labor, Flandin appointed Adrien Marquet, a fanatic protectionist and proponent of the view that the Depression could be solved simply by eliminating immigrant workers,[13] and he also created a special Interministerial Commission, directed by Radical Party leader Edouard Herriot, to review the status of the immigrant labor in France. In late November, the Herriot Commission announced that its three major goals were to curb illegal immigration; to coordinate the immigration polices of the various ministries; and to enforce existing quotas on foreign workers. New work permits were not to be granted under any circumstances, and existing permits were to be renewed only in exceptional circumstances. From now on, only foreigners who had resided in France for at least five years would be permitted to renew their permits automatically. Otherwise, renewals were to be limited to foreigners who had lived in France at least two years, and even these were to be granted only after "an extremely thorough examination."[14]

Although the Herriot Commission repeatedly proclaimed its intent to carry out its mission in a humane manner, there is little doubt that its goal was to get rid of as many foreigners as possible, either through voluntary repatriation, or, if need be, through *refoulement* and expulsion.[15] To achieve this end, the administration began to make it more difficult to obtain not only work permits, but identity cards as well. Immigrants who did not possess work permits and who could not demonstrate independent financial means were now rounded up on charges of vagabondage and ordered to leave.[16] Furthermore, on February 6, 1935, the administration issued a new decree law stipulating that foreigners' identity cards would henceforth be valid only in the department in which they had been issued, thus severely curtailing immigrants' freedom of movement. This law further mandated that foreigners requesting identity cards had to show proof of having entered the country legally, a provision few refugees could meet.[17] According to another Ministry of Labor circular, dated February 12, police were instructed not to renew identity cards of foreigners who did not possess work permits unless they had lived in France more than ten years. Without an identity card, these foreigners too lost the legal right to remain in France, and even many longtime foreign residents now became vulnerable to *refoulement* and expulsion.[18]

Finally, to ensure rigorous enforcement of these measures, the government submitted a bill to Parliament on November 20 demanding tougher prison sentences for foreigners who failed to comply with expulsion orders—instead of the current maximum prison term of six months, the government requested a minimum six-month term.[19] Although this bill never made it through Parliament, Laval's right-wing administration had announced an almost identical decree law on October 31 that mandated prison sentences of six months to two years for such infractions, after which expulsion became mandatory. From the administration's point of view, such severity had become necessary since "public opinion, justly alarmed, has demanded the imposition of restrictions on the right of foreigners to settle freely in our country and engage in commerce or hold salaried positions there."[20]

Although this crackdown was not directed specifically against the refugees, they were obviously in a vulnerable position since the majority of them had never received work permits, and even those who had could not meet the residency requirements for renewing those permits. Thus, from the point of view of Jewish organizations, these measures marked the beginning of a mass expulsion. At a Comité National meeting on November 6, 1934, Bernhard Kahn warned that the government was planning a "wholesale expulsion" of the 15,000 to 17,000 refugees currently in France.[21] Morris Troper too noted that "the authorities here are determined to rid themselves of at least 15,000 refugees," and he pointed out that refugees were being given pink slips, or *refoulement* notices, in unprecedented numbers.[22] While Troper noted that although most refugees targeted so far were of East European origin, Germans were beginning to be rounded up as well, despite the fact that repatriation for them meant being sent to a concentration camp, a fate the French government was well aware of by early 1935.[23] In desperation, the refugees spent days on end at the Préfecture de Police—the "house of tears"—in an effort to secure a reprieve from a *refoulement* or an expulsion order, even if only temporarily.[24] Rarely were these appeals successful, however, and thousands of refugees were ordered to leave the country as if they were simply immigrant workers. Those who refused, if apprehended by the police, ended up in prison, where they languished for months, only to face upon their release the prospect of undergoing the cycle of *refoulement*, expulsion, arrest, and imprisonment all over again, since they remained illegal aliens. According to a legal expert for the League for the Rights of Man, if the decree laws were not abrogated, "prison would become the sole asylum for political refugees in France."[25]

For the refugees, this crackdown represented the most serious threat to date, and it elicited a spate of protests from pro-refugee groups, including the League for the Rights of Man, the Socialist Party, the HCR, the Comité National, and the Gourevitch Committee, an independent Jewish refugee committee. These organizations inundated the Flandin administration with petitions to exempt refugees from *refoulement* and expulsion and grant them a special refugee status.[26] Moreover, every one of these groups, with the exception of the Comité National, which was reluctant to single out Jewish refugees for special treatment, petitioned the government to grant refugees work permits as well. They concurred with the position of Victor Basch, president of the League for the Rights of Man, who declared, in an open letter to the prime minister in February 1935, "It is necessary to distinguish between economic emigration and political emigration." While acknowledging that the government was perhaps justified in asking economic immigrants "to return to their countries when there is no longer work here for them," political refugees could not be treated this way. "To subject them to *refoulement*, to expel them, despite the fact that they do not have formal permission to enter a neighboring country, is an act of barbarism," Basch maintained. He furthermore insisted that the right to asylum and the right to work were inseparable, since to deny refugees the right to work was tantamount to sentencing them "to die of hunger." If the government no longer intended to uphold the tradition of asylum, it was time, Basch proclaimed, to end the cruel pretense of the current policy and "frankly close the door to the refugees."[27]

These issues came to a head in late 1934 and early 1935 during a series of parliamentary debates over the refugee issue, sparked by the introduction of the severe antiforeign decree laws. These debates are significant in that they illustrate that the government had abandoned any commitment to asylum, not only in practice, but in theory as well. They furthermore attest to the fact that the refugees had strong advocates in Parliament, especially among the socialists, but also among some members of the Radical and Communist Parties. Moreover, the arguments put forth by the pro-refugee camp, and especially by its two leading spokesmen, the socialist deputies Marius Moutet, also a member of the Chamber's Commission on Civil Legislation, and Léon Blum, the Socialist Party leader, clearly foreshadow the refugee program later adopted by the Popular Front.

The case they put forth rested on three major points. First, they maintained that *refoulements* and expulsions were being carried out by the police in an excessively brutal and arbitrary fashion, without regard for refugee status. Second, they insisted that the problem of unwanted refugees could not be solved through punitive police measures, since these people had nowhere to go. As Moutet declared, to sentence them to "perpetual prison," was not only a waste of taxpayers' money, but also constituted "an inhumane situation that cannot endure."[28] Above all, they concurred with Basch that the government needed to distinguish more carefully between economic and political immigration. The conflation of these categories, and especially the practice of getting rid of all foreigners without work permits or independent financial means, had resulted in thousands of refugees being sent back to countries where their lives were in danger and in scores of others being sent to jail. Moreover, as Blum pointed out, the right to asylum could not be made dependent on wealth; to do so was to erect "the wall of money of the exile" (*le mur d'argent de l'exil*) an obvious play on the famous "wall of money" represented by France's 200 wealthiest families.[29] Most refugees, Blum insisted, were "precisely those who crossed the border alone, naked, without resources."[30]

Third, the pro-refugee camp challenged Herriot's contention that the right to asylum had no connection whatsoever with the right to work. Without the right to work, they insisted, asylum remained a hollow promise.[31] Because according to their estimates only about 13,000 refugees had so far requested work permits, the integration of these refugees into the national labor force could not possibly harm French workers. As an alternative to the current policy, Blum and Moutet proposed that refugees who constituted a real security risk be placed in labor camps, perhaps in the colonies, where they could be kept under police surveillance. In order to guarantee that true refugees not be expelled, they proposed the creation of a consultative commission, composed of representatives of diverse ministries, together with representatives of the various refugee committees, to screen the dossiers of individuals claiming refugee status.[32]

During these debates, the minister of the interior, Marcel Régnier, a member of the conservative wing of the Radical Party, staunchly defended the administration's point of view. In response to Moutet's charge that the government seemed more motivated by short-term economic interests than by a sincere commitment to asylum, Régnier responded that it was his "mission" to ensure that France not "become the refuge for the rest of the world's undesirables." Since France had retained relatively open borders, while most of her neighbors had closed theirs, "We have been invaded to such an extent that extremely serious incidents have taken place and court sentences against foreigners have been constantly on the rise." It was not the government's aim, Régnier insisted, to abandon the tradition of asylum. But due to the economic crisis and intense job competition, there was no choice but to subject political refugees to "the ordinary regime"—that is, those possessing work cards would be allowed to stay, together with those who could support themselves independently; all others would be asked to leave.

When Sabinus Valière, a socialist deputy, asked whether that meant that impoverished refugees were no longer eligible for asylum, Régnier replied in the affirmative: "If they don't have the means to live, yes. We don't have to nourish them. There are plenty enough unfortunate Frenchmen without our having to ensure the existence of foreigners." Moreover, in response to Moutet's proposal to create a consultative commission to screen the refugees, Régnier declared such a body to be unnecessary, since the Herriot Commission was already performing this task. When Moutet retorted that many real refugees were nevertheless being expelled and that some had committed suicide when confronted with the threat of imprisonment, Régnier's icy response was: "Alas, Frenchmen commit suicide too."[33]

The pro-refugee position received a boost when the Senate Foreign Relations Committee, headed by Henry de Jouvenel, issued a resolution in early 1935 sharply condemning the administration's refugee policy and calling for a more humane alternative that would protect bona fide refugees from arbitrary arrest and expulsion.[34] Régnier refused to budge, however, especially since his views had widespread parliamentary support, even among moderate circles. Herriot himself, who in 1933 had denounced Nazi antisemitism and had demanded a liberal refugee policy,[35] now clearly believed that the Depression could be solved only by eliminating foreign workers, and if refugees got caught up in the net of *refoulements* and expulsions, that was an unfortunate but unavoidable consequence.[36] At one point during these debates, Herriot even argued that any foreigner who had committed the most minor crime, such as writing a bad check, deserved to be expelled, whether or not a refugee.[37]

Furthermore, according to the *Journal Officiel*, the official record of parliamentary debates, Régnier's remarks drew widespread applause not only from the right wing of the Chamber, but from the center as well, and there is little doubt that a broad segment of the Radical Party shared his views.[38] Indeed, when compared to the statements of right-wing deputies during these debates, Régnier's remarks seem almost tepid. Xavier Vallat, the conservative deputy from the Ardèche who later became Vichy's first commissioner-general for Jewish questions, had insisted that even tougher anti-foreign police measures were necessary since foreigners had instigated every scandal and act of terrorism in recent years. Vallat furthermore reminded the Chamber that among these scoundrels, "there aren't many Christians." While he insisted that he was not personally opposed to "France . . . remaining a land of asylum," the overly generous asylum policies of the administration had transformed France into "a manure field that gives rise to a blossoming of scandals that is simply too nauseating . . . !" In an angry retort, Jacques Doriot, the popular mayor of the Paris suburb of Saint-Denis, who was still a left-wing deputy from the Seine despite his recent ouster from the Communist Party, pointed out that none of the foreigners mentioned by Vallat was a refugee. But that was precisely the point. For the political center and right, the distinction between immigrants and refugees had become completely blurred.[39]

Whether France would continue to uphold the right of asylum, however, was being put to the test at the very moment these debates were going on. By the late fall of 1934, Pierre Laval, who had been appointed foreign minister on October 13, made it clear that he would not object to the return of the Saar to Germany, a policy that stood in stark contrast to that of his predecessor, Louis Barthou, who had taken a hard-line policy toward Germany and almost certainly would have lobbied to secure a plebiscite vote either in favor of annexation to France or the maintenance of the status quo—that is, the existing League of Nations mandate. Barthou, however, had been assassinated in October, together with the Yugoslavian king, and Flandin, egged on by Laval, embarked on a policy of appeasement vis-à-vis the Nazis, of which the abandonment of the Saar was the first step.[40]

Like subsequent attempts at appeasement, this concession came at a high price: the recognition that there would be a renewed exodus of refugees from these territories. Although the Saar had been under a League of Nations mandate for the past fifteen years, the international community expected France to receive the bulk of the refugees, in part because many of them had been French citizens or Saarlanders who had worked for the pro-French cause, and in part because France had been the major beneficiary of the League of Nations mandate, having enjoyed exclusive rights to the Saar coalfields and having incorporated the Saar into its customs union. Thus, while the League agreed to provide financial credits for the resettlement of the 6,000 to 8,000 refugees expected to flee in the event of a pro-German vote, initial arrangements for receiving these refugees were left up to the French government.[41]

Although the French response to the Saar refugee crisis has frequently been hailed by historians as an example of French generosity,[42] the actual reception accorded these fugitives was profoundly ambivalent. To be sure, the Herriot Commission, which had been given the task in November of arranging the absorption of the refugees,[43] proclaimed on December 18 that "in principle, we cannot refuse to accord generously the right to asylum on our territory to Saarlanders who, because of their sentiments and political attitudes have reason to fear the return of the Saar to the Reich," and Laval publicly affirmed this pledge before the League of Nations on January 17.[44] It was decided that anyone with either a French passport or a visa from the French consulate in Saarbrücken would automatically be granted asylum, with the exception of non-naturalized East Europeans and Germans who had taken refuge in the Saar after the Nazi seizure of power.

As in the past, East Europeans were to be repatriated to their countries of origin, although it was decided, after some hesitation, that Nansen refugees would be accepted.[45] Germans not from the Saar were divided into two groups. The first consisted of political refugees and Jews from elsewhere in Germany who had fled to the Saar after the Nazi seizure of power and were now considered to be at great risk. These people were to be directed immediately to a special reception center in Strasbourg, the abandoned military barracks of Lizé-Nord, where they were to be turned over to the jurisdiction of the HCR, which had promised to resettle them in Latin America. The other group consisted of Germans who had been *refoulés* or expelled from France in the past and were still considered undesirable there; these people, the majority of whom were communists, were to be denied entry altogether.[46]

Aside from these groups, all other Saar refugees, including the region's Jewish population, which numbered about 5,000, were to be accorded asylum as long as they acquired a visa in advance.[47] Among these prospective refugees, the Jews, it should be noted, were considered a fairly desirable group. Not only were they materially well off, but according to the Treaty of Rome, which went into effect on March 1, 1935, they had the right to transfer their property and assets abroad, in sharp contrast to the restrictions on the export of capital pertaining to refugees elsewhere in the Reich, and they were granted a one-year grace period to liquidate their affairs. During this grace period, the Treaty of Rome further prohibited the Nazis from implementing antisemitic legislation and engaging in acts of violence against the local population.[48]

Despite these plans for a liberal asylum policy, the French began to renege on their commitments almost as soon as the refugees began to arrive. On the day after the plebiscite, Flandin announced that he did not expect a refugee crisis to materialize since he was "persuaded that the German Government . . . is fully aware how to respect the rights of minorities and in so doing [will] prevent any emigration from the Saar."[49] At this moment, however, thousands of individuals had already descended upon the French consulate in Saarbrücken in a desperate effort to secure visas. Although the consulate had every intention of granting visas as liberally as possible, it was unable to handle the flood. According to Guy Brun, the vice-consul in Saarbrücken, the consular staff was working around the clock to process visa applications, and it had even recruited local school teachers to help with this task. By the end of the first week, the consulate had succeeded in processing 8,019 visas. Still, Brun noted, many who needed visas had not yet received them, and on January 18, 1935, he requested that some of these people, mostly political activists, be allowed to cross the border without visas, since their lives were in immediate danger.[50]

As a result of this frantic run on the consulate, estimates of the magnitude of the anticipated exodus shot up dramatically. Some officials reported an expected influx of 40,000 individuals, a figure far higher than the initial League of Nations estimate, and Brun predicted that as many as 100,000 to 150,000 persons would eventually emigrate.[51] As these reports filtered in, the French government began to exert mounting pressure on the League to take full responsibility for the relief effort as well as the eventual resettlement of the refugees. On January 18, it submitted a memorandum to the League stating that France "cannot continue to assume these burdens and cannot leave the door open to an immigration into its territory if it is not assured of an effective collaboration from the League of Nations."[52] When the League rejected this request, citing a lack of funds, the Ministry of the Interior retaliated by closing the border completely on January 24.[53] The Ministry furthermore contemplated the expulsion of the 400 German refugees from the Saar currently held in the Lizé-Nord camp in Strasbourg, despite the fact that this group was considered most at risk by the HCR.[54]

Whether the decision to close the border was carried out for "home consumption," as the *New York Times* suggested, or whether the minister of the interior, together with his security chief, began to fear a deluge of refugees, many of whom were communists, is not entirely clear.[55] What is clear, however, is that the closing of the border set off a wave of panic through the refugee population, and greatly antagonized a significant sector of French and international public opinion, as well as the Foreign Ministry, including the French vice-consul in Saarbrücken and the League of Nations–appointed Saar governing authorities, none of whom had been consulted in this matter. Foreign Ministry officials were furious. The herculean efforts of the consulate to review visa applications had now been "reduced to nothing," since even visa holders were being turned away at the border as if they had no papers at all.[56]

At the same time, the Foreign Ministry pointed out that this reversal of policy had severely damaged France's reputation abroad, especially since the government had publicly committed itself to ensuring asylum for Saar refugees. In an internal memorandum of January 25, the Quai d'Orsay noted that although it too believed that ultimate responsibility for the refugees resided with the League, the League's refusal to accept responsibility did not relieve France of its obligations. For these people, whose lives were in grave danger, France served as the sole escape route out of Germany. "Under these conditions," the Foreign Ministry noted, "we could not fail to be held responsible by international opinion if serious incidents were to occur, in which partisans of the status quo or reattachment to France would be the victims." Moreover, this memorandum noted, on the day of the border closing "a state of agitation had been provoked in Saarbrücken by the news that the French border authorities had decided on a massive *refoulement* of refugees who had arrived with visas."[57] The Saar Governmental Commission, presided over by Sir Geoffrey-George Knox, similarly protested to Laval, claiming that it "could not believe the measures just taken by the border authorities have met with the approval of the government of the Republic, especially since these measures seem to contradict the solemn declarations made by Your Excellency at the Meeting of the League of Nations Council on January 17, 1935."[58] Worst of all, as Brun noted, this decision had dire consequences for the refugees themselves. At the border, women were throwing themselves under trucks in order not to be sent back, and several police officers in charge of processing the refugees walked away from their posts, sickened by the heartrending scenes.[59]

In response to this outcry, Régnier was forced to reverse the border closing on January 25, only one day after the policy had been put into effect.[60] Nevertheless, even then, he attempted to implement a secret policy whereby only 6 percent of Saar refugees holding visas would be allowed to cross the border.[61] Once again, the Foreign Ministry was livid, claiming that such a quota negated the selection process conducted by the consulate and in practice amounted to a renewed closure of the border.[62] The Ministry of the Interior was again forced to retreat, and on January 30 the borders were reopened to visa holders. Nevertheless, the selection process at the border remained rigorous. According to a Foreign Ministry report of March 13, 12,063 persons with visas had presented themselves at the border in the weeks immediately following the plebiscite, but only 5,538 of these had been accepted, and of these another 586 had been *refoulés* after undergoing an initial screening process at one of the reception camps.[63] By this date, the Foreign Ministry noted that only a few hundred Saar refugees with independent financial means were residing in France, as well as 4,902 indigent refugees, of whom 750 were Germans and 220 French citizens, a far cry from the 40,000 originally predicted.[64]

France thus received the refugees, albeit reluctantly. The question of whether they would be allowed to stay, however, had not yet been resolved. Although Foreign Ministry spokesmen admitted that the majority of Saar refugees could be absorbed without great difficulty,[65] the administration nevertheless remained committed to getting rid of as many of them as possible, no matter how few their number. As René Massigli, chief of the French delegation to the League of Nations, declared, although France had a moral obligation to grant asylum to refugees who had worked for the pro-French cause, it did not have to keep them forever.[66] This strategy was most apparent with respect to the granting of work permits. Although the Herriot Commission had decided to send Saar refugees without independent financial means to agricultural departments in southwestern France, it asserted from the start that these refugees could remain there only temporarily.[67] The majority of the refugees were ultimately to be sent to Latin America, a task for which the League had promised financial credits, while efforts were also made to send political refugees to the Soviet Union and Jewish refugees to Palestine.[68]

Not everyone in the administration agreed with this policy. The Foreign Ministry believed that France had no choice but to absorb the majority of Saar refugees and that the persistent efforts to send them away were futile. As Foreign Ministry officials pointed out, no more than 100 refugees had expressed interest in going to Latin America, and Great Britain remained as reluctant as ever to grant Palestine certificates to refugees already in France.[69] Moreover, as the Foreign Ministry recognized, the cost of sending these refugees to Latin America, even with a credit of 200,000 Swiss francs from the League, was certain to exceed the cost of allowing them to remain in France. Finally, the Foreign Ministry insisted, in an argument that would become even more compelling in the years to come, it made little sense to send these refugees away when France's southwestern departments were suffering a severe population shortage due to massive urbanization and a persistently low birthrate.[70]

The minister of the interior, together with the Herriot Commission, stood firm, however, and refused to grant work permits for more than three-month periods, even for refugees engaged in agricultural pursuits.[71] As L.-O. Frossard, who became minister of labor in June of 1935, explained, "it is important to avoid any measure that might convey the impression that the [situation of] the Saarlanders is being stabilized on our territory, in order to safeguard the rights of our country vis-à-vis the League of Nations, upon whom the definitive solution to the Saar refugee problem depends."[72] The only group of Saar refugees that from the start was granted permission not only to remain in France but also to settle wherever they wished, with the exception of Alsace and Lorraine, were those who could demonstrate independent financial means, a group that included most Jews.

Although several hundred Saar refugees eventually left for Palestine, the Soviet Union, and Latin America, and especially Paraguay,[73] the majority stayed in France, despite the strenuous efforts of the Ministry of the Interior to get rid of them. In large measure, they remained because of the scarcity of emigration options. But they also remained because their situation began to improve in the fall of 1935. In September, the League of Nations, with the consent of the French government, brought the Saar refugees under the Nansen regime, and they were henceforth protected against arbitrary *refoulement* and expulsion.[74] Moreover, with the advent of the Popular Front in the spring of 1936, their situation, especially with respect to work permits and naturalization, would improve significantly, as did that of other German refugees already settled in France.[75] In addition, the refugees from the Saar were ultimately treated as a somewhat privileged group. In July 1935, the Parliament exempted Saar refugee doctors from the provisions of the Nast Law, allowing them to practice in France, although lawyers were denied similar benefits despite an appeal from the Foreign Ministry on their behalf.[76]

Although the Saar refugee crisis was ultimately resolved on a positive note, the reception of these refugees was by no means the straightforward process frequently depicted by historians. Nearly every promise originally made to these refugees had been broken along the way, although the Foreign Ministry invariably intervened to repair the situation. This episode further reveals the utter lack of coordination among the various ministries responsible for refugee policy, despite the fact that the Herriot Commission had been created in part to remedy this problem. In the case of the Saar refugees, the Ministry of the Interior, and especially the Sûreté Nationale, repeatedly assumed a hard-line position, arguing in favor of a complete closure of the border and massive *refoulements*, including even refugees who had been granted visas, whereas the Foreign Ministry remained committed to upholding France's treaty obligations and believed that it had a moral duty not to abandon these people, on whom France had relied for many years to support its interests in the Saar. This ministerial chaos, as we shall see, ultimately led pro-refugee groups to demand the creation of a special Ministry of Immigration that would coordinate refugee policy. It also fueled demands, especially on the left, for the creation of a special immigration statute that would lay out the rights of immigrants in general and refugees in particular so that they would no longer be vulnerable to arbitrary arrest and expulsion.[77]

Aside from the Saar refugees, who were accepted in a less than hospitable manner, the attitude toward other refugees from Germany hardened significantly in 1935. As we have seen, the new anti-immigrant decree laws of 1935 regarding the issuance of work permits and identity cards, as well as the exclusion of immigrants from a variety of professions, resulted in massive *refoulements* and expulsions, which deeply eroded the right to asylum.[78] Even refugees previously protected by international guarantees, such as Nansen refugees, began to feel threatened. In November, the minister of the interior reported mounting complaints from several prefects regarding the large number of stateless foreigners, "especially certain Central European nationals," who were "without resources, incapable of finding work, frequently undesirable and who it is impossible to expel." Although the minister refused to sanction their expulsion, claiming that "it is morally impossible to send them back to their country of origin, where they risk incurring severe condemnations," he nevertheless added that his office had already taken measures, such as making it more difficult for them to claim French-born children, in an effort to persuade them to leave.[79]

This hard-line attitude was apparent in naturalization statistics as well. Although 24,763 foreigners had been naturalized in 1933, that figure dropped to 17,090 in 1934, and to 15,293 in 1935, the lowest level since the 1927 naturalization law, which had reduced the residency requirement for citizenship from ten to three years, had gone into effect.[80] In July 1935, the HCR high commissioner, James G. McDonald, denounced the increasingly hard-line policies of all European nations of asylum, and France was undoubtedly at the forefront of his thoughts: "The refusal of the right to work and the destitution which follows in certain cases can only drive the victims to despair," McDonald declared. "Cases of suicide and the death of children through malnutrition are not rare, and it is surprising that not more have been driven to subversive activities." Above all, he noted, in light of their small numbers, these refugees posed no appreciable economic threat.[81] McDonald's exhortations fell on deaf ears, however, since only one month later France embarked on another massive round of *refoulements*, which again included many refugees who had previously been promised asylum and whose papers were in perfect order.[82] Moreover, these *refoulements* were carried out despite desperate appeals from German Jewish leaders, who informed French diplomats that the returnees were being sent to concentration camps.[83]

In light of this determination to rid the country of immigrants and refugees already there, it is not surprising that the government had no desire to welcome further refugees from Germany. Already in the spring of 1935, the

Ministry of the Interior had sent out a directive to the police and prefects stating, "My attention has recently been drawn to the German nationals condemned to sterilization by their government who might try to seek refuge on our territory. To avoid such an eventuality, I have the honor of informing you that there is good reason *to oppose by all means possible the entry of these individuals into our country.*" These people, the ministry insisted, were to be "*mercilessly* refused entry into France."[84] Moreover, as we have seen, every effort was made to separate German refugees coming from the Saar from longtime Saar residents to ensure that the former not be permitted to remain.

Yet it was the administration's response to the prospect of renewed Jewish immigration after the declaration of the Nuremberg Laws on September 15, 1935, that offers the best test of how hard-line this policy had become. Notwithstanding Nazi claims that these laws were intended to stabilize the situation of German Jews, French diplomats were fully aware that this legislation marked the beginning of a new and more serious stage in their persecution. According to Charles Corbin, France's ambassador in Britain, these laws "have practically made impossible any future, and nearly any present, for Jews across the Rhine," and he warned that "several hundreds of thousands of individuals" would seek to emigrate.[85] Similarly, the French vice-consul in Munich, who only months before had dismissed Jewish fears as unfounded, now reported that "one can easily understand that . . . the Jews may not be satisfied with the new charter the Aryans, in their magnanimity, wish to accord them," and he too predicted a renewed Jewish exodus. He furthermore noted, together with French intelligence services in Alsace, that growing numbers of Jews were being incarcerated and sent to concentration camps and that some had even been murdered at Dachau.[86] Thus, for French officials, the Nuremberg Laws laid to rest any lingering suspicions that German antisemitism might be a marginal phenomenon destined to subside. As Christian de Vaux Saint-Cyr, the French consul in Munich noted, every one of his contacts who knew Hitler personally was "persuaded that he will never make any concession on the Jewish question. The Chancellor is above all an antisemite."[87]

This knowledge, however, did nothing to soften the administration's attitude toward Jews seeking to escape, and soon after the Nuremberg Laws were announced, the administration took steps to ensure that these decrees "not provoke an exodus of German nationals, especially Jews, not to mention foreign Jews currently living in Germany." In sharp contrast to the policy enacted after Hitler's seizure of power, the Foreign Ministry, in a highly confidential circular of October 10, 1935, urged French consular officials to issue visas only with extreme circumspection and in strict conformity with the restrictive guidelines laid out at the end of 1933. Border surveillance was to be reinforced "to discourage any attempt at illegal immigration." As the Foreign Ministry explained, "It seems superfluous . . . to insist on the inconveniences and risks of this new emigration following the 1933 exodus, whose repercussions we have now been able to assess completely."[88] Similarly, in late November, the Ministry of the Interior insisted that "the entry of new refugees into France remains formally prohibited regardless of the motive invoked."[89]

This hard-line position was apparent at the League of Nations as well. Just days after the Nuremberg Laws were announced, Bérenger delivered a speech in which he claimed that "France can no longer accept financial sacrifices on behalf of the German refugees, who little by little must return to . . . their countries of origin."[90] These remarks delighted the Nazi press, which pointed out how far Bérenger had moved from his 1933 position, in which he had sought to "transform the refugee question into an arm of combat against 'German fascism.'" His change of heart, these German papers argued, had little to do with financial considerations. Rather, it stemmed exclusively from France's "disagreeable experiences over time vis-à-vis the victims of 'German fascism,' who initially had been received with great fanfare."[91] Notwithstanding these taunts, no one within the administration objected to Bérenger's remarks, in sharp contrast to the situation that had prevailed during the Saar refugee crisis. As Corbin advised in early 1936, despite mounting public outrage over the Nuremberg Laws in the West, and especially in Britain, it was imperative that France stay the course: "All evidence suggests that France is saturated, and the economic crisis we are experiencing does not enable us to foresee the moment when we might once again reveal a more liberal attitude with respect to the admission of foreigners." Any long-term solution to the Jewish refugee crisis, Corbin noted, now depended on the Anglo-Saxon countries with their wealthier Jewish communities.[92]

By 1935, pro-refugee activist Henri Levin could state unequivocally that "today we are witnessing . . . the application of a policy toward foreigners that is the exact opposite of that formerly practiced."[93] Not only was France determined to take no further newcomers, but every effort was being made to rid the country of foreigners already there, including the 10,000 to 12,000 German Jews who had remained in France since 1933, not to mention the thousands of East European Jews who had been forced to flee Germany as well.[94] At the end of January 1935, the government announced plans to close down the military barracks that had hitherto housed many of the German refugees,[95] and although both the JDC and the HCR would have preferred that these refugees be settled permanently in France, the

Comité National, as we will see, towed the government line and insisted that the majority of them leave, although it did endeavor to ensure that they not be sent back to Germany.

Two prominent refugee activists, the mathematician Emil Gumbel, and the journalist Berthold Jacob (who, in a much publicized incident had been kidnapped by the Nazis in March of 1935 but was subsequently released), reported in November that the majority of refugees in France "have received orders of expulsion, and it is only because the French do not take their bureaucracy too seriously that all of them have not been shipped across the border."[96] Moreover, as we have seen, since most refugees could not be sent away, they generally landed in French jails as a result of the decree laws. A spokesman for the League for the Rights of Man and Citizen poignantly described their plight: "Hunted down in countries under dictatorships, turned away from those countries still free, the political exile no longer knows where to go. If he resides in France and France expels him, his only choice is to commit suicide or refuse to obey an expulsion order."[97]

Yet if the goal of this policy was to rid France of its refugee population, it was becoming clear, at least to some officials, that the policy was not working. Although the Foreign Ministry had tried throughout 1934 and 1935 to persuade the HCR to assume a greater share of responsibility for the refugee crisis, including the reemigration of refugees already on French soil, this effort at "internationalization" had proven a dismal failure. Other countries had no wish to receive these refugees, and the HCR had no leverage to force them to do so, largely because the European democracies, including France, had refused to give the HCR any independent political power or, for that matter, even a budget.[98] Hence, although several of France's representatives at the HCR, especially Jacques Helbronner, who also played a key role in the Jewish relief effort, continued to insist that France would not serve as a "dumping ground," and that even refugees already in France would have to leave,[99] other French diplomats at the League, such as René Massigli and Joseph Paganon, who was appointed minister of the interior in June 1935, began to recognize that the League would never relieve France of her refugee burden.[100] As Paganon noted, the goal of the HCR was not to help France get rid of her refugees, but "to stabilize the existing situation"—that is, to pressure refugee-receiving countries, such as France, to absorb their existing refugee populations so that the HCR could concentrate on the more pressing problem of finding havens for refugees still leaving Germany. Although Paganon acknowledged that such a policy was "unfavorable toward those rare countries like our own, which had committed the imprudence of welcoming the foreigners too generously," he nevertheless conceded that refugees already in France, whose lives were in danger, could not be returned to their native countries.[101]

Hence, in sharp contrast to Régnier, Paganon was willing to consider several options that would allow at least a portion of the refugees to stay in France. In response to pressure from the Gourevitch Committee, he was, for the first time, willing to investigate the possibility of establishing agricultural settlements for refugees in southwestern France.[102] Moreover, he issued two circulars in November exempting stateless foreigners and refugees from expulsion, as mandated by the decree law of October 30, 1935, except if they had committed felonies or engaged in subversive behavior.[103] To be sure, many refugees, especially East European Jews, continued to be expelled, since the Sûreté Nationale refused to recognize them as stateless.[104] Still, the mere fact that such a circular had been issued shows that the administration was beginning to perceive a need to separate the refugees from the rest of the immigrant population.

Moreover, the administration in early 1936 finally decided to ratify the League of Nations convention of October 28, 1933, which protected Nansen refugees against arbitrary *refoulement* and expulsion, although the final stages of this process were concluded only after the election of the Popular Front.[105] More significantly, it agreed to a League request to extend Nansen refugee status to German refugees in anticipation of the merging of the HCR and the Nansen Office, whose mandate expired in 1938.[106] Once again, this decision marked a considerable shift away from the administration's previous stance that under no circumstances should a special international status be accorded German refugees because such a status might attract even more refugees to France, in addition to making it nearly impossible for the government to expel them.[107] Some French diplomats also argued that such a move could needlessly embroil France in political complications with Germany since it would appear that France was allowing itself to be transformed into a haven for the anti-Nazi resistance.[108] Nevertheless, under the more liberal premiership of Albert Sarraut, who took office in late January 1936, the administration began to move away from this hard-line view, which was becoming untenable for practical as well as humanitarian reasons. Moreover, at the end of 1935 Paganon even announced his willingness to countenance a limited naturalization of certain groups of refugees in order to make them eligible for military service.[109]

Although certain sectors of the administration were beginning to realize that there was little choice but to regularize the legal status of the remaining refugee population, only the political left was willing to argue that the refugees deserved the right to work as well. Still, the question of how to achieve this goal without provoking an uproar among the those middle-class groups that felt threatened by refugee competition remained unresolved. A possible solution had been raised during this first phase of the refugee crisis—the settlement of refugees in agricultural regions, either in the colonies or in southwestern France. As we will see in Chapter 7, these schemes, with the exception of the settlement of Saar refugees in the southwest, did not go beyond the planning stage in these years, in part because of opposition from the official Jewish community, and in part because the Foreign Ministry and the Ministry of Colonies feared that such schemes would attract even more refugees to France. Nevertheless, these proposals had considerable support across the political spectrum. On the right, they were seen as a less costly alternative to prison; on the left, they were perceived as a humane solution to the refugee problem, one that provided a way out of the perennial conundrum of how to assure refugees the right to asylum and the right to work without granting them work permits, a move that would inevitably provoke popular outrage.[110]

For those in the administration less concerned with finding a more humane solution to the refugee question, a more insidious alternative began to be bandied about as well—the idea of sending indigent refugees who could not be expelled to internment camps, preferably in the colonies, where they would be placed under police surveillance and subjected to forced labor. As Charles Magny, director of the Sûreté Nationale, explained in a press interview in November 1934, the sole solution to the "lamentable state of affairs" created by the inability of the administration to expel "undesirable" refugees was to send them "to a concentration camp," where they would be "subjected to hard labor for a fairly long period of time." "For whomever penetrates even a little into the question of foreigners in France," Magny stressed, "this is the sole solution before which certain nations have not recoiled."[111] In the spring of 1935, Régnier began to look into this possibility, but such plans were dropped when Paganon took over in the fall because he believed that internment would be declared unconstitutional by the Council of State.[112] Due to his reluctance, and especially the Popular Front's electoral victory, such schemes were temporarily shunted to the back burner. Nevertheless, the idea of camps was by no means dead. Instead, it would resurface in 1938 when the refugee crisis reached a second acute phase, and it was ultimately incorporated into the Daladier administration's anti-immigrant decree laws.

Thus, on the eve of the Popular Front, the administration had clearly reached an impasse. While many on the political right continued to advocate a hard-line policy, the political left—socialists as well as communists—were increasingly disgruntled over the anti-immigrant decree laws and the abandonment of France's traditional commitment to refugee asylum. Moreover, by the end of 1935, several officials from within the administration itself, such as Paganon, were beginning to push for a more humane solution to the problem, one that would not force refugees into prison or concentration camps but would instead allow the majority of those who had already arrived in France to remain there. The problem, as always, was to reconcile this desire for a more humane solution with the popular consensus not to allow refugees to work, especially in those middle-class professions widely perceived to be overcrowded: commerce, artisanry, and the liberal professions.

In light of this dilemma, the Popular Front would be forced to search for new solutions. The colonial and agricultural schemes that had been raised during this period, but that had never received much attention, would be revived. At the same time, the new left-wing coalition would endeavor to implement a more humane policy insofar as the allocation of identity cards, work permits, and naturalization were concerned. Whether such a policy could be successful, especially in light of middle-class opposition, is the question we will return to in Chapter 6. Before doing so, however, we will need to examine two other facets of the refugee question between 1933 and 1936: the question of public opinion outside the arena of parliamentary institutions, and the role of the Franco-Jewish community.

CHAPTER FOUR

The Great Invasion I, 1933–36

We have already examined some of the ways in which popular opinion, particularly through the medium of middle-class professional organizations, influenced the formulation of official refugee policy between 1933 and 1936. It nevertheless remains worthwhile to examine the broad outlines of the popular debate over the refugee question, in part to analyze the major themes of this debate, but also to assess the shifting nature of the political coalitions that lent their support to the pro- and anti-refugee causes. As we will see, by 1936, when the Popular Front came to power, every theme in the anti-refugee arsenal was already in place. By this time, extreme-right-wing spokesmen commonly referred to the influx of German refugees as an "invasion" that threatened to destroy the country from within. Politically, these spokesmen insisted, the refugees constituted a threat, in part because of their ingrained German character, which gave rise to fifth-column fears, but most significantly because of their left-wing sympathies, which threatened to exacerbate Franco-German relations abroad and to embitter relations between left and right at home.

Economically, the refugees were perceived as dangerous, not so much because they threatened to steal jobs from French workers, but, as we have seen, because they threatened to compete with the French middle classes. These fears were further heightened by the urban character of this immigration, since middle-class competition was fiercest in the cities and since cities were considered fertile breeding grounds for communist insurrection. And although France's persistent population deficit led the nation's top demographic experts to argue in favor of continued immigration and against the mass expulsions of immigrants carried out by the administrations of Flandin and Laval, these same experts nearly always deemed Jewish refugees undesirable and unassimilable, in view of their urban and middle-class character and their alleged left-wing politics.

While these anti-refugee themes were largely in place by 1936, the coalition of groups that supported these claims changed significantly over time. For the period between 1933 and 1936, the debate over the refugees broke down fairly neatly along right/left lines, with the extreme right taking the lead in advancing the anti-refugee cause while a broad-based coalition of liberals and leftists articulated the pro-refugee position. In between, there was a mass of more moderate public opinion that expressed some degree of ambivalence. Although they shared many of the concerns of the far right about the refugees, particularly insofar as they believed that the refugees constituted a threat to the security of the French middle classes, these spokesmen nevertheless did not, on the whole, favor a complete closure of the borders.

After 1936, however, the makeup of these coalitions would change significantly. Although the right/left dichotomy would continue to hold, increasing numbers of moderates began to move into the anti-refugee camp, propelled by growing fears of war, which they, like their counterparts on the far right, tended to blame on the refugees and the Jews in general, as well as by a visceral hatred of the far left, which was invariably identified with the Jewish socialist leader Léon Blum. As a result of these factors, which will be examined in greater detail in Chapter 12, by the end of the decade even many moderates began to demand a complete halt to refugee asylum, resorting to the paranoid and hysterical rhetoric of "invasion," previously the prerogative of the extreme right. Still, as we shall see, the pro-refugee camp, while diminished in size by the late 1930's, was never decimated completely, and indeed, it continued to score important political victories as late as 1939. Notwithstanding the commonly held view that the pro-refugee camp was weak and ineffectual, in reality this camp remained a vibrant force throughout the decade. It was only as a result of the military defeat of 1940 and Vichy's coming to power that this camp's voice was ultimately silenced.

That the anti-refugee campaign between 1933 and 1936 was led primarily by the forces of the far right is not surprising in view of their traditionally xenophobic and antisemitic attitudes. To be sure, one might have expected the far right's deep-seated Germanophobia to have encouraged it to show some sympathy for the victims of Nazi persecution. As several commentators pointed out, the barbaric face of Nazi antisemitism seemed to confirm the traditional right-wing analysis of the German threat—an analysis that during the 1920's had contrasted sharply with that of the British, the Americans, and French liberals like Aristide Briand. Nevertheless, the leagues and parties of the far right, in contrast to some of their more moderate conservative colleagues, refrained from exploiting Nazi antisemitism to further their anti-German vendetta.[1] Instead, their antisemitism took priority over their anti-German sentiments, a trend that may well have contributed to the eventual decision of these groups to abandon their previously unyielding stance toward Germany in favor of a more conciliatory approach. Already by the summer of 1932, the Action Française, according to a police report, was watching events in Germany closely "to pursue more vigorously the battle against the *'métèques'* and the Jews, whose number in Paris is growing incessantly."[2] Similarly, as soon as the refugees began to arrive, the literary critic Paul Morand admonished the government to make sure that other countries absorbed their appropriate share. Otherwise, he warned, France would be submerged by a wave of antisemitism that would hit not only the newcomers, but even the long-established Jewish community.[3]

To make the case that the refugees, though few in number, constituted a serious economic and political threat, extreme-right-wing spokesmen constantly stressed the nation's alleged political and economic weaknesses. Politically, a popular theme of these years was that the refugees, despite their anti-Nazi sympathies, remained intrinsically German and could therefore be expected one day to betray their French benefactors. As Gaston Le Provost de Launay, an influential member of the Paris Municipal Council and head of the Bonapartist Committee of the Seine, declared in a 1933 petition to the prefect of police, these refugees "remain Germans at heart" despite their current disagreement with the Hitler regime.[4] The warhorse of the Action Française, Léon Daudet, went further and suggested that they constituted a potential reservoir of traitors. So eager were these "Semitic emigrants" to "return to grace in the eyes of the German authorities" that they were certain to "place themselves at the command of the latter in the event of war and invasion."[5] J. Gouilloud, president of the Ligue du Bien Public, similarly reminded his compatriots that these refugees, who "only yesterday were our enemies in arms . . . are likely to become so again tomorrow."[6] Even government officials occasionally endorsed this view. The prefect of the Haut-Rhin, for example, refused to grant a residence permit to a German woman who wanted to join her German Jewish fiancé in Alsace, claiming that "she remains a good German and the antipathy she currently displays [toward Germany] is directed solely against the Hitler regime."[7]

Such suspicions quickly gave rise to charges that the refugees were engaged in nefarious pro-Nazi espionage. In January 1934, the Paris police received an anonymous letter signed "a good French woman who is warning you as all patriots ought to do" insinuating that the refugees were necessarily spies given their well-to-do demeanor and frequent phone calls to Berlin.[8] Léon Bailby's extreme-right-wing paper, *Le Jour*, similarly speculated that the largely middle-class Jewish refugees living in the Paris suburb of Neuilly were spies since they lived in relative affluence, despite the fact that the Nazis had blocked their bank accounts in Germany so that they could not transfer their assets abroad and despite the fact that they had been denied work permits in France. In the event of a Franco-German war, Bailby insisted, echoing Daudet, there was no doubt that these refugees would return to Germany.[9] Even some Jews, such as the publicist Emmanuel Berl, criticized the administration's policy of allowing refugees to enter France without controls as foolish since "numerous spies and agents" had infiltrated their ranks.[10] When the émigré journalist Berthold Jacob was kidnapped by the Nazis in Switzerland in 1935 after having been lured there by a former member of the German Social Democratic Party, the Parisian daily, *Le Matin*, ran the headline: "Beware of the German Socialists." Who, *Le Matin* asked, could be better suited than the socialists to serve as Nazi agents abroad?[11]

As this headline suggests, however, it was the left-wing character of the refugees that elicited the most vehement reaction from the far right. While *L'Action française* relentlessly harped on the theme of a Germanic-Jewish-Bolshevik invasion, it was the two papers owned by the perfume magnate François Coty, *L'Ami du peuple* and *Le Figaro*, that seized the lead in propounding this view.[12] Sending these Jewish Bolsheviks to France was, Coty maintained, a premeditated German plot designed to destroy France from within: "In their secret councils and even in their public meetings, they [the Germans] have investigated what measures to take so that the dreadful immigrants can find housing and resources in France while awaiting the Great Evening."[13] To prevent this doomsday prophecy from becoming reality, Coty advised the government to erect a "cordon sanitaire as in the case of plague or cholera" and to herd those refugees already in the country into concentration camps.[14] So great were Coty's fears of German-Jewish bolshevism that he even opposed the effort to secure an academic chair for Albert Einstein, insisting that the intent of this maneuver was to "install communism at the Collège de France."[15]

While Coty's rhetoric was by far the most inflammatory, the demand that the refugees abstain from political activity on French soil and that they, because of their left-wing views, had brought their unfortunate fate upon themselves, became standard themes of the French right by 1936. In 1933, Le Provost de Launay railed in the Paris Municipal Council against the refugees and their left-wing patrons in the Ligue Internationale Contre l'Antisémitisme (LICA; International League Against Antisemitism) who, he stated, were engaging in violent anticlerical diatribes. "We cannot allow this German immigration to Paris to serve as a pretext," he proclaimed, "for the renewal of the revolutionary or anti-Catholic campaign." If the refugees did not want "to render their situation intolerable," Le Provost de Launay sternly warned them to exercise "extreme discretion in their choice of protectors."[16]

Directly referring to the participation of many refugees in the anti-right-wing street demonstrations of February 12, 1934, Gaëtan Sanvoisin of *Le Figaro* lamented that "Hitler has sent us some 50,000 German Jews who are, for the most part, extremely dangerous revolutionaries."[17] The well-known psychiatrist and publicist, Dr. Edouard Toulouse, similarly wondered why the refugees had come to France rather than the Soviet Union since "every Jew is open to communist ideas and the Bolshevik leaders aren't suspected of being antisemitic."[18] In a 1935 series on the refugees, a journalist for *Le Matin*, Jean Lassere, claimed that the majority of refugees were in fact "dubious personages" whose flight from Germany was heralded by the German people as a "deliverance." These refugees, Lassere argued, would be inclined to foment social revolution, since only through such an upheaval could they even contemplate restoring their former positions. And while conceding France's desperate need for "new blood" to compensate for its serious population shortfall, Lassere insisted that "certain races are unadaptable." The task that lay ahead, therefore, was to choose new immigrants "with discernment."[19]

Together with this fear that the refugees would shore up the ranks of the revolutionary left in France, right-wing spokesmen also expressed concern that the refugees would seek to encourage France to declare war against Hitler to satisfy their personal lust for revenge. The clearest formulation of this theme in the early 1930's was Jérôme and Jean Tharaud's popular essay, *Quand Israël n'est plus roi*, which appeared at the end of 1933. Describing their recent travels through Central Europe, the Tharaud brothers claimed that the Jewish refugees they had encountered in Prague had no qualms whatsoever about "setting Europe on fire in order to appease Israel." One refugee, who before his exile had been the director of a major pacifist paper in Germany, was quoted as having called on France to launch a preemptory military strike against Germany: "In three years, it will be too late," he declared. "By then she [Germany] will have attacked you, and you'll be lost." Einstein too the Tharauds insisted, had undergone a similar transformation. "Yesterday an integral pacifist, today he declares that every free man is duty-bound to take up arms to defend his liberty against the barbarism issuing forth from across the Rhine." In light of this newfound Jewish bellicosity, the Tharauds warned the refugees, and indeed Jews in general, to be more discreet in their political behavior. Otherwise, they predicted, there would be an unprecedented antisemitic backlash for which the Jews would have only themselves to blame.[20] The right-wing publicist Alfred Fabre-Luce fully agreed and insisted that in light of the refugees' "spirit of revenge . . . antisemitism or anti-marxism might appear legitimate movements of defense."[21]

Complaints regarding the destructive nature of the refugees spilled over into the social and cultural realms as well. Not only were the refugees, together with other foreigners, charged with engaging in drug trafficking and a host of other criminal activities, but they were also accused of having imported a range of previously unknown exotic diseases and of clogging French hospital beds at taxpayers' expense.[22] Culturally too they were depicted as a disintegrative element. Camille Mauclair, art critic for *L'Ami du peuple*, excoriated German modernist artists and claimed that their creations were "frightful, completely lacking in taste or talent." "It is no accident," Mauclair declared, "that the vast majority of critics and art dealers of the avant-garde are Jews."[23] Other commentators warned that the aesthetic physiognomy of the nation was at stake. The refugees were ruining the "tidy and graceful visage" of Paris, according to Sanvoisin,[24] while E. Gascoin bemoaned the fact that the neighborhood around the Hôtel de Ville, the traditional Jewish quarter of Paris, had become a "veritable caravansary of all the scum from the Near East."[25]

In Alsace, according to historian Robert Redslob, the influx of the refugees was having the unfortunate effect of causing High German to become once again the lingua franca of the province, a development "fraught with danger." Nowadays, Redslob proclaimed, *Hochdeutsch* could be heard everywhere:

It's posted in streets and public places; it's spoken there without the least hesitation, I'd say even with a commanding tone and with those blasting voices peculiar to [the taste] of the other side of the Rhine, which resound like the clarion calls of a conquering army. Ah! How painful it is for us, Alsatians, to hear once again those accents that remind us of the militarism and harsh oppression of Antan! One must believe that we have been condemned to bear until our last breath those fifes and drum voices.

If the government did not stop this invasion immediately, Redslob warned, "Soon we will no longer be in our own home. Our country will revert back to being a land of Germanic colonization, as before the war."[26]

Although these political, cultural, and social arguments had widespread currency on the far right, undoubtedly the most compelling anti-refugee argument prior to 1936 was the economic one, and on this score even some moderates, while paying continued lip service to the tradition of asylum, began to edge closer toward the anti-refugee camp. The issue here, as we have seen in Chapter 2, was not so much that the refugees would steal jobs from French workers, although this theme certainly carried some weight since far-right-wing spokesmen were always eager to win support from the popular classes. According to press reports in the fall of 1933, a group calling itself the Association des Travailleurs Français, almost certainly a fictitious front for one of the extreme-right-wing leagues, distributed tracts in Paris that read: "French workers, veterans, 45,000 Germans who fifteen years ago shot at you from over there are today seizing your jobs in French factories. Isn't it time to react?"[27] Similarly, *L'Ami du peuple* blasted the government for welcoming the German refugees while "thousands of Frenchmen are unemployed . . . and dying of hunger!"[28]

In sharp contrast to the economic complaints lodged against other immigrants in France, however, the principal complaint against the refugees was less that they threatened the jobs of French manual laborers than that they posed a competitive threat to the French middle classes: merchants, artisans, and liberal professionals. Although several scholars, such as Gérard Noiriel and Richard Millman, have tended to minimize the importance of antisemitism as a separate strand within the wider phenomenon of xenophobia, the fact is that this particular argument invariably assumed a strong antisemitic tinge.[29] There is no need to reexamine the protectionist demands of the various middle-class professional associations, but it nevertheless remains worthwhile to survey briefly the extent to which these demands won support across the political spectrum. Not surprisingly, it was once again the extreme right that led the way in calling for legislation to protect the beleaguered middle classes against competition. Already at the end of 1933, *L'Action française* charged that German Jewish refugees were using "unfair" and "dishonest" business practices to undersell their French competitors. Citing the example of a German refugee firm that had used the innovative marketing technique of sending clients sample handkerchiefs with an envelope enclosed for return payment, *L'Action française* declared that "French merchants would gladly dispense with this kind of competition."[30]

In June of 1933, the Paris police reported that right-wing journalists were up in arms over the proposed creation in Paris of a new chain of *prix uniques*, or discount retail stores, by a consortium of German Jewish refugees, while in Alsace a similar refugee initiative ignited a virulent antisemitic backlash.[31] Moreover, *L'Action française*, in addition to its outspoken support for the protectionist, xenophobic, and often blatantly antisemitic demands of medical and law students, also served as the principal forum for a wide range of other middle-class grievances against the refugees. In early 1934, for example, it published a letter from the director of a secondary school railing against Jewish refugees who were competing with French youths for jobs as tutors: "Although they are not allowed to take salaried employment, these refugees . . . ingratiate themselves, insinuate themselves, shove themselves to the forefront everywhere, and since they work for extremely low wages, it is impossible to wage any struggle against them."[32]

Expressing similar concerns in the Paris Municipal Council, Le Provost de Launay submitted a written question to the prefect of police in June 1933 asking: "What is the total number of German Jews who have arrived in the Paris region at the height of the past few months? What is that of doctors, lawyers, artists, bankers, businessmen, and those belonging to all categories of the liberal professions? To what extent will they be able to resume in Paris the occupations they held in Germany?" While conceding that it was desirable for France to keep a few German doctors, chemists, industrialists, and intellectuals, the masses of refugees, Le Provost de Launay insisted, simply could not stay. These refugees threatened to compete in already over-crowded commercial and liberal professions.[33] Moreover, as we have seen, right-wing deputies in the Chamber repeatedly sponsored legislation aimed at protecting doctors, lawyers, artisans, and eventually merchants from the allegedly "un-French" business practices of the refugees that allowed them to undersell their competitors.[34]

While this campaign in favor of protectionist measures for the besieged middle classes was clearly led by the extreme right, it nevertheless elicited some support among moderate politicians and publicists even before 1936. To be sure, the vast majority of centrists on the left as well as on the right sought to distance themselves from these xenophobic campaigns. For some conservatives, like the editors of *Le Temps* and *L'Ordre*, this opposition was based on a principled rejection of protectionism in favor of free trade. In November 1934, *Le Temps* cautioned the Flandin government not to carry out the mass expulsions of immigrants, claiming that the majority of the 356,000 French workers on government assistance would never take the jobs currently held by immigrant workers. The drive to eliminate the for-eigners was so appealing, *Le Temps* declared, precisely because it offered a panacea for an enormously complicated economic problem, and it warned the population not to be duped: "Whatever measures it adopts, the government must not delude itself as to their effectiveness. To attempt to remedy the unemployment crisis by eliminating one portion of the workers is to attack the symptoms and not the illness itself. The causes of unemployment and its remedies lie elsewhere."[35]

Le Temps also opposed legislation to restrict the creation of new *prix uniques* and shoe manufacturing firms in the spring of 1936. Such restrictions, *Le Temps* declared, encouraged waste and inefficiency and ultimately led to the establishment of corporatism, an economic system it condemned as offering unfair protection to established firms at the expense of consumers.[36] Emile Buré, the conservative editor of *L'Ordre*, similarly denounced the French business community's "stupid fear of overproduction." "Economic Malthusianism," Buré declared, "is the most serious threat to capitalism." If French entrepreneurs "wanted to remain in a capitalist regime, they would have to accept that regime's rules of the game."[37]

Several center-right spokesmen, such as the highly respected publicist Wladimir d'Ormesson, nevertheless argued that some foreigners were preferable to others and that only those deemed economically useful ought to remain. For d'Ormesson, the "useful" immigrants were those who had lived in France many years and were engaged in manual labor, especially agriculture. D'Ormesson, however, joined the far right in excoriating the more recent arrivals, or "nomads" as he called them, who flocked to the overcrowded cities, and especially to "that monstrous hypertrophy—the Paris metropolitan area." These foreigners, he charged, engaged in terrorist acts and "imported their revolutionary movements here . . . which inject disorder into our ranks and poison into our souls."[38] Thus, although d'Ormesson renounced the idea of expelling all foreigners, he nevertheless insisted that these "newcomers" had to be gotten rid of. Another publicist, E. Gascoin, similarly recognized the continued need for foreigners in France, especially in light of the country's low birthrate. Yet, Gascoin shared d'Ormesson's view that some immigrants were more desirable than others, and he too singled out the recent newcomers, and especially the refugees, as the least desirable of all, citing their disproportionate representation among the criminal classes as well as the health risk they posed to the native population. Why, Gascoin wondered, did France alone have "to accept definitively all those expelled by Hitler, the Bolsheviks together with everyone else, while every other country had rejected them"? Were not these exiles "the tainted ones, the debris of humanity chased out of the Reich by the threat of sterilization?"[39]

Such anticapitalist, anti-urban, and anti-left-wing rhetoric was also prevalent on the clerical right, especially among that segment of clerical opinion that regarded itself as philosemitic. The Reverend Joseph Bonsirven, for example, a prominent Jesuit and member of the missionary order Notre Dame de Sion, whose frequent articles on the "Jewish Question" were supposedly intended to refute antisemitism as antithetical to Christianity, in reality shared many of the antisemitic assumptions of the radical right, particularly insofar as Jewish immigrants were concerned. Bonsirven fully supported the protectionist demands of the medical and law students, claiming that Jews, and especially recently naturalized ones, were disproportionately represented among these professions; the medical faculty, he noted, "was on its way toward becoming a fief of Israel." Furthermore, he argued, the protectionist campaigns of the medical and law students were not really antisemitic since they were directed not against "the honest and conscientious Jew," but only against "the parvenus or . . . the Polish, Romanian, Russian, [or] German Jews, who shamelessly indulge in communist propaganda and display a clear intention to take over every available job in France."[40] According to Bonsirven, by means of their obstreperous behavior and left-wing views, these immigrants themselves were responsible for antisemitism. And although he differed from the far right in believing that the solution to the "Jewish problem" resided in assimilation, Bonsirven nevertheless insisted that this goal could be realized only by sharply curbing future Jewish immigration and naturalization.[41]

Among liberals, such anti-middle-class and anti-urban attitudes had far less saliency, in part because most of them rejected the assertion that the middle-class professions were really overcrowded, and in part because they could not accept restrictions that curtailed not only the rights of foreigners, but also those of naturalized citizens. Thus, although a significant segment of the Radical Party was willing to endorse restrictions on foreign wage laborers, and the 1934 party platform actually incorporated a plank calling for the gradual repatriation of nearly all foreign workers, the attitude toward middle-class protection was more reserved.

Still, there were a few Radical politicians who lent support to these campaigns. The most influential of these was Emile Roche, one of the party's leading spokesmen and executive editor of *La République*, a principal organ of Radical opinion. In 1934, Roche had supported the demand to alleviate the impact of the Depression by repatriating hundreds of thousands of foreign workers, and although he did not express quite the same enthusiasm for the demands of lawyers and doctors, he nevertheless conceded that native-born citizens deserved priority in those professions as well, a position that contrasted sharply with *La République*'s general editorial line.[42] Paul Elbel, the Radical Party deputy from the Vosges, also supported the protectionist demands of French merchants. In a 1934 article entitled "Undesirables," which appeared in the Radical paper *L'Oeuvre*, Elbel argued that the problem of unfair competition from foreign merchants was no less serious than that of foreign workers. For Elbel, foreign merchants, like foreigners in general, fell into two categories—the good and the bad. The "good" foreign merchants were those who had lived in France many years, and were upstanding and respectable taxpayers. The "bad" were the recent arrivals who engaged in "unfair" business practices and declared bankruptcy without thinking twice. For these "undesirables," Elbel declared, there was only one solution: expulsion, regardless of whether they were refugees.[43]

A few journalists of Radical persuasion also expressed misgivings about the economic behavior of the refugees. Although the Radical paper *Le Quotidien* had been staunchly pro-refugee in 1933, and several of its commentators continued to express pro-refugee sentiments until the paper's demise in 1936,[44] others, such as Romain Roussel, distanced themselves from this position. Roussel, who in 1935 wrote a major series on foreigners, was clearly less hostile to immigrants in general than he was to the Jews among them, and his fierce anticapitalism led him to call for severe restrictions on all Jewish immigrants, refugees or not. Roussel fully supported the Medical Association's restrictionist campaign, and he agreed with its antisemitic assertions regarding the allegedly dishonest and fraudulent practices of Romanian Jewish doctors as well as their inferior quality.[45]

Moreover, although Roussel staunchly supported the rights of foreigners to work in France, he fiercely opposed the efforts of German Jewish refugees to open new businesses and industries. These enterprises, he insisted, would inevitably compete with French firms, notwithstanding the disclaimers of their founders, and he added, in an apt summary of the Malthusian point of view:

Insofar as German Jews are concerned, it is still permissible to suppose that most of them who claim to have been exiled by Hitler's policies are, in reality, not terribly desirable people. . . . In an era in which the public powers ought to have the courage and legal right to restrain freedom of commerce, the generator of overproduction and unemployment, the government instead seems disarmed when faced with their [the refugees'] initiatives.[46]

The sole economic contribution of this "enormous mass of parasitic elements," was, Roussel insisted, "to augment the already too numerous layers that exist between producers and consumers."[47] Similarly, for Carmen Ennesch, a correspondent for the Radical paper *L'Ere nouvelle*, which also remained largely pro-refugee during this period, the principal cause of mounting public hostility toward the refugees in 1934 was the high proportion of East Europeans among them. Due to their low standards of living, these immigrants, Ennesch suggested, had "work[ed] veritable miracles to ensure that their interests triumphed." But, she added, this success was invariably won "at the expense of the indigenous population."[48]

The view that the immigrants fell into two categories—the "desirables" and the "undesirables"—and that the refugees, together with the East European Jews who had arrived during the previous decade, were the least desirable of the lot, was not simply a vague sentiment that received occasional articulation in the press. Rather, it attained "scientific" respectability through the theoretical writings of France's two foremost demographic experts: Georges Mauco and Dr. René Martial. Both Mauco and Martial staunchly rejected demands by the radical right to halt immigration entirely. From their perspective, it was an unfortunate but irrefutable truth that France could not survive without immigrants in light of the nation's huge population deficit, a legacy of the 1.4 million lives lost during the First World War as well as the persistently low birthrate, which averaged 15.7 per 1,000 between 1931 and 1935, and was the lowest in all of Europe.[49] Despite the Depression, which conveyed the impression that there were too many people for too few jobs and led to heightened tensions between French and foreign workers, Mauco and Martial both pointed out that severe labor shortages continued to plague certain sectors of the economy, especially in the agricultural south. Due to rampant urbanization, many rural areas had suffered severe population losses in recent years, and in some regions, foreigners actually constituted the majority of the labor force. Moreover, they were both well aware of the fact that the army desperately wanted to speed up the rate of naturalization in order to increase military recruitment. Indeed, 1934 marked the first of the so-called *années creuses*, or lean years, during which recruitment was expected to drop sharply as the extremely small classes born during First World War would be called up.[50]

In light of these military and economic concerns, Mauco and Martial recognized that a complete ban on further immigration and naturalization could prove disastrous. They therefore condemned as irrational and counterproductive the mass repatriations and expulsions of immigrants implemented during the Flandin and Laval administrations. Instead, they suggested a policy of selective immigration. What they wanted was for the government to create a special Ministry of Immigration that would instill rationality and coordination into the otherwise chaotic immigration process. Businesses and industries would be allowed to recruit only immigrants with skills deemed economically useful, and the government would play a far greater role in steering immigrants to those regions of the country where there was a demand for foreign labor. At the same time, they expressed the hope that the new Ministry of Immigration would safeguard the nation's ethnic, as well as its economic and military, health by accepting only foreigners considered assimilable.[51]

Given that these theoreticians of selective immigration made no allowances for refugee asylum, the question inevitably arose of whether Jewish refugees could be made to fit the mold of the economically and ethnically desirable immigrant, and on this score the consensus tended to be negative. Both Mauco and Martial voiced extreme skepticism regarding the quality of Jewish refugees in particular, and their views once again suggest the degree to which antisemitism took on a life of its own apart from xenophobia in general, even among many moderates. Mauco, more than any other immigration expert during the interwar period, insisted repeatedly that France could not cut off the flow of immigration completely. Nevertheless, his views toward Jewish immigrants were extremely negative and devoid of any sympathy for their plight. For Mauco, what made a particular category of immigrants desirable had less to do with race per se than with economic and cultural affinities. The only immigrants he considered desirable were nonurban manual laborers, and Jews clearly did not fit this category. He fully endorsed the claims of doctors and lawyers, merchants, certain groups of artisans, and members of the entertainment industry that their professions were overcrowded, largely because of an overabundance of Jewish immigrants "more suited to business and intermediary dealings than to manual labor."[52]

And while praising the majority of immigrants in France as "laborious" and "useful" workers, Mauco joined Roussel in excoriating bourgeois, urban immigrants as "parasitic intermediaries who interpose themselves between producer and consumer."[53] These primarily Semitic foreigners, among whom Mauco counted Armenians, Greeks, and Arabs, in addition to Jews, constituted "a depressing or dissolving influence on the French collectivity."[54] Mauco moreover warned that the problem of Jewish competition in particular would not disappear soon since "France remains the last available refuge in Europe and since the influx of Jews into the liberal, commercial, and artisanal professions is caused in part by actions taken by other countries to avoid precisely this [problem]."[55] If the government did not address this situation immediately, Mauco predicted, France would soon be submerged by an unprecedented wave of xenophobia and antisemitism.[56]

For Mauco, the dilemma posed by Jewish immigrants was not exclusively economic; it also had significant cultural and ethnic ramifications. In order to determine which groups of immigrants were most desirable, he devised an ethnic and national hierarchy that ranked immigrants according to their levels of assimilability. Although assimilability for Mauco was essentially a cultural matter, having to do with similarities in language, religion, history, customs, and so on, he also insisted that these cultural attributes were linked to a geographical factor—the proximity between the immigrant's place of origin and the eventual host country. Thus, the most assimilable immigrants, according to Mauco, were from countries bordering France, with the exception of Germany, while the least assimilable were from countries farthest away. Hence, the Swiss, the Belgians, the Luxemburgers, the Italians, and the Spaniards ranked among the most desirable immigrants, whereas the Slavs (Poles, Russians, Czechs, and Yugoslavs), the Levantines (Arabs and Armenians), the Africans, and the Jews were relegated to the bottom rungs of the ethnic ladder. Since these "exotics," as

Mauco referred to them, bore within themselves customs, habits, and passions completely contrary to the French way of thinking, their integration into French society was deemed "physically and morally undesirable."[57] And in an effort to intermingle the cultural and economic arguments, Mauco insisted that working-class and peasant immigrants were "more accessible to education and assimilation" precisely because they were "less evolved" than their urban bourgeois counterparts.[58]

Mauco was therefore not opposed to immigration per se, but only to the immigration of urban, bourgeois foreigners who, in the 1930's, were almost exclusively Central and East European Jews. Still, he did not close the door altogether to Jewish refugees. Expressing a view that clearly foreshadowed his subsequent input into the Serre Plan, a scheme devised in early 1938 to settle illegal East European Jewish immigrants in agricultural colonies in southern France, Mauco argued that Jewish immigrants could in fact assimilate, but only if they left the cities and transformed themselves into farmers and manual workers. This end, he believed, could be accomplished through a rigorous program of vocational retraining, and he maintained that since Jews in ancient times had devoted themselves to pastoral occupations, there was no reason they could not do so again. If, however, they refused, Mauco warned that their behavior would inspire "the same political and economic repercussions of which they have always, in every country, been the first victim." Thus, from his vantage point, one of the first tasks facing any newly created Ministry of Immigration would be "to concern itself with the professional redistribution of the refugees, for the most part Jews, who flock to the cities and urban professions where their competition provokes a backlash."[59]

Dr. René Martial, France's leading ethnologist, took this theory of selective immigration one step further. Martial completely agreed with Mauco that France needed to encourage immigration in light of rural depopulation and the low birthrate, and he condemned the anti-immigrant policies of Flandin and Laval as a "barbarous illogicality." At the same time, however, he joined Mauco in warning that too many undesirables were being allowed to enter the country: after the First World War, he declared, "the faucet was opened too wide and the good flowed in together with the bad."[60] Thus, Martial too favored a more selective immigration policy in order to separate the wheat from the chaff.

Where Martial differed from Mauco, however, was in his linking of assimilability not to geography but to race. To be sure, like other French eugenicists, Martial did not accept the concept of pure races, and he acknowledged that the French themselves were the product of extensive racial mixing. As Martial envisioned it, the term "race" was as much a cultural as a biological concept, embracing "latent or manifest psychological traits (especially language), and anthrobiological traits, which over time (history) come to constitute a distinct unity."[61] Nevertheless, Martial did believe in what he called "resultant-races"—peoples that resulted from interracial mixing, or "grafting," as he called it. What determined whether two races could mix harmoniously ultimately depended on whether they shared similar genetic makeups, which Martial believed could be determined by comparing their respective blood type coefficients—that is, the frequency of people with one blood type as opposed to the others. Supposedly, according to Martial, type A blood was more prevalent in the West, while type B was more prevalent in the East, and he warned that mixing peoples of significantly different blood types would have grave consequences: "The marriage of a French man and a Chinese woman might be happy, but what about the value of their descendants?" For him the issue was not so much whether a certain race was superior to another, but whether "it could be successfully crossbred with the French, and if this crossbreeding would not yield maladjusted or mentally ill offspring."[62]

As was the case with Mauco, it was not immediately clear where Jewish immigrants stood in Martial's pseudoscientific scheme. Jewish groups took Martial to task for his idea that races and blood types were one and the same, and as Dr. Julius Brutzkus pointed out in 1938, Jews were in fact not a homogenous race and their blood types varied depending on where they lived.[63] In the case of Jews, however, Martial did not rely on his pseudoscientific theory at all; instead, he fell back on cultural and economic arguments to illustrate that the Jews constituted one of the least desirable groups of immigrants. In a 1933 speech, Martial railed against the refugees for having "an oriental mentality that frequently nullifies our intentions as well as our efforts, especially insofar as the application of the municipal sanitary code is concerned." And he continued, "the majority [of them] have the instinct for fraud at the same time as they have one for business. Many of them are . . . smugglers."[64] Elsewhere, he noted that the ultimate proof of France's complete lack of a rational immigration policy was the "uncontrolled admission of German refugees fleeing Hitlerian persecutions."[65] That Martial's attitude toward Jews relied more on prejudice than science is further demonstrated by the fact that he held Christian Poles to be assimilable, despite significant differences between their blood type coefficients and those of the French, while he considered all Jews to be nonassimilable, despite frequent similarities between their blood type coefficients and those of the French.[66]

On the eve of the Popular Front victory in 1936, therefore, two types of solutions to the refugee problem were beginning to emerge. On the far right, there was a general consensus that the influx of refugees, even more than the influx of immigrants in general, had to be halted completely. As Paul Morand stated, "it is necessary to apportion the proper dosage before the catastrophe, not afterward," and he warned that if the influx of foreigners was not curbed immediately, the French "will suddenly disappear from their own soil, as if they had fallen through a trapdoor."[67] A few, like Daudet, were willing to push this argument even further, demanding not only a special legal statute for immigrants and refugees, but also one for Jews in general, French and foreign alike. While Daudet would have exempted a small number of Jews, namely those who belonged to the Action Française, the vast majority of them, he maintained, were unassimilable and alien. These Jews, Daudet declared, "have abused French hospitality in their attempt to dominate us, to expropriate us, and to expel us from our traditions, customs, and religious and political convictions."[68]

To be sure, the majority of right-wing political leaders, like Colonel François de La Rocque, head of the largest and most influential of the nationalistic leagues, the Croix de Feu, were reluctant to conflate French Jews, including long-established Jewish immigrants, with the more recent Jewish arrivals. Not only did these right-wing leagues have a number of influential Jewish supporters, but also many of their leaders sincerely believed that Jews who had fought for France in the First World War had truly become one of the nation's "diverse spiritual families."[69] Nevertheless, none of these far-right-wing spokesmen had the slightest qualm about lambasting the more recent arrivals, and Daudet's leap from the refugees to Jews in general clearly foreshadowed the future direction of extreme-right-wing thought on this issue.

Among moderates, on the other hand, the idea of selective immigration had made significant headway, and the writings of Mauco and Martial did much to give this theory a veneer of "scientific" legitimacy. Yet although some adherents of this view, like Martial, were willing to call for a complete halt to Jewish immigration, the more prevalent tendency was to follow Mauco in leaving the door slightly ajar for asylum seekers. In the spring of 1935, for example, the playwright and publicist Jean Giraudoux argued that continued immigration was essential to the nation's long-term vitality, in light of the persistent demographic problem. While expulsion and repatriation might seem an appropriate policy for 1935, Giraudoux declared, it would seem less appropriate in 1936, and "it would become downright dangerous for 1950." At the same time, Giraudoux did not hesitate to call for the expulsion of recently arrived immigrants who engaged in financial speculation or in "facile agitation" and who "denature the country by their presence and their action." These immigrants, many of whom were East European Jews, "swarm toward every one of our arts or new industries as if

undergoing a process of spontaneous generation reminiscent of an outbreak of fleas on a newborn dog." Hence, Giraudoux too favored the creation of a Ministry of Immigration to weed out the undesirables.

Significantly, however, Giraudoux refused to relegate the refugees to the
"undesirable" category, a position he would renounce by the end of the
decade. Instead, he argued that as long as the League of Nations had not yet
found an international solution to the refugee problem, it would be un-
conscionable for France to turn away these helpless victims of persecution.[70] Moreover, whereas Mauco had proposed sending the refugees to the
south to become farmers, a solution that was in fact adopted with regard
to the Saar refugees, other adherents of selective immigration, including
Giraudoux, advocated sending the refugees, together with other surplus
immigrants, to the colonies, which were widely regarded to be in need of
settlers. Still others, like the former Minister of Justice Henry Lémery,
agreed with Minister of the Interior Marcel Régnier that the colonial solution might serve a punitive function as well. As Lémery declared, refugees
who persisted in meddling in French domestic politics deserved to be expelled, but "if the entire world rejects them, Guiana was always there to take
them in."[71]

Although these negative or ambivalent attitudes toward refugees were
on the rise after 1933, they by no means went uncontested. A prevailing
stereotype about the 1930's is that there was not a single party or political
organization that was willing to defend the principle of refugee asylum. According to Timothy Maga, "By 1939 anti-refugee sentiment transcended all
party lines and the refugees had no party to which they could turn for protection."[72] Michael Marrus and Robert Paxton have similarly argued that
no political party in the 1930's put forth the economic argument in favor of
refugees—that is, the notion that they constituted a potential economic asset and not a liability since they promised to create new businesses and industries and enlarge the pool of consumers, thus stimulating industrial and
commercial growth.[73] Ralph Schor too, in his survey of popular opinion
toward immigration during the interwar years has stressed the deepening
xenophobia on the political left, despite the persistence of pro-immigrant
rhetoric at the official level.[74] And in more general terms, Hannah Arendt
has charged that by the end of the 1930's France "had no more true Drey-
fusards, no one who believed that democracy and freedom, equality and
justice could any longer be defended or realized under the republic."[75]

While it is irrefutable that certain groups on the left did exhibit some ambivalence toward immigrants in general, and toward Jewish refugees in particular, the notion that no party or political organization spoke out in their
favor is vastly overblown. Moreover, if the refugee issue provides any gauge
of republican loyalties, Arendt's charge must be dismissed as a myth. The

fact is that there was a broad-based coalition of groups—including the Communist and Socialist Parties; the trade union movements, the Confédération Général du Travail (CGT) and the Confédération Générale du Travail Unitaire (CGTU); the League for the Rights of Man and Citizen; the liberal wing of the Radical Party; some moderate conservatives; and the Catholic left as well as several individual clerical spokesmen—that assumed the pro-refugee mantle in 1933 and, for the most part, adhered to this position steadfastly up through 1940. To be sure, many Radicals and moderate conservatives defected from the pro-refugee camp by the end of the 1930's, inspired by fears that the refugees would drag France into a war and that their ever-increasing numbers would only shore up the strength of the radical left. Still, much of the core of pro-refugee support remained intact. That these groups did not in the end succeed in guaranteeing the right of asylum had little to do with any alleged moral compromises on their part. Rather, their failure ultimately stemmed from the defeat of republican forces following the military debacle of June 1940 and the subsequent emergence of Vichy.

Throughout 1933 and into 1934, these groups, often working in tandem with Jewish organizations, sponsored numerous mass meetings to protest Nazism and to press for a generous public reception of the refugees. Although the Socialist Party clearly took the lead in pressing the government to grant generous terms for asylum and to keep the borders open,[76] this effort had considerable support in other quarters as well. In April 1933, the Radical newspaper *L'Ere nouvelle* noted with satisfaction that "thanks to [the government's] quick and efficient measures, those German Jews chased from their homes are finding a generous welcome in France." In October, it even recommended that the government subsidize the Comité National, claiming that the private relief initiatives were proving insufficient.[77] Several sections of the Radical Party, including those in Alsace, similarly urged the government to extend a warm welcome to the refugees, and the national leadership of the Radical and Radical Socialist Party, then presided over by Edouard Herriot, passed a strongly worded resolution condemning Nazi antisemitism. Referring to France's historic legacy of Jewish emancipation, this resolution affirmed that: "The Radical and Radical Socialist Party . . . energetically protests the unjustifiable mistreatment to which German Jews have been subjected, assures them of its sympathy, and demands . . . that measures be taken to safeguard their material, intellectual and moral well-being."[78]

In another speech, Herriot further pledged "that republican France, loyal to the teachings of Montesquieu, the Abbé Grégoire, and so many others, welcomes the exiles with . . . sympathy and respect."[79] Radicals also followed their colleagues further to the left in voicing indignation over the suicide in Paris of a 13-year-old refugee girl, Sonia Rosenzweig, following a 1933 incident in which a French merchant allegedly humiliated the girl's brother and, when she protested, had her dragged off to the police, who in turn threatened to throw her into prison. From the perspective of the Radical daily *L'Oeuvre*, there could be little doubt that this xenophobic incident had caused the young girl's death. When some of the paper's readers complained that too much sympathy was being shown toward the Jews, the editors retorted that their position was "Neither pro-semite nor anti-semite. It's humane, and that's all. If being humane is no longer to be French . . . we too might just as well stage a public bonfire where the works of all our great writers will be burned."[80]

Clerical opinion in 1933 was no less sympathetic. In early April, the press reported that anti-Nazi tracts had been posted on church doors calling upon Christians to protest that "in the year 1933 after Jesus, men, women, and children are daily being beaten and tortured . . . simply because they are Jews!" The tract then appealed to Christians and Jews to "reunite to combat those crimes unworthy of our civilization."[81] Also in the spring, Cardinal Jean Verdier, archbishop of Paris, appealed to all Christians to pray for the persecuted German Jews—an act that, according to Jacques Helbronner, was unprecedented in the history of the Church—and he personally assured Chief Rabbi Israël Lévi that French Catholics fully backed the anti-Nazi protest movement.[82] In Nice, the left-leaning bishop, Monsignor Paul Rémond, repeatedly denounced Nazi "barbarism" against the Jews in his sermons, and he publicly offered to assist those who fled.[83] Another prominent cleric, Monsignor Achille Liénart, the cardinal of Lille, provoked the wrath of the Action Française when he aided the local Jewish community in its refugee relief effort.[84]

Moreover, a number of Catholic clergy participated actively in the protest meetings against Nazi racism, including Abbé Jean-Marie Desgranges, the Abbé Paul Viollet, and the Reverend Dieux.[85] In Alsace, the archbishop of Strasbourg took the unusual step of joining the left-wing LICA in a fund-raising drive on behalf of the refugees, with the intention of using part of the money to assist Catholic refugees.[86] Among Protestants, the protest movement was equally strong. The French Council of Protestant Federations, led by Pastor Marc Boegner, issued a public statement in the spring of 1933 denouncing Nazi antisemitism, and a number of leading Protestant ministers participated actively in the anti-Nazi protest meetings.[87]

In addition to these moral protests, left-wing political organizations launched a campaign to establish a network of mutual aid associations aimed specifically at helping political, rather than religious or racial, refugees get back on their feet and find jobs in France. The most prominent of these was the Matteotti Committee, which had been established by the socialists in the 1920's to assist Italian émigrés, but there was also the communist Secours Rouge International.[88] Similarly, the juridical bureau of the League for the Rights of Man and Citizen served as the chief vehicle through which the refugees could secure the necessary papers to regularize their legal status.[89] Moreover, a broad-based coalition, which included even many centrists, such as the prominent Parisian deputy Louis Rollin, worked assiduously throughout 1933 and 1934 to secure posts for refugee scholars at French universities. It was in fact Louis Marin, deputy of the Meurthe-et-Moselle and head of the conservative Republican Federation, who spearheaded the parliamentary campaign in May 1933 to secure a chair for Einstein at the Collège de France.[90]

This effort was abetted by assistance from several professional organizations as well. In the spring of 1933, a group of university professors submitted a proposal to the minister of education to create a number of assistantships and lectureships in lycées for unmarried German refugee professors. These positions, they insisted, would incur no government expenditures aside from the provision of room and board.[91] The Fédération Générale de l'Enseignement (General Federation of Education) also appealed to its members to help refugees locate jobs as translators, researchers, and tutors,[92] and the Ligue d'Action Universitaire Républicaine et Socialiste (LAURS), a left-wing student organization, and the Fédération Nationale des Etudiants de la Ligue des Droits de l'Homme (National Federation of Students of the League for the Rights of Man) sponsored a drive to create a university center to provide free French lessons to refugee students and to help them acquire equivalency diplomas.[93]

This coalition led a vigorous campaign to defend the right of asylum not only on moral grounds, but also on economic grounds, a trend that refutes the assertion that the economic argument in favor of the refugees was never advanced. In the spring of 1933, the middle-class backlash against the refugees was not yet widely anticipated, and many shared the belief of Pierre Paraf, a LICA activist and frequent columnist for the liberal paper *La République*, that the refugees constituted a potential boon to the French economy. Whereas other immigrants did in fact compete for jobs with French workers, the refugees, Paraf argued, posed no such threat, given their middle-class status and concentration in commercial and liberal professions. Moreover, Paraf insisted, those refugees who could get at least part of their capital out of Germany, such as the Leipzig furriers and the Nuremberg toy manufacturers, were certain to generate jobs by transferring their businesses and industries to France. Finally, Paraf pointed out, the refugees, through their access to previously untapped foreign markets and their familiarity with foreign languages, promised to contribute significantly to the expansion of French international commerce.[94]

Paraf, who happened to be Jewish, was by no means alone in advancing this view. Among non-Jewish publicists, it was almost certainly Pierre Dominique, the brilliant and highly respected editor-in-chief of *La République*, who emerged as the most outspoken proponent of this view. Dominique insisted that Jewish refugees constituted the cream of German society, and he frequently compared them to the French Huguenots. As he declared in April 1933, "Let's open our doors! The opportunity being offered France is one we ought to leap at! At the end of the seventeenth century, the elector of Brandenburg civilized his country thanks to our Protestant refugees: by receiving and welcoming the German refugees with open arms, France will undoubtedly enlarge her sphere of influence in the world."[95]

Even in 1935, as the protectionist campaign was forging ahead full steam, Dominique continued to insist that the German refugees constituted an economic asset. Just as the United States had achieved greatness in the nineteenth century by having successfully assimilated successive waves of immigrants, France today, he declared, was being granted a similar opportunity. In response to those who insisted that the immigrants stole jobs, Dominique advised his readers:

To speak once again about large-scale public works projects. To remember that North Africa is at our door; to remind ourselves that each new French subject is not simply another mouth to feed, but that his presence creates work by creating consumption, and that reinforcing France by a million men is not giving her a million more unemployed. Let's naturalize, not with a turn of the wrist, [but] with intelligence, but let's naturalize, and without losing quality, we'll acquire that which we currently lack—quantity.

While acknowledging that he was likely to be accused "of wanting to ruin the doctors, starve the workers, take the side of the *métèques*—perhaps even that of the Jews," Dominique nevertheless maintained that in light of France's demographic problem, there was simply no choice.[96] Socialist activist Magdeleine Paz, similarly stressed the role of foreigners as consumers, and she urged France to follow the example of Holland, where German refugees had created 5,000 new jobs by the end of 1934.[97]

In light of this economic defense of the refugees, it is not surprising that this coalition led a vigorous, though ultimately unsuccessful, protest against Malthusian thinking and legislation. Left-wing Radicals and socialists, as well as the Catholic left, repeatedly pointed out the fallacious reasoning behind the demands of the medical and law students and their parent organizations. As Paraf noted, the claim of some student leaders that foreign medical students constituted 80 percent of the student body, when in reality they constituted only about 40 percent, was arrived at by counting naturalized citizens as foreigners, a practice Paraf excoriated as a "juridical and moral error."[98] Jean d'Alsace, writing in the left-wing Radical paper *La Lumière*, similarly noted that the so-called *pléthore médicale* was a complete myth: there was no surplus of doctors, he claimed; rather, there was an uneven distribution of them, a point that seemed confirmed by persistent shortages of doctors in rural areas and in the colonies. Moreover, according to d'Alsace, despite the repeated disclaimers of xenophobia and antisemitism on the part of the student leaders, the spokesmen knew full well that the implementation of their demands would mean the closure of the borders to all future refugees.[99] Writing in the left-wing Catholic review *Esprit*, Dr. Claude Leblond similarly blamed this student-led agitation for having introduced "racial pride" into France, and Dr. Armand Vincent insisted that the *pléthore médicale* represented nothing more than "the appetite for gain, the pursuit of ever larger clienteles." He further warned that "after chasing out those of foreign origin, we'll proceed to the negroes, the mixed bloods, the Jews, etc. . . . and once a purely aryanized medical profession has been established, there will be so few doctors that every one of them will be able to sell his services for the price of gold."[100]

   This coalition also sought to combat the legislative onslaught against the employment of foreigners in the civil service and the medical profession. The *Cahiers des droits de l'homme* (the organ of the League for the Rights of Man and Citizen), *Le Populaire* (the organ of the Socialist Party), and *La Lumière* all argued that the crackdown on foreign students in these professions would have disastrous consequences for France's reputation abroad. From their perspective, however, the most pernicious aspect of this legislation was that it stripped even naturalized citizens of the right to practice these professions for a fixed number of years. The state, they charged, was in effect condoning the creation of a "second-class" citizenry, and in doing so, it was desecrating a sacred republican tradition, the guarantee of full equality before the law to all citizens, regardless of when they had been awarded their citizenship.[101] Moreover, according to the *Cahiers des droits de l'homme*, these legislative reforms encroached significantly on the right to asylum, since all foreigners preparing for careers in these professions would now find themselves unemployed, and under current administrative policy unemployed foreigners were vulnerable to *refoulement*.[102] To highlight the nefarious impact of the July 19, 1934, law, *Le Populaire* reported in December of 1935 that a Hungarian-born Jewish officer in the French army committed suicide after finding his career path blocked by this law.[103]

   The socialists sought to overturn these laws in Parliament as well. Just after the passage of the July 19, 1934, law, a delegation representing Socialist Party lawyers filed a brief that described the law as being "of purely racist inspiration" and demanded its repeal. Moreover, they claimed that the law's retroactive character was patently unconstitutional. At the very least, they argued, naturalized citizens who had served in the army or who had performed other exceptional services for the state deserved to be awarded exemptions. In December 1936, a group of socialist and Radical deputies submitted a parliamentary bill to this effect, and indeed, this law was modified once the Popular Front came to power.[104]

Despite this noteworthy record, the left's reception of the refugees was not entirely free of ambivalence, particularly insofar as Jewish refugees were concerned. Within the trade union movement, as Rita Thalmann and Ralph Schor have shown, there was considerable dissension between the leadership and the rank and file of the labor movement on the question of foreign workers in general, and this dissension ultimately influenced the attitude of the labor movement toward the refugees as well. Whereas the leadership of both the CGT and the CGTU consistently defended the rights of immigrant workers throughout the 1930's, the membership of both these movements was often blatantly xenophobic and, like the far right, blamed the Depression primarily on the presence of foreigners.[105] Already in late 1931, the Paris police reported that the rank and file of the CGTU, and especially the building trade unions, had become extremely xenophobic, despite the persistent efforts of the union leadership to keep these antiforeign sentiments in check.[106] Moreover, specifically referring to the refugees, Communist Party activist Eugène Hénaff called on French workers in November 1933 to welcome their newly arrived German comrades and to "break the existing xenophobic currents."[107] Similarly, Emile Farinet, a socialist activist, urged French workers to exhibit greater generosity toward the refugees, and he admitted that it was "not only because they are Germans that we internationalists are shirking our duty to extend mutual assistance."[108]

The Jewish refugee committee, as we have seen in Chapter 2, had observed as early as May of 1933 that labor unions were already expressing concern about the possibility of the refugees working illegally in sweatshops for nonunion wages. It therefore recommended that every effort be made to ensure that the refugees strictly obey existing labor laws.[109] Léon Jouhaux, head of the CGT, even appealed to the League of Nations' International Labor Organization in 1933 to ensure a fair and equitable distribution of the refugees among the various member states in order to avoid fierce competition for a limited number of jobs.[110]

In addition to these economic fears, political factors further encouraged left-wing ambivalence toward the refugees, especially within the French Communist Party. Although *L'Humanité*, the party's official mouthpiece, expressed considerable concern over the fate of the political refugees, it made a sharp distinction between them and Jewish refugees, who, it suggested, were less worthy of sympathy. As Ralph Schor has pointed out, Communist Party activists rarely attended protest meetings that focused specifically on Nazi antisemitism, nor did they single out Jews as targets of Nazi persecution.[111] Indeed, the French Communist Party, as did the Communist Party elsewhere, took antisemitism seriously only to the extent that it believed it masked the true aim of Nazism and fascism: the oppression of the working class. Insofar as a small segment of the German Jewish population belonged to this class, the Communist Party was willing to consider them victims. But since the vast majority of Jewish refugees were bourgeois, communist theory mandated that they receive no special consideration. Moreover, the communists simply could not believe that Hitler would ever betray his capitalist allies, even those among them who were Jews. As J. Koepplin explained in *L'Humanité* at the time of the Nazi anti-Jewish boycott of April 1933:

For the wealthy, everything can ultimately be arranged. . . . Large-scale Jewish finance, just like large-scale Jewish industry, has so far escaped the boycott. Germany in the throes of depression will hesitate before delivering a mortal blow to itself. The spirit of class is stronger than that of racism. Well-known [commercial and industrial] specialists, just like famous artists, will be welcomed across the border, but the common people—the workers, the employees, the unemployed—what will be their future after the organized and "legal" pogrom of April 1? . . . To be a Jew is already a serious matter, but to be Jewish and communist constitutes a mortal danger.[112]

Emigrés themselves often propagated this view. Rudolf Leonhard, for example, while admitting that Jews were being persecuted, lamented the degree to which international attention had focused on this tiny minority, all the while ignoring the far greater suffering of the oppressed German workers.[113]

This left-wing ambivalence was further fueled by the long-standing tendency among communists to identify Jews with capitalism. Since the Communist Party attributed the triumph of Nazism to capitalist machinations, and since Jews constituted a powerful element within the German capitalist class, French communists, as well as some anarchist groups, drew the bizarre conclusion that Jewish capitalists bore a major share of responsibility for Hitler's rise to power. In an article of April 1933 titled "In the Financial District Where Nazis and Jews Have Reached a Common Front," *L'Humanité* proclaimed:

Who's been saying that the Jews are being persecuted? . . . Those on the stock market are still the masters here, and no one would dream of disturbing their peace and quiet or their business affairs with a decree from Hitler. Here we have the *union sacrée* [between capitalism and Nazism] under the sign of the swastika. Wasn't it the banker Schroeder who arranged the Hitler–von Papen interview that led to the formation of the current cabinet? . . . Weren't Jewish bankers and industrialists among the most zealous financial backers of the national fascist movement?[114]

Similarly, the police reported that at a LICA-sponsored anti-Nazi protest meeting in the spring of 1933, the left-wing Zionist lawyer Yvonne Netter, who was herself of Jewish origin, abruptly interrupted the proceedings to declare: "I accuse the Jewish capitalists of having given Hitler financial support, and they are partly responsible for his success."[115] Even the more moderate *Le Populaire* occasionally reiterated this theme. Describing conditions at a Jewish shelter in Paris just as the refugees were beginning to arrive, one anonymous author could not refrain from adding that "in leaving that shelter, witness to so much misery, I couldn't help but think of the Jewish capitalists who aided Hitler early on in his career."[116]

Foreign policy considerations encouraged left-wing ambivalence as well. Still steeped in the pacifist traditions of the 1920's, *L'Humanité* complained in September 1933 that the excessive international attention given to the fate of German Jews was merely a pretext behind which the capitalist West was fomenting an imperialist war against its traditional enemy, Germany. One communist journalist, perhaps following the Tharaud brothers, even cited Einstein's abrupt turn from pacifism to rabid anti-Germanism as conclusive proof of these aggressive intentions.[117]

Similar foreign policy concerns tempered the pro-refugee enthusiasm of other left-wing and liberal groups as well, albeit in a far more modified form. Writers for the Christian Democratic *L'Aube*, as well as the Radical papers *La Lumière* and *La République*, repeatedly stressed throughout 1933 and 1934 that under no circumstances did they want their pro-refugee stance to be perceived as a clarion call for a more aggressive anti-German foreign policy. Jeanne Ancelet-Hustache of *L'Aube*, who throughout the 1930's was one of the most sympathetic pro-refugee spokesmen, warned in the spring of 1933 that France should not allow itself to be transformed by the refugees into a symbol of the anti-Nazi resistance since this role would undermine efforts to achieve Franco-German rapprochement. Criticism of Nazi domestic policy, she argued, "even if justified, always raises the nationalist thermometer several degrees."[118]

Albert Bayet, one of the most prominent leaders of the left-wing of the Radical Party, similarly explained that although antisemitism might well be "the first symptom of Germany's return to barbarism," the Radical Party would nevertheless stand by its traditional motto, "Peace above all." "Even with Hitler," Bayet maintained, "France must endeavor to save the peace, because war is the supreme evil, . . . the apparent cause of the material and moral crisis which today has convulsed the world."[119] Although Bayet called upon his fellow democrats to fight Nazi antisemitism, he insisted that in the "civilized world" there was only one appropriate weapon: "the word." Explaining his personal decision to negotiate with the Germans despite Hitler's anti-Jewish and anti-leftist crackdown, another prominent Radical, Bertrand de Jouvenel, declared that while the émigrés deserved pity, the French had to refrain from "sharing their passions" so as not to ignite another war, which would undoubtedly be the world's last.[120] Even Daladier, according to the newspaper of the LICA, the *Droit de vivre*, had railed in 1933 against the excessive influence of Jewish journalists in the press, declaring that their constant harping on the evils of Nazism severely diminished prospects for Franco-German reconciliation.[121]

Despite this ambivalence, when the Flandin and Laval administrations initiated their antiforeign crackdown in late 1934 and 1935, these liberal and left-wing groups for the most part set aside their hesitations and rallied around the effort to overturn the anti-immigrant decree laws and to secure a special refugee statute that would guarantee not only the right to asylum, but also the right to work.[122] This effort was part of a broader program to protect foreign workers in France against arbitrary expulsions and *refoulements*, and these liberal and left-wing parties and associations argued insistently that the Depression could not be cured on the backs of the foreign workers. At the same time, they recognized that refugees constituted a distinct category of foreigners, since for them *refoulement* or expulsion almost certainly meant incarceration or even death. As a result, they insisted that special legislative measures be enacted to protect refugees specifically. The League for the Rights of Man, in response to the various refugee influxes of the 1920's, had already articulated a program by the early 1930's designed to achieve this end. This program called for an end to arbitrary *refoulements* and expulsions, with judicial rather than administrative review for questionable cases; the limitation of expulsion to cases involving crimes against national security or the public order; the provision of a special legal document, similar to the Nansen passport, that would identify refugees and allow them to travel freely; and, perhaps most significantly, the exemption of refugees from existing regulations governing the right of foreigners to work.[123] For, as Marius Moutet and Léon Blum insisted time and again during the Chamber debates over refugee policy in 1934 and 1935, it was sheer hypocrisy to talk about the right to asylum without guaranteeing the right to work.[124]

By 1935, as thousands of refugees were being thrown into prison, left-wing groups as well as émigrés themselves began to submit even more elaborate proposals for a refugee statute. One plan that attracted significant attention was put forth by the German émigré playwright Ernst Toller in March 1935 and called on the government to guarantee both the right of asylum and the right to work for those German refugees still remaining in France. Toller appealed to the French government to join Jewish and other private relief agencies to provide a package of 16 million francs ($2.4 million) for refugee assistance, since the Comité National was clearly unable to bear this burden alone, and he also called on the government to provide the refugees with at least 2,000 work permits. Although Toller admitted that this expenditure might at first appear steep, he insisted that in the long term such an investment was well worthwhile since it would lead to the creation of new jobs and new consumers. Toller furthermore drew up a legal refugee statute that became the central rallying point for the pro-refugee coalition. In addition to those points already incorporated into the program advanced by the League for the Rights of Man, Toller proposed that those enterprises in which refugees provided all or part of the capital investment be allowed to hire up to one-third of their personnel from among the refugees; that the legal definition of refugee status be more clearly articulated; that a consultative commission made up of government officials, pro-refugee advocates, and refugees be created to review the dossiers of asylum seekers; and that naturalization procedures be facilitated for those individuals granted refugee status.[125]

By the fall of 1935, with the Toller program in hand, the pro-refugee camp began to step up its lobbying efforts to secure a refugee statute. The socialists, the League for the Rights of Man, and the LICA all hailed the idea of a consultative commission and claimed that only by guaranteeing the right to asylum could the government effectively end the "vicious circle" of imprisonment, *refoulement*, and reincarceration that occurred whenever refugees shoved across the border were shoved back again, only to resume their illegal existences.[126] In the fall of 1935, pro-refugee activists founded a new organization, the Amis des Travailleurs Etrangers, whose secretary-general was Magdeleine Paz,[127] and in January 1936 they created the Centre de Liaison des Comités pour le Statut des Immigrés, a federation of 27 immigrant and refugee organizations whose secretary-general was Henri Levin, the vice president of the LICA.[128]

The Amis des Travailleurs Etrangers was a member of the Centre de Liaison, and both organizations shared similar goals: the education of the public, including trade unionists, regarding the benefits of immigration; the education of foreign workers with regard to French labor legislation so that they would be less inclined to accept illegal work; the streamlining of the relief effort to reduce overlap among existing refugee organizations; and the enactment of more humane immigration legislation, including a general immigration statute, to ensure that economic immigrants be carefully selected and steered only to economic sectors where they were needed, as well as a special refugee statute that would encompass the guarantees outlined by the League for the Rights of Man and Toller.[129] To diffuse these aims among the public at large as well as among the immigrant community, the Centre de Liaison created a newspaper, *Fraternité*, and in June of 1936 it sponsored an international conference in Paris to bring together refugee committees from around the world to draft a proposal for an international refugee statute to be submitted to the upcoming League of Nations refugee conference, scheduled to be held in Geneva in July.[130]

Although the creation of the Centre de Liaison was primarily a socialist inspiration, the communist refugee aid society, Secours Rouge International, participated, and the influential communist senator Marcel Cachin was one of the organizers of the 1936 International Refugee Conference in Paris. Furthermore, a group of communist deputies, led by Georges Lévy, deputy of the Rhône, submitted a bill to Parliament in July of 1936 condemning the antiforeign decree laws as "vexatious and inhumane measures" and demanding an immigration statute, including provisions for asylum seekers and the creation of a consultative commission. This bill was passed into law in early 1937, and it served as a foundation stone for the new refugee policy of the Popular Front.[131]

In addition to the demand for a refugee statute, these groups also began to examine agricultural and colonial solutions as a way of circumventing the perpetual problem of having to reconcile the right to asylum with the perceived economic threat the refugees posed to French workers and middle-class professionals. In September 1935, a German refugee wrote to *L'Oeuvre* describing the grim fate of those refugees who had remained in France. He pointed out that whatever money or relief most of the refugees had hitherto lived on had now been exhausted. Thousands of refugees faced the threat of imprisonment, and refugee women were increasingly forced into prostitution simply to make ends meet. In the end, this refugee speculated, there was only one way to spare the refugees a future of famine and crime: to send them either to the colonies or to the agricultural departments of the southwest, where severe labor shortages prevailed.[132] Marguerite d'Escola of *L'Aube* fully agreed. Bemoaning the fact that France had "colonies without settlers"—the deserted farmlands of the southwest—she insisted that these lots "could still provide asylum for entire families of farmers." Why, she asked, should these fields be left fallow when "whole tribes" were searching the world over for bed and board.[133] Léon Jouhaux, writing in the CGT paper, *Le Peuple*, also claimed in 1935 that the current policy of expelling foreigners en masse was ludicrous in light of the fact that French businesses had never ceased to import foreign workers. While Jouhaux agreed that removing the foreigners from the overcrowded urban centers was a worthwhile goal, he saw no reason why foreigners already in France, including the refugees, should not be granted priority in receiving jobs as manual laborers and farm workers in the provinces.[134]

Thus, on the eve of the Popular Front victory, the battle lines between the pro- and anti-refugee camps were clearly demarcated. On the radical right, opinion was overwhelmingly negative, and the refugees were consistently portrayed as a serious threat to the economic, cultural, and political well-being of the nation. Right-wing groups, as well as the professional corporations, frequently employed the psychological mechanism of inversion to prove that they, and not the refugees, were the true victims of Hitler's rise to power. Already in 1933, *L'Action française* lamented that as a result of the government's overly generous refugee policy, "the French have once again become victims of an appeal to their pity and generosity."[135] The conservative deputies from Alsace and Lorraine who submitted legislation in 1934 demanding protection for artisans against immigrant competition similarly declared that "France has been cruelly hit and duped" as a result of its overly generous hospitality. Did not French artisans too have a right to a bare minimum of economic security?[136]

On the other side of the battle line, the pro-refugee coalition, which included the majority of left-wing and liberal groups together with a few moderate conservatives and individual members of the clergy, rejected the idea that foreigners caused the Depression, and they pressed relentlessly for the implementation of a general immigration statute as well as a special refugee statute that would guarantee the right to asylum as well as the right to work. While some members of this coalition, most notably the trade unions, were willing to see some restrictions imposed on future economic immigration into France, they were not willing to countenance an assault against the rights of foreigners already in France; nor were they willing to tolerate any erosion of the right to refugee asylum. They were, however, willing to join their more conservative colleagues in considering agricultural and colonial solutions as a way around the perennial dilemma of seeking to reconcile the economic rights of refugees with those of French citizens.

Finally, as we have seen, a large segment of the population stood between these two camps. Many of these people became advocates of the idea of "selective immigration." To be sure, even pro-refugee spokesmen favored selective immigration insofar as it applied to economic immigration. In 1931, the League for the Rights of Man, for example, declared that it favored an immigration policy that would select out those immigrants who were "morally healthy [and] socially useful."[137] Nevertheless, the League never wavered from its position that the refugees constituted a special case, and that asylum could not be made conditional on the refugees' particular economic skills. On the other hand, the centrist advocates of selective immigration lumped the refugees together with all other immigrants and argued that they deserved no special protection. The sole criterion deemed applicable for selection was whether an immigrant was economically, or even racially, desirable. The question thus facing refugees, from this vantage point, was whether they could transform themselves into desirable immigrants — that is, manual laborers, and especially farm workers. While some theorists of selective immigration, such as Mauco, were willing to give the refugees the benefit of the doubt, others, such as Martial, were less generous.

With the Popular Front victory, however, this configuration of opinion began to change, with a significant segment of the pro-refugee camp splitting off and moving toward the center or even into the anti-refugee camp. This shift, as we will see in Chapter 12, was due less to the particular nature of the Popular Front's refugee policies than to the general perception that the Popular Front represented a radical departure in French politics, ushering in an era of radical left-wing hegemony. Such fears of "bolshevization" radicalized not only the political right, but they also gave a strong rightward shove to a large segment of moderate opinion, which previously had stood firmly in the pro-refugee camp. Thus, although in the short term the Popular Front inaugurated a new era of refugee policy, in the long term the alienation of a considerable segment of centrist opinion from the pro-refugee camp had repercussions that endured beyond the Popular Front's brief life span.

CHAPTER FIVE

Loyalties in Conflict
French Jewry and the Refugee Crisis, 1933–May 1936

An analysis of French refugee policy during the years prior to the Popular Front would be incomplete without a discussion of the role played by the French Jewish community, especially since that role has long been a matter of controversy. During the 1930's, refugee groups, together with French sympathizers, frequently accused the native Jewish establishment of having abandoned them. More recently, this view has been reiterated by Maurice Rajsfus in his scathing polemic *Sois Juif et tais-toi!*, as well as by Jean-Baptiste Joly in a more subdued essay, "L'Aide aux émigrés juifs: Le Comité National de Secours."[1] Not only did the native Jewish community fail to provide adequate philanthropy, these critics maintain, but, more importantly, it also refused to press the French government to pursue more liberal refugee policies. According to this view, French Jewish elites, fearful of an antisemitic backlash and desirous of proving that they placed their national loyalties above their Jewish ones, even went so far as to pressure the government to close the borders.

Most historians who have studied the issue, however, including David Weinberg, Paula Hyman, and most recently Catherine Nicault, have been more circumspect. While conceding that French Jews may not have accomplished a great deal on the political front, these scholars insist that in reality there was little choice. From their perspective, it was the French government that set the limits—which by the late 1930's had become very narrow indeed. They therefore argue that French Jews had control over one aspect of the refugee question only—philanthropy. And with regard to that endeavor, it is likely that they accomplished as much as could be expected.[2]

In this chapter, we will reexamine this debate with particular reference to the years prior to the Popular Front's coming to power. Although the attitudes of the native Jewish elites toward the refugees underwent a considerable evolution during the 1930's, a trend we will examine in Chapter 13, available evidence suggests that with respect to these early years, the harsh assessment put forth by Rajsfus, Joly, and other critics of the Franco-Jewish establishment is in fact correct. Despite the very real constraints imposed upon Jewish leadership as a result of government policy, French Jewish leaders could have done a good deal more, both politically and even in terms of providing philanthropy. Contrary to the view that the Jewish leaders were merely responding to pressure exerted by the government, it is clear that several individuals within the Franco-Jewish establishment played a far more active role. In particular, Jacques Helbronner, whose activities during these years have strangely been ignored, not only lobbied incessantly for a more restrictive refugee policy in his capacity as Jewish spokesman— he was vice president of the Central Consistory as well as a member of the executive committee of the Comité National, the principal relief committee between 1933 and 1935—but, more importantly, he even held key posts in the government that enabled him to exert a direct influence over the formulation of official refugee policy itself. Most significantly, Helbronner, who was already a member of the Conseil d'Etat, was appointed in 1934 to succeed Henry Bérenger as France's chief delegate to the Advisory Council of the League of Nation's High Commission for Refugees (HCR).

To be sure, the hard-line views espoused by Helbronner and his supporters were not shared by all native Jews involved in the relief effort. Within the ranks of the committee itself, Helbronner's most outspoken opponent was Raymond-Raoul Lambert, the secretary-general of the Comité National and, from 1934 on, the editor-in-chief of the *Univers israélite*, the principal mouthpiece of French Jewry.[3] Lambert, as we shall see, consistently upheld a more moderate position, one decidedly more sympathetic to the refugees themselves. Nevertheless, during this first phase of the refugee crisis, it was Helbronner's views that prevailed—a situation that had dire consequences for those refugees who had found asylum in France. The proposition that France would serve only as a *gare de triage*, a way station for refugees en route to final destinations elsewhere, was therefore not simply a policy foisted upon the Jewish community by an increasingly restrictionist government. Rather, it was a goal embraced quite willingly by one important and influential sector of the native Jewish establishment itself.

To better understand the emergence of these positions, it is useful to look back at the early history of the Jewish relief effort. In the early months following Hitler's rise to power, there were few signs of the difficulties soon to emerge. During this period, French Jewish leaders fully encouraged the government's generous reception of the refugees and did everything possible to ensure that this goodwill continue. Throughout March and April of 1933, Jewish leaders engaged in a flurry of activities on behalf of the refugee cause. Prominent Jewish journalists such as Hippolyte Prague, editor-in-chief of the important Jewish journal the *Archives israélites*, enthusiastically encouraged German Jews to come to France. France, he declared, would become their "veritable Eldorado," and he predicted that the influx of new-comers would rejuvenate French Jewish institutions.[4]

Simultaneously, Jewish groups sponsored mass rallies and demonstrations throughout the spring of 1933 to protest Nazi antisemitism and to win popular support for the refugee cause. To be sure, it was primarily groups with strong ties to the immigrant Jewish community—the International League Against Antisemitism (LICA) and the Federation of Jewish Societies of France (FSJF)*—that took the lead in organizing these events in conjunction with liberal and left-wing allies.[5] Nevertheless, despite some initial reluctance, native elites, including prominent representatives of the French rabbinate, soon joined in.[6] Perhaps most importantly, the major institutions of native French Jewry—the Central Consistory and the Alliance Is-raélite Universelle—jumped into the fray with respect to organizing a refugee relief campaign.[7] Admittedly, they were not the only ones: throughout the early spring of 1933, no less than 15 refugee committees—some sponsored by Jewish organizations, others by a wide range of political groups—cropped up in Paris alone to assist refugees with a wide range of problems, including housing, food, job placement, emigration possibilities, and legal advice.[8] Still, it was the committee created by the French Jewish establishment, initially called the Comité d'Aide et d'Accueil aux Victimes de l'Anti-

---

*The LICA was a nonsectarian organization dedicated to combating antisemitism. It was established in 1928 by Bernard Lecache, the son of East European Jewish immigrants. Although not officially affiliated with any political party, the LICA had a definite left-wing bent. On the LICA in the 1930's, see especially Hyman, pp. 205, 230, and passim; Weinberg, pp. 26–27, 164–65; Epstein, pp. 80–125, and passim. The journal of the LICA was the *Droit de vivre* (*DdV*).

The Fédération des Sociétés Juives de France (FSJF, Federation of Jewish Societies of France), created in 1913, consisted of 85 immigrant societies by the mid-1930's. The FSJF was founded to coordinate immigrant welfare, to provide the immigrants with a greater say over charitable and welfare activities (previously dominated by native French Jews), and to help the immigrants adapt to French life. On the FSJF, see Hyman, pp. 80, 85–87, 207–16; Weinberg, pp. 29–30, and passim.

sémitisme en Allemagne (Aid and Reception Committee for the Victims of Antisemitism in Germany) and reorganized and renamed the Comité National Français de Secours aux Réfugiés Allemands, Victimes de l'Antisémitisme in July, that emerged as the most important source of refugee assistance and was recognized by the government as the Jewish community's principal mouthpiece on refugee issues.[9] To ensure that borders remain open, the Alliance Israélite Universelle (AIU) promised authorities that it would undertake full financial responsibility for the refugees, guaranteeing that they would not become public charges.[10] Thus, during these first weeks of the refugee influx, French Jewry gave every appearance of having made a wholehearted and long-term commitment to the refugee cause.

By the summer of 1933, however, this wave of optimism and goodwill was beginning to give way to deep-seated apprehensions. To a large extent, the problem was a financial one. No one—neither the government nor the official representatives of French Jewry—had expected an exodus of the magnitude or duration of that which took place in 1933. Despite the Alliance's assurances that the refugees would not become public charges, the task of having to sustain a prolonged fund-raising campaign proved beyond the endurance of French Jewish institutions. By June 1933, the Comité d'Aide et d'Accueil was caring for 5,799 refugees in Paris alone. No fewer than 400 persons per day knocked on its doors seeking some form of assistance, and of these, approximately 125 per day were first-time clients.[11] Expenses mounted quickly—by the summer of 1933 the Committee's budget was approaching 900,000 francs ($225,000) per month.[12]

The French Jewish community during these years was ill-equipped to meet these demands. To be sure, there were several extremely wealthy families, most notably the Rothschilds, who were able to pour huge sums into refugee relief; indeed, they paid a full third of all the Committee's expenses in 1933.[13] Yet, nearly one-half of France's total Jewish population of about 260,000 was of recent immigrant origin and could barely afford major donations.[14] In response, French Jewish leaders began a desperate search for outside funding. France's chief rabbi, Israël Lévi, organized a fund-raising campaign in the United States and warned potential American donors that "a catastrophe is at the gate."[15]

At the same time, the Comité National, notwithstanding its initial promises of economic self-sufficiency, began to appeal directly to the government for assistance. Indeed, no sooner had the Committee been created in July of 1933 than its acting president, Robert de Rothschild, notified the minister of the interior, Camille Chautemps, that it was teetering on the verge of bankruptcy. Without an immediate infusion of public funds, Rothschild threatened, the Committee would be forced to close its doors, throwing the 3,500 refugees currently on relief out on to the streets. Deprived of food and shelter, he warned, "these unfortunates in their distress risk disturbing the public order."[16]

Such desperate appeals had the desired effect. The Comité National found a major American donor: the Joint Distribution Committee (JDC), American Jewry's principal international relief organization, which feared that the government would close the borders if the Comité National withdrew.[17] The administration too, despite continued refusals to grant direct financial assistance, nevertheless made available several unused military barracks and hospitals—the camp at Saint-Maur, the bastions at the Porte d'Orléans and the Porte d'Italie, and the Andral Hospital—to serve as temporary refugee housing for over 700 refugees, supplementing the use of hotels.[18] As a result of this outside assistance, the worst-case scenarios predicted by Lévi and Rothschild were, at least for the moment, averted.

Budgetary factors were not the Committee's sole source of concern, however. Cultural and political problems also plagued the relief effort. One particularly thorny issue was the all too visible Germanness of the refugees. In July 1933, journalist Janine Auscher reported that many French Jews, fiercely patriotic, were reluctant to give money to the relief campaign since they regarded the refugees as "above all . . . Germans, thus our former enemies."[19] Moreover, French Jewish elites repeatedly reproached their wealthy German coreligionists for refusing to bear a greater share of the relief effort. According to one well-known journalist, Jacques Biélinky, himself of East European immigrant background, wealthy German Jews, brought up in a Prussian culture that had done little to inculcate the virtue of charity "had opposed all [the Comité National's] solicitations with an icy refusal."[20] Jacques Helbronner too railed against those German Jews who were gambling away their fortunes on the Riviera while their French coreligionists back in Paris were working night and day to assist the less fortunate victims of the Nazi persecution.[21] Attempts at persuasion ultimately gave way to force: according to a report in the *Tribune juive*, the major organ of Alsatian Jewry, the Comité National actually petitioned the government to expel one wealthy German banker who had repeatedly refused to make a contribution.[22]

East European Jews living in France were scarcely more sympathetic. Resentful of the fact that they had been looked down upon by their German coreligionists, some were not altogether displeased that the tables were now turned. As one journalist noted:

Many German Jews, extremely patriotic and extremely conscious of their dignity, rose up not long ago against the immigration of East European Jews who might have harmed their considerable social standing and reinforced the impact of anti-

Jewish propaganda. Today, they are the ones harming the situation of their coreligionists and reinforcing the antipathy toward Jews that exists in the countries where they seek to settle. Thus, the hostile attitude assumed by German Jews toward the immigrants has now suddenly turned against themselves.[23]

Summing up this dilemma, another journalist declared:

At the beginning, it is true, German Jews found a warm and generous welcome. But since then a good deal has changed. French Jews complain that the newcomers have brought with them the particular faults of the Germans. Too noisy, too convinced of the superiority of German civilization. In brief—veritable "Boches."

Immigrant Jews from Eastern Europe, for their part, always mistrustful of the "Yekkes" (German Jews) have at times reproached them for their lack of solidarity. Moreover, people often distinguish, just as many antisemites do with respect to Jews in general, between each individual considered separately and the group to which he belongs. People admit that there may be "chic types" among the German Jews; nonetheless, they retain a [negative] opinion of them as a whole.[24]

Political tensions drove yet another wedge into relations between the native French Jewish elites and the refugees. Already in April of 1933, Chief Rabbi Lévi had counseled Jews to abstain from mass demonstrations to protest Nazi antisemitism.[25] Ostensibly motivated by the fear that such demonstrations might inspire an even harsher Nazi crackdown against those Jews who remained in Germany, there is little doubt that Lévi had domestic considerations in mind as well. The strongly left-wing cast of the protest rallies and demonstrations tended to make many French Jews, who frequently attributed the rise of antisemitism to the disproportionate influence of Jews in the Socialist and Communist Parties, extremely uncomfortable and fearful of an antisemitic backlash.[26] A number of spokesmen for the Jewish establishment therefore felt compelled to warn the refugees that they had better behave. Expressing the irritation felt by many native French Jews, Rabbi Ernest Ginsburger declared: "It seems that they [the refugees] apparently do not understand that they must observe a reserve, a discretion, I'd dare say even a prudence of which they should not make a spectacle. Who knows whether this effacement, this modesty would not have been better for their cause?" Even the "Pollaks," he maintained, had conducted themselves better. Although they too had been persecuted, they had found in France a happy and peaceful refuge "without meetings, without grandiloquent appeals to justice, to humanity, to history, to the universal conscience." "Reduced almost entirely to their own devices," he continued, these Poles "knew how to create an honorable position; they acquired for themselves esteem and consideration, engaged in economic and social philanthropic activities, and, conscious of their debt, sacrificed their

blood for France at the time of danger as fearless volunteers for war."
"Couldn't their conduct and their economic activities serve as examples
to the new refugees," Ginsburger asked, "or must we call into question
their much vaunted capabilities, their intelligence, their science, [and] their
initiative?"[27]

Political discord surfaced even at the Comité National itself, to the consternation of the native Jewish establishment. Due to the ever growing volume of requests for refugee assistance, Lambert reinforced security at the
Committee in the spring of 1933 to prevent disturbances from erupting
among the impatient crowds that gathered daily outside on the street; in
July, he even requested a police presence to help maintain order.[28] Incidents
nevertheless broke out. In late May, according to Lambert, two refugees
"whose incorrect behavior, threats, and revolutionary remarks, have created unrest in the street" ultimately assaulted several employees of the Committee. Following a police investigation, these troublemakers were deported.[29] In August, a food riot erupted at the St. Maur camp, one of the
caserns donated by the government, and in the fall a full-fledged riot against
the Committee broke out at the Andral Hospital. The left-wing protesters
charged that the Committee had betrayed every promise it had made to the
refugees. The food was disgusting, the pocket money woefully inadequate,
and the Committee's personnel mean-spirited. But the Committee's worst
crime was having herded the refugees into military caserns, which the protesters and their communist supporters alleged were no better than Nazi-
style concentration camps. "The administration of the Committee," their
tracts proclaimed, "has lost our confidence and has shown itself to be from
the lowest- to the highest-level functionary a band of swindlers." Robert de
Rothschild's response was swift and sharp. He demanded that the police expel the ringleaders who "not having the least recognition for the hospitality offered by our country, continue to engage in propaganda of a clear communist tendency."[30]

By the end of 1933, the relationship between the refugees and the Comité
National was sorely strained. Refugees deeply resented the steady diminu-
tion of financial support as well as the patronizing and condescending tone
of those in charge of the relief effort. French Jewish leaders, for their part,
expressed shock and anger at the impertinence and, above all, the ingratitude of the newcomers. As Ernest Ginsburger again pointed out, French
Jewry had certainly done its humanitarian duty, but, he asked, had the refugees done theirs?[31] If they truly appreciated the hospitality offered them, it
was now time that they show more tact and discretion—that they give up
what Lambert called, "that gregarious mentality, that need to band together in the service of slogan-brandishing associations."[32] Or as Robert de
Rothschild matter-of-factly put it: "If they are not happy here, let them

leave. They are guests whom we have warmly received, but they should not go about rocking the boat."[33]

Yet all of these problems, troublesome as they were, could have and probably would have been surmounted had it not been for the single most difficult challenge that confronted the Comité National in this period—the severe job shortage that resulted from the Depression and the government's ensuing retreat from its initially liberal position.[34] As we have seen, no sooner had the refugees begun to arrive than a host of middle-class professional groups—artisans, merchants, and liberal professionals—raised the hue and cry that the refugees posed a grave economic threat. As a result of their incessant demands for protection, the government began to erect a formidable barrage of legislation aimed at keeping foreigners, including the refugees, out of these middle-class professions, in addition to the already extant legislation limiting their role as industrial workers.

The question that arises with respect to French Jewish elites is not simply how they reacted to this radical shift in policy, but whether and to what degree they may have played some role in bringing it about. To be sure, the Depression imposed very real and severe limitations on relief work—for it was clear that the Ministry of Labor intended to grant the refugees work permits on an extremely limited basis.[35] Whether the new immigrants were indeed harmful to the French economy was a matter of considerable debate, as is true in contemporary society as well. It is indisputable, however, that there existed a strong popular perception that they constituted a serious economic threat. French Jewish leaders therefore felt that if they were to avoid the charge of being unpatriotic, of placing their Jewish interests above their commitments to the French people as a whole, they had no choice but to address these concerns. In a speech of June 30, 1933, in which he officially announced the opening of the Comité National, Robert de Rothschild proclaimed that French Jews were bound by a double obligation. Not only did "the most simple duties of humanity command" them "to welcome them [the refugees], [and] to help them secure new means of existence," but no less important was the duty French Jews owed the French people, who had so graciously offered their hospitality: "There is at this moment in our country an unemployment crisis that we must take care not to aggravate since French opinion would not support—and rightly so—that these Germans, no matter how worthy they are of being treated with kindness, become here an object of preferential treatment."[36] Fernand Corcos, a prominent French Zionist and member of the League for the Rights of Man and Citizen, similarly maintained that "if French workers were to run up against jobs taken without discernment by Germans, the most regrettable misunderstandings could arise."[37] Heeding these concerns, Senator André Honnorat, director of the Comité des Savants, which supervised the placement of refugee intellectuals, deemed it "dangerous to welcome too many German Jews to France"; to do so "would provoke a backlash of jealousy among unemployed French intellectuals."[38]

The economic crisis and the protectionist backlash that ensued had therefore considerably narrowed the range of possibilities available to the Comité National. Nevertheless, French Jews still had choices and continued to exercise influence over government policy—for the government conferred with the Committee at every step of the way. The dilemma they faced was how to use this influence to balance the dual obligations to which Robert de Rothschild had alluded. Achieving this reconciliation would prove no easy matter, for it was not at all clear which side of the balance would be stressed. Despite the fact that native French Jews have frequently been depicted as a homogenous group, they did not speak with a single voice, and it was precisely over this question of how to balance these conflicting obligations that a major dispute arose within the ranks of the Committee. Essentially, two viable options were available: either the Committee could adopt a hard-line position, abandoning any commitment to the refugees in order to opt for what it perceived to be the best interests of France, or it could pursue a more moderate course, striving to arrive at a true accommodation between the interests of the refugees on the one hand and those of the French public on the other. These two positions crystallized around two of the central figures within the Committee: Jacques Helbronner, who represented the hard-liners, and Raymond-Raoul Lambert, the Comité National's secretary-general, who represented the more moderate path.[39] The outcome of the battle between these two would have profound repercussions, influencing not only the nature of the relief effort but also, more significantly, the formulation of French official refugee policy itself.

As foremost spokesman for the hard-line position, Helbronner, whether he represented the Comité National or the French government at the League of Nations HCR, never failed to put forth the most extreme anti-refugee position possible. From his point of view, there was no question of conflicting loyalties. French Jews had one obligation, and one obligation only, and that was to France. In June of 1933, at a meeting of Jewish organizations, he demanded of his colleagues: "What do you plan to do with these masses [of refugees]? We're in a period of unemployment, we cannot encumber our [liberal] professions, nor are there jobs in factories or in commerce for this afflux of labor that has descended upon us." He then went on to add:

France, like every other nation, has its unemployed, and not all the Jewish refugees from Germany are people worth keeping. . . . If there are 100 to 150 great intellectuals who are worthy of being kept in France since they are scientists or chemists who have secrets our own chemists don't know . . . these we will keep, but the 7, 8, or perhaps 10,000 Jews who will come to France, is it really in our best interest to keep them?[40]

Several years later, Helbronner reiterated this position, openly bemoaning the fact that the borders had been too open in 1933. From his perspective, France had received too many of "the riff-raff, the rejects of society, the elements who could not possibly have been of any use to their own country." These individuals, he declared, were simply "a bunch of nonentities of no use to any human agglomeration."[41]

Given Helbronner's utter disdain for the refugees, it is not surprising that he made use of every opportunity to press the government to implement the most restrictive policy possible. At the Interministerial Commission meetings convened by the government in the fall of 1933 to discuss strategies for dealing with the Jewish refugee question, Helbronner—who represented the Comité National there together with either Edmond or Robert de Rothschild—lobbied the government vigorously to close the borders as tightly as possible, and he vetoed every proposal that would have enabled Jewish refugees to have remained in France. When one minister suggested that the refugees should be sent to industrial centers outside Paris where they might find better job opportunities, Helbronner objected—in light of their grievances, the refugees would be ripe for communism.[42] Furthermore, although initially willing to consider the settlement of refugees in rural France, by 1934 Helbronner adamantly opposed this proposal as well. France, he maintained, was not a country of colonization. When the JDC tried to persuade French Jewish leaders to at least investigate possibilities for agricultural placement, Helbronner protested vehemently:

From the political point of view, the projects envisioned likewise raise serious objections: whether it's a question of settlements in small groups or in large masses, it's to be feared that, due to the special conditions under which these settlements will be undertaken, as well as to the language [and] particular customs of the elements to be settled, these projects would only create an atmosphere of hostility in the designated regions and among the French peasants that could degenerate into a more or less blatant antisemitism.[43]

Helbronner's views, which were shared by Robert de Rothschild and Louis Oungre, director of the Jewish Colonization Association (JCA), provoked Bernhard Kahn, the JDC's European director, to remark bitterly in 1935: "For permanent agricultural settlement, I am sorry to say, we have not found the necessary support among French Jewry. This would have been a partial solution to the refugee problem in France. It is almost tragic that the obstacles put in the way of such an undertaking have been so far insurmountable."[44]

For Helbronner, there was only one solution to the dilemma: emigration.

As the government's delegate to the Advisory Council of the HCR, Helbronner never failed to put forth in the most unequivocal terms the view that France could serve as a transit country only—a *"gare de triage."* France, he repeatedly insisted, had done her duty; it was now time for the international community, and particularly the League of Nations, to do theirs. Even the vast majority of refugees already in France (with the exception of the 100–150 intellectuals he considered useful) would, he insisted, have to go.[45] Helbronner's attitude, it should be noted, infuriated James G. McDonald, the HCR high commissioner, as well as Bernhard Kahn, both of whom were firmly convinced that in light of the bleak prospects for finding new immigration possibilities, the countries of first asylum would have to make a considerable effort to absorb a significant portion of their refugees. As Kahn put it, "The idea that the majority of these refugees are only temporary visitors must be radically changed if the refugee problem were ever to be solved." Indeed, the JDC was so eager to see the refugees already in France settled there permanently that it even offered to pay the Comité National five pounds sterling for every refugee successfully placed in a job, and it encouraged the Committee to create loan banks to help refugees embark on small-scale business ventures, which remained unregulated by antiforeign restrictions.[46]

By mid-1934, however, such constructive solutions were becoming increasingly difficult to find, a problem Kahn attributed not only to the attitude of the French government and people, but to the influence of the hardliners on the Committee, who he believed were exploiting the xenophobic climate to achieve their own ends. These individuals, he charged, had from the beginning striven "to get rid of the refugees," and to achieve their goal they "disapprove [of] every attempt to help the refugees constructively, no matter what the project may be."[47] Madeleine Coulon, secretary-general of the Comité pour la Défense des Droits des Israélites en Europe Centrale et Orientale, also known as the Gourevitch Committee, similarly pointed her finger at Helbronner, together with his predecessor, Bérenger, who had been appointed to serve as the Comité National's honorary president in late 1933. Writing in 1936, Coulon maintained that those who "should have boldly defended the refugees' rights of residence and work" had instead used their governmental positions to "push to the extreme the theory that France serve as a simple transit country for Jewish refugees and that, with the money collected in France and abroad to save the lives and the dignity of the refugees, they had steered them, so as to get rid of them all, to Paraguay."[48]

Helbronner, to be sure, was not the sole spokesman for the Committee, and his most outspoken opponent was Raymond-Raoul Lambert, who in 1933, at the age of 39, was the foremost representative of the younger generation of native Jewish leaders. Ironically, Lambert has been the Jewish leader most vilified by critics of the native Jewish establishment, and especially by Rajsfus.[49] In reality, however, there is no convincing evidence to support this point of view. Indeed, Lambert was probably more sensitive to the plight and needs of the refugees than any of his colleagues, perhaps because of his greater sympathy for Zionism[50] as well as his profound familiarity with the German language and culture—he had taught in Saxe-Meiningen before the First World War, and from 1920 to 1924 he served the French government in Bonn as assistant to the high commissioner for the Rhineland.[51]

Throughout the 1930's, Lambert toiled to bring about a true accommodation between the needs of the refugees and what he perceived to be the best interests of France. In sharp contrast to Helbronner, who consistently rejected every attempt to find constructive solutions to the refugee problem, Lambert worked tirelessly from 1933 through 1935 to find job opportunities for the refugees that would have permitted them to remain in France. In the spring of 1933, he propounded an extremely liberal position that closely paralleled ideas being floated by the League for the Rights of Man, the LICA, and the Socialist Party. In an article that appeared in the influential Jewish journal *La Revue juive de Genève*, Lambert proclaimed:

> There is a difficult but admirable project to be realized. There are those who object that unemployment is raging, that the employment possibilities are extremely limited, that the Depression has necessitated in every enterprise a reduction of personnel. We, however, will by no means despair. We will enlighten opinion and the higher-ups will not fail to lessen the severity of certain regulations. The presence in France of new technicians, of new scientists, of new artists could bolster the productive force of the country and perhaps give rise to useful industries. Just the other day someone mentioned to me a plan for the agricultural colonization of a vast domain in the south of France; someone else told me of a study by an entrepreneur who wants to create toy workshops so as to compete with Nuremberg; another declared the possibility of establishing the fur trade in Paris to take the place of Leipzig. Perhaps these are exaggerations or wild fantasies; but all this at least goes to prove the existence of certain possibilities that we mustn't scorn.[52]

Lambert quickly realized that this task would not be so simple; nevertheless, throughout the summer and fall of 1933 he lobbied the Ministry of Labor ceaselessly to secure as many work permits as possible, even for refugees of East European origin, despite the fact that the administration had already excluded this category from refugee status.[53] And in November, facing a severe shortage of funds and an increasingly reluctant government, Lambert declared that it was now time to "be done with the period when one thinks solely of feeding and lodging the unfortunates." French Jews now had to think more seriously about constructive solutions, particularly in agriculture and industry.[54] Unlike Helbronner, who had categorically ruled out agricultural settlements, Lambert was willing to consider such schemes. To be sure, he too vehemently opposed large-scale colonization projects, fearing that the creation of unassimilated ethnic enclaves would prevent the successful integration of the refugees and would offend French sensibilities.[55] Nevertheless, he was more than willing to support the small-scale settlement of refugees in rural areas, and he endorsed the creation of agricultural training centers to ensure that refugees eligible for this type of work be carefully selected and receive proper training.[56] Lambert's efforts to secure work permits did not always bear fruit, and by mid-1935 only 2,403 refugees had been placed in jobs, primarily in domestic service and agriculture.[57] Yet the fact that his requests for work permits regularly exceeded the number granted indicates that the administration, and not Lambert, was responsible for this problem.

Lambert's commitment to the refugees led him to criticize even the government when he felt it had reneged on its original promises. According to a report of the British embassy in Paris:

The committee [there is no doubt that here the writer is referring to Lambert's role] is stated to be very dissatisfied with the attitude of the French authorities, who originally, for political reasons, welcomed the refugees but now make it virtually impossible for any of them to obtain work here. When with great difficulty the committee finds some opening, the French authorities refuse to grant a "permis de travail" [work permit] or waste so much time about it that the job has been filled by someone else meanwhile.[58]

In January 1934, when the authorities began for the first time to expel refugees whose papers were not in order, Lambert sent off a sharply worded protest to the government. "After the splendid effort offered by France in favor of the unfortunates," he declared, "it would be unjust if excessively severe measures were to come and destroy so considerable an achievement that has contributed to enhancing the prestige of hospitable France throughout the world."[59]

But perhaps the strongest testimony to Lambert's efforts is the fact that he won the praise of the refugees themselves. In an article of July of 1934, sharply critical of the Comité National, the *Pariser Tageblatt*, the foremost émigré newspaper, went to great lengths to exempt Lambert from its scathing attack:

His power of work within the relief organization is as great as his goodness of character and his affability toward the émigrés seeking assistance. Naturally, he can do nothing to counteract the bitter necessity of empty coffers; however, even those who suffer a refusal, those who are turned away by him, will always retain the feeling of having spoken to a humane and obliging man. Unfortunately, one cannot say as much for a good number of employees and even directors of Comité National services, even when they are German émigrés themselves.[60]

To be sure, Lambert was by no means an extreme radical on refugee matters. There were other groups, most notably the Gourevitch Committee, that pushed much further than Lambert both in terms of criticizing government policies publicly and with regard to advocating more innovative proposals for refugee settlement—including mass colonization schemes, either in France itself or in the colonies, or the idea that the government ought to allocate 8,000 to 10,000 work permits to refugees in exchange for the equivalent number of jobs refugee-owned firms had supposedly created for French workers.[61] Lambert also seems to have accepted certain government policies, such as weeding out East European refugees and distinguishing between "economic" and "political" refugees, without much protest, although it is important to note that he did initially intervene on behalf of refugees of East European origin.[62] Moreover, he concurred with Helbronner that a major priority of the Comité National should be emigration and repatriation.[63] Finally, Lambert, like nearly all native spokesmen, was obsessed with the problem of assimilating the refugees as quickly as possible. In December 1934, Lambert excoriated those refugees "still incapable of constructing a French sentence" and who stubbornly refused "to renounce any of their former habits." He furthermore advised them that "it is better to change oneself than to try to reconstruct a world not dependent on us."[64] Still, the fact remains that Lambert fought valiantly for constructive solutions to the refugee problem, and this effort set him sharply apart from his hard-line colleagues.

Unfortunately for the refugees, however, Helbronner, by early 1934, had clearly gained the upper hand. Emigration and repatriation became the sole priorities of the Comité National, and relief, to the extent that it was continued at all, was henceforth to be allocated on a short-term basis only to tide the refugees over until they could depart. According to the Comité National's financial report from June 1933 until December 1934, "after having fed the refugees," the most urgent task was "to evacuate them to those countries of immigration capable of receiving them: Palestine, Brazil, etc., so that our labor market, already so anemic as a result of the Depression, not be overburdened by this afflux of foreign workers."[65]

Most significantly, the Comité National even began to ship the refugees back to Germany. As one Comité National employee noted, "At the beginning of 1934, the emigration service of the Committee received a strict order to get rid of the refugees by sending them wherever: to Africa, to America, or even to Germany. We 'repatriated' even those people who no longer possessed anything, we paid for their railway ticket and sent them back to

Germany."[66] This policy was by no means undertaken surreptitiously; Robert de Rothschild announced it publicly in January of 1934: "We must likewise expect to repatriate certain elements to their countries of origin. Conditions even in Germany are improving and atrocities are, for the moment, nonexistent. Besides, life in this country too—as everywhere—is difficult due to the Depression."[67] By December, the Committee reported that it had repatriated 616 of its clients in 1934 alone, including 417 to Germany and the Saar.[68] The time had therefore come to renounce constructive solutions once and for all.[69]

In light of this single-minded emphasis on emigration, there seemed, at least to the hard-liners on the Committee, no compelling reason to continue the relief effort any longer. Indeed, to do so would only encourage further waves of refugees to seek asylum in France, an eventuality many Jewish leaders believed would inspire even greater antisemitism. As a result, in the spring of 1934 the Committee announced plans to liquidate those charity cases still on the books, including the 250 refugees still living in the casern at the Porte d'Orléans, and in July it closed its doors altogether to further requests for material assistance. One year later, it shut down even its administrative and juridical services. Accurately assessing the situation, a police report of October 1934 noted: "M. Robert de Rothschild, vice president of the Jewish Consistory of Paris, who has contributed abundantly toward the assistance program for the German émigrés is now said to have declared that he no longer wishes to continue that effort."[70] Clearly, the French Jewish establishment was abandoning all efforts to reconcile its competing loyalties to the refugees, on the one hand, and to France, on the other. In this struggle, French national interests, at least as they were conceived by the hard-liners within the Committee, dominated. The refugees were, quite simply, to be abandoned.

The émigré community was up in arms. Both the *Pariser Tageblatt* and the *Pariser Haynt*, the major organ of the Yiddish immigrant press, launched scathing attacks on the policies of the Comité National.[71] A. Alperin, the *Pariser Haynt*'s leading editorialist, charged that the Committee's claim to have successfully liquidated the refugee problem by the summer of 1934 was, to put it mildly, ludicrous: "Is it possible to find anyone to affirm that there is no longer a need for the Committee? That all the refugees are satisfied? We know exactly what this liquidation signifies—get out and go off to wherever we shove you. It's not surprising that the list of those on assistance has dropped to 500. What will become of all the other refugees? Better not ask!"[72]

Georg Bernhard, editor of the *Pariser Tageblatt* and president of the Federation of German Emigrés in France, was no less outraged. In a speech delivered in October 1934, he thanked the French government for its hospitality but then proceeded to excoriate "the attitude of his French coreligionists, who, with the exception of a small number, including the Baron de Rothschild, have not made the necessary effort to come to the assistance of the Jewish refugees."[73] Indeed, the anger and fear of the future were so great that 200 refugees, including the well-known writer Egon Erwin Kisch, staged a demonstration outside the Comité National in late July 1934 to protest the closing. According to a police report, the demonstrators "criticized the functioning of the Comité National, which they accused of having squandered the money that, according to them, was entirely of foreign origin. The French Jews, they claimed, had done nothing to help their coreligionists and had never made the least effort to facilitate their stay in France."[74]

The refugees were by no means alone in their harsh denunciations of the Comité National's irresponsibility and indifference. The JDC and the HCR seconded these attacks. Ironically, it was the JDC that had initially proposed the liquidation scheme. However, it had something altogether different in mind. According to Bernhard Kahn, the JDC had promised in late 1933 to continue subsidizing the Comité National, but only on condition that the Committee lobby the government as vigorously as possible to keep the borders open and make every conceivable effort to place the refugees in constructive employment.[75] But, as we have seen, Kahn believed the hardliners had systematically undermined these goals, and when the Committee announced its intended closing, he was outraged. On July 25, 1934, he cabled the New York office that the "French liquidation plan had not [had the] full results expected. This failure entirely due to [the] attitude of [the] French Committee." On August 1, he cabled again that "desperate refugees threatening with desperate acts."[76]

McDonald too had lost patience with the Committee. Indeed, he paid an unannounced visit to the Committee's office just prior to its closing, and to the chagrin of several administrators, publicly addressed the delegation of refugee protesters.[77] In early 1935, he told Louis Oungre, the French director of the JCA and Helbronner's closest ally, that he

did not agree with Dr. Oungre's idea that the more that is done in France, the less will be the chances of the League's assuming responsibility. No efforts should be spared to obtain concessions for the refugees from the French government and the governments of the other countries. They must be shown clearly that there is no sense in shoving refugees from one frontier to the other. A plan of emigration should be proposed for those who can emigrate and who are really not desired in France. For the others *cartes de travail* [work permits] should be stubbornly demanded, calling on France's tried and true hospitality. As to further emigration, it must be admitted that the opportunities at the present time are very meager.[78]

Even the Paris Consistory, whose vice president was none other than Robert de Rothschild himself, expressed grave concern. The Consistory's secretary-general, Albert Manuel, himself a member of the Comité National's executive committee, informed Rothschild in June 1934 that as a result of the Committee's planned closing, desperate refugees were flocking to the central Synagogue to demand assistance. The Consistory, Manuel pointed out, was in no position to take on this financial burden, and he begged Rothschild to reconsider the Committee's closing in light of the disastrous impact it would have on other Jewish institutions.[79]

These protests proved of no avail, however, and the doors of the Committee remained firmly shut. But the great tragedy of this period was still to come, since beginning in the fall of 1934 the more conservative governments of Pierre-Etienne Flandin and Pierre Laval initiated the harshest antiforeign crackdown to date. As we have seen, in the aftermath of the assassination of the Yugoslavian king and of Foreign Minister Barthou by a Ustache terrorist in October, French authorities, seeking to rid the country of the hordes of "undesirables," resorted for the first time to a policy of mass expulsion. Residence permits were increasingly denied and requests of refugees who had entered France either without papers or on short-term visas were now routinely rejected. According to new decree laws announced in November, all foreigners who did not possess residence permits could now be forcibly expelled.[80] At the same time, the government was making it more difficult than ever to acquire a work permit; even permits already in circulation were to be renewed only in exceptional circumstances.

In 1935, the Laval government pushed through yet another series of decree laws sharply limiting for the first time the right of foreigners to engage in artisan trades and peddling. These laws affected not only the refugees, but also threw out of work thousands more immigrants, many of whom had been in France for years, including large numbers of East European Jews employed in the garment trades.[81] Without a work permit, it was impossible to acquire a residence permit, and without a residence permit, foreigners faced the very real threat of expulsion.[82]

This government crackdown provided the occasion for the final round in the battle between the hard-liners and the moderates on the Committee. Not surprisingly, the position put forth by Helbronner was that Jewish organizations had no right whatsoever to intervene with the government. According to one report: "Mr. Helbronner insists on the general character of the problem of the stateless refugees and upon the necessity of not turning it into a Jewish question. . . . Given the evolution of the issue at present, any intervention in favor of the stateless refugees from the Jewish side could only compromise the program undertaken by the Viscount Cecil [of the HCR] regarding a more general plan."[83] Helbronner even went so far as to remind Jewish organizations that Jewish refugees were in fact a "privileged" category of foreigners, and they therefore had no cause to complain.[84]

Helbronner's remarks that a more vigorous pro-refugee policy would have interfered with HCR plans were made in bad faith, however, since McDonald himself had already protested against the policy of expulsion to the French government, and he had encouraged Jewish organizations, including the Comité National, to do the same.[85] Bernhard Kahn similarly warned the Committee not to act as the government's "sheriff" with regard to the execution of expulsion orders. American Jews, he threatened, would halt all further contributions to the French relief campaign if they were to discover the deplorable policies their money was actually supporting.[86]

Once again, Lambert took a diametrically opposed position. As he saw it, the government's crackdown amounted to a direct assault against Jewish refugees in particular, an assault that he warned would have dangerous and long-lasting repercussions. In two important articles that appeared in late 1934 and early 1935, Lambert lashed out against both French official policy and the passivity of French Jewry.[87] Contrary to Helbronner's appeals that Jewish organizations remain silent, Lambert proclaimed: "This situation must preoccupy our organizations and our official representatives, since the considerable number of Jewish immigrants in France turns this question of foreigners into a specifically Jewish question. The first victims of the new measures are the Jewish refugees from Germany, Poland, and Romania, for whom the associations are seeking settlement possibilities in new countries." If the government truly desired the refugees to emigrate, he pointed out, these new measures were making that goal illusory. The problem was that once a refugee failed to obey an expulsion order, he was in infraction of the law and thus began to amass a criminal record. Under these circumstances, no country was prepared to grant that refugee an entry visa. Lambert therefore proclaimed:

> It's necessary that the authorities no longer refuse to grant departure extensions [to those expelled] and that they understand the tragic problem of the stateless refugees. . . . These uprooted unfortunates, who have lost their nationality of origin (Polish, Russian or Romanian) as a result of war, successive migrations, or political upheavals, find themselves physically unable to obey an expulsion order. No country will grant them an entry visa; they are thus subject to the sad obligation of remaining in France illegally, if the negotiations of the charitable organizations that care for them are not successful in steering them toward Palestine or South America.

Lambert then went on to discuss the fact that "the new measures hit the immigrant Jews established in France for many years, of whom several even have French children. Some are artisans, others entrepreneurs, and it is no exaggeration to say that more than 5,000 persons in Paris find themselves in these straits." If Jewish garment workers were to lose their work permits as well, thousands more desperate individuals would, he predicted, be forced into dependency on the relief committees. He thus implored "the authorities not [to] ignore the tragic destiny of the stateless foreigners for whom no frontier can be opened."[88]

Lambert then turned his attention to the pathetic role of French Jewry itself. French Jews, he charged, had all too readily believed the popular myth that foreigners stole jobs from French workers and thus created unemployment. In reality, he argued, "unemployment was not the cause of the Depression, but rather its consequence," and Jewish organizations, he suggested, had been wrong to "submit themselves docilely to the pressure of every political party, without exception, that demands more severe protective measures for our national work force, whether it be the Radical Party at its last party congress or the labor unions that protect their own unemployed." It was now time to wake up, he proclaimed, and he called upon the Central Consistory and the Alliance Israélite Universelle "to prove to the immigrant Jews that French Judaism will not refuse to comprehend its imperious duty." "If one allows this storm to pass over simply by bowing one's head," he continued, "who would be able to assure us that in several years someone wouldn't dream of remedying an even more severe economic depression by revising those naturalizations granted after the war?" Contrary to prevailing opinion at the time, Lambert was convinced that "the situation of German Jewry remains very serious despite the apparent tranquillity."[89] Nor did he have any doubts that a pro-German vote in the upcoming Saar plebescite, scheduled for January 1935, would provoke yet another mass influx of refugees to France.[90] Lambert therefore warned French Jews that they had no alternative but to prepare for worse times ahead: "In so doing, we will have greater authority and more facilities to receive those unfortunates the future holds in store for us."

Lambert apparently won a short-term victory—the Comité National ultimately joined other major Jewish organizations, including the Federation of Jewish Societies of France and the Gourevitch Committee, in protesting the decree laws and calling on the government to honor France's longstanding tradition of political asylum.[91] Indeed, this initiative soon paid off; in early February, Edouard Herriot, the head of Flandin's newly created Interministerial Committee on Immigration, assured the Comité National that the refugees' right to asylum would henceforth be guaranteed but that under no circumstances would they be allowed to work.[92] In the aftermath of this commitment, perhaps aware that nothing more could be done with regard to the issue of work permits, Lambert retreated from his earlier insistence on constructive solutions. In a Comité National report from the summer of 1935, he announced that the Committee was henceforth abandoning its efforts to settle the refugees permanently in France and was now focusing its efforts entirely on emigration. He even went on to praise the French government's policies: "They [the government authorities] have never failed to give us the most valuable encouragements and to facilitate our task to the greatest degree possible." While it was true that "the general measures, taken since October of 1933 with regard to foreigners, have rendered the stay and the settlement of refugees in France more difficult," it was nevertheless the case, he argued, that these measures "have not hit the refugees any more cruelly than other foreigners in France." He added:

Moreover, the authorities have never dreamt of denying a right of asylum that conforms to our tradition. But in light of the barriers erected against the emigration from Germany by every country, France finds itself obliged to make its policy conform to the necessity in which our country finds itself, that is, to remain with respect to this immigration only a *gare de triage*. The only elements that will be permitted to settle definitively are those whose political refugee status can be proven and who bring to our country's economy undeniable talents that cause no harm to our national labor force.[93]

Despite this apparent capitulation, there are signs that Lambert did not feel altogether comfortable with having to articulate the hard-line position. Indeed, just after the Nazis proclaimed the Nuremberg Laws in September of 1935, he openly expressed a sense of extreme frustration and helplessness. In an article titled "Appeal to the Chief Rabbis of Europe," Lambert admitted, "We can no longer expect any action from Geneva, where religious and political persecutions are passed off as questions of secondary importance." The only hope, he claimed, was that "those large Jewish organizations, those that are not in a state of lethargy, obstinately continue, each one within its own domain, the positive action that attenuates miseries, that holds out hope to the youth, and might, little by little, save those families who already have or may still be able to flee the Hitlerian hell." But cognizant of the woeful inadequacy of this prescription, Lambert felt it necessary to offer another consolation: "One must now act in the spiritual realm," he proclaimed. This would be a job for the rabbis, not for the beleaguered relief organizations.[94] Lambert's point was unmistakable. In the absence of both emigration possibilities and opportunities for constructive settlement in the countries of first asylum, world Jewry could do little more for the future victims of Hitlerian antisemitism than to offer prayers and spiritual guidance.

Lambert's defeat and the Comité National's subsequent withdrawal from the scene had dire consequences for those 15,000 to 17,000 refugees still remaining in France in late 1934 and early 1935.[95] According to a report of the German Commission, a refugee-directed committee that handled juridical and administrative assistance:

There can be no divergence of opinion with respect to the present situation. The misery is frightful and the despair of the people unutterable. The cases of suicide have multiplied during the last weeks. The refugees, driven to the bottom by hunger and despair, threaten to cede to provocations of crime and corruption. We are constantly being told by those to whom assistance has been refused that they find themselves before the alternatives of stealing or begging. Thefts, and what is more frequent, cases of petty larceny, are the consequence of this state of affairs, and serve only to injure the cause of immigration and of Jewry in general. . . . Never since the beginning of the immigration has the distress of the refugees been so poignant.[96]

Another report dating from late 1934 noted that as a result of the complete absence of job opportunities, even many middle-class refugees who previously had been able to support themselves, were becoming "entirely proletarianized and reduced to living in the poorest quarters of Paris." Prostitution was on the rise, and the majority of the refugees "are restless, undernourished and terribly nervous. . . . The uncertainty of their future is constantly haunting them."[97] In the spring of 1935 the *Jüdische Rundschau*, one of the principal organs of German Jewry, published letters from several young German refugees who complained bitterly of "the moral isolation and the quasi-total solitude in which they suffer, above all in France. The first year, the mass of refugees received at least some material assistance. At present, this assistance has dried up, and the majority now find themselves in a frightful situation, without means, without friends."[98] So intolerable had the situation become that many refugees were even requesting to be sent back to Germany.[99] As one of the JDC's representatives put it, with no prospect of a better future in France, "they would rather go back to Germany and suffer among their friends."[100]

To be sure, the French Jewish establishment by no means bears the primary responsibility for the desperate straits in which the refugees found themselves by 1935. This responsibility clearly rests with the French government. Nevertheless, one sector of French Jewry—those I have called the "hard-liners"—played an influential and very direct role in the formulation of official policy itself, pressing the government at every step of the way to pursue the most restrictionist policy possible. These Jewish leaders, in weighing what they perceived to be their mutually contradictory obligations to the refugees on the one hand and to the French government and people on the other, felt compelled to opt for the latter. As a result, the refugees were left virtually defenseless. As David Wyman has shown with regard to the American case during the period of the Holocaust, the role of native Jewish elites, although not the primary determinant of refugee policy, remains a factor that cannot be discounted.[101] Indeed, due to Helbronner's pivotal position at the HCR, French Jews may have been in a more strategic position to influence the direction of refugee policy in these early years than their coreligionists elsewhere in the West.

The response of people like Helbronner and his allies must be assessed against the background of growing antisemitism during this period. Yet, their tendency to blame antisemitism entirely on the refugees and the immigrants betrays a serious misunderstanding. As some French Jews, including Lambert, were beginning to realize, the existence of antisemitism had little to do with Jewish behavior, whether it be the behavior of the refugees or that of left-wing Jews like Léon Blum.[102] Nevertheless, many French Jews could not accept this proposition and felt that their own well-being and acceptance into French society was being seriously undermined by an ever-swelling foreign Jewish presence.

It is clear that French Jewish elites, at least during this period, failed even with respect to providing philanthropic assistance to the refugees. The closing of the Comité National had nothing to do with government pressure. Rather, it reflected a conscious decision undertaken independently by the hard-liners within the Committee. Indeed, as we have shown, philanthropy itself had become highly politicized. To be too generous, according to Helbronner and his allies, would only have encouraged greater numbers of refugees to have fled to France. The hard-liners furthermore feared that if French Jewry appeared overly solicitous of the refugees' welfare, antisemitic resentment and charges of dual loyalty would inevitably result. Consequently, from the hard-liners' point of view, it was simply easier to abandon all efforts on behalf of the persecuted victims of Nazism. To do so would prove once and for all that French Jews always put their French interests above their Jewish interests.

Finally, it is also clear from this analysis that the native/immigrant paradigm that has dominated much of the historiography of twentieth-century French Jewry may not be adequate for understanding the wide range of native Jewish opinion. When it came to the refugee question, the native establishment, as we have seen, was sharply divided, and these differences ultimately resulted in the implementation of vastly divergent policies. Despite the fact that the hard-liners, led by Helbronner, triumphed during this first phase of the refugee crisis, their victory would prove short-lived. As we will see in Chapter 13, once the Popular Front came to power, the hard-liners were excluded from the relief effort altogether, and the moderates, led by Lambert, assumed the reins of leadership.

Under Lambert's guidance, the relief effort that emerged was based on the ideas he had been propagating since 1933—constructive solutions that would allow a sizable portion of the refugee population to remain in France, and even to find work. While the Popular Front would prove relatively sympathetic to these goals, the more conservative administration of Edouard Daladier, which came to power in the spring of 1938, was far less amenable. As a result, the Committee, for the first time since the beginning of the refugee crisis, would find itself in direct confrontation with the administration over refugee policy. Unlike Helbronner, however, Lambert did not perceive any conflict between his French and his Jewish identities. For him, both were linked to a vision of a liberal and republican France, and to the degree that the administration's refugee policies began to waiver from that vision, especially in the aftermath of the Anschluss, the Munich crisis, and Kristallnacht, Lambert was fully prepared to meet that challenge head-on.

CHAPTER SIX

Refugee Policy During the Popular Front Era

By early 1936, France's refugee policy was in a state of utter disarray. Nearly every relief committee had disappeared from the scene, due to lack of funds, bureaucratic obstacles, or sheer ill will, as was the case with the Comité National. Moreover, the administration's policy was incoherent and riddled with contradictions. Although the hard-line policies pursued by Flandin and especially Laval had reduced the size of France's immigrant and refugee population, they had not been able to transform France entirely from a nation of asylum into one of transit. The fact was that many of the refugees, who numbered only between 8,000 to 10,000 by early 1936, could not be expelled, no matter how harsh the police sanctions applied. Quite simply, these people had nowhere to go. Despite the fact that these individuals had once been promised asylum, they increasingly found themselves facing the cruel prospect of imprisonment for their failure to obey an expulsion order.

This situation, as we have seen, ultimately inspired pro-refugee groups to create the Centre de Liaison des Comités pour le Statut des Immigrés to fight for a refugee statute that would protect refugees against arbitrary expulsion and *refoulement*, in addition to creating a more humane legislative statute for immigrants in general. At the same time, it also led many high-ranking officials, such as Joseph Paganon, who served as minister of interior from June 1935 through January 1936, to question the wisdom of the hard-line strategy, not only on humanitarian grounds, but on practical ones as well, since the cost of imprisoning thousands of illegal immigrants and refugees had become a considerable drain on public coffers. As a result, by late 1935 and early 1936, growing numbers of officials as well as publicists were beginning to consider alternative solutions, including the establishment of agricultural settlements either in the colonies or in southwestern France or the creation of forced labor camps. Moreover, although a more liberal administration came to power in January 1936, led by the Radical politician Albert Sarraut, this regime too was unable to formulate a more coherent refugee policy, although it did alleviate the most severe aspects of the antiforeign decree laws, at least insofar as refugees were concerned.[1]

The electoral victory of the Popular Front in May 1936 reawakened hopes that the refugee problem might yet be resolved in a liberal manner. For the refugees, who by late 1935 had become thoroughly demoralized and deeply pessimistic with regard to the future, the advent of the new regime heralded a new beginning. Had it not been precisely those same socialists now in power, individuals such as Marius Moutet, Salomon Grumbach, Jules Moch, and Léon Blum himself, who had most ardently championed not only the right of the refugees to asylum, but even their right to work? "During those first months of the victorious Popular Front," the refugee writer Manès Sperber recalled, "the émigrés experienced more than at any other time in their existence the feeling of being at home in France."[2] It was now time to test whether an administration clearly sympathetic to the refugees would be able to confront those powerful middle-class lobby groups, which had insisted the only cure for the Depression was to rid France entirely of immigrant competitors.

What then were the refugee policies of the Popular Front, and did they differ significantly from the policies of preceding administrations? This question, although not yet the subject of a major scholarly study, has nevertheless stimulated heated debate in recent years. On the one hand, historians such Jean-Charles Bonnet and Rita Thalmann have been sharply critical of the Popular Front's achievements. Although Bonnet admits that the Popular Front manifested substantially more good will than the administrations of 1934 and 1935, he nevertheless suggests that the new government failed to implement any major substantive changes in refugee policy, less because it was insensitive to the problem of refugees and foreigners than because the regime quickly became overwhelmed by other problems. As a result, according to Bonnet, while the Popular Front may have ushered in a more humane tone, there was little improvement in practical terms: most of the harsh antiforeign legislation from 1934 and 1935 remained in place, although it was applied in a more humane fashion.[3] As Bonnet notes, one of the Popular Front's principal spokesmen on refugee matters, Marius

Moutet, who served as Blum's minister of colonies, ruefully admitted in 1939 that the Popular Front, while having alleviated the most severe aspects of the antiforeign decree laws, had ultimately failed to "consider the question of foreigners in France as a major question of economic and political import."[4]

Thalmann is even more critical. While recognizing the effort of the Popular Front to regularize the status of refugees from Germany already in France, she contends that Blum's refugee policy was characterized above all by a fierce determination to keep out future newcomers, and in this sense, she claims, the Popular Front merely continued the harsh policies of Flandin and Laval.[5] Attempting to refute these criticisms, Marcel Livian, who served as secretary-general of the Socialist Party's immigration commission during the years in question, alleges that Bonnet and especially Thalmann have vastly underestimated the regime's many positive accomplishments. True, Livian admits, the Popular Front may not have accomplished all that was initially expected of it. Nevertheless, he argues, that failure was due more to its brief tenure in office than to any deliberate ill will.[6]

The debate between Bonnet and Thalmann on the one hand and Livian on the other reflects the fact that the legislative policy of the Popular Front toward refugees from Germany was in reality more ambivalent than previously assumed. Thalmann is entirely correct to note that the Popular Front retained a hard-line policy with regard to future newcomers, a strategy designed to stabilize the size of the refugee population at its existing level. But if one focuses primarily on the way the new government treated German refugees already in France, Livian's more positive assessment is largely borne out: the Popular Front significantly improved the refugees' legal status, offering them an amnesty that effectively guaranteed them protection against arbitrary *refoulement*, expulsion, and imprisonment. Moreover, as Livian points out, the regime even strove to grant the refugees work permits, a policy that was sharply at odds with that of previous conservative administrations.

In light of the fact that the Flandin and Laval governments had been determined not only to close the borders to future newcomers, but to get rid of the vast majority of refugees already in France as well, these changes cannot be dismissed as minor and superficial. Rather, they constituted substantial reforms that afforded this one important segment of the refugee population the necessary security and freedom to begin the task of rebuilding their lives. Moreover, the fact that much of the anti-immigrant legislation of previous years remained on the books, as Bonnet rightly notes, is not necessarily a reflection of the Popular Front's lack of resolve to undo this state of affairs. Instead, bureaucratic obstructionism from within the civil service, persistent lobbying on the part of anti-refugee groups, and perhaps above all, a lack of time, may have proved more decisive in stymieing the realization of a more liberal legislative program.

But to fully understand the Popular Front's policy toward Jewish refugees, it is also necessary to look beyond the legislative front. To compensate for its inability to implement major legislative initiatives on the refugee question, the Popular Front adopted a second strategy that has received far less attention. This strategy consisted of the attempt to realize those alternative settlement schemes that had already been floated in 1934 and 1935: the creation of agricultural settlements for the refugees, either in the French colonies or in the depopulated regions of southwestern France. Given the depth of protectionist sentiment in France, even many of the staunchest pro-refugee advocates considered these extraparliamentary solutions the only means of reconciling the apparently antithetical interests of the refugees with those of the French middle classes. By removing refugees from cities and retraining them as peasants and artisans, pro-refugee spokesmen hoped to overturn the perception that the refugees necessarily constituted an economic threat.

Moreover, the scope of these schemes was far broader than that of the Popular Front's legislative initiatives. These schemes were intended not only for refugees already settled in France, but for future refugees as well, including East European Jews. Hence, a more comprehensive view of the Popular Front's achievement, one that considers both its legislative and administrative accomplishments as well as these colonial and agricultural schemes, which we will examine in Chapter 7, suggests that the Popular Front made a sincere and concerted effort to resolve the refugee problem in a humane way consistent with the programs advanced by the left-wing pro-refugee lobby since 1934. By approaching the issue from this dual perspective, it becomes clear that the Popular Front's policies, despite numerous shortcomings, constituted a sharp and significant break, not only in tone but also in substance, with the policies of preceding governments. It may be true that the refugee question did not constitute the Popular Front's foremost priority, but it was by no means a question that was ignored.

The ambivalent position of the Popular Front vis-à-vis the refugee question became apparent as early as the summer of 1936, when the new government was called on to ratify a new League of Nations' agreement on German refugees, "The Provisional Arrangement Concerning the Status of Refugees Coming from Germany." Plans for this new international accord had been underway since the late fall of 1935, and especially after the German refugee crisis had deteriorated sharply in the aftermath of the Nuremberg Laws, a situation that was greeted by the increased use of *refoulement* and expulsion by every one of Germany's neighbors. In November, the sec-retary-general of the League appointed a Committee of Experts to draw up provisions that would guarantee refugees from Germany an internationally recognized legal status, similar to that of Nansen refugees. The committee's report, which appeared on January 3, 1936, recommended that German refugees be granted the same international legal status as Nansen refugees — that is, that they be granted identity certificates, which would protect them against expulsion and *refoulement*, as well as internationally recognized travel documents. It further suggested that the Nansen Office and the High Commission for Refugees (HCR) be merged into a single administrative unit, in anticipation of the scheduled closing of the Nansen Office in 1938.[7] For the time being, however, the two offices were to remain separate, and the League appointed a new high commissioner, Sir Neill Malcolm, to re-place James G. McDonald, who had resigned in protest in December over the League's failure to deal with the refugee crisis and in particular to pres-sure the German government to stop the persecution of the Jews.[8] Once in office, Malcolm's first and foremost task was to plan a major intergovern-mental conference on the German refugee question that would consider the recommendations put forth in the Committee of Experts' report.[9]

Malcolm worked quickly, and in the late spring he announced that an in-ternational conference on the German refugee question would be held in Geneva on July 2–4. Throughout 1935, the French government, as we have seen, had expressed considerable ambivalence about the idea of merging the Nansen Office and the HCR, largely because it feared that granting refugees from Germany a status similar to that of Nansen refugees would only en-courage more refugees to come to France and might infringe on French sovereignty by limiting the government's authority to expel unwanted for-eigners. By early 1936, however, perhaps in response to Laval's departure from the Foreign Ministry, the Quai d'Orsay for the most part dropped these objections. As long as the sovereign right over expulsion was main-tained, the ministry was now willing to grant asylum to the few thousand German refugees still remaining in France. It also recognized that the merger of these two refugee offices would almost certainly be more efficient and would probably cause less irritation to the German government than maintaining a separate office to deal with German refugees only. Many of the thornier aspects of this accord had therefore been hammered out in ad-vance of the Popular Front's coming to power.

After it had been signed by France together with six other European na-tions on July 4, many refugee activists complained that the new accord did not live up to many of the recommendations put forth in the Committee of Experts' report. Indeed, this failure led one young Czech Jewish journalist, Stefan Lux, to stage a dramatic protest by committing suicide on the floor of the League's General Assembly on July 3.[10] Nevertheless, this accord marked an important step forward toward the realization of a major goal of pro-refugee advocates: the creation of an internationally recognized legal status for refugees from Germany. After defining a "refugee coming from Germany" as "any person who was settled in that country, who does not possess any nationality other than German nationality, and in respect of whom it is established that in law or in fact he or she does not enjoy the protection of the Government of the Reich," the agreement went on to describe the new legal status these refugees would receive. They were to be granted identity certificates that would protect their bearers from arbitrary expulsion, *refoulement*, and imprisonment. These certificates would also serve as internationally recognized travel documents, essentially taking the place of passports. Finally, the accord paved the way for the signatory nations to grant an amnesty to those refugees whose situation had hitherto been illegal: they too were to be permitted to apply for the identity certificates on condition that they report to the authorities of their respective countries of residence by a fixed date. Although this accord was only provisional, Malcolm had every intention of getting a final draft of this accord ratified at a second refugee conference to be held in the near future.[11]

Although pro-refugee groups in France hailed this accord as a major step forward, they nevertheless criticized several of its key provisions. As they pointed out, the definition of who qualified for the new refugee status was extremely narrow. Whether refugees who refused to turn in their German passports for the new travel certificates were to be excluded remained unclear. More seriously, the accord unequivocally excluded refugees of East European origin, despite the fact that they constituted a sizable contingent of the refugee population. According to the left-wing deputy Paul Perrin, president of both the Centre de Liaison des Comités pour le Statut des Immigrés and secretary-general of the newly created Bureau International pour le Respect du Droit d'Asile,* "Those banished from Germany, chased out by Hitlerism, but of Polish or Romanian origin, must now abandon all hope of ever being granted the documents in question."[12] Furthermore, the accord did not ban expulsion and *refoulement* altogether, as pro-refugee advocates had hoped. Rather, it explicitly stated that such measures, although

---

*This organization, created by the Conférénce Internationale pour le Droit d'Asile, held in Paris on June 20–21, 1936, served as an international umbrella organization for all German émigré associations. A major aim of the organization, which was headquartered in Paris, was to lobby the League of Nations for a more secure refugee status. See Livian, *Le Parti socialiste*, pp. 94–95; Albert Grzesinski, "Zentralvereinigung der deutschen Emigration," *PT*, no. 33 (July 14, 1936): 1; CDH, "Bulletin de la Ligue des Droits de l'Homme," *CDH*, Mar. 1, 1937: 151–52.

strongly discouraged, could still be carried out if a refugee posed a threat to national security or the public order, an obvious concession to concerns voiced by the various European foreign ministries, including the Quai d'Orsay.[13]

Similarly troubling was the fact that the new accord made no explicit provisions regarding the right to work, although the two major refugee conferences held in Paris in June to articulate the demands of the refugees themselves to the Geneva Conference—the International Conference for the Right to Asylum, organized by the Centre de Liaison pour le Droit d'Asile, and the HICEM/HIAS* Jewish emigration conference—had explicitly demanded such a provision.[14] Furthermore, the accord had no binding power whatsoever, and it even contained a clause that allowed the signatories to denounce its provisions at any time. Finally, it was unclear whether the new refugee status applied only to individuals who had already left Germany or to those who might flee in the future as well. Malcolm's introductory comments strongly suggested the more restrictive interpretation. In light of the Depression, he declared, certain countries, especially those bordering Germany, had already announced that "it is impossible for them to receive any more refugees, even temporarily." He thus reiterated a theme that had been stressed in the Committee of Experts' report as well: "The action of the League of Nations in favor of refugees should be confined to persons having left their country of origin."[15]

Not surprisingly, the French government prior to the Popular Front's electoral victory had taken a leading role in pressing for this restrictive interpretation, and the Popular Front, as Thalmann notes, did nothing to alter this stance. Indeed, one of the new government's delegates to the conference, Jean Longuet, a prominent Socialist Party member and the grandson of Karl Marx, had been instructed by the Foreign Ministry to address this issue directly at the conference. In a speech during one of the preliminary meetings to the conference, Longuet declared:

The French government regards the undertakings which it is about to assume as applying to persons who are at the present moment refugees. It could not—any more than any other government—blindly assume obligations which it could no longer discharge if the number of future refugees increased beyond the absorption capacity of countries of refuge.

*HICEM was the foremost international Jewish emigration organization, headquartered in Paris. It grew out of a 1927 merger of three Jewish emigration associations: the Jewish Colonization Association (JCA), established in Great Britain in 1891 by Baron Maurice de Hirsch to assist East European Jewish emigrants and to foster colonization schemes; the United Committee for Jewish Emigration (Emigdirect), formed in 1921 in Prague to facilitate emigration from the Soviet Union and Eastern Europe; and the American-based Hebrew Sheltering and Aid Society (HIAS). See Marrus, *Unwanted*, pp. 67–68.

It was not for the present Conference to foresee hypothetical eventualities. It would be failing in its mission if, by thoughtless promises, it encouraged emigration movement which in the end would aggravate the present general economic unrest.

Its object is to face present realities and try to stabilize them as much as possible.[16]

So clear was the intent of Longuet's statement that Bernhard Kahn, always an astute observer, noted regretfully that "all our fears were well founded. This declaration says that the situation of the refugees must be crystallized as it is today. There is no hope for refugees who may come from Germany later."[17]

If doubts still remained regarding the fate of future newcomers, they were quickly dispelled in the following weeks when the government began to enact the measures to implement the new accord. To be sure, the Presidential Decree of September 17, 1936, which officially created the identity certificates for those legally considered "refugees coming from Germany," made no specific mention of this issue.[18] This decree stipulated that all refugees who had been in France prior to August 5, 1936, the date the Geneva Accord went into effect, and who qualified as "refugees coming from Germany" could apply for the new certificates through their local prefectures. An amnesty was to be extended to formerly illegal refugees, and they too were urged to apply for the new certificates. The cost of the certificates was set at a modest 20 francs, with an additional fee for travel documents. But in a goodwill gesture, the government waived these charges altogether for indigent refugees. Finally, the decree set November 1, 1936, as the deadline for filing applications for the certificates, although this deadline was later extended to January 31, 1937.[19] Hence this decree, while offering extremely generous terms of asylum to refugees already in France, made no specific mention of the fate of those who might arrive later.

Yet it was precisely this issue that preoccupied the new socialist minister of the interior, Roger Salengro. In a circular issued on August 14, 1936, Salengro declared that the Geneva Accord "has as its aim *to stabilize the existing situation* of the refugees by covering and granting an amnesty for the past, but not to make any commitments with respect to the future by having to accept future immigrations." All refugees who had come from Germany between January 30, 1933, and August 5, 1936, whether or not they had entered the country legally, were declared eligible to apply for the new certificates and were henceforth granted a complete amnesty. On the other hand, however, Salengro instructed the police to prevent "in the most absolute manner every *new* admission of refugees who come from Germany, but whose situation is irregular [that is, without a visa or passport]."[20] In a subsequent circular issued on September 23, Salengro further declared:

"The request of every foreigner who has come to France since August 5, 1936, must be considered unacceptable. The necessary measures will be taken in these cases." He also warned that all refugees from Germany who failed to apply for the new refugee status—that is, by not exchanging their German passports for the new identity and travel documents—would continue to be regarded as illegal aliens and remain vulnerable to *refoulement* and expulsion.[21]

In order to screen the applicants for the new refugee status, the minister of the interior created the Consultative Commission in July, a move that fulfilled one of the long-standing demands of pro-refugee advocates. This eight-person commission, which included some of the most prominent refugee activists, consisted of an equal number of French citizens and refugees. Albert Grzesinski, a German socialist who had previously served as the Berlin chief of police and as Prussian minister of the interior, was appointed president. Raymond-Raoul Lambert, representing the Comité d'Assistance aux Réfugiés (CAR), a new Jewish relief organization created in July 1936 to replace the now defunct Comité National, was appointed secretary-general, and Paul Perrin was named vice president. The other German members were Georg Bernhard, the highly respected editor of the *Pariser Tageblatt* and president of the Federation of German Emigrés in France; Theodore Tichauer, of the German League for the Rights of Man and Citizen and vice president of the Association of German Jewish Emigrés; and Willi Münzenberg, the German Communist Party leader. In addition to Lambert and Perrin, the other French members were Emile Kahn, secretary-general of the League for the Rights of Man, and Germaine Melon-Hollard of the Quaker refugee committee, the International Service of the American Friends Service Committee.

The screening process was by no means intended to harass refugees or ensure that as few as possible applied for the new certificates. Rather, the minister of the interior hoped that such scrutiny, carried out in part by the refugees themselves, would encourage the weeding out of false refugees, and especially Nazi agents, thus permitting the government to treat authentic refugees as liberally as possible. The creation of the Consultative Commission thus marked an important milestone; never before had the government called upon the refugees themselves to play so central a role in the implementation of refugee policy, and there is no doubt that the commission strove to the best of its abilities to defend the interests of the refugee population.[22]

Although Livian has argued that the Consultative Commission had the right not only to review the dossiers of refugees arriving after the August 5 deadline, but also those of refugees already in France by this date, the available evidence does not support this interpretation. Rather, it lends credibility to Thalmann's thesis that the Popular Front, despite its ostensible commitment to refugee asylum, was fiercely determined to keep future newcomers out, regardless of the motives impelling them to flee. As Paul Perrin declared in December 1936, "Whatever the legitimacy of their requests, all German refugees who, for political, religious, or racial reasons, were forced to leave their country before January 30, 1933, or after August 5, 1936, are excluded from the benefits of the September 17, 1936, decree instituting the new identity documents." Moreover, Perrin noted, "the administration has also notified those who 'slipped into' France after the final deadline that they can expect to be subjected to the rigors of the law."[23] Jewish refugee organizations too counseled their clients that "under no circumstances could immigrants coming from Germany or other neighboring countries after August 5, 1936, or likely to enter French territory at some time in the future, be eligible to take advantage of these benevolent measures, aimed at stabilizing the present situation."[24]

Uncertain as to how to proceed with regard to refugees who had arrived after the August 5 deadline, Grzesinski requested clarification from the Ministry of the Interior in late October. At that time, the chief of the Sûreté Nationale, Bouvier, informed Grzesinski that this issue exceeded the "competence of the Commission and that further instruction from the government will have to be requested." It was true, Bouvier noted, that refugees arriving outside the prescribed dates, though not automatically eligible for refugee status, could petition the government for asylum on an individual basis, and he added that "the authorities would examine every individual case with benevolence."[25] Yet, it was clear that such cases were to be considered exceptions. Moreover, the fact that Grzesinski was still requesting clarification of this matter in June 1937, just prior to his resignation as president of the Consultative Commission, stands as further proof that not a single refugee who arrived after the August 5, 1936, deadline had yet come before the Commission.[26] Bouvier's assurances were further vitiated by the fact that it remained virtually impossible to acquire a visa from a French consulate in Germany. Anyone arriving from Germany without a visa after the August 5 deadline was automatically considered an illegal alien and was therefore vulnerable to immediate *refoulement*.

So harsh were the government's visa policies that in September 1936, the premier himself ordered an investigation into whether the Foreign Ministry was systematically denying visas to German Jews. These suspicions were, of course, well founded since the harsh visa policies enacted after the Nuremberg Laws had never been abrogated.[27] Under these circumstances, the chance that an individual request for asylum would ever reach the minister of the interior was slim indeed.

Why then did the Popular Front, ostensibly committed to the tradition of political asylum, assume such a hard-line stance vis-à-vis future newcomers? Livian has suggested that the government was concerned about the infiltration of Nazi agents, and it therefore desired to submit all newcomers to a particularly rigorous screening process.[28] Aside from Livian's word, however, there is little evidence to support this claim, and fears that the refugees constituted a fifth column of spies were in fact rarely mentioned in diplomatic or intelligence reports from this period. One might also hypothesize that the virtual closing of the border arose from the widespread belief that the refugee crisis was about to taper off, especially in the wake of the Nuremberg Laws, which many contemporaries believed would mark the final stage in the Nazi persecution of the Jews.

Yet, available evidence again suggests that no one in the Foreign Ministry held this view. Rather, the Quai d'Orsay was firmly convinced that the Nuremberg Laws signaled the beginning of a new and more serious phase in the anti-Jewish crackdown, which would lead to a renewed mass Jewish exodus on a scale far greater than even that of 1933. As one internal Foreign Ministry memorandum from the summer of 1936 explained, the German refugee problem was unique: unlike other refugee crises that "arise from situations created by events that have already elapsed and that can then be assumed to be over," the German case was "a problem in the process of evolution." Although the number of refugees was at the moment manageable, one could not forget "the million individuals, who, although still in Germany, remain candidates for emigration and will be seeking a way out." The memorandum concluded, "Thus, the problem of German refugees has far more serious demographic ramifications than any other refugee problem has ever had, and it must therefore incline us toward prudence."[29] At the same time, another Foreign Ministry official instructed the French ambassador in Moscow to investigate whether German Jews might be permitted to settle in the recently created Jewish colony of Birobijan in the Russian Far East. As this official declared:

Positive signs lead us to think that in the near future, and no doubt after the close of the Olympic games, Germany will resume at an accelerated rhythm the execution of those measures she had formerly declared with regard to the Jews. The application of this program will inevitably result in a massive aggravation of emigration. . . .

As for ourselves, however strong our desire to come to the assistance of the victims of Hitlerian ostracism, we would scarcely be in a position to accept their settlement on our territory, even in a provisional capacity.[30]

It is therefore clear that the Popular Front, while willing to absorb refugees already in France, was no less determined than its predecessors to transform France into a transit nation only, at least with respect to future newcomers. It accepted the view that had been strenuously put forth by

Bérenger and Helbronner that France had already done more than its share. The League of Nations may have failed to bring about a more equitable distribution of the refugees who had arrived in 1933, but such a failure could not be allowed to recur in the future. Indeed, from the perspective of the Popular Front, it was imperative that the size of the refugee population be stabilized at the existing level. Otherwise, those refugees already in France could never be integrated.[31] In essence, as we will see, the Popular Front's refugee policy was based on a compromise: refugees already in France were to be granted a new legal status, the right to work, extensive social and welfare benefits, and even naturalization, but only on condition that future influxes of refugees be kept to a bare minimum.

Any measured evaluation of the Popular Front's refugee program must therefore include not only an examination of these hard-line policies toward future newcomers, but also an examination of the liberal measures aimed at improving the status of refugees already in France. The fact that Salengro made every effort to ensure that the Geneva Accord be implemented as liberally as possible constitutes one important sign of the administration's goodwill toward refugees already in France. As noted earlier, the Presidential Decree of September 17, 1936, put a stop to arbitrary expulsions and *refoulements*, thus eliminating what hitherto had constituted the gravest threat to the security and well-being of the refugees. As soon as the accord was signed, Salengro warned the prefects that from now on expulsion should be resorted to only in extreme circumstances and only after conferring directly with his office; even refugees who had previously received expulsion orders were to be treated "with the greatest benevolence."[32] Later in the fall, when Salengro learned that some prefects were systematically refusing to deliver application forms for the identity certificates to refugees who had previously been sentenced to expulsion or *refoulement*, he issued a sharp reprimand: "This manner of acting totally contradicts the spirit of the regulation instituted, since its aim is precisely to necessitate a reexamination of the situation of refugees residing in our country illegally."

By the same token, Salengro repeatedly reminded the prefects of "the importance attached to the fact that the refugees be carefully instructed regarding the various formalities they must fulfill and that the greatest possible publicity be given to the principal provisions of the new regime."[33] Such measures included the publication of bilingual versions of the decree together with all necessary explanations in the émigré and general press. Indeed, so concerned was Salengro that the decree had not been publicized adequately that he extended the deadline for filing applications three times.[34] Moreover, the administration issued a new decree law on October 14, 1936, that abrogated article 4 of the decree law of February 6, 1935, according to which a foreigner's identity card was valid only in the department in which he or she had applied for it, thus sharply curtailing their freedom of movement.[35]

The impact of these measures was felt immediately. Over the summer of 1937 the League for the Rights of Man and Citizen noted with satisfaction that the number of interventions it had undertaken with the minister of the interior on behalf of refugees unjustly expelled or *refoulés* had dropped off markedly since the Popular Front had come to power. And although the League continued to criticize the Presidential Decree of September 17, 1936, as too narrow, the *Cahiers des droits de l'homme* nevertheless admitted that "thanks to the Popular Front, foreigners residing in France today enjoy a security and guarantees they have never before known."[36] Similarly, in the wake of Salengro's tragic suicide in November 1936, the Consultative Commission issued a communiqué that clearly went beyond the perfunctory condolence:

Roger Salengro's death is an immense loss for the German emigration. The Germans who have had to flee their country, who have sought and found asylum in France, had in him a sincere friend. In spite of his many duties . . . as minister of the interior, Roger Salengro found time to think of those who, far from their country, requested his protection, and he assured them of it through many valuable initiatives and measures.

With the rest of France, we consider his death a great misfortune. We have lost a big-hearted man and an affectionate comrade; we will remain loyally devoted to his memory.[37]

The Popular Front's effort to improve the legal status of the refugees was complemented by a commitment to deliver on the Socialist Party's long-standing promise to provide refugees with the right to work. This commitment, it must be stressed, went well beyond the terms of either the Geneva Accord or the Presidential Decree of September 17, 1936, neither of which mentioned the right to work. In June 1936, at a preparatory meeting for the Geneva Conference, government ministers concurred that insofar as refugees already in France were concerned, "the French government is prepared to go even further than the present project in making a declaration regarding the granting of work permits to the refugees."[38] Longuet was therefore instructed to couple his harsh pronouncements regarding the fate of future newcomers with an extremely liberal statement regarding the right to work. After stating that the aim of the present conference was "to face present realities and try to stabilize them as much as possible," Longuet declared:

In order to prevent individuals being placed in situations which are extremely distressing and to restore to refugees, together with the right to work, a sense of their dignity and independence, it [the French government] is prepared to give the most generous consideration to all applications for labor permits addressed to it by refugees who have obtained the certificate which the Conference has just instituted.[39]

So astonishing was this statement in light of the French government's previous attitude toward the right to work that Bernhard Kahn, despite his grave apprehensions over the fate of future newcomers, acknowledged that "the whole atmosphere of the conference was very favorable to the refugees, especially the French delegates, of whom Longuet . . . was one. They spoke in really human terms of the refugees. It was quite a relief to hear these French delegates after the others (Heilbronner [sic]) who represented the French government in the governing body of the High Commission."[40] Elsewhere, Kahn reported, "it must be noted that M. Longuet was the representative with the most human understanding of the whole question and who advocated the most human arrangement possible."[41]

Just after the publication of the Presidential Decree of September 17, 1936, another prominent socialist deputy, Salomon Grumbach, who had just been appointed by the Foreign Ministry to head a newly created subcommittee on the refugee question at Geneva, reiterated Longuet's commitment in no uncertain terms. Speaking for the French delegation at the League of Nations on September 27, 1936, Grumbach proclaimed that "in spite of the Depression, in spite of the unprecedented costs borne by the Jewish relief organizations, most notably the Bérenger-Rothschild Committee [that is, the Comité National], the French government is happy to have applied measures that assure German refugees in France a definitive legal status." To demonstrate its good faith, Grumbach continued, the Ministry of the Interior had already created the Consultative Commission, whose members included a number of refugees. Moreover, he declared, "work permits will be granted to refugees on the basis of priority. The French government thus offers an example of international solidarity which, it hopes, will be followed by other countries of asylum."[42]

Such resounding endorsements of the right to work signaled a radical break with the policies of the past and marked the first time a French government had publicly declared itself in favor of "constructive solutions" for the German refugees. To be sure, in allocating these work permits, "every consideration was to be given to the prior rights of French workers and to union control," as one internal Foreign Ministry memo noted; nevertheless, the memo continued, important benefits were to be gained. Not only would a more liberal attitude regarding work permits put an end to the persistent problem of illegal work, but also it would "persuade American organizations to consent to the allocation of financial credits that would relieve French associations of the burden the refugees presently constitute and would permit the creation of new enterprises that might also hire unemployed French workers."[43]

As we have seen, these were precisely the advantages pro-refugee groups had been emphasizing for the past three years, and so dramatic a shift in government policy went far to revive the hopes of international relief organizations such as the JDC and the newly created Council for German Jewry* that refugee assistance might finally be put back on the track of "constructive work"—job training and placement. "For the first time," Kahn observed, "the outlook for the refugees here is somewhat better. The French government understands that it cannot emigrate the 10,000 refugees who are in France and that a large majority must be absorbed in the economic life of the country."[44] Thus, Kahn proclaimed, "it is no longer only a question of short-term assistance, but rather of a constructive effort on behalf of refugees who are unable to emigrate."[45]

While such governmental pledges augured well for the future, it is necessary to assess whether and to what degree they were translated into practice. To be sure, numerous obstacles remained: nearly all the laws passed in recent years limiting the rights of foreigners to work as wage earners or salaried employees, artisans, or liberal professionals remained in place. As a result, historians such as Bonnet and Thalmann have concluded that the Popular Front's commitment was meager at best.[46] Considerable evidence suggests, however, that while the final results of the Popular Front's commitment may have fallen short of initial expectations, the Blum government's efforts was by no means negligible. As Livian points out, although the restrictive legislation regarding the right of foreigners to work remained on the books, the Ministry of Labor tried to interpret these laws broadly so as to ensure the maximum distribution of work permits.[47]

What evidence is there to support the contention that the Popular Front made a credible effort to secure work permits for refugees covered by the Presidential Decree of September 17, 1936? First, there are numerous testimonies from organizations such as the League for the Rights of Man and the League of Nations, in addition to Jewish organizations, that praised the government's achievement. Indeed, there had already been a marked improvement during the tenure of Ludovic-Oscar Frossard, an independent socialist, at the Ministry of Labor from the summer of 1935 until the summer of 1936. As the League for the Rights of Man reported in July 1936:

*The Council for German Jewry was founded in early 1936 and was to serve as a central coordinating organization for international relief and emigration activities. The Council, which was headquartered in London, worked closely with the JDC, the JCA, and the Jewish Agency for Palestine, as well as with refugee committees in individual countries. See Simpson, *Refugee Problem*, p. 187; Bauer, *My Brother's Keeper*, pp. 155, 157; Ronald Stent, "Jewish Refugee Organisations," in Werner Mosse, coord. ed., Julius Carlebach et al., eds., *Second Chance: Two Centuries of German-Speaking Jews in the United Kingdom* (Tübingen, Ger., 1991), p. 592.

As of last June, many refugees who had obtained the authorization to reside in France had not been able to obtain work cards, despite all our efforts. But since the arrival of M. Frossard at the Ministry, a far more liberal policy has been established; the granting of work permits to political refugees has become the norm. Working together with the services of the Main-d'Oeuvre Etranger [the bureau of the ministry dealing with immigrant labor], we have been able to regularize the situation of many of the exiles, who, until now, have not had the opportunity to earn a living.[48]

Frossard's successor, Jean Lebas, received similar high praise. During the summer of 1937, the League for the Rights of Man noted that "it is less difficult for those foreigners authorized to reside in France to acquire work cards." Of the 594 requests for work permits the League had submitted in 1936, 436 had been approved, and in 1937, of the 233 requests submitted, only 45 were denied.[49] The refugee expert Sir John Hope Simpson likewise noted that nearly all the German refugees who had received the new identity certificates had had no problems in obtaining work permits. More than 800 of them, he claimed, had received work permits in 1937, a sharp increase over the 138 permits granted to refugees in 1935.[50] The new HCR high commissioner, Sir Neill Malcolm, also singled out France for special praise. In his report to the General Assembly of the League in September 1937, Malcolm noted that although the number of refugees in need of charitable assistance had risen significantly in almost every European country during the past year, France had experienced a sharp decline. This trend, Malcolm claimed, was due "not only to departure for overseas countries, but also to the Government's action in making the final settlement of a certain number of refugees residing in France possible. This action had enabled private organizations to delete from their lists the names of a certain number of refugees to whom they'd been granting assistance."[51]

Jewish organizations were especially effusive in their praise of the Popular Front's policies, and their reports confirm Malcolm's view that job placement, not emigration, was the principal cause of the declining number of refugees on the relief rolls. Jewish emigration from France had in fact tapered off sharply in 1936: whereas the HICEM had helped 2,948 persons emigrate from France in 1935, that figure dropped to 1,541 persons in 1936.[52] While this decline could perhaps be attributed to shrinking settlement possibilities abroad, HICEM clearly believed that it was due to the new policies of the Popular Front. According to a HICEM report for 1936, "Since France ratified the Geneva Arrangement of July 4, 1936, the heavy task with which the Committee had been charged has been brought back to more manageable proportions." Moreover, the report continued, "the reduction in the number of emigrants transported is explicable, on the one hand, by the decline in the number of German refugees and, on the other hand, by the more benevolent attitude of the national authorities toward foreigners in general, and consequently, toward the protégés of the Committee as well." According to this report, over 800 work permits had been accorded to Jewish refugees by the end of 1936, a substantial increase over the 138 granted the previous year.[53] Moreover, Lebas's orders to the prefects to renew existing work permits routinely, as opposed to the deliberate harassment of refugees seeking to renew work permits in 1935, did much to ease the burden on Jewish refugee organizations.[54]

Finally, with Lebas's encouragement, German refugees were allowed to enroll in special professional training schools, an effort that was funded by private organizations. Describing these programs in early 1937, a JDC spokesman proclaimed that "as a result of cooperation between the JDC and the French Committee for Professional Retraining,* groups of intellectuals and former professional people have been afforded training opportunities with the professional schools of the French state railways, hotel management, rural trade, and handicraft and horticultural schools, and the results of this training have been highly encouraging."[55] The director of the French state railroad program concurred, since he too reported, "The success of the enterprise has exceeded all expectations."[56] Thus, the Popular Front's effort to allocate work permits to refugees from Germany had apparently made a difference.

That the prerogatives of foreign workers, and especially the refugees, were being given greater consideration is further confirmed by the way the Ministry of Labor responded to the ongoing grievances of the various middle-class professional associations. In March 1937, artisans in rural areas complained that the decree law of August 8, 1935, restricting the right of foreigners to work as artisans was not being enforced strictly enough; as a result, they insisted, they were facing competition from foreigners who "disguised as agricultural workers, in fact carry out repair and maintenance work."[57] In May of the same year, the Chambre de Métiers of the department of the Seine, with the support of the Confédération Général de l'Artisanat Français, similarly demanded "an extremely restrictive application of this decree law, estimating that the number of authorizations accorded to artisans . . . is already too high and that consequently no new artisan cards should be delivered in the department of the Seine."[58]

*The Centre de Reclassement Professionnel (CRP; also known as the Centre Industriel de Réeducation Professionnelle [CRIP]) was created in Apr. 1936 after the collapse of the vocational retraining organization Agriculture et Artisanat. The philosophy of this committee was to provide vocational training to refugees by placing them in existing French technical institutions, rather than in separate schools. Justin Godart, who had served as president of Agriculture et Artisanat, served as president of the CRIP as well. "Memo on Interview with Mr. Chantal, Secretary General of the Centre de Reclassement Professionnel," Mar. 5, 1937, *JDC*, no. 601. See also CRIP pamphlet *Reclassons*, pp. 5–6, in *JDC*, no. 601.

The Ministry of Labor rejected this proposal, however. "Without losing sight of the interests of French artisans, whom the decree law of August 8, 1935, was specifically intended to protect," a Ministry spokesman explained, "it remains the case that my Department cannot be held to so rigid a rule." From the Ministry's point of view, "a massive refusal of all requests for artisan cards . . . risks provoking violent reactions on the part of certain foreign countries . . . and might stimulate reprisals against our own nationals residing and working in those countries." Hence, although local Chambres des Métiers would retain the right to veto applications for artisan cards, as stipulated by the decree law of August 8, 1935, the Ministry also declared that these vetoes could be overturned if, in the prefect's opinion, a particular foreigner deserved special attention.* From now on, any contested dossiers were to be forwarded directly to the Ministry's office, where the final decision would be made. The Ministry also stipulated that foreign artisans who had resided and worked in France well before the law of August 8, 1935, went into effect were to be granted special consideration.[59]

The Confédération des Syndicats Médicaux too continued to press for even more restrictive legislation against foreign and recently naturalized citizens, despite the passage of the Nast Law in July 1935. Now, however, these complaints fell on deaf ears. In late 1936, Dr. I. Querrioux, speaking at the general assembly of the medical association's western and northern suburbs, warned that the Nast Law had too many loopholes since it exempted students enrolled in medical schools prior to the date of its promulgation and allowed them to convert their university diplomas to *diplômes d'Etat* automatically. As a result, he proclaimed, over 2,000 foreign doctors would eventually be able to practice in France, a trend with pernicious consequences in light of these foreigners' dubious moral character. He furthermore added that he had been informed through a reliable source that the prime minister was considering exempting at least 1,000 German refugee doctors from all extant legal restrictions, enabling them to compete unhindered against French doctors.[60]

Other spokesmen for the profession warned that far too many foreign doctors were circumventing the Nast Law by finding employment as medical assistants, dentists, or midwives. According to Dr. de Roux of Montpellier, "Jewish doctors from across the Rhine have found sponsors who want to see them authorized to compete with French doctors . . . and our nationals are already being ejected from auxiliary posts, to no one's objection."[61] Georges Cousin, a right-wing deputy and cosponsor of an earlier

* "Privileged categories" included foreigners employed as artisans prior to Aug. 8, 1935, and belonging to one of the categories outlined by the Ministry of Labor circular of May 7, 1936, including being married to a French citizen, having a son who served in the army, etc.

bill to curtail the right of naturalized citizens to practice medicine, called on the Chamber of Deputies to put a stop to these practices. "The Poles, the Romanians, the so-called orientals," Cousin proclaimed, "change their residence just like their marital status or their nationality. Before justice, whose delays are unfortunately all too well known to us, has extended its arms, they are out of reach. On occasion, you will rediscover them practicing in a provincial locale, where certain placement offices or certain medical journals have procured them as replacements."[62] So pervasive was this protectionist sentiment that even veterinarians sought to restrict the numbers of foreigners allowed to practice their profession.[63] Yet, under the new Parliament elected in 1936, the Confédération des Syndicats Médicaux was unable to push through a single legislative initiative.

The Popular Front similarly strove to improve the situation of foreigners in general and refugees in particular by speeding up the process of naturalization. Although some historians, such as Jean-Charles Bonnet and Barbara Vormeier, have argued that the naturalization policies of the Popular Front did not mark a significant break with those of the preceding government,[64] considerable evidence suggests the contrary. According to the League for the Rights of Man, the naturalization process had slowed down significantly just prior to the Popular Front's coming to power. "In 1934," the *Cahiers des droits de l'homme* noted, "M. [Henry] Chéron, at that time keeper of the seals, made it known that he would not admit any interventions with regard to naturalizations." As a result, "Foreigners complained to us that requests they had submitted years ago had not yet been decided upon, and that requests based on the most serious qualifications have been rejected."[65]

By the summer of 1937, however, this situation had been reversed, largely as a result of the efforts of the new minister of justice, Marc Rucart, a prominent Radical Socialist and well-known freemason. In the fall of 1936, Rucart's office issued a report condemning the slow pace of naturalizations and the tremendous backlog that had accumulated, a situation Rucart deemed "intolerable" in light of France's low birthrate and mounting defense needs. To remedy this state of affairs, Rucart successfully petitioned for a special appropriation from the Finance Ministry to hire additional personnel to handle this backlog.[66] In the spring, the minister of justice reiterated his pledge to streamline the naturalization process, stressing in particular the military's growing demands for new recruits. At a banquet of the Union Fraternelle des Vosgiens de Paris, Rucart declared: "I have wanted naturalization policy to take into account, above all else, the needs of national defense. I believe it is now time to facilitate the accession to French nationality of all able-bodied and perfectly honest adults under the age of 30 who have been deemed suitable for military service."[67] Rucart's efforts met with success. In the summer of 1937, the *Cahiers des droits de l'homme* noted with satisfaction:

For the last year [naturalization] requests have been examined with an eye toward reconciling the interest of the petitioner with that of the general public. The keeper of the seals has boasted of contributing one battalion per month to the national defense force simply by allowing the 1927 naturalization law to operate normally, an achievement for which our professional patriots cannot forgive him. All requests from young men who could lend their collaboration not only to national defense, but also to the economic activity of the country; all requests from those who, having founded and raised a family in France and having thus demonstrated their intention of settling definitively on our soil, are being examined in a favorable light.[68]

The number of naturalizations did in fact increase during the Popular Front, a trend that was hailed by the left and excoriated by the radical right. Although naturalizations fell to 28,951 in 1936, a 15 percent decline in comparison to the previous year's level of 34,119 — a decline almost certainly attributable to the delayed impact of the hard-line policies implemented in 1934 and 1935 — this trend began to be reversed in 1937. In that year, 31,330 foreigners were naturalized, an 8.2 percent increase over the previous year, and in 1938, 48,630 foreigners were naturalized, a 55 percent increase over the previous year.[69]

Although Vormeier has argued that these policies did little for German refugees, since they constituted only a tiny fraction of these cases, the number of Germans involved was not insignificant.[70] According to an official study published in 1942, 4,635 of the 108,911 foreigners naturalized during the three-year period between 1936 and 1938 were German. Given that there were 58,100 Germans living in France in 1936, and only 8,000 to 10,000 refugees, this figure is by no means inconsequential. Moreover, according to a Ministry of Justice report from the spring of 1938, some 1,515 German refugees had been naturalized between June of 1936 and December of 1937. Vormeier dismisses this figure as unremarkable, but it in fact represented between 15 and 19 percent of all German refugees living in France.[71]

But the Popular Front's dedication to the goal of speeding up naturalizations can be seen above all in Rucart's effort to break the restrictionist stranglehold of the middle-class professional associations, especially those of lawyers and doctors. On August 28, 1936, the Popular Front significantly modified the July 19, 1934, law that prohibited even naturalized foreigners from practicing law and certain other civil service professions for ten years following their naturalization. The retroactive character of the law was dropped, exempting foreigners already naturalized when the law was passed. At the same time, foreigners who had completed five years of military service were also exempted. "This will at least permit naturalized youths not to have to see their careers shattered by that long wait," *Le Popu-laire* noted with approval.[72]

At the same time, Rucart took steps to weaken the grip of the Con-fédération des Syndicats Médicaux over the naturalization process.[73] Al-though the former chancellery had instructed the prefects to consult with the local medical association before recommending the naturalization of any foreign doctor, this right, Rucart pointed out, had been egregiously abused. In a circular to the prefects he declared:

It has been brought to my attention that certain professional associations have profited from the requests for their opinions [regarding naturalization dossiers] that have been forwarded to them, by arrogating to themselves the right to call in the candidates for appointments and then proceeding to submit them to grueling in-quiries into their backgrounds, and particularly into their professional antecedents and their families, in a way that constitutes an abuse by these groups that must be ended immediately.

To rectify this situation, Rucart requested the prefects to remind the lead-ers of these professional associations to limit their comments strictly to the professional aptitude of the candidates, "the only issue of concern to them."[74] These measures apparently did not suffice, however, because dur-ing the summer of 1937 the *Cahiers des droits de l'homme* reported that the provisions permitting the medical association and its student affiliates to play an advisory role in naturalization procedures had been rescinded altogether.[75]

The culmination of the Popular Front's legislative effort on behalf of refugees was the ratification on October 20, 1936, of the League of Nations Convention of October 28, 1933, dealing with Nansen refugees, and the re-gime's subsequent attempts to extend these same benefits to German refu-gees.[76] According to this convention, which went into effect on Decem-ber 3, 1933, Nansen refugees received, in addition to internationally recog-nized travel and identity documents, far-reaching social benefits, including most favored nation status with regard to eligibility for social assistance (unemployment insurance, health insurance, pensions, and so on); disabil-ity pay in case of industrial accidents; the right to attend French educational institutions; and the right to work. With regard to this last point, the con-vention stipulated that "the restrictions ensuing from the application of laws and regulations for the protection of the national labor market shall not be applied in all their severity to refugees resident in the country." But for certain categories of refugees—those who had resided in the country for at least three years; those married to a citizen; those having one or more children who were citizens; and veterans of the First World War—restric-tions on the right to work were to be lifted altogether.[77]

This accord went far toward granting Nansen refugees a legal status nearly equivalent to that of French nationals, and no sooner had it been ratified than the government began to consider how to extend these same rights to German refugees. In April 1937, the undersecretary of state for the Foreign Ministry, Pierre Viénot, whose office was responsible for coordinating refugee matters during this period, convened an interministerial meeting to discuss ways by which these two groups of refugees—Nansen refugees and "refugees coming from Germany"—could be granted a single juridical status, as the Committee of Experts had recommended in early 1936. In part, the French government was motivated by the desire to prepare for the upcoming Intergovernmental Conference in Geneva, and in particular it wanted to consider Malcolm's draft proposal for a new accord that would encompass these recommendations.[78] But it also wanted to correct anomalies in the way the July 4, 1936, Geneva Accord was being implemented. Although the French government had committed itself to the goal of according the refugees from Germany the right to work, Viénot had to admit that "this right is badly regulated. In many departments refugees from Germany have a great many difficulties in acquiring the right to work."[79]

To remedy such abuses, Foreign Ministry officials even recommended the creation of a permanent work card that would be valid for all officially designated refugees—Nansen or German—so that they would no longer have to contend with the circuitous and often frustrating procedures involved in acquiring a work permit.[80] Moreover, the undersecretary of state even suggested that these refugees be exempted from the quotas imposed by the law of August 10, 1932, limiting the number of foreigners who could work as wage laborers and salaried employees.[81] At the same time, the army chief of staff, more eager than ever to recruit foreigners, submitted a proposal to eliminate altogether restrictions on the right to work for foreigners who had completed their military service, whether or not they had been naturalized.[82]

These liberal proposals, which went well beyond the rights accorded by the October 28, 1933, convention, were ultimately shelved, however, due to the staunch opposition of the Ministry of Labor.[83] Nevertheless, the ministries were able to agree that the social benefits as well as the right to work accorded by this convention should be extended to refugees from Germany. As a result, the French delegation to the Geneva Conference of February 8–10, 1938, convened by the HCR to finalize the terms of the Provisional Agreement of July 4, 1936, once again put forth a liberal point of view. The definition of a "refugee coming from Germany" was expanded to include, in addition to German citizens, persons who were officially stateless at the time they had fled Germany, and firm guarantees were adopted to prevent the *refoulement* of refugees to Germany.[84] Most significantly, this new accord granted German refugees the same social, welfare, and labor benefits as had been accorded Nansen refugees by the October 28, 1933, convention.[85]

The new accord, known as the "Convention Concerning the Status of Refugees Coming from Germany," in many ways epitomized the Popular Front's effort to normalize the status of German refugees and to integrate them into the national community. The French delegation to the League of Nations, which still included Longuet, signed this accord on February 10, 1938, but it was ratified only after the Second World War.[86] With the fall of Chautemps's cabinet in April 1938, the Popular Front came to an end, and, as we shall see, the subsequent administration of Edouard Daladier, confronted by a massive new wave of German and Central European refugees, returned to the hard-line approach. As a result, the social benefits offered by this convention were never put into practice.[87]

To conclude, the Popular Front's policy toward the refugees from Germany consisted of two distinct components: an extremely hard-line attitude toward future newcomers on the one hand, and a fairly liberal policy toward German refugees already established in France on the other. Although these two policies might at first appear contradictory, in the eyes of the administration, they were entirely complementary. As the various circulars issued by both the Ministry of the Interior and the Foreign Ministry illustrate, there was widespread consensus among French officials that a more liberal policy, including a more generous distribution of work permits and even the extension of social security and unemployment insurance, could be attained only by stabilizing the size of the refugee population at its current level. Such liberal measures, government officials believed "can apply only to refugees actually settled in France and not to those who might be brought here in the future by new Hitlerian persecutions."[88]

Thus, while making a significant effort to integrate those refugees already in France into the country's social and economic life, the Popular Front continued to endorse the view that with regard to future newcomers, France could serve as a transit country only. To be sure, there is a certain paradox here: to deliver on the liberal promise that the right to asylum had to include the right to work, the Popular Front reneged in part on the traditional notion of asylum as safe haven. True, as noted above, individuals could continue to apply for asylum to the Ministry of the Interior on an individual basis, but it was clear that every precaution would be taken to prevent yet another mass influx of refugees. From the perspective of the administration, however, this hard-line policy was intended to teach the League of Nations a lesson. Although the League had failed to achieve an equitable distribution of refugees the first time around, such a lapse could not be allowed to recur. While this strategy might appear indifferent or hard-hearted toward Jews still trapped in Germany, it nevertheless marked a significant advance over the policies of the Flandin and Laval administrations. Those administrations, as we have seen, sought not only to close the borders to future newcomers, but to rid the country of refugees already settled there as well.

It is also true that the Popular Front's refugee policies did not live up to initial high expectations, as expressed both by the refugees themselves as well as by French pro-refugee activists, including many members of the government. As Bonnet and Thalmann have suggested, the Popular Front, while it may have modified some of the harshest aspects of anti-immigrant measures implemented in 1934 and 1935, failed to overturn these measures altogether. This failure, however, cannot be attributed solely to lack of trying. On numerous occasions, left-wing deputies proposed legislative initiatives challenging existing restrictive regulations that made it difficult and often impossible for foreigners to acquire work permits, and even high-ranking government officials, such as Viénot, had favored exempting Nansen and German refugees from the provisions of the August 10, 1932, law, which sharply restricted the right of employers to hire immigrant labor.

Fearful of the backlash such measures would elicit, the Ministry of Labor firmly opposed these initiatives, and the persistent lobbying of the various middle-class professional associations doomed to failure any more sweeping efforts to overturn these restrictive laws. At the same time, it is clear that the Popular Front did attempt to break the stranglehold held by various middle-class professional associations over the distribution of work permits, and even over naturalization. The Ministry of Justice in particular, especially under Rucart, endeavored to implement more liberal naturalization policies, despite fierce opposition from the medical profession. Livian is therefore correct to point out that while the existing legislation was never abrogated, the Popular Front made every effort to interpret these laws as liberally as possible.

Bureaucratic obstructionism from within the ranks of the civil service, and especially among the prefects, further stymied the Popular Front's pro-refugee effort. Indeed, this problem partially accounts for the fact that by the summer of 1937, the Consultative Commission had received only 3,014 dossiers, of which 2,490 had been recognized as "veritable refugees."[89] As Paul Perrin noted, far too many prefects were violating Ministry of the Interior directives by failing to publish bilingual translations of the Presidential Decree of September 17, 1936, by ignoring the decree's amnesty provisions, and by disregarding applications for the new identity certificates that came through the mail. Such administrative sabotage, Perrin declared, had disastrous repercussions: "In practice, matters have proceeded far less quickly and in conditions that are all too often regrettable. It seems that on top of excellent intentions and quite substantial though incomplete [legal] texts, we have merely constructed a reality that is for the most part deceptive when it comes to juridical assistance available to German refugees." He therefore called on Popular Front ministers to rein in those among their subordinates who were flagrantly violating both the spirit and the letter of the new refugee policies.[90]

In the final analysis, however, these obstacles merely slowed the process by which the status of German refugees was liberalized; they by no means blocked it altogether. As the numerous testimonies of pro-refugee and Jewish groups contend, despite all the shortcomings, a great deal was achieved during the Popular Front's brief stint in office. Among contemporary pro-refugee activists, nearly all would have agreed with the British refugee spokesman Norman Bentwich, who declared in February 1938 that "when the Popular Front won its electoral victory, France regained her traditional mood of generosity to the victims of persecution. The condition of the Germans in France . . . has sensibly improved."[91]

One dimension of the Popular Front's policy remains to be considered: the effort to settle refugees in agricultural settlements, either in certain French colonies or in southwestern France. Once this nonlegislative strategy is taken into account, the Popular Front's pro-refugee effort appears in an even more favorable light, as we will see in Chapter 7.

CHAPTER SEVEN

Breaking the Impasse
Colonial and Agricultural Schemes During the Popular Front Era

Although the Popular Front under Léon Blum succeeded in improving the legal status of the refugees from Germany, two major obstacles to any long-term resolution of the refugee crisis remained—the problem of obtaining work permits and the reception of East European Jews. No one had spoken out more strongly than Blum, Marius Moutet, Salomon Grumbach, and other socialist leaders in insisting that the right to asylum was meaningless without the right to work. But their own government, despite its good intentions, was unable to perform significantly better than its predecessors with regard to providing constructive employment opportunities. Moreover, East European refugees had been completely excluded from the benefits of the Geneva Accord of July 4, 1936, and the Presidential Decree of September 17, 1936, which had normalized the legal status of refugees with German citizenship. In light of the sharply deteriorating situation of East European Jewry, especially in Poland, the repatriation of these individuals was becoming increasingly unpalatable. Many Popular Front spokesmen therefore realized that if the persistent contradiction between the needs of the refugees on the one hand and the protectionist demands of the French workers on the other was ever to be resolved, more radical solutions would have to be found.

Two ways out of this impasse were ultimately envisioned: first, the settlement of Jewish refugees in French colonies, and particularly on the island of Madagascar, a solution put forth most vigorously by Blum's minister of colonies, Marius Moutet; and second, the settlement of refugees in agricultural colonies in southwestern France, an alternative advocated by Philippe Serre, who served as undersecretary of state for immigration in Chautemps's cabinet in late 1937 and early 1938. That both these plans were intended not only for refugees from Germany but above all for Eastern European Jews indicates that the Popular Front understood that solutions to the Jewish refugee problem could no longer be confined to the relatively small group of German refugees. On the other hand, the significant attention paid to these colonial and agricultural schemes suggests that even the most liberal, pro-refugee regime was either unable or unwilling to challenge the wall of French protectionism head-on. Circumvention, not confrontation, was the preferred course of action. By removing Jewish refugees from cities and transforming them into peasants and artisans, Popular Front spokesmen hoped to defuse the principal anti-refugee charge that the refugees constituted a serious economic threat. They thus hoped to bring about that reconciliation between humanitarian concerns and economic interests that had hitherto proved so elusive.

During Blum's premiership, colonial solutions held center stage. Agricultural schemes, despite support in late 1935 from the minister of the interior, Joseph Paganon, were temporarily relegated to the back burner. The idea of settling Jewish refugees in French colonies was by no means new. Proposals to send refugees to colonies or territories under French mandate had been bandied about since 1933. At the first Interministerial Meeting on Refugees in May 1933, J. Gaston Joseph, a spokesman for the Ministry of Colonies, had suggested that German refugee doctors might be sent to North Africa in view of recently imposed restrictions on the practice of medicine by foreigners in France.[1] A few doctors were sent to Tunisia, but after they were expelled in late 1934 by the Tunisian bey, renowned for his antisemitism and xenophobia, these efforts came to an end.[2]

Several Jewish groups, most notably the Gourevitch Committee, with the backing of the High Commission for Refugees (HCR) and the Joint Distribution Committee (JDC), also endorsed the idea of colonial settlements, claiming that the refugees, particularly those arriving with capital, would create new businesses and industries, thus enhancing France's commercial prowess. Yet the Ministry of Colonies as well as the Foreign Ministry, particularly during Pierre Laval's tenure in office,* remained firmly opposed, citing the Depression and the specter of Arab antisemitism, which, Laval argued, would turn these territories' indigenous populations irrevocably against France. When approached on the question of colonial settle-

---

*Laval served as minister of colonies from Feb. 9, 1934, until Nov. 8, 1934, and as foreign minister from Oct. 13, 1934, until June 7, 1935.

ments, the Foreign Ministry's standard response was to repeat Laval's dictum that "at present there are . . . no possibilities whatsoever for German Jewish refugees to immigrate to our colonies."[3]

By 1935, however, certain elements within the administration were beginning to exhibit greater sympathy for the idea. In February, the minister of the interior, Marcel Régnier, had publicly expressed a willingness to look into colonial settlements for refugees who could not be expelled and who lacked financial means.[4] Régnier was motivated not by humanitarian considerations, but by financial ones, since he, along with other conservatives, resented the growing tax burden incurred by having to keep these refugees in prison. Claiming that his administration "attached the greatest importance" to this question, Régnier instructed his minister of colonies to investigate possibilities for settling refugees in overseas territories, especially French Guiana, New Caledonia, and the New Hebrides.[5] By November 1935, both the Ministry of Colonies and the Ministry of the Interior, now under Paganon's jurisdiction, rejected this idea, however, citing the prohibitive costs of sending the refugees so far away, as well as climatic and health problems, especially in Guiana, which served as a penal colony precisely because of its harsh living conditions.[6]

The most promising of these schemes during the early years of the refugee crisis was the notion of sending German Jews to Syria, then under French mandate. It was once again the Gourevitch Committee that served as principal lobbyist for this scheme.[7] Proposals to settle Jews in Syria had been put forth by the World Zionist Organization in the 1920's, but without success, since the French Foreign Ministry, despite sympathy for Zionist aspirations, feared any action that would irritate the Arabs.[8] The idea resurfaced in 1933, however, in response to the refugee crisis. In November, the *Tribune Juive*, the principal organ of Alsatian Jewry, cited an article by Emile Schreiber that favored the settlement of 50,000 German Jews in Syria and claimed that such an initiative would have positive economic and cultural benefits since these Jews would import capital to the region and would serve as a francophile element.[9] Yet, when approached by the Gourevitch Committee about this scheme, the high commissioner of Syria, Count Damien de Martel, as well as other officials at the Quai d'Orsay, expressed strong opposition, citing Arab and Turkish opposition, fears of Zionist irredentism in southern Lebanon, and concerns about the emergence of an antisemitic movement, which, they claimed, would create instability and inflame Arab opinion against France.[10]

By mid-1934, Martel began to soften, however, telling the Gourevitch Committee that he would consider its proposal if certain conditions could be met, including winning the support of local Arab notables; promising that priority would be granted to refugees already in France, especially those with large sums of capital (at least 100,000 francs, or $15,000); and ensuring that the refugees not be Zionists and not settle near the Palestine border.[11] After a concerted lobbying campaign to win local Arab support, as well as efforts to persuade the JDC to fund the project, the Gourevitch Committee claimed that it was ready to implement the plan by the end of the year. In December, a number of sources, including Martel himself, even announced that a small-scale settlement plan, involving no more than 10,000 refugee families, "was on the verge of beginning to be realized."[12]

Despite this progress, the plan apparently fell out of favor, and in September 1935 Bernhard Kahn reported that "so far no real results have been achieved."[13] While the Quai d'Orsay may have been swayed to dismiss this plan by the fierce opposition of native Jewish leaders, who argued that colonial settlements of any kind were dangerous "mirages" likely to end in failure and disillusionment,[14] it is more probable that the Foreign Ministry's decision was motivated by escalating Arab-Jewish tensions in Palestine, which came to an explosive head in the 1936 Arab general strike. Given this anti-Jewish animosity, any action that threatened to turn Arab opinion against France would have seemed foolhardy, despite the Gourevitch Committee's argument that a Jewish presence in Syria would serve as a stabilizing factor by shoring up support for the local Christian population.[15]

These colonial schemes began to be pursued in a serious way only after the Popular Front came to power, and it was Marius Moutet, the noted pro-refugee activist and Blum's minister of colonies, who emerged as their principal promoter. Prior to the Popular Front's electoral victory, it had been primarily conservatives, such as Régnier, who had been most vociferous in supporting these schemes. The socialists too were beginning to move in this direction, however. According to an intelligence report from February 1935, the Association des Emigrés Israélites d'Allemagne had drawn up a list of refugees who desired to go to the colonies, and among the plan's most avid supporters it ranked Moutet, Blum, Longuet, and Pierre-Bloch.[16] Moreover, during the parliamentary debates of February 1935, Moutet had endorsed Régnier's proposal to create work camps in North Africa for refugees considered a national security risk.[17] In January 1936, the minister of the interior reported that Moutet was planning to create a legislative committee devoted to the defense of refugees in France, and he noted that Moutet "is of the opinion that a great many refugees could be usefully employed in our colonies."[18] Similarly, the central committee of the League for the Rights of Man endorsed colonial schemes in late 1935 as the most humane alternative to mass expulsion and imprisonment.[19]

After the Popular Front came to power, these vague sentiments began to coalesce into concrete plans, largely as a result of the aggressive lobbying efforts of several of the smaller Jewish committees—most notably the Gourevitch Committee, which emerged with greater prominence after the Comité National's retreat in 1935, as well as the World Jewish Congress and the Société d'Emigration et de Colonisation Juive (Emcol).[20] Not only did these organizations launch vigorous propaganda campaigns to convince French officials that the refugees would constitute a valuable economic asset,[21] but they also carried their message directly to local colonial administrators. In October 1936, the French Zionist leader and president of the Fédération des Sociétés Juives de France (FSJF), Marc Jarblum, acting as a delegate to the World Jewish Congress, met privately with the governor-general of Madagascar, Léon Cayla, to discuss settlement possibilities on the island. Cayla, who for years had been seeking to attract settlers to Madagascar,[22] informed Jarblum that Jewish refugees would be welcome, but only on two conditions: first, that they come exclusively as farmers, so as to prevent competition with local merchants and artisans, and second, that they settle in less populated and less desirable regions.[23] Boris Gourevitch too met with Cayla on November 16, and according to Gourevitch's account of the meeting, Cayla informed him that if the Jewish settlers were to accept the conditions already presented to Jarblum, Madagascar could absorb as many as 10,000 refugees.[24] Cayla's willingness to entertain this plan ultimately convinced Moutet that the idea merited further investigation.

In early 1937, these Jewish organizations scored a major breakthrough. On January 16, the *Petit Parisien*, reported that Moutet, after "an interview . . . with representatives of various Jewish groups," had announced that the French government was ready to seek a colonial solution to the Jewish refugee problem. As Moutet declared: "I'll be very happy if, on the one hand, I can make a useful contribution to the work of colonization, and if, on the other hand, I can assist the many people whose undeserved misery . . . is attributable to political and religious passions and racial prejudice."[25] The example of Palestine, Moutet claimed, proved that Jews were "perfectly suitable for agricultural work, which is the basis of every colonization enterprise."

But at the same time, Moutet warned against exaggerated illusions. Such a colonization scheme, he claimed, would have to be conducted on a very small scale, and rigorous precautions would have to be taken: a thorough preliminary investigation into the geographic and climatic conditions would have to be conducted, colonists would have to be selected with extreme care so as "to avoid the repatriation of the unfit," and Jewish organizations would have to coordinate their efforts to mobilize the necessary financial resources. Among the colonies Moutet mentioned as most suitable for Jewish settlement were New Caledonia, the New Hebrides, French Guiana, and Madagascar, where the local administration, he noted, had already expressed strong support. To supervise this investigation, Moutet assigned two members of his staff, J. Gaston Joseph and Paul Bouteille, and he informed Jewish organizations that the French government would provide the requisite technical expertise and facilities to carry out the scientific appraisals.

While Moutet's proposal stirred considerable excitement in France itself, especially within the Jewish community, in Poland it created a sensation. Since the First World War, the situation for Polish Jewry, which numbered about 3.5 million by 1935—10 percent of the total population—had deteriorated steadily.[26] A succession of Polish regimes, riding a wave of nationalism, had pursued programs of "polonization," the attempt to create an indigenous Polish middle class at the expense of other national minorities, and especially the Jews, since Jews had historically dominated Polish commerce. During the early 1920's, as a result of pressure from Roman Dmowski's National Democratic (Endek) movement, Jews were barred from civil service posts and progressively ousted from their roles as economic middlemen. This process was accomplished by nationalizing government monopolies traditionally dominated by Jews, such as tobacco and wood; by implementing economic boycotts against Jews in commerce, artisanry, and the liberal professions; and by limiting Jewish enrollment in secondary schools and universities.

With the onset of the Depression, the economic plight of the Jews worsened dramatically, and most sources concurred that by the mid-1930's, a full one-third of Polish Jewry did "not possess the most rudimentary economic foundations."[27] After the death of Marshal Josef Pilsudski in 1935, this situation deteriorated even further. The new regime that came to power, headed by Marshal Edouard Rydz-Smigly, embarked on a policy of state-sponsored antisemitism, initiating ghetto benches in universities, supporting anti-Jewish economic boycotts, and banning *shehita*, the Jewish method of slaughtering beef and poultry to make it kosher. Moreover, this regime actively encouraged the wave of anti-Jewish pogroms that erupted at the end of 1935 and continued through 1937.[28] As economic opportunities declined and emigration possibilities dried up, the Zionist slogan that the Jews of Poland were "a people without a future" seemed about to be realized. The Anglo-Jewish paper, *The Jewish Chronicle*, described Polish Jews in 1937 as "a helpless minority sunk in squalid poverty and misery such as can surely be paralleled nowhere on the face of the earth. Today it is generally agreed that one-third of the Jewish population is on the brink of starvation, one-third contrives to maintain a mere existence, and the rest are fortunate in securing a minimum of comfort."[29]

From the point of view of the Polish government, there was only one solution to this dilemma—the mass emigration of the Jews. As the French ambassador to Warsaw, Léon Noël, noted in August 1936: "Poland is a relatively overpopulated country. . . . Given that it is a country without capital, Poland must seek to solve its population problems . . . through an intensification of emigration."[30] In September, Noël added that "with regard to the Jewish question . . . Polish public opinion and the [Polish] government itself envision no solution other than emigration. It is believed here that the departure en masse of the Jewish population would permit the Poles to exercise all the professions (liberal professions, commerce, artisan trades) over which the Jews now possess a quasi-monopoly."[31] Although the Polish government had previously hoped to encourage Jewish migration to Palestine, the Arab general strike of 1936 and the British government's subsequent decision to curtail Jewish immigration to Palestine caused the regime to seek relief elsewhere.[32]

In 1936, Poland's foreign minister, Colonel Joseph Beck, began to demand that the League of Nations include East European Jews among those officially considered refugees so that they might be resettled abroad as well.[33] At the same time, he began to press France and Great Britain to cede one of their colonies to Poland so that it could be used as a "dumping ground" for Poland's "surplus" Jewish population. When the Polish delegate to the League of Nations first put forth this proposal in September 1936, Noël reported that "the idea has arisen altogether naturally . . . that it is up to those countries that possess vast colonial territories to create a sort of second homeland where the Jews of Central Europe could settle." The Polish government was even so bold as to suggest that the Western democracies pay for this population transfer.[34]

Great Britain remained impassive to these pleas, fearing that such concessions would only encourage the Polish government to expel its Jewish population en masse. France proved more receptive, however, hoping that some concession on this score might conciliate its East European ally and prevent it from slipping into the Nazi camp. In the fall of 1936, Blum and his foreign minister, Yvon Delbos, broached this subject with Beck directly. It is therefore not surprising that Polish governing circles seized upon Moutet's speech of January 16 as the long-awaited answer to their petitions, even though Moutet never specifically mentioned either Poland or Polish Jewry. The day after Moutet's declaration, Noël reported that the Polish press was abuzz with the news, and that every major newspaper had reprinted the *Petit Parisien* article. "The news concerning a project to settle Jewish colonists in certain French colonies . . . is provoking a sensation in Warsaw as great as the Jewish problem itself," which, he noted, was "more than ever the order of the day."[35] Moreover, Noël informed the French foreign minister that even prior to the publication of Moutet's statement, Beck had approached him to ask whether France might assist Poland in evacuating its entire Jewish population. When Noël proceeded to warn Beck against "excessive illusions," Beck replied that he was simply trying to offer "hope for the future to a generally miserable population that has the feeling of being trapped in a situation with no way out."[36]

The Polish reaction caught Moutet and his staff off guard, and they acted swiftly to quell speculation that France intended to serve as Poland's handmaiden in the wholesale evacuation of Polish Jewry. At the end of January, Moutet's deputy, Bouteille, met with Jewish representatives and went out of his way to stress that the initial project was to be carried out on an extremely limited scale: no more than 10 families were to be settled in 1937; 30 in 1938; and 50 in 1939—a far cry from Beck's desire to evacuate Poland's entire Jewish population.[37] Moreover, Bouteille stipulated that prospective colonists would have to possess at least 100,000 francs, further limiting the scope of the settlement. Finally, and most significantly, he insisted that the colonists be drawn exclusively from the pool of refugees already in France.[38] As the French Zionist paper *La Terre retrouvée* reported in early February, Moutet "is not actually concerned about an immigration of Jews from foreign countries where tremendous pressure to emigrate is felt. The Minister does not want the immigration possibilities to French colonies to be exaggerated, and for illusions to take hold."[39] So too the bulletin of the Centre de Documentation et de Vigilance, the recently created self-defense organization of the native Jewish establishment, stated that at this meeting, "Mr. Bouteille finally added that the French government has learned that certain governments have the impression that the implementation of this project could help them get rid of their Jewish subjects; such an eventuality is entirely without foundation. The enthusiastic commentaries of the antisemitic Polish press are therefore without foundation."[40]

These caveats did little to dampen Polish enthusiasm, however, particularly since Bouteille's comments had been made in private before an exclusively Jewish audience. By April, the Polish government, eager to forge ahead, had already designated a three-member team to investigate conditions for Jewish settlement on Madagascar. The delegates included Commander Mieczyslaw Lepecki, a representative of the Polish government and president of the Polish Colonization Society, and two Jews—Leon Alter, the director of the Warsaw branch of HICEM, and Salomon Dyk, a prominent agronomist from Tel Aviv. Although two earlier surveys of settlement possibilities on the island—a 1926 Polish government survey to investigate the island's suitability for Poland's surplus peasant population and a Japanese study of the following year—had recommended against mass settlement schemes, Rydz-Smigly's government was nevertheless determined to proceed. As historian Yehuda Bauer has noted, "If it was not suitable for Poles, it might still be good enough for Jews."[41]

Moutet met with the Polish team in early May, just prior to its departure for Madagascar, and he subsequently held a press conference to clarify the French government's intentions vis-à-vis the Polish mission. Unfortunately, Moutet's remarks had the opposite effect, perhaps because he himself was unclear as to what the mission was intended to achieve. On the one hand, the minister of colonies reported that he had warned the Polish team that "this attempt cannot be interpreted as if we wanted to provoke a major population exodus, which, to say the least, would be singularly premature." On the other hand, Moutet made it clear that he personally had no objections to Madagascar serving as a haven for Polish Jews, a statement that flew in the face of Bouteille's earlier insistence that the plan was designed exclusively for Jews already in France. As Moutet declared:

The Polish government has asked us if it might be possible to permit the settlement of certain of its nationals in our overseas possessions. In response to such a request, we have replied that we perceive only advantages, on condition that we are talking about a serious colonization effort that could justify the investment of sufficient resources and attract competent persons to work in what would essentially be agricultural production. In favoring such an enterprise, we would like to show our liberality toward friendly nations that lack colonial territories of their own in which to settle their nationals.

Moreover, when one correspondent asked whether the minister of colonies might consider similar concessions to Germany with regard to its Jews, Moutet replied: "Why not? We are ready, I repeat, for any peaceful collaboration, on the condition *sine qua non* that the political status of our colonies or territories under mandate not be resubmitted to question and that we not be asked to redraw the map of Africa."[42]

Native French Jewish organizations were dismayed. Raymond-Raoul Lambert, the former secretary-general of the Comité National and the editor-in-chief of the *Univers israélite*, had already published an article in January 1937 denouncing the Madagascar Plan in no uncertain terms. Lambert's concern stemmed in part from the government's intention to sponsor a collective emigration scheme, rather than helping individual refugees settle on their own initiative. This decision, he believed, would lead to the creation of unassimilable ethnic enclaves that would impede integration and provoke antisemitism. But Lambert's overriding fear was that the French initiative, though motivated by generous sentiments, would inadvertently send a green light to every regime in Eastern Europe that Jews could be expelled with impunity. He therefore warned that "the goodwill of the French government justifies neither the policy of eviction practiced by certain governments with regard to the Jews, nor their projects of mass evacuation contrary to the rights of man and citizen."[43]

Moreover, for Lambert, together with many other French Jews, these colonial schemes constituted a dangerous "mirage"—a deceptively easy remedy to the enormously complicated "Jewish problem" in Eastern Europe. Such facile solutions were almost certain to fail and would ultimately arouse profound disillusionment among all parties concerned. Lambert thus warned Jacques Fouques-Duparc, now the foreign minister's chief of staff, that French Jews were "deeply worried over these rumors, which were likely to awaken among the masses of the Polish Jewish population unrealizable hopes, thus provoking an exodus for which France will sooner or later have to pay." Fouques-Duparc in turn reported that French Jews "strongly desire that these rumors be denied in some appropriate manner."[44] Louis Oungre, director of the Jewish Colonization Association (JCA), voiced similar opposition to the plan. According to Oungre, the JCA had conducted its own survey of conditions in Madagascar and had determined the place unfit; Lambert even appended a copy of this report to his appeal to Fouques-Duparc. Oungre reiterated these pessimistic conclusions at a meeting of Jewish organizations in January 1938. Besides the insalubrious climate, he now invoked the specter of diplomatic complications as well. The French government, he claimed, would never allow Jews to immigrate to Madagascar since "this would probably raise a political problem, at a time when colonies were being discussed in connection with Germany."[45]

The JDC was similarly displeased by the way the Polish government had manipulated this affair, and during the spring and summer of 1937 it took steps to regain the diplomatic offensive. In late May, Charles Liebman, vice chairman of the Refugee Economic Corporation, an organization set up by the JDC to survey land settlement possibilities for refugees, met with the French ambassador in Washington, Georges Bonnet, to discuss prospects for sending Jewish refugees to French colonies.[46] Two weeks later, Kahn followed up this discussion by meeting with Moutet himself, and he informed him that the JDC and the Refugee Economic Corporation would carry out their own survey of conditions on the island. In June, Kahn and Joseph Rosen, president of the Agrojoint, the JDC affiliate in charge of Jewish agricultural settlements in the Soviet Union, reported that the French government was reluctant to deal with the Polish Committee and "would prefer to deal with a private reliable Jewish organization and would offer such an organization better facilities for investigation than the Polish Committee may be accorded." Under these circumstances, they recommended that Jewish organizations proceed with their own investigations.[47] The JDC subsequently allocated $12,000 for a preliminary survey, and in September it sent its Cape Town representative, Max Sonnenberg, to Madagascar to head the investigation.[48]

Apparently, the JDC's initiative had the desired effect: Kahn and Rosen elicited from Moutet a promise that if they implemented their plan, the French government would be prepared to make a significant investment of capital "at least matching the investments of the Jewish organizations with respect to capital improvements in the districts where immigration would take place." Moreover, Moutet went out of his way in late June to stress that despite rumors in the Polish press, the French government had no official connection with the Polish mission. "There is . . . no link whatsoever," he reiterated, "between the dispatch of this mission and the Polish chief of state's famous evacuation plan."[49]

Despite the JDC's effort and Moutet's repeated qualifications, the Polish government remained staunchly committed to seeing its own plan through to the end. When the Polish team returned from Madagascar in September, rumors abounded that its investigation had yielded extremely favorable results. In early October, Léon Noël reported that the members of the commission were preparing their final report and that he had received official assurances that "their impressions were . . . highly favorable and their conclusions positive."[50] Later in the month, Polish shipping companies notified the French ambassador that "the emigration movement of Polish colonists to Madagascar seems about to enter into an active phase in the near future."[51] In November, squabbles even broke out between French and Polish shipping companies over whose boats would transport the Jews to Madagascar.[52]

Moutet too appeared ready to proceed with the scheme, although he again warned the members of the Polish team, with whom he conferred on November 22, that the French government would allow only a very limited immigration, and under no circumstances would it tolerate a mass expulsion of Polish Jews.[53] Similarly, Delbos, during a trip to Eastern Europe in December 1937, assured the Polish government that France would do everything possible to open up colonies for Poland, "but that France would never lend a hand to assist with an emigration planned solely for Jews whom the Poles intend to coerce into leaving Poland as a superfluous population."[54] As usual, however, the Polish government had other plans; in mid-January, Noël reported that the entire Polish press—including official government mouthpieces—"take pleasure in conversing with their readers in terms likely to make them believe that this migration has already been decided upon in principle and that a great many people could be involved."[55]

This flurry of preparations notwithstanding, neither the Polish nor the JDC plan ever materialized, due to a coalescence of factors. First, it was becoming increasingly clear that the Polish government had completely misrepresented the findings of its own investigative commission, and it was precisely because the three members held sharply divergent views that no formal report was ever published. Not surprisingly, it was Commander

Lepecki, the sole non-Jew in the delegation, who offered the most optimistic assessment. In a lecture delivered in early February 1938 and subsequently reprinted in the semiofficial *Gazeta Polska*, Lepecki claimed that the central district of Madagascar, an area of high plateaus consisting of about 66,000 square miles, was climatically suitable for the settlement of European Jews, and he recommended that one district in particular, Ankaizinana, be set aside for immediate settlement. This territory, he maintained, was capable of supporting up to 15,000 families, or approximately 40,000 to 60,000 individuals, and he estimated that it would cost 30,000 francs per family, less than the cost of settling a single family in Palestine.[56]

The two Jewish members of the team were far more pessimistic, however. According to a December 1937 report in the German Zionist paper, the *Jüdische Rundschau*, Alter and Dyk agreed with Lepecki that the region best suited for European settlement was the area of the central high plateaus, but they insisted that "there is no possibility at all for a massive immigration to Madagascar." At best, Alter believed that no more than 500 families could be settled, and Dyk set the figure even lower. If conditions in Madagascar were indeed so favorable, they asked, why "had the French government not been able to settle its own unemployed workers there?"[57] Furthermore, in Alter's opinion, the colonization of Jews presented special problems "since they consist of an urban element which is not bound to the soil and which requires a long period of instruction and assistance to prevent them overrunning the whole island, which could eventually lead to their being deported from Madagascar." Alter and Dyk warned their coreligionists, "You will not find fertile and cultivable land in Madagascar, even if enormous sums of money are placed at your disposal, even if a competent and responsible organization were to be created for that end."[58] Alter in fact had publicly denounced the Polish government's intentions as antisemitic. During the summer of 1937, he had declared, "There is no overpopulation problem in Poland; if the necessary reforms, economic as well as social, were undertaken, the rural population's buying power would be augmented and . . . the preliminary foundation for the industrialization of Polish towns would be laid, which in turn would permit the natural absorption of the excess peasant population."[59]

Polish Jews shared this lack of enthusiasm, but for them, as for their French coreligionists, it was the project's political ramifications to which they objected most. Already in June of 1937, Dr. Arieh Tartakower, one of Polish Jewry's most prominent spokesmen, had denounced the plan in no uncertain terms, proclaiming, "We will not leave because Poland is our country."[60] The major Jewish Polish-language daily, the *Nasz Przeglad*, similarly condemned the scheme as "an excellent occasion to throw the Jews out of the civilized world," and the Warsaw Yiddish paper, the *Haint*, claimed that the French initiative "attests to a great naïveté. It funnels water to the mill of antisemitism. . . . The departure of several tens of thousands of Jews will not resolve the Jewish question in Poland."[61] In March 1938 Noël reported:

If certain Jewish organizations headquartered outside of Poland are disposed to take an interest in this project, as the minister of colonies seems to believe, the Jews of Poland have until now been altogether hostile. It would in fact be a mistake to believe that the idea of a Jewish colonization in Madagascar emanates from Polish Jews; in reality it was born in antisemitic circles. Under these circumstances, it is not surprising that Polish Jews see in this emigration a kind of project for their collective expulsion, and they consequently react to it as such.[62]

Like Lambert, Noël too warned the French government to act quickly to squelch Poland's exaggerated expectations for this project. Otherwise, both Jewish and non-Jewish opinion in Poland "will turn against us and eventually reproach us either for not having sufficiently warned the interested parties and Polish [public] opinion against these chimerical projects, or for not having done everything necessary to carry this project through to completion."[63]

The hostility of the Polish Jewish population was not the only problem, however. Significant opposition to the plan was beginning to emerge in Madagascar itself. To be sure, a significant minority of public opinion supported Cayla's view and welcomed the prospect of Jewish immigration. As Isac Béton wrote in *Le Colonisé*, a major organ of the settler community: "Far from considering the persecuted Jews as dangerous competitors, the colonial population will see in them a promise of prosperity for their country."[64] The *Echo du Sud* similarly declared that if the Jews could accomplish for Madagascar what they had for Palestine, their presence would be warmly welcomed.[65]

But the majority of local papers simply reprinted articles from the extreme-right-wing metropolitan press that used antisemitism to stoke the flames of settler discontent. The *Journal de Madagascar*, the principal daily of French settlers, reprinted articles from *L'Action française* warning that Madagascar was about to become "the 'human trash bin' for all Europe's undesirables."[66] The Popular Front's sole aim was to strengthen the local communist movement by erecting "a phalange of unfortunates, justifiably revolted by the contrast between the implacable reality and the false hopes with which they had deluded themselves."[67] Georges Roux, writing in the right-wing *L'Emancipation national*, similarly wondered why Moutet was doing so much to help the "judeo-moldo-valaques," when "nothing is being done for French settlers."[68] And Jacques Perret, writing in *Je suis partout*, complained that the Jews would never confine themselves to agriculture. Rather, their natural instincts would draw them back to those "parasitical trades"—commerce and usury—for which "we already have many Greeks, Syrians, and Hindus who conduct business quite well."[69]

But ultimately it was the criticism of Marcel Olivier, the island's former governor-general, that carried the greatest weight in terms of local opposition. In February 1938, Olivier published an article in the Parisian weekly *L'Illustration* that emphasized the island's unhealthy climate and fully endorsed the pessimistic assessments of Alter and Dyk as opposed to the "evasive optimism" of Lepecki. Olivier insisted that in view of these unpropitious conditions, "the only charitable thing to do was to bar the route to the floodtide of immigration." Otherwise, he claimed, these settlers would soon be digging their own graves. Moreover, he warned, if France did nothing to stop Beck's insidious maneuver, other nations would jump on the Polish bandwagon. Indeed, he noted, the January issue of Julius Streicher's *Der Stürmer* had already been emblazoned with the headline "Madagascar: The Jews Are Our Misfortune." And during an interview with the Tharaud brothers, the head of the Romanian government, Octavian Goga, had brandished this issue of *Der Stürmer*, demanding: "Couldn't they [the Jews] be sent off to some distant place! Somewhere, on an island . . . from where they couldn't leave? . . . Madagascar, for example." Olivier thus concluded:

> If we really possessed vast habitable and deserted domains in Madagascar or elsewhere, wouldn't our millennial generosity spontaneously create there a secure refuge where the eternal wanderers of Israel could . . . come ashore? Whether chased out of Poland, Romania, or any other country, momentarily France, in accordance with its traditions, would greatly desire to make such a sanctuary available for them.
>
> But we nowhere possess such a Canaan. And that is precisely what we need to try to make Mr. Streicher, as well as Mr. Goga, understand.[70]

Yet even this local opposition might not necessarily have killed the plan had it not been for Moutet's departure from the Ministry of Colonies on January 18, 1938—the result of a cabinet reshuffle. True, Moutet returned to his post briefly during Blum's second cabinet from March 13, 1938, until April 10, 1938, and rumors began to surface that Moutet intended to resurrect this project.[71] Ultimately, however, there was simply no time. Since neither of Moutet's successors—Théodore Steeg and Georges Mandel—evinced the slightest sympathy for the plan, the Madagascar scheme was, for all intents and purposes, shelved by the end of January. Only weeks after taking office in January 1938, Steeg, in response to a query from a Romanian Jew regarding the possibility of settling in Madagascar, reiterated every criticism ever leveled against the plan: "It's to be feared that the Jewish elements desirous of settling in the colonies are composed above all of workers, small artisans, or merchants, none of whom are in the least prepared to work the land." He continued, "Soon after their arrival, rebuffed by difficulties, they would be inclined to practice that small-scale commerce that the Syrians, Hindus, and Chinese exercise in certain parts of Africa at the expense of the local economy and the natives." Besides, Steeg claimed, the plan was simply too costly, and he reiterated Noël's arguments that "the administration that would favor such an immigration movement would have to bear responsibility for the failures that would inevitably give rise to [hostile] press campaigns and would damage France's colonizing effort, already the target of so many unjust attacks from abroad." And finally, in what constituted an apparent victory for Louis Oungre, Steeg recommended that all requests from East European Jews desiring to emigrate to colonies henceforth be directed not to the Quai d'Orsay, but rather to the JCA, which had already demonstrated so much success in settling Jews in South America.[72]

It was, however, not Steeg but Georges Mandel, appointed by Daladier to serve as minister of colonies on April 10, 1938, who dealt the scheme the harshest blow. As a result of the refugee crisis sparked by the Anschluss— Germany's annexation of Austria on March 13, 1938—interest in Madagascar revived, not so much in France, where the Foreign Ministry had in fact instructed its embassies on April 8 that the plan was no longer on the docket, but rather in Great Britain, where the Foreign Office in particular was eager to alleviate pressure on the British government with respect to Palestine. On April 6, the British M.P. Captain Alan Graham raised the question of Jewish settlement in Madagascar in the House of Commons, claiming that this plan promised to relieve "Palestine of further congestion and friction consequent upon a renewed exodus of Jews from Central and Eastern Europe." Initially, the Foreign Office replied that "while His Majesty's government would naturally be sympathetic to any proposal for such immigration [to Madagascar] which had the approval of the French government, they do not contemplate approaching the French government in the matter."[73] The British colonial secretary, William Ormsby-Gore, deeply disturbed by the plight of the refugees, refused to drop the matter, however. On April 26, he petitioned the British foreign minister, Lord Halifax, to approach the new French foreign minister, Georges Bonnet, to see whether France might reconsider Madagascar as a haven for Jewish refugees, especially those fleeing from Austria. As Ormsby-Gore explained:

To please the F.O. I have agreed to a drastic cutting down of the number I personally would like to see allowed to go to Palestine—but if the F.O. objects to Jewish refugees going to Palestine in order to try and placate the Arabs (I am sure it won't achieve that end), at least we ought in view of the Balfour Declaration to give any influence we can to find them homes of refuge from religious and race persecution elsewhere. Madagascar is large, healthy, undeveloped and sparsely populated. I get so many appeals from the Jews to help find somewhere for them now that the gates of Palestine are so nearly closed against them. No one wants these wretched hunted people, and Madagascar seems to me a chance.[74]

Halifax complied, and on May 2, he informed Ormsby-Gore that Bonnet had promised "to look into [the matter] with a desire to be helpful."[75]

Officials at the French Foreign Ministry forwarded Halifax's request to Mandel, who replied on May 25 with an uncategorical refusal. Mandel's hostility to the plan far exceeded Steeg's, and it is likely that Mandel—a political conservative, an ardent patriot, and a highly assimilated Jew—was motivated in part by a desire to avoid even a hint of acting on behalf of Jewish rather than French national interests.[76] Mandel may also have been influenced by some of his contacts in the native Jewish establishment, since his line of reasoning mirrored their own.[77] Like Lambert, Mandel argued that the Madagascar Plan would have dangerous political repercussions: "In effect, if we accord Jewish emigrants from Poland, Romania, Germany, Austria, [and] Hungary, special advantages, we thereby recognize the existence of a Jewish problem. We therefore risk encouraging precisely those same persecutions and coercive measures that gave rise to the exodus of these Jewish populations in the first place." Indeed, he pointed out, recent approaches by the Romanian authorities to see whether they too might be able to deport their Jews to Madagascar illustrated all too clearly the inherent dangers of such schemes.[78] Moreover, Mandel followed Louis Oungre in raising the specter of revanchist claims. As he stated:

Perhaps it would be foolhardy to receive Jews who come from countries that have formulated colonial claims on our overseas territories, such as Germany and Poland. Since, let's suppose that in the more or less distant future, the Jewish settlers succeed in establishing an important and prosperous community, wouldn't it be possible to expect that the governments of those states where the settlers came from originally might end up by claiming that colony inhabited by its former subjects?

Finally, Mandel reiterated the climatic and financial difficulties that would have to be overcome. In particular, like Lambert, he worried about what would happen in case of failure: "Toward which country would they be directed? Upon whom would the costs of repatriation and support fall?" He thus concluded, "It would be more than imprudent to show ourselves to be favorable to Jewish colonization projects. To do so would risk provoking, from every angle, far more dangers than advantages." In the meantime, Mandel promised that other alternatives would be explored.[79] To ensure that this message reached its intended audience in Poland, the Foreign Ministry, at the behest of Noël, inserted an article over the summer in *Le Temps*, the Quai d'Orsay's semi-official mouthpiece, to announce that France had dropped the plan once and for all.[80] With this announcement, the JDC postponed its own survey of conditions in Madagascar as well.

While Moutet was busy finalizing plans to send Jewish immigrants to Madagascar during the fall and winter of 1937, the Popular Front, led since

June by a new premier, the Radical politician Camille Chautemps, advanced another radical proposal for solving the Jewish refugee crisis—the creation of large-scale agricultural settlements in southwestern France. Chautemps's personal interest in agricultural schemes dated back to the early months of the refugee crisis, when he had served as minister of the interior. At the first meeting of the Interministerial Commission on German Refugees in May 1933, he had declared that the principal obstacle to any long-term solution to the Jewish refugee problem was the absence of jobs in middle-class professions, and he called on the refugees to reform their occupational distribution. At the same time, he suggested that the government explore the possibility of agricultural settlements for refugees, and the minister of agriculture was subsequently instructed to "try to place the refugees in agricultural centers, especially in those parts of the country where there is a shortage of agricultural labor or where fallow land still exists."[81]

Despite this support, this idea never took root prior to 1936. In the spring of 1934, with the support of the Ministries of Agriculture and Labor and the Corsican General Council, the Comité National and several smaller refugee committees sponsored the settlement of ten Jewish refugees in Corsica to work as agricultural laborers. If successful, this effort was to be followed by a larger settlement of up to 500 refugees on the island.[82] This effort ended in failure, however, and within weeks the refugees involved had all returned to the metropole. In part, this failure was due to bad planning—apparently, the refugees had not been provided with adequate training, and as soon as they arrived they began to complain to the Comité National, their sponsor, of the harsh working and living conditions.[83] This scheme also encountered political opposition. Although it had enthusiastic support from the Corsican General Council, which welcomed the refugees as an economic boon as well as a possible antidote to the predominance of Italian immigrant laborers, who were frequently anti-French,[84] other politicians, especially the province's influential deputy, François Piétri, were fiercely opposed and lobbied to kill the plan. Piétri may have feared, together with other Foreign Ministry officials, that any increase in the island's immigrant population was dangerous, regardless of their nationality.[85]

In addition to the Corsica scheme, several smaller refugee committees, including the ORT, Renouveau, Agriculture et Artisanat, and the Hechaluz,* which prepared Jewish youth for immigration to Palestine, also

---

*These committees worked closely with one another and trained several hundred refugees for jobs in agriculture and artisanry. The ORT, which in Russian stood for Obshchestvo Rasprostraneniya Truda sredi Yevreyev (Society for Spreading [Artisan and Agricultural] Work [among Jews]), was an international Jewish organization devoted to the vocational retraining of Jews in skilled trades and agriculture. The Renouveau was founded in Paris in Sept. 1933 and began operations in 1934. It was directed by Dmitri

strove to create agricultural settlements for refugees in depopulated regions of the southwest, where other groups of immigrants, especially Italians, Russians, and Poles had settled in recent years.[86] These schemes had the support of the Ministry of Labor and local officials who appealed to the administration to permit the refugees to settle in the southwest to compensate for the huge rural outmigration that had taken place there in recent years.[87] They also had the support of the HCR, the Gourevitch Committee, the LICA, the Zionists, and most importantly the JDC, which by mid-1934 had poured nearly a half a million francs into these experiments.[88]

By 1935, however, most of these projects had run aground. The original sixteen refugee families who had settled in the ORT colony of Villeneuve in southwestern France had dwindled to a mere eight. The refugee committee Agriculture et Artisanat, which sponsored vocational retraining for refugees, was liquidated at the end of the year, and the Renouveau's training farm, the Château Born, faced foreclosure in 1936.[89]

These settlements failed in part because of mismanagement,[90] but political factors were also to blame. Despite their support from the Ministries of Agriculture and Labor, the Foreign Ministry opposed these schemes, fearing that they would convey a willingness to maintain the refugees perma-

---

Marianoff, Albert Einstein's son-in-law. Several members of the Consistory sat on its board of directors, including Julien Weill, the chief rabbi of Paris, and William Oualid. In Sept. 1935, when Marianoff emigrated to the United States, this committee was turned over to the religious Zionist organization, Mizrachi. The Agriculture et Artisanat was created in 1933 and worked with the Comité National to offer vocational retraining to the refugees living in the caserns. After its liquidation at the end of 1935, it was supplanted by a new committee, the Centre Industriel de Rééducation Professionnelle (CIRP) in Apr. 1936. The Hechaluz, which worked closely with these other committees, trained refugees to work the land in preparation for emigration to Palestine. At the beginning of 1936, it had three kibbutzim, or training farms, in France: Haolim in the Moselle; Hassela in Gers, and Namshir in Haute Garonne. This last kibbutz was liquidated in 1936.

On the ORT's activities in France, see "Emigranten, die sich 'umstellen': Ein Besuch beim 'ORT,'" *PT*, Feb. 15, 1936: 3. On the Renouveau, see J. Biélinky, "Pour la ferme-école du 'Renouveau,'" *UI*, June 8, 1934: 321; "L'Oeuvre du 'Renouveau,'" *UI*, Dec. 7, 1934: 199; "Renouveau: An Association to Foster Jewish Interests in Agriculture" [pamphlet], *JDC* no. 602; Charles Riveau, "Rapport sur la ferme école du Renouveau," *Les Cahiers du Renouveau*, 1er année, no. 4 (Mar. 1935): 121–26; Mauco, *Mémoire*, p. 77. On the Agriculture et Artisanat, see "Ce qu' 'A et A' fait pour la jeunesse juive," *La Terre retrouvée*, no. 8 (Apr. 25, 1934): 9; Agriculture et Artisanat, "Plans of 'A et A' for 1935," *JDC* no. 601; "Berufsumschichtung in Frankreich," *PT*, no. 298 (Oct. 6, 1934): 3; Bauer, *My Brother's Keeper*, pp. 140–41. On the Hechaluz, see Joseph Walden, "Hehalouts en France en 1936," *La Terre retrouvée* 6, no. 13 (Apr. 1, 1937): 8; A. C., "Bei jüdischen Pionieren im Elsass," *TJ*, 15ème année, no. 38 (Sept. 20, 1933): 647; "Auf Landarbeit im Elsass," *PT*, no. 280 (Sept. 1934): 3; "Memo concerning 'A et A' and Hechaluz, May 31, 1934," *JDC* no. 602; *Emigrés français*, p. 133.

nently, a notion that contradicted its desire to transform France into a transit nation only. Already in the fall of 1933, the Quai d'Orsay had vetoed a proposal put forth by one Jewish organization to purchase an abandoned plot in the department of Lot for some 200 refugee families.[91] Around the same time, the Foreign Ministry also rejected the visa applications of several German Jews who desired to enroll in French agricultural training schools, declaring: "It seems we have no interest in favoring the creation of German agricultural colonies on our soil, nor of augmenting the number of candidates for jobs that are already too scarce and are reserved for our own agronomists."[92] Moreover, when Justin Godart, president of the Agriculture et Artisanat, asked whether his organization might help settle Saar refugees on farms in southern France, the Foreign Ministry refused, claiming that these refugees would not be allowed to remain.[93] In light of this attitude, these committees, in order to operate at all, had to promise that their clients would be recruited exclusively among refugees already in France and that they would ultimately emigrate elsewhere.[94]

More serious, perhaps, was the fact that the government, after promising these refugees the right of residence, never followed through on this promise. According to Bernhard Kahn, the sixteen families who had created the ORT colony of Villeneuve had invested 30,000 to 40,000 francs apiece in this endeavor on the basis of government assurances that they would be granted the right to stay. These refugees never received their residence permits, however, and many of them were deported during the anti-immigrant crackdown of late 1934 and 1935.[95] In the spring of 1936, the Hechaluz also reported that it was liquidating one of its settlements because so many of its clients had been deported.[96]

Finally, due to the opposition of the native Jewish establishment, these initiatives had little chance of success, especially since they could not raise the requisite funding. To be sure, the Comité National was not averse to placing individual refugees in agricultural jobs; indeed, the vast majority of work permits allocated to male refugees between 1933 and 1935 were for jobs in the agricultural sector, and the Comité National even subsidized the work of the Agriculture et Artisanat.[97] Nevertheless, the leadership of the Comité National, and especially Helbronner, remained staunchly opposed to large-scale agricultural collectives. When the Corsica scheme failed, the Comité National faced bitter recriminations, not only from the refugees, but also from prominent Jews, such as the Zionist poet André Spire.

After this episode, the Committee understandably became wary of these schemes.[98] In 1934, after Jean Dobler, the French consul in Cologne, charged the Hechaluz with having forged agricultural contracts to smuggle refugees into France, the leaders of the Comité National, which had been implicated in this deception, were furious and announced that the Ministry of Agriculture had decided that "no further agricultural contracts can be delivered in France to the refugees."[99] Moreover, although some Jewish leaders, especially in Alsace and Lorraine, favored the creation of agricultural collectives as a means of reinvigorating traditional Judaism,[100] the majority of them shared Helbronner's concern that large-scale agricultural collectives would prevent assimilation and foster antisemitism among the peasantry. Several Jewish leaders, especially Helbronner and Louis Oungre, also shared the Quai d'Orsay's view that constructive solutions to the refugee problem should be avoided altogether, since such schemes only attracted even more refugees to France.[101]

Despite these manifold difficulties, the government began to reconsider these proposals after Joseph Paganon became minister of the interior in June 1935. Régnier had pursued the idea of colonial settlements as an alternative to the expulsion and imprisonment of thousands of refugees for infractions of the decree laws, and his more liberal successor endorsed agricultural settlements for precisely the same reason. Paganon was determined to find a way out of the vicious cycle of *refoulement*, expulsion, and imprisonment, since he realized that these refugees could not return home. As in the case of the colonial settlement schemes, it was once again the Gourevitch Committee that set the ball rolling. In October 1935, the committee sent a delegation to meet with Paganon to discuss the possibilities for agricultural settlements. According to the head of this delegation, General Brissaud-Desmaillet, who represented the Société de Géographie Commerciale et d'Etudes Coloniales, "the minister of the interior declared that he wanted to find a realistic and humane solution for these serious problems [that is, expulsions]. The establishment of agricultural farms for Jewish refugees in the southwest of France seems desirable to the minister."[102]

In late November, Paganon informed Justin Godart, the president of the Gourevitch Committee, that "if American financial support for such an initiative is not a myth" (an obvious allusion to JDC assistance), the government was prepared to authorize such settlements, particularly in Lot-et-Garonne, but on two conditions only: first, that the refugees restrict themselves exclusively to agriculture and abstain from commerce altogether, and second, that "these agricultural workers must be recruited from among the refugees *actually present on our territory*, [since] the entry into France of new foreign refugees remains formally prohibited, whatever their alleged motive."[103] Yet, this plan too never materialized, in part because the question of residence permits for prospective settlers remained unresolved, and in part because the Popular Front during Blum's premiership focused primarily on colonial schemes.

Still, the idea of creating agricultural centers for refugees was by no means dead. Although the Jewish refugee situation in France had been fairly stable from the summer of 1936 through the summer of 1937, conditions thereafter deteriorated sharply. To some extent, this situation was due to the general crackdown against foreigners initiated by the Chautemps government in the fall of 1937. Not only had approximately 300,000 Spanish republican refugees crossed the border into France during the first year of the Popular Front, saddling the government with a heavy financial burden,[104] but a series of bombings took place in 1937 that were widely attributed to foreign agitators. The bombing at the rue de Presbourg in Paris on September 11, which destroyed the offices of the Confédération Général du Patronat Français (French Employers Federation) and the Union des Industries Metallurgiques de la Région Parisienne (Union of French Metallurgists of the Paris Region) and left two dead, provoked a harsh official response. Although initially blamed on the French left, the police soon shifted responsibility to an Italian émigré, Luigi Tamburini, allegedly an agent of the Italian secret police.[105]

Desiring to quell criticisms that the Popular Front had been too lenient with foreign agitators in the past,[106] Chautemps delivered a speech on September 15 in which he warned foreigners not to meddle in France's domestic affairs. Although France would continue to grant asylum to "honorable refugees" in "accordance with its traditions of generosity and liberalism," it was now time to submit those immigrants who "indulge in maneuvers hostile to our country and our system of government" to more rigorous police surveillance. To achieve this end, the administration would, according to Chautemps, "create a true 'legal statute for foreigners' that would offer serious guarantees" to those worthy of asylum, while weeding out "those unworthy of our hospitality." Indeed, Chautemps noted, he had already instructed his minister of the interior to appoint an interministerial commission to draw up this new immigration statute.[107]

Chautemps's threat of a renewed crackdown against "undesirables" was in no way directed against Jewish refugees. Nevertheless, concurrent events focused attention on them as well. For one thing, the Ministry of the Interior as well as the Foreign Ministry expressed growing concern about the possibility of a new influx of refugees from Germany. Although article 4 of the February 6, 1935, decree law prohibiting refugees from changing their domicile without the prefect's prior permission had been abrogated in October 1936, this regulation was reinstated in March 1937 for the three frontier departments of the Bas-Rhin, the Haut-Rhin, and the Moselle. As one Sûreté National official explained, conditions "there necessitate a rigorous control and . . . a strict limitation on foreign immigrants." In particular, he pointed to the security risk posed by German refugees, and he instructed the prefects of these departments to "be especially severe toward German subjects [who] all too often want to settle close to their country of origin,

in places where their massive settlement is dangerous in every respect." Foreigners who had moved into the region since October 1936 were to be thoroughly investigated, and those deemed "undesirable" were to be "invited"
to move to the interior."[108]

In the fall of 1937, a security police commissioner in Lorraine similarly
complained that too many German Jews were entering the region illegally
after having exchanged their property in Germany for property in France,
a tactic that allowed them to escape with at least a portion of their wealth.
Some of these refugees, he insisted, were almost certainly German spies.[109]
Moreover, French diplomats were convinced that the exodus from Germany was bound to worsen. In December 1937, the French consul in
Nuremberg noted that the increasingly strict application of the Nuremberg
Laws by the Nazis "could only precipitate the recent movement of emigration that has taken place in recent months." Other consuls were also predicting a renewed Jewish exodus in light of stricter German border controls—Jews, even those who had left on short-term visas, were no longer
being allowed to return.[110]

But the German Jewish refugee problem paled besides a more immediate dilemma: the influx of some 15,000 to 18,000 illegal refugees during the
summer and fall of 1937, of whom at least 80 percent were East European
Jews, primarily Poles. Having come to France on tourist visas, ostensibly to
visit the 1937 World's Fair, the vast majority of these immigrants stayed on
once their visas expired, thus joining the ever-growing ranks of clandestine
foreigners.[111] The minister of the interior, Marx Dormoy, who happened to
be both a socialist and a Jew, was infuriated by this incursion. Dormoy
agreed completely with the policy of his predecessor, Roger Salengro, prohibiting the entry of further foreigners to France. As early as July, Dormoy
railed against "the risks of a massive immigration of undesirables," and he
maintained that under no circumstances would these newcomers be eligible
for political asylum: "It's not at all a question of refugees but rather of individuals without work and without resources in search of jobs, whatever
they might be. In order to achieve their ends, they make use of every pretext and resort to every subterfuge. All these immigrants are now beginning
to submerge our commercial and artisanal professions, thus imposing a
heavy burden upon our general economy." The minister of the interior
therefore called on border police to "redouble their vigilance to prevent the
entry of all foreigners whose [legal] status is irregular," and he instructed
police to expel all immigrants who had slipped through the cracks in recent
months. Yet, in a reaffirmation of socialist traditions, Dormoy tempered his
remarks by adding that "these instructions do not affect authentic political
refugees—who in reality are relatively few in number—and . . . they in no
way affect the right to asylum, which we have always recognized."[112]

The police greeted Dormoy's crackdown with relief. From their perspective, the Popular Front had been far too lenient with illegal foreigners, and they had complained incessantly that existing regulations, especially expulsions, had not been enforced strictly enough. Moreover, the prefect of police had been piqued that the minister of tourism had never consulted him regarding security measures to curtail illegal immigration at the time of the World's Fair. Emboldened by Dormoy's newfound zeal, the police now proposed their own program to deal with "undesirables." In a report sent to the minister of the interior on July 23, 1937, the prefect of police outlined three principal strategies: the implementation of more stringent border controls; the immediate expulsion of all illegal refugees, unless they could offer irrefutable proof that they were political refugees; and the channeling of refugees out of Paris to facilitate police surveillance.[113] Dormoy obviously took these suggestions to heart: pro-refugee activists reported a dramatic rise in the number of expulsions and *refoulements* in the fall of 1937,[114] and on December 8 he submitted a report to the Cabinet recommending that every foreigner entering France be required to obtain a visa from a French consulate, which would then have to be verified by the prefect of police within 48 hours after crossing the border.[115]

The task of implementing the third and most radical of the recommendations—the effort to drive the refugees out of Paris—was left to Chautemps's new undersecretary of state for immigration, Philippe Serre, a prominent Radical deputy from the Meurthe-et-Moselle. The principal aim of Serre's office, officially created on January 18, 1938, was to draw up a general statute for foreigners that would clearly distinguish between "useful" and "undesirable" immigrants and set up an administrative machinery to implement these new regulations.[116] Three new councils were to be established: the Superior Council of Foreigners, to coordinate the immigration policies of the various ministries and to make the final determination as to which immigrants were to be given permanent refugee status; the Consultative Commission of Refugees, to be composed of pro-refugee activists who would screen the dossiers of foreigners applying for asylum and recommend to the Superior Council those it considered worthy; and the Commission of Border Surveillance, to coordinate immigration policies at the border.[117]

Although none of these plans made any specific mention of Jews, the 12,000 to 15,000 East European Jews who had entered France illegally during the 1937 World's Fair nevertheless became the principal target of the Serre Commission's activities. To solve the irritating problem of clandestine Jewish immigration, Serre, together with his chief of staff, the renowned ethnologist and immigration expert, Georges Mauco, devised a radical plan. What they suggested was to channel the entire population of illegal

Jewish immigrants away from Paris and other urban centers to the depopulated regions of southwestern France, where they would be resettled on large-scale agricultural collectives.[118]

While this idea had appealed to the prefect of police for security reasons, Serre and Mauco found it attractive for its purported economic benefits. Above all, they hoped that diverting Jewish refugees to the countryside would ease competition between Jewish immigrants and French workers. As Mauco explained to Jewish leaders in the spring of 1938, labor unions, especially in the leather, garment, and metal trades, had been complaining bitterly of "unfair" competition from illegal refugees, who often worked in sweatshops for substandard wages and for hours far surpassing those permitted by union contracts. "The French government," Mauco maintained, "feels compelled to give way to this pressure, but would like to do it in a systematic and humane way."[119] Apparently, Mauco's claims were not exaggerated; petitions from these unions appeared regularly in the socialist press, and in some cases, these unions even demanded that the borders be closed to further immigration altogether. In an interesting sidelight, it must be noted that these tensions were not simply the result of a conflict between East European Jewish immigrant workers on the one hand and native French workers on the other. Rather, it was precisely those unions dominated by more established East European Jewish immigrant workers that pressed these demands most aggressively. As the Union des Syndicats Parisiens argued, illegal immigration had to be curtailed precisely to protect the hard-won gains of unionized immigrant workers.[120]

Such distinctions, however, were of scant importance to Serre and Mauco, for whom the nagging problem of illegal competition from newly arrived immigrant workers had to be resolved once and for all. Since their scheme depended entirely on the willingness of the Jewish community, and especially the JDC, to finance the operation, they approached the Central Consistory in February and requested that it convene a delegation of representatives of the major Jewish organizations involved in refugee work so that details of the plan could be hammered out.[121] The Consistory complied, and in March a delegation of representatives from the Consistory, the CAR, the HICEM, the Comité Central d'Assistance aux Emigrants Juifs (CCAJE), the JDC, the FSJF, and the ORT entered into negotiations with Mauco.

What Mauco offered Jewish leaders was nothing less than a clear-cut ultimatum: either they could comply with the plan and pay for this mass population transfer, or they could finance the wholesale repatriation of the recently arrived Jewish immigrants. If Jewish leaders agreed to the agricultural resettlement plan, Mauco recommended that the JDC put up 20 million francs to launch the project. In return, he promised that all refugees sent to the agricultural centers would be granted agricultural work permits and political refugee status. Once resettled, these refugees would be prohibited from leaving the centers; otherwise, Mauco warned, they would be "ruthlessly expelled." Refugees who refused to leave the cities, together with those deemed unfit for agricultural work, would suffer the same fate. Finally, Mauco emphasized that the extension of political asylum to these refugees by no means signaled a more liberal refugee policy in general.[122] Indeed, he claimed, in the future only well-known political activists would be eligible for refugee status.[123] As another Ministry of Labor spokesman declared:

The project under consideration is of limited scope and is aimed only at recent immigrants already in France. In any case, the project must not provoke any new influx of immigrants, and it behooves us to insist on this point. We desire merely to relieve the labor market without having to resort to massive expulsions, and, at the same time, to relieve the congestion in the cities in favor of the depopulated countryside. That is the double goal of the project actually under study.[124]

Aside from the obvious economic benefits, Serre even maintained that this plan would eliminate antisemitism altogether. By congregating in the "already encumbered professions,"[125] East European Jews were themselves "unconsciously responsible for the one truly serious and dangerous form of antisemitism: that of certain working class circles faced with this competition." Once transformed from a "competitive" into a "complementary work force," Serre insisted that the scourge of antisemitism would inevitably disappear.[126]

Mauco's ultimatum presented Jewish leaders with a grave dilemma, especially since the majority of them had vehemently opposed agricultural collectives for refugees in the past. Ironically, the one group that had embraced the idea—the Gourevitch Committee—was barred from these negotiations. Lambert, backed by the Central Consistory, had vetoed its participation, insisting that it was "*pro-Jewish* and represented nothing."[127] Exactly what Lambert meant is not entirely clear, although there is no doubt that he, together with the Consistory, viewed the Gourevitch Committee as a threat to their status as sole representative to the government on refugee affairs. In using the term "pro-Jewish," Lambert was suggesting that the Gourevitch Committee, unlike the CAR and the Consistory, did not have French as well as Jewish interests in mind, and therefore had no claim to representation. Although Jewish leaders who did participate in these negotiations were not initially enthusiastic about Mauco's proposals, the threat of mass expulsion persuaded at least some of them to reconsider.[128]

As these negotiations progressed, three main positions began to emerge. Not surprisingly, the hard-line view was put forth most vigorously by

Jacques Helbronner, who represented the Consistory. As in the past, Helbronner remained staunchly opposed to any constructive solutions to the refugee problem; he therefore recommended that the settlement scheme be rejected, and he endorsed the idea of expelling all recently arrived East European Jews. William Oualid, representing the CCAJE, and Edouard Oungre, representing the JCA, adopted an intermediate stance. Although willing to accept the settlement of individual refugees on existing farms, they remained firmly opposed to large-scale agricultural collectives, claiming that such colonies would invariably provoke xenophobia and anti-semitism.[129] Oungre therefore refused to lend any financial support to the resettlement scheme, and Oualid sided openly with Helbronner, proclaiming that repatriation was the preferred course of action.[130]

Finally, there were leaders like Jarblum and Lambert for whom any discussion of mass expulsion was out of the question. As Jarblum explained to Serre privately, Jewish organizations would never use money raised for relief purposes to carry out such ignominious ends. Hence, for Jarblum there was no alternative but to comply with the Serre Plan. But Jarblum welcomed the scheme with a certain enthusiasm as well, since it constituted the first time the government had been willing to extend refugee status to East European Jews, even if only to a limited degree.[131] Most significantly, Lambert, who had always been sympathetic to the idea of small-scale farms, was now willing to countenance large-scale collectives as well. Indeed, according to Mauco, Lambert was "very enthusiastic" about the plan, an attitude he attributed to Lambert's relative youth.[132]

Since Kahn too was vehemently opposed to mass repatriation,[133] Jarblum and Lambert ultimately prevailed, signifying the growing influence of the moderates, and especially Lambert, over refugee matters. In late March, Robert de Rothschild drafted a statement proclaiming that French Jewish organizations "register with satisfaction the government's intention to carry out a new repartition of a number of foreign Jews in our country," and he added that they, in conjunction with the JDC, would carry out a technical study of the proposed project and provide up to 3 million francs for the initial experiment.[134] To be sure, this amount fell far short of the 20 million francs initially requested by Mauco. But the JDC, despite its long-standing support for agricultural settlements in France, wanted to proceed with caution. As Kahn stated, "there can be no question of raising fantastic sums for fantastic schemes."[135]

Despite these preparations and the support of the prime minister and minister of the interior,[136] the Serre Plan suffered the same fate as its colonial counterpart; it too collapsed when the government sponsoring it fell from power. By the spring of 1938, the Popular Front had disintegrated, and in early April a new government came to power led by Radical Party leader

Edouard Daladier. Daladier not only dropped Serre's plan, but he also eliminated Serre's office altogether.[137] The new prime minister was almost certainly swayed in this decision by the Foreign Ministry's vehement opposition to the plan. Already in March, the Foreign Ministry had informed Serre that it considered the extension of refugee status to East Europeans a dangerous precedent likely to encourage further immigration. It furthermore opposed the creation of an immigration statute, arguing that the current case-by-case approach was ultimately more restrictive.[138] In light of the dramatic worsening of the Jewish refugee crisis sparked by the Anschluss, it is likely that Daladier wanted to avoid any action that could suggest French willingness to accept new refugees on a permanent basis. As a result, Daladier's government, as we shall see in Chapters 8 and 9, returned to the hard-line tactics of expulsion, *refoulement*, and imprisonment. Still, the colonial and agricultural schemes did not disappear altogether; at the end of 1938 and in 1939 both these ideas were revived, albeit in modified form.

In terms of assessing the Popular Front's effort on behalf of refugees, the fact that both Moutet and Serre failed to carry their plans to fruition reveals little about the government's commitment to finding a humane solution to the Jewish refugee problem. The discontinuation of both these plans had more to do with ministerial instability and the Popular Front's brief tenure in office than with any lack of resolve. These colonial and agricultural schemes do, however, reveal much about of the attitudes of Socialist and Radical Party leaders toward the Jewish refugee issue. While Popular Front spokesmen from both these parties apparently believed that the German Jewish refugee problem could be solved by granting the relatively small group of German refugees the right to asylum and, whenever possible, even the right to work, the continuing influx of East European Jews, whose legal status was often irregular, continued to pose problems. Moutet clearly agreed with those critical of the July 4, 1936, Geneva Accord for having failed to include Jews of East European origin, and he obviously felt that France's humanitarian obligation extended to them as well. Chautemps and Serre, while less motivated by humanitarian concerns, were nevertheless persuaded by the incessant complaints of labor unions that the East European Jewish problem could no longer be ignored. For many Radical and socialist politicians, the traditional strategy of considering East European Jews as economic rather than political refugees was becoming untenable in light of the upsurge of antisemitism throughout Eastern Europe. From their perspective, a broader solution to this aspect of the refugee problem had to be found.

While the schemes put forth by Moutet, and to a lesser extent Serre, illustrate the Popular Front's relatively liberal attitude toward Jewish refugees, especially when compared to the policies of the conservative Bloc National governments of 1934 and 1935, these plans also reflect the constraints within which even the most pro-refugee regime had to operate. Both plans accepted Malthusian premises as a given, and neither Blum's nor Chautemps's coalition displayed any willingness to confront head-on the deeply entrenched forces of French protectionism. Moreover, although not remaining true to the letter of Salengro's 1936 circulars, which had stipulated that France would receive no further refugees after August 5, 1936, both plans nevertheless remained faithful to the spirit of these circulars. Neither Moutet nor Serre was willing to countenance the settlement of additional refugees, whether from Central or Eastern Europe, in major metropolitan centers. Even Popular Front leaders who did not believe the refugees constituted a serious competitive threat to French labor were nevertheless acutely aware that the refugees were perceived as such by much of the French public. Hence, Popular Front politicians seeking to reconcile France's humanitarian obligation to the refugees with its commitment to the French labor force envisioned only one solution: diverting the refugees to the colonies or the provinces, where they would be retrained as agricultural workers.

Many liberal politicians fully agreed with Serre and Mauco that such an economic regeneration of the Jews would even eliminate the scourge of antisemitism. As Pierre Viénot, undersecretary of state in Blum's first cabinet, declared: "It's absolutely indispensable that the Jewish immigration orient itself toward those professions in which its entry will not provoke those same political and economic repercussions of which, in every country, it has always been the first victim."[139] The socialist refugee leader Rudolph Breitscheid similarly proclaimed that he was "fully aware of [French labor's] terrible fear of competition from foreign workers, but I also believe it would be possible to come to an understanding with the CGT if the immigration were steered toward agricultural regions where there is a permanent shortage of French workers."[140] Hence, for growing numbers of pro-refugee spokesmen as well as refugees themselves, a thoroughgoing occupational and geographical redistribution of the refugees offered the only viable alternative to a regime of harsh restrictionism.

The Popular Front, in the final analysis, did a great deal to alleviate the plight of Jewish refugees. For refugees with German citizenship, it implemented a significant program of legislative reforms that regularized their legal status and protected them against arbitrary expulsion and arrest. Furthermore, as the plans of Moutet and Serre illustrate, the Popular Front also intended to grant political asylum to those refugees who were not German citizens or who had arrived in France after the August 5, 1936, deadline, but in these cases, this privilege was to be extended only on condition that these refugees go to the colonies or to the agricultural provinces of the southwest.

In light of this array of initiatives, the claims of Bonnet, Thalmann, and others that the Popular Front was either indifferent to the refugees or that it failed to bring about a significant reform in refugee policy are clearly exaggerated. Nevertheless, it must also be stressed that the Popular Front's attitude toward future newcomers did not differ significantly from that of its predecessors. Like them, the various Popular Front coalitions took vigorous steps to discourage future influxes of refugees, and the government continued to maintain that France in the future would serve as a transit country only. Although the continuation of this hard-line policy toward future newcomers may seem hard-hearted, it was motivated, as we saw in Chapter 6, by a desire to pressure the League of Nations to devise a plan to redistribute future refugees more equitably than in the past, since even pro-refugee activists believed that France had already borne a disproportionate burden. Moreover, as the Serre Plan reveals, by 1938 the government was prepared to resort to coercion to force both the refugees and their native Jewish sponsors to comply with plans for the geographical and occupational restructuring of the Jewish immigrant population. This trend augured ill for the future. Under Daladier, this element of coercion would quickly overshadow whatever humanitarian impulses had initially inspired Popular Front refugee initiatives.

The Deluge
From the Anschluss to Evian

Every successive wave of émigrés has washed up here . . .
Paris is everyone's last hope and last chance.
Erich Maria Remarque [1]

The year 1938 marked a sharp deterioration in the Jewish refugee situation. When Edouard Daladier became premier on April 10, whatever alternative strategies the Popular Front had devised to reconcile working- and middle-class demands for economic protection against immigrants with a more humane refugee policy fell by the wayside. In response to Foreign Ministry objections that the Serre Plan would only encourage further immigration, Daladier not only dismissed these agricultural settlement schemes but dismantled the office of undersecretary of state for immigration altogether. Moreover, as we have seen, Daladier's new minister of colonies, Georges Mandel, staunchly refused to consider Moutet's colonial plans, especially with respect to Madagascar.

Precisely at this moment, however, the refugee crisis was reaching crisis proportions. In Germany itself, Hitler was embarking on an anti-Jewish crackdown that would ultimately culminate in Kristallnacht. At the same time, Hitler's incursions into Austria and Czechoslovakia provoked unprecedented floods of refugees. Finally, Italy, together with most East European nations, inaugurated antisemitic programs of their own, prompting thousands more Jews to seek asylum in the West.

In France, the prospect of yet another huge influx of refugees stimulated renewed and more strident demands for economic protection against immigrant competition. But it also generated growing security concerns. Although fifth-column fears and charges of Jewish warmongering became widespread only at the time of the Munich crisis in September, more general security considerations, linked especially to fears of foreign inspired terrorism and internal subversion, increasingly influenced Central European refugee policy. Indeed, it was a combination of economic and security considerations generated by the Austrian refugee crisis, the worsening situation of German Jewry, and the growing demand of East European Jews for asylum that stimulated the Daladier administration to formulate new policies over the spring and summer aimed at blocking the entry of new refugees and forcing out thousands of illegal aliens already there. Although government officials publicly expressed sympathy for the plight of the refugees and insisted that France was continuing to grant refugee asylum, the policies implemented ran directly counter to these assertions. By the time of the Evian Conference in July, France had abandoned even the pretense of remaining a nation of asylum.

The refugee policies of the Daladier administration must be seen against the backdrop of the worsening international situation. The events of the spring of 1938 shattered forever the assumption underlying Popular Front refugee initiatives—the notion that the Central European refugee population could be stabilized. The creation of Léon Blum's second cabinet on March 13 coincided with the Anschluss, Hitler's annexation of Austria. Thus, when Daladier became premier in April, a major refugee crisis was already brewing. Whereas the Nazis had introduced antisemitic policies in Germany over several years, in Austria these measures were enacted almost overnight. As a French police report from mid-April noted, "What has occurred over the course of these last weeks in Austria with regard to the Jews far surpasses the antisemitic measures taken in the Reich. . . . The misery that has overtaken Vienna's Jewish population is indescribable."[2] Moreover, Hitler decided to use Austria as the testing ground for his most recent anti-Jewish policy—forced emigration. Under the supervision of Adolf Eichmann, the Nazis began in early June to expropriate the property of Austria's Jewish population, which numbered slightly under 200,000.[3] It also sought to force the Austrian Jewish community to pay for its own emigration. While some Austrian Jews resorted to suicide, the vast majority, together with a smaller number of non-Jewish anti-Nazi dissidents, fled to the West.[4]

Hitler also intensified the anti-Jewish crackdown in Germany itself. In early 1938, the Nazis announced their intention to aryanize the approximately 40,000 businesses still remaining in Jewish hands. By the year's end, they declared, "not a single Jewish firm in Germany would continue to exist and not a single Jew would be receiving a salary."[5] The anti-Jewish boycott was renewed, and on April 26 Reich Minister Hermann Göring called for an inventory of all Jewish property, initiating the first stage in the complete expropriation of Jewish wealth.[6] In the spring and summer, the government further limited Jewish economic activities and imposed even harsher restrictions on the amount of money Jewish emigrants could withdraw from the country. Moreover, beginning in late 1937, Jews who departed Germany, even on short-term visas, had to pledge never to return under pain of being sent to a concentration camp.[7] In the spring, the Nazis carried out their first major anti-Jewish raid, which ended with the arrest of some 4,000 Jews. Yet as France's ambassador to Germany, André François-Poncet, warned, these measures did not mark the end of the Nazi "policy of extermination." The Nazis, he claimed, were bent on "ruining the Jews . . . and ridding Germany of them definitively. . . . Before long existence will become absolutely impossible for the Jews of Germany, and they will have no choice but to emigrate from the Reich."[8]

Elsewhere in Central and Eastern Europe conditions for Jews were deteriorating as well. Having failed to persuade the League of Nations or the other Western nations to assist in the forced evacuation of Polish Jewry, the Polish government began to resort to strong-arm tactics. On March 31, 1938, the government of Marshal Edouard Rydz-Smigly announced a law depriving Polish nationals who had lived outside the country more than five years of their citizenship. This law, which went into effect only in late October, did not specifically mention Jews. There is, however, no doubt that Jews were the intended target since the Polish government was determined to prevent the return of the thousands of Polish Jews currently being expelled from Austria and Germany. At the same time, this law threatened to strip Polish Jews elsewhere in the West of their citizenship as well, thus creating another mass of stateless refugees.[9]

The governments of Romania and Hungary followed suit. In January, the extreme-right-wing government of Octavian Goga in Romania enacted legislation barring Jewish participation in a wide range of professions and stripping Jews naturalized after 1918 of their citizenship, a measure that affected approximately one-third of the nation's 700,000 Jews. For these now stateless Jews, Romanian authorities proclaimed their nation's desire to serve "only as a temporary asylum until means of forcing them to leave . . . have been found."[10] These laws ultimately proved to be short-lived; in February the Romanian courts declared them unconstitutional, and Goga's government fell. Nevertheless, with the threat of discrimination hanging over them, many Romanian Jews decided to flee. In Hungary, the pro-German government of Prime Minister Kálmán Darányi issued measures sharply curtailing Jewish economic activity, and it too began to denaturalize large numbers of Jews. In January, 1938, the government declared that Jews from the northeastern provinces who could not prove Magyar ancestry back to 1851 would be deprived of their citizenship, and several months later it followed the Polish example and stripped Hungarian Jews living abroad of their citizenship.[11]

These developments threatened to send an unprecedented flood of Jewish refugees to France, and the Daladier administration realized that if France was to avoid a deluge, far tougher immigration policies would have to be implemented. So preoccupied was Daladier with illegal immigrants that he even used the occasion of his inaugural address to announce his intention to initiate harsh measures to force them to leave.[12] At the same time, new restrictions were to be enacted to prevent additional refugees from crossing the border. While these policies did not officially abrogate the right to asylum, their intent was clearly to whittle away that right as much as possible.

The administration's first major effort to head off a new refugee crisis was the decree law of May 2, 1938, which in some respects grew directly out of Serre's efforts to devise a statute to distinguish "desirable" from "undesirable" immigrants. Despite the fact that the number of legal immigrants in France had actually declined since the early 1930's,[13] the new minister of the interior, the Radical politician Albert Sarraut, declared in the preamble to this decree that the security and economic well-being of the nation were threatened by "the ever-growing number of foreigners residing in France," an obvious allusion to the recent influx of refugees. France, according to Sarraut, had no intention of closing its doors, and he affirmed that the decree law "does not in the least endanger the traditional rules of French hospitality." Nevertheless, the new minister of the interior noted, France had received too many undesirables in recent years, and these people would have to leave. To achieve this end, a rigorous selection process would be implemented to distinguish the "foreigner[s] of good faith, who maintained an absolutely correct attitude vis-à-vis the Republic and its institutions," from the "'clandestine' foreigners, irregular guests . . . unworthy of living on our soil." While the former would be granted asylum, the "undesirables" would be ruthlessly expelled.[14]

To get rid of illegal foreigners, or "clandestines" as they were called, a host of new regulations was declared. Foreigners who lacked visas or identity cards, or those carrying false papers, were subject to stringent fines of 100 to 1,000 francs and automatic prison sentences of one month to one year. Individuals who helped illegal aliens enter the country or remain there were subject to the same sanctions. Failure to comply with an expulsion order now elicited a far harsher sentence than it had in the past. Previously, this crime had been punishable by up to six months in jail, but the minimum sentence was now fixed at six months and the maximum at three years. Moreover, although foreigners in the past had generally been able to obtain temporary extensions of their residence permits when these permits expired, this was no longer the case; now these immigrants became vulnerable to immediate *refoulement*. Finally, the decree law gave the police extensive new powers to deal with foreigners. Whereas expulsion had previously been the prerogative of the minister of the interior, that power was now extended to the police and the prefects, who received substantial financial credits to cover the costs of their new responsibilities.[15]

These harsh measures were tempered, however, by two articles that seemed to guarantee a modicum of asylum. Article 10 gave newly arriving foreigners the right to file a declaration of refugee status with the police within 48 hours after crossing the border, thus allowing them, at least in theory, to be considered for refugee status. This article also permitted foreigners who faced expulsion to request an administrative hearing if they had entered France legally, had ever possessed a valid identity card, and had never incurred a criminal conviction. Moreover, in a major policy shift, article 11 stipulated that foreigners who had been expelled but were unable to depart were not to be sent to prison. Instead, following a suggestion first put forth in 1935 by Minister of the Interior Marcel Régnier, these foreigners were to be sent to an assigned residence under police surveillance. This option had become imperative, Sarraut explained, because the government had "tried in vain to solve the [refugee] problem internationally."[16] Moreover, as his predecessors had learned, keeping these refugees in jail indefinitely was neither politically nor economically feasible.

Whether the decree law was informed by traditional economic concerns linked to the Depression or by political factors, especially fifth-column fears, has recently been the subject of some debate.[17] Although Sarraut did in fact cite a combination of economic and security concerns in the preamble to this decree, security considerations were clearly paramount in his mind, although they were linked far more to the threat of internal subversion than to fifth-column fears per se. In this sense, the May 2, 1938, decree law stemmed directly from Chautemps's antiforeign crackdown in the fall of 1937. In a circular of April 14, 1938, Sarraut explained to the prefects and police that tougher immigration measures had become necessary because "the influx of foreigners, who . . . have come to seek refuge on our soil" has greatly aggravated "problems regarding French security and public order." As a result, "methodical, energetic, and swift action [is necessary] to rid our country of the too numerous undesirable elements who circulate and agitate here in complete contempt of [our] laws and regulations, and who intervene inadmissably in squabbles or political and social conflicts that concern only ourselves."[18]

In another circular of May 4, Sarraut instructed the mobile police to crack down on the criminal element among the foreign population. These people, he maintained, had recently carried out a wave of "assassinations, murders, armed assaults, aggravated robberies, [and] swindles."[19] Similarly, in an interview with the newspaper *Marianne* in mid-May, Sarraut declared that France could no longer "offer shelter on our soil to foreigners who mock our laws, or who profit from our hospitality to foment extremist agitation in our country." French security, Sarraut promised, "would destroy 'clandestine' foreigners once and for all," and "unmask the spies and political agitators swarming throughout our land."[20]

While Sarraut's preoccupation with security matters is clear, it nevertheless would be wrong to dismiss traditional economic concerns altogether. Unlike most other Western nations, France remained mired in the Depression. When Daladier took office, official unemployment was still 393,000 and industrial production remained below the 1929 level.[21] Moreover, Radical Party leaders had always expressed sympathy for middle-class protectionist demands, and now that they had returned to power, they revived the strategy of seeking to remedy the Depression on the backs of the country's immigrants. Soliciting the cooperation of customs agents in the enforcement of the decree law, Sarraut explained that this anti-immigrant crackdown was necessary, "to assure control over a foreign population that is becoming excessive and among whom certain elements weigh upon our general economy." He then proceeded to denounce "immigrants of all nationalities who, by escaping all verification, successfully infiltrate and eventually constitute an unassimilable mass of often defective individuals, who possess uncertain resources [and] equivocal morality."[22]

Similarly, in mid-May the minister of the interior ordered police to stiffen procedures by which foreigners could renew their identity cards. Too many of them, he maintained, had received multiple extensions, allowing them to remain in France permanently "to the detriment of our artisans and small-scale commerce."[23] At the same time, the Foreign Ministry directed French consuls abroad to "refuse visas altogether to artisans and small-scale merchants whom they suspect of wanting to settle in France."[24] Although these circulars made no specific mention of Jews, there is little doubt, given the professional categories mentioned, that they were the principal target.

The administration's persistent preoccupation with economic considerations is further revealed by another decree law announced by the minister of commerce, Fernand Gentin, on June 17, 1938, which for the first time imposed limits on the right of foreigners to engage in commerce. This law, the fruit of years of intensive lobbying by the Chambers of Commerce and the General Confederation of the Middle Classes,[25] stipulated that foreigners could not be inscribed in the commercial registry or establish commercial or industrial enterprises without first obtaining a special merchant's card from the police. These cards were to be issued only after the police had consulted the local chambers of commerce regarding the "desirability" of the proposed foreign-owned enterprise, thus granting to merchants powers analogous to those already accorded artisans and doctors. This law also permitted the extremely xenophobic and antisemitic Chambers of Commerce to set quotas on the numbers of foreigners permitted to work in certain commercial professions, similar to the quotas already in place for industrial wage laborers and artisans.

In November, another decree law stipulated fines of 100 to 2,000 francs and prison sentences of one to six months for infractions of the June 17 decree.[26] Such harsh measures were necessary, Sarraut insisted, "to protect French commerce, which is ever more invaded by foreign elements."[27] Moreover, in an effort to curtail the large number of illegal foreigners involved in peddling and artisan trades, especially in the garment, leather, hatmaking, and fur industries—that is, those sectors dominated by East European Jews—the Ministry of the Interior imposed a residency requirement of five years on foreigners applying for merchants' or artisans' cards beginning in the fall of 1938, and these cards were henceforth limited to their department of residence.[28]

Aside from the issue of motive, the key question about the May 2, 1938, decree law is whether Sarraut was sincere in his proclaimed intention to uphold France's commitment to refugee asylum. On this issue, the record is ambiguous. On the one hand, some evidence suggests that Sarraut, at least at this stage, meant what he said. Why else would he have reaffirmed this commitment on numerous occasions, not only in public, but in internal memos as well? In a circular of April 14, Sarraut reiterated a pledge that would reappear in the preface to the decree law, informing the prefects and police that "no matter how grave the results may be, our country has no intention of renouncing the spirit of liberalism and humanity that constitutes one of the most noble aspects of its genius." He then stipulated that "it is not the government's intention to submit the entire . . . foreign population to an annoying surveillance or to limit the liberties it enjoys in our land."[29]

In another circular, dated May 18, the minister again warned the prefects and police not to expel foreigners en masse. Rather, this circular insisted, many foreigners in an irregular situation deserved to have their status normalized since they were often "political refugees whose conduct is beyond reproach" or well-intentioned workers who in better economic times would have been granted a work permit. It was therefore imperative to distinguish common criminals and "infamous agitators" from "those whose sole sin is that they failed to comply with administrative formalities." To ensure that the decree law be carried out in a "spirit of justice and humanity," Sarraut instructed the prefects to conduct fair and scrupulous investigations into every case.[30]

The inclusion of articles 10 and 11 also suggests the government's commitment to providing some degree of political asylum. Indeed, when the decree law first appeared, several pro-refugee advocates expressed relief that it was not as draconian as they had initially feared, and some even welcomed it as an improvement over the previous regime. According to Emile Kahn, secretary-general of the League for the Rights of Man, the fact that foreigners from now on had merely to declare themselves refugees at the border implied that the long-standing distinction between German and Nansen refugees, on the one hand, and other foreigners, including East Europeans, on the other, no longer applied. Moreover, Kahn praised article 11 for finally recognizing that expulsion was an inappropriate punishment for illegal refugees. These foreigners, he declared, would "no longer be obligated to choose between perpetual prison and death."[31] The Radical Socialist deputy Henri Guernut, another pro-refugee advocate and former secretary-general of the League for the Rights of Man, likewise applauded article 10 for providing refugees who had received expulsion orders with the right to request an administrative hearing. This liberal measure, Guernut insisted, reflected Sarraut's Dreyfusard past.[32]

Whatever Sarraut's intentions, the Sûreté's harsh and often arbitrary implementation of the decree law suggests that the crackdown against the "undesirables" was to take precedence over any guarantees of the right of asylum. Already in late April, the *Petit Parisien* reported that the police were conducting antiforeign raids in the Paris region and that hundreds of foreigners had been arrested and expelled.[33] In early May, just days after the decree law was announced, Emile Kahn decried these indiscriminate roundups. "Pass by the Prefecture of Police," he declared, "The unfortunates, who have been summoned imperiously, wait trembling that someone might call them. They are shoved, in batches, before anonymous civil servants, who, with a single word, will decide their fate. No discussion is allowed, nor are any explanations to be given: 'So and so? Refoulement. . . . So and So? Expulsion, You have 48 hours in which to leave.'"[34] The Jewish community too was appalled at the zeal of the police. When the prefect of the Bas-Rhin requested the Strasbourg Jewish Consistory's aid in apprehending illegal foreigners, suggesting that it submit daily lists of newly arrived refugees seeking assistance, the chief rabbi of Strasbourg flatly refused, claiming that Christian associations had not been asked to do the same.[35]

Moreover, even the few putatively liberal provisions of the decree law, especially articles 10 and 11, were either implemented improperly or not at all. Notwithstanding the guarantees afforded by article 10, most refugees were unwilling to declare themselves to police at the border, either because they feared being sent back to Germany[36] or because they feared, not without reason, that their petitions for refugee status would be denied. Having failed to comply with the 48-hour stipulation, these refugees lost the right to an administrative hearing if they later received an expulsion order. They also lost the right to be sent to a detention center as mandated by article 11.

Yet that too made little difference, since article 11 remained a dead letter, at least until the end of 1938. Initially, Sarraut had been eager to implement this provision, and he had even drawn up a list of possible locations for these detention centers. But the Ministry of the Interior soon became aware of the disadvantages inherent in this measure. On August 25, 1938, the head of the Sûreté, Jean Berthoin, who was also Sarraut's personal chief of staff, issued a circular instructing the prefects and police to use article 11 only with great circumspection. An overly liberal application of this measure, Berthoin insisted, would create a security problem by congregating all the "notorious undesirables" in a few locations. Moreover, Berthoin argued, article 11 would ultimately attract even greater numbers of immigrants to France. Immigrants disguised as refugees would flock to France, and once there, they would declare themselves stateless and demand the right to stay. To prevent France from becoming a magnet for "undesirables," only foreigners able to offer irrefutable proof of being political, and not economic or religious, refugees would be allowed to remain. All others, which obviously included the vast majority of Jews, were now to be expelled. Moreover, refugees covered by article 11 were henceforth required to prove that they had endeavored to leave the country by having applied to at least three different foreign consulates for a visa.[37] In November, Sarraut instructed the prefects to threaten these consulates with diplomatic sanctions if they persisted in withholding these visas, and he even offered to pay the refugees' transportation costs in full.[38] Given Sarraut's misgivings about article 11, it is not surprising that it took months before the promised detention centers were established, to the chagrin of pro-refugee advocates, who perceived these centers as the only means by which refugees could avoid the dreaded fate of expulsion or imprisonment.[39]

At the same time, the harsh visa policy implemented after the Anschluss as well as the beefed up police presence at the border leave no doubt that the administration was determined to keep out further newcomers. Although this strategy in some respects marks the continuation of the policy put in place by Salengro in 1936, the closure of the borders in 1938 had more serious repercussions. Indeed, during the last weeks of Blum's ministry in March, it appeared that France would pursue a relatively generous policy toward Austrian refugees, a factor that supports the liberal interpretation of the Popular Front's refugee policy. Although refugees from Austria holding East European passports continued to be turned away,[40] those with Austrian passports were allowed in even if they had only transit visas. Furthermore, although many refugees entered through Alsace, where they were forbidden to remain unless they had relatives there or were deemed economically useful, these refugees were nevertheless allowed to proceed unhindered to the French interior with the help of local Jewish refugee committees.[41]

Yet before Blum left office, security officials had expressed consternation over this state of affairs, and when Daladier became premier, their views prevailed. Already in March, the prefect of police, dismayed by security reports of an impending invasion of Austrian refugees, recommended to the Sûreté Nationale that the Austrians be placed under tighter surveillance and that they be required to register with the police within 48 hours after their arrival, instead of having two months to register, as their transit visas provided.[42] Furthermore, the prefect of police renewed his efforts to ban refugee settlement in the department of the Seine, and right-wing deputies submitted a bill to this effect in the spring of 1938.[43] Hence, although the initial influx of Austrians was considerably smaller than the government or the Jewish community had expected, with police reporting the presence of only about 600 Austrian Jews by mid-April,[44] the government nevertheless launched a fierce crackdown against these newcomers. On April 15, the Sûreté instructed the police to verify existing information about the restaurants and cafés where Austrian refugees gathered.[45] A few days later, the press began to report massive roundups of foreigners in and around Paris. These arrests were followed on April 30 by a new Ministry of the Interior directive calling for tighter police surveillance over Austrian refugees in particular. These measures were necessary, the ministry explained, to "avoid a massive and uncontrolled invasion [of our country] by émigrés of all sorts."[46]

This circular, which incorporated most of the suggestions put forth by the police and reveals that even article 10 of the decree law had originally been conceived as a surveillance measure, mandated that all Austrians arriving after March 14 report to police headquarters within 48 hours, whether or not they possessed visas. There, they would fill out questionnaires providing information about their family members, financial resources, and family relations in France. This information was to be compiled into a census, and to keep track of new arrivals in the future, a special stamp was to be placed in their passports designating them as "ex-Austrians." At the same time, the ban on refugee settlement was extended to the departments of the Seine and the Seine-et-Oise, in addition to the frontier departments of the northeast. Austrian refugees who had arrived without papers were to be placed under heightened surveillance, and in the future they would have to offer proof of having been persecuted by the Nazis. Under no circumstances were non-Austrian nationals to be allowed to enter, thus continuing the long-standing exclusion of East Europeans. Finally, Austrian refugees were forbidden to work without the prior approval of the Ministry of Labor. Refugees who failed to comply with these regulations were to be expelled immediately.

Even these measures, restrictive as they were, still permitted a modicum of asylum. But as the refugee crisis worsened over the summer—with the Foreign Ministry predicting the arrival of 30,000 German Jews and 400,000 to 500,000 Austrians[47]—Sarraut moved to close the borders altogether. As the prefect of the Gironde explained, the administration was determined to avoid "having to accept any refugees other than those already in France."[48] This new hard-line policy was in part designed to send a signal to the Nazis that the increasingly common practice of "dumping" German Jews across the border into France would no longer be tolerated.[49] In early June, the new foreign minister, Georges Bonnet, protested this policy directly to Wilhelmstrasse, and Sarraut sent police reinforcements to the border to prevent refugees without papers from entering.[50] In July, Sarraut instructed the prefects of the border departments, in clear contravention of article 10 of the decree law, to bar access to France of all foreigners coming from Germany without papers; these "supposed political refugees or deserters," as the minister now referred to them, were to be *refoulés* immediately, even if that meant sending them back to Germany.[51]

To further beef up border surveillance, Sarraut issued yet another decree law on August 12 creating a special border police to root out illegal immigrants.[52] This police presence obviously had an impact since both the press and Jewish organizations reported at the end of the summer that Jewish refugees were being turned away at the border in droves, although individuals able to prove their status as political refugees were apparently allowed in.[53] As the Strasbourg Jewish refugee committee grimly noted, Jewish refugees now faced a painful dilemma: "In Germany, the concentration camp awaits them; in France, they face the threat of prison for illegal entry."[54]

While Sarraut applied himself to the antiforeign crackdown at home, the Foreign Ministry initiated harsh restrictions on the distribution of visas, making legal immigration all but impossible. As long as Blum remained in power, Austrian Jews had been able to acquire entry visas, although as we have seen, such visas were unnecessary since simple transit visas sufficed.[55] Once Daladier took power, this situation changed, however. According to one police report, on April 12, 1938, just two days after Daladier assumed office, French consulates in Austria were instructed "to no longer deliver visas to Austrian subjects." Only Austrians who already held U.S. visas were to be allowed in, a concession to American diplomatic pressure.[56] French consulates elsewhere in Central Europe received similar instructions to "stop the influx of refugees of Austrian provenance into France."[57] At the same time, Jewish organizations began to complain that German Jews were being denied entry visas routinely, except for those able to export significant sums of wealth.[58]

Meanwhile, the government was more determined than ever to prevent East Europeans from acquiring visas, despite the dramatic rise of state-sponsored antisemitism in Eastern Europe. In an effort to stave off a deluge of stateless refugees, the Foreign Ministry instructed Léon Nöel on May 19 to protest the Polish law of March 31 and to "indicate to the Polish government that . . . the French authorities would not hesitate to take all expedient measures to avoid the presence of individuals in France who could become stateless as a result of its actions."[59] Sarraut had in fact already taken action on this front. Despite official Polish assurances that Polish Jews in France were not the intended targets of this decree, the Ministry of the Interior nevertheless issued a circular on May 3 instructing the prefects and police to expel all illegal Poles in the country, the vast majority of whom were Jews.[60] As Nöel counseled, "More than ever, our consulates and police services must exercise extreme vigilance if we intend to stop the progressive invasion of our country by undesirable elements."[61] At the same time, the Foreign Ministry was contemplating similar measures to prevent an influx of Hungarian and Romanian Jews. As one Foreign Ministry spokesman explained, these Jews "were undesirable individuals, whose presence and activity can only be prejudicial to the country from every point of view. Not only are the vast majority of them bearers of physiological and moral defects that pose a health risk to our compatriots, but they will become public charges from the moment they cross the border."[62]

These hard-line attitudes began to coalesce in the weeks immediately preceding the Evian Conference, which was scheduled to be held in early July. In late March, President Franklin D. Roosevelt had called on the international community to convene a conference to deal specifically with the Central European refugee problem, since neither Austrian nor East European Jews were covered under the existing High Commission for Refugees (HCR) mandate.[63] At the very least, Roosevelt hoped a new international initiative would bring the Austrians under the juridical umbrella of the HCR, making them eligible for benefits accorded to the German refugees by the Geneva Accords of July 4, 1936, and February 10, 1938.[64] Roosevelt had initially intended this conference to be held in Switzerland, but the Swiss declined, supposedly because they feared drawing attention to their own increasingly restrictive refugee policies.[65] The Americans then turned to France, which agreed, almost certainly because Blum was still premier and because his foreign minister, Joseph Paul-Boncour, had always been sympathetic to the refugees.[66] As the location, the French government selected the southeastern resort town of Evian-les-Bains.

The administration began to hammer out a strategy for this conference only after Daladier came to power. Aware that the American intention was to pressure West European nations, including France, into absorbing at least a portion of the Austrian refugees, the Foreign Ministry convened two interministerial meetings in June to formulate the French response.[67] Of the ministries represented, only the spokesman for the Ministry of Labor expressed any willingness to accept the Austrians. But even he acknowledged that under existing economic circumstances, these refugees could not be permitted to work.[68] The Foreign Ministry adamantly ruled out "the possibility of admitting an important contingent of immigrants into the metropolitan territory in a permanent capacity." It nevertheless remained open to the suggestion, which it was certain the Americans would advance, that at least some of the refugees be settled in French colonies.[69]

But on this score, the minister of colonies stood firm; in correspondence with the Foreign Ministry on June 21, Mandel reiterated the objections he had already put forth in his letter of May 28, proclaiming that "Jewish colonization in our overseas domains would, from every respect, pose more numerous dangers than advantages."[70] By the same token, the spokesman for the Bureau of Algerian Affairs, a branch of the Ministry of the Interior, continued to oppose sending refugees to Algeria: "Given the acuity of the anti-Jewish problem in Algeria," he explained, "the arrival of new Jewish elements could not fail to rebound dangerously on the [antisemitic] campaigns currently taking place." Furthermore, he added, it would be unwise to send these primarily urban refugees, most of whom "came from the city of Vienna, the center of the socialist and communist movements," to an agricultural country such as Algeria. "These new elements . . . could not fail to stimulate the growth of the proletariat in cities where there is at present no industry and only minimal commerce, and they would only increase the number of unemployed who . . . remain public charges."[71]

Not surprisingly, however, it was the chief of the Sûreté, Berthoin, who argued most adamantly that France could absorb no further Austrian immigration "no matter how minimal it might be."[72] According to Berthoin, although the economy had been able to assimilate immigrants who had arrived just after the First World War, "It's not at all the same for those who have recently arrived on our soil. In effect, as a result of the economic depression from which we are suffering, our country is less and less able to accommodate itself to the influx of merchants or artisans who come almost exclusively from Central or Eastern Europe."[73] Any relaxation of immigration restrictions in favor of the Austrians, whose "professional apti-

tudes are analogous to those of [the refugees] who came from Germany"
would, he insisted, endanger "the economy and the social equilibrium of
our country."

From Berthoin's perspective, the only conceivable role France could play
with respect to an international solution to the refugee problem was to
serve as a nation of transit. To be sure, this was not a new concept, but
Berthoin was defining it more narrowly than ever before. From his perspective, France could accept only refugees who had already obtained entry
visas for other countries, since any others were unlikely to leave. Moreover,
France would grant residence permits only to individuals deemed useful to
the national economy or the "intellectual patrimony of our country." The
so-called "waste products of the entire Austrian or German immigration"
would no longer receive consideration.[74] Berthoin thus summed up the
position of the minister of the interior by proclaiming:

> In order that French policy in this regard be coherent, it is important, after rein-
> forcing the controls over all the entry routes into our country . . . to *refouler* with-
> out mercy and prohibit the entry of all refugees from Austria who either have not
> received prior authorization to settle in France or who do not possess documents
> and means of existence that would permit them to enter another country.
>
> In other words, under no circumstances could France consent to open her bor-
> ders unconditionally and without limitation to individuals solely on the basis of
> their claim to be refugees. In effect, our present state of saturation with respect
> to the issue of foreign immigration can no longer permit us to adopt so liberal a
> policy.

If these conditions were met, Berthoin added, the minister of the interior
would be prepared to drop his objections to extending the benefits of the
July 4, 1936, and February 10, 1938, Geneva Accords to Austrians already
residing in France legally, since this group represented only a fraction of the
entire Austrian refugee population.[75]

Berthoin's proposals, which amounted to a virtual death sentence to the
right to asylum in France, became the core of the Foreign Ministry's platform going into Evian. At the conclusion of these preliminary meetings,
the Foreign Ministry requested every ministry to compile statistics demonstrating France's past contributions with respect to the refugee problem in
order to prove that France could do no more.[76] Armed with these statistics,
Henry Bérenger, who had been reappointed by Daladier to serve as chief
spokesman on refugee matters at the League of Nations and was now serving as honorary chairman of the Evian Conference, lost no time in setting
forth his government's position. In his speech at the conference's opening session on July 6, Bérenger proclaimed that France had absorbed over
200,000 refugees since the end of the First World War. On the basis of this

figure, which included not only Central European refugees, but Nansen, Italian, and Spanish refugees as well, he proceeded to state that France had done more than any other nation in the world to solve the refugee problem. Although France would "remain true to the long-standing tradition of . . . hospitality . . . to the extent permitted by her geographical position, population and resources," it "had [now] reached, if not surpassed, the extreme point of saturation." Although individual requests for asylum would continue to receive consideration, Bérenger made it clear that further large-scale influxes of refugees would not be permitted in the future.[77]

Given this attitude, it is not surprising that the Quai d'Orsay was not altogether disappointed by the paltry results of the conference. Of the 32 nations represented, only one—the tiny Dominican Republic—had agreed to take any Jewish refugees at all.[78] Moreover, although the conference had voted in favor of bringing Austrian refugees under the juridical umbrella of the Geneva Accords of July 4, 1936, and February 10, 1938, thus granting them the same legal status as Germans, this measure was never ratified and therefore had no binding power.[79] The sole concrete achievement of the conference was the creation of the Intergovernmental Committee on Refugees (IGCR), a permanent international committee that was to operate independently of the HCR so that it could negotiate directly with the Germans, a prerogative not available to the HCR. The aim of these negotiations was not to stop the persecution of the Jews, as the League of Nations had endeavored to do just after Hitler's seizure of power. Rather, it was to persuade the Germans to grant departing Jews the right to withdraw at least a portion of their wealth, a concession deemed essential for their eventual resettlement.[80]

To be sure, the Foreign Ministry, which had always called for international solutions to the refugee problem, would have preferred Canada, Australia, and Latin American countries to have opened their doors. At the same time, the ministry was pleased that pressure had not been brought to bear on France to have absorbed any more refugees. As one Foreign Ministry official noted: "Evian . . . does not impose any imperative obligations on the participating states. More specifically, there is no particular reference to the contingents of refugees each country would have to admit. In this respect, the French delegation has succeeded completely in maintaining its point of view and in having successfully avoided . . . precise commitments."[81] The French delegation had also succeeded in averting any discussion of colonial settlements. And in concert with the British, it had fended off pressure from East European heads of state, Jewish organizations, and the United States to include the question of East European Jews on the conference's agenda.[82]

Although the Foreign Ministry failed to defeat Roosevelt's proposal to create the IGCR, an effort it had undertaken out of fear that this new committee might try to impose new financial and even moral obligations on its member states, it nevertheless stifled an American plan to headquarter the new committee in Paris.[83] If such a committee were established there, a Foreign Ministry memo noted, the French capital "would witness the expansion of every ethnic, religious, or political organization that concerns itself with every minority and political opposition group. Our efforts to put an end to the activities of irresponsible foreign bodies on our territory would thus be annihilated." Finally, the memo noted, sounding a theme that would assume greater importance in the coming months, the creation of such a committee in Paris was likely to embroil France in foreign policy complications: "Is it in France's interest to appear as the refuge of all the misfits and . . . everyone Germany considers its natural enemy? An element of cultural and racial antagonism will be permanently introduced into Franco-German relations."[84] In view of these objections, the executive committee of the Evian Conference ultimately agreed to headquarter the IGCR in London rather than in Paris.

By the end of the summer, the administration's hard-line policy was in place, and Sarraut and Bonnet had every reason to believe that the Jewish refugee problem was under control, at least insofar as France was concerned. At the opening meeting of the IGCR in London on August 3, 1938, Bérenger reiterated that France had "reached the saturation point that will not permit her to accept new refugees without causing a rupture to the equilibrium of her social body. . . . The absorptive capabilities of every people has a limit. This limit has long been exceeded in France. She said so at Evian: she repeats it in London."[85]

The question, however, was whether the harsh visa policies and the tough police measures embodied in the decree laws would suffice to stop future influxes of refugees. As the administration soon realized to its dismay, the deluge of refugees was only just beginning. Moreover, as fears began to grow that the refugees were seeking to drag France into an undesired war, Sarraut, Bonnet, and Daladier became more resolved than ever to stand by the hard-line approach. By the fall, as we will see in Chapter 9, French refugee policy became infused with a siege mentality. In the minds of the nation's top officials, it was no longer so clear whether it was Hitler or his victims who constituted the greatest threat to French peace and security.

CHAPTER NINE

The Impact of Appeasement

In the fall of 1938, several new and potentially explosive ingredients were added to the mix of long-standing economic and security concerns that had encouraged restrictionist policies in the past. As Europe edged closer to war, fears began to arise in popular and governmental circles that the refugees might be serving as a fifth column of Nazi spies. But even more important was the fact that the majority of Central European refugees already in France were openly hostile to Hitler and vehemently opposed the government's policy of appeasement. This stance pitted them, together with a small minority of anti-*munichois* journalists and politicians, against the majority of French citizens, who desired peace at any price.

The charge that the refugees, and to some extent French Jews as a whole, were warmongers bent on embroiling France in a vendetta against Hitler gained widespread currency at the time of the Munich crisis. As Arthur Koestler noted in his memoirs, the refugees' anti-Nazi opinions "condemned us to the always unpopular, shrill-voiced part of Cassandras. Nobody likes people who run about the streets yelling 'Get ready, get ready, the day of wrath is at hand.' Least of all when they yell in a foreign accent."[1] As suspicions that the enemy within might constitute an even greater threat than the enemy without took hold, a note of defensiveness, paranoia, and even overt racism began to creep into official debates over the refugee question and reinforced administrative resolve to stand by the hard-line approach.

Only weeks after Henry Bérenger's speech in London, there were fresh indications that the government might not be able to stave off further incursions of refugees. In October, the Nazis ratcheted up the level of anti-Jewish persecution in Germany and Austria another notch. According to a Reich Ministry of Interior ordinance of October 5, all German and Austrian Jews were ordered to turn in their passports so that they could be stamped with the letter "J." This measure came about in response to a Swiss request to label the passports of Jews coming from "Greater Germany," since Switzerland, which had no visa requirement for Germans, could more effectively bar their entry.[2] But ultimately, this innovation assisted the Germans in preventing the return of Jewish émigrés.[3] In some respects, this measure merely formalized a practice in place since early 1938 whereby departing Jews had to sign a written pledge to abandon their property and never return. Nevertheless, as the French consul in Vienna noted, the new passport decree was significant because it constituted the final stage in the denaturalization of German Jews, transforming them into a mass of stateless refugees.[4]

Hitler's incursions into Czechoslovakia, which culminated in the Munich Agreement of September 29–30, sent thousands more Jews into exile. Nearly 200,000 people fled the annexed Sudeten territories, of whom about 15,000 were native Czech Jews, and another 4,000 to 5,000 were German or Austrian refugees, including many East Europeans, who had fled Germany in recent years. Yet, as refugee organizations noted, many of Czechoslovakia's 354,000 Jews were likely to flee in the near future because the new rump Czech state, already being chiseled away by Poland and Hungary, seemed likely to fall into German hands.[5]

At the same time, Mussolini, in an attempt to solidify his recent alliance with Germany, stunned the international community by initiating an anti-semitic program of his own. A decree of September 7 not only restricted the professional, economic, and educational opportunities of Italian Jews, native and foreign alike, but it also revoked the citizenship of Jews naturalized after 1919 and ordered them, together with foreign Jews, to leave the country within six months. This law affected some 15,000 Jews, of whom some 6,000 were German and Austrian refugees.[6] As the Quai d'Orsay knew full well, these Jews too would almost certainly seek refuge in France.

The situation of East European Jews deteriorated even further in the fall and winter of 1938. In December, the Romanians, imitating their German mentors, mandated that Romanian Jews exchange their passports for unrenewable travel certificates in an effort to prevent departing Jews from returning.[7] On October 6, the Polish government also began to implement the March 31 decree, which denaturalized Polish citizens who had lived abroad more than five years and had not renewed their passports. Aware that this measure was intended to prevent the return of the 70,000 Polish Jews still living within the boundaries of "Greater Germany," the German Foreign Office retaliated on October 26 by expelling these Jews. On October 27, the Gestapo rounded up 17,000 Polish Jews and began to transport them to Poland. Determined to prevent their return, the Polish government closed the border, leaving these Jews stranded in horrendous conditions in the no-man's-land of Zbaszyn.[8]

In France, the prospect of a renewed influx of foreign Jews sparked more profound anxiety than ever before, especially in light of the refugees' alleged pro-war proclivities. At the time of the Munich crisis, these sentiments exploded in open violence. As French troops anxiously mobilized for war, riots, targeted at immigrant Jews, erupted in Paris, as well as in Rouen, Dijon, Lille, Nancy, and in towns and cities throughout Alsace and Lorraine.[9] According to the account of one Jewish defense organization: "Foreigners, Jews have been molested, despoiled, and battered on the streets of Paris, accused of sometimes having shouted 'Vive la guerre!' and sometimes even 'Vive Hitler!'"[10] The International League Against Antisemitism (LICA) reported that Jewish shops in the Montmartre district of Paris, as well as in Strasbourg and Metz, were pillaged "on the pretext that the Jews had fled to the rear."

At the same time, the fact that 15,000 foreign Jews had enlisted for military service provided another pretext for attack.[11] As the LICA noted, Jews were damned either way. If they enlisted, people said: "Naturally, the Jews desire war!" And of those who might be waiting to see how events turn out before enlisting: "Naturally, the Jews are shirking their military service!"[12] In Dijon, a particularly violent incident broke out: a crowd of 500 persons sacked and pillaged the shop of a Polish Jew named Lerner, since he had allegedly shouted "Vive la guerre!" The crowd became so unruly that Lerner and his family had to be escorted out of town secretly by the police. Georges de la Fouchardière, a popular columnist for the Radical daily *L'Oeuvre*, went so far as to suggest that the Lerners deserved worse than pillaging; they deserved to be hanged![13]

In this atmosphere of war hysteria and mounting antisemitism, the government firmed up already stringent visa policies. French consulates in Germany and Austria began to follow the Swiss example of using the "J" stamp on Jewish passports to deny visas, since they knew that the bearers of these passports would never be allowed to return, notwithstanding Nazi protestations to the contrary.[14] Even individuals whose passports had not been stamped were now to be subjected to thorough investigations into their "ethnic situation," since they too were almost certainly Jews who would not be allowed to return.[15] Outraged by such discriminatory practices, the left-liberal paper *La Lumière* accused the Foreign Ministry and its consulates abroad of flagrant complicity with Nazi racism.[16]

Domestic considerations, and especially the ongoing campaigns of merchants and liberal professionals for government protection against immigrant competition, also encouraged a more restrictive visa policy. On September 24, the minister of the interior, Albert Sarraut, in response to complaints especially in Alsace and Lorraine, instructed the prefects of the three northeastern frontier departments, who played an advisory role in the granting of visas, that they could henceforth veto visa applications from any foreigner who posed a competitive threat to local business interests. As a result, visa applications of Austrian and German refugees, which in the past had usually been approved as long as the refugee in question proceeded to the interior,[17] now began to be routinely denied. According to these prefects, these refugees did not merit visas since they would "enlarge the already considerable number of ex-Austrian refugees who have found asylum in our country and would compete against French business firms."[18] Once a refugee's visa application had been turned down, entry into another department became nearly impossible.

This exclusionary mood was evident in the government's response to Czech refugees as well. Although the international community had expected France and Britain to have made special provisions to receive Czech refugees after the Munich crisis since they were considered largely responsible for the Czechs' plight, this did not turn out to be the case. Although France and Britain provided a package of £14,000,000 in grants and loans to be used in part for Czech refugee assistance,[19] the French government moved swiftly to impose a visa requirement on Czechs, whose entry into France had previously been unrestricted.[20] It also turned a deaf ear to pleas from Czech diplomats and representatives of the World Jewish Congress to grant the 15,000 Jews expelled from the Sudetenland at least temporary visas.[21] As these spokesmen noted, these Jews faced virulent antisemitism both in the new Czech rump state, which began to block their entry as of early October,[22] and in the newly autonomous Slovak state, which decreed that all non-Slovak Jews would have to leave after January 31, 1939.[23]

In October, France and Britain finally agreed to allocate 310 and 350 visas respectively to Czech refugees deemed in grave danger, a tiny number considering that at least 50,000 were expected to flee.[24] But while Britain made good on its promise, France procrastinated, so that by early 1939, only 100 visas had actually been issued.[25] So niggardly was French conduct in this matter that even the British Foreign Office complained that "France, as Czechoslovakia's ally, might be expected to have made a rather more generous contribution to this problem than they appear to have done up to the present time."[26]

Moreover, to the limited extent that France was prepared to grant visas to the Czechs, Jews were specifically excluded, despite the fact that they, unlike their German counterparts, had been accorded the right to take their property with them, a provision that ought to have made them "desirable" refugees.[27] On October 25, the government convened a special interministerial meeting to discuss the Czech refugee crisis and consider a request to grant visas to a preliminary list of 100 Czech refugees drawn up by the Confédération Générale du Travail (CGT) president, Léon Jouhaux.[28] The Ministry of the Interior used this occasion to reiterate its view that "the saturation point has been reached, if not surpassed"; it therefore opposed granting even this minimal number of visas.

Camille Chautemps, now serving as deputy prime minister, was less categorical. Nevertheless, he too voiced concern about granting visas to "individuals whose political tendencies present a danger to our social order." Chautemps further recommended that Jews be excluded from consideration altogether since he believed it was the government's obligation "to ensure that an influx of Jews not provoke difficulties of a racial order in our country." While acknowledging that the country desperately needed certain categories of foreign workers—agricultural workers, miners and metallurgy workers, and, most surprisingly, rural doctors—Chautemps stressed that "our borders cannot remain open to intellectuals, merchants, or manual laborers who would rapidly become charges of the French state." With reference to the doctors, the deputy prime minister noted that although many refugee doctors would be glad to go to rural areas, such projects had to be abandoned due to the opposition of the Ministry of Public Health as well as the fiercely protectionist doctors' association. In light of these pressures, Chautemps concluded, "We cannot, in principle, receive Czech refugees."[29] The effects of this policy were soon apparent. Shortly after this meeting, the Czech consul in Paris reported that the vast majority of Sudeten refugees had gone to Great Britain rather than to France, although some 2,000 Czech refugees, of whom at least 60 percent were Jews, had crossed into France illegally. He further observed that "visas [to France] cannot be obtained by Jews, but much more easily by non-Jews, political refugees," a view confirmed by the Joint Distribution Committee (JDC) as well.[30]

As these stringent visa policies were being deployed, Albert Sarraut further intensified his crackdown against illegal refugees already in France. At the time of Czech crisis, police surveillance over Central Europeans was stepped up significantly. According to a police report of September 15, German and Austrian refugees congregated nightly in the cafés on the *grands boulevards* in the Montmartre-Poissonnier district:

These German-speaking foreigners mix into the customers' conversations and the international political situation is at times discussed with great animation. Violent criticisms are directed against Hitler and the totalitarian states, and even the attitude of the French government is judged without sympathy. . . . Those who speak out criticize our government's lack of courage and insult the German head of state. "War against Germany is not only inevitable," they claim, "but necessary."

These debates became so heated that fistfights occasionally broke out. While the police acknowledged that most of the refugees "remain passive," it was nevertheless the case that "some trouble making elements have slipped in among them, who . . . seek to foment incidents." They therefore recommended that refugees be prevented from congregating on street corners and in cafés.[31]

The internal crackdown began in earnest, however, only after the Czech Crisis. In the wake of the mobilization order of September 27, the LICA reported that police in the 3rd, 10th, and 20th arrondissements had "arrested . . . , without cause, men who had foreign appearances and accents, [and] brought them to the police station, where they insulted them and roughed them up. Without interrogation or any form of due process, they were slapped, knocked around, and called 'dirty Jews' and other specifically antisemitic epithets."[32] On October 12, the Ministry of the Interior issued a circular ordering the expulsion of all refugees who did not have visas or passports, and who had not declared themselves at the border. This decree, whose impact was retroactive, was targeted specifically at Austrians who had entered France illegally after the May 2 decree law and who had become stateless as a result of the new German passport measures. Moreover, the ministry for the first time justified this measure by invoking fifth-column fears. As Berthoin proclaimed: "This severity has become indispensable" since the Germans intended to exploit France's tradition of asylum "to introduce into our country the less desirable elements, or possibly even false refugees assigned to carry out intelligence missions."[33]

Sarraut followed this expulsion decree by enacting a number of police measures targeted specifically at Central European refugees. In October, the police announced a "decongestion policy" with respect to refugees in the Paris region, and at the same time the Ministry of the Interior extended the ban on refugee settlement to include the departments of the Eure, the Eure-et-Loire, the Loiret, the Oise, the Seine Inférieure, the Seine-et-Marne, and the Seine-et-Cire.[34] Although Austrian refugees had been banned from the Paris region since the spring, this ban had apparently not been enforced. After the Munich crisis, this situation changed, however, perhaps in response to shrill demands by right-wing politicians such as the Paris municipal councilor, Charles Trochu, to purge the capital of recent Jewish arrivals.[35] In November, the *New York Times* reported that the police had initiated a full-scale campaign to drive the Austrians out of Paris,[36] and the Sûreté simultaneously informed Jewish leaders that reception centers would be created at the borders to absorb refugees "who have been *refoulés* from Paris and other regions that are currently oversaturated."[37]

To escape these roundups, refugees began to flee Paris on their own, and a number found their way to the refugee colony at Chelles on the outskirts of the capital. This colony, which was sponsored by the new Jewish refugee committee, the Comité d'Assistance aux Réfugiés (CAR), had been created in the spring, when the refugee ban went into effect. The approximately 700 refugees who resided in Chelles by the end of the year lived either in private homes purchased by the CAR, or in barracks, and received occupational retraining from the ORT while they awaited visas from abroad. Since Chelles was located in the department of the Seine-et-Marne, which had been included on the list of banned departments in the fall, local authorities at one point had tried to expel the refugees. But due to the intervention of the CAR and the JDC, as well as protests from local merchants, who in an interesting twist saw these refugees not as competitors, since they were forbidden to work, but as valued customers, the central government ultimately prevailed upon municipal authorities to overturn this expulsion decree.[38]

Sarraut hoped to bring this crackdown to a conclusion with the decree law of November 12, 1938. This law, while still directed primarily at illegal immigrants, constituted a serious assault on the rights of naturalized foreigners as well, and reflected once more the minister's deep-seated belief that France was being corroded by an enemy within. In an effort to "exercise absolute control over the access into our territory and to render illegal entries practically impossible," Sarraut announced the creation of a special border police to be financed entirely from fees paid by foreigners for residence permits and identity cards. Article 25 of the decree law mandated the creation of special centers or camps where foreigners considered dangerous to national security but who could not be expelled were to be detained. As Sarraut explained, police surveillance at these detention centers was to be far more rigorous than what he had initially envisioned for the assigned residences prescribed by article 11 of the May 2, 1938, decree law.

In addition to these police measures, this decree included several provisions that infringed directly on the civil and political rights of naturalized citizens. In an effort to prevent *mariages blancs*—marriages arranged solely for the purpose of acquiring citizenship—foreigners were no longer permitted to marry French citizens unless they had resided in France legally for a minimum of one year. Given that it was virtually impossible to acquire legal residence, this law in effect banned all marriages between foreigners and French citizens. Article 10 also stipulated that naturalized foreigners would be stripped of their citizenship if they engaged in activities injurious to national security, evaded military service, or committed a crime carrying a prison sentence of more than one year. According to article 20, recently naturalized foreigners were denied an automatic right to vote; from now on, they would have to wait an additional five years before exercising that right.[39]

To be sure, these measures fell short of proposals put forth in recent months by right-wing parliamentarians. In April, Moïse Lévy, the senator from the Haute Saône, had called for even longer waiting periods before granting naturalized citizens the right to vote, and in October, the conservative deputy from the Moselle, Robert Schuman,* had submitted a bill recommending a rollback in all naturalizations granted since 1919.[40] Nevertheless, the decree law of November 12 marked an important stage in the institutionalization of a two-tiered system of citizenship, a trend that had begun with the 1934–35 legislation limiting the rights of naturalized citizens to practice certain professions.

Sarraut and Daladier expected this decree to resolve once and for all the problem of illegal foreigners in France, and Daladier used the occasion of the Radical Party Congress in late October to rail once more against the interference of refugees in French internal affairs.[41] Events of early November, however, propelled the refugee issue to the forefront of public attention and imbued charges of Jewish warmongering with unprecedented urgency. Just as Georges Bonnet, the administration's most ardent champion of appeasement, was secretly concluding plans for a bilateral nonaggression pact with Germany, an illegal Jewish refugee committed a crime that threatened to shatter forever Bonnet's dream of Franco-German rapprochement. On November 7, Herschel Grynszpan, a seventeen-year-old German-born Polish Jewish youth, shot and killed the third secretary of the German embassy in Paris, Ernst vom Rath. Grynszpan's alleged motive was to retaliate for the expulsion from Germany of Polish Jews, including his parents, at the end of October.

Outraged by vom Rath's murder, the Germans used this incident as the pretext to launch the Kristallnacht pogrom of November 9–10. In this assault, 91 German Jews were killed, 267 synagogues were burned, over 7,000

---

*Robert Schuman served as deputy of the Moselle from 1919–40 and again from 1946–51, when he became a leading figure in the Mouvement Républicain Populaire (MRP), a French Christian Democratic party. Throughout his career he held numerous cabinet posts, including undersecretary of state for refugees in Paul Reynaud's cabinet in 1940, and after the Second World War he served as minister of finance and minister for foreign affairs, in addition to serving briefly as prime minister in 1947–48. He is best known for his role in framing the Schuman Plan, which established the European Coal and Steel Community in 1951 and provided the foundation for the creation of the European Common Market in 1957. Schuman's hostility to immigrants in the 1930's was typical of many politicians in Christian Democratic parties, especially in Alsace and Lorraine.

Jewish stores were plundered, and 35,000 Jews were arrested and sent off to concentration camps.[42] The Nazis inflicted a similar wave of terror in Austria, where an additional 20,000 Jews were arrested and some 2,000 were sent to Dachau.[43] Following these atrocities, the Nazis implemented another round of anti-Jewish legislation designed to ghettoize and despoil the remaining Jewish population.[44] According to Robert Coulondre, the new French ambassador in Berlin, the situation of German Jewry had reached a new abyss. If a Jew were ever again to kill a Nazi official, the Gestapo, he predicted, "would not hesitate to annihilate in a sea of blood those they call the descendants of Judah."[45]

The assassination of vom Rath and the anti-Jewish riots in Germany and Austria that followed placed the French government in a quandary. In and of itself, Grynszpan's act did not necessarily endanger Franco-German relations. Bonnet took immediate steps to prevent the assassination from having political repercussions, and he assured the Germans that the government in no way condoned Grynszpan's act. French police promptly arrested and interrogated Grynszpan, and Bonnet sent a medical team to try to save vom Rath's life. In an additional show of goodwill, Bonnet even attended vom Rath's funeral service in Paris.[46] Such conciliatory gestures elicited a show of gratitude from the German government, which, while lashing out at international Jewry, went out of its way to exonerate France. As Hugues de Montbas, the French chargé d'affaires in Berlin, declared, "everything has been arranged in Berlin to ensure that this affair not have repercussions of any sort on the political and diplomatic realm."[47] At the same time, however, Montbas reported that he had been warned by the German Foreign Office as well as the state-controlled German press that "nothing would have happened if the control of foreigners at our borders and their surveillance in the interior had been rigorously exercised, and above all if refugees of all sorts did not enjoy here, by means of their intrigues, a tolerance and even a certain encouragement thanks to which they believe everything is permissible."[48] Not surprisingly, the Nazi press applauded the November 12 decree law, and especially the creation of concentration camps for undesirable refugees, as a step in the right direction.[49]

Although Bonnet successfully absolved the French government of responsibility for Grynszpan's crime, the repercussions of Kristallnacht on his plans for appeasement were not so easily smoothed over. In Britain and the United States, there was a tremendous public outcry in reaction to the Nazi anti-Jewish violence, and for the first time, even proponents of appeasement cast doubt on the sincerity of Hitler's declarations of peaceful intentions. According to the *New York Times*, Europe could not "expect any real appeasement so long as this unappeasable force wrecks the plans for universal appeasement."[50] From now on, the paper counseled, "appeasement of Germany should be continued only as she corrects her brutal policies toward the Jewish racial minority."[51] The *Yorkshire Post* similarly proclaimed that until Germany exhibits some moderation and international goodwill, "it is impossible to understand how anyone who is either himself not hopelessly duped or is seeking to dupe others can talk seriously of producing a European appeasement."[52] Moreover, the German ambassador in London reported that even formerly pro-appeasement circles in the British government were shocked by Germany's treatment of the Jews. "Their confidence in the possibility of an Anglo-German understanding is shaken; their effectiveness is crippled," he stated. "Chamberlain's opponents have lost no time in exploiting the fresh anti-German wave to criticize him and to renew their contention that collaboration with a country in which such brutalities are possible must be rejected for ideological reasons."[53]

In response to this public outcry, Chamberlain himself roundly condemned Germany's anti-Jewish persecutions before the House of Commons and issued a formal protest against the malicious German accusation that British statesmen were behind the assassination of vom Rath.[54] In the United States, Roosevelt declared that he "could scarcely believe that such things could occur in a twentieth-century civilization,"[55] and to demonstrate the depth of his displeasure, he even recalled the American ambassador from Germany.[56] Moreover, in an effort to match words with deeds, Chamberlain and Roosevelt stepped up IGCR negotiations to seek an international solution to the ever-worsening refugee crisis.[57] As the *New York Times* reported, British and American leaders now agreed that "there can be no real appeasement, no peace in the world, while hundreds of thousands of refugees are dumped homeless, stateless and penniless on the doorsteps of neighboring countries."[58]

In contrast to their British and American counterparts, Daladier and Bonnet refused to allow Kristallnacht to deflect them in any way from their pursuit of appeasement. To be sure, French diplomats in Germany were as outraged as everyone else by the anti-Jewish violence, and several speculated that Kristallnacht would put an end to any talk of Franco-German rapprochement. According to Montbas, Nazi leaders "seemed to have dealt the final blow to a policy of moderation and international understanding . . . and this at a time when . . . one would have thought that the spirit of the Munich accord would finally triumph." The entire diplomatic corps, he noted, now believed that "if nothing happens to alter the internal evolution of the Third Reich, a European conflict could well be inevitable."[59] The French consul in Karlsruhe similarly declared that he and his colleagues "had always viewed with skepticism the generous efforts of the French to arrive at an understanding with this people." He then expressed his personal hope that "the events of these past few days might lead to the reestablishment of the united front of democratic peoples that twenty years ago steadfastly brought about the triumph of civilization over barbarism and brute force."[60] Even Coulondre, one of Bonnet's most staunch supporters, noted that "the treatment inflicted in Germany upon the Jews whom the Nazis intend to extirpate completely like malevolent beasts illuminates the utter distance that separates the Hitlerite conception of the world from the spiritual patrimony of the democratic nations."[61] He thus advised the Foreign Ministry "not to expect an excessive spirit of conciliation from the German side."[62]

Bonnet ignored this counsel, however. Instead, he sought to speed up the pace of negotiations with Germany to ensure that the furor over Kristallnacht not incur any delays. So eager were the French to forge ahead that when Coulondre paid his first official visit to Germany's foreign minister, Joachim von Ribbentrop, on November 19, he made no allusion to the anti-Jewish atrocities. Rather, the French ambassador reassured Ribbentrop that French public opinion fully supported Bonnet's drive to achieve Franco-German reconciliation.[63]

Whether Bonnet still had public support was no longer certain, however, especially after November 23, when he first revealed details of the proposed Franco-German declaration and Ribbentrop's intended visit. As the foreign minister's critics on both the left and right pointed out, Daladier was alone among Western leaders not to have condemned the Nazi atrocities. According to the socialist *Le Populaire*, "The price official circles attach to the accord with Germany would explain the incredible silence they are observing in the presence of the pogroms across the Rhine."[64] On the right, Henri de Kérillis, the conservative deputy from the Seine and editor of the daily *L'Epoque*, similarly blasted Bonnet's attempt to achieve Franco-German rapprochement at the expense of the Jews. Bonnet's policy, Kérillis claimed, could have only one result: the estrangement of an increasingly "Hitlerized" France from its democratic allies.[65]

Bonnet met particularly fierce opposition in the Foreign Affairs Commission of the Chamber of Deputies. There, the socialist deputy Salomon Grumbach declared that France's silence "has provoked in all governmental and parliamentary circles in the United States and Great Britain a considerable astonishment and has done little to boost our country's moral prestige of abroad."[66] Fernand Laurent, a prominent conservative, also pushed through a resolution that called on the administration to take up with Chamberlain and Halifax, scheduled to arrive in Paris on November 23, "the persecution [in Germany] of which certain racial and religious minorities are the victims."[67]

Even Daladier's cabinet did not support Bonnet. At the November 23 cabinet meeting, several ministers protested that "it was neither safe nor desirable" for Ribbentrop to come to Paris at this time. Mandel, according to the *New York Times*, opposed not only the timing of Bonnet's policy but the substance as well and feared that a separate Franco-German pact would weaken the Little Entente (France's alliances with Czechoslovakia, Romania, and Yugoslavia) and isolate France from its Anglo-Saxon allies. The minister of education, Jean Zay, also pressed Bonnet not to allow Ribbentrop to come to Paris. If the pact had to be signed, Zay recommended that a lower ranking German official, such as the German ambassador, be given that honor. Anatole de Monzie, the minister of public works, and César Campinchi, the minister of the Navy, similarly suggested that the signing ceremony be held in Strasbourg or even London to avoid violent protests in Paris.[68]

Opinion abroad was no less critical. Although Chamberlain announced that he welcomed this agreement, which closely resembled one his own government had signed with the Nazis just after the Munich crisis,[69] there is little doubt that the British were taken aback by Bonnet's timing. According to the American chargé d'affaires in Paris, Britain's ambassador to France, Sir Eric Phipps, expressed veiled disapproval of Bonnet's policies. As Phipps declared, "The atrocious treatment of Jews in Germany had of course shocked opinion in England as it had in America and it had slowed up the effort at appeasement with Germany. When a country, however, had determined upon a definite line of foreign policy as the French had there was nothing to do but go ahead with it."[70] The London *Times*, hitherto the most adamant supporter of Chamberlain's appeasement policy, similarly declared that "the conclusion of the agreement between France and Germany is by no means assured of a general welcome. M. Bonnet's critics are already expressing indignation that he should have seen fit to establish closer relations at a moment when the conscience of the whole world has been shocked by the persecution of the Jews."[71]

In the United States, the acting secretary of state, Sumner Welles, rejected Bonnet's request that the American government express public approval of the Franco-German accord, if only through a press statement. In view of the strained relations between the United States and Germany, Welles informed the French ambassador in Washington that such approval would be inappropriate.[72] Even the Italian government expressed surprise that "the recrudescence of antisemitic persecutions in Germany did not lead to the ruin of the project of the Franco-German declaration."[73]

Despite this barrage of criticism, Bonnet refused to be deterred. Instead he lashed out against the Jews and the communists, whom he believed were orchestrating the campaign against him. Describing a phone conversation with the French foreign minister on November 11, Phipps reported that "M. Bonnet is rather perturbed at the growing antisemitic feeling. He says it's due to the fact that the public is realizing more and more that prominent Jews here desired war at the time of the last crisis." The British ambassador then added in a confidential aside that Bonnet had summoned Baron de Rothschild "to warn him . . . that the impression must not be allowed to grow that the French Jews want war in order to avenge their luckless brethren in Germany." Bonnet then accused French Jewish leaders of having used "funds intended for the relief of refugees in France . . . to subvention certain bellicose organs of the press," although he told Phipps that this practice had now stopped.[74]

Later that month, Bonnet similarly informed the German ambassador in Paris that "even the agitation about our measures against the Jews and the sharp personal attacks by certain international circles on him would not deter him from continuing an understanding with us, which was supported by more than ninety percent of the French nation and against which only the Jews and communists were crying out."[75] Bonnet's admonitions to Jewish leaders to curb Jewish warmongering almost certainly accounts for the controversial statements made by Julien Weill in the conservative daily *Le Matin* on November 19. In this interview, the chief rabbi of Paris sought to allay fears that French Jews might seek to exploit anti-German sentiment in the wake of Kristallnacht "to embark on a [refugee] initiative that might in any way impede efforts currently underway to achieve Franco-German rapprochement."[76]

Bonnet eventually had his way, and Ribbentrop arrived in Paris on December 6 to sign the "no war" declaration.[77] Even then, however, the French foreign minister ignited further controversy. Although the Ministry of Justice had refused to support a proposal put forth by Bonnet to limit press criticism of foreign heads of state—an obvious concession to German pressure[78]—Bonnet nevertheless took exceptional measures to curb anti-German publicity. All posters protesting the Franco-German talks were banned,[79] and according to one German refugee, "Many political émigrés were sent to small provincial towns for the duration of Ribbentrop's stay in Paris."[80] The *New York Times* reported that Bonnet had even rerouted Ribbentrop's train at the last moment to avoid potential anti-German demonstrations.[81]

But above all, Bonnet ignited a furor when he failed to invite Georges Mandel and Jean Zay—the two ministers of Jewish origin—to the state dinner in honor of Ribbentrop on the evening of December 6, a move that prompted *Le Populaire* to speculate that "Hitler was already dictating the law in France."[82] In his post-war memoirs, Bonnet explained that Mandel and Zay had not been invited because they held minor portfolios and that official protocol did not require every minister to be present.[83] Yet Bonnet's explanation smacks of insincerity, especially since Mandel's post at the Ministry of Colonies was by no means irrelevant to Franco-German relations in light of Germany's keen interest in colonial concessions. Furthermore, the fact that Campinchi refused to attend the reception because he was outraged by Bonnet's failure to have invited Mandel and Zay suggests that the foreign minister's concept of proper protocol was not universally shared. According to Otto Abetz, head of the German Foreign Office's French department, Daladier himself was none too pleased on this occasion, although whether his displeasure stemmed from the controversy over the "Aryan dinner" or his growing unease with Bonnet's policies is not clear. In any event, Abetz recounted in his memoirs that at Ribbentrop's dinner party, "Daladier presided over the meal with an expression of defeat and the members of his cabinet observed an embarrassed silence."[84]

Just as Kristallnacht did nothing to alter Bonnet's plans for appeasement, it did little to influence France's refugee policy, at least in the short run. In the immediate aftermath of the pogrom, the French authorities were more determined than ever to prevent new waves of refugees from infiltrating into France, despite fervent appeals by several French diplomats to reopen the border. As the French consul in Nuremberg noted, "All foreign countries are closing their borders and refusing them asylum. If the governments of the great democratic powers remain deaf to the appeals of these unfortunates and do not take immediate measures to help them, it is certain that the sole refuge of German Jews will be death, and the coming days will register a wave of mass suicides."[85]

Notwithstanding Bonnet's post-war claims that he welcomed Jewish refugees in the wake of Kristallnacht,[86] contemporary evidence suggests this was far from the case. According to Phipps's account of his phone conversation with Bonnet on November 11, in which the later had complained of Jewish warmongering, Bonnet had "spoke[n] bitterly about the large numbers of undesirable foreigners in France, and pointed out that nearly all the recent political assassinations here had been committed by such foreigners. He said that the French government meant to take stringent measures in this connexion, to expel many of these undesirables and to place a number in concentration camps. France could no longer serve as a dumping ground."[87]

Moreover, despite the fact that Bonnet had assured the British after Kristallnacht that France would grant visas to refugees whose lives were in danger,[88] Bonnet did nothing of the sort. The Jewish press reported that in the wake of Kristallnacht, it had become more difficult than ever for refugees to acquire visas. According to *Samedi*, "France no longer admits German Jews—with the exception of a very few special cases." French consulates "do not deliver the aforesaid visa until after making lengthy inquiries, with the aid of detailed questionnaires, about the character of the applicant, [and] especially about his religion, his 'race' and that of his parents and grandparents. . . . If someone has Jewish blood in his veins, the consul wants to know everything, just like a vulgar Nazi police commissioner."[89] The Austrian socialist press similarly condemned France's restrictive visa policy after Kristallnacht as "an undeniable success for Goebbels . . . a triumphal path in preparation for Hitler's victory."[90]

Bonnet's reluctance to extend even the slightest concession to the refugees was apparent within the IGCR as well. Although in October Bérenger had recommended that France support the IGCR in light of renewed refugee crises,[91] Bonnet apparently disagreed. According to reports of American officials, France's financial contribution to the IGCR was nonexistent and Bérenger was frequently out of touch with the committee, sometimes failing even to attend meetings.[92] Bérenger's behavior was not simply a reflection of his irascible character, as many IGCR members believed. Rather, he was acting in response to Bonnet's instructions. According to a Foreign Ministry memo of November 21, France's goal within the committee was to avoid further commitments of any kind, since "the problem of German Jewish emigration is now assuming truly disquieting proportions." While France could continue to serve as a transit country for refugees who had already secured visas for other countries, under no circumstances could it provide permanent refuge or even provisional asylum to refugees who did not have visas in hand.[93]

Moreover, Bérenger and Bonnet were afraid that if the IGCR were to succeed in its goal of persuading the Germans to relax the currency restrictions on departing Jews, France would be inundated with yet another wave of refugees. Thus, as early as August, the French, together with Germany's other West European neighbors, warned IGCR director George Rublee that if his negotiations with the Nazis were to succeed, they would not allow Jewish refugees to pass through their territories. As Rublee noted, "The French have been particularly emphatic in stating that this emigration must go from German ports directly to the countries which have offered places of settlement."[94] At the IGCR meeting on December 2, Bérenger fended off another proposal, endorsed by Britain and the United States, that would have required Germany's West European neighbors to grant temporary asylum to all refugees from German-occupied territories.[95] This maneuver provoked Rublee to complain that "the attack on the Jewish community in Germany on the one hand and the indifference of the particular governments to the fate of the victims on the other has brought the affairs of the Intergovernmental Committee to a critical stage."[96]

Responsibility for France's hard-line policy after Kristallnacht cannot be attributed to Bonnet alone, however. Rather, it was Sarraut's fierce crackdown against illegal immigration that had the most immediate impact. As we have seen, the decree law of November 12 reinforced border controls, and German Jews trying to escape to France after Kristallnacht were by no means exempted from these regulations. In mid-November, the press reported that French border police had refused to grant entry to German Jews who had arrived without visas, and several of these individuals had subsequently been shot by the Nazis.[97] When the Intercomité des Oeuvres Françaises des Réfugiés, a newly formed federation of refugee committees, intervened on behalf of some 50 to 60 refugees apprehended near Strasbourg, they were informed by two of Sarraut's deputies that "France is presently saturated with refugees." Although these refugees were eventually allowed in, the Ministry of the Interior warned Jewish leaders that from now on "a serious sifting out" would be conducted at the border.[98]

Moreover, in a highly unusual move, Sarraut began to turn away even refugees holding French visas. This extraordinary measure was necessary, Sarraut explained, "to guard against the threat of a massive immigration of undesirable elements . . . who believed it to be their duty to trick our consuls with regard to the duration and the true reasons for their sojourn in our country."[99] In reality, this measure was almost certainly prompted by the new German passport requirements as well as by the fact that several consular officials, acting on their own conscience, were granting Jews visas despite official policy.[100] At the same time, the minister sent urgent telegrams to the prefects of the northeastern border provinces instructing them to bar the entry of German Jewish children in particular,[101] notwithstanding Daladier's recent declaration that France would join Britain, Belgium, and Holland in absorbing a contingent of refugee children.[102] In an effort to highlight the degree to which France had deviated from its traditional policies of asylum, Bernhard Kahn, the European director of the JDC, pointed out at a refugee conference in mid-December that although the Ministry of the Interior had received some 78,000 applications for visas, "no entry permits are being granted."[103]

The French made two concessions to international opinion, however. First, in response to mounting pressure from the United States that France allow refugees to settle in its colonies, Bérenger announced at the IGCR meeting on December 2, according to Rublee's account, that "if all the other participating government's of the Evian Committee would make a specific contribution, France would consider the settlement in Madagascar and New Caledonia of 10,000 persons but not (repeat not) persons of German origin." What Bérenger meant, according to Rublee, was that France would absorb 10,000 non-German refugees in its colonies and another 10,000 German refugees in metropolitan areas, including those who "had crossed the frontier illegally in the last few weeks and were now lodged in various jails." German refugees, Bérenger had argued, "could not settle . . . in the colonies or mandated territories because the government in Germany might change and then they would have a minority problem on their hands."[104] This stipulation was obviously a concession to Mandel, who had long been concerned with the possibility of revanchist claims if German refugees were to settle in French colonies. It nevertheless came as a surprise to the Americans, who had believed that a French concession in this matter would have involved German and Austrian Jews.[105] Still, the British and Americans viewed Bérenger's proposal as a major breakthrough, particularly since Mandel had staunchly opposed such schemes in the past and because the plan provided for the settlement of 10,000 German Jews in metropolitan France.[106]

Bonnet's second concession was to accede to a British request, made during the Anglo-French discussions in November, that he raise the Jewish refugee issue with Ribbentrop during his visit to Paris. Specifically, the British were hoping that Bonnet could help the IGCR persuade the Nazis to relax the severe restrictions on the amount of capital German Jews could transfer out of the country so that they might be resettled more easily abroad, especially since a colonial deal now seemed in the offing.[107] Bonnet did in fact raise the issue, but the manner in which he did so conveyed the impression, both to Ribbentrop as well as to the British and Americans, that he cared less about helping the refugees than about preventing their influx into France. In his memoirs, the French foreign minister claimed that he had attempted to broach the subject with Ribbentrop on December 6 but that Ribbentrop had refused to discuss the matter in an official capacity, claiming it was a purely internal affair.[108] Yet, according to a contemporary account by Edwin C. Wilson, the American chargé d'affaires in Paris, Bonnet had personally told him that "he had not mentioned the matter at all to Ribbentrop on the first day of the latter's visit December 6 because the Ambassadors and certain experts were present and he was certain that Ribbentrop would refuse to discuss it in their presence."[109] In any case, Bonnet decided to wait until the afternoon of December 7, when he was scheduled to meet with Ribbentrop for unofficial discussions.[110]

According to Ribbentrop's version of this conversation, sent directly to Hitler on December 9, Bonnet had told him:

how great an interest was being taken in France in a solution of the Jewish problem. To my question as to what France's interest might be, M. Bonnet said that in the first place they did not want to receive any more Jews from Germany and [asked] whether we could not take some sort of measures to keep them from coming to France any more, and in the second place France had to ship 10,000 Jews somewhere else. They were actually thinking of Madagascar for this.

Ribbentrop then responded, "We all wished to get rid of our Jews but that the difficulties lay in the fact that no country wished to receive them, and further, in the shortage of foreign exchange." Although these comments were clearly intended to discourage speculation that Germany might entertain the IGCR proposal, Ribbentrop nevertheless agreed "that a German well versed in the Jewish problem should sometime confer in a private capacity with a deputy of an international committee, in order to examine the question of the Jewish emigration from Germany in its practical aspects."[111]

Other versions of this conversation substantiate the view that Bonnet's main aim was to prevent further refugees from coming to France. According to Wilson's report to the State Department, based on Bonnet's own version of these negotiations:

Ribbentrop began by stating that there were two categories of Jews—bad Jews and good Jews. All the Jews in Germany were bad Jews; they had come from the east, poverty stricken and diseased. . . . On the other hand other countries such as France and Great Britain had the good Jews and it was because of this fact that these countries had failed to understand the strong feeling against the Jews in Germany and the necessity for Germany to rid itself of them.

Bonnet then explained that "he had no wish to mix into German internal affairs but that Germany was creating a problem for other countries by forcing them to accept people whom Ribbentrop himself had referred to as bad Jews and that the settlement of this problem would be greatly facilitated by some cooperation from Germany." Bonnet asked Ribbentrop whether "the German government would agree to send a representative to meet representatives of the London Refugee Committee informally on some neutral territory to discuss the whole problem." Ribbentrop finally agreed, but stipulated that the German representative, "who would not be a Jew," would meet IGCR officers only in an unofficial capacity and in a neutral country.[112] In yet another version of these discussions, relayed to the British Foreign Office by Phipps, Bonnet had informed Ribbentrop "that France could not go on admitting Jews indefinitely."[113]

The strategies embraced by Bonnet and Sarraut following Kristallnacht suggest that France was more determined than ever to uphold the hard-line approach. Although initially motivated by economic protectionism and security concerns, by the end of 1938 foreign policy considerations had emerged as a key determinant of French refugee policy, particularly insofar as these interests were related to Bonnet's pro-appeasement drive. The refugees now loomed as a double threat: not only did they endanger the national economy by stealing jobs from French workers and competing with the middle classes, but they now endangered the nation's vital security interests as well. As we have seen, officials at the highest levels of government, including Bonnet himself, apparently believed that the refugees, acting in concert with native Jews and communists, were seeking to embroil France in an undesired war.

At the same time, however, several politicians and publicists were beginning to question whether the hard-line approach could achieve its goals: preventing refugees from entering the country and forcing those there to leave. As in the past, the majority of refugees had nowhere to go, and French police, despite intensive efforts to seal the borders, were unable to do so. As a result, thousands of immigrants continued to stream into France illegally in late 1938 and early 1939, despite the new restrictions. The major question facing the administration in 1939 with regard to Central and East European refugees was therefore whether to maintain the hard-line approach, despite its inability to curb the influx of refugees, or whether to resurrect the more constructive approaches of the past, especially the colonial and agricultural settlement schemes advanced by the Popular Front. At the same time, new pressure groups, especially the military, were beginning to lobby the administration to relax refugee policies since they were eager to incorporate more foreigners into the armed forces. As the year drew to a close, there were therefore hints, however faint, that the hard-line tactics of 1938 might not be appropriate for the future.

CHAPTER TEN

The Crosscurrents of 1939

As 1939 commenced, the Daladier administration seemed intent on abiding by the hard-line policies of 1938, especially since the Jewish refugee crisis showed no signs of abating. In March, the Nazis seized the rump state of Czechoslovakia, and the Italian deadline for the expulsion of non-naturalized Jews expired. Nazi pressure on Poland to return the free city of Danzig to Germany also increased in the spring of 1939, while the various regimes of Eastern Europe continued to implement their own antisemitic programs. Most significantly, France now faced a major refugee crisis from an entirely different quarter: nearly half a million Spanish refugees fled across the border in January and February after the defeat of the republican forces by Franco.[1] This "invasion," as it was referred to even by the mainstream press, reinforced the public perception of a nation overrun by alien hordes of left-wing revolutionaries and fortified the administration's resolve to seal the borders.[2]

Powerful countervailing forces were at work as well, however, and although these forces ultimately did nothing to alter the administration's attitude toward future newcomers from Central and Eastern Europe, they did eventually lead to a liberalization of policies toward refugees already in France. First, it was becoming clear that the decree laws were not accomplishing their goal of preventing new refugees from crossing the border and forcing illegal ones already in France to leave. Despite Sarraut's efforts to shore up the police presence at the frontier, France was unable to seal her borders completely. As a result, thousands of Central and East European refugees continued to stream into the country illegally, exacerbating the problem of clandestine refugees, which the decree laws were intended to solve. These refugees could not be expelled; nor was the Foreign Ministry able to persuade other nations to take them, despite persistent efforts to do so. Thousands of them therefore ended up in jail, at considerable expense to French taxpayers. Those who eluded prison often did so by resorting to the burgeoning underground network of false paper operations, further fueling the charge that they constituted a criminal element fully deserving of the harsh punishments meted out by the decree laws.

Yet, the tragic fate of refugees who landed in jail as well as the harsh measures implemented at the border provoked a backlash of pro-refugee sympathy among certain sectors of public opinion. Many in France were convinced that the majority of refugees arrested as a result of the decree laws were not common criminals, but had been transformed into such by these laws. Law enforcement officials—police and especially judges—began to express growing unease at having to enforce legislation they considered unjust, particularly in the aftermath of Kristallnacht. Moreover, a number of journalists, politicians, and Jewish community leaders banded together to wage a campaign to overturn the decree laws, arguing that France, by enforcing these laws, was joining the ranks of the persecutors. While these groups conceded that France was saturated and could not absorb further massive influxes of refugees, they nevertheless insisted that France had an obligation to extend at least temporary asylum to the victims of Nazi persecution. They therefore called for a return to the more humane refugee policies of the Popular Front, including an amnesty for refugees already in France, the reconstitution of the Consultative Commission to sift out authentic refugees, and the revival of colonial and agricultural settlement schemes.

But whereas the pro-refugee campaign had previously been inspired by humanitarian sentiments, there were now compelling pragmatic considerations as well. First, as pro-refugee spokesmen argued, there was no reason the refugees could not be made economically useful by training them to be agriculturists and sending them to work either in the underpopulated regions of southern France or in the colonies. As nearly everyone acknowledged, France needed to boost her population, and a well-coordinated immigration policy, one that steered foreigners away from congested cities and toward the depopulated countryside, offered an important solution. Ultimately, this view impelled the Daladier administration to resuscitate the Serre Plan, which it had rejected in the spring of 1938, and to a lesser extent the Popular Front's colonial schemes. A second consideration was the military's growing need for manpower as France began to prepare for war. As pro-refugee advocates never ceased to point out, expelling refugees or throwing them into jail made little sense when France badly needed bodies to shore up its armed forces, particularly because France's population numbered 40 million as opposed to the German population of 60 million. The Military High Command itself, desperate for new recruits, began to press the administration to speed up the naturalization process and to facilitate the enlistment of non-naturalized foreigners. At the same time, the fact that many refugees had economic skills that might prove useful in wartime was a consideration the administration could no longer ignore.

The government therefore faced a significant challenge in the spring and summer of 1939. On the one hand, there was considerable pressure from pro-refugee groups as well as the military to recognize the failure of the decree laws and to turn what had previously been considered a liability—the presence of thousands of illegal aliens—into an economic and military asset. On the other hand, the administration still had to contend with ongoing pressure from the anti-immigrant protectionist lobby. Not only did the Chambers of Commerce and doctors' association continue to oppose any modification of the decree laws, but they also demanded more stringent economic measures against foreigners as well as tighter naturalization procedures. Still reluctant to confront these protectionist forces head-on, the Daladier administration again sought a compromise, but the half measures implemented ultimately satisfied no one. As a result, when war was declared in September, the legal status of the refugees, although improved, had not been fully resolved, and the refugees were left suspended between hope and uncertainty regarding the future.

In the early months of 1939, however, there were few signs that a liberalization of refugee policy was in the offing. According to a Joint Distribution Committee (JDC) report, French consulates throughout Europe continued to deny prospective refugees visas, and in January immigration restrictions and border controls were further intensified, making illegal immigration more difficult than ever.[3] After the Nazi invasion of Czechoslovakia in March, additional police reinforcements were sent to the border,[4] and Sarraut subsequently ordered a crackdown on refugees residing in France on only transit visas or international transit cards issued by navigation companies. From now on, he declared, refugees wanting to enter France solely to emigrate elsewhere would have to show entry visas for their final destinations prior to crossing the border, and shipping companies were instructed to sell tickets only to individuals holding such visas.[5] In early 1939, immigration to the French Antilles was similarly suspended in view of the influx of hundreds of Jewish refugees from Italy.[6] Moreover, in marked contrast to England, Holland, and Belgium, which all agreed to accept contingents of refugee children after Kristallnacht, France, at least initially, refused to make such a concession, despite the fact that Jewish organizations had agreed to accept full responsibility for them. If war were to break out, the JDC claimed, the government had expressed concern that these children might be abandoned by their benefactors, becoming "a burden to the state at a very critical moment."[7]

At the same time, fifth-column fears were increasingly playing a role in the hardening of refugee policy. In the spring, the French minister in Luxembourg acquired a list of 64 German refugees allegedly under the "protection" of the Nazi Gauleiter, Dr. Diehl, of whom at least 30 percent were Jews seeking to enter France. According to the prefect of the Bas-Rhin, "This confirms that many of the so-called German refugees remain in the service of their country and that their installation in France, especially in the border departments, constitutes a real danger to national defense."[8] The minister of the interior also rejected the request of the chief rabbi of France, Isaïe Schwartz, to permit 200 elderly German Jews to be settled in Alsace after Kristallnacht, claiming that these refugees threatened national security since there were already too many Germans in the border provinces.[9]

Despite these efforts, the decree laws failed to achieve their goals of preventing refugees from entering the country and forcing those there illegally to leave. All too often, the laws had precisely the opposite effect. Because of France's geography, it was nearly impossible to seal the borders, no matter how many police Sarraut stationed there. The Gestapo persisted in dumping refugees across the border, notwithstanding Bonnet's protests to the German Foreign Office, and this practice rarely met resistance on the French side. As one JDC report of July 1939 noted, the German police guided the refugees to the French border at night and then waited until "the guards change or when by some trickery the guards are induced to leave that part of the border without leaving any watch to replace them." Other refugees, this report continued, "have been put on busses or taxis, and as harmless travelers are put over the borders."[10]

At the same time, many border police simply looked the other way. Some acted out of venality, as was the case of Inspector Augustin Francal, who was charged with having extorted huge bribes, and perhaps even sexual favors, from refugees fleeing Italy in exchange for smuggling them across the border.[11] But others were motivated by humanitarian concerns. As the JDC again noted, "Even if the police . . . saw some of these illegal entrants, they were so moved by their plight that they did not obey the orders of their superiors to send these people back, and brought them instead to the nearest Jewish refugee committee."[12] Raymond-Raoul Lambert, secretary-general of the Comité d'Assistance aux Réfugiés (CAR), declared: "We know the frontier through which they come in, and the French authorities know it as well; even the Gestapo know. The French turn back one person as a formality, and then let the others in."[13] No matter how harsh the decree laws, the fact was that most Central European refugees were not about to be deterred. As one commentator explained, they "know our prisons are preferable to Hitlerian concentration camps."[14]

Moreover, once the refugees entered France illegally, the decree laws failed to achieve their second major goal—forcing the refugees to leave. Quite simply, there was nowhere for them to go. Expulsion was becoming increasingly difficult due to the tough immigration policies of France's neighbors as well as the growing reluctance of Latin American countries to accept Jewish newcomers, despite Sarraut's attempt to threaten them with diplomatic sanctions if they did not open their doors.[15] So too the U.S. consulate in Paris was one of the most restrictive in Europe, and even refugees who had been promised visas were frequently put off indefinitely, to the consternation of French refugee committees.[16] As a result, France found itself saddled with an ever swelling population of clandestine immigrants. By the end of 1938, it was estimated that as many as 42,000 of the almost 60,000 Central and Eastern European Jewish refugees in France were illegal.[17] Among recently arrived refugees, the proportion of "illegals" was even higher, with the CAR reporting that 90 percent of all the refugees registered between July and November of 1938, mostly Austrians, had entered the country clandestinely.[18]

Since the government had not yet established detention centers for refugees who were arrested but could not be expelled, these refugees continued to be sent to jail. On January 25, the minister of justice reported to Parliament that as many as 8,405 refugees had been imprisoned for some infraction of the decree laws since the decree law of May 2nd had gone into effect, at a cost to taxpayers of 1,770,954 francs ($632,500).[19] At the same time, the administrative machinery for dealing with refugee matters was unable to cope with this deluge. Refugees trying to regularize their legal status or obtain an extension of the standard two-week residence permit had to queue up for days at the Prefecture of Police in Paris,[20] and, as the Gourevitch Committee noted, "The life of police employees has become an inferno, in view of the fact that each one of them has to talk to several hundred people daily, and examine their cases."[21] Judges too were overwhelmed, sometimes hearing up to 60 cases per day.[22] But what most overloaded the system was the fact that the refugees, once released from prison, were forced to return to an underground existence since they had no means of regularizing their legal status.[23] They were therefore trapped in what critics of the decree laws referred to as an "infernal cycle"[24] in which repeat offenders were "steered to the border, where they were shoved back by the neighboring country; [and] again imprisoned."[25]

Ironically, by sentencing the refugees to a life of perpetual criminality, the government diminished their chances of departing, since individuals with criminal records generally became ineligible for entry visas to other countries.[26] This policy often had absurd consequences, such as the case of a certain H. Kann, who received a prison sentence for not having complied with an expulsion order, despite the fact that he had applied for a visa to no fewer than 42 foreign consulates.[27] Thus, as one journalist noted, the decree laws had the paradoxical result of ensuring that "these unfortunates condemned by us are forced to stay here. The punishments they are hit with will become increasingly severe, and their prison stays longer and longer."[28]

Refugees seeking an escape from this "infernal" cycle had only two options: suicide,[29] or resorting to the burgeoning network of false passport and visa operations, an option that ultimately involved the refugees in even more compromising criminal activities. These operations, nearly always run by other foreigners, frequently worked in tandem with corrupt Latin American consulates and extorted huge sums of money from desperate refugees for documents that usually turned out to be invalid.[30] Some refugees resorted to even more serious crimes. A particularly sensational incident occurred in the spring of 1939, when one refugee brutally murdered another for refusing to lend him money to get his mistress out of prison, where she was serving time for some infraction of the decree laws.[31]

And finally, the decree laws failed because growing numbers of law enforcement officials began to balk at having to enforce measures they considered unjust. Border police, as we have seen, frequently looked the other way, and in one instance a police chief requested a transfer, claiming that he could no longer bear to watch refugees being turned away at his border station.[32] Even the prefect of the Haut-Rhin, who had never evinced much sympathy for Jewish refugees, finally yielded to pressure from the Mulhouse Jewish refugee committee in March to stop shoving refugees into Switzerland. The Swiss government had recently declared that all illegal refugees who could not be returned to France would be sent back to Germany, a practice even this die-hard official found difficult to stomach.[33] Similarly, the Paris police, while continuing to arrest refugees involved in the trafficking of false papers, nevertheless conceded that the refugees could scarcely be blamed "for accepting the services of these rotten intermediaries since through them alone can they count on the possibility of a future, a life. . . . These shady agents succeed precisely where . . . international conferences have run aground."[34] On the French Riviera too, according to Rabbi Maurice Liber, refugees arriving from Italy "unanimously recognize the gendarmes, mobile guards, and mountain rangers who have detained them on this side of the border to be kindhearted, compassionate, understanding, and charitable men."[35]

Judges expressed even greater frustration, and in particular they complained of not being allowed to take extenuating circumstances into account in the sentencing of refugees for violations of the decree laws. According to the Gourevitch Committee, the president of a criminal court resigned in protest after he was forced to sentence a 72-year-old German professor to prison for some minor infraction of the decree law.[36] A judge in Compiègne similarly pleaded with the government to allow judges to take extenuating circumstances into account, claiming that "it is not only in the Gospel that one needs to know how to separate the wheat from the chaff."[37] In another case, when a court sentenced the renowned German Jewish lawyer Erich Frey to prison for having failed to comply with an expulsion order, despite the fact that Frey had applied to no fewer than 11 consulates for a visa, the magistrates reportedly hung their heads in shame.[38] And in Nice, where thousands of refugees from Italy were being smuggled across the border, judges regularly refused to send these people to jail as long as the Jewish refugee committee would guarantee their financial support.[39]

While the growing incidence of refugee criminality invited charges by the right-wing press, and even centrist papers such as *L'Oeuvre*, that France was being "invaded" by "the international underworld," it had the opposite effect on a broad spectrum of public opinion.[40] Many in France were beginning to realize that the vast majority of refugees had been transformed into common criminals solely as a result of the decree laws. As one French Jewish lawyer pointed out, the "sole crime" these foreigners had committed was to have "been considered adversaries of totalitarian regimes in their respective countries."[41] Furthermore, the critics of the decree laws charged, by cracking down on all refugees without exception, France was sliding into the camp of the victimizers. As the Gourevitch Committee stated, "Those who are persecuted in Germany drink the bitter cup of exile to the dregs and the democratic state adds to the persecution inflicted by the totalitarian government."[42] One liberal journalist went so far as to charge the decree laws with having introduced Hitlerian racism into France.[43]

To be sure, these critics agreed with the administration that France could not permanently absorb another large-scale influx of refugees. Addressing the annual convention of the International League Against Antisemitism (LICA) just after Kristallnacht, Léon Blum himself proclaimed, "Naturally, these unfortunates cannot stay here forever, that's understood. Naturally, it will be necessary to find stable and durable solutions." Nevertheless, Blum insisted, the government, together with the French Jewish community, had an obligation to provide these refugees with "asylum for one night"—until they could find more permanent homes elsewhere.[44] *Le Populaire* reiterated this theme several months later when two Central European Jews attempted suicide after being denied residence permits: "Sad, very sad, is the situation of these refugees who ask only to live honestly under a more clement sky than that which exists in their own country. Do we have the right to refuse them?"[45]

Inspired by this moral outrage, a broad-based coalition of groups, led by the Socialist Party; the Centre de Liaison pour le Droit d'Asile, which included the League for the Rights of Man and Citizen and the Confédération Générale du Travail (CGT); the Association des Amis de la République Française, a newly formed organization seeking to improve relations between foreigners and French citizens;[46] the Gourevitch Committee; and the CAR, which unlike its predecessor, the Comité National, was willing to challenge the government head-on, orchestrated a campaign to reform the decree laws and to reinstate the more liberal refugee policies of the Popular Front. Their demands included the implementation of articles 10 and 11 of the May 2, 1938, decree law so that authentic refugees might be considered for asylum; the reconstitution of the Consultative Commission to weed out the "desirable" from the "undesirable" refugees; the creation of special transit camps to provide refugees waiting to emigrate elsewhere with vocational training in agriculture and artisanry; the granting of a general amnesty to refugees already in France; a provision allowing judges to take extenuating circumstances into account in sentencing refugees; and automatic extensions of residence permits and identity cards as well as the creation of a special travel certificate so that refugees could move about freely.[47] A revival of these Popular Front initiatives made sense not only on humanitarian grounds but on practical ones as well. As the conservative deputy Louis Rollin argued in a much publicized petition to the government, throwing Jewish refugees into jail was not only inhumane but counterproductive, especially since the CAR had agreed to support refugees willing to go to the proposed transit camps.[48]

By the end of 1938, this campaign began to score some successes. In mid-December, the government, apparently embarrassed by international criticism of its harsh refugee policies in the wake of Kristallnacht, agreed to a request from the Alliance Israélite Universelle (AIU) to accept 250 refugee children under the age of 15, and it promised that 1,000 refugee children would eventually be accepted on condition that they not go to Paris but instead settle in children's homes in the provinces.[49] Moreover, although the chief rabbi of France, Isaïe Schwartz, and Louise Weiss, a prominent journalist and feminist leader who was emerging as a key spokesperson on refugee matters,[50] failed to persuade the administration to allow refugees over the age of 60 to enter France freely, they did convince the government in early 1939 to permit a contingent of elderly Jews just expelled from old-age homes in the Palatinate to resettle in Lunéville and Nancy.[51]

Most important, at the end of December, Louise Weiss persuaded Bonnet to create a government-sponsored refugee committee devoted specifically to Central Europeans, the Comité Central des Réfugiés, subsequently referred to as the Bonnet Committee because Bonnet served as president.[52] As to the foreign minister's motives for creating this committee, there is little doubt that they were self-serving. Although Bonnet claimed in his post-war memoirs that he had acted out of humanitarian concerns—to assist Jewish refugees victimized during Kristallnacht[53]—internal Foreign Ministry memoranda suggest that his real goal was to deflect mounting American and British criticism of France's harsh refugee policies. In a speech of January 14, 1939, in which he publicly announced the creation of the new committee, Bonnet grossly inflated the number of refugees in France. Although Jewish organizations estimated the number of the Central European refugees at between 40,000 and 60,000, a figure Bonnet himself had cited to the Foreign Affairs Commission of the Chamber of Deputies on December 14, he now claimed that France had absorbed 200,000 of them since 1933, half of whom had arrived in recent months.[54] He furthermore claimed that France had already done more than its share and could not accept a "new appreciable contingent of immigrants." Thus, just as Bonnet was announcing the new refugee initiative, he felt compelled to reiterate the restrictionist refrain: "We cannot . . . through overly massive admissions [of refugees] into France, condemn to misery and degradation that social category of our own compatriots whose conditions of existence have already been seriously compromised by the abuses of an insufficiently controlled immigration."[55]

Yet Bonnet sorely underestimated the willpower and initiative of the secretary-general of the new committee, Louise Weiss. Weiss was determined not to serve as Bonnet's lackey, and she and her coworkers labored indefatigably to overturn the government's existing refugee policy. As she declared in an interview with the *Univers israélite* in December 1938, the committee had four principal goals: to coordinate the work of the diverse private refugee committees and to serve as a liaison between them and the government; to find employment for refugees and to press the government to relax restrictions against the creation of foreign-owned enterprises, especially those that promised to create jobs for French workers; to acquire collective visas for refugee children; and, most important, to secure an amnesty from the decree laws for Central European refugees already in France. In a show of independence from the administration, Weiss sharply condemned the current practice of sending refugees to prison solely because they had "fled with insufficient passports and visas from countries where their existence entailed the danger of death."[56]

Weiss's efforts, however, would never have made headway had there not been compelling pragmatic reasons for reforming the decree laws and perhaps abolishing them altogether. As Europe edged closer to war, growing numbers of politicians and publicists were beginning to insist that France's low birthrate necessitated a more sane immigration policy, one that would boost the size of the nation's population, particularly in the depopulated countryside, and allow foreigners, including the refugees, to serve in the armed forces. These considerations, together with the apparent failure of the decree laws, ultimately persuaded the government to revive the agricultural and, to a lesser extent, colonial settlement schemes for Central and East European refugees that had been dismissed when Daladier came to power in 1938. They also paved the way for new legislation facilitating the enlistment of foreigners in the army, eliminating some of the restrictions on foreigners seeking to create new businesses and industries, and rationalizing naturalization procedures. Taken collectively, these reforms seemed to augur a return to the more liberal refugee policies of the Popular Front. As advocates for these reforms argued, it was "a political and economic absurdity" for France to ignore the military and economic benefits its large immigrant population had to offer.[57]

The first sign of this policy shift was the revival of the Serre Plan at the end of 1938. This plan, put forth by Chautemps's newly appointed undersecretary of state for immigration in late 1937 and early 1938, had called for the creation of agricultural settlements for thousands of East European Jewish refugees who had arrived illegally in 1936 and 1937.[58] Yet precisely because it offered a constructive solution to the refugee problem, one that would have allowed a portion of the refugees to remain, the Daladier administration had rejected it, eliminating Serre's office altogether. The Daladier administration instead opted for a hard-line approach to rid the country of the refugees altogether. By the year's end, however, as the failure of the decree laws was becoming apparent, the alternative approaches devised by the Popular Front began to regain some luster.

Economic considerations also encouraged renewed interest in Serre's proposal. Local administrators, especially in the underpopulated areas of southern France, were demanding immigrant labor for agricultural needs, and in 1939 their claims attracted considerable attention with the publication of a comprehensive survey by Albert Demangeon and Georges Mauco on the role of immigrant labor in French agriculture. According to this study, French agriculture could not survive without a continued influx of foreign labor. The authors furthermore insisted that there was nothing wrong with this dependence as long as these immigrants were rapidly assimilated. Indeed, in light of the country's low birthrate, Demangeon and Mauco insisted that the government was morally obliged to encourage immigration, since it alone offered a cure, at least in the short term, for the nation's ongoing demographic problem.[59]

Despite Mauco's involvement with the Serre Plan, this survey made no mention of using Jewish refugees in this capacity. Nevertheless, several local officials, a number of journalists, and for the first time the native Jewish community seized on this idea as a way out of the perennial obstacle to any liberalization of refugee policy—the charge that these urban and middle-class refugees constituted a competitive work force. As Serre himself had argued, if foreign Jews could be transformed from a "competitive" work force into a "complementary" one, composed of manual and agricultural laborers, this dilemma might yet be resolved.

Thus, in the wake of Kristallnacht, the idea of creating agricultural settlements for Jewish refugees in southern France began to garner widespread popular support. To be sure, the extreme right continued to assail any measure that would grant even temporary asylum to the refugees. Jacques Saint-Germain, for example, warned of "a terrible decline of our racial potential" if Jewish immigrants were allowed to buy land and settle in the south.[60] Similarly, when the CAR purchased some property in Burgundy to build an agricultural center for refugees in early 1939, the far-right-wing *Choc* asked whether "our Burgundy was going to become a Zionist colony."[61]

These opinions represented a minority view, however, and the majority of publicists across the political spectrum expressed enthusiastic support for the idea. According to Jeanne Ancelet-Hustache, an influential commentator for the Christian Democratic *L'Aube*, it was ludicrous for large landowners to recruit seasonal migrant laborers every year "while we have so many refugees right here who could well die of hunger." Although Ancelet-Hustache noted that Jewish refugees would need extensive professional retraining, she insisted that the recent example of Palestine proved that urban middle-class Jews could be transformed into farmers.[62] Franz Gravereau, writing in the *Petit Parisien*, similarly proclaimed that Jewish agricultural settlements would "put an end to the anguish of these unfortunates, who have been searching the world over for a hospitable land," while they would "give new life to deserted villages, to houses in ruin, to uncultivated lands."[63] The CGT too hailed the idea. Reiterating the labor movement's long-standing support for agricultural solutions to the refugee problem, Léon Jouhaux declared that such colonies would reconcile three hitherto contradictory goals: safeguarding the welfare of French workers; meeting the needs of the national economy; and providing the refugees with the right to asylum.[64]

At the other end of the political spectrum, Henri de France, the Count of Paris and the claimant to the throne, also endorsed this cause. Refuting his former sponsor, the royalist Action Française, with whom he had broken ranks in 1937, the Count insisted that Jewish refugees could provide "the necessary hands to carry out those specific and urgent tasks for which there are insufficient numbers of French workers."[65] Within the administration itself, individuals such as Marcel Paon, director of the Ministry of Argiculture's labor bureau and a longtime advocate of these schemes, together with the prefects of southwestern provinces, were similarly supportive of the idea.[66] Summing up this emerging consensus, one journalist declared: "Jewish exiles are seeking to work the land, and the land of southwestern France needs hands to care for it."[67]

Aside from these economic benefits, the revival of the Serre Plan offered political and cultural advantages as well. The time, money, and energy spent on policing refugees could now be funneled into more constructive forms of refugee relief.[68] Overcrowded jails could be relieved, and Paris and other major urban centers could be "disgorged" of surplus refugees.[69] The government further hoped that these centers would provide the refugees with agricultural and artisanal skills necessary for their eventual reemigration.[70] Even *Le Temps*, which had previously endorsed the decree laws as the best method of dealing with the refugee problem, now admitted that "the land is . . . the best school for assimilating foreigners and for integrating them into French life." To be sure, the paper affirmed its long-standing belief that "the influx of émigrés from every country and every race risks modifying fundamentally the physiological and psychological organism of our country, of upsetting our traditions, of modifying the image of France." It nevertheless conceded that steering immigrants toward rural areas offered the best means of "dealing with these inconveniences and transforming these sometimes terrifying invasions into a happy influx of new blood."[71]

Several publicists emphasized the salutary effects such a policy would have on Jews themselves. According to the philosemitic Catholic writer Joseph Bonsirven, "Israel will be infinitely less vulnerable when it can thrust down deep and thick roots into the land, the source of stability and morality."[72] The influential Radical journalist Pierre Dominique similarly argued that antisemitism would disappear once these "hypercivilized" Jews, who "too readily partake in our quarrels," were transformed into "peasants, artisans, workers and above all Frenchmen without an excessive taste for politics."[73]

Given that Jewish leadership had now come around to supporting these schemes—a trend we will examine in Chapter 13—the government, in the weeks after Kristallnacht, reopened negotiations with Jewish leaders to draw up a blueprint for implementing this plan. Needless to say, the government's aim here was not the same as the Jewish community's: it envisioned these centers exclusively in terms of preparing refugees to emigrate,[74] whereas Jewish leaders hoped that the vocational retraining would enable some of the refugees to stay. These differences notwithstanding, both sides agreed that in the short-term the creation of provincial centers offered the best way of emptying the prisons of refugees and "relieving congestion in the cities without creating xenophobia and antisemitism in rural areas where it did not previously exist."[75]

In mid-November, the minister of the interior summoned William Oualid, who represented the Comité Central d'Assistance aux Emigrants Juifs as well as the Intercomité des Oeuvres Françaises des Réfugiés (Intercommittee), a recently formed federation of refugee committees, to meet with the director of the Sûreté Nationale, Amédée Bussières, and one of his assistants, Combes. According to Oualid's account, Bussières and Combes began this meeting by reiterating the government's position that France was "saturated" and could serve as a transit country only.[76] To ensure this goal, the minister of the interior planned to erect "reception centers" at the border where incoming refugees would be submitted to a rigorous screening. Those deemed worthy of asylum, which almost certainly meant those already holding visas for other countries, would be sent to the newly created provincial centers in southwestern France, where they would be joined by thousands of refugees "who were to be ejected from Paris and other overly saturated regions."[77] At these "Sheltering and Reeducation Centers," as they were to be called, refugees would receive professional retraining, paid for and coordinated by the Jewish community.

By August, the CAR, with considerable assistance from the JDC, had established five major provincial centers: Martigny-les-Bains in the Vosges, Argenteuil in the Seine, Ste. Radegonde and the Villa Pessicarl in Nice, and a center in the Corrèze.[78] There were several smaller initiatives as well, such as the center of the Jewish scout movement, the Eclaireurs Israélites de France (EIF), near Dijon, the Château de Bures for Sudeten Refugees in the Seine-et-Oise, and the Emil Gumbel Interconfessional Center in Lyons, named after the world-renowned refugee mathematician who had been granted a chair at the University of Lyons.[79] Jewish organizations estimated that it would cost a minimum of 500 francs ($200) per month to maintain a single refugee at one of these centers,[80] and either the Centre Industriel de Rééducation Professionnelle (CIRP) or the ORT was to sponsor the vocational retraining.

Although this effort began slowly—by August, there were only 385 refugees in the five major centers—there were plans to absorb hundreds more in the near future.[81] Moreover, the suburban refugee center in Chelles outside of Paris was expanded considerably: by July it was providing vocational retraining and assistance to some 800 refugees.[82] To induce refugees to come to these centers, the Jewish community announced that refugees willing to move would have priority in receiving assistance.[83] At the same time, the CAR persuaded the government to offer 50 percent reductions in train fares.[84] Most importantly, the Jewish community elicited a promise from Sarraut that refugees in these centers would be granted a complete amnesty from the decree laws.[85]

By the spring of 1939, Jewish organizations were working hand in hand with the government to ensure the success of the initiative. In Paris, Louise Weiss lobbied hard to win the cooperation of high-ranking government officials,[86] and at the Ministry of Agriculture, Paon urged his colleagues to support these ventures.[87] These efforts obviously met with success—in Dijon, local officials regularly recruited agricultural workers from the provincial office of the CAR,[88] and in Nice, the municipal authorities donated a chateau to the Jewish relief committee to be used for refugee accommodations and vocational retraining.[89] To facilitate job placement, the government called for the creation of a detailed census listing each refugee by occupational specialization.[90] So pleased was the administration with these efforts that by the end of the summer it promised to find jobs in metropolitan France for 20 to 25 refugees per month, beginning in November, who had been trained to build motors at the Argenteuil center.[91] Moreover, the refugees sent to the new centers seemed relatively happy with their new status. In the spring, the CAR reported that the refugees at Chelles, "who but a short time ago had the pallor of city dwellers, appear sunburned and healthy, happy and eager in their new work."[92] The *Univers israélite* similarly observed that the refugees at Martigny "once again expected to become architects of their own destiny."[93]

In addition to the agricultural schemes, the administration also revived the Popular Front's colonial initiatives in an effort to find alternatives to the decree laws. Although Mandel had fiercely opposed these schemes in the past, even he began to reconsider his position in light of a variety of domestic and international factors that coalesced in late 1938. First, on the domestic front, the same public outrage that had encouraged the administration to revive a variation of the Serre Plan in the weeks following Kristallnacht stimulated renewed interest in Popular Front colonial initiatives as well. The issue had in fact resurfaced at the time of the Evian Conference. In an editorial in *La République*, the influential Radical Party spokesman Emile Roche reiterated the view that in light of continued high unemployment, metropolitan France was "saturated" and could accept no further immigrants. On the other hand, however, Roche believed it was in the national interest to encourage "an immigration accompanied by capital likely to create employment opportunities, new markets, or new trade possibilities" in French overseas territories, and he called on the government to reconsider this option.[94]

At the time, Roche's argument did not stimulate much debate, but after Kristallnacht it garnered considerable support. In late November, Emile

Buré's influential conservative daily, *L'Ordre*, called on the government to follow the British lead in seeking a colonial solution to the refugee problem. "In Madagascar," the paper noted, "a significant number of Jewish households could be settled who would soon rediscover the joy of living through work and love of a new country."[95] In early 1939, Y. Grosrichard, a journalist for *L'Oeuvre*, similarly wondered whether positions might not be found in certain French colonies "for engineers, for doctors, instead of turning them into useless, uprooted souls."[96] Not everyone was so enthusiastic, of course. *L'Action française* reiterated its view that "it would be inadmissable to deliver up merchants, French colonists as well as natives of Indochina or Madagascar, to the claws of German Jewish usurers."[97] But such views held little sway, and the public on the whole seemed eager to reexamine these options in an effort to reconcile humanitarian impulses with perceived national interests.

International factors too sparked fresh consideration of these schemes. In the immediate aftermath of the Evian Conference, the Roosevelt administration—through the new mechanisms of the IGCR and the President's Advisory Committee on Political Refugees (PAC),* as well as the State Department itself—pressed both Britain and France to reexamine colonial settlement plans. Roosevelt had in fact wanted the colonial question raised at Evian, and in June 1938, the State Department sent a representative from the embassy in Paris to discuss with Foreign Ministry officials the possibility of settling refugees in Madagascar.[98] Ultimately, however, the United States caved in to British and French demands that the colonial question not be raised at the conference; to do so, the Europeans had argued, would only have encouraged East European countries to expel their Jews.[99] After Evian, however, Roosevelt refused to let the issue drop. Already in September, Myron C. Taylor, the U.S. representative to the IGCR, recommended that France settle 30,000 Central European refugees in its colonies over the next five years. It would be up to the French government, Taylor suggested, to provide the land, while Jewish organizations would cover the costs of emigration and vocational retraining.[100] Furthermore, from mid-October on, Assistant Secretary of State Sumner Welles repeatedly told Saint-Quentin, France's ambassador in Washington, that the United States was still interested in Popular Front colonial initiatives, especially the Madagascar Plan.[101]

In the weeks following Kristallnacht, the United States stepped up this

*The PAC was a quasi-governmental committee created by Roosevelt in 1938 to help devise new refugee policies. Its chairman was James G. McDonald, the former HCR high commissioner, and its executive secretary was George L. Warren. On the PAC's activities, see Wyman, *Paper Walls*, pp. 47–48, 138–39, 142–48, 199–201; and Wyman, *Abandonment*, pp. 133–34, 198, 263, 315.

pressure significantly, and given widespread public support in Europe for a new international refugee initiative, it finally succeeded in wrenching several concessions from its European allies. When Chamberlain denounced the German atrocities of Kristallnacht before the House of Commons on November 21, he promised that Britain would seriously examine the possibility of colonial solutions.[102] At the same time, Welles elicited a pledge from Bonnet and Daladier "to conduct a study without delay of the possibilities of settling a certain number of Jewish refugees in French colonies."[103] Privately, Daladier even informed Welles that France was now prepared to accept 40,000 Jewish refugees in Madagascar.[104] Furthermore, when British leaders, acting in concert with the Americans, raised this issue during the Anglo-French talks on November 24, Bonnet himself assured them that France intended to absorb a certain number of Jewish refugees in its colonies on condition that the United States and Britain accept similar numbers of refugees.[105]

Foreign policy considerations relating to France's East European allies, especially Poland, also stimulated renewed interest in the Madagascar Plan. After the Munich crisis, the Germans made a concerted effort to woo Poland away from its Western allies, and one of their strategies was to promise the Poles a share of the colonial spoils they expected to wrest from the West. On October 25, 1938, Josef Lipski, Poland's ambassador to Germany, informed Colonel Josef Beck that Germany was prepared to work together with the Poles "in questions having to do with colonies and Jewish emigration in Poland."[106] Soon afterward, on November 9, Hitler informed Göring, without having broached the subject with the French, that he had decided "to throw the ball back into the court of those powers that have raised the Jewish problem, with the aim of really settling the question of Madagascar." On January 5, Hitler himself told Beck: "If the western powers were to show greater comprehension for German demands relating to the colonies, I would perhaps assign a territory in Africa to serve not only for the settlement of German Jews, but for that of Polish Jews as well."[107]

Seeking to retain the Polish alliance, the French ambassador there, Léon Noël, previously a staunch opponent of the Madagascar Plan, began to reconsider. In early 1939, Noël alerted the Foreign Ministry that Polish public opinion was unanimous in believing that the "Jewish Problem" could be solved only through mass emigration,[108] and for the first time he conceded that the official Polish position on this issue "seemed reasonable enough" since "the Jewish question could only get worse." If Jewish emigration were prevented, Noël argued, antisemitism would fester and Poland would become fertile turf for German propaganda. Besides, if France were to help Poland resolve this issue, France itself could deter an influx "of miserable and unassimilable elements whose settlement on our soil must irrefutably be avoided."[109] Noël therefore recommended that France undertake some diplomatic initiative to help the Poles get rid of their Jews. While his first suggestion was that France exert greater pressure on Latin American countries to open their doors, he also suggested that the government consider granting Poland a colonial concession, possibly Madagascar.[110]

In light of these domestic and international factors, the government decided to give the colonial option a second chance. At the IGCR meeting in London on December 2, 1938, Bérenger made his dramatic announcement that France would accept 10,000 Jewish refugees in French colonies on condition that the United States and Great Britain absorb similar numbers of refugees. This concession, as we have seen, was limited to non-German refugees in an attempt to appease Mandel's fifth-column fears. In return, however, Bérenger promised that 10,000 German refugees currently being held in French jails would be allowed to remain in metropolitan France.[111] Other destinations were also under consideration. Throughout the fall of 1938, Mandel's staff met on several occasions with private promoters of Jewish colonization schemes, as well as with George Warren, executive secretary of the PAC, and American representatives of the IGCR, to discuss the possibility of sending Jews to French Guiana,[112] an option urged by the French shipping line which was hoping to recoup some recent losses on its South American routes.[113] These negotiations ultimately proved successful: on Christmas day 1938, Warren reported that Mandel had agreed to allow Central European refugees to immigrate to French Guiana but that for political reasons Mandel deemed it wise not to stress the Jewish nature of this migration.[114]

As a result of this shift in policy, the Jewish community, which was now prepared to lend support to these schemes as well, began to organize a small-scale Jewish immigration to French Guiana in January 1939.[115] The Ministry of Colonies would provide the land, and the Intercommittee, with some JDC support, was to cover all expenses relating to emigration and vocational retraining.[116] The actual blueprint for settlement was provided by the maverick Jewish nationalist Henry (Kadmi) Kohen, who had written a detailed pamphlet on the subject several months earlier.[117] On January 31, a mass rally was held in Paris to win support for this project,[118] and on February 10 the first contingent of ten refugees departed for South America, including several engineers and doctors from the Austrian refugee colony at Chelles. Twenty more refugees were scheduled to depart in March and April.[119]

By the spring, other projects were also under way. In February, Mandel signaled to the French minister in Bucharest, who had recently complained of being "besieged by letters" from Jews wanting to settle in French colonies, that the ministry was now prepared to consider a limited migration of Romanian or Hungarian Jews to French colonies on condition that they be economically self-sufficient.[120] In March, Mandel promised Louise Weiss that 100 Jewish families were to be settled as farmers in Madagascar,[121] and he similarly promised Wenzel Jaksch, the head of the Czech Social Democratic Party, that several hundred Sudeten refugees would be allowed to go to New Caledonia and Madagascar on condition that they possess 10,000 francs ($4,000) apiece.[122] In late May, the Intercommittee called on all refugees in France to register with a view to possible settlement in French Guiana, New Caledonia, and Madagascar,[123] and by the summer technical missions were on site to assist with refugee settlement.[124] In mid-July, a major new initiative was announced when deputy François de Tessan revealed at an ORT reception that he had just been informed by Bonnet and Mandel that 25,000 to 40,000 refugees were about to be sent to Madagascar and New Caledonia.[125] To be sure, there were some minor setbacks, such as the return of three Austrian refugees from Guiana in the summer of 1939. These refugees were not only disillusioned by the harsh conditions, but according to *Je suis partout*, they claimed to have been swindled by the group's Hungarian leader.[126] Nevertheless, the prevailing sentiment remained optimistic, and by the end of the summer, neither the government nor the Jewish community envisioned any insurmountable obstacles.

As these agricultural and colonial schemes were getting under way, military exigencies too encouraged a more liberal refugee policy. As pro-refugee forces had long argued, the availability of a large pool of foreigners could significantly boost the army's manpower, and the economic skills of the refugees could help the country gear up for war. According to Pierre Dominique, the chief promoter of this campaign, "if 300,000 soldiers could be salvaged" from the country's three million foreigners, "we need to salvage them, and quickly."[127] For Dominique, it was "a matter of life and death" that all male immigrants of military age be inducted into the armed forces immediately for the standard two-year term of service, with the exception of the Spanish refugees, whom he considered dangerous anarchists and communists. He furthermore advised that foreigners who had already completed military service in another country be required to serve in the reserves. In return, Dominique called on the government to grant these foreigners immediate naturalization and full civil and political liberties. At the same time, he recommended that foreigners who refused to serve be ordered to leave. Or, if expulsion proved impossible "for fear of being sent before a firing squad," they were to be sent to concentration camps in France and set to work on public works projects. To emphasize the link between military prowess and demographic vitality, Dominique presciently predicted that if the French refused to remedy their "demographic decadence," and especially the shortage of manpower in their army, they were soon likely to find themselves living under German rule.[128]

Dominique's campaign ultimately bore fruit and resulted in new legislation expanding the obligations of foreigners serving in the French army. Already in January, the conservative deputies Henri Pichon and Jean Goy had appealed to the prime minister in the name of the Union Nationale des Officiers Anciens Combattants, the French veterans' association, to integrate France's three million foreigners into the armed forces.[129] On February 24, these deputies submitted a resolution to the Chamber of Deputies

requiring foreigners who live on our soil to reinforce our military power and to participate in the execution of our national defense obligations. It is just to request foreigners, who live off our resources and benefit from our well-being, to participate in the same capacity as Frenchmen. This measure could be quite useful considering that the number of foreigners eligible for mobilization could reach about one million and could thus noticeably augment our military power.[130]

This resolution further recommended, in accordance with Dominique's views, that foreigners who refused to serve be sent to concentration camps.

In response to these pressures, and with the support of the army chief of staff, the Cabinet issued a decree law on April 12, 1939, that greatly expanded the obligations of foreigners with regard to military service. Although Nansen refugees had been subjected to the same military obligations as other Frenchmen in 1937,[131] the April 12, 1939, decree was the first measure that affected the military status of all foreigners in France. According to this decree, foreigners between 18 and 40 years of age who had been in France more than two months were now allowed to contract an engagement in the French army during peacetime, whereas previously they had been allowed to serve only in the Foreign Legion. Moreover, all stateless foreigners as well as those enjoying the right of asylum (in other words, Nansen refugees together with the German beneficiaries of the July 4, 1936, Geneva Accord) between 20 and 48 years of age were subjected to the same duties as other Frenchmen in wartime—that is, a two-year term of service—while in peacetime they were required to furnish two years of *prestation*, or civilian, service related to national defense.[132] Two additional decree laws, of July 20 and 22, mandated that all foreigners covered by the April 12 decree who had not yet registered for military service do so immediately, and it implemented a general census of foreigners to ensure proper registration.[133] Although no mention was made of the rights foreigners would receive in return, it was widely expected that swifter naturalization would be the reward.

Public opinion on both the left and the right generally applauded these new measures. Although a few isolated voices on the extreme right criticized these laws, claiming that the majority of foreigners were communists "ready, in the event of war, to take the place of mobilized nationals and . . . to provoke trouble on the homefront," their views had little currency.[134] Even *L'Action française*, while it opposed the induction of foreigners into the armed forces, was nevertheless willing to countenance the creation of special foreign battalions within the Foreign Legion to be sent to North Africa to work on military-related projects.[135] Mainstream opinion was considerably more enthusiastic and concurred with conservative daily *Le Matin* that "whoever requests asylum in France must sign up to serve to the extent of his capacities and means."[136] According to the socialist *Le Populaire*, the decree law would "contribute to easing the atmosphere created in France at the time of the events of last September, when the spirit of xenophobia began to make itself felt among certain stratum of the population." Most significantly, *Le Populaire* hailed these decrees as a sign that "our leaders have begun to understand that the foreigners here are a necessary and even indispensable element."[137]

Jewish organizations were especially enthusiastic and perceived these decrees as signaling a major shift in policy toward refugees. In its December newsletter, the Centre de Documentation et de Vigilance (CDV), the Consistorial-based self-defense organization, had lavishly praised Dominique's program, and in February it argued that the massive enlistment of foreigners at the time of the Munich mobilization, including some 15,000 Jews, had demonstrated that they were "ready to defend, weapons in hand, the country many of them considered their new *patrie*."[138] Lambert expressed similar excitement, proclaiming: "One cannot be too pleased about these dispositions. To be sure, this is not yet the long awaited statute of refugees. It is, however, proof that the efforts of qualified organizations have not been in vain and that the government has decided to resolve this most delicate of problems."[139]

Even the more skeptical immigrant periodical *Samedi* applauded these measures. While conceding the "brutality" of Dominique's recommendation to intern or expel foreigners who refused to serve, *Samedi* nevertheless acknowledged that his program "conforms to French national interests . . . and . . . to the interests of the great majority of foreigners." At the same time, however, *Samedi* reminded the government that obligatory military service for foreigners was acceptable only if accompanied by complete equality of rights. If justly implemented, *Samedi* declared, this legislation would entail the full integration of foreigners and an end to all discriminatory legislation, including the regime of work cards, identity cards, and residence permits, as well as the restrictive quotas on foreigners in a various professions.[140]

Military exigencies were also reflected in a decree law of April 21 governing the economic status of foreigners in France: "The Decree to Favor the Establishment in France of Industries of National Interest." Sponsored by the minister of commerce, Fernand Gentin, this decree was the fruit of the persistent lobbying of Louise Weiss and the Bonnet Committee. As Weiss and her colleagues never tired of pointing out, Holland and Great Britain, despite restrictive immigration policies, had succeeded in attracting refugees with valuable economic and technical skills, to the detriment of France. To achieve this end, Britain had accorded these foreigners a host of privileges, including swifter processing of applications for residence permits, five-year irrevocable residence permits, the promise of naturalization after five years, two-year commercial tax exemptions, rent-free factories in certain industrial regions, long-term credit at low interest, and three-year residence permits for industrial foremen on condition that their number not surpass 10 percent of the number of British workers hired. As an additional incentive, foreigners considered capitalists were given £5,000 ($1,050) in government start-up funds, and special grants were made available to "every foreigner who consents to form a partnership with a British citizen in order to establish a productive industry in some depressed part of the country." As a result of these policies, it was estimated that Britain had significantly reduced her dependence on imports, had created some 45,000 jobs for British workers, and had siphoned off some 60 percent of the most productive elements among the Austrian refugee population.[141]

Although France had hitherto ignored these potential advantages out of deference to native business interests, Weiss's vigorous lobbying, together with the looming threat of war, finally convinced Gentin that France needed similar legislation. As the preamble to this decree stated:

The present circumstances have impressed upon us an imperious duty to utilize all forces that could be a factor for progress or useful elements of prosperity.

Our economic system, based upon the principle of freedom of trade and industry, recognizes the right of anyone, French or not, to create an industry. By contrast, current regulations governing the right of foreigners to reside in France subjects the initiatives of foreign industrialists to constraints incompatible with the confidence and stability that the creation of all new enterprises requires.

For this reason, we first of all want to make known the desire of France to facilitate the establishment on its soil of industries likely to increase in times of peace its power for expansion, and in times of war its capacity for resistance.[142]

The government was especially eager to attract foreigners who might contribute to the armaments industry—technicians, chemists, and engineers.[143] Administrative procedures for granting residence permits to "economically useful" immigrants were to be simplified, and to achieve this end a special interministerial committee was to be created composed of six members—three from the Ministry of Commerce and one apiece from the Ministries of the Interior, Labor, and Foreign Affairs—to screen the dossiers of foreign entrepreneurs interested in settling in France. Furthermore, in a gesture that augured well for the pro-refugee cause, Gentin invited the Bonnet Committee to participate in the screening process in an advisory capacity.[144]

To be sure, this measure still fell short of current British legislation. According to article 1 of the decree, all foreigners eligible for residence under these new conditions were still subject to the gamut of legislation governing the status of foreigners in France, including the requirement that they obtain a special merchant's card, as stipulated by the decree laws of June 17 and November 12, 1938. Nor was any mention made of swifter naturalization procedures. Most significantly, the decree law included a major concession to native business interests. After alluding to the maze of bureaucratic obstacles currently facing foreign entrepreneurs in France, the preamble of the decree law went on to state that new foreign-owned enterprises would be authorized only if they "provide guarantees to already established enterprises that they will not be the object of new and unjustifiable competition on the domestic market." Once again, the Chambers of Commerce were to be brought into the screening process, evoking the prospect that the majority of applicants would be rejected.

Still, pro-refugee advocates applauded this measure as a step in the right direction. According to R. de Saint-Pourçain, a contributor to *Esprit*'s special July issue on immigration, Gentin deserved praise for rising above sectarian interests and for creating a single interministerial committee to deal with immigration issues.[145] The German émigré paper the *Pariser Tageszeitung* similarly hailed this decree as an important step toward ending the bureaucratic runaround as well as the constant threat of *refoulement* and expulsion that plagued the refugee community.[146]

The government also began to tackle the thorniest of all problems related to immigration—naturalization policy—upon which all other policies ultimately depended. Given the low birthrate as well as the decreasing population in many parts of the country, government circles were increasingly receptive to the views of Mauco, Dominique, and others that a more rational immigration policy was imperative to strengthen the nation for war. Thus in late February 1939, the administration created a High Committee on Population, under the direction of the minister of justice, Paul Marchandeau. This committee was to develop a selective immigration policy that would centralize the naturalization process in the hands of a single administrative body under the auspices of the Ministry of Justice. According to a preliminary plan put forth in early March, the new committee would take periodic censuses of the entire French population, paying particular attention to the ethnic and professional makeup of each region. After assessing these regional needs, the committee would steer new immigrants to areas in need of workers with particular professional skills. From now on, French consulates would grant visas only with these regional requirements in mind. Foreigners who received visas would enter the country at specific border crossings where special commissions would be set up to verify their visas, grant them identity cards, and direct them to assigned residences in their designated departments. After a waiting period of five years, or three in exceptional circumstances, these foreigners could apply for naturalization, but their applications would now have to be approved not only by the Ministry of Justice, but by a regional tribunal as well.[147]

Finally, in yet another move that suggested a significant liberalization of refugee policy, the Bonnet Committee and the CAR, working in conjunction with the JDC and the Jewish emigration society, HICEM, persuaded Sarraut in June to join Belgium, Holland, and Great Britain in accepting a contingent of the 907 refugees stranded on board the Hamburg liner S.S. *Saint-Louis*, which had been wandering the seas for weeks after having been denied the right to disembark in every country, including Cuba, despite the fact that the passengers held Cuban visas.[148] Sarraut's acceptance of the *Saint-Louis* refugees was by no means unconditional. According to a State Department report, "the French refused to accept any Poles at all" since they feared that these stateless refugees would never leave. They furthermore insisted that the majority of refugees they did accept have U.S. visas in hand to ensure their imminent departure from France.[149] Thus, of the 224 refugees granted provisional asylum in France, 162 already possessed U.S. visas, and all the refugees were steered to the various provincial refugee centers.[150]

Later in June, Jewish refugee committees again prevailed upon Sarraut to grant provisional asylum to 96 German and Czech refugees trapped on board the S.S. *Flandre*, "on condition that Jewish organizations be enlisted to take care of them and to facilitate their reemigration."[151] Sarraut's generosity in these instances did not go unnoticed, even by his critics. According to Louise Weiss, Sarraut's "republican credentials had been bolstered," and both she and Lambert praised Sarraut for having refused a JDC offer to provide $500 cash guarantees for each refugee.[152]

These reforms, complemented by several related measures, such as the decree law of April 12, 1939, which increased surveillance over foreign associations in France in order to root out Nazi and fascist propaganda,[153] and the Marchandeau Law of April 21, 1939, which outlawed religious and racial defamation in the press,[154] augured well for the pro-refugee cause and instilled momentum into the campaign to eliminate the decree laws altogether and secure an amnesty for Central European refugees in France. Indeed, it appeared by the late spring of 1939 that the government was poised to make a major concession. Not only had more radical organizations, such as the Gourevitch Committee and the LICA, repeatedly petitioned Daladier and Sarraut to overturn the decree laws and grant asylum to those fleeing religious and racial persecution,[155] but even mainstream native Jewish leaders, such as Lambert and Rothschild, were demanding an end to this regime.[156]

At the same time, nonsectarian groups, such as the Centre de Liaison and the Amis de la République, stepped up their lobbying as well. In May, a delegation from the Centre de Liaison, including the prominent socialist deputy Pierre-Bloch as well as the Centre's director, Henri Levin, met with Sarraut and submitted a memorandum demanding a new statute for foreigners in France in view of the new decree laws mandating military service for foreigners.[157] As Pierre-Bloch declared in *Fraternité*, the CGT paper for immigrant workers, thousands of foreigners were waiting to enlist, but feared coming forth since they were not in compliance with the decree laws.[158] On May 9, the Amis de la République sponsored a rally in Paris that called for an end to the government's anti-immigrant economic policies and an amnesty for "victims of racism." "It's unacceptable," Robert Lange, former vice president of the Radical Socialist Party, declared, "that those who will be called on to defend France, first find asylum in her prisons." The next day, the Amis de la République sent a delegation to meet with Sarraut.[159]

While these delegations were petitioning the government in early 1939, the Bonnet Committee was busy drafting an amnesty proposal. In April, the executive committee, working together with Alexis Léger, secretary-general of the Foreign Ministry, adopted a motion demanding "urgent reform" of the decree laws,[160] and on May 15, the committee sent a delegation—including Louise Weiss; Albert Lévy, director of the CAR; and Isaïe Schwartz, the chief rabbi of France—to petition the minister of justice to overturn the decree laws and grant an amnesty to refugees who had been unjustly arrested so that they could "reconstruct their lives on a dignified and stable foundation . . . in France or elsewhere." Prison, this petition declared, was "neither an equitable nor a humane solution" since it rendered impossible the reemigration of the refugees as well as their ultimate assimilation. The time had therefore come "to show clemency and enact . . . those measures that will save the . . . lives of thousands of innocents and will be consistent with our generous national tradition."[161] In June, the Intercommittee, of which the Bonnet Committee was a member, seconded this proposal and called on the government to extend the amnesty provisions of the September 1936 Presidential Decree to Central European refugees who had arrived after that date.[162]

These appeals ultimately reached the highest levels of government. In the

Chamber of Deputies, the conservative deputies Louis Rollin and Louis Marin, together with the powerful Foreign Affairs Commission of the Chamber of Deputies, implored Sarraut and Marchandeau to implement the amnesty plan.[163] In response to this pressure, Rollin was informed by Léger in March that the Foreign Ministry would do everything possible "to ameliorate, to the extent compatible with our national exigencies, the fate of this category of foreigners whenever they have been regularly admitted to our territory."[164] More significantly, the *Univers israélite* reported in early May that Bonnet himself had "expressed a desire to take charge personally of the effort to consolidate and render infinitely more humane the legislation targeting the refugees." The *Univers israélite* thus expressed the hope that in the near future there would "be a modification of the legislation whose application has revealed itself to be both unjust and contrary to the traditions and interests of the country."[165]

The debate over amnesty came to a head on June 8, when the Parliamentary Commission on Civil and Criminal Legislation introduced an amnesty bill in the Chamber of Deputies. Speaking on behalf of this bill, Charles Valentin, a conservative deputy, condemned the decree laws as "cruel," "merciless," and "inhuman," and called on the minister of justice to allow judges to be able to take extenuating circumstances into account in their sentencing.[166] Most significantly, this proposal called for an amnesty for political and religious refugees who had committed no crimes other than having violated the decree laws. As Marius Moutet, who had helped frame this proposal, declared, "Everyone who frequents the antechambers of the courts knows . . . the revolt of judges in the presence of laws they are mandated to apply without being permitted to proportion their application, laws whose automatic character outrages their conscience and their humanity." Moutet also pointed out the deleterious consequences of imprisoning female refugees, since it had been rumored that frightful abuses were taking place in the women's detention centers. It was therefore time, Moutet insisted, for the government to devise a more humane and rational immigration policy, one that would utilize the talents and skills of Hitler's victims while preventing the infiltration of criminals and spies.

The administration's response to the amnesty bill was fairly conciliatory in light of its previous hard-line stance. Marchandeau, who had been sent to Parliament to represent the administration's point of view, surprisingly agreed with Valentin that the decree laws were excessively severe and did not adequately distinguish "desirable" from "undesirable" foreigners. The minister even went so far as to admit that "there isn't a single member of this Assembly who couldn't cite the case of some particularly respectable foreigner, whose conduct on French soil has been irreproachable, who has been condemned unjustly by virtue of this law."[167] He therefore claimed that he and Sarraut were ready to ensure that "persons of good faith, whose conduct here has been irreproachable" would no longer be subject to "truly shocking prison sentences." And on June 24, the decree law of May 2, 1938, was in fact amended to allow judges to take extenuating circumstances into account.[168]

Contrary to the hopes of pro-refugee advocates, however, Marchandeau refused to go further. As he declared during this debate, granting an amnesty to all refugees who had violated the decree laws would endanger French national security and "leave our country vulnerable to an invasion, which was not at all desirable." While willing to admit that some foreigners had been treated unfairly under the decree laws, Marchandeau insisted that many remained "undesirables" deserving of harsh treatment. Thus, while the government was ready to amend certain aspects of the decree laws, it was not prepared to dispense with them altogether.

This legislative defeat did not mark the end of the amnesty campaign, however. Despite the administration's reluctance to annul the decree laws altogether, subsequent developments show that it was willing to concede, albeit in a behind-the-scenes fashion, nearly all the demands of the pro-refugee campaign, at least insofar as Central European refugees already in France were concerned. On June 29, the minister of the interior convened a meeting between his secretary-general, Jean Berthoin, and the leaders of the Groupement de Coordination, presided over by Robert de Rothschild, aimed at implementing a plan that bore an uncanny resemblance to the Serre Plan. At this meeting, the administration announced that it would offer an amnesty to all German and Central European refugees sponsored by the Groupement on condition that these refugees be sent to the provinces and be provided with vocational retraining in agriculture or artisanry to prepare them for eventual reemigration. As Sarraut noted in a July 16 letter to Rothschild, current emigration possibilities were reserved almost exclusively for farmers and artisans.

Moreover, Sarraut strongly urged the refugee committees to create collective agricultural settlements rather than insist on the placement of individual refugees on existing family farms, as had been their practice previously. Not only were collective settlements more conducive to carrying out the professional retraining efforts, but, Sarraut insisted, they would also prevent refugees from returning to the cities "where there is a tendency for them to become encrusted in a milieu conducive to the exercise of all sorts of business activities for which they continue to feel a natural propensity." If this were to occur, Sarraut claimed, "the result will be an irritation of public opinion that in turn creates a climate ripe for the propagation of xenophobic remarks." Once again, Jewish organizations were expected to pay for this scheme, and Sarraut recommended that the money set aside for the Serre Plan the previous year—presumably the three million francs promised by the JDC—be used to finance this endeavor.[169]

Finally, Sarraut set forth one last condition: that Jewish organizations do everything within their power "to no longer solicit the introduction of new foreigners—except for . . . exceptional cases in which the life of the concerned is in question, *and to reserve possibilities for overseas settlement exclusively* for refugees who are, at this moment, benefiting from our hospitality."[170] Despite the apparent absurdity of such a demand, given that Jewish organizations had no means to prevent refugees from entering the country, it was nevertheless in keeping with previous amnesty plans, such as the Presidential Decree of September 17, 1936, and the Serre Plan, both of which limited their provisions exclusively to refugees already in France.[171]

Although the Groupement's written response to Sarraut's letter is missing from the archival record, subsequent refugee committee reports demonstrate that Jewish organizations accepted the government's plan in full. According to an Intercommittee report from the end of the summer, the pace of both individual and collective settlement efforts in the provinces had been accelerated. As we have seen, there were nearly 400 refugees residing in the centers by the end of the summer, and plans were under way to send more in the near future. Vocational retraining efforts had been intensified as well: 700 refugees had successfully completed ORT programs, and the CIRP had retrained 122 pupils in the Paris region and 91 in the provinces.

Most significantly, the Intercommittee report noted, the government has "agreed to grant the refugees admitted to these centres a privileged regime under the guarantee of the organizations."[172] In return, Jewish organizations did make an effort to prevent further refugees from seeking asylum in France. As Lambert declared at a JDC-sponsored migration conference in Paris in late August, "Due to the international situation, to the ever growing number of attempts to enter the country clandestinely and illegally, we cannot request any new entries into France at the present moment. Jewish organizations have obtained a privileged treatment for refugees already in France on condition that they not intervene on behalf of new entries." To be sure, he noted, the refugee committees "would continue to do our duty and defend the refugees as energetically as possible." But he insisted that from now on they would consider France a "provisional asylum" only.[173]

By the end of the summer, a modus vivendi had therefore been worked out between the refugee committees and the administration. As early as June, the JDC noted a marked improvement in the relations between the CAR and the authorities, commenting that with regard to refugee placement "a more liberal regime [is] coming into effect."[174] At the same time, however, Jewish organizations observed an intensification of the police crackdown against illegal refugees at the border. In late May, the CAR reported that "following the international tension, surveillance at the French borders . . . has been reinforced considerably, and as a result, illegal immigration has become increasingly difficult, if not impossible."[175] In June, the JDC similarly reported that "the police are becoming more severe and recent refugees . . . were [being] arrested."[176] Although initially baffled by this discrepancy,[177] the JDC soon realized that it constituted the cornerstone of the administration's policy. While pro-refugee advocates would certainly have preferred to keep the borders open, they nevertheless realized that Sarraut's amnesty proposal constituted the best deal possible under the circumstances.

Yet even the status of refugees in France remained problematic, notwithstanding the optimistic assessments of the JDC and the refugee committees. Although the Jewish refugee committees had overcome their initial hesitations about the creation of collective refugee settlements in the provinces, it was clear this process would take years. Furthermore, whole categories of refugees remained outside the agreement. Whereas Sarraut's amnesty proposal specifically mentioned German and Central European refugees, the question of the East European immigrants remained undecided, despite strenuous attempts by Lambert to ensure their inclusion.[178]

More importantly, the myriad loopholes that riddled the liberalized immigration laws of the spring prevented these policies from having much effect. On the economic front, the impact of the April 21, 1939, decree aimed at facilitating the establishment of foreign-owned businesses and industries that could strengthen the economy and prepare the nation for war was severely hampered by the virtual veto powers exercised by the xenophobic and protectionist Chambers of Commerce. Even Louise Weiss, despite her pivotal role in the framing of this law, could not persuade Gentin to stand up to these protectionist forces. Writing of her efforts to secure visas for a group of Sudeten Jewish jewelers who hoped to reestablish their businesses in France, Weiss recounts:

Their industry represented an annual turnover of several billions. These remarkable businessmen succeeded in escaping with their order books, their specialized workers, their tools and sufficient funds to invest elsewhere. They proposed to the French government that they settle in the Doubs or the Jura where they would promise to employ a maximum of local workers. From every point of view, their contribution would have signified a fantastic windfall for France. Thanks to them, the Franche-Comté would instantly have supplanted Czechoslovakia as the principal supplier of rosaries and semi-precious necklaces to all the world's believers, to all the world's coquettes. The decision depended upon the Minister of Commerce who first wanted to consult with the Chambers of Commerce and the workers syndicates of Dôle and

Besançon, whose members lived . . . from similar, but artisanal activity. The vipers hissed. The executive power was so weak that it recoiled, and as a result . . . the country thus lost an enormous source of wealth.

Ultimately, these jewelers found asylum in England, leading Weiss to comment bitterly that "the British were not so stupid."[179] This experience was by no means unique. On August 25, the German émigré paper the *Pariser Tageszeitung* pointed out that the decree law of April 21 had scarcely had any impact: nearly all the petitions submitted by foreign merchants and industrialists had been rejected, and only fifteen cases to date had received favorable consideration.[180]

Nor was the government ready to stand up to the medical lobby, which successfully hampered efforts to send refugee doctors to the provinces and colonies, despite a growing consensus that these regions were suffering severe shortages of physicians. As we have seen, Chautemps admitted this shortage during negotiations over the Czech refugees in October 1938. He nevertheless refused to send Czech refugee doctors to rural areas, citing the opposition of the Confédération des Syndicats Médicaux.[181] The administration's deference to the medical establishment is further reflected in its handling of a request from the League of Nations in late 1938 that France, together with several other member states, absorb twelve refugee doctors from the free city of Danzig, which had been governed by the League since the Treaty of Versailles, but whose return to German rule now seemed imminent. Although Britain readily agreed to take three of the doctors, France initially refused to take any, citing "the extremely severe regulations governing the practice of medicine." Nevertheless, a Foreign Ministry official sympathetic to the League's request, citing France's "obligations toward the Jewish population of Danzig" since France had been the chief guarantor of Danzig's free status, recommended that these refugees be sent to Togo or Cameroon, which as mandates were not subject to the legislation regarding foreign doctors. He further recommended that these refugee doctors be employed as medical assistants rather than full-fledged doctors so as to prevent any "inadmissible competition." Yet even this request was satisfied only in part; the Ministry of Colonies ultimately permitted two refugee doctors to go to Cameroon as medical assistants.[182]

Furthermore, to the chagrin of pro-refugee advocates, the government made no effort whatsoever to grant rights to foreigners in exchange for military service. Just days after the April 12 military decree law was announced, *Le Populaire* pointed out that the new decree law stood in flagrant contradiction to two other recent government rulings: the exclusion of foreigners from the right to receive gas masks and their exclusion from civil evacuation plans. Now that foreigners were subject to the same obligations as all other

French citizens, *Le Populaire* argued that they deserved to be granted equality of rights. Pointing out the cruel impact such continued discrimination would have, especially on schoolchildren, the socialist daily declared:

At school, these students will become *métèques*, pariahs. If they are young, they will arrive home in tears, or if they are already old enough to understand, they will be exasperated. . . . What sentiments will they have toward their fatherland?

On the other hand, what attitude will this foster among French children of "pure race," who, upon seeing their young comrades treated this way, will tend to regard them as criminals and people condemned to death![183]

More significantly, despite the fact that 10,000 foreigners had registered for military service within three days after the April 12 decree law went into effect, the promise of swifter naturalization never materialized.[184] In June, the CGT organ *Le Peuple* wondered why foreigners, who were now being required to pay the "blood tax" like other citizens, had not been given the same rights. To correct this inequity, *Le Peuple* called on the government to simplify and speed up the naturalization process.[185]

But in raising the question of naturalization, the CGT had hit on the principal obstacle to further reform. Despite growing support for increased immigration and swifter naturalization for foreigners considered assimilable, especially those willing to serve in the army, certain corporate groups, primarily the Chambers of Commerce and the Confédération des Syndicats Médicaux, were determined to block any liberalization on this front. These corporations not only pressed to halt further naturalizations, but they also demanded a rollback in naturalizations already granted. In late 1938, the Paris Chamber of Commerce, apparently dissatisfied with the decree law of June 17, 1938, passed a resolution calling for even tighter restrictions on the right of foreigners to engage in commerce, including a ban on the creation of new foreign-owned businesses, the imposition of higher taxes on foreign-owned firms, a ban on further naturalizations, and a review of all naturalizations granted during the past ten years.[186] In January 1939, it further called on the government to grant the Chambers of Commerce a decisive veto over the granting of merchants' cards.[187]

Similar campaigns reached fever pitch in Alsace and Lorraine. In November 1938, the Bas-Rhin General Council submitted a proposal to the prefect demanding a thorough review of all naturalizations granted in recent years and the nullification of naturalizations previously granted to "undesirables."[188] In February 1939, the Metz Chamber of Commerce called on the government to make it illegal for naturalized foreigners to frenchify their family names for at least ten years after their naturalization; otherwise, it insisted, "hordes of immigrants" would be free to pursue "unfair competition."[189] This proposal was almost certainly provoked by a recent bill submitted to parliament aimed at speeding up the assimilation of foreigners by requiring "a name change of every naturalized foreigner whenever the name of the naturalized citizen does not sound French."[190]

The Lyons Chamber of Commerce similarly passed a resolution in June that, while recognizing the country's need to increase its population "due to our weak birthrate," nevertheless maintained that too many recent naturalizations had been carried out "without sufficient inquiry." These abusive naturalizations, it insisted, were "especially prejudicial to our country's commerce and industry that suffers as a result of unfair competition." The Lyons Chamber of Commerce therefore followed its Parisian counterpart in demanding veto power not only over the allocation of merchants' cards, but over each and every decision regarding the naturalization of potential competitors.[191]

The Chambers of Commerce were joined in this campaign by the staunchly protectionist Confédération des Syndicats Médicaux. In early 1939, *L'Action française*, which frequently spoke on behalf of the Confederation, published a letter from a certain Dr. Tournay claiming that Jews constituted approximately 80 percent of all recently naturalized doctors and medical students. This fact proved, according to Tournay, that the real problem facing the medical establishment was not that of foreign doctors, but of foreign Jews in particular. Citing a speech he had delivered to the general assembly of the Paris Medical Syndicate on November 30, 1938, Tournay criticized the administration for "having betrayed and defied us" by having refused to confer upon the medical associations a decisive veto over naturalizations. He therefore called for a public boycott of all doctors and medical students who had been "naturalized in spite of the unfavorable opinion of our syndicates."[192]

This same syndicate lambasted the government in the summer of 1939 when it believed that a number of foreign medical students who had passed their *agrégation** in France were about to be permitted to practice. Notwithstanding the fact that the minister of education quickly denied this rumor, this syndicate nevertheless seized on this occasion to demand a complete ban on the conferral of medical diplomas to foreign students. As the syndicate's president, Dr. Boelle, declared, far too many foreigners had been granted the right to practice medicine in France in recent years either because they possessed a diploma in medicine from a recognized foreign university or because "government authorities have pronounced too many abusive naturalizations, without taking into account the opinion of the medical syndicates." Above all, Boelle noted, "a sizable number of doctors,

---

*The *agrégation* is a competitive exam for admission to the teaching staff of public secondary schools or faculties of law, medicine, and pharmacy.

political refugees, abuse our generous hospitality by practicing openly and illegally." To underscore his charge that many of the naturalizations carried out in recent years had been "abusive," Boelle claimed that 78 percent of the 431 doctors and medical students who had requested naturalization during the Popular Front "belong to an ethnic minority of their country of origin and install themselves here in order to find a better life." The time had therefore come for the government to grant the medical syndicates a decisive veto over the naturalizations of doctors and medical students.[193]

Although denounced by left-wing commentators as motivated exclusively by greed,[194] these middle-class protectionist campaigns elicited support from a number of prominent politicians and eventually influenced administrative policy at the highest level. Over the summer of 1938, Emile Béron, a deputy from the Moselle and a longtime advocate of restrictions on foreign merchants, appealed to the Ministry of the Interior to investigate foreign merchants in the region, especially German refugees working as traveling salesmen. Most of them, he claimed, were not refugees at all, but were agents of German firms who used their refugee status to elicit sympathy from prospective clients, thus giving them a competitive edge over native firms. The prefect of the Bas-Rhin firmly denied Béron's charges, claiming that he had already reviewed the credentials of foreign merchants in the region, but the Sûreté Nationale was clearly sympathetic to Béron.[195]

Moreover, as we have seen, another deputy from the Moselle, Robert Schuman, presented an appeal to the Chamber of Deputies in November 1938 protesting the behavior of certain foreigners, including naturalized citizens, during the September mobilization. To correct these abuses, Schuman recommended a revision of all naturalizations granted since 1919, a ban on further naturalizations, and a ban on the practice of commerce in the frontier departments by naturalized citizens not subject to mobilization.[196] Similarly, the prefect of the Moselle, in response to a Ministry of the Interior circular of November 15, 1938, requiring the prefects to assess the economic importance of various categories of foreigners in their departments, recommended that future naturalizations be restricted to foreigners engaged in manual labor, since those in commerce "offer an exaggerated competition to our own nationals." He then went on to add that:

Special mention must be made of Jews from Poland or other East European countries. Coming to our region mostly as industrial workers, a profession they have little inclination for, these foreigners have succeeded, little by little, in insinuating themselves into certain branches of small- and large-scale commerce. It moreover seems, in my opinion, that this penetration has been a decisive factor in the rise of the antisemitic campaign in my department.

A judicious limitation of *naturalizations* of foreigners belonging to this category, who are, furthermore, extremely refractory to assimilation, would be . . . desirable in every respect.[197]

When the conservative deputies Louis Marin and Fernand Laurent called for a reform of the 1927 naturalization law in December 1938, they too justified this measure by claiming that "recently naturalized foreigners constitute in commerce as well as in certain liberal professions, and especially in medicine, inadmissible competition to French citizens."[198] And in the spring of 1939, the right-wing deputy Raymond Lachal submitted a bill "obliging foreign merchants, industrialists, and artisans settled in France to practice their profession under their own family name."[199]

These protectionist demands ultimately influenced the administration's new naturalization policy, particularly because Marchandeau, chairman of the newly created High Committee on Population, had close ties to the protectionist lobbies, as he had demonstrated during his stint as minister of commerce in 1935.[200] The new committee's task was to devise a "selective" immigration policy aimed at liberalizing immigration and naturalization procedures for immigrants whose skills were deemed valuable to the national economy. Determining what these skills were, however, was a highly subjective process, which these corporate pressure groups successfully exploited to their advantage. On February 15, 1939, the secretary-general of the Confédération des Syndicats Médicaux publicly proclaimed that the Confederation had achieved its goal, since there had been significantly fewer naturalizations of doctors and medical students in recent weeks. He furthermore proclaimed that the Confederation's vice president, Dr. Alexis Giry, had recently met with Marchandeau and, according to Giry's account, Marchandeau had informed him that he too believed that "the naturalizations carried out during the last few years have introduced, especially into the medical profession, undesirables from every point of view." To remedy this situation, Marchandeau declared that he had "in principle decided that there will be no further naturalizations of foreign [medical] students and doctors." To be sure, as the secretary-general acknowledged, this commitment was only a gentlemen's agreement. Nevertheless, the fact that Marchandeau never denied it suggests it was true.[201]

Marchandeau was not the only high-ranking official who exhibited open sympathy for these groups' racist sentiments. As we have seen, during deliberations over the Czech refugee question in October 1938, Chautemps had declared that "we need to ensure that an influx of Jews not provoke difficulties of a racial order in our country."[202] Similarly, during an interministerial meeting in April devoted to a discussion of possible reforms in the naturalization process that might be considered by the High Committee on Population, Emile Charvériat, director of the Bureau of Political Affairs of the Foreign Ministry, declared that the racial aspect of the immigration question could no longer be ignored. "Is it really in France's best interest to augment appreciably the actual proportion of Jews in the population and to naturalize Jewish émigrés who come from Poland, Romania, and Germany?" Charvériat asked. "Without lapsing into an antisemitism that would be unworthy of our country, one could estimate that in this respect and even in the interest of French Jews themselves, extreme prudence is called for."[203] In light of such attitudes, it is not surprising that the committee never succeeded in bringing naturalization policy into line with the new military decree laws regarding foreigners.

By endeavoring to accommodate these contradictory pressures, the administration's immigration policy fell into a state of disarray on the eve of the war. In response to growing economic and especially military exigencies, together with the recognition that the decree laws had failed, the administration had begun to move toward a liberalization and a rationalization of refugee policy. On the other hand, the administration's unwillingness to confront protectionist interest groups, such as the Chambers of Commerce and the Confédération des Syndicats Médicaux, meant that every reform contained a loophole that could ultimately be used to subvert its original intent. Moreover, the growing pervasiveness of racial thinking, even at the highest levels of government, made it virtually impossible to rationalize naturalization procedures. In light of these contradictory pressures and the administration's indecision, it is not surprising that when war broke out the administration had not yet determined what sort of immigration policy best reflected the national interest. Indeed, there was no consensus over what the national interest entailed. Whether and to what degree these issues would be clarified in the cauldron of war is the question to which we now turn.

CHAPTER ELEVEN

The Missed Opportunity
Refugee Policy in Wartime

> Contemporary history has created a new kind of human
> being—the kind that are put in concentration camps by
> their foes and internment camps by their friends.
>
> Hannah Arendt[1]

When France declared war on September 3, 1939, the contradictions that
had riddled refugee policy during the previous months became even
sharper. The military and economic decree laws announced in the spring
suggested the government's intention to utilize the refugees in the event of
armed conflict, either by recruiting certain categories of them directly into
the armed forces or by using them as *prestataires*—civilian auxiliaries recruited for noncombatant defense work. When war broke out, however,
these plans fell by the wayside. Instead, due to fifth-column fears the government resorted to a policy of internment for Central European refugees,
now declared "enemy aliens." Moreover, despite the need for workers on
the home front, the government made it more difficult than ever for businesses and industries to hire foreigners in order to appease popular fears
that foreigners would steal jobs from men called up for military service.

Nevertheless, until the German invasion of the Low Countries in May of
1940, pressures militating in favor of a more liberal refugee policy continued to operate. In response to public pressure at home and abroad, the government created *criblage*, or sifting, commissions to review the dossiers of
all internees to determine which were Nazi sympathizers and which were
loyal to the Allied cause. Moreover, despite considerable delays, efforts
were eventually made to utilize the refugees militarily. Certain groups of
refugees—the Poles and the Czechs—were allowed to join their respective

national legions. Others, depending on their age and fitness, were given the option of joining the Foreign Legion or enlisting for *prestataire* service. At the same time, some restrictions regarding the use of foreign labor were dropped, making it easier for foreigners not interned to find employment, and by the late fall of 1939, provisions had finally been made for the families of internees serving in the Foreign Legion or *prestataire* formations to receive military allocations.

This progress was brought to an abrupt halt by the German invasion, however. In response to a second wave of fifth-column hysteria, the government resorted again to wholesale internments of Central European refugees. These internments were far more comprehensive than those of September, and for the first time included women. It was only at this moment, when France was most in need of additional manpower, that the effort to utilize the refugees in the war effort was abandoned altogether. Whether a more determined and efficient use of the refugees would have made any difference to the outcome of the battle for France is impossible to know. What is clear, however, is that the government lost a significant opportunity to draw on an important and highly spirited source of anti-Nazi fighting power. Military exigencies ultimately gave way to fifth-column suspicions, procrastination, bureaucratic ineptitude, and even overt xenophobia and antisemitism, suggesting that the administration never gripped the urgency of mobilizing every available resource. From the vantage point of the refugees, this missed opportunity became emblematic of the political ineptitude and lack of determination that led to the debacle of June 1940.

Although the internment of "enemy aliens" was certainly a possibility with the outbreak of war, it was by no means predestined.[2] Until September 1, there were numerous indications that France intended to treat German, Austrian, Czech, and Saar refugees with considerable leniency and to permit them, together with the large number of stateless refugees, including many East European Jews, to serve in the armed forces. According to a police report of February 1939, only White Russian émigrés were suspected of strong pro-Nazi sentiments. Germans, on the other hand, were regarded as politically reliable. Despite their strong sense of German identity, these refugees, this report maintained, felt they had been "cast out of the 'German national body,'" and regarded "a European conflagration . . . [as] a generalized form of civil war."[3]

Moreover, the government did nothing to deter the Central European refugees who, together with thousands of other foreigners, turned out en masse to sign up for military service. Already in the spring, just after the proclamation of the April 12, 1939, decree law, both the police and the press reported thousands of foreigners volunteering,[4] and in September this trend reached a crescendo. Only days after the outbreak of the war, French military authorities admitted that they were unable to cope with this deluge, and they turned the registration process over to private associations, such as the Amis de la République and the International League Against Antisemitism (LICA).[5] According to the newspaper *L'Epoque*, the Amis de la République registered over 1,000 foreigners per day in September, and the Jewish War Veterans registered over 9,000 Jewish immigrants for regular army service as of October 8 and another 9,000 for duty in the Polish and Czech Legions.[6] This registration drive was enthusiastically endorsed by various émigré associations. German refugees, the Fédération des Emigrés d'Allemagne en France declared, "will fulfill their duty with the same devotion, the same spirit and the same courage as other Frenchmen."[7] As émigré writer and journalist Leo Lania explained, for these refugees "who had lost . . . everything . . . faith in France was the only barrier between themselves and bottomless despair."[8]

Despite this outpouring of pro-French loyalties, the government ultimately chose to ignore the provisions of the April 12 decree law and instead fell back on a policy treating foreigners in general and Central Europeans in particular as potential "enemy aliens." On September 8, Prime Minister Daladier declared that "foreigners are authorized to enlist for the duration of the war in the Foreign Legion and the Foreign Legion only."[9] This order came as a bitter pill for most foreigners because they wanted above all to serve in the regular army, and service in the Legion, even if "only" for the duration of the war rather than the regular five-year stint, was not an attractive option given the Legion's harsh disciplinary regime and its reputation as a haven for hardened criminals.

An even more severe fate lay in store for German, Austrian, Czech, and Saar refugees. On September 4, a decree was announced ordering all males from "Greater Germany" between the ages of 17 and 50 to report to designated assembly centers; ten days later, this age limit was extended to 65. Those summoned were told to bring a two-day supply of food, as well as blankets, underwear, and eating utensils. All other "Greater German" subjects—men and women—were ordered to report to police headquarters or city halls to register and apply for new identity papers, and they were henceforth forbidden to leave their neighborhoods without police authorization.[10] Most seriously, the government froze the bank accounts of those refugees detained, inflicting severe economic hardship on their families.[11]

Although the refugees had been told to prepare for a 48-hour stay, most were detained for at least ten days and sometimes up to a few weeks.[12] At the Colombes Stadium outside of Paris, it took several days to register the 10,000 refugees who reported. Living conditions were abysmal. A single water pump served the entire camp population, and water was strictly rationed. Food consisted of dry bread and pork liver pâté; kosher food was unavailable. Large pails were set up in the corners of the stadium to serve as toilets, and the refugees had to sleep in the open air. Chaos reigned outside the camp as well. Government officials refused to release any information to desperate wives and relatives who congregated outside the camp daily, and journalists were strictly banned, although a few smuggled themselves in.[13]

Within days, the scope of the internments was widened considerably. On September 9, Albert Sarraut, still minister of the interior, issued another decree law that allowed even naturalized foreigners to be stripped of their citizenship on the mere suspicion of involvement in activities injurious to national security.[14] Another decree law, issued on September 17, 1939, authorized police to arrest all politically suspect foreigners and either expel them or send them to an internment camp.[15] Armed with these decrees, the police initiated a fierce crackdown against hundreds of foreigners in France, most of whom were stateless communists or left-wing dissidents who, as a result of the Nazi-Soviet nonaggression pact of August 23, had been transformed overnight into enemies of the state.[16] Males were initially brought to the Roland Garros tennis stadium, and women were sent to the Petite Roquette prison in Paris.

By mid-September, it became clear that the vast majority of detainees were not about to be released soon. Aside from the Czechs, who were freed in October so that they could join the Czech Legion,[17] the detainees were offered the choice of enlisting in the Foreign Legion or being interned. Although the Ministry of Defense stipulated that the Germans were to be allowed to sign up only for the regular five-year term of service, Austrians were to be allowed to serve for the duration of the war.[18] In practice, however, it appears that everyone was offered only the five-year term of service.[19] As one refugee complained bitterly to Emile Buré's conservative but pro-refugee paper *L'Ordre*, the choice of internment or the Legion was "cruel" and "undeserved," since nearly all male refugees of military age had already volunteered for regular army service.[20] Fearing that enlistment in the Legion would foreclose this possibility, most refugees opted for internment.[21]

At the end of September, therefore, the military began to redistribute the approximately 18,000 detainees, of whom about 5,000 were Austrians and the rest Germans, to one of the 80 or so internment camps throughout the country.[22] Some of these camps, like St. Cyprien, Argelès, Barcarès, and Gurs, had been erected in March to absorb the half million Spanish refugees who had flooded across the border.[23] Others, like Rieucros in the Lozère, which held politically suspect women, had served since January as detention centers for foreigners considered dangerous to national security but who could not be expelled.[24] Still other camps, particularly in the north, had been hastily improvised in September for the sole purpose of absorbing Central European refugees.[25]

The worst camp was almost certainly Le Vernet in the Ariège, which housed politically suspect foreign males. Of the approximately 900 refugees interned there in mid-October, the majority were either Spanish or Central and Eastern Europeans, including many who had fought in the International Brigades. By December, after most of the Spaniards had been inducted into the Foreign Legion, one relief committee estimated that 80 to 90 percent of the remaining inmates were Jews.[26] According to Arthur Koestler and others, those sent to Le Vernet were treated more harshly than German POWs. The camp was cordoned off by barbed wire, the guards carried whips, and the inmates' heads were shaven. Despite the rigorous work discipline, work clothes were not provided, and the inmates were sent out in rags. To maintain a military character, the camp held four roll calls a day and visits from friends and relatives were strictly forbidden. The barracks were overcrowded, unlit, and poorly insulated, and the sole furnishings consisted of bare wooden planks that served as beds. Except for the food, which Koestler noted was "less substantial and nourishing" than that in Franco's prison,[27] French authorities provided nothing: blankets, eating utensils, soap, clothing, even furniture, had to be provided by private relief agencies. "As regards food, accommodation and hygiene," Koestler commented, "Vernet was even below the level of Nazi concentration camps." And although inmates were not deliberately tortured, the sum total of suffering experienced here was, according to Koestler, not appreciably different.[28]

Although this harsh disciplinary regime was unique to Le Vernet, living conditions at the other camps were not perceptibly better. At Meslay-du-Maine in the Mayenne west of Paris, neither barracks nor tents had been set up when the first detainees arrived. According to Leo Lania, only the long ditch that served as the latrine had been prepared in advance. It was three weeks before a hot meal was served, and fresh water was even scarcer than at Colombes.[29] Although Meslay may have been more primitive than other camps, it was by no means exceptional. Furniture, heat, and lighting were everywhere lacking. At many camps, there were no beds, and refugees had to sleep on straw. As one former German statesman testified, "No means to wash oneself; no canteen was ready, and I am no longer a youngster to lie on straw and hard stone floors."[30] By early November, the Joint Distribution Committee (JDC) reported that refugees were dying due to the lack of heat and winter clothing.[31] Family visits and mail were extremely limited, and the overcrowded conditions and lack of solitude drove many to the breaking point.[32] By contrast, the camp food was considered even by inmates to be "very good—both as to quality and quantity," and relief committees also noted that the guards generally treated the internees with respect, as opposed to conditions at Le Vernet.[33]

Beyond these material deprivations, however, the greatest torment for many refugees was the conviction that France had betrayed them. As Lion Feuchtwanger explained, the sole reason he had remained in France since his emigration there in 1933 was to participate in the impending battle against Hitler. Now he commented bitterly, "The French not only refused any cooperation from us German anti-Fascists, they locked us up."[34] Compounding this disappointment, internees were not even allowed to participate in noncombatant defense work. Instead, they were either left idle or given what seemed senseless work unrelated to the war effort.[35] The French government, Koestler lamented, "did not want us, even as cannon fodder."[36] Moreover, while most refugees recognized the government's need to sift out the fifth columnists among them, the inordinately long delays in implementing this process eventually provoked anguished protests. In his famous plea on behalf of the refugees, *L'Allemagne exilée en France*, the émigré writer Ernst Erich Noth warned in the fall of 1939 that if the sifting process were not completed quickly, France would lose a vast reservoir of fighting power. At the same time, he pointed out, the internments were providing grist for the Nazi propaganda mill, which delighted in showing that the West despised the refugees no less than the Germans.[37]

Given that the vast majority of Central and Eastern European refugees were known to be anti-fascist, why did France decide in favor of wholesale internments? This question cannot be settled definitively even today since the government has not yet released all pertinent archival records. Nevertheless, it is striking that France alone of the major Western powers resorted to such a policy during the period of the "phony war." Belgium and the Netherlands, although they too had camps for illegal refugees, did not indiscriminately intern all German and Austrian males in September 1939. Similarly, Great Britain did not resort to mass internments until May 1940, after the German invasion of the Netherlands. Instead, to guard against a possible fifth-column threat during the "phony war," the British set up 112 tribunals to review on a case-by-case basis the dossiers of German and Austrian refugees, who in the meanwhile remained free. After the completion of this review process, less than 1 percent of the 55,000 refugees in Britain were detained. The rest were encouraged to find employment, and some were even permitted to work in national defense industries.[38]

Why then did France act so swiftly in this matter? First, there can be no question that fifth-column fears, while hugely overblown, were not entirely fanciful.[39] The police reported in October that at least some of the refugees still crossing the border illegally from Italy were "suspect individuals and probably . . . in the pay of Germany who hide their true designs under false identities."[40] In December, the minister of the interior alerted the border police that he had just received word that Nazi spies were infiltrating enemy countries disguised as Jewish refugees and bearing passports marked with a "J."[41] Some historians have dismissed these claims as utter nonsense or, more seriously, as a smoke screen behind which Daladier's already "fascisticized" government could lock up its foreign enemies on the left.[42] Yet even many pro-refugee spokesmen as well as the majority of refugees themselves admitted the existence of some spies among the refugees.[43] The fact that the majority of them had entered the country illegally further contributed to fifth-column fears. In contrast to Great Britain, where all refugees had been screened when they applied for visas, without which it was impossible to enter the country,[44] in France only the few thousand refugees whose dossiers had been reviewed by the Popular Front's Consultative Commission had already been screened. Moreover, as Michael Miller has pointed out, the proliferation of false passport and visa schemes made refugees a propitious target for fifth-column suspicions.[45]

Some analysts have also argued that the mass internments of September were triggered in part by the military's long preparation for such an exigency, and that the General Staff was unable to differentiate the situation in 1939 from that of the First World War, when Germans had also been interned.[46] As one contemporary observer put it, in the eyes of the French military, "a boche is always a boche."[47] Moreover, the fact that the Sûreté Nationale had instructed police even before the outbreak of war to separate recently arrived refugees—"Jewish Germans, Austrians, Poles, etc.,"—from longtime resident immigrants might suggest some advance planning. From now on, these refugees were no longer to receive renewable identity cards, but only temporary residence permits that required them to report to the police every few weeks.[48] Finally, the fact that France already had a camp network made mass internments more likely there than in Britain.

Yet none of these explanations fully accounts for the government's decision to intern Germans and Austrians in September. While some evidence suggests that internments were a conditioned reflex to the outbreak of war, other factors indicate that this policy had not been planned far in advance. The police report of February 1939, which described German émigrés as generally trustworthy, as well as the military registration of Germans and Austrians up until September, suggests that this policy was motivated by more immediate concerns. That no preparations had been made for mass internments prior to the outbreak of war further indicates the improvised nature of this policy. Except for Rieucros and those camps already in place for the Spaniards, most of the camps were erected at the last moment in great haste.[49] Furthermore, although the British began to implement their *criblage*, or sifting, process almost immediately, it was months before the French began to review the internees' dossiers.[50]

It therefore seems that some specific event occurred on the eve of the war that tipped the scales in favor of a policy of mass internments, and there can be little doubt that this incident was the Nazi-Soviet nonaggression pact. While the government may previously have felt confident in recognizing friends and foes, the signing of the nonaggression pact on August 23 cast a cloud of suspicion over all foreigners in France as well as over Communist Party members, citizens and foreigners alike. Already on August 22, as news of the pact became known, the minister of the interior issued a circular instructing prefects to inscribe in the *Carnet B*, the list of politically suspect foreigners, all foreigners who had ever received expulsion or deportation orders for national security reasons. On August 28, this list was expanded to include "all naturalized foreigners whose loss of citizenship has been envisaged," and on September 9 the government issued a decree law that enabled it to strip suspect individuals, French or foreign-born, of their citizenship.[51]

Furthermore, the government unleashed a fierce crackdown against the Communist Party: on September 26, the party was legally dissolved and its publications banned, and the following January, Communist Party deputies, despite having voted for military credits, were forced to forfeit their seats in Parliament.[52] To be sure, many communists, especially among the émigrés, denounced the pact and proclaimed their loyalty to France,[53] but their appeals fell on deaf ears. Whether the government was indulging in a witch-hunt, as many émigrés and contemporary historians have claimed,[54] or whether it truly believed that the communists constituted a serious security threat remains unclear. The fact is, however, that the Comintern had instructed its followers to sabotage the war effort and spread defeatist propaganda,[55] and in light of this order, the administration's response seems not unreasonable. Seeing the internments largely as a response to the nonaggression pact also helps explain why the government felt compelled to resort to mass roundups, despite the fact that the dossiers of several thousand refugees had already been scrutinized. While these individuals may have been screened for possible pro-Nazi leanings, pro-communist sympathies may not have received close attention.[56]

In addition to interning German and Austrian refugees already in the country, the government, in conjunction with British authorities, proceeded to force all German and Austrian male nationals of military age to disembark from neutral ships, despite the fact that those detained were nearly always Jewish refugees bearing visas for either the United States or some Latin American country. According to international law, belligerents had the right to remove enemy aliens from neutral ships if those aliens were thought to be possible members of the enemy's armed forces. As the JDC explained, "The French authorities, naturally, were anxious to eliminate every possibility for agents of the German government to go overseas, and the Jewish refugees unfortunately were caught up in the[ir] nets."[57] Men removed from these ships were subsequently directed to internment camps; the women and children were allowed to proceed.[58]

In light of the internments as well as the seizures at sea, the situation for German and Austrian refugees did not look bright in the fall of 1939. Nevertheless, several pressure groups continued to lobby the government to ameliorate camp conditions and to utilize the refugees in the war effort, and their efforts eventually yielded some success. Jewish relief agencies, for example, demanded access to the camps in order to bring desperately needed relief. They further pressed the government to stop those activities—such as blocking internees' bank accounts and seizing refugees from neutral ships—that were costing them huge sums of money by making the victims' families entirely dependent on charity.

These organizations also protested the government's failure to pay military allowances to foreigners serving in the armed forces,[59] and they lobbied the government to lift newly imposed restrictions on the right of foreigners to work, which had a particularly harsh impact on the families of internees. Just after the outbreak of war, the government, in an effort to compensate for the labor shortfalls following the mobilization, had decided to suspend the decree law of August 10, 1932, which had imposed quotas on the number of foreigners eligible to work in certain industries. On September 20, 1939, however, it reversed this measure by imposing new restrictions on the hiring of foreign workers in response to popular fears that foreigners would steal the jobs of mobilized soldiers.[60] From now on, foreign workers were required to obtain special work permits from the local branch of the Ministry of Labor, at a cost of 400 francs, even if they already had work permits.[61] This measure threw thousands of foreigners out of work, including many women who had been forced to become self-supporting as the result of the internments.[62]

France's refugee policies also came under attack both at home and abroad. Foreign governments, and especially the United States, were stridently critical of French and British seizures of refugees from neutral ships, and at the Washington Refugee Conference in October, President Roosevelt himself condemned these seizures and called on France and Britain to allow Jewish emigration from Germany to proceed unhindered.[63] After a particularly inflammatory incident in December in which it was reported that a French submarine commander had boarded an Italian liner and had demanded the disembarkation of Jews in particular, France's ambassador in

Washington, René Saint-Quentin, wired the Foreign Ministry for verification. Such claims, he maintained, "are presented by the American press in a way that incites pity, which borders here on indignation." Furthermore, he noted, "American opinion does not easily comprehend that Jews fleeing Nazi persecution are being prevented from utilizing immigration visas they applied for up to 18 months or even two years ago."[64] Although the Quai d'Orsay denied these charges, such incidents nevertheless embittered Franco-American relations in the early months of the war.[65]

The foreign press, especially in the United States, was similarly critical. Already in October, the French Foreign Ministry had instructed its embassies and consulates to stress that camp conditions were not as terrible as depicted in the foreign press and that a *criblage* process had been implemented to screen the internees so that those judged friendly to the Allied cause could be released.[66] As long as the internments continued, however, these efforts at damage control had only limited success. In January, the *New Republic* carried a vitriolic piece titled "France Copies Hitler." "France," it declared, "is supposed to be fighting this war for democracy. Some people in America would be more willing to accept this point of view if it were not for the shocking treatment the French are now giving to foreign Jews."[67] To stanch such criticism, Saint-Quentin inaugurated his own propaganda campaign, and when a letter sympathetic to French refugee policy finally appeared in the *New York Times*, he claimed his efforts had been vindicated. He further sought to discredit the negative publicity surrounding the camps by attributing it entirely to Communist Party sources.[68]

On this count, Saint-Quentin was mistaken, however, since there was a groundswell of criticism at home as well, which was by no means limited to left-wing circles. In the Chamber of Deputies, two of the most outspoken pro-refugee advocates, the socialists Marius Moutet and Salomon Grumbach, used their positions on the influential Commissions on Civil and Criminal Legislation and Foreign Affairs to attack the government's policy. As Moutet proclaimed in November, the internments, while perhaps justifiable in September, were no longer so today, and he called on the government to speed up the *criblage* process and follow the British example of allowing nonsuspect refugees to remain at liberty, but under police surveillance. If the administration hoped to avoid further tarnishing France's image abroad and to maintain the loyalties of the refugees eager to fight for France, it would have to end the "bureaucratic delays, xenophobic prejudices, [and] obtuseness," that until now had impeded all progress on this issue.[69] Significantly, Moutet's position had support not only on the left, but among prominent conservatives as well, such as Emile Buré of *L'Ordre* and Wladimir d'Ormesson of *Le Figaro*.[70]

Aside from the moral issue, the domestic debate also focused on the practical problem of how France might better utilize the huge population of foreigners in general, including the internees, in the war effort. After the declaration of war, popular pressure to recruit foreigners into the military became more vociferous than ever. In late September, Senator André Honnorat, a longtime pro-refugee advocate, appealed to the administration to allow the internees to serve in the army, or at least in the Foreign Legion for the war's duration. Otherwise, he claimed, the combative spirit of the refugees would be lost forever. Honnorat further contested the government's ban on foreigners serving in regular regiments. At the very least, he argued, foreigners who had resided in France for many years deserved to be exempted.[71] The conservative daily *L'Ordre* concurred and lambasted the authorities for allowing the huge reservoir of foreign manpower to go to waste. If the army refused to enlist nonnaturalized foreigners, every effort should be made to speed up naturalization procedures, particularly for longtime foreign residents, many of whom had already requested naturalization.[72] Most significantly, this view was endorsed by the Ministry of Defense, which pressed relentlessly to speed up the naturalization process so that at least some of the 64,000 foreigners who had volunteered for military service might be incorporated into the regular army. At the same time, the ministry also called for swifter recruitment of the internees into the Foreign Legion.[73]

These pressures came to a head on December 8, when Moutet and Grumbach brought the refugee question to a debate on the floor of the Chamber. Speaking on behalf of the Commission on Civil and Criminal Legislation, Moutet asked the administration to clarify a number of issues: What was the situation of the wives and families of the internees? Were the internees who had signed up for the Foreign Legion being granted military allowances and pensions, and would they eventually be naturalized? Were those still in the camps "interned" or merely "detained"? And what would happen to those previously guaranteed asylum, such as Saar refugees or the beneficiaries of the July 4, 1936, Geneva Accord? Alluding to the recent spate of criticism from abroad, Moutet concluded his speech with a ringing denunciation of the internments: "We must not allow public opinion abroad to perceive France as more cruel toward the victims of Hitler than Hitler himself. We cannot permit those who have escaped Hitlerian concentration camps to remain interned in French camps. That would be too unjust and too cruel!"[74]

Sarraut, who spoke on behalf of the administration at this debate, prefaced his remarks by attacking foreign governments that had criticized France's refugee policies. Given their own restrictionist policies, the minister of the interior declared, they had no right to lecture France. He then proceeded to explain that the internments had initially been necessary since the administration had no means of identifying genuine suspects. Nevertheless, Sarraut admitted that the arbitrary nature of the internments "may have created painful situations," and he announced that the government was now prepared to remedy this situation. *Criblage* commissions had been set up, and Sarraut noted that 7,000 of the original 15,000 internees had already been released. And while conceding that these commissions did not always operate as efficiently and fairly as possible, he nevertheless promised to correct this situation in the near future. In the end, the minister's message was clear: the administration shared the goals of the reformers, and it was prepared to liquidate nearly all the camps and recruit as many internees as possible into the Foreign Legion.[75]

Although Sarraut's figures were inflated—Jewish organizations estimated the number of refugees remaining in the camps as of mid-December at about 10,500[76]—there is little doubt that the administration intended to accomplish the goals set out by the minister. In an attempt to meet the demands of Jewish relief organizations and to "forestall the dangerous influence of propaganda from abroad and of the deliberate campaign against the Centres,"[77] the military authorities in charge of the camps encouraged the creation of a new refugee committee in mid-November, the Commission des Centres de Rassemblement, funded primarily by the JDC but also by the Groupement de Coordination, a coalition of French refugee organizations created in the fall of 1938.[78] Albert Lévy, director of the Jewish relief committee, the Comité d'Assistance aux Réfugiés (CAR), served as president, and Robert de Rothschild served as honorary chairman. Most significantly, the new commission was brought under the aegis of the Ministry of Public Health, and an official of that ministry, Félix Chevrier, was appointed secretary-general.[79]

The humanitarian impact of the commission's work was felt almost immediately. By the end of November, it had spent over 600,000 francs ($222,000) on blankets, shoes, clothing, medicines, and even heating and furniture.[80] Moreover, during the coming months, Chevrier and his associates visited every camp to assess the material conditions as well as the state of morale among the internees. So improved were camp conditions by the end of the year that the *New York Times*, the League of Nations High Commission for Refugees (HCR), and the Red Cross all commended the government on these efforts.[81] Refugee memoirs, too, attest to this change. Leo Lania reported that those refugees still at Meslay were brought to a new camp in December that, to his amazement, had real barracks, bunks with straw pallets, benches, tables, and running water. For a small fee, it was even possible to get a hot shower.[82]

By the end of 1939, many of the problems Jewish organizations had experienced were on their way toward being resolved. In late October, the Groupement and the Jewish emigration organization, HICEM, were granted permission to enter the camps to facilitate the emigration of the internees, especially those who had already been granted U.S. visas or quota numbers. Camp officials cooperated fully in this effort, and the government even created two special camps for internees awaiting departure — one near Le Havre and the other near Bordeaux. By the end of the year, some 250 internees had emigrated with their families, and HICEM expected many more to leave in the near future.[83]

Furthermore, the question of military allowances was finally settled in November with the announcement that all foreigners serving in the army, including the Legion, were henceforth to receive payments equivalent to those of French soldiers.[84] The internees also won the right to sign up for the Legion only for the war's duration rather than for the full five-year term of service.[85] At the same time, the administration began to ease up on employment restrictions for foreigners who had skills useful to national defense.[86] Finally, by early 1940 the government bowed to pressure from the U.S. State Department, as well as from French Jewish organizations and the HCR, to stop seizures of refugees at sea. Although French naval officials continued to check the identities of German nationals on board these vessels, once it was certified they were bona fide refugees, they were allowed to continue their journeys.[87]

Paralleling these reforms, Sarraut also revamped the *criblage* process in an effort to make it more fair and efficient. Already in September, the Ministries of Interior and Defense had set up regional *criblage* commissions to begin reviewing the internees' dossiers and determining which individuals were loyal.[88] Yet by all accounts, these tribunals worked at an inordinately slow pace. Although certain categories of refugees had been designated as early as mid-September as likely candidates for release — refugees with French wives or children, refugees who had enlisted in the Foreign Legion, and refugees personally recommended by the minister of the interior — it was weeks before further action was taken on their behalf.[89] Moreover, at least to the refugees, the process seemed completely arbitrary. As Koestler pointed out, one factor alone seemed to make any difference: having a *piston*, or an influential personal intercessor.[90] Koestler ultimately turned to Léon Blum, while others appealed to other high-ranking politicians. Ironically, members of the administration, such as Saint-Quentin, frequently intervened on behalf of individual refugees.[91] Intellectuals were especially fortunate in that they had the patronage of the influential Pen Club, whose assiduous efforts to secure their release were nearly always successful.[92]

After the chaos of the initial weeks, it was clear that measures would have to be taken to speed up the *criblage* process. In October, Sarraut ordered the prefects to stop the arbitrary arrests that had resulted in many innocents being sent to Le Vernet and Rieucros.[93] At the same time, in an effort to coordinate the process, the administration established the Central Interministerial Criblage Commission in Paris, which included representatives from the General Staff, the Foreign Ministry, and the Ministry of the Interior.[94] Even then the rate of release was "discouragingly slow"—according to an advisor to the Central Interministerial Criblage Commission, aside from those internees who had French wives or children, no more than 100 persons had been released by early November.[95] Leo Lania calculated that had the commission continued to operate at this pace, reviewing only 40 to 50 dossiers per week, it would have taken three to four years to complete the process.[96]

To remedy this situation, the Central Interministerial Criblage Commission decided in early November that whole categories of refugees were to be released, except for those interned at Le Vernet and Rieucros. These categories included all refugees over the age of 40 who either were married to French citizens or had French children, were former Legionnaires, had applied for French citizenship before the war with favorable recommendations, or were recipients of the Legion of Honor or the Médaille Militaire. Still other categories were to be released unconditionally regardless of age: refugees with sons currently serving in the army, those not medically fit, those who had acquired some citizenship other than German prior to the mobilization, and Saar refugees who had completed military service. In December, these lists were expanded to include all refugees with visas to emigrate abroad, plus Saar, Rhineland, and ex-Austrian refugees over 48 years of age.

Refugees remaining in the camps were to be granted several options. Men between the ages of 17 and 48 judged physically fit were encouraged to join the Foreign Legion, and Saar refugees of military age were allowed to join the regular army. Refugees over 48 years of age, or those who refused to join the Legion, were to sign up for *prestataire*, or noncombatant labor, service.[97] The government therefore seemed intent on fulfilling its promise to liquidate the camps, with one or two exceptions for those refugees still considered suspect. All others were supposed to be released, recruited into the Legion, or drafted into *prestataire* service—in which case, they were supposed to be transferred to other camps set up specifically for this purpose.

As several refugees pointed out, the idea of releasing whole categories of refugees contradicted the administration's initial rationale for having interned the refugees, since the mere fact of having a French wife or child by no means precluded one's being a Nazi agent.[98] Nevertheless, faced with negative publicity campaigns at home and abroad, as well as the army's incessant demands for more bodies, the administration calculated that urgent action was necessary to expedite the *criblage* process, even if a few Nazis went free. Once the new *criblage* regulations went into effect, the pace at which internees were released accelerated tremendously. By February, only 6,428 were left in the camps, and only 29 camps remained in existence.[99] In April, the military declared the sifting process over for refugees being considered for *prestataire* service,[100] and Jewish relief organizations reported their first drop in expenditures since the outbreak of the war.[101]

The administration's most significant reform, and the one on which the success of the *criblage* system depended, was the decision to utilize the internees, alongside foreigners in general, to participate in the war effort. Yet this was the issue that inspired the greatest ambivalence in administrative circles, and ultimately the General Staff allowed xenophobia and antisemitism to take precedence over military exigencies. That this would occur, however, was by no means immediately apparent, since during the fall and winter the Ministry of Defense launched a concerted effort to encourage internees to sign up either for the Foreign Legion or for *prestataire* service.

Although *prestataire* service became obligatory for internees not enlisted in the Legion only on December 21, 1939,[102] the military had authorized the use of labor brigades composed of internees already in September. These battalions sometimes performed work directly related to national defense, such as constructing air raid shelters, but they were usually used to supplement the work force in areas plagued by labor shortages after the mobilization, such as road building, mining, and harvesting crops.[103] In January, 1940, *prestataire* service became compulsory for internees of military age who had not enlisted in the Legion, as well as for stateless refugees and beneficiaries of the right of asylum who had not been interned. Those who signed up were now transferred to special camps, where living conditions were appreciably better. Most significantly, the military declared that the *prestataires*, who numbered about 5,000 in the spring of 1940, would be treated on a par with French soldiers: they were to receive equivalent military allocations for themselves and their families, in addition to pensions and regular leaves.[104] In February, the army even negotiated a deal with the CAR to allow a few internees with specialized technical skills to work in national defense industries.[105]

The General Staff made an even greater effort to enlist refugees in the Foreign Legion. To accommodate these foreigners, the army created special units, the Régiments de Marche des Volontaires Etrangers (RMVE). Although incorporated into the framework of the Legion proper, these regiments had their own command structure and differed from other Legion regiments with regard to personnel.[106] The majority of those who joined the RMVE were either Spanish refugees, stateless refugees (mostly Central and East European Jews), or Polish Jews, who had not been welcome in the Polish Legion.[107] To encourage foreigners to enlist in the RMVE, the government granted them special dispensations, such as exemption from having to carry the special identity card for foreigners, automatic and free extension of residence permits, and temporary amnesty from expulsion or *refoulement* orders.[108] The one inducement not granted, however, was the promise of eventual naturalization, a failing that elicited widespread public criticism on the center right as well as on the left.[109]

The fate of the "enemy aliens" interned in the camps was slightly different. Whereas the Czechs were quickly released so that they could join the newly formed Czech Legion, Germans and Austrians were initially barred from the Foreign Legion. The General Staff soon changed its mind on this issue, however. Already in September, the internees were being recruited for five-year terms of duty, and in late October the Ministry of Defense issued a decree allowing Germans as well as Austrians to volunteer solely for the duration of the war.[110] Recruitment nevertheless proceeded slowly, largely because the majority of refugees, with the exception of die-hard communists, still nurtured the dream of serving in the regular army. Camp commandants frequently resorted to cajolery and coercion to persuade refugees to sign up. According to Leo Lania, many refugees enlisted solely because they needed the military allocations to support their now destitute families. Heinz Pol too claimed that some internees were told that their property would be confiscated if they did not sign up, and others were threatened with hard labor, imprisonment, and even expulsion to Germany.[111]

Once the refugees realized that they were not going to be permitted to join the regular army, and as the benefits extended to those serving in the Legion improved, the Legion became more attractive. According to Pol, 70 percent of the internees at his camp ultimately volunteered, and many were so eager to serve that they finagled their way in even after failing their medical examinations.[112] By December, the flood of volunteers had become so great that the Sûreté Nationale agreed to allow the LICA into the camps to assist with the registration process, and the *New York Times* reported that the Legion could not absorb all the internees who had signed up.[113] By the spring, no fewer than 9,000 internees had enlisted in the Legion,[114] to the immense satisfaction of the French public. When the first contingent of 600 Germans departed for North Africa on December 29, 1939, shouts of "Down with Hitler!" had reverberated through the harbor. For these men, *Paris-Soir* noted approvingly, Hitler was "not only the enemy of the Allies, but Germany's own worst enemy."[115]

Despite the General Staff's zeal in getting foreigners and internees mobilized as quickly as possible, problems persisted. As we have seen, the General Staff lobbied vigorously to speed up the naturalization process, at least for the thousands of foreigners who had applied for citizenship prior to the war's outbreak. On this issue, however, the General Staff encountered staunch resistance from the new minister of justice, Georges Bonnet, whom Daladier had finally edged out of the Foreign Ministry. Bonnet, it is true, attempted to appease the generals by issuing a circular on October 22 that ordered the prefects to accelerate naturalization procedures for foreigners whose applications were already in the pipeline, and especially for those between the ages of 18 and 45 who had resided in the country legally for at least five years. But following the policy outlined by his subordinate at the Foreign Ministry, Emile Charvériat, back in April, Bonnet insisted these benefits be restricted to foreigners considered "assimilable"—that is, those with desirable professional skills, especially in agriculture, and those from "countries bordering France, with the obvious exception of German nationals."[116]

Although Bonnet's concessions significantly increased naturalizations—44,498 adult men and women were naturalized in 1939, an 89 percent increase over the previous year's total of 23,544—the General Staff remained dissatisfied.[117] In November, General Louis Colson, the army chief of staff, complained to Bonnet that the government was not adequately publicizing the new naturalization procedure, and he insisted that all foreigners be included, not merely those from countries bordering France. It was urgent, he stressed, to remedy this problem in order not to dampen the fighting spirit of these foreigners and "to satisfy a public opinion impatient to see foreigners fulfill their obligations to the country."[118] During a parliamentary debate over the issue in December, Bonnet conceded that there were important military reasons to quicken the naturalization process. He nevertheless argued for caution, since far too many "undesirables" had been naturalized in recent years, and he again insisted that "racial affinities" and occupational skills be taken into account.[119] On December 26, Bonnet issued a circular that encompassed these new guidelines, but he refused to go any further.[120]

Even the military was not immune to such prejudices, however, as its treatment of refugees, and especially Jews, within the ranks of the Legion and the RMVE units shows. From the beginning, the Legion commanders, with the complete support of the General Staff, insisted that former internees be treated differently than veteran legionnaires. In October, it was decided that the new recruits were to be stationed exclusively in North Africa or Indochina,[121] and in December, General Maurice Gamelin, commander-in-chief of the army, declared that they would be kept in segregated units, contrary to the long-standing Legion practice of creating units of mixed national backgrounds. This decision was justified on the grounds that the army would have been remiss "to neglect the security measures required by the regrouping of enemy subjects among whom dangerous elements may have slipped in."[122]

Legion commanders were furthermore obsessed by the need to control the proportion of Germans among their ranks. Already in November, the commander of overseas operations began to worry that if the majority of German internees were eventually recruited into the Legion, they would constitute nearly one-third of Legion troops, creating a "troublesome disequilibrium."[123] It was therefore decided as early as October that the proportion of Germans allowed to serve in North Africa be limited to 25 percent.[124] Ironically, this level was reached in May 1940, just at the time of the German invasion. According to an internal Defense Ministry memo, the proportion of Germans was now about 24 percent of all North African troops, and "it would be dangerous to increase it any further." "Under these conditions," the memo continued, "it seems desirable to put a definitive stop to enlistments of Germans in the Legion for the duration of the war." Hence, at the very moment the army most needed additional troops the Legion Command actually began to ship German recruits back to the metropole, where they were either incorporated into *prestataire* formations or, if considered suspect, interned.[125] At the same time, the Foreign Ministry similarly instructed its embassy in Switzerland not to extend visas to German refugees wanting to come to France to fight in the Legion.[126]

Specifically antisemitic attitudes among Legion and RMVE commanders were even more pronounced. In his book *Jews and the French Foreign Legion*, historian Zosa Szajkowski, himself an East European Jew who served in one of the RMVE units, wrote, "The attitude toward Jews was not exactly friendly." Jewish legionnaires, he claimed, were convinced that the officers "did not want an almost completely Jewish regiment," a concern that stemmed from the fact that Jews constituted as much as three-quarters of the troops in several RMVE units.[127] Documentation from the French military archives bears out Szajkowski's claims. In evaluating the caliber of the different nationalities under his command, Sergeant Major Mazzoni, commander of the Legion training camp at Barcarès in southern France, ranked East European Jews at the bottom of the camp hierarchy. "With a few exceptions," he noted, "I do not think we can nurture great hopes for this category of enlistees."[128] Captain Pierre-Olivier Lapie, commander of the 13th demi-brigade, often referred to as "the troop of intellectuals," because of the high proportion of Jews, commented that his soldiers, while "excellent in study, in application, in calculations . . . were detestable in drill, in marching, in fatigue duties, and in discipline, always complaining."[129] Szajkowski too recounts that Colonel Besson, commander of the

12th regiment, informed his troops that other officers had refused to work with them because of the large number of Jews.[130]

These attitudes filtered up to the highest levels of the Legion command and ultimately influenced recruitment policies. On January 10, 1940, the Legion Command issued secret orders "to refuse from now on the enlistment of Jews in the Legion under a variety of pretexts." Future troop reinforcements from the RMVE to the Legion proper were "not to include any Jews." As for the 900 Jews already in the Legion, they were to be transferred into the less prestigious RMVE, together with "a hundred non-Jews (the least skilled, so as to remove from this operation any taint of being a measure targeted exclusively at Jews.)"[131] In February, the commander-in-chief in North Africa, General Charles Noguès, who subsequently threw in his lot with Philippe Pétain, reaffirmed these orders, declaring that he wanted "to see the Jewish candidates categorically kept out of the Legion."[132] The impact of these decisions was discernible immediately, since, as Szajkowski describes, when new Legion units were being assembled at the training camp at La Valbonne, near Lyons, Jews were systematically separated from the other new recruits and sent away, leaving "a terrible impression on the remaining Jews."[133]

Such attitudes may have reflected military considerations rather than antisemitism per se, as Douglas Porch has recently speculated in his history of the Foreign Legion. That Legion commanders perceived the largely middle-class, highly educated, and generally older Jewish recruits as poor fighting material is not surprising. The Jewish recruits, Porch notes, "were deeply out of sympathy with the culture of the barracks in which social acceptance was earned after a novitiate of bullying, brawling, drinking and womanizing."[134] Furthermore, many Legion officers looked askance at the ideological motivations that had impelled these Jews to join the Legion. From their perspective, the Legion was supposed to be a strictly mercenary army, aloof from the political fray.[135] These officers may also have feared rivalries between these refugees and veteran legionnaires, whose politics often veered toward fascism.[136]

Yet while discrimination against Jewish recruits may have stemmed in part from antibourgeois and anti-intellectual biases, it is difficult to dismiss as anything other than antisemitism the constant barrage of insults suffered by Jewish legionnaires. Szajkowski's sergeant, for example, referred to all the Jewish volunteers as "Salomon" and frequently shouted: "This is the Legion, not a synagogue!" In light of this evidence, as well as the harsh treatment meted out to Jewish legionnaires after the fall of France, Porch too admits, "It is difficult to escape the conclusion that antisemitism was the principal motivation in the Legion's desire to exclude Jews."[137]

These problems were not readily apparent to the public, however, and even the administration's most severe critics, such as Moutet, were willing to concede by the spring of 1940 that considerable progress had been made toward speeding up the *criblage* process, incorporating the refugees into the *prestataire* units and the Legion, and liquidating the camps.[138] These efforts came to an abrupt halt on May 10, 1940, however, when the *Wehrmacht* invaded the Low Countries. As German troops headed toward France, a wave of fifth-column hysteria swept the country that far exceeded anything that had surfaced in September, and the government again resorted to mass internments.

On May 13, General Pierre Héring, military governor of the Paris region, ordered the reinternment of all "Greater German" subjects between the ages of 17 and 55; two weeks later, this age limit was extended to 65. Moreover, women up to the age of 55 were, for the first time, also included.[139] On May 14, posters went up throughout the metropolitan area ordering all men from "Greater Germany" to report to the Buffalo Stadium with a two-day supply of food, cutlery, and a maximum of 30 kilograms of baggage, and women were ordered to report to the Vélodrome d'Hiver on May 15.[140] In the course of these roundups, it was estimated that some 8,000 "Greater German" subjects were apprehended in the Paris region, of whom at least 5,000 were Jews.[141] By the end of the month, these internment orders were extended to the provinces. Furthermore, the 10,000 refugees from Belgium, Holland, and Luxembourg, who had streamed across the French border in flight from Hitler's armies, were also steered to the internment camps.[142]

Why the administration of Paul Reynaud, which had just come to power in March, resorted to this second round of internments can be explained only by the wave of fifth-column hysteria that swept the country following the German invasion. This time, however, France was not acting alone. Even Great Britain interned its "enemy alien" population in May in response to fifth-column fears, which had been raised to fever pitch by rumors that the Netherlands' defeat had been brought about in part by internal German subversion.[143] The French decision may nevertheless seem somewhat puzzling in that nearly all the refugees, with the exception of the recent arrivals from Belgium, Holland, and Luxembourg, had supposedly been screened by the *criblage* commissions. On the other hand, most of the refugees had been released only because they belonged to one of the categories fixed by the government in November, and the vast majority had never been screened individually. The government may also have wanted to appease popular apprehensions regarding the refugees, who were increasingly identified with their Nazi victimizers.

All contemporary refugee accounts attest to the depths of anti-German sentiment that surfaced in May. As trains transported refugees to internment camps in the south, crowds of onlookers threw stones and branded the refugees as Nazi spies.[144] One refugee actually expressed relief at being sent to a camp, claiming, "It's our only defense against the popular indignation."[145] After a nightmarish journey to St. Cyprien, during which Belgian refugees traveled for three days in sealed cars without food or water, one Belgian refugee reported, "I have never seen such a fear of spies, no, not even in 1914."[146] French officers too now treated the refugees as outright criminals. According to Koestler, while being escorted to the Buffalo Stadium, he was told by one French officer that "we're going to line you up and shoot you ourselves before the Germans come."[147]

Yet the decision to go ahead with the internments was motivated not merely by the need to appease public opinion. Rather, Georges Mandel, a staunch conservative of Jewish background who became minister of the interior on May 18, was dead-set on weeding out potential fifth columnists, including those who had infiltrated the émigré population. Hence, although many historians and even some refugees have minimized Mandel's responsibility for the crackdown in May, the action must be seen as an integral aspect of his anti-fifth-column crusade in general. Unlike his predecessors, Mandel for the first time energetically pursued potential traitors on the extreme right as well as the communist left, and among the notorious right-wing Nazi sympathizers he arrested were Charles Lesca, director of *Je suis partout*; his collaborator, Alain Laubreaux; the Baron Robert de Fabre-Luce; and the antisemitic publicists, Paul Ferdonnet and Jacques Saint-Germain.[148] Supposedly, Mandel even considered arresting Pierre Laval, Pierre-Etienne Flandin, and Jacques Doriot for making defeatist remarks, but he stopped short when it became clear that Reynaud disapproved.[149]

Despite this focus on the extreme right, Mandel gave no respite to the communist left or the foreign population. On May 26, the *New York Times* reported that Mandel had just arrested the wives of two missing Communist Party leaders, André Marty and Gabriel Péri, for having engaged in defeatist propaganda, and it added: "Under M. Mandel's direction, raids have been multiplied in the Paris region. More than 2,000 cafés and public establishments were visited and 62,000 persons questioned in these raids or on the streets. This resulted in the arrest of 500 individuals and 334 foreigners have been sent to concentration camps."[150] By pursuing this anti-leftist campaign, Mandel furthermore sent a clear signal that he concurred fully with the conclusions of an internal Sûreté Nationale memorandum issued on May 14, 1940, just prior to his taking office. In this memorandum, titled "German efforts to weaken French morale," the director of the Sûreté proclaimed that "the defeatism born of German inspiration and communist propaganda are, in reality, two forms of a vast demoralization campaign that must be repressed with equal attention and equal rigor," and he recommended that certain groups be placed under heightened surveillance, including "the foreign colonies, among whom the intelligence services from across the Rhine may easily have found contacts, and in particular German women who, for the most part, have not been interned."[151] Interestingly, Mandel's fifth-column fears did not extend to the Italian immigrant population. Despite preexisting orders that Italians too were to be interned en masse if Italy declared war, which occurred on June 10, these orders were canceled due to the economic "perturbations" that were expected to ensue. In the end, only individual Italians considered suspect were sent to the camps.[152]

As the Germans advanced southward, capturing Paris on June 14, the fate of the refugees became a living hell. For those in the camps, living conditions deteriorated sharply. The two major camps, St. Cyprien for men and Gurs for women, were disease-ridden and overcrowded, and they became even more so as they absorbed growing numbers of refugees evacuated from camps in the north. St. Cyprien, nicknamed the "hell of Perpignan" by its former Spanish inmates, was the worst. Lacking vegetation, the place was regularly besieged by sandstorms. During the day, the heat and sun were intolerable, and at night temperatures dropped close to freezing. Sanitary conditions were abysmal: toilet paper was unknown, and the water was infected with typhoid. As one refugee reported, "Dysentery is raging to the point of insanity." The barracks remained unlit, and there were no mattresses.[153] Another refugee complained to relatives in the United States that "German concentration camps were as sanatoria compared to this."[154]

Moreover, there was now no hope of release. When a delegation of former premiers and left-wing members of Parliament petitioned Reynaud on May 16 to release the anti-Nazi refugees in the camps, the prime minister allegedly "received the delegation ungraciously and replied that he had far more important things to attend to."[155] Similarly, when an official from the Ministry of Information protested that he could not perform his job, which entailed decoding secret Nazi radio emissions, without his German émigré collaborators, his petition too was denied.[156] "For the moment," the Foreign Ministry noted, "the competent military authorities are refusing to liberate any German subjects from the camps."[157]

As Nazi victory seemed imminent, a veritable panic seized those refugees trapped in the camps, who now faced the nightmarish prospect of being turned over wholesale to their German persecutors. Not surprisingly, German advances emboldened some refugees to reveal themselves as Nazi sympathizers. "Hitlerites," Feuchtwanger commented, "seemed to sprout more numerously the nearer Hitler's armies came."[158] The overwhelming majority of refugees were petrified, however, and pleaded with camp commanders to be released. The government had made no provisions for the internees in the advent of a German victory, and camp commanders were left to their own devices. Most ultimately followed the dictates of their consciences and complied with refugee demands, but others refused, claiming that they could not disobey orders.[159]

When the armistice was finally announced on June 22, 1940, the refugees initially reacted with relief, but this sentiment soon gave way to despair as the terms, particularly of article 19, became known. This article stated that "the French Government is obliged to surrender upon demand all Germans named by the German Government in France, as well as in French possessions, Colonies, Protectorate Territories and Mandates."[160] The terror inspired by article 19 as well as the profound hopelessness evoked by Hitler's triumph sparked a wave of suicides. Among the most prominent refugees who took their lives were the literary critic Walter Benjamin, the writer and art historian Carl Einstein, and the playwright Walter Hasenclever.[161]

Paradoxically, many refugees chose to remain in the camps, calculating that they were safer there than roaming the countryside without resources and contacts.[162] For those who escaped, however, the logical solution, after having located their families, was to get out of France as quickly as possible. A fortunate few were able to board the last British ships departing from Bordeaux.[163] The vast majority flocked to Marseilles, where they tried desperately to procure overseas, and especially American, visas, with which they were then able to obtain transit visas for Spain and Portugal. In those days, as relief worker Varian Fry noted, the U.S. consulate was generally cooperative, and visas were not particularly difficult to come by. A more significant problem was securing a French exit visa, without which it was impossible to leave the country legally. Fortunately, for many refugees this requirement was rarely enforced.[164] Still, the process of securing these papers usually took several weeks, and in the meantime a cloud of uncertainty hung over the refugees. As Fry observed, so great was the tension that refugees trapped in the south "believed that every ring of the doorbell, every step on the stair, every knock on the door might be the police come to get them and deliver them to the Gestapo."[165]

Refugees who served in the *prestataire* service, the RMVE, or the Legion proper, although exempted from reinternment, did not fare significantly better. While some *prestataires* succeeded in escaping to Great Britain, the majority fled south, often with assistance from the British, where they joined the masses of other foreigners.[166] And although the Legion proper did not fight on French soil, RMVE units ultimately did. At first, it seemed that the antisemitism and xenophobia most refugees had previously encountered vanished with their arrival at the front. For the first time,

Szajkowski noted, Jewish recruits were treated as human beings.[167] Nevertheless, once the military situation began to deteriorate, antisemitism resurfaced with a vengeance. According to Hans Habe, who served in the 21st RMVE, the response of one general to the news that 500 soldiers had been lost in the battle of Ste. Menehould was simply, "Five hundred Jews the less." Habe also argued that the Army Command deliberately used the RMVE troops as cannon fodder to protect French forces. As he states in his memoir, *A Thousand Shall Fall*, the generals deliberately blew up the lines of retreat "to keep the Germans busy massacring us, in order to gain as much time as possible for the troops retreating southward."[168]

That there was a massacre is beyond dispute; unofficial sources after the war testified that as many as 80 percent of the 21st regiment had been declared missing in action.[169] Whether this massacre was deliberately planned remains uncertain even today. What is certain, however, is that these troops were sent into battle with badly outdated equipment and with no logistical support. Szajkowski states that his regiment wore First World War uniforms and carried antiquated guns dating back to 1907 or earlier, while Habe was issued an 1891 Remington.[170] According to Porch, the equipment of the 12th REI (Régiment étranger d'infanterie) was in such paltry shape that it had to be held together with string—hence the Germans nicknamed it the "string regiment." Moreover, these troops were never provided with adequate air, artillery, or tank support.[171]

Despite the abysmal quality of their armaments and munitions, these troops fought with courage and fortitude. Habe, who himself was not Jewish, claimed that the East European Jews with whom he fought were the most heroic of the lot. From his perspective, the French Army was thoroughly demoralized, from top to bottom, and the soldiers in the field had not a clue what they were fighting for. French soldiers, according to Habe, were simply amazed that anyone would have volunteered to fight, and he claimed that their favorite slogan was "Run for your lives!" Jewish recruits, on the other hand, knew precisely what they were fighting for, and they fought with a vengeance that surprised many of their commanders.[172] In a report issued after the armistice, the commander of the 12th REI commented that "the Polish Jews, who by nature are not very courageous, have performed their duty; one of the wounded refused to allow himself to be evacuated."[173] Years later, General Brothier remarked: "In observing the behavior of our Jewish volunteers, later I better understood why, in the Israeli army, familiarity and slovenliness went so well with courage and a redoubtable efficiency."[174] To be sure, these assessments were still riddled with ambivalence toward Jews. Nevertheless, precisely because of this ambivalence, the praise is that much more compelling. According to Porch, "the conduct of the Legion and the RMVE in the battle for France in 1940 ran from very credible to spectacular. What the regiments lacked in military skill they made up in courage and tenacity."[175]

France's military defeat, however, brought an end to any prospect that the situation of the refugees might improve. Indeed, as we know, under the Vichy regime their prospects declined sharply. Nevertheless, it is essential to remember that nothing was determined until May, and even then the administration's policy was more one of confusion than deliberate persecution. As we have seen, those countervailing forces that had characterized French refugee policy throughout the 1930's continued to operate even during the "phony war." To be sure, fifth-column fears, heightened by the Nazi-Soviet nonaggression pact, resulted in the mass internments of September and May. Between those dates, powerful counterpressures, including military demands for more manpower as well as international and domestic criticism of the internments and the seizures of refugees at sea, persuaded the administration to release the majority of refugees and to utilize them either in the Foreign Legion or in the *prestataire* service. As a result, the situation of the refugees improved dramatically by the spring of 1940, and relief organizations had every reason to expect that the camps, with one or two exceptions, would be liquidated in the near future. Only in May, when Mandel inaugurated the second wave of mass internments, did it become clear that fifth-column fears would prevail over efforts to utilize the refugees constructively in the war effort. Hence, although Reynaud ultimately opted for a hard-line position, it is essential to remember that the situation between September and May remained one of considerable fluidity.[176]

In the long run, however, there is also no doubt that by having failed to implement a more complete mobilization of the refugee population for the war effort, France wasted an enormous reservoir of manpower, talent, and professional skills. Whether a more farsighted use of foreigners in general and refugees in particular might have enabled France to win the war will obviously never be known. There can be no question, though, that France's chances of victory would have been improved had it made better use of the millions of foreigners residing on French soil, many of whom were eager to serve and often possessed valuable technical and professional skills. Instances such as that cited by Porch, in which a French intelligence officer was forbidden from using immigrant cryptographers until they had enlisted in the Legion, or another case in which a German refugee industrialist released from the camps was barred from returning to his factory since it was engaged in defense work, could only have weakened French military preparedness.

Similarly, as Porch has suggested, French defenses might have been bolstered had the army allowed regular Legion regiments to fight on French soil.[177] That xenophobia and antisemitism were allowed to obstruct military efficiency in these ways strongly suggests that the administration was not prepared to mobilize every available resource for the sake of winning the war. To have done so would ultimately have entailed a radical liberalization of naturalization procedures, a proposition the administration was not ready to countenance, despite some support for such a measure in Parliament and the press.

But aside from this issue of manpower and talent, it is also necessary to ask whether the internments and the persistence of xenophobia and antisemitism tell us anything about the larger causes for France's defeat. As the rich memoir literature from this period suggests, many refugees perceived their experiences to be emblematic of the larger problems that ultimately brought about the country's demise. For Lion Feuchtwanger, for example, the internments were due not to deliberate malice or persecutory zeal on the part of the government. In speaking of his experiences at the camp of Les Milles, he repeatedly stressed that "there was never a case of beating, of punching, of verbal abuse." Rather, as he saw it, it was the very muddledness of French policy, the fact that French statesmen did not have their priorities straight, that led to the internments and ultimately to the defeat. Even if the initial internments were justified, the fact that the refugees were allowed to languish in the camps for months afterward, despite the fact that they could have been put to use for the war effort, was, Feuchtwanger believed, the result of "pure thoughtlessness, a lack of talent for organization." Whereas the German devil was one of sadism, the French devil assumed a more congenial, but no less pernicious form—that of bureaucratic ineptitude, irresponsibility, and a "genteel indifference to the sufferings of others," summed up by the motto, "Je m'en fous," or "I don't give a damn." For Feuchtwanger, this "je m'en foutist" attitude was responsible not only for the ill-conceived refugee policies of the Daladier administration, but for the military debacle as well.[178]

But while Feuchtwanger put the primary blame on bureaucratic ineptitude, others saw the internments as a sign of the deep defeatist mentality that had penetrated the bureaucracy, the population at large, and perhaps most significantly, the army command. According to Koestler, the internment of the anti-Nazi refugees was only one of many signs that the government hated its enemies on the left, particularly the foreigners, far more than its enemies on the right. As Koestler explained, military officers frequently blamed the war not on Hitler, but on Léon Blum & Co.—the socialists and communists, the refugees, and the Jews—and no one believed any longer in fighting to save democracy and freedom. Rather, the prevailing sentiment among the population as a whole, and among the troops as well, was "Il faillait en finir" ("It was necessary to get it over with"). A desire to preserve the status quo and be left in peace, together with the failure to see fascism and Nazism as significant threats to democracy, especially in comparison to communism, ultimately brought about what Koestler, together with Heinz Pol, referred to as the "suicide" of France.[179]

Hans Habe too perceived defeatism to be rampant among the ranks of the military. While his own commander, Lieutenant Saint-Brice, did his utmost to fight the Germans, Saint-Brice's superiors, according to Habe, wanted peace at any price and simply delivered their country over to the Germans. As one captain allegedly told Saint-Brice, "He loved France more than he loved Hitler, but . . . he loved Hitler more than Léon Blum." On another occasion, Saint-Brice explained that the real reason for France's defeat was not the state of her weaponry or munitions, but rather that "this was a war of Frenchmen against Frenchmen. And no one told us."[180] Alfred Döblin too recorded in his memoirs that after the initial mobilization in September, he never witnessed any enthusiasm for fighting among French soldiers. He furthermore noted that many of the soldiers returning from the front in June were actually glorifying Hitler.[181]

Despite the subjectivity of these accounts, the extent to which they concur in their assessments of administrative and military weaknesses, as well as on the pervasiveness of a defeatist mentality, is striking, and there is no doubt that the refugee experience afforded these writers a unique vantage point from which to survey the larger historical forces at work. Yet these accounts would also agree that the experience of refugees during the 1930's, while perhaps a prelude to what was to come during the Vichy era, nevertheless remained distinct from that experience.

Just as Feuchtwanger claimed that the nature of French refugee policy from September 1939 through June 1940 was not one of deliberate malice, in contrast to the situation in Germany, the same could also be said when comparing the refugee policies of the Daladier and Reynaud administrations to those of the Vichy regime. While xenophobia and antisemitism colored some of the policies under Daladier and Reynaud, these forces generally remained submerged. Under Vichy, however, deliberate malice and outright antisemitism surfaced almost immediately, and all notions that there might still be constructive solutions to the refugee crisis, solutions that would allow at least a portion of the refugees to live freely in France, were shelved once and for all. Under Vichy, in contrast to the situation at the end of the 1930's, there was simply no one left to argue the liberal line. Given the sharp deterioration of the economy following the defeat as well as the psychological need to find scapegoats, it is not surprising that the refugee population, which had so enthusiastically endorsed the war, became a principal target of popular indignation and administrative wrath. Already in September 1940, one Belgian refugee trapped in southern France lamented: "The democratic ideal, which seemed to be the essence of France itself, has yielded to xenophobia, [and] to poorly understood totalitarianism."[182]

CHAPTER TWELVE

The Great Invasion II, 1936–40

After having surveyed the political situation of the refugees until the fall of the Third Republic in June 1940, it is useful to return to the theme of public opinion, which after 1936 continued to serve as a constant impetus in the formation of refugee policy. From 1933 until 1936, as demonstrated in Chapter 4, anti-refugee sentiment was primarily the domain of the far right. Afterward, however, it became common currency even among many moderates. Two factors account for this shift. First, according to the British ambassador in Paris, Sir Eric Phipps, Léon Blum's election in 1936 had ignited a resurgence of antisemitism, unprecedented since the Dreyfus Affair. Phipps noted in the spring of 1938:

> As to M. Blum, members of the Right political parties and of the "monde," disturbed by the successes of the Left at the polls, and by the legislation introduced under successive Front Popular Governments, are apt to centre their political animosities on him personally, and, because he is a Jew, to abuse Jews in general. Such attacks are commonly heard at Paris dinner tables. Those responsible for them come, of course, mainly from circles where the fear of Communism leads to a certain sympathy for authoritarian régimes, and are perhaps not uninfluenced by the anti-Jewish movement in Germany.[1]

To be sure, this particular aspect of the antisemitic revival was not directly connected to the refugees. Nevertheless, it had profound implications for them as well. The refugees, as we have seen, had enthusiastically embraced the Popular Front and benefited tangibly from its liberalized refugee policies. Moreover, because Blum was both a socialist and a Jew, it was widely assumed that he shared their point of view, especially in foreign policy matters relating to Germany.

No less important in impelling many moderates into the anti-refugee camp was the sharp deterioration of the international situation, which provoked a growing fear of war. After the Germans remilitarized the Rhineland in 1936, and especially after the Anschluss and the Munich crisis of 1938, antiwar fever gripped the French population, and those eager to embrace the appeasement policies of the foreign minister, Georges Bonnet, tended to share his view that Hitler's victims—the refugees, the Jews, and the communists—and not Hitler himself, were responsible for bringing Europe to the brink of war. Moreover, as many contemporary observers noted, antiwar sentiment frequently masked a deep-seated fear that war would lead to social revolution at home, and ultimately to communist hegemony. By the end of the 1930's, it was widely believed that the enemy within—the left—was a far greater menace than the enemy without, a theme encapsulated in the popular slogan, "Rather Hitler than Blum."[2]

Since the refugees were perceived as leftists and warmongers, every stage of Nazi expansion had the paradoxical effect of hardening public opinion against them. Although Ralph Schor has recently claimed that refugee asylum was never seriously challenged in the 1930's,[3] considerable evidence suggests that by the time of the Munich crisis, the principle of asylum had been abandoned by all but a tiny minority of the French public. Even those who continued to argue in favor of "selective immigration," as opposed to a complete closure of the borders, increasingly excluded Jews from the list of desirable immigrants. Still, the pro-refugee camp, though diminished in size, never abandoned the struggle to keep the borders open. Instead, it launched a vigorous campaign to reinstitute the liberal policies of the Popular Front, and in 1939 its efforts, as we have seen, were crowned with some success. As this coalition maintained, support for the refugee cause and opposition to antisemitism were integral elements of the broader campaign to preserve democracy and republican values. That their cause ultimately failed was due not to any wavering of their republican sympathies or to any flirting with xenophobia and antisemitism, as has frequently been maintained. Instead, their defeat was due to the military debacle of 1940, which brought an abrupt end to republican France.

The Popular Front victory of May 1936 sharply polarized French political life, and Blum's opponents lost no time in using antisemitism to attack the new government. In Alsace, the electoral campaign had assumed such a fierce antisemitic cast that the Consistory of the Haut-Rhin felt compelled to call for government intervention, a move the left liberal paper *La Lumière* claimed was "without precedent in the annals of republican justice."[4] Violent antisemitic diatribes surfaced even on the floor of the Chamber of Deputies. In June, Xavier Vallat, deputy of the Ardèche and a prominent member of the Croix de Feu, the right-wing league headed by Colonel François de La Rocque, explained before Parliament why he had not voted for Blum. Addressing his remarks directly to the new prime minister, Vallat declared: "There's another reason that prevents me from voting in favor of the ministry of M. Blum: that's M. Blum himself. Your ascendance to power is incontestably a historic date. For the first time this old Gallo-Roman country will be governed by a Jew."

When the president of the Chamber, Edouard Herriot, demanded a retraction, denouncing such language as "inadmissable in a French tribune," Vallat not only refused, but went on to declare that Jews could never be truly French:

I have no intention of forgetting the friendship that binds me to my Jewish comrades in arms. Nor have I any intention of denying to members of the Jewish race the right to acclimate here, just like everyone else who has come here to be naturalized. Nevertheless, I must say . . . out loud what everyone else is thinking to themselves—that in order to govern this peasant nation that is France, it is preferable to have someone whose origins, no matter how modest, disappear into the bowels of our soil, rather than a subtle talmudist.

While the left banks of the Chamber vehemently protested Vallat's remarks, silence prevailed elsewhere, suggesting that Vallat's assertion of speaking for the majority was indeed correct.[5]

Several years earlier, Vallat had expressed similar views. In private correspondence with a Jewish war veteran, he had explained that while some Jews were perhaps not Bolsheviks, the fact remained that "the immense majority of your coreligionists are found enlisted in the ranks of the international and revolutionary army for which they increasingly furnish the most frightening leaders. Léon Blum personifies them to such a degree that he's currently turning members of his own group into antisemites. That man isn't French; his thought isn't French."[6] Echoing such sentiments, Senator Joseph Caillaux, a spokesman for the right-wing of the Radical Party, tarred Blum as foreign and unfit to govern because he "didn't have enough French earth on the soles of his shoes!"[7]

These smear campaigns extended to the entire Popular Front, and opponents of the new government repeatedly charged that Blum had stacked his cabinet and administration with Jewish appointments. In reality, the number of Jews holding high-ranking posts was not excessive. Blum's first cabinet (June 4, 1936, to June 21, 1937) included four Jews besides himself:

Jules Moch, Cécile Léon Brunschvicg, Marx Dormoy, and Jean Zay, who was half-Jewish. His second cabinet (March 13, 1938, to April 8, 1938) also included four Jews: Moch, Dormoy, Zay, and Pierre Mendès France. Nevertheless, the perception that Jews dominated persisted. According to Phipps, it was commonly believed that Marius Moutet, Blum's minister of colonies, was Jewish, and historian Steven Schuker has recently identified Ludovic-Oscar Frossard, who served as minister of propaganda in Blum's second cabinet, as a Jew, an identification not substantiated elsewhere.[8]

More important, however, was the fact that Blum's personal entourage did include several Jews, such as André Blumel and Georges Boris, and even the Jewish socialist deputy Pierre-Bloch admitted that Blum had appointed large numbers of Jews to lower level administrative posts. According to a 1937 letter sent by a "prominent Catholic personality" to *La Juste parole*, a recently created "philosemitic" journal (an organ of Catholic opinion devoted to fighting antisemitism), French youth felt that they had been "eliminated from positions for the benefit of Jews who have only just become French and scarcely even know how to speak our language." During Blum's second cabinet, La Rocque, who now headed the nation's largest right-wing party, the Parti Social Français, railed against the premier's "adulterated" government, which "has literally filled cabinet posts, and all other important and well paid positions, with a Jewish clientele that is all too often revolutionary, sometimes German or just recently naturalized, and nearly always ostentatious and indiscreet."[9]

Although the French Jewish community vigorously refuted these charges, it too feared a resurgence of antisemitism. As Phipps reported, when Blum "first came into power, one of the Rothschild family had expressed the hope to a member of my staff that M. Blum would avoid doing so." The ambassador similarly noted the unconfirmed rumors that the chief rabbi of France had intervened personally with Blum to dissuade him from assuming office. According to André Blumel, the chief rabbi had even offered Blum a lifetime pension equivalent to his salary as head of state if he would agree to step down.[10]

Aside from Blum's election, the Popular Front's refugee policies further fanned the flames of antisemitism. In August of 1936, *L'Action française* railed against the recently signed Geneva Accord that granted an amnesty to German refugees already in France and protected them against arbitrary expulsion or deportation:

What is one to think of this measure? In this country, stricken with unemployment, the idiots who govern us have opened our borders to everyone Germany is trying to get rid of. France has therefore become the refuge of undesirables.

Besides, how many of these allegedly persecuted individuals and refugees are in reality spies working on behalf of Germany?[11]

At the same time, as we have seen, spokesmen for the liberal and commercial professions stepped up their demands for increased protection against the newcomers, and they specifically attacked the overly generous naturalization policies of the new government. Other commentators blamed the mass strikes of 1936 on foreign machinations. According to the *Revue de deux mondes*, this labor strife was "the result of a skillfully prepared organization, operating according to methods imported from abroad, [and] implemented by ringleaders who . . . were purveyors of orders emanating" from Moscow. By having granted asylum to "elements expelled by governments more concerned with their national health," France had become the "victim of its imprudent generosity."[12] Most strikingly, even some Radicals endorsed these demands. In October 1937, Herriot railed against foreign merchants who "abuse the right to asylum and import a policy of 'dumping,'" and he denounced the excessive number of foreign workers "who constitute a veritable danger for the national labor force." Most significantly, he joined his colleagues to the right in castigating the overly generous naturalization procedures of the Popular Front. Such indiscretion, he warned, could have dangerous political as well as economic repercussions.[13]

The most portentous charge against the refugees, however, was that they were seeking to drag France into an undesired war. Although this charge was by no means new, it acquired added poignancy in the aftermath of the Nazi invasion of the Rhineland in March 1936. Already at that time, a British embassy official in Paris reported that "In political circles of [the] centre and right and even in the press, allusion is being made to a Jewish conspiracy to drag the country into a war at the behest of Moscow, and I should not be surprised if there were to be an increase of anti-Jewish agitation within the next few days." The next day, this same official reported that La Rocque had recently delivered a speech in which he had declared that "France must not allow herself to be rushed into war with Germany by an oligarchy of Jewish financiers or by the partisans of the Soviet alliance."[14]

In October, Edmond Jaloux, a member of the Academie Française, gave further credence to these claims in an article titled "The Undesirables," which appeared in the conservative daily *L'Echo de Paris*. According to Jaloux, the refugees in France were not only inciting revolutionary discord, but they were also seeking to drag the nation into a war to satisfy their personal lust for revenge. Indeed, from Jaloux's perspective, these aims were intertwined:

Among the refugees settled here, some are working on behalf of universal revolution and would like to drag us into a social cataclysm, the consequences of which cannot be foreseen. But others are seeking to incite a hatred toward their respective countries among our own population. If we want peace, it is not beneficial that so many Italians, and especially so many Germans, *constantly incite French groups to turn against their respective countries*. We have even seen them request that France . . . declare war on Germany in order to get rid of Chancellor Hitler!

If the French were determined to "destroy their own house," that was their prerogative, "but it's our right, too," Jaloux maintained, "to demand that those in charge of the demolition not be recruited among outsiders." Moreover, Jaloux warned, these refugees were more dangerous than previous generations of immigrants. They were:

already formed, embittered, [and] irritable. Most often expelled from their native countries for their political attitudes, they will perpetuate and pass down from one generation to the next the echo of their quarrels, their partisan passions, their revolutionary myths, their frenzied discontent. Such individuals can never be made into true Frenchmen; at the least sign of trouble, their tumultuous heredity will reemerge and inflict upon us untold harm, either through treason or by preparing for war.

As a result, Jaloux declared, these refugees could never "become soldiers ready to die for us."[15] Fears such as Jaloux's ultimately led some right-wing deputies in 1936 to demand the mandatory expulsion or internment of all foreigners under 50 years of age in the event of a military mobilization.[16]

The theme of Jewish warmongering, carried out under the aegis of Léon Blum and his German émigré cohorts, also figured prominently in the most violent antisemitic diatribe of the pre-Munich period, Louis-Ferdinand Céline's *Bagatelles pour un massacre*, published in 1937. This book, written by a former medical doctor, was described by Phipps as "400 pages of hysterical abuse of the Jews as the corrupters of all healthy French institutions." The Jewish defense organization, the Centre de Documentation et de Vigilance (CDV), attributed Céline's rantings to Nazi subsidies as well as to the fact that he had received two unremovable bullets to his head during the First World War. Nevertheless, this work was enormously influential in extreme-right-wing circles.[17]

Like his intellectual predecessor, the late nineteenth-century antisemitic leader Edouard Drumont, as well as Céline's contemporary German counterpart, Hitler, Céline railed against Jewish domination. In contrast to Drumont, however, who had aimed his most venomous barbs at the Rothschilds, Céline's target was Léon Blum and his Jewish Bolshevik allies. Following the Popular Front victory, Céline charged that France had become "a colony for Jewish international power." Bolshevism was nothing more than a Jewish plot to rule the world, and to further their revolutionary goals, the Jews were prepared to plunge the world into yet another world war, more devastating than that of 1914–18. While such an upheaval might satisfy the thirst for revenge of "those little Jews [who had been] kicked out of every good German job," it was not in France's interests: "A war for the joy of the Jews! That would really enflame their gangrene, their worst buboes. I can't imagine any humiliation worse than having to die for the yids; from my view, nothing would be more ignoble and degrading."[18] Given a choice between Jewish and German domination, Céline had no doubt which was preferable: "As for me, I make no distinction whatsoever between the Jewish army of Blum and the boche army of Falkenhayn. . . . They're the same humiliation, the same shackles, the same debasement, the same shame. . . . There's absolutely no difference . . . between the Jewish peace and the German peace. . . . And, I prefer the German peace any day."[19]

Despite this hysterical anti-refugee rhetoric from the extreme right, and increasingly from the conservative right as well, the debate over the refugees remained relatively subdued during the Popular Front, since their numbers tapered off significantly during these years. In 1938, however, this situation changed dramatically as a result of the Anschluss, the Munich crisis, and Kristallnacht. These events created thousands of new refugees, and for the first time the refugee crisis was extended beyond Germany's own borders. At the same time, they signaled a sharp deterioration in the international situation, bringing Europe ever closer to war. Although the economic concerns that had figured so prominently in the refugee debate prior to 1936 continued to be aired, these fears were increasingly subsumed by growing political anxieties, and especially the fear that the refugees, together with their "Bolshevik" comrades in the Popular Front, were seeking to embroil France in a war for their own ends. By the end of 1938, these fears impelled even many formerly pro-refugee advocates to join the anti-refugee camp. And notwithstanding the military and economic exigencies that encouraged a more lenient refugee and immigrant policy with the approach of war, these fears paved the way for the fifth-column hysteria that swept the country in September 1939.

Not surprisingly, the extreme right, and especially the Action Française, still "carried the ball" when it came to the anti-refugee campaign.[20] Every political charge that had been leveled before the Popular Front—that the refugees constituted a potential fifth column and were fomenting war to further their own ends—was now instilled with fresh urgency. At the time of the Munich crisis, *L'Action française* flatly stated that "the French do not want to fight—neither for the Jews, the Russians, nor the Freemasons of Prague,"[21] and it declared that the émigrés, notwithstanding their anti-German rhetoric, were in reality seeking to strengthen the Reich so that they could recover their lost fortunes and positions. When the German diplomat Ernst vom Rath was assassinated in France, *L'Action française* seized the occasion to blast the Daladier administration's lax surveillance at the border, which had permitted an illegal refugee like Grynszpan to commit his odious crime. Was France destined to remain forever "the battlefield for all the *métèques* [foreigners] of Europe and the entire world, and will we always have to pay the consequences for acts as heinous as the one that occurred yesterday? . . . The great city of Paris is fed up with having to serve as the garbage dump for the entire cosmopolitan criminal underground. There are limits to the right to asylum."[22]

Even Kristallnacht failed to evince any sympathy. While acknowledging that Jews had been victimized, their suffering, Maurras insisted, had been wildly exaggerated: "Synagogues have been burned, stores have been ramshackled and even pillaged. Large enough numbers of Jewish troops have been expelled. But people are crying out as if there have been numerous deaths. There were no deaths. People say: *pogrom*. Pogrom means a massacre of Jews. Jews haven't been massacred. To be beaten up is one thing. To be massacred is another."[23] Why, Maurras wondered, was everyone making such a fuss over the Jews, when no one had protested other recent atrocities, such as the persecution of the Spanish Catholics or that of the Rhineland separatists by the Weimar government? Above all, *L'Action française* warned that Kristallnacht serve neither "as a pretext for us to be inundated with Jews . . . nor as a pretext for war." "The prestige of France," Charles Maurras declared, "isn't threatened when one burns down a synagogue somewhere. One can burn them all. It's not our business and it has no impact whatsoever on us. No diplomatic intervention, no war for the Jews."[24]

Others on the far right followed suit. During the Munich crisis, *Je suis partout*, the mouthpiece of the young guard of the extreme right, railed against German Jews who congregated in the cafés on the Champs Elysées: "At all the tables, the usual combinations, cinematographers and stock brokers, devote themselves to one topic only: will France finally attack Hitler? These brazen fellows, chased out of Berlin or Vienna, have no hope other than returning to their homes, to reestablish their dominance over the Kurfürstendamm or the Ring. They cling to this hope with a frenzy."[25] After the crisis subsided, *Je suis partout* even suggested that the Jews be made to pay for the mobilization.

At the time of vom Rath's assassination, Lucien Rebatet railed against the refugees, whom he referred to as "those animals" and "a band of filthy lice vomited up by Poland." Ultimately, however, all Jews were to blame: "That the Jews feel the need to settle their quarrels with the Germans, that's entirely comprehensible. But that they've chosen Paris for this end, that's intolerable. That the Jews have come to poison our already difficult and perilous relations with the Germans by shooting their revolvers at [German] diplomats here, that's simply going too far." To ensure that justice be meted out, Rebatet called on the authorities to turn Grynszpan over to the Germans.[26] Moreover, right-wing pacifists increasingly accused anyone opposed to their views of being in the pay of the Judeo-communist conspiracy. In December 1938, the powerful right-wing industrialist François de Wendel accused Henri de Kérillis, executive editor of *L'Epoque* and the sole conservative deputy to have voted against the Munich Accord, of being "a scoundrel completely in the hands of the left and the Jews who are up-in-arms over antisemitism."[27] *Le Matin* too attributed the pro-war fever to "an occult force"—the refugees and ultimately the Soviet Union—whose sole goal was to drag Europe into an "apocalyptic battle."[28]

For the extreme right, there was one solution only: to abolish the right to asylum altogether. The decree laws were wholly inadequate, and as Raymond Recouly wrote in *Gringoire*, although the Nazi treatment of Jews was deplorable, "it is . . . impossible to receive on our territory . . . all the Jews chased from their countries without provoking a violent reaction."[29] The right-wing daily *Le Journal*, which at the time of the Evian Conference had compared the incursion of refugees into France to the fifth-century barbarian invasion of Rome, called on the government to "purge" the "undesirables who have swollen the ranks of the international underworld." Recognizing that the majority of these "undesirables" could not be expelled because they had been banned from their native countries, *Le Journal* recommended that they be placed for the time being in concentration camps in France.[30] This view was endorsed by Rebatet as well. At the time of the Anschluss, he had declared that "sooner or later the concentration camp will become a necessity in a country that remains open to the scum of the entire continent." If tighter immigration policies were not implemented immediately, "a blind pogrom—brutal and liberating—would at some time or another take care of everything."[31]

These extreme-right-wing demands for more stringent immigration policies were linked to renewed calls for both a general immigration statute, which would impose severe restrictions on the rights of foreigners in France, and a specifically Jewish statute. In October 1938, Maurras proposed a special statute for immigrants that called for the expulsion of all foreigners involved in political or criminal activities, a ban preventing foreigners from acquiring property, discriminatory treatment of foreign workers, special taxes on foreigners, a revision of all naturalizations granted since 1936, and a waiting period of two to three generations before naturalized foreigners would become eligible for full political rights.[32] A similar program was endorsed by La Rocque's Parti Social Français as well. After the Munich crisis, the Alsatian branch of the organization decried the fact that "Jews with neither hearth nor home have invaded Alsace by the thousands, to the great detriment of our laborious population." It therefore proposed an immigration statute that, in addition to Maurras's program, called for a revision of naturalizations granted since 1918, a complete ban on naturalized citizens holding public office, and a twenty-year waiting period before naturalized citizens could hold culturally influential posts, including the practice of law, medicine, journalism, as well as positions in the media and the arts.[33]

Although La Rocque himself sought to tone down the extreme anti-semitism of the Alsatian branch's program, there is little doubt that he too embraced these anti-immigrant provisions.[34] *Je suis partout*, meanwhile, complemented its anti-immigrant demands with a call to restrict Jewish rights in general because, it maintained, no matter how assimilated they had become, Jews always remained foreigners. In March, Rebatet argued that undesirable foreigners, who, he insisted, were nearly always left-wing Jews, be separated from the desirable ones—the Swiss and the Belgians, for example.[35] Moreover, Rebatet, together with his confrere at *Je suis partout*, Robert Brasillach, drew up a special "Jewish statute" that called for a ban on Jewish immigration; the withdrawal of citizenship from all Jews; the exclusion of Jews from public office; the imposition of a *numerus clausus*, or quota, on Jews in the liberal professions, commerce, cinema, and the press; and a requirement that all Jews carry a special identity card. While this statute provided exemptions for individual Jews who had performed exceptional services to the state, it mirrored Nazi racial legislation in that it covered half Jews as well.[36]

Nor were such demands aired only in the extreme-right-wing press. They also had considerable support among the far-right-wing delegates to the Paris Municipal Council—Pierre Dailly, Henri Torchaussé, Charles Trochu, Georges Lebecq, and especially Louis Darquier de Pellepoix, director of the Rassemblement Anti-Juif, a federation of antisemitic organizations, and executive editor of the antisemitic papers *La Rafale* and *La France enchaînée*. From 1936 on, this coalition clamored for the adoption of an immigrant statute directed primarily at Jews, as well as for a more general Jewish statute. Such a statute would impose a *numerus clausus* on Jews in various professions, levy special taxes on Jews, and strip all Jews—French and foreign alike—of their citizenship.

Although this campaign made little headway, it may have played some role in persuading the government to implement the ban on refugee settlement in the department of the Seine in the fall of 1938. Most significantly, Darquier de Pellepoix, who eventually became commissioner-general for Jewish affairs under Vichy, accomplished what was clearly his major goal: the introduction of virulent antisemitism into the Municipal Council's proceedings. On one occasion, after he provoked an acrimonious debate over Jewish naturalizations, the Hôtel de Ville became the scene of a violent melée.[37] On another, when he protested the fact that the president of the Municipal Council, Le Provost de Launay, had sent congratulations to the newly appointed chief rabbi of France on behalf of the entire council, Le Provost de Launay himself, who was no great friend of the Jews, publicly rebuked Darquier for his outrageous antisemitic behavior, which, he claimed, was promoting a spirit of national divisiveness.[38] According to the *Droit de vivre*, the organ of the LICA, the provocations of Darquier and his right-wing colleagues had transformed the bulletin of the Municipal Council, the official transcript of the council's minutes, into an antisemitic propaganda sheet, financed at taxpayers' expense.[39] In one instance, Le Provost de Launay actually excised Darquier's antisemitic remarks from the bulletin, deeming them unfit for a government publication.[40]

While the tone of the extreme right's rhetoric over the refugees, and increasingly over Jews in general, became more hysterical as the threat of war became imminent, their program was entirely consistent with their stance since 1933. What most distinguished the debate in 1938 and 1939 from earlier years is the degree to which many moderates, including not only conservatives but also many Radicals and a few dissident socialists, began to move into the extreme-right-wing camp. On the conservative right, this shift was perhaps most noticeable in the attitude of *Le Temps*. Usually considered the semiofficial mouthpiece of the Quai d'Orsay, this paper had expressed considerable sympathy for the refugees in 1933 and 1934. By 1938, however, *Le Temps* advocated complete closure of the borders for all but a few exceptional individuals, notwithstanding its repeated assertions that the right to asylum remained inviolable. For *Le Temps*, the refugee issue had important economic, social, and political consequences that threatened the very existence of the nation. With regard to the economic aspect of the refugee problem, *Le Temps*, which had vigorously opposed protectionist anti-immigrant legislation prior to 1936, completely reversed its position. Average citizens, *Le Temps* declared, were rightfully concerned about "the competition these foreigners pose in commercial matters and in the labor market, as well as in the domain of the liberal professions." Given that these foreign "competitors" often failed to comply with "professional rules and regulations imposed by our nationals," it was only just that their entry be barred.[41]

Socially too France's excessively generous refugee policy had grave consequences. At the time of the Evian Conference, *Le Temps* echoed Béranger's declarations almost verbatim, declaring that France was "already saturated with foreigners," and that in the future it could serve as a transit country only.[42] It was not only the right, but the duty of every nation to ensure that "a certain physical, moral and intellectual equilibrium not be abruptly disrupted by a pronounced influx of elements too different and sometimes unassimilable."[43] These foreigners did not constitute an element "of order and prosperity, but, to the contrary, they encumber the labor market, press our police to the limit, overburden our relief services, and at times even mar the physical appearance of our cities."[44] A policy of selective immigration, one that would weed out the good from the bad elements, was therefore imperative. While there was no question of France needing to increase the size of its population, for economic as well as military reasons, it was precisely because of the chronically low birthrate that the issue of selection had become so pressing. As *Le Temps* declared:

Quantitatively, . . . a country as unprolific as ours cannot afford to accommodate an influx of foreigners that will sharply reduce the numerical proportion between natives and foreigners. We are all too well aware that our low fertility constitutes an argument in favor of a policy of demographic growth carried out via a policy of wisely conceived and closely supervised naturalizations. But enough is enough, and besides, the qualitative aspect of the problem counsels us to be prudent in this regard. The unfortunate fact is that, alas, it is not the elites of Europe . . . who are flocking to us.[45]

To ensure that at least a modicum of social homogeneity be preserved, *Le Temps* even suggested that the 1927 naturalization law, which extended citizenship automatically to children of foreigners born in France, be revised, all the while insisting that foreigners be obligated to perform military service.[46]

Despite these socioeconomic concerns, *Le Temps*'s decision to opt for a hard-line position on the refugee question was almost certainly motivated by political factors. Following the assassination of vom Rath, the paper railed against the hordes of "undesirables," who, like Grynszpan, had "used our territory to indulge in either the most shady sorts of political maneuvers, or in the most criminal acts, without giving the least thought . . . to . . . French interests." It was intolerable, *Le Temps* declared, that France remained "the *only* country in the world where political refugees from all nations are free to come settle their quarrels, [and] to carry out . . . kidnappings, and murders, which . . . disrupt order, embarrass public authorities, [and] trample underfoot public law and common law." To stanch this "positively invading" influx, two measures needed to be adopted instantly. First, there had to be better police surveillance over refugees already in the country. It was necessary to "expel without hesitation everyone who is not absolutely above reproach." Second, tougher border controls needed to be adopted to keep out future newcomers. *Refoulement*, *Le Temps* argued, ought to become the norm rather than the exception. Public opinion was fed up with "political refugees who, by definition, are future recipients of public assistance or future delinquents, competitors to workers or French intellectuals . . . , and whose contradictory ideologies, by clashing with one another on our soil, cannot but create disorder, encourage violence, [and] cause blood to flow."[47]

With the influx into France of the Spanish republicans in early 1939, these concerns became truly alarming. No longer could there be any doubt that what *Le Temps* feared above all was that these refugees were carriers of left-wing ideologies. Together with other conservative papers, *Le Temps* described the flight of the half million Spanish republicans across the border as a military invasion. "A foreign army has today penetrated our soil," *Le Temps* declared,[48] and it warned that although "no one would contest the fact that the vast majority of these expatriates are brave people, worthy of respect, . . . a few of these guests . . . have introduced a mentality against which we have to guard ourselves."[49] To "preserve our country physically and morally from a veritable invasion," it was imperative to adopt a more rational and selective immigration policy, even if this meant excluding legitimate refugees. The presence of so many political refugees, whether "nazis, fascists, antifascists, or communists, would become terrifying if France were to have to respond to an act of aggression."[50] If government measures were not enacted soon, "xenophobic and antisemitic movements would become widespread."[51] As *Le Temps* lamented, "Our liberalism, sometimes carried too far, must now give way to our security."[52]

These views were echoed by other conservative papers as well. According to *L'Intransigeant*, Grynszpan's crime constituted "additional testimony to our weakness," and in an editorial titled "Enough Foreigners," the paper's editor asked whether the government was finally prepared "to take . . . radical measures to stop the invasion of France by foreign hordes." While France boasted of being hospitable, it was supposed to be intelligent as well, and it was now time to adopt a more selective immigration policy so that only those "who were physically and morally intact" be admitted.[53] The *Journal de débats* concurred, and in the aftermath of vom Rath's assassination declared it intolerable that other countries felt free to "empty their rubbish into our garbage bin."[54] Stéphane Lauzanne of *Le Matin* similarly advocated granting asylum to Jewish refugees only on condition "that they faithfully observe French laws, French traditions, [and] the French spirit. . . . To adhere to France is not to adhere to parties of social subversion which dream of overthrowing it. To serve France is not to serve Franco-Russian bolshevism."[55] *L'Epoque* too, despite Kérillis's outspoken opposition to antisemitism, nevertheless perceived all foreigners, including the refugees, as a grave threat. France, according to one of the paper's commentators, was undergoing a "pacific invasion." Not only were foreigners disproportionately represented among the criminal classes, but the recently naturalized among them had helped elect "those deplorable tyrants of

May 1936." Moreover, if war were to break out, France would now be in the unfortunate position of having "500,000 revolutionaries at our backs."[56]

Clerical opinion too, which in the early 1930's, despite some ambivalence, had generally been sympathetic to the refugee cause, grew increasingly hostile after the Popular Front. In 1938, a number of clerical spokesmen even went so far as to demand a *numerus clausus*, not only for Jewish immigrants but for all Jews, French and foreign alike. The most controversial of these appeals was issued by Joseph Rossé—deputy from the Haut-Rhin; president of the Alsatian autonomist party, the Union Populaire Républicaine (UPR); and director of the powerful Catholic press consortium, Alsatia, which published the *Elsässer Kurier*. At the time of the Munich crisis, Rossé wrote a series of articles for this paper titled "An Open Word to Our Fellow Jewish Citizens" in which he expatiated on the reasons behind the recent outburst of antisemitism in Alsace. Rebutting left-wing claims that antisemitism in the border provinces was being whipped up by Nazi agitators, Rossé insisted that this phenomenon was due exclusively to indigenous factors. Among these factors, he cited the recent influx of German refugees, Jewish domination over the region's cultural and economic life, Jewish warmongering and reports that Jews had fled to safety during the mobilization, and the disproportionate role of Jews in the Popular Front and their long-standing support of anticlerical legislation.

In an article of October 2, paternalistically titled "What Do We Expect from True Jews?" Rossé cited but one example of the way in which Jews had become overbearing. Jewish lawyers, he claimed, had constituted only 10 percent of the Alsatian bar in 1918, whereas today they represented over 30 percent. As a result of this "colossal increase," he declared, "many Christian lawyers have been pushed to near starvation, so they revolt and antisemitism begins to take hold." Once antisemitism was recognized as "a reaction to an aggressive semitism," the solution to the "Jewish problem" became clear:

Since it is highly unlikely that the Jews themselves will be able to impose the necessary restrictions on their own society, the impetus must come from outside—and, if necessary—from the legal realm. The introduction of a numerus clausus will almost certainly spare us from a wave of popular uprisings in which the masses will demand, with justification, the implementation of measures similar to those already in effect in Germany and Italy. The Jews have the same right to live as the Christians, but not any privilege.[57]

Rossé's statements ignited a storm of controversy, especially after the Christian Democratic paper *L'Aube*, which was generally sympathetic to Jews, published a letter by Rossé on October 14 in which these ideas were set forth for the broader public.[58] Emile Buré, the conservative editor of

L'Ordre, criticized Francisque Gay, *L'Aube*'s executive editor, for having provided Rossé with a platform for his antisemitic views, and he blasted Rossé's contention that he was merely acting in the Jews' own best interest. "The good apostle," Buré charged, "dreams of setting fire to the temple of Israel in order to save it from the flames of antisemitism."[59] Rossé, Buré insisted, was nothing more than the Alsatian equivalent of Konrad Henlein, the Sudeten German leader, and there could be no doubt that "in our recovered provinces, antisemitism is the harbinger of hitlerism." *La Lumière* too condemned Rossé's antisemitic attacks as an expression of "the best hitlerian propaganda,"[60] and according to *Le Populaire*, in light of Rossé's stature, antisemitism in the recovered provinces could no longer be dismissed as a marginal phenomenon, the work of a few German-paid agents. The real reason for Rossé's anti-Jewish campaign, it maintained, was to wean voters away from even more extreme antisemitic parties, such as Joseph Bilger's Bauernbund (Peasant Front).[61]

That other leading clerical spokesmen shared Rossé's views suggests, however, that more was at stake than Alsatian electoral politics. *La Croix*, the principal organ of Catholic opinion, with close ties to the Vatican, published two articles in the fall of 1938 that closely mirrored Rossé's views. On September 1, in a general exposition of the Jewish problem in Europe, Léon Merklen, the paper's executive editor, again blamed Jews themselves for antisemitism. In times of revolution and social crisis, Merklen argued, "many Jews, out of a spirit of vengeance or revenge, side with the instigators of disorder." Moreover, he claimed, the manifold faults of the Jews provided "sufficient motives for defiance and hostility against them." Among these faults, he listed, "their tendency to monopolize, their habit of pushing themselves into influential posts, . . . their solidarity that transcends [national] borders, . . . their practical racism . . . [and] their materialist conception of life." Although Merklen acknowledged the Church's opposition to the sort of violent antisemitism common in Germany, Austria, and Poland, he nevertheless admitted:

The Church accepts the fact that Christians need to adopt measures of defense against their [the Jews'] invasion into civil or political life. She has never condemned the *numerus clausus* in effect in East European universities, nor has she ever set up obstacles to state-sponsored projects aimed at restricting the participation of Jews in civil service positions or the liberal professions to their proportion in the population.[62]

A few weeks later, Jean Guiraud, the paper's former executive editor, reiterated the claim that although the Church could not condone violent antisemitism, nonviolent forms of anti-Jewish discrimination, such as those endorsed by the medieval Church, were perfectly acceptable: "All countries and all societies have the right to defend themselves against the introduction of foreign elements which foster their disintegration, and it was this right she [the Church] used against the Jews." These medieval precedents, Guiraud contended, could "serve us well in studying the situation of foreigners in France [today] and in suggesting what measures might justifiably be used against those who are undesirable."[63] Even more liberal Catholics, such as Stanislas Fumet, executive editor of *Le Temps présent*, noted that nations had the right "to defend themselves against an excessive percentage of Jews in a country's high level positions." Citing the disproportionate role of Jews in Léon Blum's cabinets, Fumet insisted that "the *numerus clausus* is perhaps not an arrangement to be rejected."[64]

Although most Catholic spokesmen stopped short of advocating a full-fledged *numerus clausus*, they generally agreed that Jews had become excessively dominant, that they were bearers of revolutionary and anticlerical ideologies, and that they were responsible for the worst excesses of capitalism. In a 1937 statement explaining his decision to join the patronage committee of the newly created philosemitic journal, *La Juste parole*, the Catholic novelist and publicist François Mauriac declared that although antisemitism was a "sin against charity," one nevertheless had to admit that:

Israel is at times partly responsible for the instinct of defense it evokes among certain nations in certain historical epochs. . . .

The Jews cannot perpetuate themselves, marry amongst themselves, jealously isolate themselves from Christians, without evoking a reaction of defense and hostility.

They cannot monopolize international finance without making others feel they are being dominated by them. They cannot sprout up wherever one of their own has been successful (Minister Blum), without evoking hatred because they themselves have indulged in [anti-Christian] reprisals.[65]

"The fight against antisemitism," Mauriac declared, "must begin among the Jews themselves." And although he rejected the idea of a *numerus clausus*, he nevertheless called on Jews to behave with greater "tact" and "sensibility" so as not to offend their Christian neighbors.[66]

The Catholic journalist Robert d'Harcourt expressed similar ambivalence. Shortly after the Evian Conference, d'Harcourt called for a more restrictive refugee policy. Concurring with Bérenger that France had reached the "saturation point," d'Harcourt opined "that when the volume of foreign immigration reaches . . . the 'flash point,' . . . considerations of hospitality, tradition, and even humanity cannot intervene. A people cannot consent to their own self-destruction out of an obligation to love their neighbor. Faced with the dilemma—firmness or suicide—there can be no hesitation . . . , since suicide itself constitutes on assault on the moral order."

Besides, d'Harcourt added, the political inclinations of the recent arrivals could not be ignored: "Many toxic elements have slipped into France since the war. . . . Revolutionary marxism has found its bullion of natural culture in the disintegrative elements other countries have rejected. The totalitarian states have very generously made us a present of their bacilli. . . . As Catholics, we have often come face to face with the threat of the marxist spirit of disintegration, which is frequently supported by the Jew." Although d'Harcourt did not reject the tradition of asylum altogether, he nevertheless insisted that some refugees—"our own," that is, our "Catholic brothers"—merited priority over others. That the recently created Mauriac Committee, established especially to assist Austrian Catholic refugees, was funded almost exclusively with Rothschild money was not, of course, mentioned in d'Harcourt's article.[67]

Such ambivalence was apparent even in the philosemitic press. Just prior to vom Rath's assassination, Oscar de Férenzy, the editor of *La Juste parole*, argued that despite the moral imperative to help the refugees, France could no longer accept them all. It was simply too dangerous, he declared, since they were "alien to our language, our culture, [and] our customs. Moreover, they were likely . . . to become a crushing burden on our public assistance organizations . . . and were almost certain to embrace extremist doctrines, which, alas, already count far too many devotees." Thus, Férenzy concluded, "the right to asylum includes limits before which even Christian charity must bow."[68]

Yet a final cause for the lack of sympathy among Catholics was a deep resentment arising from the anticlerical campaigns of the past, which they blamed on the socialists, the League for the Rights of Man and Citizen, and the Jews, whom they identified with the two other groups. As long as the 1901 ban on religious congregations remained in effect, why, these Catholics wondered, should they feel any obligation to help Jewish refugees? As one provincial Catholic paper stated, "Before lauding the right to asylum at international conferences, our politicians would do well to allow the French religious [congregations] to return to France."[69] *La Croix du Rhône* similarly published a letter recommending that any demand that France open its doors to Jewish refugees be coupled with a demand to "welcome back the French religious exiles. Let's open our home to the banished of the world, but our own have a place here as well."[70]

Such sentiments surfaced even in the Radical press. Attempting to bridge the long-standing divide between Radicals and Catholics in order to fight the Marxist left, Léo-Abel Gaboriaud, a leading editorialist for the right-wing Radical paper *L'Ere nouvelle*, blamed the fantastic surge of antisemitism in Alsace on the "stupid and odious" anticlericalism of the Jews. He therefore counseled them, and especially the refugees, to abstain from any behavior that might cause "the inhabitants of the countries that . . . are offering you hospitality . . . to believe that you intend to supplant them in every high-ranking position and to deprive them of their most cherished liberties."[71] So intense had this bitterness become that when one Protestant minister tried to persuade several Alsatian Catholic leaders to sign a petition protesting Nazi antisemitic excesses at the time of Kristallnacht, they refused, citing the fact that the Jews, and especially the government of Léon Blum, had not spoken out against the persecution of Catholics in Spain.[72]

Still, the increasingly negative attitude toward Jewish refugees and Jews in general among many conservatives and Catholics was not altogether surprising in light of their fervid anticommunism and hostility to the Popular Front. That these trends surfaced also among Radical circles and dissident left-wing groups came as a far greater shock to the native Jewish community, as well to foreign observers like Phipps, who saw them as symptoms of the rapid diffusion of antisemitism in France.[73] Mounting xenophobia among the ranks of the Radical Party was already apparent at the party congress of southwestern federations in January 1938. A motion adopted here called for a rigorous ban on foreign workers who did not have work permits as well as the *refoulement* of all illegal aliens. And while exempting political refugees from these provisions, this motion made the right to asylum conditional on their complete abstinence from all political activity: "It's not a matter of France behaving in a xenophobic fashion, but merely of engaging in self-defense."[74]

The Radical newspaper *L'Oeuvre*, which for the most part had been extremely pro-refugee earlier in the 1930's, also adopted an increasingly harsh stance. When the May 2, 1938, decree law, which imposed new restrictions on foreigners, was announced, *L'Oeuvre* still expressed a generally pro-refugee view. Although it hailed the decree law as necessary, claiming that too many undesirables had entered France in recent years, it nevertheless insisted that the right to asylum had to be guaranteed for true refugees—"the stateless people and the 'underdogs of the world' . . . who have not been able to find any other country of asylum."[75]

By the fall, however, the category of those refugees *L'Oeuvre* considered "undesirable" expanded considerably. In two articles in October and November 1938, Paul Elbel, who represented the Vosges in the Chamber of Deputies and who had just resigned as president of the Radical faction in the Chamber, warned that antisemitism in Alsace was reaching dangerous proportions, providing an "admirable field of maneuver . . . for Hitlerian propaganda." For Elbel, the principal cause of this antisemitism was the recent influx of Jewish refugees. Although he praised the behavior of the native Alsatian Jewish community as beyond reproach, the same could not be said of the more recent arrivals. As a result of the centuries of persecution they had suffered, they had been forced "to live from second-hand dealing and often from usury. Not all of them are easy to assimilate." The fact that they had arrived at the height of the Depression made their assimilation especially difficult. "These immigrants," Elbel contended, "have neither the discretion to earn their living penuriously, nor the tact to die of hunger. They attempt to make it in business. Some of them succeed, and sometimes ostentatiously. . . . They rent either the most elegant shops or sordid little boutiques, depending on their resources. They settle in cities where apartments are scarce, and thus contribute to soaring rents."

Moreover, Elbel claimed, their behavior at the time of the Munich mobilization had greatly antagonized local opinion. "Many of them, exempted from all military obligations, were able to conserve matériel untouched by the requisitions, and could thus continue their business activities profitably at the very moment the majority of Frenchmen were forced to suspend theirs." Such abuses had to be stopped. Otherwise, Elbel maintained, this "distressing" and "offensive" antisemitism, by providing a wedge for the infiltration of Nazi propaganda, would eventually threaten French national security. To remedy this situation, Elbel proposed a three-pronged program: first, he called for more stringent limits on immigration, especially into the border provinces; second, he demanded that Jewish immigrants show more tact and renounce "a too rapid enrichment"; and third, he called for the immediate implementation of a "statute for foreigners." The aim of such a statute would be to ensure that all beneficiaries of the right to asylum be subject to the same obligations as citizens, including military service. Xenophobia and antisemitism would disappear, Elbel claimed, only when the refugees ceased to appear "as a sort of privileged island."[76]

Other Radical papers followed suit, and by the end of year their anti-refugee diatribes were scarcely distinguishable from those of the far right. Just after the Evian Conference, Maurice Ajam, writing for *La Dépêche de Toulouse*, the principal organ of provincial Radical opinion, applauded the increasingly restrictive immigration and naturalization policies adopted by the government. "Although racism may be folly," he declared, with respect to immigration, "a wise nationalism is indispensable to the nation's general well-being." Moreover, Ajam insisted, Jewish refugees were especially undesirable, since unlike other foreigners, they refused to assimilate. While acknowledging the patriotism of Jews who fought for France during the First World War, the fact remained that the Jews, who "always marry among themselves . . . constitute a race opposed to the descendants of the Gallo-Romans, the Celts, the French, and all the admirable mixed breeds who have made France such a prodigiously interesting country."[77]

In a series of articles in *La République* just after the Evian Conference,

Emile Roche too reiterated his earlier prognostications that any new refugee influx could "provoke discontent among our liberal and commercial professions from which Jews would be the first to suffer the consequences." "Not one unemployed French worker," he declared, "should be the price of our generosity." After the Munich crisis, he again warned refugees not to become involved in French politics: "France's affairs have nothing to do with you. Don't share your quarrels and hatreds with those who have welcomed you."[78]

Roche's colleague, Pierre Dominique, went even further. Like Georges de la Fouchardière of *L'Oeuvre*, Dominique too claimed that the crowds were not unjustified in attacking immigrants who, like the Lerners in Dijon, had stayed behind at the time of the mobilization. Moreover, Dominique concurred with Elbel that it was now up to the government to demand that foreigners, and especially beneficiaries of the right to asylum, bear the same duties as other French citizens, including military service; otherwise, they deserved to be expelled.[79] After the assassination of vom Rath, Dominique's ire was further aroused, and he declared that in spite of France's continued need for immigrants, a more selective immigration policy, such as Martial had advocated, was imperative. Manual workers, artisans, and peasants were, according to Dominique, "useful" immigrants, but the "hypercivilized" Jews were a different story. They competed in the "overencumbered" liberal professions and commerce, and intervened in French domestic quarrels. While they might still be transformed into "useful" immigrants if they were resettled in the countryside, he nevertheless insisted that if they remained in the metropolitan centers, and especially in Paris, xenophobia and antisemitism would continue to soar.[80]

Among papers of Radical opinion, *L'Ere nouvelle*, which represented the right wing of the party, far exceeded its peers in expressing anti-refugee, and increasingly antisemitic, views, despite the fact that its executive editor, the former secretary-general of the Radical Party, Albert Milhaud, was himself a Jew. The reasons why *L'Ere nouvelle* embarked on this path, completely reversing its earlier pro-refugee stance, can only be ascribed to the paper's fierce hostility to the Popular Front, and to Léon Blum specifically—a hostility that was increasingly expressed through the medium of antisemitism—as well as to its fervent pacifism. Already in the spring of 1938, at the time of Blum's second ministry, Phipps noted with some surprise that "a Socialist Radical and freemason organ such as the *Ere nouvelle* recently published an article by M. [Gaston] Riou, the Secretary of the Foreign Affairs Commission of the Chamber, attributing to M. Blum 'the anarchy which has given the handle to antisemitism.'"[81] Moreover, in response to the Evian Conference, the paper explicitly stated what Bérenger had only implied—that is, that "the saturation point of Jewish elements has largely been attained," and it called on the Soviet Union to take a greater share of the refugees, since so many were bolsheviks anyway.[82]

But the paper's most visceral anti-refugee diatribes surfaced during the Munich crisis and in the weeks that followed. In an editorial of September 22, 1938, Gaboriaud railed against the legions of clandestine Jewish refugees who had arrived in recent years; their covert aim, he declared, was nothing short of the destruction of France:

> Those who have come here . . . invoking the right to asylum, have engaged in a slow, painstaking, but ardent task of reversing all our hierarchies, our disciplines, and our values, in order to substitute, amid the anarchy they hope to create, their own hierarchy and their own values! Their values! Their hierarchy!
>
> Everywhere they tend to push the French out of all prestigious posts . . . all the disciplines that have constituted their grandeur, in order to better destroy them.

To curb these dangerous excesses, Gaboriaud called on native Jews to join their Christian compatriots to stop "the dangerous invasion of wanderers who have besieged us . . . [and] to . . . advise those who sin through their excessive behavior . . . that they had better not push the citizens of this country into having to impose a numerus clausus."[83]

After vom Rath's assassination, *L'Ere nouvelle* carried this theme even further. In its editorial of November 8, the paper declared that Grynszpan's crime illustrated that stepped-up police measures alone could no longer solve the refugee problem: "In truth, there are far too many people here who are foreign to our soil, to our mentality, to our national preoccupations: they contribute nothing. Quite the contrary. This cannot endure." Alleging that their Dreyfusard credentials gave them the right to speak freely on all Jewish-related issues, the editors claimed that the time had now come to implement a more radical refugee policy. Once again, *L'Ere nouvelle* called on the native Jewish community to help in this endeavor. It would be up to them to ensure "that the other Jews, those fleeing their countries of origin, cease coming here and injecting among us a mentality analogous to that of many immigrants to Palestine. How? By what means can they implement this enterprise? From our point of view, there is only one that is sure and effective: the numerus clausus." Such radical measures had become necessary, *L'Ere nouvelle* declared, because of mounting complaints from various professional associations, and especially "from doctors from large cities or the Paris suburbs who have provided us with stupefying statistics regarding the proportion of Jewish doctors and foreign Jewish doctors in the medical corps of the large urban centers." As a first step toward restructuring the occupational distribution of Jews, *L'Ere nouvelle* recommended that the native Jewish community set up vocational retraining schools for refugees already in the country to transform them into manual laborers and farmers: "Civilization is founded upon manual labor. . . . That is what ennobles man."[84]

L'Ere nouvelle's appeal to Jews to impose quotas on themselves sparked yet another heated controversy in the press. Although *L'Action française* condemned the *L'Ere nouvelle* for being excessively liberal, leaving the door open for some Jews to assimilate by transforming themselves into farmers,[85] the left-wing press expressed shock and outrage, and even suggested that the *L'Ere nouvelle* might be in the pay of the Nazis. Nicolas Paillot of *La Lumière* sharply condemned *L'Ere nouvelle*'s call for a *numerus clausus* as the first step toward the intrusion of Hitlerian antisemitism into France. It was scandalous, Paillot declared, for "a paper that claims to be radical to make distinctions among citizens according to religion or . . . race!"[86] *Le Populaire* concurred, claiming that *L'Ere nouvelle* had even surpassed the Action Française in its support for discriminatory legislation modeled on that of czarist Russia or Nazi Germany. The implementation of racial or religious quotas was intolerable "in our France where all men are 'free and equal before the law.'"[87] Jeanne Ancelet-Hustache of *L'Aube* further warned that *L'Ere nouvelle*'s demand was only one of many symptoms that a resurgence of antisemitism was in the offing. In Germany, she declared, antisemitism had also begun modestly, with demands for legal restrictions against Jews, but before long this campaign had escalated into full-fledged persecution. She therefore cautioned her countrymen not to "slip into the same excesses as . . . our neighbors. . . ."[88]

Most surprisingly, several voices further to the left joined the anti-refugee and anti-Jewish chorus. At the time of the Munich crisis, the socialist deputy Armand Chouffet railed against his Jewish colleagues Salomon Grumbach and Jules Moch, claiming that he had "had enough of the Jewish dictatorship over the party. . . . I won't march off for the Jewish war." Another socialist activist, Ludovic Zoretti, blamed Blum personally for the mounting war fever in the fall. The French, he proclaimed, "have no desire to kill millions of men, to destroy an entire civilization, solely to make life easier for 100,000 Sudeten Jews." Even Paul Faure, executive editor of *Le Populaire* and secretary-general of the Socialist Party, attributed Blum's increasingly militant stance toward Germany to his Jewish background: "Blum would have us all killed for his Jews," he declared.

Among the neosocialists, who had split with the party in 1933 and were fiercely pacifist, such views were especially pronounced. Adrien Marquet, who subsequently became Vichy's first minister of interior, declared that French soldiers could not be allowed to die in a "war for the USSR and Jewry."[89] Dissident Radicals too, most notably Gaston Bergery, also blamed Jews rather than Hitler for the deteriorating international situation.

Writing in his paper, *La Flèche*, just after Kristallnacht, Bergery noted the tremendous surge of antisemitism in recent months. While abjuring anti-semitism personally, Bergery suggested that the phenomenon was not entirely unwarranted. As a result of the number of Jews in Blum's ministries, people believed the country was being governed by a Jewish "camarilla." Moreover, Jewish warmongering in recent months had inflamed public opinion. The Jews wanted war, Bergery stated, "less to defend the direct interests of France, than to crush the hitlerian regime in Germany—that is to say, millions of Frenchmen and Europeans would die solely to avenge a few dead Jews and several hundreds of thousands of unfortunate Jews."[90]

As this survey of opinion shows, the theme of refugee invasion, primarily the prerogative of the far right prior to 1936, had made deep inroads into moderate opinion by the end of the decade. To be sure, among most moderates the idea of selective immigration continued to hold sway, and to this extent their views remained distinct from those on the far right. There is no doubt, however, that the category of immigrants considered "useful" and "desirable" had shrunk significantly, and Jewish refugees were nearly always excluded, at least insofar as they retained their urban and middle-class character. Mauco, for example, while stepping up his appeals to the government to increase immigration, claiming that French agriculture could not survive without immigrant labor and pointing to increased military needs, nevertheless expressed growing doubts regarding the assimilability of Jewish refugees in particular. In 1939, he railed against these refugees whom he now condemned as a semicriminal element because they had entered the country illegally.

Furthermore, Mauco claimed, the refugees' tendency to "flock to cities and urban activities where they compete with the French" had a "depressing and dissolving influence on the French collectivity." Since the majority of them were "physically and especially mentally diminished as a result of anguish," this trend was especially acute, and unlike peasants and manual laborers, their "previous formation . . . stands opposed to a real and profound frenchification." Mauco therefore insisted that henceforth only "useful" and "desirable" immigrants be accepted—that is, peasants, artisans, and manual laborers who could easily be steered to the provinces. He never explicitly stated that such a policy would signal an end to refugee asylum, but that is precisely what he had in mind. As to refugees already in the country, although he did not recommend their expulsion, he continued to argue that the provisions of the Serre Plan be implemented—that is, that they be allowed to stay only on the condition that they go to the provinces and transform themselves into peasants and artisans, a view that was garnering growing support.[91]

This increasingly narrow view of selective immigration was also apparent in two other important works of the late 1930's: Raymond Millet's *Trois millions d'étrangers en France: Les indésirables, les bienvenus (Three Million Foreigners in France: The Undesirables and the Welcome Ones)*, which was published in 1938 and had appeared earlier that year as a series of articles in *Le Temps*, and Jean Giraudoux's 1939 treatise, *Pleins Pouvoirs (Full Powers)*, the famous playwright's meditation on the underlying causes of French decadence. Like Mauco and Martial, Millet too sharply distinguished between "the good immigration and the bad." Not surprisingly, "the good immigration" referred to manual workers, artisans, and especially peasants; these immigrants, Millet declared, were essential since they "collaborate in our agricultural and industrial production, accomplish those jobs abandoned by our own compatriots, [and] replace those children our war dead would have had and those their survivors should have had." Unfortunately, Millet lamented, the recent arrivals did not fit this profile; rather, they belonged to the "undesirable" category: urban immigrants, largely East European Jews, who "through their competition, ruin French artisanry, small commerce, [and], by transforming themselves overnight into 'intellectuals,' infiltrate the liberal professions; marry our daughters, thus spreading their physical or moral defects; invade our hospitals, our insane asylums, our prisons, and seem to have come for the express purpose of accentuating that 'French decadence,' which is the talk of all Europe."[92]

Moreover, Millet argued, many refugees bore strange diseases like tuberculosis, and Slavs and Jews in particular were prone to mental illness, causing them to clog French hospital beds at taxpayers' expense. Although Millet repeatedly abjured any racist intentions, he nevertheless admitted that the presence of these foreigners would not be so threatening if "their blood and their mentality could be intermingled with that of our own people without any danger." But, as Martial had shown, there was little probability of a harmonious racial mixing, especially in the case of Jews.[93] What France therefore needed was not to close the borders completely, but rather to implement a more selective immigration policy that would separate the "wheat from the chaff."

Although Millet stopped short of advocating the expulsion of the refugees, admitting that such a move would almost certainly be "translated into a massacre,"[94] he nevertheless suggested that France could absorb no further influxes of refugees since "the assimilation of a single foreigner lost among the French crowd is swift, [but] that of a group of foreigners is far less so."[95] He furthermore argued that naturalization be made more difficult to preserve the nation's ethnic and demographic "equilibrium." To support this argument, he cited a medical doctor who recommended that naturalizations, at least for doctors, "should never be accorded to men born outside our territory," and he apparently agreed with Martial that a fifteen-to twenty-year waiting period for naturalization was not unreasonable.[96] As to the Serre Plan, Millet expressed greater skepticism than Mauco. The government, he proclaimed, would be reluctant to send Jewish refugees to border areas given the current international tensions, and he worried that the plan would accord refugee status too liberally, since it envisioned the reconstitution of the Consultative Commission.[97] In the end, notwithstanding Millet's repeated assertions of his belief in the inviolability of asylum, his goal was clearly to bar entry to the vast majority of asylum seekers in the future. Moreover, he too warned that if the problem of the "undesirables" was not addressed immediately, France would become the scene of violent antisemitic outbreaks.[98]

Giraudoux's treatise, *Pleins Pouvoirs*, which sought to explain the deep-seated causes of French decadence, further highlighted the way advocates of selective immigration were increasingly veering toward outright antisemitism. Appointed by Daladier in the summer of 1939 to serve as high commissioner of public information, Giraudoux was by no means a rabble-rousing antisemite. Rather, he represented middle-of-the-road republicanism, and it is precisely for this reason that his views regarding foreigners seem jarring to us today.[99] Giraudoux, as we have seen, was not a newcomer to the immigration question. Already in 1935, he had advocated selective immigration as opposed to the closed-door policies of Flandin and Laval. And although he had voiced some skepticism regarding the quality of the recent newcomers, he had nevertheless maintained that France had an obligation to accept asylum seekers, at least until an international solution to the refugee problem was found.

After the refugee deluge of 1938, however, Giraudoux's views hardened significantly. As he declared in *Pleins Pouvoirs*, the primary cause of France's decline to the status of a second-rank power was not military weakness; rather it was France's demographic problem, and especially its chronically low birthrate. As long as the size of France's population lagged so miserably behind that of the Germans, France would never be able to fend off a German military threat; even the most savvy military alliances would be of no use. This demographic problem, Giraudoux argued, should have been remedied long ago, through state-sponsored natalist and eugenics policies, similar to those implemented in Nazi Germany. Unfortunately, the government had not taken this path; instead, it had compensated for the low birthrate through immigration. While there was nothing inherently wrong in this strategy, it had been carried out in an arbitrary and chaotic fashion, with no regard for the nation's economic or racial health. As a result, France now faced an "invasion" of undesirables that threatened to "corrupt a race that owes its value to selection and to twenty centuries of refinement."[100] Who were these "barbarian" hordes who had used "every persecution as a pretext to come here"? According to Giraudoux, "all the expelled, the inapt, the greedy, the ill, . . . hundreds of thousands of Ashkenazim, escaped from the ghettos of Poland or Romania . . . accustomed . . . to work in the worst conditions, [and] who drive our compatriots out of every sector of small-scale artisanry. . . . By congregating by the dozens in small sweatshops, they are able to evade every official investigation, whether for tax purposes or labor conditions."

To ensure that in the future only desirable immigrants be recruited— peasants and artisans "from those races closest to our own"[101]— Giraudoux called on the government to create a new office, the Ministry of Natural-ization. If France wanted to regain her stature as a first-class power, this problem, Giraudoux maintained, could no longer be ignored. Indeed, it de-served even higher priority than military matters: "What does it matter if a country's borders are intact if its racial borders are constantly shrinking! . . . We are in complete accord with Hitler in proclaiming that politics has not achieved its highest form unless it is racial." Thus, at the very moment statesmen and publicists were calling on the government to recruit more foreigners into the armed forces to strengthen the military, Giraudoux was advising a more cautious approach: "It's not only a problem of numbers, it's a question of quality."[102]

By the end of the decade, this assault against the refugees had expanded well beyond the ranks of the radical right, and it was beginning to spill over into a more general antisemitic campaign. This assault did not go unchal-lenged, however. The pro-refugee camp, while diminished in size, never-theless mounted a spirited counterattack and was able to claim several strik-ing successes by the spring of 1939. This camp still comprised the majority of left-wing parties, including the socialists, the communists, and especially communist intellectuals associated with the paper *Ce Soir*; the League for the Rights of Man and Citizen; the left wing of the Radical Party, repre-sented by the paper, *La Lumière*; the Christian Democrats at *L'Aube*; and Emmanuel Mounier and his colleagues at the nonconformist Christian re-view, *Esprit*. On the conservative right, the pro-refugee camp included Emile Buré, the influential editor of *L'Ordre*; André Géraud, more com-monly known as Pertinax, executive editor of *L'Europe nouvelle*; and Henri de Kérillis, deputy of the Seine and editor of *L'Epoque*, who, although not strictly speaking a pro-refugee advocate, was nevertheless an outspoken critic of antisemitism.

As these spokesmen observed, the debate over the refugees and the Jews had become bound up with the larger debate over appeasement, and as even a brief perusal of the list of pro-refugee advocates reveals, there was a re-markable overlap between this camp and the emerging anti-*munichois* op-position. From the vantage point of the pro-refugee camp, one's position on the refugee question and antisemitism more generally was becoming, as had also been the case during the Dreyfus Affair, a leading barometer of one's republican loyalties and of the degree to which one was willing to defend democracy against fascism, both at home and abroad. Ultimately, for the pro-refugee camp, this debate raised the key question regarding France's future—would it remain wedded to democracy and republican values—the values of the Declaration of the Rights of Man and Citizen—or would it slide into the Nazi/fascist coalition, toward authoritarianism, corporatism, and racism?

Kristallnacht, followed almost immediately by the signing of the Franco-German pact, brought these issues into sharp relief. For the pro-refugee camp, France's failure to respond to the wave of Nazi antisemitic persecution, and even worse, Bonnet's continued attempts to reach accommodation with Germany, symbolized the country's craven eagerness to kowtow to the Germans no matter what the price. Among the most eloquent critics of the administration's response to these events was Albert Bayet, a prominent spokesman for the left wing of the Radical Party. Although Bayet had always been a fierce critic of Nazi Germany, he had argued earlier in the 1930's that German domestic policies, no matter how abhorrent, should not interfere with international efforts to maintain the peace.

By 1938, and especially after Kristallnacht, however, Bayet could no longer abide by this position. Now he decried as shameful the silence of the government and the mass-circulation press in the face of this renewed wave of antisemitic persecution, especially in light of the swift and forceful condemnations of the British and the Americans. In France, he declared, fear of war was becoming a sort of tyranny, silencing anyone who spoke out in defense of the rights of the persecuted and oppressed: "The day before yesterday, we were told when we protested the massacres in Ethiopia, China, and Spain—'Silence! you're provoking war!' Yesterday, we were told, when we protested the mutilation of Czechoslovakia: 'Silence! You're warmongers.' Today, when we protest the ignoble persecution unleashed against helpless Jews, against their women and children, we're told: 'Silence! France is terrified.'"[103]

Besides, Bayet argued, "the true France," the majority of French people who "remain immovably loyal to the great human idea that proclaims [Seventeen] Eighty-Nine," were no less horrified by the recent anti-Jewish pogroms than their British or American counterparts, notwithstanding the quiescence of the press. If France wanted to survive, physically and morally, it would have to return to the camp of the Western democracies, the upholders of liberty, freedom, and the rights of man. Bayet then turned to his comrades on the right wing of the Radical Party, especially those affiliated with *L'Ere nouvelle*, and begged them to cease flirting with antisemitism and the far right. The fight against fascism could be won, he declared, only by re-creating a strong united front on the left: "Let's reforge, honestly and bravely, a union sacrée not with the *cagoulards*,* not with the agents of foreign fascism, but a republican union for the defense of France and its human ideal."[104]

Bayet's view that French silence in the face of Kristallnacht signaled mounting complicity with the Germans was widely shared by spokesmen on the political left. Pierre Cot, a former minister and representative of the left wing of the Radical Party, warned that France "seemed to be wavering between the camp of the Democracies and that of the adversaries of Democracy."[105] Emmanuel Mounier, although not criticizing the government's effort to reach some accommodation with the Germans, nevertheless issued a scathing condemnation of Bonnet's efforts to secure a non-aggression pact with Germany just weeks after the anti-Jewish atrocities. At the very moment Great Britain and the United States were denouncing this persecution, France, he declared, "threw out the bomb of the Franco-German Declaration; and, in an effort to sign away everything, its border police have sent back to the Gestapo 70 German Jews who crossed the border at risk of their lives." Through such craven behavior, Mounier charged, the Daladier administration was "slowly but surely selling the soul of our country . . . to the racist and totalitarian passion."[106]

Even *L'Oeuvre*, despite its sharp condemnation of Grynszpan's crime and its repeated warnings to the refugees not to turn France into a battleground for their private quarrels, sharply condemned the Franco-German pact. In an article titled "Peace Cannot Be Founded on the Pogrom," *L'Oeuvre* questioned whether "Wilhelmstrasse could really believe that Franco-German rapprochement, no matter how desirable, could be based on a French anti-semitic campaign 'in alignment' with the German antisemitic campaign."[107]

---

*Cagoulards, or "hooded ones," were members of the Cagoule, a secret extreme-right-wing paramilitary organization that planned to overthrow the Third Republic through a coup d'état. Also known as the Comité Secret d'Action Révolutionnaire (CSAR), the Cagoule was headed by Eugène Deloncle, a former Action Française activist, and received backing from the Italian fascist government of Benito Mussolini. The Cagoule, whose membership is estimated at between 2,000 and 10,000, was motivated by a visceral anticommunism and became especially active in the summer of 1936, when the Popular Front came to power. This organization was responsible for a number of assassinations, including the brutal murder in 1937 of the Italian antifascists Carlo and Nello (Sabatino) Rosselli. The Cagoule was also responsible for the rue de Presbourg bombing in Paris on Sept. 11, 1937, which the French police had blamed first on the communists and then on an Italian fascist agent, Luigi Tamburini. Although many Cagoule leaders were arrested at the end of 1937, most were released in 1939 and 1940, at the beginning of the Second World War. Several Cagoule leaders, most notably Joseph Darnand, went on in 1943 to organize the Milice, the extreme-anticommunist paramilitary organization that supported the Vichy government and waged fierce combat against the

Most significantly, in early January *L'Oeuvre* carried a sharply worded denunciation of France's response to Kristallnacht by Léon Archimbaud, one of the preeminent spokesmen for the left wing of the Radical Party in the Chamber of Deputies. According to Archimbaud, the rising tide of antisemitism in France, expressed above all by the repeated charges of Jewish warmongering, constituted a "harbinger of dictatorship" that was gradually propelling France into the Nazi camp. Antisemitism, he declared, was a dangerous diversion that turned the French against one another—toward the enemy within—instead of against the real enemy, the Germans. Whereas antisemitism had been "the exclusive domain of a small clique" before the War, it had now become a broad-based movement, with strong support even from many republicans and democrats. Vigilance was therefore necessary. While the antisemites depicted themselves as superpatriots, in reality, Archimbaud charged, they were traitors, disseminating "a foreign propaganda aimed at subverting democracy and French patriotism." [108]

Such views were articulated on the conservative right as well, albeit with far less frequency. For Emile Buré, the absence of a strong response to Kristallnacht and the subsequent signing of the Franco-German accord offered irrefutable proof of the folly of appeasement. It was shameful, he declared, that the French ambassador in Berlin "was celebrating its [Germany's] genius and the nobility of its contributions to the progress of civilization by means of assassination, torture, and the ambushing of Jews." Moreover, Buré joined Archimbaud in excoriating the Radicals in particular; Daladier's party, by having implemented such a despicable policy, had lost the right "to speak for the immortal principles of 1789!" [109]

Pertinax too decried the fact that Bonnet had "invited M. von Ribbentrop to come to Paris, just at the moment Germany had placed itself outside the pale of traditional civilization through the persecution of the Jews." [110] Kérillis agreed, and warned that the antisemitic movement in France was taking on a strong pro-German cast. If allowed to continue, this antisemitism would drive a wedge between France and its democratic allies, Great Britain and the United States. Once France fell into the Nazi camp, Europe was doomed, and antisemitism, which Kérillis believed was at the core of Nazi ideology, would swell to unprecedented proportions. "Tomorrow," he prophesized, "Nazi Germany will demand that every Euro-

---

French Resistance. The Milice was responsible for the assassinations of Georges Mandel and Victor Basch, and it collaborated with the Nazis in carrying out anti-Jewish activities. On the Cagoule, see Philippe Bourdrel, *La Cagoule: Histoire d'une société du Front populaire à la Ve République* (Paris, 1992); Soucy, pp. 46–53. On the rue de Presbourg bombing, see Chapter 7, n. 105. I also wish to thank Joel Blatt for his help in providing this information.

pean nation implement exceptional measures against the Jews or even their mass expulsion, their internment on some faraway continent, something akin to a colossal recommencement of the Babylonian captivity after the destruction of the Jerusalem Temple."[111]

This campaign had some success, especially in 1939 as the threat of war became imminent. By the spring of 1939, the massive publicity drives sponsored by the left-wing press, Jewish defense organizations, and *L'Epoque* and *L'Ordre* on the conservative right to expose the links between the extreme right—and especially antisemitic organizations—and the Nazi propaganda service, the Weltdienst (World Service), began to pay off.[112] Inaugurating its crackdown against the fifth column, the government passed the Marchandeau law in April, which banned antisemitic propaganda as inimical to the national interest. It also passed a decree law outlawing foreign associations, which was aimed almost exclusively at Nazi and fascist organizations. The first victim of the Marchandeau law was none other than Darquier de Pellepoix, who was arrested and tried in the summer of 1939,[113] but others soon followed, including the notorious antisemitic propagandist, Paul Ferdonnet, whose antisemitic radio broadcasts were beamed to France via Stuttgart during the "phony war."[114] During the summer of 1939, the government also moved against extreme-right-wing and antisemitic organizations in Alsace, and in the fall it arrested several Alsatian autonomist leaders, including Rossé, on charges of espionage.[115]

Moreover, in 1939, as the need for soldiers became more pressing, many moderates toned down their anti-refugee rhetoric significantly. Pierre Dominique, for example, despite his lashing out against the refugees at the time of the Munich crisis and especially after the assassination of vom Rath, emerged in the spring of 1939 as the foremost advocate of recruiting foreigners, including the refugees, into the armed forces. While many in France persisted in denouncing the foreigners as "the criminal underground of Europe," Dominique insisted time and again that in light of the country's low birthrate, these foreigners offered France one of the few remaining hopes of salvation. To be sure, he agreed with the far right that the Popular Front's naturalization policies had been overly generous, with the regrettable result that "the communists of Germany and Central Europe have been naturalized by the hundreds and thousands." Still, he maintained, the vast majority of foreigners were trustworthy and could be inducted into the army without problems.[116] *Le Temps* too, notwithstanding some reservations, was now willing to endorse the participation of foreigners in the armed forces after a thoroughgoing selection process.[117] Even Wladimir d'Ormesson of *Le Figaro*, while still insisting that extreme caution had to be exercised with regard to recent newcomers, nevertheless conceded in 1939 that the majority of longtime resident foreigners were loyal and ought to serve in the army. Unlike Dominique, however, he recommended that if naturalization were the reward for military service, full political rights, including the right to vote, ought to be withheld for at least another generation.[118]

At the same time, several other proposals of the pro-refugee camp began to win support among centrist and right-wing spokesmen who had hitherto voiced considerable opposition to a more liberal refugee policy. As illustrated in Chapter 10, there was mounting support for agricultural and, to a lesser extent, colonial solutions, even from several right-wing quarters. To the great chagrin of the Action Française, the Count of Paris, the monarchist heir to the throne, openly endorsed the idea of agricultural settlements for Jewish refugees,[119] and *Le Matin*, hitherto one of the most xenophobic papers, called on the government to open up French colonies for refugee settlement. Responding to the *Saint-Louis* crisis of the summer of 1939, Stéphane Lauzanne, the paper's executive editor, maintained that the international community had a moral obligation to assist these refugees; otherwise, he stated flatly, they would die, a prediction that seemed warranted in light of recent press revelations regarding conditions in Nazi concentration camps. *Le Matin* even sponsored a fund-raising drive for the *Saint-Louis* refugees, raising some 45,000 francs ($16,700), which it handed over to the Groupement de Coordination, a newly formed Jewish refugee committee. Moreover, *Le Matin* completely renounced its earlier restrictionist position regarding immigration and began to advocate a more liberal approach, at least toward refugees who might be considered economically useful. Reiterating the standard pro-refugee refrain, *Le Matin* now declared that the refugees were an economic asset, and not a liability, since they increased production and consumption, thereby creating new jobs and expanding French markets.[120]

A similar shift in attitude was apparent in the thinking of Raymond Millet. Although initially an avid supporter of the anti-immigrant decree law of May 2, 1938, Millet eventually denounced this law as unjust and cruel. In the aftermath of Kristallnacht, he declared that refugees seeking asylum in France could no longer be considered "undesirable" from a juridical point of view, since there was no question that they were fleeing persecution. Moreover, like many others at the time, Millet pointed out that although the decree law had been designed to weed out "undesirables"—"the suspects, the frauds, the 'illegals,' the irregulars"—in practice it was genuine refugees who were being targeted. These innocents either landed in jail or, if they were shunted across the border, in Nazi concentration camps, where they faced "a certain death." Millet therefore joined the pro-refugee camp in calling for an amnesty that would provide at least provisional asylum, and

he advocated "a true statute for foreigners" to replace the arbitrary and unjust decree laws.[121]

Despite this brief turnaround of opinion, the old prejudices resurfaced
almost immediately with the outbreak of war, and as we have seen, Daladier's internment policies had widespread support, even among many
moderates. Antisemitism could therefore no longer be regarded as a marginal phenomenon. As Phipps had noted, by the late 1930's, it had become
an integral part of a broader debate about the nature of French society and
French politics, surfacing repeatedly in Paris municipal council proceedings
and even in parliamentary debates. Why did so many allow themselves to
be seduced into an obsessive battle against the enemy within—the communists, the refugees, and the Jews—instead of following the advice of
Archimbaud, Kérillis, Bayet, and others to reforge the spirit of union sacrée
to fend off the real threat—the Germans? First there were cultural and social reasons for this obsession. Ironically, as we have seen, preoccupations
with questions such as which immigrants were most desirable and how
many of them could be accommodated without upsetting the "social equilibrium" were catapulted to the center stage of French politics not because
France had no need of immigrants, but precisely because she needed them
so desperately. While this need might have left the door open to the refugees, the fact was that most demographic experts and political commentators viewed Jews as a particularly undesirable ethnic group. Due to their
urban and middle-class backgrounds, they were widely perceived as a competitive threat to the French middle classes—merchants, artisans, and especially liberal professionals—and even pro-refugee advocates, like Jeanne Ancelet-Hustache of *L'Aube*, shared Mauco's view that Jewish refugees ought
to go to the provinces and transform themselves into artisans or farmers.

Moreover, because so many of the refugees had entered the country clandestinely, they were increasingly branded as criminals, even by
liberal papers like *L'Oeuvre*. At the same time, the mass nature of this influx also posed special problems. While admitting the need for new immigrants, *Le Temps*, for example, insisted that "the constant, overflow-
ing, excessive influx of foreigners to France is a fact whose consequences for
the nation *cannot . . . be favorable*." Given the country's precarious demographic situation, the arrival of these hordes posed a threat whether or not
they were assimilated. If they failed to assimilate, "they would constitute
veritable 'foreign bodies' which sooner or later would be exploited as
ethnic minorities by more or less totalitarian governments." But if they did
assimilate, "the physical, intellectual, and moral elements that constitute the
originality of the French people would eventually be profoundly affected
and adulterated."[122] Many therefore shared the view of the critic Robert

Aron, who, although a Jew, nevertheless warned that "a *métèque* is never worth the same as a true Frenchman, and that the sole durable solution to the problem of foreigners consists in supporting and defending the French birthrate."[123]

Aside from these sociodemographic concerns, political anxieties further fueled the obsession with the "enemy within." Fears of social revolution at home, inspired by the Popular Front victory, increasingly became linked to fears of war, and for many, some sort of alliance with the Nazis, or perhaps even outright subservience to them, offered the only guarantee against a communist takeover. Already in 1936, the Catholic novelist Martin du Gard had written a friend that he preferred a fascist dictatorship, and even Nazi domination, to war: "No servitude can be compared to war and all that it entails," he exclaimed, especially since "war would also mean civil war, the triumph perhaps of Communism after years of blood, ruins and unspeakable horrors."[124]

According to Pertinax, by the time of the Munich crisis such views had become widespread: "Among the so-called conservative classes . . . many have come to feel that the social peril takes precedence over the German peril, that the totalitarian states must be regarded as an assurance against Moscow, that Adolf Hitler and Benito Mussolini possess the depository of our civilization and that a war waged against them would result in an irremediable social upheaval."[125] For Kérillis, whose anticommunist credentials were beyond dispute, such fears masked dangerous defeatist tendencies. In March 1938, he cited a letter from an acquaintance predicting that the sole result of war would be social revolution. If French youth were called up, this acquaintance declared, they would undoubtedly do their duty, but "' without enthusiasm and with a sense of dread in their hearts . . . For what ideal . . . are we sacrificing our lives? . . . For France? . . . But I know only too well that war is being waged in order to bring about the sovietization of Europe.'" For Kérillis, such defeatist thinking played right into Hitler's hands, and he noted that historically, social revolutions occurred only after military defeats, but never after victories. If the French expected victory, Kérillis chided, these fears of "sovietization" had to be set aside once and for all.[126]

Such apprehensions, while most pervasive on the conservative right, had penetrated deep within the ranks of the Radical Party and, to a lesser degree, even into some socialist circles. As Serge Berstein has recently shown, the Radicals were deeply divided by the end of the 1930's. Those on the right, who shared the views of Georges Bonnet, Emile Roche, and Albert Milhaud, detested communists and socialists and had never supported the Popular Front. Like their conservative counterparts, they were increasingly willing to use any means to combat the left, including outright xenophobia and even antisemitism. Moreover, among neosocialists and even a few Socialist Party members, pacifism, anticommunism, and sheer hatred of Léon Blum were frequently expressed through the medium of antisemitism. Thus by the end of the decade, anti-refugee and antisemitic prejudices had permeated across a wide swath of public opinion.[127] To be sure, a number of liberals and leftists, as well as spokesmen of the Christian left, continued to advance the cause of the refugees and to warn of the dangers posed by antisemitism and xenophobia. Yet it is also clear that the pro-refugee faction had lost considerable political clout by the end of the 1930's, despite their brief success in the spring and summer of 1939.

Finally, there is little doubt that Jewish refugees were linked in the public mind not with other immigrants, but with native French Jews, who were themselves increasingly excoriated as foreigners. Faced with a steady barrage of extreme-right-wing accusations that he was in reality a foreigner, Léon Blum, in late 1938, decided to refute this accusation head-on. On the front page of *Le Populaire*, he declared: "I was born in Paris, the 9th of April 1872, a Frenchman, of French parents. . . . My four grandparents were all born in France, on Alsatian territory. As far as it is possible to trace the outlines of a modest family's history, my ancestry is purely French."[128] That a former prime minister should have responded to such charges, and in so public a fashion, suggests the degree to which Blum took the antisemitic threat seriously. Similarly, Georges Mandel's biographer, John M. Sherwood, speculates that Mandel, though a staunch conservative, was reluctant to assume a more visible leadership role in the anti-*munichois* opposition precisely because he feared giving credence to the charge that only the enemies within—the Jews, the refugees, and the communists—opposed appeasement.[129]

Despite persistent efforts by some Jews, such as the publicist Emmanuel Berl, to maintain a sharp distinction between Jewish refugees and immigrants on the one hand and native Jews on the other, by the end of the decade the fates of these two groups had become inextricably intertwined. This development had an impact not only on decisions made by prominent Jewish political figures, like Blum and Mandel, but it also posed a grave challenge to native Jewish communal leadership. As we will see in Chapter 13, native French Jewish leaders responded to this test with a new sense of assertiveness that contrasted markedly with their behavior during the first anti-refugee crackdown in 1934 and 1935.

CHAPTER THIRTEEN

The Politics of Frustration
The Remaking of the Jewish Relief Effort, 1936–40

While the Comité National has come under attack by historians for its failure to protest the anti-refugee crackdown of 1934–35, as well as its lackluster
performance in providing relief, its successor, the Comité d'Assistance aux
Réfugiés (CAR), has suffered no less harsh treatment. David Weinberg,
Paula Hyman, and Catherine Nicault agree that, while sustaining the relief
effort, native Jews after 1935 nevertheless bowed to the administration's
view that France was "saturated" and could accept no more refugees. They
furthermore maintain that once the government embarked on the policy of
appeasement, native Jewish leaders, fearful of appearing unpatriotic, refused to condemn this policy, despite the fact that every effort at appeasement uprooted thousands more refugees. Finally, they insist that native
Jewish elites acquiesced to the anti-immigrant decree laws of May and November 1938 without protest, further widening the rift between themselves
and more activist pro-refugee groups, such as the Gourevitch Committee.
While none of these historians would go so far as Maurice Rajsfus in arguing that the CAR actually welcomed the decree laws as a means of getting
rid of unwanted foreign coreligionists, they would almost certainly concur
with Weinberg that by 1939, "most natives had written off the refugee problem as hopeless, arguing that French Jewish organizations had done as
much as was humanly possible to care for Jews fleeing from Nazism."[1]

All of these interpretations are premised on the view that the CAR was the direct offshoot of the Comité National and that the policies elaborated between 1936 and 1940 were essentially identical to those implemented between 1933 and 1935. Yet, as we will see, the CAR, as well as several new refugee committees created by the native Jewish establishment in 1938 and 1939, were by no means extensions of the Comité National. Rather, the CAR was an entirely new committee, created under the impetus of the more liberal Popular Front. Most significantly, the leadership of this committee, together with that of its affiliates, no longer resided in the hands of hard-liners such as Jacques Helbronner and Louis Oungre. Instead, a new and more moderate leadership came to the fore, represented above all by Raymond-Raoul Lambert, the CAR's secretary-general, as well by Albert Lévy, its president and a member of the Central Consistory; William Oualid, a member of the Paris Consistory and vice president of the Alliance Israélite Universelle (AIU);[2] and Louise Weiss, a prominent journalist and feminist leader.[3]

Unlike Helbronner and Louis Oungre, whose principal aim was to get rid of the refugees, these leaders believed that French Jews had a moral obligation to help their persecuted coreligionists, and, for the first time, they focused their attention on "constructive solutions" aimed at providing the refugees with long-term assistance and vocational retraining so that at least some of them might remain in France. Most significantly, although these leaders generally abstained from criticizing appeasement directly, in contrast to their coreligionists to the left, they nevertheless launched a full-scale political drive to overturn the anti-immigrant decree laws of 1938 and secure an amnesty, at least for refugees already in France. Although the gains won during this struggle quickly dissipated with the outbreak of war, and especially with the advent of Vichy, they nevertheless indicate the degree to which Jewish leadership had abandoned the policies of the Comité National. By 1939, as a result of this pro-refugee stance, the ideological gap between the native establishment and its erstwhile critics, such as the Gourevitch Committee, had largely been overcome, ushering in a brief period of consensus, if not cooperation, over refugee matters. At the same time, the increasingly adversarial relationship developing between the Jewish community and the government, while falling short of the more tragic dimensions it would assume under Vichy, nevertheless provided native Jewish leaders with a bitter foretaste of things to come.

To understand this transition from an anti-refugee to a pro-refugee stance, it is necessary to recall briefly the dire straits into which the Jewish relief effort had fallen on the eve of the Popular Front. Except for the few loan banks initiated by the Joint Distribution Committee (JDC) in late 1934 and 1935,[4] the Comité National, under the sway of hard-liners like Helbronner, had completely disappeared from the scene. Moreover, even many of the smaller committees, such as Agriculture et Artisanat and the German

Commission, were on the brink of disintegration, due in part to mismanagement, but mainly to the demise of their sponsor, the Comité National.
According to Bernhard Kahn, the European director of the JDC (Joint Distribution Committee), the situation of the 8,000 to 10,000 German refugees still in France in early 1936 had become "desperate," and he noted
acidly, "Nobody cares about the German refugees in France."[5]

Yet the advent of the Popular Front, with its decidedly pro-refugee bent,
set the stage for a thoroughgoing reorganization of the Jewish relief effort.
The JDC, which had always favored "constructive solutions," was determined to take advantage of the new circumstances. It therefore initiated negotiations with French Jewish leaders to renew the relief effort. Initially, the
native elite displayed little interest. Robert de Rothschild reiterated the
view that French Jews had done enough for the refugees; it was now time
to pay attention to their own institutions. Furious, Kahn threatened to cut
off funding to France altogether if French Jewish leaders failed to comply
with his plan. At the same time, he promised to subsidize 50 percent of the
new committee's operational expenses.[6]

This commitment was not unconditional, however. First, Kahn insisted
that the new committee devote itself principally to constructive solutions—
job placement and training. And second, he demanded that the new committee be thoroughly restaffed. As he stated: "A new director [Albert Lévy]
has been engaged: nobody has been taken on as an employee who has been
in any way connected with the old Comité National so that its memory will
not haunt the activities of the new committee."[7] Alone of the former personnel, Lambert was permitted to stay on as secretary-general; even Rothschild, while continuing to serve as a patron, no longer held a seat on the
CAR's executive board.[8] Moreover, for the first time, representatives of the
East European and German immigrant communities—Israël Jefroykin,
president of the Fédération des Sociétés Juives de France (FSJF), and Hugo
Simon, president of the German Commission—were included on CAR's
executive board. Most importantly, Helbronner was out of the picture entirely. He was excluded from membership on the new committee, and the
Popular Front refused to send him back to his post at the League of Nations.[9] It was now Lambert who became the principal liaison between the
CAR and the government: not only was he appointed secretary-general of
the newly created Consultative Commission—a delegation of prominent
pro-refugee activists—both émigré and French—whose task it was to review the dossiers of all those applying for the new refugee status,[10] but in
this capacity he also served as key adviser to France's new delegate to the
League of Nations, the socialist deputy Salomon Grumbach, who replaced
Helbronner during this period.[11]

The CAR, which officially came into existence on July 7, fulfilled nearly all of Kahn's expectations. While continuing to work with the Jewish emigration society, HICEM, to facilitate the departure of refugees with emigration possibilities, the committee endeavored to create constructive solutions, as opposed to the "purposeless" short-term assistance of the past. As the *Univers israélite*, which was under Lambert's editorial direction, explained in August, the committee's goal was "to help refugees incorporate themselves as quickly as possible into French life by providing constructive assistance, without causing harm to the national labor force."[12] Even the tone of the fund-raising campaigns marked a radical departure from the past. In contrast to the persistent complaints of the Comité National that French Jews had reached their limit, Albert Lévy now declared: "As long as a single victim of hitlerian persecution remains in need of assistance and aid in France, we have no right to believe we have done our duty."[13]

With firm government support, many of the schemes initially floated in 1933 but subsequently dropped due to official obstruction were now revived. Under the leadership of Irène Joliot-Curie, a new Academic Assistance Council was created to help place refugee scholars in academic posts.[14] Similarly, the JDC and the Centre Industriel de Rééducation Professionelle (CIRP), which had supplanted the Agriculture et Artisanat in the spring of 1936, negotiated deals to set up vocational retraining programs for refugees with the French State Railways, as well as with schools specializing in hotel management, rural trade, and handicrafts. As a JDC spokesman told the *New York Times*, "The results of this training have been highly encouraging," and according to Raoul Dautry, then director of the French State Railways, "The success of the enterprise has exceeded all expectations."[15] To be sure, the CAR still intended for many graduates of these programs to emigrate to South America or Palestine, and the Jewish Agency even promised to give them preference with respect to the allocation of Palestine certificates. Nevertheless, several hundred CIRP trainees were able to find jobs in France. For Bernhard Kahn these developments proved immensely satisfying. As he commented in mid-1937, despite "the great difficulty we always had with the refugee committee in France, [the] new committee . . . today functions very well."[16]

This era of hope and optimism came to an abrupt end with the demise of the Popular Front. In 1938, events took a dramatic turn for the worse. Hitler's march into Central Europe; his fierce antisemitic crackdown at home, culminating in Kristallnacht; the implementation of anti-Jewish legislation in Italy; and the rise of antisemitic regimes in Eastern Europe combined to create a Jewish refugee crisis of unprecedented proportions.[17] By the end of the year, it was estimated that there were approximately 60,000 Central and Eastern European Jewish refugees in France, and the overwhelming majority of these had entered the country illegally.[18]

From the vantage point of the Daladier administration, which came to power in April 1938, these hordes of illegal aliens proved intolerable. While traditional economic concerns continued to play a role in the formulation of refugee policy, as manifested especially by the decree law of June 17, 1938, which limited for the first time the right of foreigners to engage in commerce, the administration expressed growing consternation that the refugees might be seeking to drag France into an undesired war.[19] It was therefore time, the minister of the interior, Albert Sarraut, declared, "to render impossible all illegal sojourns of suspicious foreigners."[20] To remedy this problem, the administration, as we have seen, enacted the antiforeign decree laws of May 2 and November 12, 1938, aimed at barring the entry of further refugees and routing out illegal aliens already there. Those illegal refugees who could not be expelled, either because their native countries refused to receive them or because they were in fact refugees whose lives were in danger, were to be imprisoned, or ultimately detained in internment camps, as stipulated by the decree law of November 12.

Once again, French Jews were confronted with a grave dilemma, and not surprisingly, the old divisions between hard-liners and moderates resurfaced. Yet the outcome of this round of the contest was altogether different from the result in 1934 and 1935; this time, the moderates prevailed. To be sure, the hard-liners still included some prominent spokesmen, most notably the chief rabbi of Paris, Julien Weill. In an interview with the conservative *Le Matin* just after Kristallnacht, which the Nazis claimed had been revenge for Herschel Grynszpan's assassination of the third secretary of the German embassy in Paris, Ernst vom Rath, Weill repeated the familiar refrain that France "has already done more than any other country in the world, and can no longer welcome new immigrants." Further initiatives on behalf of Jews fleeing Nazi persecution, he insisted, would have to come from the international community, and he ruled out the possibility of settling a few thousand refugees in French colonies. Finally, Weill reassured the French public that French Jewry would do nothing to torpedo the upcoming Franco-German peace talks, even if that meant complete quiescence with regard to the refugees. "No one is more sympathetic than I am to the misery and pain of the 600,000 German Jews," he declared, "but nothing seems more precious and necessary to me than the maintenance of peace on earth."[21]

Weill's statement ignited a storm of protest within the Franco-Jewish community. As usual, the sharpest criticism came from left-wing circles, immigrant and native alike, as well as from the increasingly activist youth movement.[22] Wladimir Rabinovitch (Rabi), a prominent left-wing Zionist, denounced Weill and his bourgeois supporters for having betrayed the refugees in exchange for "peace at any price, the peace of the antisemites."[23]

No less harsh was the condemnation of the Comité de Coordination des Jeunesses Juives de Strasbourg, which publicly called on Weill to retract his insidious statement; silence, they insisted, would have been preferable.[24] But perhaps the most stinging denunciation came from Léon Blum himself. At the ninth annual congress of the International League Against Antisemitism (LICA) in late November, Blum proclaimed that it was "an elementary human duty" to offer asylum to the victims of Nazi terror, and he continued:

I intend to speak my mind freely here, even if I offend the feelings of other Jews, even if I have to take a stand against the remarks proclaimed recently . . . by men who . . . try to pass themselves off as the representatives of the Jews.

There is nothing in the whole world as painful and dishonorable to me as to see French Jews today attempting to close the doors of France to Jewish refugees from other countries. . . . Perhaps your house is already full, it's possible, but when they knock on your doors, let them in and don't ask them for their identity papers, judicial records, or vaccination certificates.[25]

Most significantly, this criticism did not remain restricted to the fringes of the Jewish community, as historians have previously contended; rather, the majority of native Jewish leaders sought to distance themselves from Weill's hard-line position.[26] When the German foreign minister, Joachim von Ribbentrop, came to Paris in early December to sign the Franco-German nonaggression pact, Jules Braunschwig, a member of the AIU's executive committee, vehemently denounced the lavish hospitality French officials bestowed upon "one of the men most responsible for the frightful suffering of the Jews in Germany."[27] Moreover, the *Univers israélite*, usually unsympathetic to left-wing views, reprinted major portions of Blum's speech.[28] At the same time, the chief rabbi of France, Isaïe Schwartz, together with the leaders of Alsace-Lorraine Jewry, called upon French Jews to assist their coreligionists: "Our refugee brothers must not be forced into wandering, suicide, madness or any other act of desperation through any fault of our own. No sacrifice will be too great."[29] Even Weill's own domain, the Paris Consistory, expressed deep dissatisfaction. It too passed a resolution sharply condemning Kristallnacht and proclaimed it to be a "human duty . . . to assure every possibility of life to the unfortunate Jews. . . . The Paris Consistory will do everything possible . . . to ensure that this relief effort be completely effective."[30]

To meet this challenge, Jewish leaders thoroughly revamped the rescue and relief mission, an effort that stands in stark contrast to the collapse of the Comité National in 1934 and 1935. To better coordinate relief and fundraising efforts, Rothschild and Lambert created two new central organizations: the Groupement de Coordination, which served as a coordinating body for the 30 different refugee committees then operating in France, and the Intercomité des Oeuvres Françaises d'Assistance aux Réfugiés (the Inter-committee), which acted as the Groupement's administrative arm.[31] In December 1938, Louise Weiss prodded Foreign Minister Georges Bonnet to create yet another umbrella organization, the Comité Central des Réfugiés, or the Bonnet Committee, as it was commonly called. This committee, directed by Weiss, mediated between the Groupement and the government, channeling all administrative, legal, and juridical questions pertaining to refugee work to the appropriate government ministry.[32]

Moreover, the AIU, in conjunction with the Oeuvre de Secours aux Enfants (OSE), convinced government authorities in December to allocate 1,000 entry visas for German and Austrian children,[33] and a special committee—the Comité pour les Enfants venant d'Allemagne et d'Europe Centrale, directed by the Baronesses de Rothschild and de Gunzbourg—was created to oversee this effort.[34] The Bonnet Committee, together with the Alsatian refugee committee, launched a similar initiative to secure entry visas for 200 elderly Jews, but in this case the minister of the interior refused, claiming that the presence of adult Germans, especially in the border provinces, would constitute a security risk.[35]

Finally, the CAR streamlined and humanized its reception services. For the first time, Lambert saw to it that modern social work procedures were implemented: refugees were now given numbers so that they would not have to wait in line for endless hours, a special waiting room was installed where trained personnel were available to answer questions, and a larger facility was acquired to accommodate growing demand.[36] These reforms proved immensely successful. During its first two months of existence, the Groupement raised as much money as the Comité National had during its entire three years of operation,[37] and JDC spokesmen now praised their French colleagues for showing "greater energy and devotion than before."[38]

Those in charge did not rest content with ensuring the day-to-day survival of the refugees, however. Rather, they continued the battle for long-term constructive solutions. In an attempt to reverse the extreme Malthusianism that prevailed in France, native Jewish leaders and their Christian supporters stepped up the long-standing propaganda campaign to convince the French public that the refugees constituted an economic and demographic asset. Not only would the refugees create new jobs for French workers, but they would also bolster France's sagging population, an issue of growing concern given the country's mounting defense needs.[39] At the same time, these activists fought tirelessly to secure work permits for the refugees, even if that meant sending them to far-off provinces where certain skills were in short demand. As Louise Weiss argued to the minister of commerce in an attempt to persuade him to allow the resettlement of a group of Sudeten Jewish jewelers in the Franche-Comté, their presence "would have signified a fantastic windfall for France."[40]

These efforts failed, however, due to the government's extreme deference to the protectionist demands of labor unions and especially of the middle-class professional associations of artisans, merchants, and lawyers and doctors. By 1939, job placement had come to virtual standstill (for the month of May, the CAR placed only 11 refugees in jobs),[41] and CAR administrators expressed mounting frustration with the bizarre policies of the Ministry of Labor. "It is impossible to obtain working cards for the refugees even in trades where there is no unemployment," one CAR report noted. In Nice, positions had been available for dressmakers, domestics, furriers, and tailors, but the Ministry in Paris vetoed every one of these requests. "The policy of refusing a working card to a tailor in Nice because a tailor in Paris or Lille is out of work should be changed," CAR spokesmen insisted, "since the latter will not leave his city to work elsewhere."[42] Weiss's efforts on behalf of the Sudeten jewelers were similarly stymied because, as we have seen, the Ministry of Commerce caved in to the protectionist demands of the Chambers of Commerce and artisan associations of Dôle and Besançon. As a result, Weiss commented, France "lost an enormous source of wealth."[43] Similarly, the Confédération des Syndicats Médicaux, the professional association of French doctors, subverted every attempt to settle refugee doctors in southern France or in the colonies, despite severe shortages of medical personnel in these regions. The problem, according to William Oualid, was no longer economic but psychological. As long as France remained "mired in a jealous Malthusianism," he wrote, "there can be no hope of [economic] progress and growth."[44]

French Jewish notables still were not deterred. Instead, they displayed a willingness to consider even those radical proposals they had shunned in the past: collective agricultural settlements in southwestern France and in French colonies. Although such projects had long been supported by the Gourevitch Committee, the Zionists, and much of the immigrant and Alsace-Lorraine Jewish communities,[45] the native establishment had generally greeted these schemes with considerable reserve. Agricultural collectives, they believed, would prevent assimilation and ultimately provoke antisemitism.[46] They further maintained that colonial ventures, such as Marius Moutet's plan to settle refugees in Madagascar, might encourage East European regimes to expel their Jewish populations en masse and "awaken among the masses of the Polish Jewish population unrealizable hopes, thus provoking an exodus for which France will sooner or later have to pay."[47]

Yet the tragic circumstances of 1938 and 1939 compelled French Jews to

take a fresh look at these proposals.[48] In part, this reassessment was motivated by more vigorous government support for these schemes. In early
1938, as we have seen, Chautemps's newly appointed undersecretary of state
for immigration, Philippe Serre, had devised a scheme to resettle some
12,000 to 15,000 illegal East European Jewish refugees in the provinces, a
move designed to counter mounting complaints from labor unions that
these immigrants—who worked long hours at substandard wages—were
stealing jobs from French workers. Jewish organizations were expected to
pay for this resettlement, and refugees who refused to comply were to be
"ruthlessly expelled."[49]

Although this plan was ostensibly dropped when Chautemps's government fell from power in March, most of its major features survived. Beginning in the spring of 1938, the Daladier regime passed a series of decrees
banning refugee settlement in a number of departments, including the
Seine, and at the same time it offered 50 percent reductions in the train fares
to those refugees willing to go to the provinces.[50] Once again, Jewish organizations were expected to finance this resettlement, and in return the government assured the CAR that those refugees who went to the provincial
centers would be fully exempted from the decree laws.[51] To be sure, the
refugees were not supposed to remain in these provincial centers indefinitely. The aim was rather to provide temporary shelter until the committees could arrange for their emigration elsewhere.

At the same time, the government began to take a more favorable view
of colonial schemes. Georges Mandel, Daladier's minister of colonies, initially voiced vehement opposition to these plans, largely for the same reasons as native Jewish leaders, and indeed Mandel's background as a highly
assimilated Jew may have colored his views on this question.[52] Nevertheless, in response to mounting American and British pressure to open up
new lands for refugee settlement in the fall of 1938, and especially after
Kristallnacht, France's foreign minister, Georges Bonnet, reversed this
stance. In early December, Bonnet declared publicly that France was ready
to permit 10,000 Jewish refugees to settle in French colonies on condition
that the United States and Great Britain absorb similar contingents. And in
an apparent nod to Mandel's fears of future German revanchist claims on
French territories opened up to refugee settlement, Bonnet further stipulated that these refugees not be of German origin.[53]

Jewish leaders now realized that these ventures offered the last hope, and
they worked feverishly in late 1938 to make these provincial centers a success.[54] By the eve of the war, five centers were in operation under the aegis
of the CAR; two devoted primarily to agricultural work and the other three
to various sorts of vocational retraining.[55] Moreover, the CAR began to offer cautious support for the colonial schemes, sponsoring the emigration of

a small contingent of 30 refugees to French Guiana in the spring of 1939.[56] The CAR even appeared willing to go along with a far more ambitious plan, announced by the government in the late summer of 1939, to settle 25,000 to 40,000 refugees in Madagascar and New Caledonia.[57]

Ultimately, however, these attempts at constructive solutions were confounded, not by the obstructionist behavior of certain Jewish leaders, as had been the case in the past, but rather by the policies of the French government, and especially the decree laws. The major problem was that hundreds and perhaps even thousands of refugees—Germans, Austrians, and East Europeans[58]—were being arrested and thrown into prison for the simple crime of not possessing a visa or a passport.[59] As a result, the committees were forced to invest inordinate amounts of time, money, and energy into two administrative tasks: regularizing the legal status of the thousands of newcomers so that they would not be thrown into prison, and securing the release from prison of those who had not been helped in time.

The frustrations of this work were enormous, since every case had to be handled individually. In Nice, where thousands of refugees flocked following the anti-Jewish crackdown in Italy, one CAR official noted: "For practically all refugees, intervention is necessary because they all have some trouble or other with their papers."[60] The expenses, too, were astronomical; it cost nearly 600 francs ($220) to regularize the status of a single refugee.[61] But, as the director of the Menton committee put it, "We ask only that this price be paid to secure the admission of our brothers."[62] To be sure, most of these interventions eventually met with success. In Nice and Lyons, good relations had been established with the local magistrates, and as a result nearly all the refugees were granted provisional liberty until their situation was regularized.[63] Yet, for leaders like Lambert, who had striven long and hard to redirect Jewish philanthropy away from short-term charity toward long-term constructive work, this trend proved disheartening to the extreme. "The activity of the Committee is being turned more and more from its original purpose," the JDC reported in 1939. "It wanted to do constructive work but is forced to do charitable work instead. . . . All the efforts of the Committee are directed toward the regularizing of the papers of these people and protecting them from rigorous action by the authorities."[64]

At first, Jewish leaders sought to work within these constraints, perhaps in a last-ditch effort to prove Jewish and French interests were still one and the same. Indeed, in the fall of 1938 a bargain was struck. The government promised that it would treat all those refugees who went to the provincial centers as "privileged foreigners," exempting them entirely from the decree laws. In return, the government demanded that the committees take measures of their own to halt illegal immigration.[65] Obviously, this was an impossible demand, since it was the government, not the Jewish community, that policed the borders. Nevertheless, when officials threatened to block all further authorizations for illegal refugees already in France to remain, some Jewish leaders felt compelled to comply. At a meeting of refugee committee delegates in the spring of 1939, Lambert declared: "We must draw the attention of our German friends to the danger in France of clandestine and non-controlled emigration. The authorities are becoming very strict, and sometimes they throw it into our face that: 'How can we answer yes [to demands to regularize a refugee's status], when every month there are 1,200 clandestine entries?'"[66]

In the summer, Lambert again reported that although the committees had successfully ameliorated conditions for a large number of illegal refugees, this effort could not be continued "if . . . illegal and clandestine entries at all frontiers continue to increase."[67] Maurice Stern, president of the Intercommittee, even went so far as to propose that the Intercommittee itself create special reception centers at the borders where refugees could be screened, thus ensuring that only those worthy of asylum be allowed to enter. This proposal never saw the light of day, however, causing Stern to remark that "although we have to do our best to demonstrate to the authorities that we by no means favor illegal entries . . . whatever action we take in this regard constitutes nothing more than a platonic gesture."[68]

Yet beneath these attempts to pay obeisance to government policy, deep discontent and frustration were brewing within the ranks of the Franco-Jewish establishment. Not only did those in charge resent having to squander valuable time and resources on never-ending interventions with the authorities, but most importantly they could not accept the fundamental premise of government policy—that the refugees, simply because they had crossed the border without papers, deserved to be treated as common criminals. As Jacques Biélinky, a prominent Russian-born journalist with strong ties to the native community, declared: "It suffices to attend the correctional hearings in order to realize that in reality it is not only undesirables who are targeted . . . in the vast majority of cases, those . . . condemned are extremely brave people, perfectly inoffensive, who . . . have no notion of where to go."[69] Jewish leaders were also appalled by the stupidity of a policy that flew in the face of alleged government goals—the eventual emigration of the refugees. Once a refugee had accrued a criminal record, the possibility of acquiring an entry visa to another country was reduced to almost nil. Hence, Lambert noted, those very "measures taken to hasten the departure of persons result in making their emigration impossible."[70] Increasingly, the only alternative was to steer these refugees to the provincial centers, where they became wholly dependent on the charity of the committees.[71]

By the spring of 1939, this discontent erupted into open confrontation.

In a speech to the general assembly of the Oeuvre Philanthropique des Asiles Israélites in April, which was attended by nearly the entire French rabbinate, Joseph Lubetzki, the organization's secretary-general, declared: "Unfortunately, the draconian measures adopted by the government against the victims of racism have had the following result: the prisons of the republic have become the shelters for those Jews persecuted everywhere else."[72] Lambert too admitted: "No one can deny that the decree laws . . . have had unacceptable consequences as a result of an overly mechanical and overly severe administrative execution. It is necessary that these decrees be revised or repealed. It is inadmissible that the prisons have been populated by unfortunates who have committed no crime other than fleeing too quickly from those countries where far worse persecutions lay in store for them."[73] Even Rothschild, who never before had dared to criticize the government openly, could no longer refrain, and in the summer of 1939 he declared:

All too often we find ourselves face to face with truly unsolvable conundrums, with distressing situations that bring us to the brink of tears: certain legal dispositions sometimes render it difficult, if not impossible, for any kind of charitable and humanitarian work to succeed. What lamentable odysseys we hear of every day . . . the imprisonment of unfortunates . . . treated like common criminals, . . . *refoulements*, expulsions, and the impossibility for those who have been expelled to flee elsewhere. Is it really a Penelope's web, a rock of Sisyphus before which we find ourselves?[74]

There was only one escape from this quandary, and that was to follow the path suggested by Lambert: to demand the elimination of the decree laws and "to restore and bring back to life the [Popular Front] decree of 17 [September] 1936, which codified the right to asylum for those refugees recognized as such."[75] To be sure, more radical organizations, such as the LICA and the Gourevitch Committee,[76] had been protesting the decree laws since their inception, and on several occasions had intervened directly with both Sarraut and Daladier.[77] These efforts were of no avail, however, and native Jewish leaders ultimately recognized that they too would have to act. In February 1939, representatives of a number of private Jewish associations in France, including the AIU, complained about the decree laws to the High Commission for Refugees (HCR),[78] and in April the executive committee of the Bonnet Committee, which included Jacques Helbronner, adopted a motion demanding "urgent reform" of the decree laws. Indeed, according to the *Univers israélite*, Bonnet himself had "expressed a desire to take charge personally of the effort to consolidate and render infinitely more humane the legislation targeting the refugees. The representatives of the [refugee] associations are enormously heartened by the hope . . . that in the very near future there will be a modification of the legislation whose application has revealed itself to be both unjust and contrary to the traditions and interests of the country."[79]

This effort culminated on May 15, 1939, when a delegation representing the Bonnet Committee—including Louise Weiss, Albert Lévy, and Chief Rabbi Isaïe Schwartz—petitioned the minister of justice to overturn the decree laws and grant an amnesty to refugees who had been unjustly arrested so that they could "reconstruct their lives on a dignified and stable foundation, whether in France or elsewhere." These people, their petition declared, had been imprisoned simply because

> they are born in such and such a way, or they have been prohibited from adhering to such and such a belief, that is to say for exactly the same reasons their own countries of origin have evoked so as to despoil them, to torture them, and to hunt them down. . . . [But] prison is neither an equitable nor a humane solution. It runs counter to every effort undertaken on behalf of the refugees, whether that be to encourage their ultimate emigration or the assimilation into French life of those elements deemed desirable for our national economy.

The delegation thus implored the minister of justice to free the Jewish relief organizations from the "infernal circle" of unending bureaucratic interventions and to "show clemency and enact . . . those measures that will save the . . . lives of thousands of innocents and will be consistent with our generous national tradition."[80] In June, the Intercommittee, to which the Bonnet Committee belonged, seconded this proposal and called on the government to extend the Popular Front's amnesty provisions to Central European refugees who had arrived after the August 5, 1936, cutoff date.[81]

This campaign yielded several short-term gains. On April 12, all refugees between the ages of 20 and 48 who were either stateless or who had received refugee status during the Popular Front were declared eligible for military service, presaging a significant improvement in their legal status.[82] Moreover, on April 21, a new interministerial committee was created, under the aegis of the minister of commerce, aimed at facilitating the creation of new immigrant-owned businesses and industries. The job of screening the applicants was left to the Bonnet Committee, and candidates deemed economically desirable were to be offered incentives to settle in France.[83] And in June, the Bonnet Committee and the CAR, in conjunction with the JDC and the HICEM, prevailed upon Sarraut to grant provisional asylum to several hundred refugees from the S.S. *Saint-Louis* and the S.S. *Flandre*, both of which had been forced to return to Europe from Cuba. These refugees were to be steered to the provincial centers, and Jewish leaders had to promise that they would make every effort to ensure their rapid departure.[84]

Finally, following an intense debate in Parliament over the refugee question in June, Sarraut convened an interministerial conference on June 29 to consider a revision of the decree laws. At this meeting, Sarraut's secretary-general, Jean Berthoin, informed the Groupement that the administration was ready to offer an amnesty to all German and Central European refugees on condition that they be sent to the provincial centers, where they were to be provided with vocational retraining in agriculture and artisanry to prepare for emigration abroad. Once again, this resettlement was to be paid for by the Jewish community, and Sarraut recommended that the three million francs formerly promised by the JDC for the Serre Plan be used for this end. Finally, the Ministry, well aware that illegal Jewish immigration had reached new heights in the spring of 1939 (9,000 new arrivals had been registered by the CAR for the month of March alone), reiterated its demand that Jewish leaders discourage all further immigration. Henceforth, they were to focus exclusively on securing emigration possibilities for refugees already in France.[85]

The Jewish community, desperate to secure an amnesty, responded positively to Sarraut's requests. By the end of the summer, 400 refugees were residing in the provincial centers, and the Groupement intended to send many more there in the near future. At the same time, the ORT and the CIRP intensified their vocational retraining efforts, and the CAR even subsidized the local press in municipalities where these settlements were being established to win popular support and refute rumors that the refugees would constitute a financial burden.[86] Moreover, Jewish leaders endeavored to comply with Sarraut's request that they discourage further influxes of Jewish refugees into France. As Lambert declared at a refugee conference in late August, the "privileged treatment" Jewish leaders had secured for refugees already in France depended on their "not interven[ing] on behalf of new entries." While noting that the Jewish committees "would continue to do our duty and defend the refugees as energetically as possible," he conceded that France from now on would serve as "a provisional asylum" only.[87]

By the end of the summer, whatever tensions had existed between the Jewish community and the government seemed on their way toward being resolved. It even appeared that the last major sticking point—the question of military service—was on the verge of being settled favorably. Jewish leaders had fervently hoped that the refugees would be allowed to fight for France, optimally in the regular army, but at least in the Foreign Legion or in the civilian auxiliary, or *prestataire*, service. In the spring, Lambert had even gone so far as to lambast the government's refusal to enlist the refugees as a "cruel and illogical . . . crime against the fatherland."[88] He therefore hailed the decree laws of July 20 and 22, 1939, which mandated a census of stateless refugees and beneficiaries of the right of asylum so that they could be called upon in the event of war. For Lambert, these laws, more than any factor, proved that the pro-refugee efforts of the Jewish community "have not been in vain."[89]

The outbreak of war, however, ended all progress on this front. In September, the government, as we have seen, announced the internment of all male "enemy aliens" between the ages of 17 and 65, a decision that saddled the Jewish relief effort with an unprecedented burden. The costs of providing food and shelter to the 18,000 internees and their families were astronomical, especially since the government had frozen the internees' bank accounts. For the month of December alone, CAR expenditures came to 4.5 million francs—the equivalent of its entire annual budget for 1938. Not surprisingly, the JDC now had to subsidize 90 percent of the French relief effort.[90] Moreover, for a brief moment it appeared that political considerations might once again threaten the relief effort. On the day war was declared, the CAR closed its doors, to the great dismay of the JDC's new European director, Morris Troper. As Troper explained, "French Jewry was paralyzed. Fearful lest any activity on their part in behalf of German refugees might be construed as consorting with enemy aliens, and further that it might provide a basis for antisemitic sentiment during a period when anything might happen, French Jewry disassociated itself completely from any activity in behalf of the refugees." Yet by the next day, Troper successfully persuaded the CAR to reopen, and the relief effort was fully resumed.[91]

A few months later, once again with the support of the JDC as well as the government, which hoped to use the native Jewish community to counteract negative publicity about the internment camps in the foreign press, French Jewish leaders created a new committee to provide assistance to the internees—the Commission des Centres de Rassemblement, presided over by Albert Lévy.[92] At the same time, they lobbied vigorously to secure the release of the internees so that they could serve either in the Foreign Legion or the *prestataire* service[93] as well as to find jobs for nonmobilized refugees, a task complicated by a maze of new wartime restrictions on the employment of foreigners.[94]

Despite considerable progress in resolving these issues by early 1940,[95] with the majority of refugees being allowed to serve either in the Foreign Legion or in the *prestataire* service, these achievements too came to a standstill with the German invasion of the Low Countries in May 1940. Some 10,000 additional Jewish refugees streamed across the French border, imposing another huge burden on the relief committees. Moreover, the government's decision to reintern all "enemy aliens," men and women alike, put an end to any hope that the refugee situation would be favorably resolved.[96] Despite continued fears that pro-refugee initiatives might be perceived as unpatriotic,[97] native Jews clearly had little faith left in the government's policy. As Albert Lévy poignantly declared in May 1940, French Jews could not help but see those in the camps as "human beings, creatures of God like ourselves, our brothers, [and since] they were the first victims of the savagery of the hitlerian fury, we cannot, in good conscience, consider them enemy subjects."[98]

By the eve of the war, French Jewish leaders had come to a bitter realization: they, just as much as those refugees they were seeking so desperately to help, were trapped in France. Betrayed by their own government, they were indeed caught up in an "infernal circle." They were furthermore becoming increasingly aware that antisemitism, originally targeted primarily at foreign Jews, was beginning to encompass "the totality of the people of Israel," as Radical Party spokesman Emile Roche aptly noted.[99] Indeed, at a meeting between Jewish communal leaders and leading French Jewish intellectuals held in February 1938 to discuss strategies to combat antisemitism, Robert de Rothschild himself warned that if antisemitism were permitted to take hold in France, all Jews "would be thrown into the same sack." Another participant at this meeting, the prominent lawyer Armand Dorville, also proclaimed that Jews in the liberal professions had a special obligation to fight antisemitism since "nearly all of us belong to the liberal professions . . . and every country begins by hitting liberal professionals before the others." Even the playwright Henry Bernstein, not known for his left-wing views, called on Jews to demonstrate solidarity in the face of the antisemitic onslaught; in the end, he stated, they would all be considered "Frenchmen of the Jewish race."[100]

Notwithstanding these apprehensions, Lambert refused to abandon his faith in France, and with respect to the anti-immigrant decree laws, he counseled his coreligionists "not to judge our country according to transitory legislation." The forces of reason, he argued, would ultimately triumph.[101] Nevertheless, he warned, dramatic improvements should not be expected in the near future: "As long as Europe is living in a state of disquiet, as long as the international community fails to resume its normal activities and intercourse, we can expect no plan nor any discovery of new lands that might offer the solution for the great distress of those Jews still forced to wander."[102] In the meanwhile, French Jews would have to wait it out, and endeavor to the best of their abilities "to save those lives in danger, to dress the wounds of those who suffer and to maintain intact the spiritual discipline, whose permanence gives us reason to hope for a better future."[103] This was the policy Lambert later referred to as "holding on and holding out"[104]—the strategy of maximizing small victories, and it was precisely this policy that would guide native Jewish leaders through the more trying times ahead.

To conclude, it is abundantly clear that the policies of French Jewish notables vis-à-vis the refugees underwent a dramatic transformation during the course of the 1930's. Although the hard-liners prevailed in 1935, their position had become untenable by the late 1930's. The moderates now in charge stubbornly refused to abandon the refugees, even though that stance pitted them against their own government. Indeed, by the end of the decade, native French Jewry was doing everything within its power to ameliorate the refugees' plight, not only by providing philanthropic assistance, an enormous task in and of itself, but also by pressing the government on the political front to overturn the "monstrous" decree laws.[105] Even non-Jews took note of this transformation. As the nationally renowned journalist Raymond Millet commented in 1938, French Jews now seemed more determined "than ever to fulfill their duty of solidarity."[106]

To be sure, traces of earlier ambivalence remained, as evidenced by the CAR's publication of an extremely paternalistic manual during the summer of 1938. This manual counseled the refugees on how to behave so as not to provoke antisemitism: be polite, discreet, and modest (in particular, don't say "Everything used to be better where we came from"; avoid any involvement in French politics; and learn French and assimilate as quickly as possible ("Don't speak in a loud voice, and, if you speak in a foreign language, try not to do so in public, on the street, on public transport, or on the terrace of a café").[107] Yet ultimately, the majority of native leaders overcame this ambivalence, and never again did it seriously threaten the relief effort. Indeed, the publication of the CAR manual marks one of the last times French Jewish leaders publicly held the refugees themselves responsible in any way for antisemitism.[108] By the time of Kristallnacht, it had become altogether clear who the victims were. Hence, although the harsh assessments of native French Jewry's response to the refugee crisis are by and large justified for the period 1933 to 1935, there is little foundation for these charges with respect to the second half of the decade.

This analysis furthermore suggests that philanthropy and politics were never as distinct from one another as Weinberg, Hyman, and Nicault claim. To be sure, French Jewish notables initially sought to separate the two spheres, but it quickly became apparent that philanthropy itself had far-reaching political implications. As Helbronner noted in 1934 and 1935, to be too generous in allocating relief would only entice more refugees to seek asylum in France and would remove all pressure on the League of Nations to arrive at a more equitable international redistribution of the refugees. On the other hand, the moderates who directed the committees in the late 1930's worked assiduously on behalf of constructive solutions no matter what the cost. They too were fully aware of the political repercussions of their strategy; in their view France would have to accept at least a portion of those refugees who had sought asylum there, and with regard to the thousands of others, France was obliged to provide a humane, if only temporary, haven. To ensure this outcome, French Jewish leaders were even willing to engage in a political battle, challenging the decree laws head-on. Even the Consistories, the most politically conservative of all Jewish institutions, challenged article 7 of the November 12, 1938, decree law, which forbade foreigners who had not secured a *permis de séjour* from marrying French citizens.[109] The charge of native Jewish passivity in the face of the decree laws is therefore without foundation.[110]

Furthermore, although most accounts of French Jewry during the 1930's emphasize the degree to which the community was deeply divided over a range of issues, the analysis presented here suggests that in reality a significant degree of consensus prevailed by 1939, at least insofar as the refugees were concerned. Indeed, if one examines the various pro-refugee programs advocated at the end of the decade by a host of Jewish organizations, it becomes clear that they shared similar goals: the elimination of the decree laws; the institution of a just and humane statute for immigrants based on the Popular Front's refugee policies; a continued emphasis on constructive solutions, including agricultural and to a lesser degree colonial settlements; and, finally, a recognition that under the present economic and political circumstances, France really could serve as a transit country only. Even Léon Blum acknowledged in his speech to the LICA: "Naturally, these unfortunates cannot remain here forever, that's clear. Naturally, it will be necessary to find solutions of a stable and enduring nature. . . . [B]ut . . . as long as they're waiting to find lodging of a more certain and durable nature elsewhere, how can you refuse them shelter for one night?"[111] Indeed Blum, like many others at the time, including Lambert and Rabbi Jacob Kaplan, the future Chief Rabbi of France, went on to endorse Zionism—the creation of a Jewish homeland in Palestine—as the most desirable solution.[112] Hence, the conflict between French Jewish leaders and their government was not over whether France should serve as a permanent or a temporary haven. Rather, the debate focused on the failure of the current regime to provide even short-term shelter, and on this issue, French Jews were widely agreed, despite continued bickering over questions relating to leadership and representation.

Finally, this study sheds considerable light on the debate over French Jewish behavior during Vichy. Those organizations that emerged during the Vichy era to unify and centralize relief—the Coordination Committee, or C-Coord, established on January 30, 1941, and most importantly, the Union Générale des Israélites de France (UGIF), the French Jewish council established by Vichy on November 29, 1941—did not arise in a vacuum. Rather, they were direct outgrowths of those coordinating bodies that had come into existence in 1938: the Groupement, the Intercommittee, and the

Comité Central. Even many of the same personalities were involved, most notably Lévy and Lambert, who served, respectively, as the president and secretary-general of the UGIF in the southern zone.

Although some commentators, like Rajsfus, have charged that the UGIF collaborated with Vichy to rid France of the foreign Jews,[113] others, especially Richard I. Cohen, have recently reassessed the UGIF's activities, and Lambert's role in particular, in a far more sympathetic light.[114] Yet even Cohen underestimates the extent to which both the policies and attitudes of those involved in the UGIF had been decisively shaped by the circumstances of the 1930's. Indeed, the evidence presented here underscores Cohen's thesis that the motives of those in charge were laudable and reflected their fervent desire to sustain the relief effort, irrespective of whether they may have erred politically by seeking to work within the framework mapped out by Vichy. Indeed, for leaders like Lambert, the situation after the fall of France merely marked a continuation of the catastrophe of the late 1930's. A full year after the armistice, Lambert repeated the credo that would determine his behavior until his own deportation to Auschwitz in 1943:

During the tragic hours of the summer of 1941, there exists no grandiose project, nor any constructive solution that might be capable of saving all the unfortunates who have pinned their hopes on our organizations. Nevertheless, our incessant activity seems to us more useful than ever since every act of relief, every act of social work, every gesture, every counsel, every intervention, every donation or every loan constitutes an indispensable contribution to the appeasement of an immense suffering, no matter how inconsequential it might seem.[115]

CHAPTER FOURTEEN

The Path to Vichy
Continuities and Discontinuities in Jewish Refugee Policy

France of 1940 has nothing in common with pre-war France. A country which was proud to be a refuge for freedom, a place of shelter for all persecuted people in Europe, has now become selfish and intolerant due to the changed situation.   Walter Baum [1]

But the real question is whether France has lost her reason. Can it be true that France, the home of "Liberty, Equality and Fraternity," will willingly, of her own complete volition, douse the light of freedom which she loved, and go in for the systems of Hitler and Mussolini, with all that is so hateful in them? If that has happened, it is so strange that one must wait to learn more about it. . . .
    France must not go Nazi. Even if she must use the guillotine, she must not have concentration camps. There is a difference. "The knife is quick and means death to individuals. The barbed wire of the political prison camps is slow death for a nation."   Edwin L. James [2]

With the military defeat, the Third Republic came to an abrupt end. On June 16, 1940, the Renaud government was forced to resign, and a new government was formed at Bordeaux led by the octogenarian hero of Verdun, Henri Philippe Pétain. The first act of this government, which soon relocated to the spa town of Vichy, was to sign an armistice with the Germans that divided France into two principal zones. The Germans directly occupied the economically richest areas of the country—the north, the northeast, and the Atlantic and Channel coasts—while Vichy was ceded control over most of southern France. [3] Moreover, in a rather complicated arrangement, the Germans agreed that Vichy legislation would be valid for both the occupied and unoccupied zones, as long as it did not directly contravene German law.

In early July, the French Parliament, absent the communist deputies who had been forced underground in early 1940, as well as the 27 members of Parliament, including Edouard Daladier and Georges Mandel, who had sailed to North Africa on the *Massilia* in the hope of continuing the war, voted Pétain full powers.[4] The constitution of the Third Republic was abrogated, and the new head of state declared, "A new order is commencing."[5] The republican principles of 1789—liberty, equality, fraternity—were to be replaced by the right-wing agenda long espoused by the Action Française and its allies, an agenda summed up by the slogan "Patrie, Famille et Travail" ("Fatherland, Family, and Work"). Pétain's "National Revolution" was to be based on an authoritarian and hierarchical concept of government, Christian social values, and a corporate economic system—a third path between unfettered capitalism and socialism—that would restore economic power to professional organizations and small-scale property owners, while eliminating class conflict and labor strife. Furthermore, the proponents of the new regime believed that in order for this "true France" to emerge, the advocates of the anti-France—communists, foreigners, freemasons, and Jews—would have to be shorn of the disproportionate power and influence they had allegedly amassed over French life during the ignominious Third Republic.[6]

Since the anti-Jewish policies of the Vichy government have received considerable attention in recent years, there is no need to provide yet another comprehensive survey of this question here. Nevertheless, in light of our previous examination of the way three factors in the 1930's—government policy, public opinion, and Jewish responses—interacted to influence French refugee policy in the 1930's, it would be useful to analyze the extent to which these factors paved the way for Vichy's anti-Jewish policy. Although many contemporaries viewed Vichy's treatment of the Jews as a radical break with republican traditions, more recently scholars, especially Michael R. Marrus and Robert O. Paxton, have argued that the anti-Jewish legislation of Vichy, as well as the continued emphasis on emigration and internment, stemmed directly from policies initiated at the end of the Third Republic. As Marrus notes, in an article devoted to the continuity theme:

Vichy's anti-Jewish policy . . . drew directly upon the experience of the 1930's, notably the last two years of Republican government under Daladier. Indeed, Vichy was much less original in her initial attack upon the Jewish minority than is often assumed; Vichy ministers had a wealth of Republican precedents before them as they isolated and discriminated against the Jews, accounting in part for the nearly universal acquiescence in the laws when they were first passed in 1940 and 1941. Innovation came later, in the summer of 1942, when the Nazis' deportation programme thrust new dilemmas upon the French government and the police.[7]

While the republican precedents for many of Vichy's anti-Jewish initiatives deserve to be highlighted, the emphasis on continuity should not be pushed too far. Vichy's innovations began well before 1942, and while many of the new regime's policies did have roots in the 1930's, they acquired a new intensity and scope once Pétain came to power. This escalation occurred because the pro-refugee lobby, which had continually challenged these measures during the 1930's, sometimes with considerable success, was now silenced completely. Hence, as the ideology and program of what had been a single political faction in the 1930's became enshrined as the ideology of the state, a path was cleared to pursue these policies to a degree inconceivable under republican auspices.

In examining the issue of continuity and discontinuity with respect to government policy, we will focus our attention on three areas: Vichy's legislative assault against the Jews, its continued emphasis on emigration as the principal solution to the Jewish refugee problem, and the policy of internment. Insofar as the legislative assault against the Jews was concerned, the new regime lost little time, and the weeks immediately following the armistice witnessed a veritable cascade of anti-Jewish measures, suggesting the priority the "Jewish Question" was to receive. Moreover, as Marrus and Paxton have demonstrated, the bulk of this early legislation owed little to German prompting. Rather, as Pétain's civilian chief of staff, Henri du Moulin de Labarthète, later conceded, "Germany was not at the origin of the anti-Jewish legislation of Vichy. This legislation was, if I dare say it, spontaneous, native."[8]

Already on July 13, 1940, Pétain issued a decree stating that "only men of French parentage may belong to the Ministerial Cabinets," a decree that German radio immediately interpreted to mean the "elimination of Jews from government posts."[9] On July 22, another law was passed permitting the government to denaturalize all foreigners who had acquired their citizenship since the 1927 naturalization act; not even veterans or family members of war dead were to be exempted. Such a law had become necessary, the minister of the interior subsequently explained, because "the presence on [French] territory of many persons who emigrated from or were expelled from their countries, foreigners or persons without countries, Jews or non-Jews, constitut[es] a certain danger to peace and public order."[10]

On July 23, Vichy announced yet another decree authorizing the cancellation of citizenship and the confiscation of property of all French nationals who had departed France after May 10, 1940, without an officially "valid" reason. Although several prominent non-Jews were mentioned as targets of this law, including Pertinax, Henri de Kérillis, Pierre Viénot, and Pierre Cot, the majority of individuals singled out were Jews, including Baron Robert de Rothschild and his three brothers, Edouard, Philippe, and Henri; the bankers Léon and Maurice Stern and Louis-Louis Dreyfus, also a senator from the Alpes-Maritimes; and the deputies Jean Zay, Pierre Mendès France, and Edouard Jonas.[11] According to the French government, these individuals no longer merited French citizenship since they had shown themselves to be "Jews before they were French" by fleeing the country at the moment of military collapse.[12]

In another move that had serious implications for the propagation of antisemitism, the new government abrogated, on August 27, the Marchandeau decree of April 1939, which had banned antisemitism and racial defamation in the press. Those who had been arrested under the terms of this legislation, such as the notorious antisemite, Louis Darquier de Pellepoix, were now released and permitted to resume their antisemitic activities unhindered.[13] On October 7, 1940, the government dealt yet another blow to Jewish emancipation when it rescinded the 1870 Crémieux decree, which had granted civil rights to the Jews of Algeria.

The major thrust of Vichy's antisemitic legislation, however, was the drive to eliminate Jews from public service as well as from a wide swath of French professional life. On July 17, the new regime issued a decree limiting civil service posts to individuals born in France of French fathers, a measure that excluded many French citizens. Another law, of August 16, created a doctors' guild, the Ordre des Médicins, and forbade the exercise of medicine, dentistry, and pharmacy to all persons not born in France of French fathers. On September 10, these persons were excluded from the practice of law as well. According to a pronouncement of the new minister of the interior, Marcel Peyrouton, "The various professional organizations should take action to eliminate from their membership even French elements who by their acts or attitudes showed themselves unworthy to exercise their profession in the manner the present situation demands."[14] An even more comprehensive law, the Statut des Juifs of October 3, 1940, expanded by a second statute of June 2, 1941, codified and elaborated upon these earlier measures.

For the first time, these statutes, which were clearly modeled on the 1935 Nuremberg Laws, defined Jews in racial terms. According to the second Statut des Juifs, a Jew was defined as anyone having three or more grandparents "of the Jewish race," irrespective of whether that person had been converted, or, if that person was married to a Jew, two Jewish grandparents sufficed. These statutes then barred Jews from civil and military service positions, including judgeships, teaching and administrative posts, and army staff positions; all professions having an influence over public opinion—

theater, the press, publishing, radio, and film; and a wide range of commercial professions—banking, the stock exchange, and real estate and publicity agents. Moreover, the Council of State was now authorized to set quotas on Jewish participation in the liberal professions and educational institutions. On June 21, the number of Jewish students in institutions of higher learning was set at 3 percent; and on July 16 and August 11 respectively, the number of Jewish lawyers and doctors was set at 2 percent. Although exemptions were to be granted to individuals who had fought for France or who had performed exceptional services to the state, these exemptions were allocated only sparingly. According to Susan Zuccotti, of 125 Jewish university professors who applied for exemptions in the fall of 1940, only 10 had received them by the spring of 1941.[15]

What prompted this slew of antisemitic measures, and to what degree did they owe their existence to the antiforeign initiatives of the 1930's? The first and most obvious difference between the measures implemented in the 1930's and those implemented under Vichy is that the latter were overtly antisemitic. Even the most radical antiforeign restrictions of the 1930's, such as the civil service law of July 19, 1934, and the Nast Law of 1935, which had restricted the rights of recently naturalized citizens in the fields of public service and medicine, were never formulated in overtly antisemitic terms, despite the fact that they were indeed targeted at recently arrived Central and East European Jews. Rather, these laws were always framed as antiforeign measures, thus avoiding any hint of legalized antisemitism, which was still considered anathema during the Third Republic.

In other respects, however, Vichy's anti-Jewish legislation owed much to the antiforeign legislation of the 1930's. First, the aforementioned laws had already begun the process of rolling back citizenship by stripping recently naturalized citizens of their professional rights. By condoning this two-tiered system of citizenship, the Parliament had already in the mid-1930's done much to pave the way for Vichy's denaturalization policies. Moreover, as a recent study by Bernard Laguerre shows, Vichy's denaturalization legislation was not prompted by German pressure, at least until the summer of 1943, and was aimed overwhelmingly at Jews. Of a total of 15,154 recently naturalized foreigners stripped of their citizenship under the July 22, 1940, law, Laguerre estimates that 6,000, or 40 percent, were Jews, primarily from Eastern Europe. Given the fact that foreign Jews constituted less than 1 percent of all foreigners in France, it is clear that they were being singled out by this legislation.[16]

Just as significantly, the same corporate pressure groups—merchants, artisans, and liberal professionals, especially lawyers and doctors—were clearly behind both the antiforeign legislation of the 1930's and Vichy's anti-Jewish legislation. Although Donna Evleth has recently argued that the

Ordre des Médecins would have been content with antiforeign rather than explicitly antisemitic legislation, it is difficult not to see the influence of the former Confédération des Syndicats Médicaux, as well as its other middle-class analogues, on Vichy's anti-Jewish program.[17] For these middle-class professional associations in the 1930's, xenophobia and antisemitism were essentially one and the same, since Jews, unlike most other immigrants, were overwhelmingly concentrated in middle-class professions. Thus, in a statement justifying professional restrictions on Jews, Xavier Vallat, who had just been appointed commissioner-general for Jewish affairs at the end of March 1941, declared in a press release prior to the announcement of the second Statut des Juifs that Jews, French and foreign together, constituted 12.5 percent of the nation's doctors and 9.3 percent of its dentists.

Although Vallat justified these restrictions by alleging that Jews were "a parasitical element, dissolving and revolutionary," there is little doubt that his principal concern here was the economic threat posed by Jews.[18] Precisely how these middle-class professional associations, which were granted extensive autonomy under Vichy's new corporatist economic ideology, influenced the precise phrasing of the anti-Jewish laws, as well as the actual quotas imposed, is a question that merits further study. Nevertheless, the fact that these groups had put forth nearly all these demands in their prewar programs and had called for restrictions not only on foreigners, but also on recently naturalized citizens, and even on citizens not born of French fathers, suggests a direct influence. Moreover, as we have seen, these professional associations, especially those representing doctors and merchants, had insisted on a greater say over naturalization policy throughout the 1930's. Although the various governments of the Third Republic had granted these associations an advisory role in this matter, never had they ceded complete control. To what must have been their immense satisfaction, Vichy's denaturalization policies as well as the ousting of Jews from nearly all middle-class professions obviated the need for further concessions in this matter.

A second, less obvious inspiration for the anti-Jewish legislation was the fervent desire of high-ranking government officials to find scapegoats for the French defeat, a desire almost certainly fueled in part by the inability of Pétain and the members of the General Staff to admit responsibility for the debacle. While the republican leaders who had led France into war—Daladier, Reynaud, Mandel, and Léon Blum—were arrested, jailed, and scheduled to be tried at Riom in 1942 for having engaged France in a military contest for which it was woefully unprepared,[19] Jews too, and especially the refugees, came in for their share of opprobrium. Having been accused of warmongering in the 1930's, it was now alleged that they had caused the defeat, since they, together with their communist and socialist allies, had provoked a war merely to pursue their own personal vendetta against Hitler, despite French military vulnerability.

In an article titled "Vichy to Penalize Jews for Defeat," the *New York Times* cited at length the preamble to the first Statut des Juifs, which was framed in large measure by the antisemitic minister of justice, Raphaël Alibert. Here the new government laid the blame for the nation's humiliation squarely on the Jews, together with the Popular Front, with whom they were identified. Following a recent speech of Pétain's in which the chief of state had disclaimed any intention of seeking "reprisals for 1936," the preamble proclaimed:

In its work of national reconstruction the government from the very beginning was bound to study the problem of Jews as well as that of certain aliens, who, after abusing our hospitality, contributed to our defeat in no small measure. In all fields and especially in the public service . . . the influence of Jews has made itself felt, insinuating and finally decomposing.

All observers agree in noting the baneful effects of their activity in the course of recent years, during which they had a preponderant part in the direction of our affairs. The facts are there and they command the action of the government to which has fallen the pathetic task of French restoration.[20]

Maxime Weygand, Maurice Gamelin's successor as commander-in-chief in May 1940 and Vichy's new minister of defense, similarly blamed the defeat not on the failures of the military, but on the nation's internal sources of decay, including the low birthrate and its corollary, the excessively high rate of immigration. As he declared in a manifesto submitted to Pétain in July 1940, and signed by nearly all members of Parliament: "The decline in the birthrate, by diminishing the potential of France, has led us, from a military point of view, to defend our territory with an unacceptable proportion of North African, colonial and foreign contingents; [and] from a national point of view to effect massive and regrettable naturalizations and to hand over to foreign exploiters a portion of our soil and wealth." Whether "foreign exploiters" referred to the immigrants or to the Germans is not altogether clear, but Weygand almost certainly had Jews in mind when he condemned the excessive naturalizations in recent years, especially under the Popular Front.[21]

In addition to being charged with having caused the defeat, Jews, and especially the refugees, continued to be viewed as dangerous subversives bent on the destruction of the state. Not only had they maintained their links with Moscow, but according to one police report of November 1940, they were fomenting Gaullist, or Free French, propaganda throughout the south:

The Jews, not without skill, exploit the anglophile current, which is shared by a large segment of opinion, and they also know how to take advantage of the population's national sentiment, which reacts to the presence of demands put forth by the occupation authorities or to the various draconian measures taken by the Reich (such as the expulsion of French speaking Lorrainers). It is possible to regard all Jews as "Gaullists."

How was this Jewish underground sustained? Supposedly, diverse groups of Jews stayed in touch with one another through the frequent journeys of journalists and bankers, as well as "the numerous trips taken by agents of the OSE (Oeuvre de Secours aux Enfants [Organization for Assistance to Children]) and the ORT, organizations that have set up their headquarters in Montpellier and Marseilles, and which have also remained in contact with the anglo-saxon countries, either directly, or through Portugal." That ORT or OSE agents may have been traveling to assist the thousands of displaced Jews who had fled to the south had obviously never occurred to this agent. Rather, their suspicious comings and goings could have meant only one thing, and he therefore recommended that all Jews be placed under heightened surveillance.[22]

No one better sums up the various ideological strands of Vichy's antisemitism than Xavier Vallat, who served as commissioner-general for Jewish affairs from March 1941 until he was forced out of office by the Germans one year later, just prior to the onset of the deportations. Although Vallat's antisemitism seems moderate in comparison to that of his successor, Darquier de Pellepoix, it was nonetheless quite virulent, as any reader of his postwar memoirs, *Le Nez de Cléopâtre* (*Cleopatra's Nose*), can attest. Moreover, Vallat's brand of antisemitism, which abjured anti-Jewish violence but favored legal restrictions on Jews, was certainly more in tune with French right-wing thinking than that of Nazi-style antisemites, such as Darquier de Pellepoix or the *Je suis partout* crowd, who remained in Paris throughout the occupation and engaged in open collaboration. Whereas Vichy leaders, including Pétain himself, frequently railed against the financial "plutocracy" and "international capitalism," which they blamed, together with communism, for the decay of the Third Republic and ultimately for the defeat, Vallat made it crystal clear just who was being targeted in these attacks.[23] Vallat's postwar memoirs furthermore provide valuable insight into how attacks aimed primarily at foreign Jews easily merged into attacks on Jews as a whole, although it must be said that Vallat, even in the 1930's, never limited his antisemitic diatribes to foreign Jews. Indeed, if anyone was his principal target, it was Léon Blum, whose parents and grandparents had been born in France, as Blum repeatedly felt compelled to point out.

According to Vallat, who after the war showed no remorse whatsoever for his role in having helped implement the first phase of Vichy's anti-Jewish program, Jews were responsible for the twin evils of unfettered capitalism and communism, and as such their activities had to be curbed by the introduction of corporatism, which was intended to restrict both excessive competition and excessive egalitarianism and sought to return power to the professional associations in a system reminiscent of medieval guilds. Vallat further maintained that no matter how long Jews had lived in France, or anywhere else for that matter, they remained unassimilable, "a state within a state," as their two-thousand year history in the diaspora demonstrated. After the First World War, all the ghettos of Eastern Europe had, he claimed, "sent us their tens of thousands of young Jews, with empty pockets but insatiable greed, who skipped their traditional stopping place of Germany in their *Drang nach Westen*."

Although these Jewish immigrants might have been assimilated had they settled in the provinces and engaged in manual labor and agriculture, this had not occurred. Rather, Vallat claimed, echoing the views of ethnologists such as Mauco and Martial, they had flocked to urban centers, and especially Paris, where they had "invaded" the middle-class professions. Before the First World War, Vallat alleged, the Paris bar had counted about 400 Jews, but this number had swelled significantly every year since. The Jewish immigrant "invasion" of the medical profession was even more threatening. Out of 6,000 doctors in the department of the Seine in 1939, Vallat now claimed, going well beyond the figures he had earlier cited, that 2,000 had been Jews, mostly recently naturalized citizens from Romania and elsewhere in Eastern Europe.

Vallat furthermore charged that Jews during the Third Republic had achieved control over a number of other industries as well: banking had become a virtual Jewish fiefdom, dominated by the Rothschilds, the Worms, and the Finalys; shoe manufacturing and the textile and garment industries had also become quasi-Jewish monopolies; and the film industry as well as journalism had fallen under Jewish control. Moreover, unlike other immigrants, Jews had pushed themselves to the forefront politically, and due to "their hereditary appetite for power and domination," they had flocked to the militant parties of the left, especially Léon Blum's Socialist Party. Whereas there was only one Italian deputy for one million Italian immigrants, the Jewish population, which numbered a mere 300,000, had managed to get 14 Jewish deputies elected to Parliament, despite the fact that a system of proportional ethnic representation, which Vallat obviously favored, would have limited them to two parliamentary seats.

Finally, in case these factors did not suffice to justify Vichy's anti-Jewish agenda, Vallat fell back on the traditional argument of the Action Française that France was, after all, a Christian nation and that in implementing a program of anti-Jewish legislative restrictions, the French government was merely following the dictates of the Catholic Church. As Vallat explained, "It would be unreasonable to allow them, in a Christian State, to run the government and oppress Catholics by means of their authority. It is therefore legitimate to forbid them access to public offices; legitimate as well not to admit them to the University and to liberal professions except in fixed proportions." In contrast to Nazi antisemitism, which sanctioned physical violence and pogromlike behavior, Vichy's anti-Jewish program, Vallat maintained, "sensibly remains within the guidelines followed by the Church throughout the ages. She has limited herself solely to measures against Jewish influence in the political, economic, and cultural realms." And indeed, Vallat's assertion carries considerable weight, since, as we have seen, the French clerical press in the 1930's had enthusiastically supported the imposition of a *numerus clausus* on Jews in the liberal professions and educational institutions, and the Vatican itself, as Vallat pointed out, never protested any of Vichy's anti-Jewish measures.[24]

Beyond the legislative realm, two other important aspects of Vichy's anti-Jewish program need to be examined to assess the degree of continuity between the 1930's and Pétain's regime: emigration and internment, which remained inextricably intertwined. Vichy authorities had clearly hoped that their new order would allow them to get rid of the masses of foreign Jews who had congregated on French soil in recent years. This hope, however, was sorely disappointed, and in fact the Jewish refugee problem in the unoccupied zone was vastly compounded by the defeat and the terms of the armistice. Among the millions of French men, women, and children fleeing south at the time of the German invasion were between 165,000 to 210,000 Jews, including most of the Central European refugee population of Paris, as well as thousands of Eastern European Jews, the majority of whom were also recent immigrants.[25] While native Jews were allowed to return to Paris after the peace was signed, a German ordinance of September 27, 1940, mandated that foreign Jews who had not yet returned to their homes in Paris or elsewhere in the occupied zone would not be permitted to cross the demarcation line.[26] Moreover, as we have seen, at least 10,000 Jewish refugees from Belgium, Luxembourg, and Holland had fled to southern France at the time of the Nazi invasion of the Low Countries, and they too were not permitted to return home.[27] Finally, the army's decision to demobilize its foreign troops, including foreign Jews who had served in the war effort, added another 30,000 souls to the population of homeless, destitute, and unemployed Jews who now found themselves amassed in the south, far away from their homes and their livelihoods, and stripped of their financial assets because their property had been expropriated by the Nazis and their bank accounts blocked.[28]

But aside from Germany's refusal to allow Jews to return to their homes in the north, other German actions greatly exacerbated the Jewish refugee problem in the south, to the great chagrin of the Vichy authorities, who had hoped for greater cooperation in this matter. As we have seen, article 19 of the armistice treaty stipulated that Vichy hand over to the Germans "on demand" any German refugees on French soil, regardless of which zone they lived in. As to why Vichy agreed to this gross violation of the right of asylum, despite the international outcry it evoked, there can be little doubt that it welcomed the repatriation of German refugees on French soil, Jews and non-Jews alike. In September, the Foreign Ministry sent a directive to the prefects describing article 19 as a measure "that envisions the departure from France of the majority of German Jews."[29] Similarly, Ernst Kundt, the German embassy official appointed to head the commission sent out over the summer to inspect the internment camps and determine which refugees were to be repatriated, noted in November that the French authorities regarded the internees as "a considerable burden for the economy and a danger from the point of view of political security. . . . The French government is grateful to us for every man we relieve them of."[30]

Vichy's hopes for a mass repatriation were sorely disappointed, however. Although the Kundt Commission had determined as early as July 2 that the German government "was at bottom not interested in bringing about the repatriation of émigrés and Jews who still possessed German citizenship," it apparently took some time for this decision to filter down to the French.[31] Jewish refugees, on the other hand, quickly realized that their initial fears of being sent back to Germany were groundless. As the émigré journalist Leopold Schwarzschild, who had just arrived in the United States, reported to the Joint Distribution Committee (JDC) in September 1940:

Shortly after the armistice, German officers visited the camps and separated the interned people into Jews and non-Jews. They did not bother about the Jews at all; they told them they were not Germans and therefore, they had nothing to do with them. The first officers who came made no investigation whether these Jews were enemies of the Nazis or not. The German non-Jews, however, were again separated into those who were in France before 1933 and those who came later. Those who were in France before 1933, were immediately liberated and could go back to Germany, or occupied France or wherever they had been in France. Those who came after 1933, remained in camp and the officers had to check each case and find out why they had come to France, and under what circumstances they had left Germany.[32]

Similarly, in January 1941 the French delegation to the Armistice Commission at Wiesbaden reminded the minister of the interior that everything should be done "to accord the maximum of exit visas to German Jews requesting departure to the United States," since Germany had no interest in keeping these Jews on French soil. Only those refugees who had appeared on the Kundt Commission's lists at the end of the summer were not to be given exit visas, and nearly all of these were non-Jews. Moreover, the Kundt Commission failed to relieve France even of the majority of non-Jewish refugees. As Morris Troper of the JDC noted, most of the political refugees in whom the commission was interested had either emigrated or gone into hiding, and in the end the Kundt Commission repatriated only about 800 refugees, although among these were some of the most prominent political personalities, such as Rudolf Breitscheid, Rudolf Hilferding, and Rudolf Leonhard.[33]

Not only did the Germans fail to alleviate France's existing refugee problem, but to the dismay of Vichy officials, they significantly aggravated it by dumping unwanted Jews from German-occupied territory and even from Germany itself into the unoccupied zone. In July 1940, the Germans expelled into Vichy territory the approximately 4,000 Jews who had remained in Alsace and Lorraine after the German invasion.* These people were granted less than one hour to pack their bags and were permitted to take no more than 5,000 francs ($2,000) per person. Then, on October 22 and 23, the Nazis proceeded to expel 6,538 Jews from Baden-Württemberg, and another 1,125 from the Palatinate and the Saar. Once again, these Jews were given one to two hours' notice, and they were allowed to take only one piece of luggage and 10 Reichsmarks, the equivalent of $2.50. They were then brutally packed into cattle cars and shipped to southern France. Most of these Jews were elderly and infirm, since most younger Jews had already left Germany, and some were over 100 years old.[34] Although French police had attempted to stop these trains from crossing the demarcation line, the Germans, by tricking Vichy police into believing that the refugees on board were from Alsace and Lorraine, convinced them to allow the trains to proceed to Lyons, from where they were distributed to various internment camps in the south.[35]

This infringement of French sovereignty proved intolerable to Vichy authorities, who feared these dumpings constituted the first sign of a much larger transport into southern France of peoples deemed undesirable by the Nazis from elsewhere in their now greatly expanded Reich.[36] To guard against such an eventuality, Vichy launched an immediate and vigorous protest. In late October 1940, General Charles Huntziger, France's representative to the Armistice Commission at Wiesbaden, instructed the French delegation there "to raise a protest and declare that France cannot receive the expellees from Germany." France had not been forewarned of these

---

*The rest of the Jewish population of Alsace and Lorraine, which numbered about 29,000, had been evacuated to the interior at the time of the German invasion. See "Report on the Situation of the Jewish Religion in the Occupied Area," translation of report sent from Grand Rabbi Hirschler to Herbert Katzki, JDC, New York, in JDC no. 613 (*France, Cult and Religion*, 1942).

transports, nor did the terms of the armistice obligate it to accept these fresh incursions of "undesirables." As an internal Foreign Ministry memo noted, "It is at least inopportune, at the moment in which we are forced [to effect the emigration] of foreigners, and especially Jews, to receive thousands of German Jews on our territory." To prevent future incursions of refugees "who will be difficult to expel later," the French issued several strongly worded protests throughout the fall of 1940 and even into the following spring, and they furthermore requested the immediate repatriation of those refugees recently dumped on French soil. At the same time, they beefed up police surveillance along the demarcation line as well as along France's eastern frontier.[37]

In a manifestation of utter disdain for the French, German officials ignored these protests completely. In mid-November, General Paul Doyen, France's new chief delegate to the Armistice Commission at Wiesbaden, complained that he had not yet received a response from the Germans.[38] Nor did the Germans ever acknowledge any of Vichy's repeated requests for financial assistance to help defray the costs of maintaining these refugees on French soil. Instead, they responded to French protests by dumping even more refugees into the unoccupied zone: in mid-November, they pushed some 287 Luxembourg Jews across the demarcation line, and in March 1941, they shoved another 1,500 Jews, the last of the Jewish population of Luxembourg, into Vichy territory as well.[39] Furious, the French warned the Germans that they could not keep these refugees indefinitely, and that they might even allow the departure of certain categories of refugees hitherto barred from leaving by the Germans, such as former members of the Polish and Czech legions of military age.[40]

Faced with this ever-growing refugee problem, Vichy's first line of defense was to fall back on the strategy employed by its republican predecessors: to search for emigration possibilities. This strategy, which had not been successful in the 1930's, proved even less so after 1940, given the outbreak of war and the even greater reluctance of other nations, especially the United States, to absorb refugees from Germany or German-occupied territories as a result of heightened fifth-column fears. Nevertheless, until the first deportations of Jews from the unoccupied zone to Eastern Europe in the summer of 1942, Vichy was fiercely determined to get rid of as many refugees as possible, preferably through emigration abroad, but as a last resort colonial options were to be considered as well. To be sure, numerous problems remained, and the extraordinary bureaucratic difficulties refugees experienced in procuring exit visas, even when entry visas for other countries were already in hand, has led some historians, including Marrus and Paxton and Susan Zuccotti, to question whether Vichy was entirely serious about emigration.[41] Yet, as we will see, many of the obstacles to emigration were not of Vichy's making, and as Foreign Ministry documents suggest, Vichy officials remained resolved, up until the summer of 1942, to solve the Jewish refugee problem through emigration.

As in the 1930's, it was again the minister of the interior who led the drive for Jewish emigration. In November 1940, Peyrouton informed the minister of foreign affairs that he attached "the highest importance . . . to provoking a massive emigration of undesirable foreigners who are in excess in the French collectivity and economy," and he requested yet another detailed survey of overseas emigration possibilities. Whereas France had previously needed foreign workers, this was no longer the case due to the amputation of the country's principal industrial centers and the current high levels of unemployment. Moreover, the continued internment of these foreigners, who constituted a pool of unproductive consumers and whose numbers had been increased by the recent arrival "of several thousands of German Jews" was not a situation the government wanted to perpetuate. "The sentiment of social responsibility, [and] concern not to fall short of the rules of humanity, have imposed on us an imperious obligation," Peyrouton maintained, "to assure the immediate departure of the greatest number of them for other climates."[42]

Similarly, Pierre Laval, who continued to hold the portfolio of foreign minister while serving as deputy prime minister, informed the French ambassador in Washington, Gaston Henry-Haye, in the fall of 1940 that the refugee problem, which had already reached crisis proportions before the war, "has now reached a tragic degree of acuteness. . . . Only a more fair distribution of foreign refugees, and especially Jews, among the different countries will ease the situation."[43] And, as we have seen, the French delegation to the Armistice Commission at Wiesbaden had also begun to urge an accelerated pace of Jewish emigration once it realized that Germany had no intention of repatriating Jews.

Faced with these pressures, the Foreign Ministry renewed its efforts to persuade other countries to open their doors, and French embassies were once again instructed, as they had been in 1938, to threaten diplomatic sanctions in the event of noncompliance.[44] During the late fall of 1940, French embassies throughout Latin America sent out queries regarding emigration possibilities for Central European and Spanish refugees in France, and an especially vigorous lobbying effort was undertaken in the United States, where an emotional press campaign was raging over Vichy's internment policies. Although disgruntled by these attacks, the minister of the interior nevertheless hoped that this moral outrage might finally persuade U.S. policy makers to see that they too bore some responsibility for the refugees' tragic plight, since they had consistently refused to accept their proportional share of the refugee burden.[45]

In an additional effort to facilitate emigration, the foreign minister, once again at the urging of the minister of the interior, instructed French embassies in Spain and Portugal to press those governments to continue to grant transit visas to refugees en route to Lisbon or other points of debarkation. The Jewish refugee problem, these embassies were informed, was "of such gravity that the French government is obliged to seek out all possibilities of usable transport." To reassure Spain and Portugal that they would not have to bear any responsibility for refugees in transit, the minister of the interior was prepared to offer firm guarantees. The refugees would be transported on French trains under heavy police escorts, and the arrival of these trains would be timed to coincide with the docking of the ships in harbor so that the refugees would have no time to wander about unsupervised. The French government also promised to take back any refugees unable to depart at the last moment.[46]

Finally, in yet another effort to ensure that refugees already holding U.S. visas be allowed to depart without the usual long waits for French exit visas, waits that frequently resulted in the expiration of U.S. entry visas, Vichy set up a special internment camp at Les Milles, near Marseilles, in the fall of 1940. Only refugees already holding entry visas for other countries were permitted to go to Les Milles, and the prefect of the Bouches-de-Rhône was instructed to grant these internees exit visas without difficulty.[47] In the wake of these improvements, the Jewish emigration organization, HICEM, reported in the summer of 1941 that "the French Authorities are doing now everything possible to facilitate the departure of emigrants being in transit camps and that all Government Departments are always ready to accept any suggestion we might be able to make."[48]

These efforts to facilitate emigration were thwarted on several fronts, however, and while some of the impediments to emigration were of Vichy's own making, others were simply out of the regime's control. The first and most immediate obstacle to emigration was the bureaucratic chaos that ensued in the aftermath of the armistice. Bureaucracies, even under normal circumstances, work slowly, and in light of the administrative chaos that prevailed in the summer and early fall of 1940, it is not surprising that routine procedures, such as the delivery of exit visas, took longer than usual.[49] Moreover, Jewish relief organizations, which had always served as the principal facilitator of Jewish emigration, were similarly in a state of disarray. Having been headquartered in Paris before the war, these organizations had to restructure their operations completely after the defeat, and it took several weeks for the Comité d'Assistance aux Réfugiés (CAR) and HICEM to resume operations. Thus, the JDC reported in August 1940, "there is absolutely no [emigration] bureau to which refugees can apply for assistance."[50] Indeed, according to Xavier Vallat, one of his chief aims in establishing the Union Générale des Israélites de France (UGIF), the French Jewish Council established in November 1941, was to create a central organization devoted to expediting Jewish emigration.[51]

Vichy's emigration efforts were further stymied by German restrictions on which refugees were eligible to emigrate, restrictions that also explain why Vichy was so concerned about exit visas in the first place. As we have seen, article 19 of the armistice stipulated that the Germans had the right to request the surrender of any refugees in the unoccupied zone, and Vichy was obliged to wait until the Kundt Commission had compiled its lists before it could allow any refugees to depart. Moreover, the armistice also stipulated that male refugees of military age from countries formerly at war with Germany, such as Poland or Czechoslovakia, not be allowed to emigrate, since they were likely to rejoin the Allied war effort. This restriction yielded some paradoxical results, as Morris Troper of the JDC wryly noted in late 1940:

In Perpignan young men sitting in the cafés look enviously at men who have a patch of gray hair because that makes it possible for them to pass for 48 years of age, which is the limit of military age, and thus enables them to obtain their exit visas and Spanish transit visas. Often one hears a young man say, "If only I had his head of hair."[52]

Other problems beset Vichy's emigration initiatives as well. Due to shortages of Portuguese vessels, even refugees with overseas visas frequently experienced long delays, and in February 1942 the French government went so far as to investigate the possibility of leasing Swiss ships to transport refugees with U.S. visas from Casablanca, where they had been sent by HICEM to await transportation.[53] Vichy currency restrictions further complicated the process. These restrictions set a limit of 25,000 francs ($10,000) on the amount of money an individual emigrant could take out of the country. Since transportation costs had to be paid in U.S. dollars, the bulk of this money went toward paying the costs of the voyage itself. Well aware that refugee-receiving countries would never grant entry visas to penniless refugees, Peyrouton, eager to speed up Jewish emigration, appealed to the minister of finance to relax these restrictions in cases involving Jewish refugees. The minister of finance refused, however. Since the U.S. Treasury Department had frozen French assets after the armistice, he argued that the French government ought to convince the United States to unblock these funds specifically to finance Jewish emigration to the United States, particularly in light of that country's persistent complaints regarding France's persecution of the Jews.[54]

Yet the major impediment to emigration remained the reluctance of other countries to absorb any of France's refugees. Spain and Portugal, despite their initial willingness to serve as transit nations, grew increasingly hesitant to do so in response to German pressure, and even Peyrouton's rather extraordinary security guarantees failed to convince them to comply with French requests.[55] France's ambassadors in Madrid and Lisbon refused even to broach this matter with Spanish and Portuguese authorities, claiming that they had heard privately through high-ranking channels that such a request would be denied, since Jews were not liked in those countries, and their entry, even on transit visas, was deemed undesirable.[56] Latin American countries too wanted nothing to do with Jewish refugees. In response to the French query regarding immigration possibilities for German refugees, the Guatemalan foreign minister responded in the negative. "The Germans," he argued, "are all Jews; they will occupy the only profession they are capable of exercising: commerce, which has already been hard hit as a result of the Depression and the war. We don't want any more of them." Brazil was similarly unforthcoming. German Jews, Brazilian authorities contended, were politically subversive, engaged in commercial fraud, and were overall "refractory to assimilation."[57]

It was, however, American assistance that the French most desired, but in this respect too all illusions were quickly dispelled. In November, the French ambassador in Washington, Gaston Henry-Haye, appealed to the United States for help in dealing with Vichy's ever-growing refugee problem, especially in light of the recent dumpings of German Jews into southern France. In accord with Peyrouton's instructions, Henry-Haye even went so far as to threaten "stern measures" if the United States failed to comply. Unwilling to be "bludgeoned" into receiving more refugees, Robert Pell, representing the U.S. State Department, replied that the United States would remain firm in the face of Germany's continued efforts to dump refugees on the West. If "weakness" were to be displayed by absorbing these refugees, the Germans would send even more refugees westward. Then, Pell predicted, "the French will find not 10,000 people dumped on them but perhaps 100,000."[58] The United States remained similarly unresponsive to French appeals throughout 1941, and after the Japanese invasion of Pearl Harbor, the distribution of visas to refugees in France came to a virtual standstill.[59]

In light of these manifold difficulties, it is not surprising that Vichy experienced only modest success in its emigration initiatives. According to the JDC, only 1,400 refugees had successfully emigrated abroad with HICEM's assistance from July 1940 through May 1941, although the minister of the interior claimed that 7,000 refugees had left France as of September 1941, a figure that almost certainly included non-Jews as well.[60] Moreover, despite considerable talk of colonial solutions to the problem — an interministerial commission had recommended this alternative in August 1940, and Admiral François Darlan, who served as deputy premier from February 1941 until April 1942, was reported to have proposed a scheme to settle as many as 5,000 Jews, mostly East Europeans, on the island of Madagascar as late as September 1941—these efforts never materialized.[61] At best, Darlan succeeded in transferring a contingent of 2,000 to 3,000 Jewish refugees to Algeria in the spring of 1942, just prior to the onset of the deportations.[62] In light of this slow rate of emigration as well as the dumpings of refugees from Germany and Luxembourg onto French soil, the Ministry of the Interior actually reported a 100 percent increase in the number of internees—from 25,000 to about 50,000—between September 1940 and February 1941, although this figure subsequently dropped to approximately 15,000 by February of 1942 as a result of emigration and the incorporation of the majority of male internees into the special labor battalions for foreigners, the Groupements de Travailleurs Etrangers, or GTE.[63]

Laval's decision to collaborate with the Germans in the deportations of Jews from both zones, a decision finalized in July 1942, must be understood against the background of this emigration impasse. While Laval may well have been motivated by the desire to win greater autonomy from the Germans by demonstrating to them the value of French collaboration, the principal thesis propounded by Marrus and Paxton, it is fairly certain, as they also suggest, that he had a more basic objective in mind as well. Quite simply, he wanted to be rid of the foreign Jews, and whether the Americans or the Germans helped him accomplish that goal was ultimately of little concern. While Laval may not have been a fanatical antisemite of the Darquier de Pellepoix stripe, he was nonetheless xenophobic and moderately antisemitic, as his role in the antiforeign crackdown of 1934–35 and his staunch opposition in 1934 to Jewish refugee settlement in North Africa suggest.[64] Moreover, while Laval would almost certainly not have embarked on the murder of the Jews on his own initiative, he was nevertheless immensely pleased to see at least the foreigners among them depart. Indeed, as early as August 1940, Robert Murphy, a U.S. State Department attaché, had reported:

Vichy authorities are in the process of expelling undesirable foreigners with the announced purpose of ridding this overcrowded city of persons who serve no useful purpose. . . . Authorities declare campaign is not directed against any racial group but there is no question that one of its objectives is to cause the departure of Jews. These, Laval told me recently, were congregating in Vichy to an alarming extent. He believed they would foment trouble and give the place a bad name. He said he would get rid of them.[65]

To achieve this goal, Laval, like other Vichy officials, had supported Jewish emigration, but when that effort yielded only meager results, and when the Germans began to press Vichy in the late spring of 1942 to turn over

Jews, Laval readily complied. In response to heated United States protests over French complicity in these actions, he explained that the United States and other Western powers had left him no choice since they had never offered to help France solve its refugee problem. Despite the obviously self-serving nature of this explanation, it nevertheless rings true in light of Vichy's earlier persistent attempts to foster Jewish emigration.

This absence of alternatives was in fact the theme of two memos Laval sent to French diplomats abroad on August 9 and September 30, 1942, outlining the reasons for French collaboration in the deportations so that these officials could respond to the barrage of foreign criticism being leveled against Vichy.[66] According to Laval, the Germans had decided on the deportations primarily for security reasons, since they feared that in the event of an allied invasion of France and the opening up of a second front, these refugees would join the Allied cause.[67] But, he insisted, France had its own reasons for getting rid of these foreign Jews. After the tremendous influxes of Jewish refugees from the Low Countries, the occupied zone, and Germany in 1940, "the population of Hebrew stock has reached an excessive proportion." These stateless Jews, Laval claimed, "form a manifestly dangerous element." They "engage in the black market and in Gaullist and communist propaganda, constituting for us a source of trouble to which we must put an end." The government had therefore decided that "the only way to conjure away this danger was to repatriate these individuals to Eastern Europe, their country of origin."

As to foreign denunciations of French complicity in the deportations, Laval dismissed these as hypocritical and unjustified, since these countries "continue to close their doors to Hebrew immigration," despite France's repeated offers to hand over the refugees. Indeed, Laval claimed that he had personally given advance warning of the deportations to H. Pinkney Tuck, the U.S. chargé d'affaires at Vichy, in the expectation that the United States might still take at least some of the refugees off France's hands. Tuck's sole response, according to Laval, was to claim that the United States already had a large enough Jewish population. Finally, Laval insisted that "the operation cannot . . . be characterized as persecution in any respect." Rather, he claimed, French policy "is inspired solely by a concern for national prophylaxis, it tends only to free our soil of the presence of immigrants who have been introduced here in excessive numbers over the course of the last years." As for allegations of anti-Jewish atrocities being committed in Eastern Europe, Laval dismissed these as groundless. Finally, with respect to the fate of French Jews, Laval reiterated in both these memos that "no measure is foreseen, nor will it be, aside from the application of laws that inflict certain disabilities upon them."

Laval's claim that he had no desire to persecute foreign Jews may seem disingenuous, especially since he knew full well that the deportees to Poland were destined to suffer a terrible fate, and perhaps even death. Although reliable news of what the Nazis referred to as the "Final Solution" reached the West only in August 1942, the severe persecution of Jews in Poland had been a matter of public record for some time, and if Laval willfully chose to ignore that information, foreign, and especially American, diplomats, felt compelled to remind him of it in the hope that he might yet call a halt to the deportations. On September 15, 1942, U.S. Secretary of State Cordell Hull held a press conference in which he deplored Vichy's collaboration with the Germans in the deportation of Jews, especially from the unoccupied zone. This action, Hull declared, amounted to "the delivery of these unhappy people to the enemies who have announced and in considerable measure executed their intention to enslave, maltreat and eventually exterminate them under conditions of the most extreme cruelty. The details of the measures taken are so revolting and so fiendish in their nature that they defy adequate description." Hull furthermore added, almost certainly in reference to Laval's decision to deport Jewish children together with their parents, that he found it inconceivable that "a Frenchman could apply such inhumane measures."[68]

Hull's denunciations had little effect, however, since Laval had convinced himself that he was not engaged in an act of persecution. Rather, as he envisioned it, he was simply getting rid of undesirable foreign Jews, an effort that was consistent not only with Vichy's Jewish policy during the past two years, but even with the policies of Vichy's republican predecessors. If persecution turned out to be the unfortunate by-product of the deportations, that was none of his affair, since these stateless refugees became the responsibility of the Germans once they crossed the border. According to Tuck, who at various times over the summer had protested the "inhuman and revolting manner" in which the deportations were being carried out, Laval seemed to have "little interest in or sympathy for the fate of any Jews." Indeed, Tuck reported that Laval seemed "pleased at the opportunity presented to get rid of a considerable number [of Jews]; and that in spite of the various protests which have been made he has no intention of departing from his original plans."[69]

It furthermore seems that Laval was telling the truth when he claimed that he had offered to turn the refugees over to the Americans but that his overtures had been ignored. Aside from Laval's claim of having given Pinkney Tuck advance warning of the deportations, Henry-Haye too alleged that in a meeting with Hull just after the latter's press conference, he had given the United States another opportunity to relieve France of its refugee burden. "Alluding to the possibility of organizing a collective departure of Jews to the western hemisphere," Henry-Haye reported, "I registered no reaction on the part of (the Secretary of State)." A few days earlier, Henry-Haye similarly referred to an Associated Press report from Vichy stating that "a well informed source has declared that the head of the Government, M. Laval, had offered to send all the Jews of France to the United States, instead of sending them to Germany or Poland, if the federal government would accord the entry visas. The informant, who did not wish to be cited, declared (that this) offer was transmitted to the U.S. Chargé d'affaires when the latter made official representation regarding the massive arrests of Jews."[70] It may have been embarrassment over this gulf between words and deeds that impelled the State Department to agree precisely at this time to a Quaker request to grant 5,000 visas to refugee children from France. This plan ultimately fell through, however, when the Germans, in an effort to counter the Allied invasion of North Africa on November 8, invaded the unoccupied zone three days later, cutting off all further Jewish emigration.[71]

Just as Vichy's Jewish emigration policy exhibited both signs of continuity and discontinuity with policies initiated in the 1930's, so too did its policy of internment. Here again Marrus has suggested that Vichy scarcely needed to innovate, at least until the deportations, when the internment camps in the unoccupied zone assumed a new function, being transformed from makeshift residences for foreign Jews awaiting emigration into holding pens for Jews consigned for deportation, first to transit camps in the occupied zone, and ultimately to death camps in Poland. Yet although Marrus is correct to point out that the internment camps during Vichy's first two years of existence served many of the same purposes as the camps established under republican auspices, it is nonetheless the case that both the scale and scope of the internments under Vichy far exceeded anything that had transpired under the Third Republic. Moreover, this policy too became overtly antisemitic in intent, which had never been the case in the 1930's, despite the always present antisemitic undertones.

That Vichy's internment camps were not simply carryovers from the 1930's is illustrated by several factors. First, the refugees interned after July 1940 were not necessarily the same individuals who had been in the camps earlier, although there was a considerable overlap. Immediately after taking power, Vichy, in compliance with German demands, issued a circular ordering that the Germans interned since May not be permitted to leave the camps, with some minor exceptions. Nevertheless, as we have seen, many camp commandants had already released the refugees at the time of the German invasion, and on August 14, 1940, Vichy issued a new circular stipulating that German nationals, men and women alike, between the ages of 17 and 65, were to be reinterned.[72] In light of their fear of being turned over to the Germans, however, few refugees returned voluntarily. Many succeeded in fleeing across the Pyrenees in the hope of sailing to the United States, or they attempted to secure U.S. visas while remaining in hiding in southern France.

Moreover, for the first time, the legislation authorizing the internments assumed an overtly antisemitic cast. On September 27, 1940, Vichy issued a general internment order for all male foreigners between 18 and 55 years of age who were "in excess in the national economy." These foreigners were to be drafted into forced labor battalions, the GTE, which were direct outgrowths of the *prestataire* units established for noncombatant male foreigners during the war. On November 4, Vichy imposed rigid restrictions on the freedom of movement of all foreigners, forbidding them to leave their towns of temporary residence without advance permission from the prefect.[73] Yet, these antiforeign decrees were considered inadequate for dealing with the Jewish refugee problem, and on October 4, 1940, Vichy issued a law authorizing the internment of all "Foreign Nationals of the Jewish Race." Precisely who fell into this category was to be determined by the Statut des Juifs, which had been announced the previous day.

As a result of these laws, the scope of Vichy's internments was significantly greater than those carried out under the Third Republic. First, according to the decree of October 4, all foreign Jews, not just refugees or illegal immigrants, were to be interned, and, as we have seen, the category of "foreigners" was growing rapidly as a result of Vichy's denaturalization policies. Moreover, Jewish women were to be interned as well, which had not been standard policy during the Third Republic, with the exception of Mandel's internment order of May 1940.[74] Vichy's major innovation, however, was to intern foreign Jews irrespective of age. Never before had young children and the elderly been included in these measures.[75] Finally, the sheer scale of the internments under Vichy was far greater than it had been prior to June 1940, except for the temporary internment of the Spanish refugees in early 1939. Whereas French internment camps had held about 18,000 individuals in the fall of 1939, by January 1941, there were 51,439 foreigners interned in Vichy camps, although this figure declined significantly prior to the deportations. Of these internees, 33,910, or two-thirds, were Jews.[76]

Given the inclusion of Jewish infants and children, pregnant women, and the elderly and infirm, who were especially numerous among the German refugees dumped into the unoccupied zone in October 1940, camp conditions deteriorated far beyond what they had been before. Rampant disease and even death became common, and according to French lawyer and historian Serge Klarsfeld, nearly 3,000 foreign Jews died under the watch of French camp guards in the period prior to the deportations.[77] The horrendous conditions at the women's and children's camp of Rivesaltes provoked one relief worker to comment that "no self-respecting zoo-keeper would allow the animals in his care to be housed under the conditions prevailing here," and the Swiss press reported that children here were dying in droves.[78] Epidemics of typhoid and malaria raged at nearly all the camps due to overcrowded and unsanitary conditions.[79] And at Gurs, where the camp population swelled to over 14,000 after the unannounced arrival of the German refugees in the fall of 1940, it was reported that internees were literally starving. An American Jewish Congress memorandum of the spring of 1941 noted that "autopsies on those who have died in [this] camp have revealed bodies which were simply skin and bones, with no fat and no muscles at all." "These camps," this memorandum declared, "have shocked the whole of the civilized world. In no other one period of the history of Europe have so many innocent men, women, and children languished in confinement." A Swiss relief worker similarly referred to the camps as a "shame for France."[80]

Despite the greater scope and intensity of the internments under Vichy, there were nevertheless similarities between Vichy's policies and those of the Third Republic. In both instances, security concerns were invoked as the chief justification for the policy, and given the widespread belief among Vichy officials that foreign Jews were heavily involved in Gaullist and communist propaganda, such measures were deemed not only justified but imperative. As Henry-Haye explained to a representative of the Gourevitch Committee, now headquartered in New York City, "It would not have been possible to keep up security of the country in the troubled circumstances that accompanied the end of the conflict, without submitting to a strict control the whole of the refugees."[81] At the same time, Vichy also justified the internments as "measures necessitated . . . by imperious considerations of an economic order." The primarily East European refugees were regarded as an "unstable population, badly disciplined and one that cannot be left in a dangerous state of inactivity."[82]

The regime was furthermore determined not to repeat the mistake of its republican predecessors by allowing foreigners, and especially foreign Jews, to compete for jobs with French nationals. Although the economic argument had not been used to rationalize the internments in 1939–40, it had served as the justification for removing Jewish refugees from Paris beginning in late 1938 and resettling them in agricultural collectives in the south. The aim of these agricultural centers was in fact the same as that of the internment camps under Vichy—both were intended to serve as temporary abodes until their inhabitants could arrange for their departure. And indeed, despite the terrible conditions of internment under Vichy, there is no doubt that until the summer of 1942, Vichy officials truly believed that "the internment of these foreigners must constitute only a provisional measure preceding their emigration."[83]

Furthermore, just as the Third Republic was sensitive to international public criticism of the internment camps, so too was Vichy. Like the internments carried out by the Daladier administration, Vichy's internments similarly came under fierce attack by the foreign press, especially in the United States and Switzerland, and ultimately by those governments as well, particularly after several camp revolts were ruthlessly suppressed in the fall of 1940.[84] In response, Vichy sought to speed up emigration, but it also launched a campaign to improve camp conditions, a factor that further supports the view that these camps were not intended to torture their inhabitants, but to provide temporary shelter prior to emigration. On November 17, 1940, responsibility for the camps passed from the military to civilian control, and the regime declared that the camps should henceforth be called "shelter centers" rather than internment or concentration camps. While one relief worker ridiculed this change of name as "a charming administrative euphemism" since nothing had yet been done to improve camp conditions, the regime did inaugurate a reform program shortly thereafter and even set aside a sum of $500,000 for that purpose.[85]

One of the earliest signs of change came in January 1941, when the regime agreed to a request put forth by the Gourevitch Committee to release all internees for whom Jewish organizations could provide a 1,200-francs-per-month guarantee. These individuals were still expected to emigrate, but they would now be permitted to live outside the camps while awaiting their visas. This agreement ultimately fell through, however, since the JDC, the designated sponsor, determined that it could not afford an expenditure of this magnitude, which it estimated at $250,000 per year, or between one-third to one-half of its entire budget for France.[86]

More significantly, in April 1941 Vichy named André Jean-Faure, prefect of the Ardèche, to serve as inspector general of the camps in an effort to counter the negative publicity campaign abroad. Ironically, the official most responsible for Jean-Faure's appointment, M. Sarrien of the Foreign Ministry, blamed the Jews themselves for their horrendous situation; their barracks were so filthy, he claimed, since "they had unfortunately brought with them 'the filth' of the ghettos." Nonetheless, the Foreign Ministry was deeply concerned about the long-term impact of the camps on France's international reputation, and it hoped that Jean-Faure would be able to consolidate the camp administration and inaugurate a program of reform.[87]

Although Jean-Faure was by no means out of sympathy with Pétain's National Revolution, he was nevertheless profoundly shocked by the camp conditions. These camps, his inspection team reported, "seriously threaten the honor of France" and constituted "for foreign propaganda hostile to France, a source of severe and dangerous criticism, especially since it is well founded." Under Jean-Faure's supervision, camp facilities were improved, private organizations were given greater access to the camps, and internees began to be released in greater numbers, either through incorporation into the GTE or through emigration. At the same time, greater numbers of children were released into the care of various relief organizations.[88] Indeed, Jean-Faure intended to empty the camps altogether through these means, and he worked hard to achieve this goal right up until the deportations. And although the deportations brought Jean-Faure's initiative to an abrupt end, his work was not without effect. As Yehuda Bauer has noted, when the roundups began in the unoccupied zone in July and August of 1942, German officials were dismayed to find that the pool of available deportees being held in the camps had shrunk to only 12,000 to 13,000, due in part to Jean-Faure's efforts.[89]

To sum up this discussion of government policy, it is clear that Vichy's anti-Jewish program simultaneously exhibited signs of continuity and discontinuity with policies initiated in the 1930's. On the one hand, there is little doubt that in the area in which Marrus sees little innovation—antisemitic legislation—there was in fact a major break. While Vichy's antisemitic legislation clearly grew out of the antiforeign legislation of the previous decade, never had that legislation been framed in overtly antisemitic language, an innovation whose significance cannot be overemphasized. Moreover, the fact that this legislation was aimed at French Jews in addition to their foreign coreligionists marked a momentous innovation and further suggests the degree to which the new government perceived the "Jewish Problem" to be distinct from the question of foreigners in France. While certain sectors of public opinion had always made this distinction, never before had it received legislative expression.

On the other hand, two other Vichy initiatives relating to Jews that had roots in the 1930's—emigration and internment—while perhaps exhibiting greater signs of continuity, were now carried to new extremes. During the first two years of its existence, Vichy's emigration policy was in fact closely modeled on the emigration policies of the 1930's, and indeed, Laval even perceived the deportations as an extension of this policy. Nevertheless, the deportations did mark a major turning point, as Marrus correctly points out, but it also needs to be stressed that this was a German and not a French policy, despite the fact that France ultimately lent administrative support. Moreover, with respect to Vichy's internment policies, while the goal remained the same as in the 1930's—that is, to provide a temporary abode for refugees awaiting emigration—the scale and scope of this policy, as well as the specifically antisemitic component of it, signaled an important break with the past.

While there were continuities and discontinuities in government policy toward Jewish refugees, the same was true of public opinion, the second major theme traced throughout this book. As we have seen, public opinion played a major and perhaps even decisive role in shaping the anti-refugee and anti-immigrant agendas of various administrations during the 1930's. There is also little doubt that the animosity toward the refugees, and increasingly toward Jews in general, permeated a wide swath of public opinion in the 1930's, stretching from extreme-right-wing circles, like the Action Française or *Je suis partout*, into more moderate camps, including even factions of the Radical and Socialist Parties. Nevertheless, it has become a common assumption, articulated by Marrus and Paxton and more recently John Sweets, that Vichy's antisemitic program did not have widespread public support. Rather, as Marrus and Paxton note, the antisemitism of Vichy was "neither the work of mass opinion nor of the men at the very top." Instead, they claim, "the basic indifference of Pétain and Laval left the field to the zealots," such as Raphaël Alibert and Xavier Vallat.[90]

While there is little doubt that Vichy antisemitism was the work of powerful factions within the bureaucracy, it is fairly certain that these factions had considerable popular support, especially among groups on the right that perceived foreigners, and particularly foreign Jews, as the symbol of everything they detested about contemporary French life. Like Pétain and Weygand, these groups too blamed foreigners, and especially Central European refugees, for bringing on the war and subsequently the defeat. As Maurice Prax of the *Petit Parisien* declared in September 1940:

Through their constant and secret maneuvers, they disrupted every pacifist effort several of our ministers had attempted to achieve. . . . [T]hey devoted themselves to thwarting every effort at rapprochement and détente. They wanted war. That is to say, they wanted to obligate Frenchmen to fight for them. In order to serve their interests, their passions and their grudges, they so generously sacrificed our soldiers' blood.

The time had now come, according to Prax, to purge these "vermin" from French national life, and he demanded that the refugees be tried at Riom, together with the Third Republic's political leadership.[91] Even more moderate right-wing papers gave voice to these views. According to the Catholic *La Croix*, the Third Republic had been corroded from within well before the Germans had arrived; it had thus toppled within weeks like "a building eaten away by termites." What had caused this internal decay? Rural depopulation, the low birthrate, an excessively materialistic spirit, and the invasion of immigrants that had "submerged" France after the First World War. Now, however, these "putrefying" elements were to be eliminated, and "Providence would soon bring about the rebirth of another France. Christian and traditional France. . . ."[92]

But the complaint here was not simply that the immigrants, and especially the foreign Jews, had caused the defeat. Rather, as Colonel François de La Rocque stated, this problem had an economic dimension as well. Quite simply, due to the "hasty and unjustified naturalizations" that had occurred over the past few years, there was now an "overcongestion of Jews in certain professions."[93] And indeed, considerable evidence suggests that the middle-class groups concentrated in these professions provided Vichy's antisemitic program with a strong base of grassroots support. In his diary, Raymond-Raoul Lambert noted that the Jews' economic competitors, especially in the banking industry and the Chambers of Commerce, unashamedly applauded the Statut des Juifs, which severely curtailed Jewish participation in a wide range of middle-class professions.[94]

Furthermore, the Ordre de Médecins enthusiastically supported Vichy's denaturalization campaign, which, as we have seen, was targeted primarily at foreign Jews. And, although the Ordre itself did not call for specifically anti-Jewish legislation, since it considered the ousting of foreigners and recently naturalized citizens sufficient, several of its local affiliates openly embraced antisemitism.[95] Similarly, a number of individual doctors became leading advocates for Vichy's antisemitic program. Dr. Fernand Querrioux, who had called for restrictions on naturalized doctors already in the 1930's, published a treatise in December 1940, *La Médecine et les juifs*, in which he listed every naturalized doctor with an annotation of whether they were "probably Jewish" or "almost all Jewish." Another far-right-wing medical practitioner, Paul Guerin, hailed Vichy's first Statut des Juifs as a long-awaited antidote: "One Jew in the on-duty room can be a colleague: with two Jews, the clan is formed: with four Jews, comradeship is over. The whole story of the quota is right there."[96] French film industry spokesmen similarly acclaimed the Statut des Juifs for having liberated them from the long-standing monopoly held by the "organized band of Jews and *métèques*."[97]

This middle-class support for antisemitism extended even to the deportations. Although recent research has stressed the role of the deportations as a catalyst in turning a significant sector of public opinion against the regime, a sizable segment of the middle class apparently remained immune from this trend. According to a Foreign Ministry report from September 1942 describing the popular reaction to the deportations in Marseilles:

The reaction among the local population is extremely lively. Working class circles and ordinary people show a great sympathy toward the Jews, and unfortunately place the burden of responsibility on the French administration. It should also be noted, however, that some police agents gave advance warning to some of the Poles slated for arrest, so they could try to save themselves. The sought after foreigners have found places of refuge among some circles of liberal intellectuals where they are currently in hiding.

On the other hand, however, this report went on to note: "Merchants, industrialists, doctors, lawyers and others, who feared the competition of Jews, approve [of the deportations], even with indecency. Aside from the integral Catholics who express sorrow, the propertied bourgeoisie has shown itself to be indifferent."[98] Besides seeing their competitors eliminated in a single blow, many of these middle-class groups had also benefited tangibly from the regime's aryanization policy—the transfer of expropriated Jewish property into the hands of non-Jewish managers. And, as Donna F. Ryan has recently shown, this policy was carried out in Marseilles to a greater extent than elsewhere in the unoccupied zone.[99]

Finally, it is necessary to look briefly at continuities and discontinuities with respect to the role of the French Jewish community. That Vichy would embark on a broad-based anti-Jewish campaign, aimed at French as well as foreign Jews, should not have come as a complete surprise to French Jewish leaders. Such an eventuality had been discussed in Consistorial circles even before the war, and according to a JDC report of July 1940, Jewish leaders unanimously agreed "that the prospects for the Jewish people in France, not only the refugees . . . , but also French Jews themselves, are exceedingly discouraging."[100] Nevertheless, French Jews seem to have been caught completely off guard by the scope of Vichy's anti-Jewish legislation, which they correctly perceived as an attempt to reverse Jewish emancipation altogether.

No one better exemplifies their profound shock and dismay than Lambert, whose recently published diary constitutes an invaluable source of information for understanding the perceptions and motivations of this extremely important Jewish leader. On October 19, 1940, the day after the first Statut des Juifs appeared in the *Journal Officiel*, Lambert recorded in his diary:

Racism has become the law of the new state. What shame! I still cannot come to terms with this negation of justice and scientific truth. . . . All my illusions are shattered. I'm afraid not for myself, but for my country. This cannot endure, this isn't possible. But, from the point of view of history, this abolition of the Declaration of the Rights of Man in 1940 seems like a new revocation of the Edict of Nantes. . . .

. . . Judaism will survive as in the Middle Ages. But what suffering it is to become a second class citizen when such a fate is not deserved, especially when one had once enjoyed every liberty. Where is the free thinking spirit of France . . . slumbering at this moment?

After the publication of the second Statut des Juifs, Lambert expressed similar disbelief. "It's inconceivable," he declared, "that Frenchmen would have dared to sign such measures 150 years after the Declaration of the Rights of Man. What shame for the country! Is this truly the armistice with honor and dignity? I wonder if I might be dreaming." At one point, Lambert became so depressed that he wished he might have died fighting for France, save for his wife and three children.[101]

What prevented this despair from becoming paralyzing, however, was an awareness among many Jewish leaders, including Lambert and Albert Lévy, that their own sufferings paled besides those of their refugee and immigrant coreligionists.[102] Although these leaders have frequently been excoriated for their insensitivity to the immigrants during these years,[103] the fact is that it was only in response to the immigrants' plight that they mustered the energy to revive and revamp the relief effort.[104] To be sure, this reorganization did not proceed entirely smoothly. The CAR in Paris closed its doors in June 1940, and as we have seen, it was several weeks before it reestablished operations in the southern zone. Once established, however, the task facing the CAR was a formidable one, and by May of 1941, the CAR reported that it was caring for 14,500 individuals in addition to the internees.

At the same time, in contrast to the situation in the 1930's, there was now no hope of improvement, at least until the end of the war. The government clearly had no interest in constructive solutions, and fund-raising had become impossible due to the emigration of most wealthier Jews and the imposition of anti-Jewish disabilities, including the expropriation of Jewish property. The CAR was therefore reduced to providing short-term relief, which, while considered the bare minimum in the 1930's, had now become a task of daunting proportions. At the same time, it became almost entirely dependent on JDC financial support, which now accounted for 95 percent of the CAR's budget.[105]

Not all French Jewish leaders, however, supported the attempt to revive the relief effort, and not surprisingly this faction was led by the Consistory's vice president, Jacques Helbronner, who had expressed similar concerns in the early 1930s. The Consistory, which remained headquartered in Paris, was reluctant to involve itself in the relief effort for two main reasons. First, it did not want to be seen as too closely identified with the foreign Jews, since it believed that such an identification would only encourage the government to lump all Jews, French and foreign, together.[106] Second, it also feared that involvement in an ostensibly nonreligious activity such as relief work would only substantiate the administration's effort to define Jews on racial or ethnic lines, thus facilitating anti-Jewish rather than antiforeign discrimination.[107]

The debate over the degree of responsibility French Jews owed their immigrant coreligionists erupted during the negotiations between Vallat and French Jewish leaders regarding the creation of the UGIF in the fall of 1941, and it eventually split French Jewish leadership into two opposing camps. Whereas Lambert and Lévy were ultimately willing to cooperate with Vallat to head the UGIF in the southern zone, on condition that the council's activities be limited "primarily" to the provision of social assistance,[108] the Consistory refused to cooperate in any respect. Indeed, the Consistorial leadership, and especially Helbronner, were furious that Lambert had negotiated with Vallat without their consent. According to Helbronner, Lambert was merely engaging in an act of self-promotion at the community's expense. "It is inconceivable," Helbronner complained, "that this individual acts as if he were the chief Rabbi of France, the President of the Central Consistory, and the Vice President of the Welfare Organizations, all in one."[109]

Yet while there may have been a grain of truth to Helbronner's charges, since Lambert had long resented the dominance of the Consistory, it is clear that Lambert's decision to serve as secretary-general of the UGIF was guided by far more than personal ambition. As both Lambert's diaries and Richard Cohen's recent study of the UGIF suggest, Lambert believed that the UGIF offered the only means of providing desperately needed relief to the internees in the camps, whose existence would have become unbearable without Jewish communal support.[110] As Albert Lévy declared at the UGIF's first meeting in the southern zone in May 1942, UGIF leaders had only one goal: to act as "social workers in the service of our faith and our country."[111]

Whether the UGIF lived up to these expectations, or whether it ultimately abetted in the persecution of the Jews by blinding them to their ultimate fate and forestalling the emergence of an armed resistance movement, has long been a matter of controversy.[112] Yet, even many of the UGIF's critics acknowledged that by 1943, the UGIF in the unoccupied zone had assumed a dual function. While continuing to provide relief, the UGIF increasingly came to serve as a cover for a wide range of covert resistance activities. Moreover, just as the refugees had exempted Lambert in particular from their criticisms of the Comité National in 1934 and 1935, so too did some members of the Jewish resistance exempt him from their criticisms of the UGIF, since he was perceived as the individual responsible for having given the green light to these covert operations. Thus, while condemning the UGIF as an "odious institution," Anny Latour after the war praised Lambert as "an indisputable resistance fighter."[113] In truth, however, Latour's attempt to draw a radical distinction between Lambert and the UGIF is untenable because Lambert was the UGIF's guiding spirit up until his own deportation in the summer of 1943.

Although there are strong continuities between the 1930's and Vichy in the three areas that contributed to the formulation of refugee policy—government policy, public opinion, and the role of the native Jewish community—the advent of Vichy in 1940 was universally perceived as a radical break with the past. The major shift here came well before the deportations of the summer of 1942. Rather, it came in the fall of 1940 with the implementation of antisemitic legislation, which singled out Jewish refugees from other foreigners and, for the first time, targeted French Jews as well, reversing Jewish emancipation completely. As a result of this shift, even those policies exhibiting more continuity than discontinuity with the past, such as emigration and internment, assumed an intensity and scope that far exceeded what had transpired in the 1930's.

Similarly, with respect to Jewish responses, while the role of the native community as an intermediary between the refugees and foreign Jews in general continued, it is clear that the Jewish community lost whatever leverage it had ever exercised in the formulation of government policy. That leverage had already been severely diminished by the end of the 1930's, but under Vichy it disappeared altogether. The best Jewish leaders could now hope for was to secure some individual exemptions from antisemitic legislation and to ameliorate the plight of foreign Jews as much as possible.

It is perhaps in the area of public opinion that continuity between the 1930's and Vichy is most apparent. From the early 1930's on, the French right had taken a strong stance against Jewish refugees, claiming that these Jews constituted an economic as well as a political threat because they stole jobs from French workers and shored up the forces of the left, to say nothing of their imputed role as potential German spies. With the Popular Front's victory in 1936 and especially Léon Blum's ascension to power, this animosity, which linked anti-leftist to anti-refugee and ultimately anti-Jewish sentiments, assumed unprecedented proportions and began to attract support even among moderates, whose greatest fear was a left-wing takeover. Finally, during the Munich crisis, when large segments of the population were desperate to avoid war at any cost, this animosity broke out into open anti-Jewish hostility, since Jews, and especially the refugees were perceived, together with the communists, as the vanguard of the pro-war party. Although moderates did not generally approve of this anti-Jewish violence, they nevertheless began to join the mounting chorus of voices calling for restrictions on the occupational and residential rights of immigrant Jews.

At the same time, this right-wing agenda won strong support from a broad range of middle-class groups—the Chambers of Commerce, the Confédération des Syndicats Médicaux, and the Confédération de l'Artisanat Familial—who felt threatened by Jewish refugees and immigrants in particular and sought every means of excluding them from their ranks. Beginning with anti-immigrant attacks in the late 1920's and early 1930's, these professional groups quickly moved to an assault on the rights of naturalized citizens, and ultimately, under Vichy, to an assault on the rights of Jews, immigrant and native alike. Although even Vichy did not ultimately fulfill most of its corporatist promises, since to have done so would have catapulted France back to the nineteenth century economically, the concession of antiforeign and especially anti-Jewish measures did much to placate these aggrieved middle-class groups.[114] In this respect, the traditional explanation of antisemitism as an essentially middle-class protest movement aimed at curbing large-scale capitalism on the one hand and socialism on the other still carries considerable weight, and there is little doubt that popular support for this agenda extended well beyond the ranks of a small faction in the bureaucracy.

Yet, despite these continuities in public opinion, there was nevertheless a major shift, and that was the virtual disappearance of the pro-refugee lobby. To be sure, some isolated voices of dissent remained, but given the new constellation of power under Vichy, these voices were now denuded of any broader political support, in contrast to the situation in the 1930's. Edouard Herriot and Jules Jeanneney, presidents of the Chamber of Deputies and the Senate, respectively, had, for example, initially resisted applying the Statut des Juifs to their Jewish colleagues in Parliament, but ultimately they were forced to comply because they lacked any broader support. Similarly, at the time of the deportations, these same parliamentary leaders sent a letter of sympathy to the chief rabbi expressing their "horror" "at the measures that have just been inflicted . . . on those Jews banished by their own countries who had found asylum in ours, at the barbaric treatment to which their children have been subjected."[115] Yet once again, their protests remained isolated and ineffective because those politicians who in earlier years would have joined such a protest had now been either silenced or driven into exile.

Despite occasional wavering from republican traditions, the various administrations of the 1930's, even those tilted strongly rightward, had been engaged in an effort to balance competing interests with respect to the refugees, and as we have seen, there was no straight line between the policy articulated in 1933 and that implemented under Vichy. Rather, refugee policy in the 1930's fluctuated tremendously, swinging back and forth between more liberal and more hard-line approaches, depending on the party in power as well as the political and military circumstances at any particular time. It was therefore only as a result of the defeat, and the ensuing ascendance of a right-wing, authoritarian regime, whose ideology closely mirrored that of the Action Française, that this question was finally resolved in favor of the hard-liners. Yet, it is also necessary to remember that "hard-line" in the French context did not mean the mass murder of Jews, although some extreme antisemites clearly favored this end. Rather, "hard-line" at Vichy meant anti-Jewish discrimination, rollbacks in naturalizations, and the internment of foreign Jews in the expectation that they would emigrate. Had there not been outside German pressure, it is highly unlikely that Vichy leaders would ever have conceived of the idea of deporting Jews to their death in Eastern Europe, notwithstanding Laval's ready compliance with German demands. It is even less likely that Vichy would have turned over its own Jewish citizens voluntarily, but this subject, which continues to inspire heated debate, lies beyond the scope of the present study.

CHAPTER FIFTEEN

Conclusion

In examining the course of French policy toward Jewish refugees from 1933 through the Vichy era, it is clear that this policy was not a straight line, but rather a "twisted road," fluctuating between more liberal and more hard-line phases.[1] From a perspective of hindsight, it might appear that Vichy's harsh anti-refugee and anti-Jewish policies were the inevitable culmination of trends in the 1930's, but this is clearly not the case. While Vichy's policies were indeed rooted in the 1930's, as described in Chapter 14, it is also true that there was a diversity of views regarding the refugee problem during that decade, and it was only as a result of the military defeat of 1940 that one of these views came to prevail. It would therefore be useful to review the major findings of this study in an effort to reassess the various twists and turns of refugee policy in the 1930's, not only with an eye toward Vichy, but to understand the major determinants of refugee policy in their own right.

Refugee policy, as has been demonstrated throughout this book, was propelled by three interrelated forces: the government, public opinion, and the native Jewish community. Insofar as the government's role is concerned, two major factors—economic and political—account for the shift away from the initial liberal policy of the spring of 1933. Economic considerations linked to the Depression militated in favor of a more restrictive immigration policy. No sooner had the refugees arrived than a host of middle-class professional groups embarked on a crusade to close France's borders to further influxes of refugees. These groups furthermore used this opportunity to whittle down the rights of long-term immigrants, and even those of recently naturalized citizens, many of whom were East European Jews who had come to France after the First World War. To be sure, some government officials regarded the influx of the refugees, many of whom had valuable technical and commercial skills, as an economic asset, and they insisted that permitting refugees to create new businesses and industries would generate new jobs and bring down consumer prices. And indeed, wherever such refugee-owned firms were permitted to flourish, such predictions were borne out. Nevertheless, by 1934–35 the government had completely caved in to this middle-class pressure, adopting a hard-line policy that sharply restricted the ability of refugees, and even recently naturalized citizens, to engage in these professions.

Why were these lobby groups so successful in pressing their agendas? The most obvious answer is that the government wanted to be perceived as pursuing an activist policy to fight the Depression, and an indiscriminate anti-immigrant crackdown, which made no provision for refugee asylum, offered a facile means of achieving this end. Moreover, the chronic ministerial instability of the Third Republic, which reached unprecedented heights in the 1930's—between January 31, 1933, and June 16, 1940, there were no fewer than fifteen different cabinets—combined with the absence of a strong executive, made the government particularly susceptible to lobby group pressure. Since every major political party on the right as well as the left, including the Socialists, was heavily beholden to middle-class electoral support, even the most ardently pro-refugee politicians, such as Léon Blum or Marius Moutet, could ill afford to ignore middle-class grievances altogether.

Whereas economic factors served as the principal determinant of refugee policy between 1933 and 1936, political factors, and especially the fear that the refugees would undo the government's policy of appeasement, increasingly played a role during the second half of the decade, and especially in 1938–39, when Nazi expansion into Austria and Czechoslovakia brought France to the brink of war. Not only were the refugees viewed as potential Nazi spies, but many at the highest levels of government, including Daladier's foreign minister, Georges Bonnet, accused the refugees, together with their alleged communist allies, of seeking to drag France into a war solely to satisfy their personal lust for revenge against Hitler. Moreover, after the electoral victory of the Popular Front in 1936, it became an increasingly common belief not only among right-wing politicians, but among centrists like Daladier as well, that a principal by-product of war would be the outbreak of civil war in France, an event they believed would culminate in a communist takeover—a fate they dreaded far more than the Nazi threat.

Thus, while the economic determinants of refugee policy by no means subsided in the late 1930's, with middle-class groups demanding even more stringent restrictions against foreigners, and especially against naturalized citizens, it was primarily these security considerations, together with the growing tendency to link the refugees to the Bolshevik threat, that led to the harsh anti-immigrant decree laws of 1938. These laws effectively closed the borders to future newcomers and inaugurated a fierce crackdown against refugees already in the country illegally. These security considerations also impelled the administration to create an internment camp network as an alternative to prison for the rapidly expanding ranks of "undesirables," a category that by mid-1938 included anyone who had entered the country without papers, which comprised nearly all recent arrivals, since visas were no longer attainable. Thus, although government spokesmen, like Henry Bérenger, continued to describe France as a nation of temporary asylum—a way station for refugees en route to final destinations elsewhere—such statements no longer bore any relation to reality. By 1938–39, the doors of France had slammed shut altogether, and the thousands of refugees who succeeded in crossing the border in spite of the decree laws faced an extremely high probability of arrest or internment.

While these economic and security considerations clearly militated in favor of a hard-line stance, there were, however, important countervailing forces at work as well. Although the argument that the refugees constituted a potential economic asset made little headway after the first government crackdown of 1934–35, it did resurface for a brief moment in 1939 when the government passed a new decree law in April specifically encouraging the creation of immigrant-run businesses and industries in an effort to gear up the economy for war. Another factor encouraging a more liberal refugee policy was France's long-term population deficit. Leading demographic experts such as Georges Mauco, despite their disdain for the refugees, whom they considered unwanted competitors of the urban middle classes, were nevertheless willing to allow refugees to settle in the depopulated agricultural areas of southwestern France, on condition that they transform themselves into peasants and artisans.

Such views were furthermore translated into policy. At the end of 1938, the Daladier administration implemented a plan remarkably similar to the Serre Plan, devised earlier that year by Mauco and Chautemps's newly appointed undersecretary of state for immigration, Philippe Serre, to "decongest" the Paris region of Jewish refugees. According to the Daladier administration's scheme, further refugee settlement in the Paris region was to be banned altogether, and the Jewish refugee committee was encouraged to steer thousands of refugees to newly created agricultural collectives in southwestern France. By July of 1939, Minister of the Interior Albert Sarraut even announced the government's willingness to grant an amnesty from the decree laws to all refugees settled in these agricultural centers.

Perhaps most significantly, the nation's demographic shortfalls encouraged the military to press for a more liberal refugee policy, particularly with the onset of the *années creuses*, or lean years, when the smaller military classes born during the First World War first became eligible for conscription. That the *années creuses* coincided with the first phase of Nazi military expansion imbued this argument with particular urgency, and in April 1939, the government announced a new decree law facilitating the recruitment of foreigners into the armed forces. Moreover, the military's desperate need for recruits ultimately persuaded the administration to release the vast majority of refugees from the internment camps during the period of the "phony war" so that they could be utilized either in the Foreign Legion or in the *prestataire* (civilian auxiliary) units. Indeed, by the spring of 1940, the internment camps had been emptied almost entirely, and it was only as a result of the fifth-column fears generated by the Nazi invasion of the Low Countries in May that the refugees found themselves reinterned.

Finally, fluctuations in government refugee policy were determined in part by which party or coalition of parties happened to be in power at a particular time. Despite the Radical Party's increasingly hard-line stance, which was apparent as early as the fall of 1933, there is no doubt that government policy hardened significantly under the Bloc National governments of Pierre-Etienne Flandin and Pierre Laval. Moreover, it is undeniable that the coming to power of the Popular Front ushered in a more humane era in the treatment of German refugees in particular. To be sure, the Popular Front fell short of its original goals. While it did succeed in guaranteeing asylum to German refugees already in France, it refused to extend this guarantee automatically to refugees who might arrive in the future. Even more significantly, it failed to secure the right of the refugees to work, despite the fact that the Socialist Party and the League for the Rights of Man and Citizen had always argued that asylum without the right to work was a sham since such a policy would doom the refugees to a life of poverty and destitution.

Once in power, however, even the parties of the left realized that insisting on the refugees' right to work in addition to the right to asylum would have provoked a fierce middle-class backlash. As a result, the Popular Front was forced to seek out alternative strategies—settling refugees either in French colonies or in underpopulated regions of southwestern France. And while it is true that the harsh decree laws of 1938 were implemented by a

Radical administration, it is fairly certain that the ameliorations to this pol-icy introduced in 1939—the decree laws of April, which encouraged the in-troduction of refugee-owned businesses and industries and facilitated the recruitment of foreigners into the armed forces, as well as Sarraut's amnesty proposal of July 1939—would not have been proffered by a more conserva-tive administration.

Turning to the second major determinant of refugee policy in the 1930's, public opinion, there was clearly a tremendous groundswell of middle-class protest against the refugees, which swiftly expanded to include East Euro-pean and ultimately native Jews as well. Although historians have tended to downplay this element in the resurgence of antisemitism during the inter-war years, there is no doubt that it played a critical role. Indeed, if one ex-amines the antisemitic rhetoric of extreme-right-wing leagues, such as the Action Française or the Croix de Feu, it is apparent that their animosity toward Jews stemmed in part from their role as self-appointed defenders of the middle classes. Moreover, this antisemitism was not simply another form of xenophobia, as Gérard Noiriel and Richard Millman have recently argued.[2] Rather, although related to xenophobia, this antisemitism took on a life of its own, largely because immigrant Jews, in contrast to most other foreigners, were overwhelmingly urban and middle class. Thus, even spokes-men such as Mauco, Raymond Millet, and Jean Giraudoux who favored immigration for economic and military reasons, nevertheless relegated Jews, especially East Europeans, to the bottom rung of the ethnic hierarchy, in part because of their alleged revolutionary proclivities, but also because of their urban and middle-class backgrounds.

Such attitudes surfaced even in Parliament. In a heated debate over the Spanish refugee question in March 1939, the discussion swiftly turned to Jews and the need to protect the middle classes from their "ruinous and murderous competition." To be sure, Jews were not mentioned by name in this debate, but the professions alluded to as being in dire need of gov-ernment protection—medicine, law, commerce, and artisanry, especially leather manufacturing, hosiery, and hatmaking—were precisely those in which immigrant Jews played a disproportionate role.[3] It would therefore seem that the traditional explanation of modern antisemitism as a form of middle-class protest against excessive competition and the constant intro-duction of new production techniques should not be dismissed lightly. In-deed, the endorsement of corporatism by Vichy was intended to placate these middle-class grievances by curbing unfettered capitalism, identified with Jews, and returning economic power to the professional associations. That these promises were never realized does not reflect a lack of zeal for these ideas on the part of Vichy's leaders. Rather, it reflects the fact that Vichy economists ultimately realized that corporatism was incompatible with economic modernization and growth, elements even Vichy leaders recognized as indispensable if France were to retain its role as a great power.[4]

The other salient feature of public opinion toward refugees in the 1930's is that it was far more nuanced than previously believed. Throughout the 1930's, there were two extreme poles of opinion: one on the left, represented by the Socialists, the League for the Rights of Man and Citizen, and to a lesser extent the Communists, and the other on the extreme right, represented by the Action Française and other far-right-wing leagues. In between, however, was a large body of opinion whose views fluctuated over the course of the decade. Until 1936, the bulk of this centrist opinion was willing to tolerate some modicum of asylum. On the center-left, although many politicians bought the theory propounded by Radical Party leaders Edouard Herriot and Emile Roche that getting rid of immigrants in general was the best means of alleviating the Depression, many still believed that refugees merited special treatment and that the principle of asylum ought to be preserved. Among other centrists, like Mauco or Giraudoux, the problem was not so much immigration, which they believed was essential to French prosperity and military preparedness. Rather, to them the problem was the absence of a policy of "selective immigration," a means of weeding out "desirable" from "undesirable" foreigners. While these spokesmen clearly did not like East European Jews—whom they considered unassimilable because they flocked to the cities, competed with the middle classes, and frequently engaged in revolutionary propaganda—they were nevertheless willing before 1936 to tolerate some policy of refugee asylum, at least insofar as refugees agreed to obey French law and abstain from political activity.

After the Popular Front victory, however, this centrist position began to erode, and many of those previously willing to countenance some degree of asylum increasingly regarded the refugees as a political as well as an economic liability. The refugee cause became inextricably linked to the fate of the political left, and any group perceived as shoring up the political prowess of Léon Blum and the Popular Front was deemed unacceptable by the majority of moderates, who increasingly feared an imminent left-wing takeover. These attitudes hardened even further after the arrival of tens of thousands more refugees in 1938, following the Anschluss, the Munich crisis, and Kristallnacht. Now, the presence of these anti-Nazi refugees on French soil gave rise to fears that the refugees were seeking to drag France into an unwanted war, and these fears erupted into anti-Jewish violence at the time of the Munich crisis. After Ernst vom Rath's assassination in November at the hands of the refugee youth Herschel Grynszpan, even the two major organs of the Radical Party, *L'Ere nouvelle* and *L'Oeuvre*, demanded a complete halt to refugee asylum, and *L'Ere nouvelle* even went so far as to call for the removal of Jewish refugees altogether from the Paris region and the imposition of strict quotas on Jewish immigrant participation in a wide range of middle-class professions. Similarly, the rhetoric of centrists like Mauco and Giraudoux became increasingly shrill, relegating the vast majority of refugees to the ranks of the "undesirables." Thus, by the time of Kristallnacht, whatever moderate opinion may previously have been sympathetic to the refugee cause had dissipated almost entirely.

At the same time, however, it is essential to remember that while the ranks of the pro-refugee lobby may have shrunk over the course of the decade due to political polarization and fifth-column fears, a nucleus of pro-refugee support remained active until the fall of the Third Republic. These voices, associated above all with the Socialist Party, the League for the Rights of Man and Citizen, the Catholic left, the Communist Party, and a few isolated individuals on the conservative right, such as Emile Buré, did not compromise their views over the course of the decade.[5] Rather, they worked assiduously to achieve a refugee statute that would distinguish the rights of refugees from those of economic immigrants and would preserve the right of asylum in France. They also endeavored to secure the right to work for the refugees, but in this area their efforts were ultimately stymied. Nevertheless, the role of the pro-refugee lobby should not be underestimated. Rather, as we have seen, these groups helped persuade the government in 1939 to ameliorate refugee policy, and it was partly due to their persistent pressure that Sarraut issued his amnesty proposal in July. Moreover, these groups worked hard throughout 1939 and the early months of 1940 to improve the physical conditions in the internment camps and to secure the release of as many internees as possible. That their views were ultimately eclipsed by a more hard-line position after Vichy came to power was due not to any lapse of commitment on their part. Instead, it was due to the fact that most of the pro-refugee camp was driven into exile under Vichy, leaving only a few isolated voices, such as that of Herriot or Jeanneney, to resist the anti-Jewish policies of Pétain and Laval.

Finally, we have reassessed the role of the native Jewish community in the articulation of refugee policy during the 1930's. Although historians of French Jewry during the 1930's have traditionally divided the community into two major camps—natives vs. immigrants—it is clear that this dichotomy is overly simplistic. In reality, the native community itself was sharply divided over the handling of refugee policy. During the first phase of the refugee crisis, the years 1933–36, that faction I have called the hardliners prevailed. Represented above all by Jacques Helbronner, who not only held high positions in the Jewish community, but also served as a delegate to the League of Nation's High Commission for Refugees (HCR), these individuals pushed for the most restrictive refugee policy possible, hoping to avert an antisemitic backlash and to prove that they ranked their French above their Jewish loyalties.

As a result, the hard-liners urged the government to close the borders altogether, and they encouraged the repatriation of the vast majority of refugees already on French soil. They furthermore opposed all alternative settlement strategies, such as sending refugees to the colonies or to agricultural areas in the south. Such settlements, they argued, would create unassimilable ethnic enclaves and, due to the refugees' left-wing proclivities, would inject communism into these regions. Finally, Helbronner even succeeded in cutting off philanthropic assistance to the refugees by closing the doors of the Comité National altogether in 1934–35. This decision was not sanctioned by the government, nor did it have the backing of the Joint Distribution Committee (JDC), the Comité National's principal sponsor. Rather, it was simply a means by which the hard-liners hoped to use philanthropy for political ends. Their aim was to deter further refugees from coming to France and to force those still there to leave, even if that meant their return to Germany.

Despite the victory of the hard-liners in 1935, the election of the Popular Front in 1936 led to the creation of an entirely new refugee committee, the Comité d'Assistance aux Réfugiés (CAR), dominated by more moderate pro-refugee spokesmen—Raymond-Raoul Lambert and Albert Lévy. These individuals not only fought for a more generous policy of asylum—and indeed, Lambert even held a seat on the Popular Front's Consultative Commission—but they also fought to secure for the refugees the right to work. Moreover, in 1938–39, when the refugee crisis reached new heights, these leaders, despite initial reservations, decided to support schemes to settle refugees in agricultural areas in southern France or in French colonies in order to ensure the provision of at least temporary asylum. Most significantly, they launched a concerted political battle to overturn the harsh anti-immigrant decree laws, refuting the oft-repeated contention that the native Jewish community never undertook any political initiatives on behalf of the refugees. The fact is that the CAR worked hand-in-hand with the pro-refugee lobby, confronting the government head-on in an effort to overturn the decree laws. Sarraut's 1939 amnesty proposal, as well as the other more liberal decree laws of the spring of that year, were due in no small measure to these persistent lobbying efforts. Finally, the CAR and the other Jewish refugee committees worked assiduously during the "phony war" not only to provide relief to the internees, but to secure their release as well. Despite the manifold difficulties involved in this effort, the ultimate release of the majority of refugees by April 1940 so that they could serve in some manner in the war effort was due in part to Jewish lobbying efforts.

Ultimately, however, the coming to power of Vichy and the reinternment of the refugees put an end to this political campaign. While the Jewish community continued to lobby for an amelioration of the harsh anti-Jewish and anti-refugee policies of the Vichy government, leaders like Lambert and Lévy nevertheless realized that the most they could achieve under the circumstances was to try to save as many refugees as possible, and as a result, they channeled their remaining resources and energy into the relief effort. That many of the refugees, and especially the East European Jews, later blamed the CAR and then the Union Générale des Israélites de France (UGIF), which was a direct offshoot of the CAR, for their plight in the camps and ultimately for the deportations was due in part to the long-standing animosity between immigrants and natives, but also to the widespread tendency of Jews to blame their own leaders for policies that were in reality the work of oppressive regimes. Indeed, from the point of view of the Nazis, a principal goal of creating Jewish councils in Nazi-occupied territories was to divert hostility away from themselves and toward the Jewish leadership, who, despite their appearance of being in control, in reality had little or no power.[6] Indeed, the fact that many of the native community's most prominent leaders, including both Helbronner and Lambert, were themselves eventually deported, confirms the view that the major decisions regarding the Jews' fate were being made elsewhere.[7]

The period from 1933 through 1945 was in reality the last battle of the long civil war that began with the Revolution of 1789. The "Refugee Question," and ultimately the "Jewish Question," emerged as central themes of this battle, repeating a pattern established during one of this civil war's earlier skirmishes, the Dreyfus Affair. Although some historians have recently suggested that the focus on the "Jewish Question" under Vichy, and by extension during the 1930's, has been wildly blown out of proportion since this issue could have been of only marginal significance at the time, such interpretations miss the point.[8] Even a cursory reading of the documentary record from these periods shows that the "Jewish Question," and especially the question of foreign Jews, was not an issue of marginal significance. Rather, it was central to the political, economic, and cultural debates that raged during these years. In political terms, the refugee crisis in the 1930's posed the issue of the degree to which France would remain true to its republican heritage, including the right to asylum. But it also raised the issue of the extent to which France would compromise its democratic and liberal principles to appease the dictatorial, racist, and expansionist regime on its eastern border, a goal pursued not only to avoid a repeat of the bloodletting of 1914–18, but also to preempt the possibility of a left-wing coup at home.

Moreover, the treatment of foreign and refugee Jews raised critical questions regarding the nature of French citizenship, an issue that went to the very heart of the republican enterprise. How receptive would France remain to immigration and naturalization, since, as we have seen, notwithstanding the Depression, there was a widespread consensus that France needed new immigrants for military as well as economic reasons? Even more significantly, the debates that revolved around the professional rights of foreigners, and especially recently naturalized citizens in middle-class professions, raised questions regarding the extent to which the republic would continue to guarantee the equality of all citizens before the law. Were citizens who could prove several generations of French forebears, in addition to Christian credentials, to be granted preferential professional and political rights solely because of their birth? Or would France remain a constitutional state, in which all citizens were treated equally in the eyes of the law, regardless of their religious, ethnic, or racial backgrounds? Such debates also raised more general questions regarding whether France would continue to pursue a capitalist path of economic development since such development depended on the French Revolutionary principle of "careers open to talent." Those professional associations that favored corporatism, with its severe restrictions on the professional rights of foreigners and Jews, in essence wanted to return to the economic system of the ancien régime, with its closed guilds and sharp restrictions on economic competition.

Ultimately, these debates over the "Jewish Question" in the 1930's and 40's were inextricably bound up with the question of what sort of nation France wanted to be. Would it remain a liberal, democratic, and secular republic, open to political debate and economic modernization? Or would it become a defensive and backward-looking society, modeled on the authoritarian, hierarchical, and Christian principles of the ancien régime, a society in which rights were distributed according to the prerogatives of birth rather than individual merit? In 1940, France chose the second of these paths. But as the British historian Alexander Werth pointed out, there was a cruel irony in this choice because the triumph of the right-wing nationalist slogan "France for the French" came at the moment of the nation's greatest military defeat.[9]

It was by no means an accident that the eclipse of liberalism and republicanism in 1940 had disastrous repercussions for Jews in France. As Hannah Arendt noted some time ago, the fate of Jews in Europe was inextricably bound up with the fate of liberalism in general, since Jewish emancipation depended on the willingness of the state to guarantee individual rights before the law.[10] Nor was it an accident that those political groups opposed to liberalism focused their wrath on the Jews, since Jews, more than any other group, had become the preeminent symbol of liberalism, and indeed, of the French Revolution as a whole. Not only had the Revolution emancipated the Jews, but the consequences of this act—the granting of equal rights and liberties to that group most despised under the ancien régime—also stood as a potent symbol of everything the Revolution stood for.

For those French Jews who survived the war, most of whom had been firmly committed to liberalism prior to 1940, the introduction of anti-semitic legislation under Vichy and the regime's complicity in the deportations, which resulted in the death of about 76,000 Jews, two-thirds of whom were foreign born,[11] provoked a profound disillusionment with liberalism, and inspired many to turn to more radical alternatives, including communism or Zionism. For others, however, such as Pierre Mendès France or Raymond Aron, these same experiences reinforced their faith in liberalism, which they perceived as the sole guarantor of individual rights and freedoms.

At the same time, however, these spokesmen became increasingly aware that liberalism and democracy might not survive on their own; instead, these institutions might need to be defended through military force. One of the few Jews who recognized this need already in the 1930's was Lambert. Although frequently depicted as a naïve liberal, blind to the dangers of Nazism and the far-right-wing political forces at home, the fact is that Lambert had an astute understanding of those forces, and as early as the spring of 1938 he warned the French not to become complacent regarding their republican institutions. Even France, he predicted, was susceptible to being overtaken by "a collective delirium," which could bring to power an illiberal and exclusionary regime. But, he warned, such an event "would not be accepted without a struggle, with the blind submission of slaves. . . . For, whoever hints at the possibility of struggle, hints at the possibility of victory." Although many Jews in France, including Lambert, never lived to see that victory, the struggles of the thousands of others—refugees, immigrants, and French alike—who fought in the Resistance, helped pave the way for the reemergence of liberal and republican institutions in France after 1945.

Reference Matter

Abbreviations

ACIP	Archives, Consistoire Israélite de Paris
ADBR	Archives Départementales du Bas-Rhin, Strasbourg
AF	*L'Action française*
AFSC	American Friends Service Committee
AI	*Archives israélites*
AIU	Archives, Alliance Israélite Universelle, Paris
AN	Archives Nationales, Paris
APP	Archives, Préfecture de Police, Paris
BDIC	Bibliothèque de Documentation Internationale Contemporaine, Centre Universitaire, Université Paris X, Nanterre
CBR	Archives, Consistoire Israélite du Bas-Rhin, Strasbourg
CDH	*Les Cahiers des droits de l'homme*
CDJC	Centre de Documentation Juive Contemporaine, Paris
CDV	Centre de Documentation et de Vigilance
DBFP	*Documents on British Foreign Policy*
DDF	*Documents Diplomatiques Français*
DdV	*Droit de vivre*
DGFP	*Documents on German Foreign Policy*
FDR Library	Franklin Delano Roosevelt Library, Hyde Park, New York
FRUS	*Foreign Relations of the United States*
JDC	Joint Distribution Committee Archives, New York
JO	*Journal Officiel*

JTA	Jewish Telegraphic Agency
JTS	Jewish Theological Seminary Archives, New York
LBI	Leo Baeck Institute Archives, New York
LBIYB	*Leo Baeck Institute Year Book*
MAE	Archives, Ministère des Affaires Etrangères, Paris
MP	McDonald Papers, Columbia University, New York
NYT	*New York Times*
PH	*Pariser Haynt*
PRO	Public Records Office, London
PT	*Pariser Tageblatt* (became *Pariser Tageszeitung* after June 12, 1936)
RJG	*La Revue juive de Genève*
SDN	Société des Nations (League of Nations)
SHAT	Archives, Service Historique de l'Armée de Terre, Vincennes
TJ	*La Tribune Juive*
UI	*L'Univers israélite*

Notes

Chapter One

1. The major work on Vichy policy toward the Jews remains Marrus and Paxton. For other recent works on this subject, see A. Cohen; Kaspi; Klarsfeld; Paxton, "La Spécificité," pp. 605–19; Peschanski, "Exclusion," pp. 209–34; Ryan, *Holocaust*; Zuccotti. For useful overviews of the historiography on this subject, see Marrus, "Coming to Terms," pp. 23–41; Poznanski.

2. On France's liberal reception of immigrants in the 1920's, see J.-Ch. Bonnet, 1–190; Marrus, *Unwanted*, pp. 113–14; Schor, *L'Opinion française et les étrangers*, pp. 27–90, *passim*; Maga, *America*, pp. 3–4, 13–17; Livian, *Le Parti socialiste*, p. 10; Cross, pp. 15–17, 55–63, 122–85; Mauco, *Les Etrangers*; Noiriel, *La Tyrannie*, p. 107.

3. On France's reception of Spanish refugees, see L. Stein, pp. 5–106; Pike; Marrus, *Unwanted*, pp. 190–94. On France as a haven for Central European refugees in the 1930's, see especially Badia et al., *Les Barbelés*; Badia et al., *Exilés en France*, p. 124; Badia et al., *Les Bannis*; Bartosek et al.; J.-Ch. Bonnet; Langkau-Alex; Kantorowicz; Maga, *America*; Palmier, vol. 1; Peterson; Schor, *L'Opinion française et les étrangers*; Schramm and Vormeier; Schiller et. al.; Thalmann, "L'Emigration du IIIᵉ Reich," pp. 127–39; Adolf Wild, intro. to *Propos d'exil*.

4. On the United States, see especially Feingold; Wyman, *Paper Walls*; Wyman, *Abandonment*. On Canada, see Abella and Troper, "Line Must Be Drawn," pp. 178–209; Abella and Troper, *None Is Too Many*. On Britain, see Sherman; Kushner; London, "British Immigration Control"; London, "British Government Policy," pp. 26–43; London, "Jewish Refugees," pp. 163–90; London, "British Immigration Control Procedures and Jewish Refugees, 1933–1939," in Werner Mosse,

coord. ed., Julius Carlebach et al., eds., *Second Chance: Two Centuries of German-Speaking Jews in the United Kingdom* (Tübingen, 1991), pp. 485–517; Wasserstein, *Britain*; Wasserstein, "British Government." On the Netherlands, see Moore. On Italy, see Voigt, "Refuge." On Australia, see Blakeney. On Latin America, see Avni. On Brazil, see Lesser. For brief summaries of asylum policies of various countries, see Marrus, *Unwanted*, pp. 145–90; Palmier, 1: 201–334.

5. "Ces Immigrés à qui la nation française doit tant," *Le Monde*, Feb. 8, 1997, p. 10. See also Noiriel, *Le Creuset français*, pp. 15–124, 333–58; Noiriel, "Immigration: Le Fin mot"; Noiriel, "Difficulties"; Noiriel, "Immigration: Amnesia," p. 368. See also Brubaker.

6. Conan and Rousso, pp. 269–70. The authors actually make this contention with respect to the Vichy period, but one can extrapolate it back to the 1930's as well.

7. See Schleunes.

8. For works suggesting this view, see Thalmann, "L'Emigration du IIIᵉ Reich"; Thalmann, "L'Accueil"; Schramm and Vormeier; Vormeier, "L'Opinion française et les réfugiés et immigrés d'Europe Centrale," in Bartosek et al., *De l'exil à la résistance*, pp. 13–26; Vormeier, "Législation."

9. See Bartosek et al., table 1, p. 22; Cross, p. 168; Livian, *Le Parti socialiste*, pp. 10–11.

10. See Ministry of Interior, Sûreté Générale, reports of 1926, as well as press clippings in AN F⁷ 13518 (File: "Les Etrangers en France; main d'oeuvre étrangère, législation, 1925–1934"); Maga, *America*, pp. 56–57; "Nos Interventions," *CDH*, July 10, 1930, p. 429; "Nos Interventions," *CDH*, Feb. 28, 1930, p. 139; Schor, *L'Opinion française et les étrangers*, pp. 281–83, 477–82; J.-Ch. Bonnet, pp. 106–8.

11. On the labor shortages due to the introduction of the 40-hour work week, see Philippe Serre, Ministry of Labor, to the Inspecteurs divisionnaires du travail et de la main d'oeuvre, no. 183, Jan. 19, 1938, in APP DA 783; Cross, pp. 186–214, esp. pp. 209–10, 213–14. On the continued need for immigrant labor in 1930's, see Demangeon and Mauco; Mauco, *Les Etrangers*, pp. 90, 102, 109, 472–73, 505, 555–58; Mauco, *Mémoire*; Millet, esp. pp. 12–15, 21–22, 27–28, 126–27, 137–38.

12. "Mémoire Maklakoff," AN AJ⁴³ 1 (20 A.80817); Police report, Jan. 27, 1938, APP BA 355 Provis. 51.343-9; Simpson, *Refugee Problem*, p. 289.

13. On the Nansen regime, see Simpson, *Refugee Problem*, pp. 191–261; Solomon, pp. 15–22, 25–31; Marrus, *Unwanted*, pp. 51–121; Noiriel, *La Tyrannie*, pp. 100–106; Sjöberg, pp. 24–27.

14. Vormeier, "La Situation administrative," p. 185; Noiriel, *La Tyrannie*, pp. 114–16. Noiriel confuses the status of Nansen and German refugees.

15. On the creation of the HCR, see Marrus, *Unwanted*, pp. 158–66; Simpson, *Refugee Problem*, pp. 214–18; Tartakower and Grossman, pp. 405–12; Solomon, pp. 22–24; John P. Fox, "Great Britain"; Genizi; Sjöberg, pp. 32–37.

16. Sharf, p. 165; Thalmann, "L'Immigration allemande," p. 172.

17. Marrus, *Unwanted*, p. 142.

18. On the role of the right-wing leagues, see especially Millman; Schor, *L'Antisémitisme en France*; Soucy. On Léon Blum as a target of antisemitism, see Birnbaum; Schuker.

19. For a more in-depth examination of this subject, see Caron, "Antisemitic Revival."

20. The two major exceptions to this rule are Ralph Schor and Jean-Charles Bonnet, both of whom emphasize the role of pro-refugee opinion. See Schor, *L'Antisémitisme en France*, esp. pp. 201–325; Schor, *L'Opinion française et les étrangers*; J.-Ch. Bonnet.

21. In a speech before Parliament in June, 1939, the socialist deputy, Marius Moutet, who had been minister of colonies during the Popular Front, admitted that the Popular Front had committed an error by not taking the problem of immigration more seriously. As Moutet declared, "L'erreur en cette matière [immigration], c'est de ne pas avoir considéré en France la question des étrangers comme une grande question d'ordre politique et économique.... En 1935, au nom du groupe socialiste, j'avais déposé une proposition de loi dans laquelle, de temps en temps, on est allé prendre quelques dispositions que l'on a accolées à quelques décrets lois, sauf ensuite à ne pas appliquer même des dispositions attenuantes de la rigueur des lois à l'égard des étrangers. Mais s'est-on soucié d'examiner au fond ce vaste problème des étrangers?" See *JO*, Débats Parlementaires, Chambre des Députés, June 8, 1939, p. 1526, cited in Schramm and Vormeier, p. 233. See also Ch. 6, "Refugee Policy During the Popular Front Era," n. 4.

22. Noiriel, *La Tyrannie*, pp. 318–20.

Chapter Two

1. On the Nazi seizure of power, see Karl Dietrich Bracher, *The German Dictatorship: The Origins, Structure, and Effects of National Socialism*, translated by Jean Steinberg (New York, 1970); William Sheridan Allen, *The Nazi Seizure of Power: The Experience of a Single German Town, 1933–1935* (Chicago, 1965).

2. For an overview of Nazi antisemitic legislation in the 1930's, see Dawidowicz, *War*, pp. 63–92; Dawidowicz, *The Holocaust Reader* (New York, 1976), pp. 35–44; Schleunes, pp. 92–132.

3. On the anti-Jewish boycott, see Schleunes, pp. 62–91; Ian Kershaw, "The Persecution of the Jews and German Popular Opinion in the Third Reich," *LBIYB*, 1981, pp. 261–89. On aryanization, see Schleunes, pp. 132–68; Barkai, pp. 69–77, 108, 119, 124–30, 167, 175.

4. Marrus, *Unwanted*, pp. 129, 146; "L'Aide aux réfugiés allemands," *Le Temps*, Dec. 6, 1933; Thalmann, "L'Immigration allemande," p. 150; Lengyel. Although 25,000 is generally cited as the number of refugees from Germany in France in Dec. 1933, there may have been as many as 40,000 during the summer and early fall of the year. See "Les Réfugiés allemands en France," *Le Matin*, Aug. 5, 1933, clipped in AN F[7] 13431; French ambassador, London, to the British Foreign Office, Sept. 14, 1933, PRO FO 371/16757.C8149. On the percentage of Jews among the total cohort of German refugees, see "Report of Bernhard Kahn submitted to the [JDC] Executive Committee Meeting," Jan. 4, 1934, JDC no. 160; Marrus, *Unwanted*, p. 129; Livian, *Le Parti socialiste*, p. 12; "60,000 Have Fled from Nazis' Reich," *NYT*, Dec. 6, 1933, p. 18.

5. On France as a haven for Central European political refugees, see Chapter 1, n. 3.

6. On British and American refugee policy in the 1930's, see Chapter 1, n. 4.

7. On France's reliance on immigrant labor throughout the 1930's, see Maga, *America*, p. 56; Demangeon and Mauco; Philippe Serre, minister of labor, to the Inspecteurs divisionnaires du travail et de la main d'oeuvre, Jan. 19, 1938, no. 183, APP DA 783; P. J. Philip, "France Welcomes the Political Exile," *NYT Magazine*, Oct. 29, 1933, pp. 9, 17.

8. Report of Norman Bentwich, cited in Marrus, *Unwanted*, p. 147.

9. See n. 164, below.

10. Statement by McDonald made at session of the Permanent Committee of the Governing Body at London (doc. no. A/117), Feb. 12, 1935, MP: H 28; Walter Kotschnig, HCR, to André Wurfbain, HCR, Mar. 5, 1935, MP: H 20; "Need of Refugees Told by Bentwich," *NYT*, Apr. 10, 1935, p. 18. The figure of 13,500–14,000 reflects a high-end estimate of the number of refugees in France, including those recently arrived from the Saar. The HCR actually estimated the number of refugees in France at this time to be 8,000–10,000.

11. See especially Maga, "Closing the Door," particularly p. 435.

12. Berstein, *La France*, pp. 25–28, 48; Sauvy, 2: 18–27; Jackson, pp. 23–24, 29; Landau, pp. 28–30; Weber, *Hollow Years*, pp. 29–33.

13. On the impact of the Depression on immigrant workers, see Schor, *L'Opinion française et les étrangers*, pp. 549–631; Cross, pp. 187–88; Noiriel, *Le Creuset français*, pp. 249–94; Weber, *Hollow Years*, pp. 87–102; Schramm and Vormeier, p. 209; Livian, *Le Parti socialiste*, pp. 16–21; "Les Problèmes du chômage devant le Conseil général de la Seine," *Le Populaire*, Dec. 2, 1933, pp. 1–2, "Chômage et misère!" *Le Populaire*, Dec. 15, 1933, p. 6; "Le Problème de chômage et de la main d'oeuvre étrangère," *Le Temps*, Nov. 18, 1934, p. 8; Luigi Campolonghi, "La Grande pitié des émigrés et des proscrits," *CDH*, Nov. 30, 1934, pp. 747–57. On the fate of Polish workers in particular, see Ponty, pp. 287–318; MAE Z (Europe 1930–40) 433 (Polonais en France).

14. In the fall of 1933, the Comité National reported the following professional breakdown of the refugees:

Intellectuals/artists (including liberal professions)	25%
Engineers/specialized technicians	10%
Workers in commerce/industry	40%
Workers in small commerce/artisanry	15%
People without professions	10%

Comité National, compte rendu, spring 1933–Oct. 16, 1933, Foreign Ministry (SDN), SDN I E (Minorités) 448 (Allemagne: Minorités juives, Protection des réfugiés, HCR...), p. 59. (Also in "Aide Mémoire," Nov. 22, 1933, MAE SDN I E 448, p. 79.) For a complete professional distribution, see "Etat des professions exercées en Allemagne par les étrangers qui se sont présentés comme réfugiés d'Allemagne, du 10 avril 1933 à 7 novembre 1933," APP BA 1814 241.155-1-A (Chiappe). On the professional breakdown of the refugees, see also Thalmann, "L'Immigration allemande," p. 150; Thalmann, "L'Emigration du III^c Reich," p. 128; Schramm and Vormeier, pp. 211–12; Badia, "L'Emigration," p. 16.

For a professional breakdown of the refugees in the Bas-Rhin in the fall of 1933, see Roland-Marcel, prefect, Bas-Rhin, to the undersecretary of state to the president of the council, Direction Générale des Service d'Alsace et de Lorraine, Sept. 21, 1933, ADBR D 460 paq. 5 (36). According to the figures here, 62% of all male heads of household among the refugees were involved in commerce:

People in liberal professions, doctors, lawyers	28
Industrialists	8
Merchants	199
Students	33
Commercial employees	138
People without specific professions	135
Total	541

15. Foreign Ministry (Contrôle des étrangers), "Note pour le Ministre," Mar. 31, 1933, pp. 9–12; Pierre Arnal, chargé d'affaires, Berlin, to the Foreign Ministry (Europe), no. 338, Apr. 11, 1933, pp. 36–39, both in MAE Z 710.

16. Police report, Apr. 5, 1933, APP BA 1814 241.155-1-C. According to Maurice Moch, a spokesman for the Central Consistory, "En décidant de donner l'hospitalité à tous ces malheureux, les gouvernements de MM. Daladier et Chautemps n'entendaient pas subvenir à leurs besoins et comptaient uniquement sur la charité privée pour leur venir en aide." Moch, "Note sur les réfugiés d'Allemagne," July 2, 1971, AIU, ms. 650, boîte 12 (44). See also MAE (Contrôle des étrangers), to the British ambassador in Paris, Apr. 12, 1933, MAE Z 710 (Allemagne: Réfugiés israélites à l'étranger), pp. 51–52.

17. Paul Bargeton, Foreign Ministry (Affaires Politiques et Commerciales), to the undersecretary of state to the president of the council, Apr. 14, 1933, MAE Z 710, pp. 57–58; Foreign Ministry (Contrôle des étrangers), to the British ambassador in Paris, Apr. 12, 1933, MAE Z 710, pp. 51–52; minister of the interior, circular 222, Apr. 20, 1933, APP BA 407^P 13.112-3; "Note pour le Service Français de la SDN," Nov. 17, 1933, MAE SDN I E 448, pp. 66–68; "Comité Central [League for the Rights of Man]," "Extraits," meeting of May 4, 1933, CDH, June 20, 1933, pp. 376–78; Police report, "Renseignements concernant les réfugiés d'Allemagne," Nov. 10, 1933, APP BA 407^P 13.112-3; Police report, Summary of Measures Regarding Refugees from Germany, [fall 1933], APP BA 407^P 13.112-1; Marrus, *Unwanted*, p. 146; Livian, *Le Parti socialiste*, p. 46; Palmier, 1: 277; Schramm and Vormeier, p. 201.

18. Léger, Foreign Ministry (Contrôle des étrangers), to the French consulates in Berlin and Munich, Apr. 27, 1933, APP BA 407^P 13.112-3. On the Nansen regime, see Chapter 1, n. 13.

19. Police report, "Renseignements concernant les réfugiés d'Allemagne," Nov. 10, 1933, APP BA 407^P 13.112-3; Police report, "Note," [fall 1933], APP BA 407^P 13.112-1 (also in APP BA 1814 241.155-1-G).

20. Ministry of the Interior, Sûreté Nationale, circular no. 227, July 18, 1933; Ministry of the Interior, Sûreté Nationale, circular no. 231, Nov. 15, 1933; Police report, "Résumé des instructions ministérielles concernant les réfugiés d'Allemagne," Nov. 27, 1933, all in APP BA 407^P 13.112-1.

21. *JO, Débats Parlementaires, Chambre des Députés*, Apr. 5, 1933, p. 1893, clipped in APP BA 407 Provisoire. On Moch's interpellation of Chautemps regarding refugee policy as well as the interpellations of two other left-wing deputies, Paul Malingre and Gabriel Péri, see also Schramm and Vormeier, pp. 195–96, 200–201; Thalmann, "L'Accueil," p. 122; Police report, "Renseignements concernant les réfugiés d'Allemagne," Nov. 10, 1933, APP BA 407^P 13.112-3; Police report, "Renseignements concernant les réfugiés allemands," [fall 1933], APP BA 1814 241.155-1-A; Police report, including clippings of "Les Réfugiés israélites allemands en France," *Le Temps* and *JO, Débats Parlementaires*, Apr. 1, 1933, APP BA 1814 241.155-1-G.

22. "Le Professeur Einstein occuperait en décembre prochain au Collège de France la chaire qui lui a été votée," *Le Journal*, Apr. 14, 1933, p. 4; Mathieu, "Einstein," pp. 163–67; Weber, *Hollow Years*, p. 106. Jewish organizations around the world expressed deep gratitude to the French government for its generous reception of Einstein. See D'Aumale, French consul-général, Jerusalem, to the Foreign Ministry, teleg. no. 69, Apr. 24, 1933, MAE Z 710, p. 66; Zionist Organization of Romania, to Gabriel Puaux, ministre plénipotentiaire de la France, Apr. 19, 1933, MAE Z 710, p. 105; French chargé d'affaires, to the Foreign Ministry, no. 187, May 8, 1933, MAE Z 710, p. 104. On the right-wing press campaign against Einstein, see Chapter 4, n. 15.

23. De Monzie, to the League for the Rights of Man and Citizen, Oct. 9, 1933, cited in "Autres Interventions," *CDH*, Nov. 10–15, 1933, p. 669. See also "Pour les réfugiés allemands," *CDH*, May 20, 1933, p. 312.

24. Mordagne, pp. 2453–54.

25. "Refugee Jews in France," *Manchester Guardian*, Apr. 24, 1933, p. 9. A French translation of this article entitled "L'Accueil en France des réfugiés allemands" can be found in AIU, ms. 650, boîte 12 (43).

26. Charles Liebman to Dudley, May 30, 1933, JDC no. 617.

27. "Christians Cited for Aid to Jews," *NYT*, Sept. 18, 1933, p. 12. Ironically, Mussolini was also among those cited. See also "Wise Praises France for Assisting Jews," *NYT*, July 21, 1933, p. 5; "Reich to Protest British Criticism: 'French Are Pleased,'" *NYT*, Apr. 15, 1933, p. 6.

28. A. Kammerer, French ambassador, Brazil, to the foreign minister, Apr. 1, 1933, MAE SDN I E 446 (Minorités en Allemagne: Minorités juives...), pp. 25–27; French ambassador, Brussels, to the foreign minister, no. 252, Mar. 30, 1933, MAE Z 710, pp. 6–7. See also M. Gaillard, French minister, Egypt, to the foreign minister, no. 71, Apr. 13, 1933, MAE SDN I E 446, pp. 69–71.

29. M. A. de Fleuriau, French ambassador to Great Britain, to the foreign minister, no. 264, Apr. 6, 1933 (doc. no. 96), in DDF Ier série 3, Mar. 17, 1933–July 15, 1933, p. 175. See also de Fleuriau, to the foreign minister, Apr. 1, 1933, no. 213, MAE SDN I E 446, pp. 20–24.

30. Jeanneney, *François de Wendel*, p. 499.

31. Pierre Arnal, chargé d'affaires, Berlin, to the Foreign Ministry (Europe), no. 338, Apr. 11, 1933, MAE Z 710, pp. 36–39. See also Foreign Ministry (Contrôle des étrangers), "Note pour le Ministre, (confidentiel et très urgent)," Mar. 31, 1933, MAE Z 710, pp. 9–12; Léger, Foreign Ministry, to André François-Poncet, French ambassador, Berlin, Apr. 7, 1933, MAE Z 710, pp. 26–28.

32. Dobler, consul général de France, Cologne, to the Foreign Ministry (Europe), teleg. no. 38, Apr. 27, 1933, MAE Z 710, pp. 80–84; Dobler, to the Foreign Ministry (Europe), teleg. no. 34, May 12, 1933, p. 110; Foreign Ministry (Europe), to Dobler, no. 18, May 10, 1933, p. 107; Dobler, to the Foreign Ministry, May 14, 1933, pp. 112–20; Dobler, to the Foreign Ministry (Contrôle des étrangers), no. 59, May 24, 1933, pp. 132–36; Dobler, to the Foreign Ministry (Contrôle des étrangers), June 7, 1933, pp. 149–51, all in MAE Z 710. For the reprimand Dobler received, see Foreign Ministry (Contrôle des étrangers), "Note pour le Directeur des Affaires Politiques et Commerciales," July 13, 1933, MAE Z 710, p. 193. The French consul in Munich made a similar suggestion and was also reprimanded. Binet, French consul, to the Foreign Ministry, no. 405, June 6, 1933, MAE Z 710, p. 147; Bargeton, Foreign Ministry (Contrôle des étrangers), to Binet, June 7, 1933, MAE Z 710, p. 148. For the subsequent shift in policy, see Foreign Ministry, "Note pour M. Blanchet," Dec. 18, 1933, MAE Z 711, pp. 142–48; Police report (Sous-direction des étrangers et passeports): "Note de Cologne," [Nov. or Dec. 1933], APP BA 1814 241.155-1-A. On Dobler, see also Maga, *America*, p. 68; Schramm and Vormeier, p. 205. On Bos, see Police report, Oct. 19, 1933, APP BA 1814 241.155-1-A.

33. Foreign Ministry, to the minister of the interior, Sûreté Générale, May 5, 1933, MAE Z 710, pp. 99–100.

34. Police report, Direction de l'Administration et de la Police Générale, Sous-direction des étrangers et passeports, Nov. 10, 1933, APP BA 1814, 241-155-1-A.

35. Ministry of the Interior, Sûreté Nationale, circular no. 40, Apr. 1, 1933, ADBR D 460, paq. 5 (36).

36. Police report, Direction de l'Administration et de la Police Générale, Sous-direction des étrangers et passeports, Nov. 10, 1933, APP BA 1814 241-155-1-A.

37. François-Poncet, to Paul-Boncour, foreign minister, no. 1358, Dec. 14, 1933, MAE Z 711, pp. 139–40. On this case, see also M. Dufort, French consul, Frankfurt A/m, to Paul-Boncour, no. 102, Dec. 11, 1933, pp. 136–37; Foreign Ministry (Europe), "Note pour le Service du Contrôle des Etrangers," Dec. 20, 1933, pp. 150–51, all in MAE Z 711.

38. Fernand Leroy, prefect, Haut-Rhin, to the minister of the interior, Sûreté Nationale, Service central des cartes d'identité des étrangers, Dec. 23, 1933, ADBR AL 98 393 (unmarked dossier).

39. Fouques-Duparc, Foreign Ministry (SDN), "Note pour le Ministre," Nov. 3, 1933, MAE SDN I E 448, pp. 41–43.

40. For a discussion of this campaign, see Chapter 4.

41. On the law of Aug. 10, 1932, see *JO, Lois et Décrets*, Aug. 12, 1932; Schramm and Vormeier, p. 212; Livian, *Le Parti socialiste*, pp. 10–11; Livian, *Le Régime ju-*

ridique, pp. 107–9; Marrus and Paxton, pp. 54–55; Leven, p. 12; Feblowicz and Lamour, pp. 304–6; Guillaume, pp. 117–18. On Mar. 15, 1933, additional legislation was passed restricting the number of foreigners who could work as musical and theatrical performers. *JO, Lois et Décrets*, Mar. 31, 1933, p. 2588; "Protégeons la main-d'oeuvre nationale," *Le Figaro*, Mar. 18, 1933, p. 4; "La Protection des musiciens français," *Le Temps*, Apr. 1, 1933, p. 4; J. R., "Le Droit d'asile," *CDH*, Apr. 10, 1933, pp. 229–30; Schramm and Vormeier, p. 212; Guillaume, p. 118. This measure initially applied only to Paris, but during the summer of 1933 it was extended to all of France. See Prefect, Bas-Rhin, to the subprefect, Sélestat, ADBR D 391/24: 237. These restrictions were further tightened in early 1934. See "Questions Sociales: La Limitation de la main-d'oeuvre étrangère," *Le Temps*, Jan. 1, 1934, p. 2.

42. On the minister of labor's initial promises to grant work permits to refugees as liberally as possible see Norman Bentwich, to James G. McDonald, Feb. 22, 1934, MP: H 10; "Comité Central, Extraits, Séance du 18 mai 1933," *CDH*, June 30, 1933, pp. 376–78.

43. Already in May 1933, the minister of labor, François-Albert, warned his colleagues that an overly generous refugee policy could have deleterious political repercussions. According to the minutes of the First Interministerial Meeting on Refugees, "M. François-Albert remarque que la difficulté est surtout d'ordre politique: ces réfugiés a qui l'on va donner des cartes de travail sont susceptibles de faire concurrence à des Français." "Procès verbal de la Ier séance tenue par la Commission Interministérielle des Réfugiés Allemands," May 27, 1933, MAE Z 711, pp. 93–96. In Aug. 1933, the minister of labor declared that no special dispensations would be made to grant work permits to refugees as a group. Instead, work permits were to be allocated on a case-by-case basis. See "Les Emigrés d'Allemagne et la carte de travailleur," *Le Temps*, Aug. 14, 1933, p. 3; "Les Réfugiés allemands et la carte de travailleur," *Le Peuple*, Aug. 16, 1933, clipped in APP BA 1814 241.155-1-G.

44. For the position of the labor movement on immigrant labor see the numerous articles on this subject in *Le Populaire*, *L'Humanité*, and *Le Peuple*. See also Chapter 4.

45. Comité d'Aide et d'Accueil, compte rendu no. 2, for the period May 20–30, 1933, AIU X D 56. On this problem, see also Thalmann, "L'Immigration allemande," p. 158; Schor, *L'Antisémitisme en France*, pp. 146–47. According to Victor Basch, president of the League for the Rights of Man and Citizen, "Beaucoup d'ouvriers sont refoulés parce que, parfois, la CGT elle-même le demande, par suite de la surabondance de la main-d'oeuvre française dans certaines corporations." "Le Congrès international des Ligues de Droits de l'Homme," *CDH*, Jan. 20, 1933, p. 29.

46. E. Hénaff, "Pour empirer les conditions de vie de la classe ouvrière, le patronat tente de se servir des travailleurs immigrés," *L'Humanité*, Nov. 10, 1933; Emile Farinet, "Appel aux militants du parti," *Le Populaire*, Aug. 3, 1933, both clipped in APP BA 1814 241.155-1-G; Police report, Nov. 29, 1931, APP BA 67 Provisoire 331.500-1; Thalmann, "L'Emigration du IIIe Reich," p. 134. For an overview of the Communist Party's attitude toward foreigners in the 1930's, see Schor, "Le Parti communiste," pp. 84–86. In my view, Schor's assessment is too negative and does not sufficiently differentiate the party's position on the right to asylum as opposed

to its position on economic immigration. On the CGT's hostility to foreign workers in general see Schor, *L'Opinion française et les étrangers*, pp. 260–71, 555–76. For a more positive assessment of the CGT's position, see Cross, pp. 191–92, 207–8. For the position of the left-wing parties toward immigrant workers during the 1930's, see also J.-Ch. Bonnet, pp. 205–9, 215–16.

47. "Pour l'installation des réfugiés allemands," *La République*, June 13, 1933, p. 4. For the views of Jouhaux and the CGT, see also Jouhaux, "Main-d'oeuvre étrangère et droit d'asile," *Le Peuple*, Mar. 8, 1935, pp. 1, 2; Schramm and Vormeier, p. 204; Vormeier, "La Situation administrative," p. 191; Cross, p. 208.

48. J. Biélinky, "Paris hospitalier," *UI*, Oct. 6, 1933, p. 90; Police report, "Renseignements concernant les réfugiés d'Allemagne," Nov. 10, 1933, APP BA 1814 241.155-1-A (also in APP BA 407^P 13.112-3); Police report, "Renseignements concernant les réfugiés d'Allemagne," Nov. 28, 1933, in APP BA 407^P 13.112-1. See also Jacques Fouques-Duparc, "Aide-Mémoire," Nov. 22, 1933, MAE SDN I E 448, p. 82, and "Note pour le Service Français de la SDN," Nov. 17, 1933, MAE SDN I E 448, pp. 66–68.

On the lobbying efforts of the League for the Rights of Man, see "Rapport Moral," *CDH*, June 30, 1933, p. 414; "Comité Central, Extraits, Séance du 18 mai 1933," *CDH*, June 30, 1933, pp. 376–78; J. R., "Le Droit d'asile," *CDH*, Apr. 10, 1933, pp. 229–30. For a brief summary of the League's position regarding immigrant labor and refugees during the interwar period see J.-Ch. Bonnet, pp. 70–85.

On the lobbying efforts of the Comité National and the JDC, see "Procès verbal de la 2ème séance tenue par la Commission Interministérielle des Réfugiés Israélites Allemands," Oct. 16, 1933, MAE Z 711, pp. 37–41; "Procès verbal de la 3ème séance tenue par la Commission Interministérielle des réfugiés allemands," Oct. 23, 1933, in MAE Z 711, pp. 70–74; Ministry of Labor, Service de la Main d'Oeuvre Etrangère, to the president of the Comité National, Nov. 9, 1933, MAE SDN I E 451 (Allemagne: Minorités juives; réfugiés allemands), p. 141; "'Report of Dr. Bernhard Kahn,' submitted to [JDC] Executive Committee Meeting of January 4, 1934," JDC no. 160; Norman Bentwich, to James G. McDonald, Feb. 22, 1934, MP: H 10; Bernhard Kahn, European Director, JDC, to Mr. Stephany, Allocations Committee, Central British Fund for German Jewry, London, Mar. 8, 1934, JDC no. 617; "Report on the Activities of the AJDC, with Special Attention to the Last Five Months," Apr. 16, 1934, JDC no. 249, p. 16; Morris Troper, "Summary Report of Trip (Oct. 24, 1934, to Dec. 13, 1934), JDC no. 160, pp. 14–16. On the role of the Comité Nationale, see Chapter 5.

49. Procès verbal de la 4ème séance tenue par la Commission Interministérielle des réfugiés allemands," Nov. 13, 1933, MAE Z 711, p. 101.

50. Police report, Direction de l'Administration et de la Police Générale, Sousdirection des étrangers et passeports, Nov. 10, 1933, APP BA 1814 241.155-1-A. See also Badia, "L'Emigration," p. 30.

51. On Malthusianism, see especially Sauvy, 2: 22–23, 99, 302, 359–78, 469–70; Berstein, *La France*, pp. 12–16, 37–45; Kuisel, *Capitalism*, pp. 93–127; Kuisel, "Businessmen."

52. According to an intelligence report of June 1933 (Sûreté Générale, June 9, 1933, A-5194, AN F[7] 13430),

Antérieurement déjà au mouvement hitlérien, qui a eu pour conséquence l'exode de nombreux Israélites allemands hors de leur pays, beaucoup d'entre eux possédaient des avoirs à l'étranger.

Ces avoirs avaient été constitués par les intéressés, surtout lorsqu'ils étaient exportateurs de produits nationaux.

Ils vendaient leurs marchandises au delà des frontières du Reich à des prix souvent peu rénumérateurs, et se gardaient bien, prévoyant les mesures dont ils allaient être les victimes, de faire transférer dans les banques allemandes les sommes qui leur étaient dues.

Les fonds versés par leurs acheteurs étaient portés au crédit des exportateurs allemands dans les banques françaises.

C'est ainsi que des juifs, obligés de quitter l'Allemagne, ont pu retrouver en arrivant en France, un pécule qui les a sauvés de la misère.

La méthode dont il vient d'être parlé a été pratiquée d'une manière particulièrement active avant l'avènement d'Hitler.

Elle se poursuit encore à l'heure actuelle, mais sur un mode ralenti.

In Apr. 1933, *Le Temps* also reported that among the first wave of refugees, many "étaient des gens plutôt aisés." "Les événements en Allemagne: L'exode des israélites, Bruxelles," *Le Temps*, Apr. 6, 1933, clipped in APP BA 1815 241.155-2. On June 29, 1933, the Strasbourg Chamber of Commerce passed a resolution "protestant...avec la plus grande énergie...contre l'établissement d'Allemands,...réfugiés politiques et autres, disposant souvent de capitaux importants...dans nos départements desannexés." Foreign Ministry (Europe), "Note pour l'information du Ministre," July 21, 1933, MAE Z 710, pp. 209, 216.

53. See Chapter 4, nn. 94–104. On this theme, see also Comité pour la Défense, pp. 5–6, *passim*; Raymond-Raoul Lambert, "L'Accueil de la France," *RJG* 1, no. 8 (May 1933): 348–51; and the statements by Claude Farrère at an anti-Nazi rally, Police report, "Meeting de protestation contre les persécutions antisémites en Allemagne, organisé par le Comité Français pour la Protection des Intellectuels Juifs Persecutés, 10 mai 1933," May 11, 1933, APP BA 1815 241. 155-1-B.

54. Sûreté Nationale report, (no. A-2.840), Apr. 1, 1933, AN F[7] 13430. Similarly, Paul Bargeton, chief of the Foreign Ministry's political affairs bureau, observed that "en ce qui concerne...les représentants de commerce, il pourrait y avoir intérêt à les garder en France et à les lier à des maisons de commerce françaises dont ils augmenteraient la clientèle." "Procès verbal de la Ier séance tenue par la Commission Interministérielle des réfugiés allemands," May 27, 1933, MAE Z 711, p. 94.

55. Subprefect, Haguenau, to the prefect, Bas-Rhin, Nov. 15, 1933, ADBR D 460, paq. 12 (91).

56. Ministry of Commerce and Industry, 1st bureau, to Senator André Honnorat, June 9, 1933, ACIP B (not classified; dossier: Comité d'Accueil des Intellectuels Etrangers); Ministry of Commerce and Industry, to the Foreign Ministry, no. 5160, Dec. 15, 1933, MAE Z 711, pp. 158–59. Although the Ministry of Commerce did not

give special provisions to the Leipzig furriers, it did initially seek to attract the Nuremberg toy manufacturers. A cooperative by the name of Jou-Jou was allowed to operate out of the Saint-Maur barracks, where refugees were housed beginning in the fall of 1933. On Jou-Jou, see Margaret Hess, "Little Germany in Paris Gives a Haven to Exiles," *NYT*, sec. IX, Apr. 15, 1934, p. 11; Comité pour la Défense, pp. 6–8; Madéleine Misard, "Comment la France absorbe-t-elle l'immigration judéo-allemande?" *Excelsior*, Jan. 22, 1934, APP BA 1815 241.155-1-G.

57. Sûreté Nationale, Report, no. A-2.840, Apr. 1, 1933, AN F⁷ 13430. See also the Sûreté Nationale reports of Apr. 3 and May 24, 1933, AN F⁷ 13430.

58. "L'Installation des réfugiés allemands dans les départements recouvrés," *Le Matin*, Aug. 16, 1933, clipped in ADBR D 460, paq. 5 (36); Gaëtan Sanvoisin, "Les Réfugiés allemands dans l'Est," *Le Figaro*, Aug. 17, 1933, p. 1. See also President of the Chamber of Commerce Strasbourg, to the prefect, Bas-Rhin, May 6, 1933, ADBR D 460, paq. 5/36; Chamber of Commerce, Strasbourg, "Délibération concernant l'établissement en Alsace d'industriels et de commerçants étrangers, extrait du procès-verbal de la séance du 29 juin 1933," MAE Z 710, p. 184; Foreign Ministry (Europe), "Note," July 18, 1933, MAE Z 710, pp. 196–97; "Réunion à la Présidence du Conseil des représentants des divers départements et services intéressés [aux réfugiés allemands]," Sept. 23, 1933, APP BA 407ᴾ 13.112-1; Lucien Lamoureux, minister of commerce, 3ème bureau, to the prefects, Sept. 27, 1934, ADBR D 460, paq. 5 (33); "Les Commerçants messins protestent contre l'invasion des commerçants allemands," *L'Oeuvre*, July 16, 1933, p. 2; "Les Réfugiés allemands en France," *Le Matin*, Aug. 5, 1933, clipped in AN F⁷ 13431; "L'Installation des réfugiés allemands dans les départements recouvrés," *Le Matin*, Aug. 17, 1933, clipped in ADBR 460 paq. 5 (36); "Les Réfugiés allemands dans l'Est," *Le Figaro*, Aug. 18, 1933, p. 2; Gaëtan Sanvoisin, "Trop d'immigrants dans l'Est," *Le Figaro*, Sept. 2, 1933, p. 1; "German Jews as Competitors Harass French," *New York Herald Tribune*, Aug. 16, 1933, clipped in JDC no. 617; "Les Réfugiés politiques en Alsace," extrait de *l'Elsässer*, Dec. 5, 1933, clipped in ADBR D 460 paq. 5/36; "Les Juifs expulsés d'Allemagne," *AF*, Sept. 21, 1933, clipped in APP BA 1814 241.155-1-G; "La Question des réfugiés allemands," *TJ*, Aug. 25, 1933, no. 34, p. 565; "Les Réfugiés allemands en Alsace-Lorraine," *AI*, Aug. 31, 1933, p. 138; Schor, *L'Antisémitisme en France*, pp. 147–48, 160–61; J.-Ch. Bonnet, pp. 220–21.

59. Police report, June 13, 1933, APP BA 1844 241.155-1-C; Gaëtan Sanvoisin, "Trop d'immigrants dans l'Est," *Le Figaro*, Sept. 2, 1933, p. 1; "Les Réfugiés allemands en Alsace et Lorraine," *Le Matin*, Sept. 1, 1933, p. 2; minister of the interior, Sûreté Nationale, to the Foreign Ministry, Sept. 4, 1933, MAE Z 710, pp. 262–63; "Les Magasins à prix unique," *DdV*, Sept.–Oct., 1933, p. 5; "French Hit Jewish Shops," *NYT*, Sept. 2, 1933, p. 6; Férenzy, pp. 199–200; "Les Réfugiés politiques en Alsace," extrait de *l'Elsässer*, Dec. 5, 1933, clipped in ADBR D 460 paq. 5/36; Joseph Bonsirven, "Chronique du judaisme français: Y a-t-il un réveil de l'antisémitisme?" *Etudes* 222, Jan. 5, 1935: 98–100. On the spread of *prix uniques* in the 1930's, see Weber, *Hollow Years*, p. 52. In 1936, a law was passed banning the development of new *prix uniques*. Weber, *Hollow Years*, p. 54, Sauvy, 2: 373–74.

60. F. Peter, president, Chambre des Métiers d'Alsace, to Edouard Herriot,

minister of state, Nov. 13, 1934, ADBR D 460, paq. 5 (33). See also Chambre des Métiers, Alsace, "Résolution concernant la concurrence des étrangers," Dec. 14, 1934, ADBR D 460, paq. 7 (45); Fédération Patronale des Tailleurs d'Alsace, to the prefect, Bas-Rhin, June 23, 1933, ADBR D460, paq. 7(51); Comité Républicain de l'Industrie et de l'Agriculture of Alsace, "Rapport de M. Coullerez à M. Sarory, Président du Comité Républicain," [Nov. 1933], ADBR D 460 paq. 12(88); Fédération Patronale des Tailleurs d'Alsace, to the prefect, Bas-Rhin, Nov. 20, 1935, ADBR D 460 paq. 7(45); and "Résolution prise par la Chambre Syndicale des Fabricants de Chaussures d'Alsace et de Lorraine dans son Assemblée du 23 septembre 1933," ADBR D 460, paq. 5/12. On Peter, see also Zdatny, *Politics*, p. 85; Zdatny, "Class," pp. 128–29. On the complaints of artisans against Sarre refugees, see also Secrétariat Législatif, "Question écrite," no. 10.637, Dec. 14, 1934, MAE Z 313 (Réfugiés sarrois en France), p. 88; also in *JO*, *Documentation* (Questions écrites), *Débats Parlementaires*, *Chambre des Députés*, p. 3227, forwarded from the minister of labor to the foreign minister, Jan. 29, 1935, MAE Z 314 (Réfugiés sarrois en France), pp. 195–96.

61. Annexe no. 4148, *JO*, *Documents Parlementaires*, sect. 3, chambre 1934, 2ème session extraordinaire, pp. 131–32; J.-Ch. Bonnet, p. 220. Among the principal sponsors of this bill were the deputies from Alsace and Lorraine: Joseph Rossé, Robert Schuman, Emile Seitz, Alfred Wallach, Marcel Stürmel, and Emile Béron.

62. Petitions of the Chambers of Commerce of the Moselle, the Haut-Rhin and the Bas-Rhin, to Paul Valot, Directeur général des services d'Alsace et de Lorraine et Président du Conseil, cited in "L'Installation des réfugiés allemands dans les départements recouvrés," *Le Matin*, Aug. 16, 1933, clipped in ADBR D 460 paq. 5(36) and Gaëtan Sanvoisin, "Les Réfugiés allemands dans l'Est," *Le Figaro*, Aug. 17, 1933, p. 1. On the charge that these practices were "disloyal," see Klein Frères, Usines mécaniques alsaciennes de [Piassarta], Brosses et Pinceaux, Obernai (Bas-Rhin), to the Chambre Syndicale de la Brosserie, Paris, Dec. 18, 1933, and Klein Frères, to the prefect, Bas-Rhin, Mar. 27, 1934, both in ADBR D 460, paq. 12 (91). On the charge that these practices were communistic, see Zdatny, "Class," p. 128. On complaints regarding shortages of skilled workers, see Lucien Weyl, honorary president, Chambre Syndicale des Fabricants de Chaussures d'Alsace et de Lorraine, to President of the Strasbourg Chamber of Commerce, Aug. 22, 1935 and Sept. 2, 1935, in ADBR D 460 paq. 12 (91); Herreschmidt, president, Chamber of Commerce, Strasbourg, to the mayor of Haguenau, Ville, no. 8778, Sept. 3, 1935, ADBR D 460, paq. 12 (91); E. Roblot, prefect, Bas-Rhin, to the subprefect, Haguenau, no. 1026, confidential, Sept. 17, 1935, all in ADBR D 460, paq. 12 (91).

63. M. J. Morize, Membre français de la Commission du Gouvernement de la Sarre, to J. Paul-Boncour, Foreign Minister, July [20,] 1933, MAE Z 710, pp. 207–8.

64. See, for example, the resolution passed by the Chamber of Commerce of Strasbourg in May 1935, at the behest of the Chambre Syndicale des Fabricants de Chaussures d'Alsace et de Lorraine, calling on the government to pass legislation requiring all foreign merchants and industrialists to obtain ministerial permission to establish a firm in France. Chambre de Commerce, Strasbourg, "Procès-verbal, séance du 16 mai 1935," ADBR D 460, paq. 12 (91).

65. Italics in text. R. Weyl of R. & L. Weyl et Cie, Manufacture Alsacienne de

Chaussures, to Roland-Marcel, prefect, Bas-Rhin, Sept. 6, 1933; R. Weyl to M. Morel, Inspecteur du Travail, Sept. 6, 1933, both in ADBR D 460, paq. 12 (91).

66. Italics in text. "Résolution prise par la Chambre Syndicale des Fabricants de Chaussures d'Alsace et de Lorraine dans son Assemblée du 23 septembre 1933" (mimeog.), ADBR D 460, paq. 5 (12). On the view that overproduction, due largely to technological innovations, was the cause of the Depression, see Bernard and Dubief, p. 179; Jackson, pp. 16, 40; Sauvy, 2: 22–23, 359–78; Berstein, *La France*, pp. 41–42; Weber, *Hollow Years*, p. 35.

67. Jacques Ziring, Etablissements ASTRA, Strasbourg, to the prefect, Bas-Rhin, [Apr. 1934], ADBR D 460 paq. 12 (91); Roland-Marcel, prefect, Bas-Rhin, to the minister of the interior, Sûreté Générale, Contrôle Général, Service de Police administrative, Paris, no. 433, May 5, 1934, ADBR D 460, paq. 12 (91). For the police investigation into the refugee-owned shoe manufacturing firm of Cléo, see also Special Police Commissioner, Haguenau, to the Contrôleur Général chargé des Affaires d'Alsace et de Lorraine, no. 1295, Dec. 15, 1933, ADBR D 460, paq. 12 (91); Extrait du *Journal d'Alsace et de Lorraine*, Dec. 23, 1933, clipped in ADBR D 460, paq. 12 (91); A. Mallet, Contrôleur Général, minister of the interior, Sûreté Nationale, to the prefect, Bas-Rhin, no. 7672, Dec. 18, 1933, ADBR D 460 paq. 12 (91). The Alsatian brush manufacturer, Klein Frères, charged that the owners of one German-owned firm "fait ici en Alsace de l'antisémitisme à la Hitler." Klein Frères, Usines mécaniques alsaciennes de [Piassarta], Brosses et Pinceaux, Obernai (Bas-Rhin), to the prefect, Bas-Rhin, Mar. 27, 1934, ADBR D 460, paq. 12 (91).

68. Commissaire spécial de Haguenau, no. 1159, Nov. 6, 1933, a/s Gunzburger, ADBR D 460, paq. 12 (91).

69. A. Mallet, Contrôleur Général, minister of the interior, Sûreté Nationale, Affaires d'Alsace et de Lorraine, to Commissaires spéciaux, Sûreté Nationale, and to the prefects of the Bas-Rhin, the Haut-Rhin, and the Moselle, circular no. 101, Nov. 13, 1933, ADBR D 460, paq. 12 (91).

70. Minister of the interior, Sûreté Nationale, to the Foreign Ministry, Sept. 4, 1933, "a/s réunion de 31 août 1933 [à Metz]," MAE Z 710, pp. 262–63; Chamber of Commerce, Strasbourg, Procès-verbal, séance du 16 mai 1935, ADBR D 460, paq. 12 (91).

71. Préfecture du Bas-Rhin, Cabinet, "Note pour M. le Secrétaire Général," June 30, 1933, ADBR D 460, paq. 5 (36). See also "L'Installation des réfugiés allemands dans les départements recouvrés," *Le Matin*, Aug. 17, 1933, clipped in ADBR D 460, paq. 5 (36); "Les Réfugiés allemands dans l'Est," *Le Figaro*, Aug. 18, 1933, clipped in ADBR D 460, paq. 5 (36); "La Question des réfugiés allemands," *TJ*, Aug. 25, 1933, p. 565; "Nos Echos: La Propagande antisémite dans la Moselle," *UI*, Aug. 4, 1933, p. 513. The Nazis took great satisfaction in the fact that the refugee influx into Alsace was provoking an antisemitic backlash. See Report, Commissaire de Police, Forbach, to Contrôleur Général Affaires d'Alsace et Lorraine, Strasbourg, June 23, 1933, no. 1872, AN F[7] 13430.

72. *New York Herald Tribune*, Aug. 16, 1933, clipped in JDC no. 617; *NYT*, Sept. 2, 1933, p. 6.

73. Prefect, Moselle, to the president of the Council, Paris, Nov. 29, 1929,

ADBR AL 98 392 A. In Lorraine, according to Henri Lévi, the rabbi of Thionville, the campaign against foreign Jewish competition had become particularly vicious. Since 1930, the Fédération des Groupements Commerciaux de la Moselle had begun to attack the commercial activities of Polish Jews; in 1933, they extended those attacks to German refugees. According to the Paris Consistory, this campaign against the East European Jews had impelled many of them to flee to Paris. "Rapport sur l'activité du Comité Central d'Assistance aux Emigrants Juifs en 1932," ACIP B 127 (D-Oeuvres); "Thionville: Un sermon sur Roch-Hachana," *UI*, Oct., 27, 1933, pp. 193–95; "Tribune des Lecteurs," *UI*, Nov. 3, 1933, p. 218; "Mise au point," *UI*, Nov. 10, 1933, p. 253. On the continued battle of the merchants of the Moselle in 1934, see Camille Hocquard, president of the Fédération des Groupements Commerciaux de la Moselle, circular, "Les Commerçants de la Moselle protestent contre l'invasion des étrangers," *Le Journal des débats*, Jan. 24, 1934, clipped in AIU ms. 650, boîte 13 (46); "Les Commerçants détaillants de la Moselle s'inquiètent de l'invasion des concurrents étrangers," *Le Matin*, Jan. 23, 1934, clipped in AIU ms. 650, boîte 13 (46).

74. Alfred Wallach, a deputy from the Haut-Rhin, submitted a bill in 1933 to eliminate peddling from the region. Strasbourg Chamber of Commerce, "Délibération concernant l'établissement en Alsace d'industriels et de commerçants étrangers: Extrait du procès verbal de la séance du 29 juin 1933," MAE Z 710, p. 184; "L'Installation des réfugiés allemands dans les départements recouvrés," *Le Matin*, Aug. 16, 1933, pp. 1–2, clipped in ADBR D 460, paq. 5 (36); Gaëtan Sanvoisin, "Les Réfugiés allemands dans l'Est," *Le Figaro*, Aug. 17, 1933, p. 1.

75. Question 9531, *JO, Débats Parlementaires, Chambre des Députés*, Nov. 6, 1934, pp. 2254–55.

76. Mayor of Haguenau, Ville, to the prefect, Bas-Rhin, Sept. 11, 1935, ADBR D 460, paq. 12 (91).

77. On the decree laws regulating foreign artisans, see *JO, Lois et Décrets*, Aug. 9, 1935, pp. 8699–701; Livian, *Le Régime juridique*, pp. 125–30; Feblowicz and Lamour, pp. 82–86; L. Marcel, "La Situation des artisans étrangers," *Le Populaire*, Sept. 9, 1935, p. 1; Schramm and Vormeier, pp. 214–15. According to Livian, this law was based on a bill submitted by the Bas-Rhin deputy Michel Walter. See Livian, *Le Régime juridique*, p. 130; *JO, Documents Parlementaires, Chambre des Députés*, 1934, annexe no. 4148, pp. 131–32. The government also planned to levy a tax on all employers whose foreign work force constituted more than 5% of the total work force. See "Défendons les travailleurs immigrés," *L'Humanité*, Nov. 6, 1934, clipped in APP BA 1814 241.155-1-G.

78. Fernand Peter, president, Chambre des Métiers d'Alsace, to the prefect, Bas-Rhin, 4ème division, 2ème bureau, Feb. 18, 1936, ADBR D 460, paq. 7 (45).

79. E. Roblot, prefect, Bas-Rhin, to the minister of labor, Mar. 12, 1936, ADBR D 460, paq. 7 (45).

80. These groups repeatedly demanded such concessions, however. See, for example, Chamber of Commerce, Strasbourg, "Procès-verbal, séance du 16 mai 1935," ADBR D 460, paq. 12 (91); "Rapport fait au nom de la commission des finances chargée d'examiner le projet de loi portant fixation du budget général de l'exercice

1936, Services d'Alsace et de Lorraine," presented by deputy Charles de Lasteryie, Paris, *JO, Documents Parlementaires, Chambre des Députés*, section 3, 2ème session ordinaire, annexe no. 5586, June 28, 1935, pp. 1371–72; *JO, Débats Parlementaires, Chambre des Députés*, sect. 2, session ordinaire, vol. 2, 1935, pp. 1967–68.

81. "La Question des réfugiés allemands devant le Sénat," *AI*, June 8, 1933, p. 87; Agence Fournier, Service de l'après-midi [news service], May 11, 1933, p. 3, ADBR D 460, paq. 5/36.

82. "Procès verbal de la Ier séance tenue par la Commission Interministérielle des Réfugiés Allemands," May 27, 1933, MAE Z 711, pp. 93–96; Thalmann, "L'Immigration allemande," pp. 162–63.

83. President of the Council, minister of war (Direction Général des Service d'Alsace et de Lorraine), and the minister of the interior, Sûreté Nationale, to the prefects of the Bas-Rhin, the Haut Rhin, and the Moselle, July 1, 1933, in APP BA 1814 241.155-1-A; Police report, Direction de l'Administration et de la Police Générale, sous-direction des étrangers et passeports, July 25, 1933, APP BA 407^P 13.112-1; minister of the interior, circular, Aug. 3, 1933, APP BA 407^P 13.112-1. See also police report, Sept. 23, 1933, "Réunion à la Présidence du Conseil des représentants des divers départements et services intéressés [aux réfugiés allemands]," Sept. 23, 1933, APP BA 407^P 13.112-1; "L'Installation des réfugiés allemands en France et particulièrement dans les départements recouvrés," *Les Dernières nouvelles de Strasbourg*, Dec. 10, 1933, clipped in ADBR D460, paq. 5/36; Schor, *L'Opinion française et les étrangers*, p. 616.

84. Police report, "Réunion à la Présidence du Conseil des réprésentants des divers départements et services intéressés [aux réfugiés allemands]," Sept. 23, 1933, APP BA 407^P 13.112-1.

85. *JO, Lois et Décrets*, Oct. 31, 1935, pp. 11490–91; Livian, *Le Régime juridique*, pp. 135–38; Feblowicz and Lamour, p. 91. Minister of the interior, Sûreté Nationale, to the prefect of police, no. 26.389, July 20, 1935, APP BA 64 Provisoire 51343-5.

86. *JO, Lois et Décrets*, July 20, 1934, p. 7347; Schor, *L'Antisémitisme en France*, pp. 148–49; Noiriel, *Le Creuset français*, p. 285.

87. It is true, as Livian points out, that the 1927 Naturalization Law had barred naturalized citizens from holding elected office for ten years if they had not completed their military service, although it was possible to acquire an exemption from the keeper of the seals. Livian, *Le Régime juridique*, p. 194. Nevertheless, the law of July 19, 1934, was the first time the professional as opposed to political rights of naturalized foreigners had been restricted. On the law of July 19, 1934, see Livian, *Le Régime juridique*, pp. 204–5; Feblowicz and Lamour, pp. 200–204; Schor, *L'Antisémitisme en France*, p. 149; Leven, p. 11; Raymond Millet, "Visites aux étrangers de France" (V), *Le Temps*, May 22, 1938, p. 6; Millet, p. 75; Charles-August Bontemps, "Etudiants, méfiez-vous de toute xénophobie," *DdV*, no. 24 (Feb. 1935): 1–2; André Féry, "L'Etranglement des naturalisés," *DdV*, Feb. 15, 1936, pp. 1, 5; André Féry, "Chiffons de papier," *DdV*, Feb. 22, 1936, p. 5.

88. Schor, *L'Antisémitisme en France*, p. 149.

89. "L'Oeuvre du gouvernement du Front Populaire en faveur des travailleurs immigrés," *Le Populaire*, Feb. 17, 1937, clipped in APP BA 67 Provisoire.

90. Véricourt, pp. 352–53; Lafond, p. 16; Schor, *L'Antisémitisme en France*, p. 149.

91. Noiriel, *Le Creuset français*, p. 286; "La Seconde journée de grève des étudiants de Paris s'est déroulée sans violence," *Le Matin*, Feb. 3, 1935, pp. 1, 5; "Le Pourcentage des étudiants étrangers," *Le Petit Parisien*, Feb. 3, 1935, p. 5.

92. Noiriel, *Le Creuset français*, pp. 286–87; Comité Consultatif de l'enseignement supérieur (sous-commission Balthazard, Carnot, Gosset, Lépine, Rist), *Sections de Médecine et Pharmacie; Réforme des Etudes Médicales*, 1931, in AIU France V D 19 (dossier relatif à une loi Armbruster, 1931); Véricourt, p. 353; Lafond, pp. 33, 43. For greatly exaggerated figures of the number of foreigners in the medical faculties, see Sergent, "Etudiants," p. 816.

93. Comité Consultatif de l'enseignement supérieur (sous-commission Balthazard, Carnot, Gosset, Lépine, Rist), *Sections de Médecine et Pharmacie; Réforme des Etudes Médicales*, 1931, AIU France V D 19 (dossier relatif à une loi Armbruster, 1931); Véricourt, p. 353; Lafond, p. 43.

94. Schor, *L'Antisémitisme en France*, p. 151; Sylvain Lévi, president, Alliance Israélite Universelle, to the dean of the medical faculty, Paris, July 3, 1931, AIU France V D 19; Fernand Corcos, "Les Médecins étrangers en France et la question des étudiants roumains," *CDH*, July 10, 1931, pp. 447–48; Max Massot, "La Défaite du métèque par le médecin français," *Le Journal*, Apr. 22, 1938, p. 4.

95. On the 1857 treaty, see Comité Consultatif de l'enseignement supérieur (sous-commission Balthazard, Carnot, Gosset, Lépine, Rist), *Sections de Médecine et Pharmacie; Réforme des Etudes Médicales*, 1931, in AIU France V D 19 (dossier relatif à une loi Armbruster, 1931); Pécout, p. 41; Romain Roussel, "Les Causes du mécontentement des étudiants en médecine," Apr. 7, 9, 10, 1935, pp. 1–2, all in *Le Quotidien*; Max Massot, "La Défaite du métèque par le médecin français," *Le Journal*, Apr. 22, 1938, p. 4; Sergent, "Etudiants," pp. 819–20; Lafond, pp. 68–70, 102–3.

96. Corcos, "Les Médecins étrangers en France et la question des étudiants roumains," *CDH*, July 10, 1931, pp. 447–48. On the status of Romanian Jews during the interwar years, see Mendelsohn, pp. 171–211.

97. Comité Consultatif de l'enseignement supérieur (sous-commission Balthazard, Carnot, Gosset, Lépine, Rist), *Sections de Médecine et Pharmacie; Réforme des Etudes Médicales*, 1931, in AIU France V D 19 (dossier relatif à une loi Armbruster, 1931); "Les Etudiants étrangers et la question juive," *DdV*, no. 27 (June 1935): 2.

98. Roussel, "Les Causes du mécontentement des étudiants en médecine," *Le Quotidien*, Apr. 7, 1935, pp. 1–2. On the large number of Polish Jews coming to study medicine in France, see P. Chastand, French consul, Lvov, Poland, to the Foreign Ministry (Contrôle des étrangers), no. 4, Feb. 8, 1931, pp. 30–31, and no. 5, Jan. 23, 1932, pp. 102–4, both in MAE Z 433.

99. Comité Consultatif de l'enseignement supérieur (sous-commission Balthazard, Carnot, Gosset, Lépine, Rist), *Sections de Médecine et Pharmacie; Réforme des Etudes Médicales*, 1931, in AIU France V D 19 (dossier relatif à une loi Armbruster, 1931).

100. Corcos, "Les Médecins étrangers en France et la question des étudiants roumains," *CDH*, July 10, 1931, pp. 447–48.

101. As quoted in Sylvain Lévi, president, Alliance Israélite Universelle, to the dean of the medical faculty, Paris, July 31, 1931, AIU France V D 19.

102. Cited in Schor, *L'Antisémitisme en France*, p. 151. See also Sergent, "La Pléthore médicale," pp. 346–47, 355.

103. Cited in Roussel, "Les Causes du mécontentement des étudiants en médecine," *Le Quotidien*, Apr. 11, 1935, pp. 1–2. For other similar statements, see Véricourt, pp. 353–54; remarks of Dr. Bosc, cited in "L'Agitation antisémite au Quartier Latin," *L'Ere nouvelle*, Apr. 3, 1935, clipped in APP BA 1812 79-501-882-D.

104. Pécout, "Introduction."

105. Cited in Nicolas Lerouge, "Propos Ingenus: Xénophagie," *La République*, Mar. 27, 1935, p. 1. See also "Les Etudiants étrangers et la question juive," *DdV*, no. 27 (June 1935): 2.

106. Pécout, p. 45; Mordagne, pp. 2453–55; Jean d'Alsace, "Veut-on réglementer ou veut-on prohiber l'exercice de la médecine par les étrangers?" *La Lumière*, June 29, 1935, p. 4; Roussel, "Les Causes du mécontentement des étudiants en médecine," *Le Quotidien*, Apr. 10, 1935, pp. 1–2.

107. Dr. Leblond, "La Communauté interraciale," *Esprit*, Apr. 1, 1935, pp. 148–50; "Ceux qu'on appelle métèques," *Esprit*, May 2, 1935, pp. 325–26; Nicolas Lerouge, "Des places de médecin? En voici!," *La République*, Apr. 6, 1935, p. 1; B. de B., "La France n'a pas assez de médecins," *La République*, Dec. 25, 1935, p. 5; "Les Xénophobes contre la France," *La Lumière*, May 11, 1935, p. 3; Delcourt-Haillot, "La Pléthore médicale," *L'Aube*, Aug. 3, 1935, pp. 1–2; "Les Campagnes réclament des médecins suppléants," *L'Oeuvre*, Sept. 16, 1935, p. 2; Georges Limoux, "Futurs pionniers...ou chômeurs de demain: (VIII) Le 'Péril métèque,'" *Le Populaire*, Dec. 25, 1935, pp. 1, 2. On pro-protectionist forces who admitted the existence of this shortage, see Véricourt, pp. 355–56; "Un Problème angoissant pour les jeunes français," *Le Matin*, Dec. 20, 1933, pp. 1, 2; Sergent, "La Pléthore médicale," p. 347.

108. Dr. A. Vincent, "Il n'y a pas pléthore médicale," *Esprit*, Apr. 1, 1935, pp. 52–53; Sauvy, 2: 137; Berstein, *La France*, p. 47.

109. Schor, *L'Opinion française et les étrangers*, pp. 607–8; Schor, *L'Antisémitisme en France*, p. 151; J.-Ch. Bonnet, p. 218; Véricourt, p. 351; Jean d'Alsace, "Veut-on réglementer ou veut-on prohiber l'exercice de la médecine par les étrangers?" *La Lumière*, June 29, 1935, p. 4.

110. Lengyel, pp. 9–10.

111. Mordagne, pp. 2453–54; "Les Etudiants sont rentrés," *Le Petit Parisien*, Feb. 5, 1935, p. 5; Claude Martial, "Le Médecin naturalisé français qui n'a que le droit d'être soldat," *L'Oeuvre*, Apr. 28, 1933, pp. 1–2; Jean d'Alsace, "Veut-on réglementer ou veut-on prohiber l'exercice de la médecine par les étrangers?" *La Lumière*, June 29, 1935, p. 4.

112. Mordagne, p. 2453. De Monzie served as minister of education from June 3, 1932, until Jan. 30, 1934.

113. For a summary of these bills, see Roussel, "Les Causes du mécontentement des étudiants en médecine," *Le Quotidien*, Apr. 15, 1935, p. 2; Jean d'Alsace, "Veut-on réglementer ou veut-on prohiber l'exercice de la médecine par les étrangers?" *La Lumière*, June 29, 1935, p. 4. See also "La Pléthore des diplômes et le problème des étu-

diants étrangers évoqués à la Chambre," *L'Aube*, Feb. 23, 1935, p. 3; "Les Interpella-tions," *Le Quotidien*, Feb. 23, 1935, p. 3. For the protests of the League for the Rights of Man against these proposals, see *CDH*, Aug. 10, 1935, p. 569; "Bulletin de la Ligue des Droits de l'Homme: Nos Interventions," *CDH*, Feb. 20, 1935, pp. 111–12.

114. Huguette Godin, "Les Manifestations s'apaisent au Quartier Latin," *Le Quotidien*, Feb. 3, 1935, pp. 1, 3; "Les Etudiants en médecine de plusieurs facultés de province ont fait grève hier pour protester contre l'intrusion en France des étrangers dans les professions libérales," *Le Matin*, Feb. 1, 1935, pp. 1, 3; "La Situation des étu-diants étrangers," *Le Matin*, Feb. 16, 1935, p. 2.

115. "Echos: Les Incidents du Quartier,'" *Le Journal juif*, no. 14 (Apr. 5, 1935): 1; Schor, *L'Opinion française et les étrangers*, p. 608; Noiriel, *Le Creuset français*, p. 287.

116. "La Grève des étudiants en médecine," *Le Matin*, Mar. 31, 1935, p. 6; "Une Manifestation au Quartier Latin," *Le Figaro*, Mar. 30, 1935, p. 4; "Les Etudiants en médecine recommencent leurs protestations," *L'Oeuvre*, Mar. 30, 1935, p. 2; Claude Martial, "La Grève est fini," *L'Oeuvre*, Mar. 31, 1935, pp. 1, 2; "Trop de médecins étrangers s'installent en France," *L'Aube*, Apr. 1, 1935, p. 1.

117. Claude Martial, "Les étudiants en droit vont-ils s'en mêler?," *L'Oeuvre*, Apr. 4, 1935, p. 2; "L'Agitation antisémite au Quartier Latin," *L'Ere nouvelle*, Apr. 3, 1935, clipped in APP BA 1812 79-501-882-D.

118. Nicolas Lerouge, "Propos ingenus: Xénophagie," *La République*, Mar. 27, 1935, p. 1. See also Sergent, "Etudiants," p. 819. On several occasions, native French medical students even went out of their way to exempt West Europeans, and espe-cially Belgians, from their protests, referring to them as their "veritable compatri-ots." Huguette Godin, "Les Manifestations s'apaisent au Quartier Latin," *Le Quoti-dien*, Feb. 3, 1935, pp. 1, 3; Roussel, "Les Causes du mécontentement des étudiants en médecine," *Le Quotidien*, Apr. 11, 1935, pp. 1–2; "Les Etudiants étrangers et la question juive," *DdV*, no. 27 (June 1935): 2; Claude Martial, "Les Etudiants en médecine recommencent leurs protestations," Mar. 30, 1935, p. 2; C. Martial, "La Grève est finie," Mar. 31, 1935, pp. 1–2; C. Martial, "Les Etudiants en droit vont-ils s'en mêler?" Apr. 4, 1935, p. 2, all in *L'Oeuvre*.

119. E. Buré, "La Protestation des étudiants en médecine et ses causes pro-fondes," *L'Ordre*, Feb. 2, 1935, p. 1. On the strike, see also Schor, *L'Antisémitisme en France*, pp. 151–52; Noiriel, *Le Creuset français*, p. 287; J.-Ch. Bonnet, p. 219; Huguette Godin, "Le Mouvement gréviste des étudiants en médecine," *Le Quoti-dien*, Feb. 2, 1935, pp. 1, 3; "Un peu de fièvre au Quartier Latin," *Le Petit Parisien*, Feb. 2, 1935, pp. 1, 5; "La Grève de protestation des étudiants en médecine," Feb. 1, 1935, p. 3, and "Les Manifestations des étudiants parisiens," both in *Le Journal*, Feb. 2, 1935, p. 3; "Les Etudiants en grève tiennent un grand meeting en fin d'après-midi," *Paris-Soir*, Feb. 3, 1935, pp. 1, 7; "La Grève des étudiants est terminée," *L'Aube*, Feb. 3–4, pp. 1, 2; *Le Petit Parisien*, Feb. 2, 1935, p. 1; "French Students Strike in Protest on Foreigners," February 1, 1935, p. 44; "French Students Riot: Protest Against Foreigners in Paris Medical and Technical Schools," Feb. 2, 1935, p. 4; "Anti-Foreign Drive Dropped in Paris," Feb. 3, 1935, p. 9, all in *NYT*; various articles in *Le Temps* between Feb. 1, 1935, and Feb. 6, 1935; "Après les étudiants en médecine,

les étudiants en droit s'élèvent contre les facilités accordées aux étrangers," *Le Matin*, Apr. 3, 1935, p. 5.

120. According to a Ministry of the Interior report, as a result of both the Armbruster and Nast Laws, many Polish Jews who had received their medical degrees in France began to return to Poland. A special committee was even set up in Mar. 1934 to help them return and establish careers in Poland. Minister of the interior, Sûreté Nationale, to the Foreign Ministry, "a/s du Comité de l'Association Centrale des Diplômes Polonais," June 8, 1935, MAE Z 434 (Polonais en France), p. 209. The German émigré paper, the *Pariser Tageblatt* (*PT*), also noted that many foreign Jewish medical students were returning to Eastern Europe. "Auslandisches Studenten wollen Paris verlassen," *PT*, Apr. 3, 1935, p. 3.

121. Sergent, "Etudiants," pp. 819–20. According to Sergent, the 1857 agreement was modified so that "le nombre annuel des diplômes donnant le droit d'exercer la médecine en France, ne dépasserait pas le maximum du nombre des diplômes qui avaient été decernés, dans une même année, avant 1914, maximum évalué à 10." See also Pécout, p. 41.

122. On the Nast Law, see Schor, *L'Opinion française et les étrangers*, pp. 609–10; Livian, *Le Régime juridique*, pp. 140–45, 205; Feblowicz and Lamour, pp. 208–9; J.-Ch. Bonnet, p. 219; Pécout, p. 51; Lcvcn, p. 11; Max Massot, "La Défaite du métèque par le médecin français," *Le Journal*, Apr. 22, 1938, p. 4; Jean d'Alsace, "Veut-on réglementer ou veut-on prohiber l'exercice de la médecine par les étrangers?" *La Lumière*, June 29, 1935, p. 4; Delcourt-Haillot, "Le Pléthore médicale," *L'Aube*, Aug. 3, 1935, pp. 1–2.

123. Fouques-Duparc, "Note, a/s réfugiés allemands, Visite de M. Mantoux," Sept. 6, 1933, MAE SDN I E 447 (Allemagne: Minorités juives), pp. 89–93.

124. Foreign Ministry (Europe), "Note," July 21, 1933, MAE Z 710, pp. 211–15 (also in SDN I E 447 [Allemagne: Minorités juives, 73rd Session du Conseil...], pp. 55–59).

125. Foreign Ministry, Direction Europe: "Note a/s israélites allemands," July 20, 1933, MAE Z 710, pp. 206–7. See also Foreign Ministry (Europe), "Note a/s israélites allemands," Sept. 5, 1933, MAE Z 710, pp. 267–68. For other diplomatic reports on the worsening situation of German Jewry during the summer and fall of 1933, see J. Dobler to the Foreign Ministry (Europe), no. 59, July 8, 1933, MAE Z 710, pp. 178–81; MAE (Europe), "Note," July 18, 1933, MAE Z 710, pp. 196–97; Foreign Ministry (Europe), "Note," July 21, 1933, MAE Z 710, pp. 211–15; Bargeton, Foreign Ministry (Europe), to Roger Cambon, chargé d'affaires, London, Sept. 8, 1933, MAE Z 710, pp. 280–85; R. Cambon to the British Foreign Office, Sept. 14, 1933, PRO FO 371/16757. C8149, pp. 11–14; P. Arnal, chargé d'affaires de France, Berlin, to J. Paul-Boncour, foreign minister, no. 1059, Sept. 27, 1933, MAE SDN I E 447.

126. "Procès verbal de la 2ème séance tenue par la Commission Interministérielle des Réfugiés Israélites Allemands," MAE Z 711, Oct. 16, 1933, MAE Z 711, p. 41.

127. Timothy Maga has argued that when Chautemps replaced Daladier as

prime minister in Oct. 1933, he restored a liberal refugee regime that, according to Maga, remained in place for the next five years until Daladier returned as prime minister. There is no basis whatsoever for this claim. See Maga, "Closing," p. 431.

128. Foreign Ministry (Europe), "Note," July 18, 1933, MAE Z 710, pp. 196–97.

129. Foreign Ministry (Europe), "Note," July 18, 1933, MAE Z 710, pp. 196–97; Foreign Ministry (Europe), "Note," July 21, 1933, MAE Z 710, pp. 211–15; Foreign Ministry (Contrôle des étrangers), "Note pour la sous-direction d'Europe," Aug. 12, 1933, MAE Z 710, p. 231; Foreign Ministry (Contrôle des étrangers), to consulates in Vienna, Prague, Copenhagen, The Hague, Luxembourg, and Berne, Aug. 14, 1933, MAE Z 710, pp. 236–37.

130. Report, Sûreté Générale, Oct. 3, 1933, AN F[7] 13431 (also in APP BA 1814 241.155-1-A; MAE Z 710, pp. 110, 210, 229). See also "Procès verbal de la 2ème séance tenue par la Commission Interministérielle des Réfugiés Israélites Allemands," Oct. 16, 1933, MAE Z 711, pp. 37–42.

131. Ministry of the Interior, Sûreté Nationale, circular, Aug. 2, 1933, no. R 5, ADBR D 460, paq. 5 (36) (also in MAE Z 710, p. 234 and APP BA 407[P] 13.112-1]; Schor, *L'Opinion française et les étrangers*, p. 616. See also Police Report, Nov. 10, 1933, "Renseignements concernant les réfugiés d'Allemagne," n.d. (Nov. or Dec. 1933), APP BA 407[P] 13.112-1 (also in APP BA 1814 241.155-1-A); "Aide-Mémoire a/s réfugiés allemands en France," Nov. 22, 1933, MAE SDN I E 448, pp. 76–84; Police Report, "Résumé des instructions ministérielles concernant les réfugiés d'Allemagne," Nov. 27, 1933, APP BA 407[P] 13.112-1.

132. Foreign Ministry (Contrôle des étrangers), to Consulates in Berlin, Munich, Vienna, Prague, Copenhagen, The Hague, Brussels, Luxembourg, Berne, Aug. 8, 1933, MAE Z 710, p. 233.

133. Foreign Ministry (Contrôle des étrangers), to the minister of the interior, Sûreté Nationale, Oct. 19, 1933, AN F[7] 13431. See also Police report, "Résumé des instructions ministérielles concernant les réfugiés d'Allemagne," Nov. 27, 1933, APP BA 407[P] 13.112-1; Police report, "Renseignements concernant les réfugiés d'Allemagne," Nov. 10, 1933, APP BA 407[P] 13.112-1; "Aide-Mémoire a/s réfugiés allemands en France," Nov. 22, 1933, MAE SDN I E 448, pp. 76–84; Schramm and Vormeier, p. 201. For the Foreign Ministry's response to Victor Basch, see Foreign Ministry (Contrôle des étrangers), to Victor Basch, president, Ligue des Droits de l'Homme, Nov. 20, 1933, MAE Z 711, pp. 84–86; "Comité Central, Extraits, Séance du 21 décembre 1933," *CDH*, Jan. 30, 1934, pp. 65–66.

134. "Procès-verbal de la 3ème séance tenue par la Commission Interministérielle des Réfugiés Allemands," Oct. 23, 1933, MAE Z 711, pp. 70–74; Blanchet, Foreign Ministry (Contrôle des étrangers), to French diplomatic agents in Europe, confidential memo, "a/s réfugiés d'Allemagne," Dec. 22, 1933, MAE Z 711, pp. 152–56.

135. Of the German Jewish population, which numbered about 500,000 in 1933, there were 98,787 Jews of foreign origin. The majority of these, some 56,480, were Polish. Bauer, *My Brother's Keeper*, p. 244. According to statistics compiled by the Comité National (Germany Emergency Relief, "Summary of Income and Expenditure of Organizations Occupied in Refugee Work Subsidized by the AJDC During

1933 and Jan.–June 1934," JDC no. 181.), the breakdown of the refugees according to citizenship was as follows (the first figure refers to the period up to Dec. 31, 1933, the second to the period Jan. 1–June 1, 1934):

German citizens	5,279	894
Polish citizens	3,332	717
Stateless persons	2,067	647
Others	563	26
Total	11,241	2,284

According to Ministry of the Interior, Sûreté Nationale, circular no. 40 of Apr. 1, 1933, if France were to accept these "non-Allemands sans ressources et sans papiers…il ne sera plus possible par la suite de [les] refouler vers l'Allemagne." ADBR D 460, paq. 5 (36). Also, at the first meeting of the Interministerial Commission on German Refugees held in the spring of 1933, Guy La Chambre, the undersecretary of state for the president of the council, noted that "de nombreux israélites polonais qui s'étaient fixés en Allemagne sont entrés en Alsace par la Sarre; il y aurait lieu de s'entendre avec la Pologne pour permettre leur rapatriement." "Procès verbal de la Ier séance tenue par la Commission Interministérielle des Réfugiés Allemands," May 27, 1933, MAE Z 711, p. 94. With regard to refugees with Nansen passports, see minister of the interior, Sûreté Générale, to the prefect, Bas-Rhin, June 22, 1933, ADBR D 460, paq. 5/36; Ministry of Foreign Affairs (Europe), "Note," July 18, 1933, MAE Z 710, pp. 196–97; Foreign Ministry (Europe), to the president of the League for the Rights of Man and Citizen, Sept. 7, 1934, MAE Z 434, p. 56.

On the basis of figures supplied by the Comité National, a police report of June 30, 1933, claimed that of the 4,900 refugees who had arrived in Paris as of Mar. 1933, 50% were German Jews, 40% Poles, and 10% stateless. The same report noted: "Suivant les dernières instructions reçues, les soi-disant réfugiés israélites polonais font l'objet d'une mesure de refoulement lorsque leurs passeports n'ont pas été visés par les autorités françaises en Allemagne." APP BA 1814 241.155-1-A. In late 1934, Bernhard Kahn, the European director of the JDC, estimated the proportion of East European Jews among the refugees at 60%. Kahn to Baerwald, Nov. 6, 1934, JDC no. 601. According to the HCR, of the 60,000 Jews who fled Germany by the end of 1933, 16,520, or 28%, were non-German citizens, mostly Poles and stateless persons. "60,000 have fled from Nazis Reich," *NYT*, Dec. 6, 1933, p. 18.

136. Of a total of 5,600 Polish and stateless Jews in France as of Dec. 1933, it is estimated that only 1,190, or 21%, were born in Poland. M. Kramarz, "Les Juifs polonais réfugiés d'Allemagne," *UI*, Dec. 29, 1933, p. 477.

137. According to Bernhard Kahn, an additional reason for France's wariness with respect to allowing refugees with East European passports to work was that according to the terms of reciprocal treaties France held with several East European nations, these refugees would become eligible for unemployment insurance after six months on the job. Bernhard Kahn to M. Stephany, Central British Fund for German Jewry, London, July 25, 1935, JDC no. 602 (France, "Organisations"). French Jewish organizations fully accepted this policy of repatriating Jewish refugees of East European origin. As a JDC official noted: "Repatriation, especially of those with

Polish passports, is regarded in the present circumstances as desirable." Joseph L. Cohen, "Report on Hicem and the French National Committee for German Refugees," Aug. 8, 1933, JDC no. 617. See also M. Moch, "Projet d'organisation pour l'accueil et l'établissement des juifs allemands en France," May 26, 1933, AIU ms. 650, boîte 12 (44), and "Résolution" [taken by Jewish refugee committees], [spring 1933], LBI, AR-C 1698/4099.

138. Blanchet, Foreign Ministry (Europe), "Note pour la sous-direction des Chancelleries et du Contentieux, a/s naturalisation des étrangers d'origine polonaise," Mar. 21, 1931, MAE Z 433 (Polonais en France), pp. 36–37 (also in MAE Z 330 [Religion israélite. Immigration de juifs polonais dans les colonies françaises...], pp. 30–31). For other negative assessments of East European Jews by French officials, see Police report, Oct. 24, 1933, APP BA 1814 241.155-1-A; A. Mallet, Contrôleur Général, Sûreté Nationale, Strasbourg, to the director of the Sûreté Nationale, Cabinet, Paris, May 24, 1933, ADBR D 460, paq. 5/36; Laroche, French ambassador, Poland, to the Foreign Ministry (Europe), no. 34, May 15, 1934, MAE Z 433, p. 234; Laroche, to the Foreign Ministry, no. 353, May 15, 1934, MAE Z 330, pp. 78–83; Laroche to the Foreign Ministry, Aug. 13, 1934, MAE Z 434, pp. 16–22. In these reports, Laroche claims that the Polish government has made "des efforts très méritoires...pour améliorer la situation des israélites dans ce pays" and that those Jews who claimed to have been persecuted in Germany had been persecuted not as Jews, but as left-wing dissidents who had sought to foment a communist revolution at the time of the Russo-Polish war. The minister of labor also perceived these Jews as military defectors rather than refugees. See minister of labor, to the Foreign Ministry, Sept. 2, 1933, MAE Z 433, pp. 186–87. For a further discussion of this hostility, see Chapter 4.

139. On the protest of the Polish embassy in France, see Foreign Ministry (Contrôle des étrangers) to the Polish ambassador in France, Dec. 7, 1933, MAE Z 711, pp. 126–27. The Polish Consul in Strasbourg similarly protested as early as May of 1933. Commissaire Spécial des Ponts du Rhin et du Port de Strasbourg, to the prefect, Bas-Rhin, May 2, 1933, ADBR D 460, paq. 5/36. On McDonald's protest in Apr. 1934, see "McDonald in Poland on Refugee Problem," *NYT*, Apr. 19, 1934, p. 19. On the Comité National's intervention, see minister of labor, to the Foreign Ministry, Sept. 2, 1933, MAE Z 433, pp. 186–87. On the intervention of the League for the Rights of Man and Citizen, see Basch, to the foreign minister, Mar. 10, 1934, MAE Z 433, p. 192. See also Foreign Ministry, to Basch, Apr. 21, 1933, p. 203; League for the Rights of Man, to the Foreign Ministry, June 30, 1934, p. 258; League for the Rights of Man, to the Foreign Ministry, July 27, 1934, p. 271; and Foreign Ministry (Europe), "Note," Aug. 13, 1934, pp. 24, 54, all in MAE Z 434. The League for the Rights of Man and Citizen ultimately asked the Polish government to grant an amnesty to Polish Jewish refugees from Germany who were being expelled from France so that they could return to Poland. Basch, to the president of the Council of Ministers of the Polish Republic, Aug. 22, 1933, MAE Z 433, p. 193. In Sept. 1934, the French Foreign Ministry, for the final time, informed the League for the Rights of Man and Citizen that East European Jews would not be eligible for special refugee status. Foreign Ministry (Europe), to the president of the League for the Rights of Man, Sept. 7, 1934, MAE Z 434, p. 56.

140. J. Biélinky, "La Situation des 'Ostjuden' réfugiés en France," *UI*, Oct. 27, 1933, pp. 186–87. See also J. Biélinky, "Une réunion de réfugiés polonais," *UI*, Nov. 10, 1933, p. 257; Foreign Ministry (Contrôle des étrangers), to the Foreign Ministry (Europe), Sept. 11, 1933, MAE Z 710, p. 275; Police report, Oct. 1933, APP BA 1813 241.155-B; Comité pour la Défense, especially p. 8; Comité pour la Défense, "Memorandum sur la situation économique des israélites en Pologne," sent to the Foreign Ministry, Apr. 6, 1934, MAE Z 330, pp. 70–75; *Pariser Haynt* (trans. into French), Oct. 26, 1933, ACIP B127 (extracts, Yiddish press).

141. Dobler, to the Foreign Ministry (Europe), no. 38, Apr. 27, 1933, pp. 80–84. See also Dobler, to the Foreign Ministry (Europe), teleg. no. 34, May 12, 1933, p. 110; Dobler, to the Foreign Ministry, May 14, 1933, pp. 112–20; Dobler, to the Foreign Ministry (Contrôle des étrangers), no. 63, June 7, 1933, pp. 149–51, all in MAE Z 710.

142. Foreign Ministry, (Contrôle des étrangers), to Binet, French Consul, [Munich], June 6, 1933, p. 148; Foreign Ministry (Contrôle des étrangers), "Note pour le Directeur des Affaires Politiques et Commerciales," July 13, 1933, p. 193, both in MAE Z 710.

143. M. V., Police report, "Note de Cologne," [Nov. or Dec. 1933], APP BA 407[P] 13.112-1 (also in APP BA 1814 241.155-1-A [Réfugiés Allemands, Chiappe]); Foreign Ministry, "Note pour M. Blanchet," Dec. 18, 1933, MAE Z 711, pp. 142–48; Blanchet, Foreign Ministry (Contrôle des étrangers), to French diplomatic agents in Europe, Confidential, "a/s réfugiés d'Allemagne," Dec. 22, 1933, MAE Z 711, pp. 152–56.

144. For reports on the worsening situation for German Jews, see Dobler, to the Foreign Ministry (Europe), no. 59, July 8, 1933, MAE Z 710, pp. 178–81; Foreign Ministry (Europe), "Note," July 21, 1933, MAE Z 710, pp. 211–15; Cambon, to the British Foreign Office, Sept. 14, 1933, PRO FO 371/16757.C8149, pp. 11–14; Cambon, to the Foreign Ministry (Europe), Sept. 17, 1933, MAE SDN I E 447, pp. 109–10; P. Arnal, French chargé d'affaires, Berlin, to the Foreign Ministry (Europe), no. 1059, Sept. 27, 1933, MAE SDN I E 447.

145. These conditions were first laid down in Feb. 1934. See F. Leroy, prefect, Haut-Rhin, to the minister of the interior, Feb. 21, 1934, ADBR AL 98 397 B. See also M. Telie, Gérant, French consul, Frankfurt a/M, to the Foreign Ministry, May 26, 1934, and M. Prochte, Commissaire Spécial, St. Louis, Report on Georges Sobernheim, May 16, 1934, both in ADBR AL 98 393; F. Leroy, prefect, Haut-Rhin, to the Ministry of the Interior, Sûreté Nationale, "a/s Hans Schiffmann," Oct. 22, 1934, and F. Leroy, prefect, Haut-Rhin, to the Ministry of the Interior, Sûreté Nationale, "a/s George Lindemann," July 18, 1934, both in ADBR AL 98 393; Leroy, to the minister of the interior, Sûreté Nationale, "a/s Leon Aronssohn," Aug. 4, 1934, Leroy, to the minister of the interior, Sûreté Nationale, "a/s Charlotte Manasse," Aug. 4, 1934, Leroy, to the minister of the interior, Sûreté Nationale, "a/s Rose Samson," Feb. 21, 1934, and Leroy, to the minister of the interior, Sûreté Nationale, "a/s Moïse Feller," Mar. 22, 1934, all in ADBR AL 98 397 B.

In a major report on the status of refugees in France, the minister of the interior reiterated this point: "Il [the foreign minister] accorde, semble-t-il la qualité de réfugié politique au seul étranger qui a été victime de violences matérielles, à l'exception de celui qui a quitté son pays dans la crainte de dangers éventuels." Minister of the interior, to the president, Commission des Affaires Etrangères de la Chambre des Députés, Nov. 1935, MAE SDN I M (Questions Sociales) 1806 (Office Nansen), p. 190.

146. G. Oudara, Directeur Commissaire spécial de Police (Renseignements Généraux), to the prefect of police, Paris, Oct. 9, 1933, APP BA 1814 241.155-1-A. See also Oudara, to the prefect of police, "a/s des étrangers se disant réfugiés d'Allemagne," Oct. 21, 1933, APP BA 1814 241.155-1-A; A. Mallet, Contrôleur Général, Strasbourg, to the director, Sûreté Nationale, Paris, May 24, 1933, ADBR D 460, paq. 5/36.

147. Police report, "Direction de l'Administration et de la Police Générale, sous-direction des étrangers et passeports," Nov. 10, 1933, APP BA 1814 241-155-1-A. See also G. Oudara, Directeur Commissaire spécial de Police (Renseignements Généraux), to the prefect of police, Paris, Oct. 9, 1933, and Oudara, to the prefect of police, "a/s des étrangers se disant réfugiés d'Allemagne," Oct. 21, 1933, both in APP BA 1814 241.155-1-A; P. Roland-Marcel, prefect, Bas-Rhin, to the Contrôleur Général, Chargé des Services Généraux de Police d'Alsace et de Lorraine à Strasbourg, Aug. 8, 1933, ADBR D 460, paq. 5/36.

148. On the Bernheim Affair, see Marrus, *Unwanted*, p. 160; Simpson, *Refugee Problem*, pp. 214–15; Dawidowicz, p. 246 n.

149. For France's outspoken condemnations of Nazi antisemitism and its initial desire to see the Minority Rights Treaties imposed on Germany, see Foreign Ministry (Europe), "Note pour la Direction des Affaires Politiques et Commerciales," Mar. 29, 1932 [sic, 1933], p. 49; Jacques Fouques-Duparc, "Note, a/s le traitement des juifs par l'Allemagne et la protection des minorités," Apr. 1, 1933, pp. 11–19; Fouques-Duparc, "Note pour le Ministre," Apr. 5, 1933, pp. 29–31; Foreign Ministry (SDN), "Note a/s position de la France dans le débat sur la question juive en Allemagne," May 21, 1933, pp. 216–19; Foreign Ministry (SDN), "Mémoire," May 26, 1933, , pp. 220–22; Massigli, Foreign Ministry (SDN), to the Foreign Ministry, teleg. no. 698, May 27, 1933, p. 172; Foreign Ministry (SDN), "Question I: Pétition Bernheim," May 27, 1933, pp. 177–78; Massigli, Foreign Ministry (SDN), to the Foreign Ministry, teleg. no. 721, May 30, 1933; Société des Nations, "Soixante-treizième session du Conseil," Procès verbal, 6ème séance, May 30, 1933, pp. 207–10, all in MAE SDN I E 446. Foreign Ministry (SDN), "a/s 73ème Session du Conseil, Note pour le représentant de la France," June 3, 1933, p. 8; Foreign Ministry (SDN), "Note pour le Ministre des affaires étrangères," June 3, 1933, p. 7; Massigli, to the Foreign Ministry, June 13, 1933, pp. 39–42; Massigli, to the Foreign Ministry, June 13, 1933, pp. 42–45; Paul-Boncour, to Léon Blum, June 15, 1933, p. 47; Fouques-Duparc, "Note, a/s réfugiés allemands, visite de M. Mantoux," Sept. 6, 1933, pp. 89–93, all in MAE SDN I E 447; "League Will Hear Jews on Oppression by Nazis," *NYT*, May 21, 1933, p. 1; "Au Conseil de la Société des Nations," *Le Temps*, May 31, 1933; "Germany Rejects Report to League that Her Laws Violate Silesian Treaty," *NYT*, May 31, 1933, pp. 1, 8; "La Situation des Juifs allemands devant la Société des Nations," *AI*, June 8, 1933, p. 89.

150. Massigli, to the Foreign Ministry, teleg. no. 848, Oct. 3, 1933, MAE SDN I E 447, pp. 175–76; Société des Nations, "Quatorzième session ordinaire de l'assemblée, Sixième Commission, Procès verbal provisoire de la 5ème séance tenue le mardi 3 octobre 1933," Foreign Ministry, SDN I E 447, pp. 204–5; "Recommandation adoptée par le Comité de la 6ème commission," [Oct. 1933], MAE SDN I E 447, p. 114; "Reich Bars Jews in Minority Pact," Oct. 4, 1933, p. 16, "Briton Denounces Nazi Racial Views at Geneva Session," Oct. 5, 1933, pp. 1, 13, "France Stiffens Plan on Minorities," Oct. 6, 1933, p. 12, "Bérenger on Minorities," Oct. 6, 1933, p. 12, all in *NYT*; "Les Persécutions des Juifs en Allemagne sont évoquées devant la SDN," Oct. 4, 1933, p. 3, "M. Henry Bérenger [déclare] au nom de la France le droit des juifs persécutés en L'Allemagne," Oct. 6, 1933, p. 3, both in *Le Populaire*; "La Question juive a été posée devant l'assemblée de Genève," Oct. 4, 1933, p. 3, "Le Problème juif devant l'Assemblée de Genève," Oct. 6, 1933, p. 3, both in *L'Oeuvre*; "A l'Assemblée de la SDN," Oct. 4, 1933, p. 8, "Les Minorités ethniques et la question juive," Oct. 6, 1933, p. 8, both in *Le Temps*; "Le Débat sur la question des minorités à Genève," *L'Ordre*, Oct. 6, 1933, p. 1; "Juifs d'Allemagne et Minorités," *L'Humanité*, Oct. 6, 1933, p. 3; "Un Grand débat sur la question juive à la Société des Nations," Oct. 13, 1933, *UI*, pp. 120–22; "Israël devant la SDN," *Cahiers juifs*, no. 7 (Jan. 1934), pp. 72–75. In his speech, as reported by the *NYT*, Bérenger declared:

Are the Jews a minority or are they not a minority is the question that has been argued. I believe the Jews themselves do not agree on the answer. If you ask French Jews you will find hardly any to declare themselves a minority. They call themselves French citizens like the others. I am as convinced as Dr. von Keller [the head of the German delegation to the League] that if a few years ago one had put the same question to the German Jews, they would not have wished to call themselves anything but Germans. . . .

Had it been otherwise, it is only too clear that in 1919 the Jewish delegation that drew up the first draft text to inspire the peace conference in establishing minority treaties would have asked this protection for German Jews, which they did not ask because it seemed to them unnecessary and anachronistic. They felt they were assimilated and assured of their situation by the tradition of a century of liberalism.

But no matter how true these facts are, we must also admit the idea admitted by all others that, in the modern sense, there is a minority as soon as there is a legal discrimination. A Jewish minority could not have existed as such in Germany, but this minority is created when discriminations are made against German Jews. There is an unescapable dilemma for us all, and once we are in it you should understand that we cannot in the debate which you yourselves have raised fail to accord the Jewish minority some sentiments of human solidarity and justice that you ask in favor of other national minorities outside Germany. . . .

You have done us the pleasure, Honorable Delegate of Germany, of invoking here the name of Aristide Briand, and I feel I am continuing here his tradition. . . . That is why, in the name of the French Republic, inheritors of the principles of the revolution that proclaimed the rights of man and of citizens without distinction of race, religion or origin, the French delegation moves this resolution.

Jewish organizations effusively thanked Bérenger for his tough stand at the League. See "Nos Echos: L'Alliance remercie M. Henry Bérenger," Oct. 20, 1933, "France: Une lettre du Comité des délégations juives," Nov. 17, 1933, pp. 287–88, both in *UI*; *Le Temps*, Oct. 11, 1933, p. 3. For a good summary of France's position through Oct. 1933, see Foreign Ministry, "Note pour le Ministre, a/s le rôle de la France dans les discussions relatives aux problèmes allemands devant la dernière Assemblée," Nov. 6, 1933, MAE SDN I E 448, pp. 48–52.

151. Schramm and Vormeier, p. 227; "Daladier Delays Answer to Hitler," Oct. 16, 1933, *NYT*, p. 3.

152. Foreign Ministry, to French diplomatic personnel in Rio de Janeiro, Ottawa, Santiago, Lima, Addis Ababa, Cairo, Tehran, and Peking, Urgent Telegram, May 22, 1933, MAE Z 710, pp. 126–27 (also in MAE SDN I E 446, pp. 148–49); Thalmann, "L'Immigration allemande," pp. 164–65. For the responses, which came in late May and June, see MAE SDN I E 451 (Allemagne: Minorités juives, réfugiés allemands).

153. Edouard Daladier, Président du Conseil, to the Foreign Ministry, Aug. 24, 1933, MAE SDN I E 447, p. 80; Jacques Fouques-Duparc, "Note," Aug. 30, 1933, MAE Z 710, pp. 256–58 (also in MAE SDN I E 447, pp. 83–86).

154. Foreign Ministry (SDN), "Note, a/s la question juive en Allemagne devant les Commissions de l'Assemblée," Oct. 1, 1933, MAE SDN I E 447, pp. 161–71.

155. R. Cambon, French chargé d'affaires, London, to the British Foreign Office, Sept. 14, 1933, PRO FO 371/16757. C8149, pp. 11–14; Cambon, to the Foreign Ministry, Sept. 17, 1933, MAE SDN I E 447, pp. 109–10; Foreign Ministry (SDN), "Note, a/s la question juive en Allemagne devant les Commissions de l'Assemblée," Oct. 1, 1933, MAE SDN I E 447, pp. 161–71.

156. J. V. Perowne, to Cambon, Sept. 18, 1933, PRO FO 371/16757.C8149, pp. 7–9.

157. "Procès-verbal de la 3ème séance tenue par la Commission Interministérielle des Réfugiés Allemands," Oct. 23, 1933, MAE Z 711, pp. 72–73.

158. Jacques Fouques-Duparc, Foreign Ministry (SDN), "Note," Aug. 24, 1933, MAE Z 710, pp. 249–53 (also in MAE SDN I E 447, pp. 77–79); Fouques-Duparc, "Note," Aug. 30, 1933, MAE Z 710, pp. 256–58 (also in MAE SDN I E 447, pp. 83–86); Foreign Ministry (SDN), "Note," Sept. 20, 1933, MAE Z 710, pp. 288–89 (also in MAE SDN I E 447, pp. 111–12); Massigli, to the Foreign Ministry, teleg. no. 808–10, Sept. 29, 1933, MAE Z 710, pp. 289–91 (also in MAE SDN I E 447, p. 146); Foreign Ministry (SDN), "Note, a/s la question juive en Allemagne devant les Commissions de l'Assemblée," Oct. 1, 1933, MAE SDN I E 447, pp. 161–71; Fouques-Duparc, Foreign Ministry (SDN), Confidential Report, "La Question des étrangers et des réfugiés et la SDN," Apr. 2, 1935, MAE SDN I M 1806, pp. 19–23; Report, "Chief Points of Interviews A. W. [André Wurfbain] Had in Paris on May 15, 1935," May 16, 1935, MP: HP 4.

159. [Massigli], Foreign Ministry (SDN), "Diplomatie Paris," teleg. no. 888–90, Oct. 10, 1933, MAE SDN I E 447, pp. 266–67 (also in MAE Z 711); Massigli, Foreign Ministry (SDN), to the Foreign Ministry, teleg. no. 898–99, Oct. 12, 1933, MAE Z 711, p. 20; Foreign Ministry, "Note pour le Ministre, a/s le rôle de la France

dans les discussions relatives aux problèmes allemands devant la dernière Assemblée," Nov. 6, 1933, MAE SDN I E 448, pp. 48–52; Fouques-Duparc, "Note," Nov. 8, 1933, MAE SDN I E 448, pp. 53–54.

160. [Massigli], Foreign Ministry (SDN), "Diplomatie Paris," teleg. no. 888–90, Oct. 10, 1933, MAE SDN I E 447, pp. 266–67; Massigli, Foreign Ministry (SDN), to the Foreign Ministry, teleg. no. 875–76, Oct. 7, 1933, MAE Z 711, pp. 10–12 (also in MAE SDN I E 447, p. 256); Foreign Ministry, "Note pour le Ministre, a/s le rôle de la France dans les discussions relatives aux problèmes allemands devant la dernière Assemblée," Nov. 6, 1933, MAE SDN I E 448, pp. 48–52. There was clearly some division within the French delegation to the League of Nations over how much autonomous power the HCR should have. Massigli and Fouques-Duparc wanted a relatively weak high commissioner, whereas Salomon Grumbach and Yvon Delbos wanted a stronger high commissioner with an independent budget and greater powers to mandate receiving countries not to expel refugees arbitrarily. Delbos even suggested that the countries of asylum be forced to grant work permits to refugees. See S. Grumbach, "L'Allemagne est isolée à Genève," *La Lumière*, Oct. 14, 1933, p. 8; Massigli, Foreign Ministry (SDN), to Foreign Ministry, teleg. no. 875–76, Oct. 7, 1933, MAE Z 711, pp. 10–12. The views of Grumbach and Delbos would become more influential during the Popular Front.

161. On the creation of the HCR, see Chapter 1, n. 15.

162. On the desire for a weak HCR, see n. 160, above. On the ambivalence of the French delegation, see Foreign Ministry (SDN), to the Foreign Ministry, teleg. no. 889, Oct. 10, 1933, MAE Z 711, p. 15; Massigli, Foreign Ministry (SDN), to the Foreign Ministry, teleg. no. 875–76, Oct. 7, 1933, MAE Z 711, pp. 10–12 (also in MAE SDN I E 447, p. 256); "Procès verbal de la 2ème séance tenue par la Commission Interministérielle des Réfugiés Israélites Allemands," Oct. 16, 1933, MAE Z 711, pp. 37–42.

163. Several of Bérenger's figures here are exaggerated. He claimed that 30,000 refugees had come to France, 5,000 more than the HCR estimated. Also, the figure of 4,000 refugees placed in jobs is greater than the figures cited by Jewish organizations. According to JDC statistics, compiled from the reports of the Comité National, only 1,263 refugees had been placed in jobs by Dec. 31, 1933. See Germany Emergency Relief, "Summary of Income and Expenditures of Organizations Occupied in Refugee Work Subsidized by the AJDC During 1933 and January–June, 1934," JDC no. 181. According to a reliable Jewish periodical, 1,147 refugees had been placed in jobs as of Nov. 30, 1933. See Bernard Schönberg, "L'Aide aux réfugiés allemands," *RJG*, no. 5 [Feb. 1934]: 183. It is true, however, that since refugees who worked as artisans, merchants, or commercial employees did not have to obtain work permits, the number of refugees who actually held jobs was probably greater than 1,263.

As to the number of scholars placed, Bérenger's figure is accurate, although it needs to be said that these scholars were not placed in regular positions, but rather in low-level posts as assistants or lab technicians, or as lycée teachers (B. Schönberg, "L'Aide aux réfugiés allemands," *RJG*, no. 5 [Feb. 1934]: 183). France's record on the placement of refugee scholars was in fact dismal in comparison to that of other countries. According to the annual report of the *Journal of the American Medical Association*, a total of 650 Jewish intellectuals had left Germany prior to June of 1935: 287 had obtained stable posts, of whom 76 were in the United States, 57 in Great Britain, 38 in Turkey, 30 in Palestine, and none in France. A total of 366 had received temporary posts: 155 in Great Britain, 58 in the United States, and only a few in France.

With specific reference to doctors, according to German government statistics, a total of 1,307 Jewish doctors left Germany by 1935: 13% went to the United States, 38% to Palestine, and only 7% (91 persons) to France. See *Journal of the American Medical Association* 105 (1935): 448, 1048 ff, cited in Dr. Horace Goldie, "A Propos de 'La Race française' du Dr. René Martial," *La Terre retrouvée* 8, no. 4 (Dec. 25, 1935): 22–23.

164. Minutes, HCR, Conseil d'Administration, 1st session, Minutes of the 5th and 6th meetings, Dec. 7–8, 1933, LBI, AR 7162, box 5 (Collection: HCR, Minutes, Dec. 1933–Dec. 1935). See also "Suisse: La Conférence pour les réfugiés allemands," *Havas*, Dec. 8, 1933, clipped in MAE Z 711, pp. 131–32; "America Is Chided on Reich Refugees," *NYT*, Dec. 9, 1933, p. 8; "L'Aide aux réfugiés allemands," *L'Aube*, Dec. 9, 1933, p. 3; "L'Aide aux réfugiés allemands," *Le Temps*, Dec. 10, 1933, p. 2; "Possibility of New Exodus of Jews from Reich Revealed at Meetings of M'Donald's Refugee Commission," *Jewish Chronicle*, Detroit, Dec. 15, 1933, clipped in JDC no. 250. For the position paper on which Bérenger based his remarks, see Jacques Fouques-Duparc, Foreign Ministry, "Aide-Mémoire," Nov. 22, 1933, MAE SDN I E 448, pp. 83–84.

165. Bérenger delivered a two-part lecture titled "Hitler et Israël" at the Théatre des Ambassadeurs in Paris on Nov. 18 and 26, 1933. See Police report on Bérenger's speech, "Israël devant la S.D.N.," Nov. 19, 1933, APP BA 1814 241.155-1-A (réfugiés allemands, Chiappe); "Hitler et Israël," *L'Ordre*, Nov. 19, 1933; "M. Henry Bérenger parle aux Ambassadeurs d'Hitler et d'Israël," *L'Oeuvre*, Nov. 19, 1933, p. 5; "Une Conférence de M. Henry Bérenger sur Hitler et Israël," *Le Quotidien*, Nov. 19, 1933, p. 2; "Sees Anti-Semitism Deeprooted in Reich," Nov. 19, 1933, *NYT*, p. 15; "Hitler et Israël," *Paix et droit*, no. 9, Nov. 26, 1933, MAE Z 711, pp. 107–10; "Hitler et Israël: Une Conférence de M. Henry Bérenger," Nov. 30, 1933, *AI*, pp. 183–84; "Une Conférence de M. Henry Bérenger," Nov. 24, 1933, *UI*, p. 312; "Israel devant la S.D.N.," *Cahiers juifs*, no. 7 (Jan., 1934): pp. 72–75. Bérenger subsequently published an extended version of this speech, titled "France, Allemagne, Israël," in W. Simon, pp. 201–4. The quote in the text here appears on pp. 201–2. On Dec. 12, 1933, Bérenger delivered another hard-line anti-German speech to an audience of French Zionists, in which he railed against antisemitism. See Police report, "Réunion organisée à mémoire de Leo Motzkin, ancien président du Comité des délégations juives," Dec. 12, 1933, APP BA 1813 241.155-B.

166. Breitscheid, to Paul Hertz, Oct. 24, 1933, cited in Langkau-Alex, pp. 36–37.

167. Police report, Oct. 30, 1933, "Note sur les réfugiés d'Allemagne," APP BA 1814 241.155-1-A.

168. For complaints by the Comité National that it was running out of money, see secretary-general, League for the Rights of Man, to the director of public assis-

tance, Aug. 22, 1933, APP BA 1815 241.155-1-D; Police report, Sept. 16, 1933, APP BA 1815, 241.155-1-D; Police report, "Réunion à la Présidence du Conseil des représentants des divers départements et services intéressés [aux réfugiés allemands]," Sept. 23, 1933, APP BA 407^P 13.112-1; "Procès verbal de la 2ème séance tenue par la Commission Interministérielle des Réfugiés Israélites Allemands," Oct. 16, 1933, MAE Z 711, pp. 37–41; Comité National, "Compte rendu de l'activité du Secrétariat Général jusqu'au 16 octobre 1933," MAE SDN I E 448, p. 9 (also in AIU, France X D 56 [226]).

169. On the discussion over the use of the barracks, see "Procès verbal de la 2ème séance tenue par la Commission Interministérielle des Réfugiés Israélites Allemands," Oct. 16, 1933, pp. 37–41, "Procès verbal de la 3ème séance tenue par la Commission Interministérielle des Réfugiés Israélites Allemands," Oct. 23, 1933, pp. 70–74, "Procès verbal de la 4ème séance tenue par la Commission Interministérielle des Réfugiés Israélites Allemands," Nov. 13, 1933, pp. 99–104, all in MAE Z 711; Police report, "Les Réfugiés allemands dans la région parisienne," Nov. 1933, APP BA 1814 241.155-1-A; Police report, "Renseignements concernant les réfugiés d'Allemagne," Nov. 28, 1933, APP BA 407^P 13.112-1; "Création du Comité National Français de Secours aux Emigrés Allemands, Victimes de l'Antisémitisme," *UI*, June 30, 1933, pp. 350; "In einer Pariser Emigrantenkaserne," *TJ*, no. 50 (mid-Dec., 1933): 865–66; Fouques-Duparc, "Aide-Mémoire," Nov. 22, 1933, MAE SDN I E 448, pp. 76–84; Schramm and Vormeier, p. 197; Badia, "L'Emigration," pp. 32–33.

170. Lengyel, pp. 9–10.

171. On the influence of lobby groups in the 1930's, see Jackson, p. 20.

172. On the Popular Front's policies in general, see Chapters 6 and 7.

173. Paxton, *Vichy France*, pp. 243–49.

Chapter Three

1. For a brief synopsis of the Stavisky Affair, see Cobban, 3: 140–46; Berstein, *La France*, pp. 69–77; Weber, *Hollow Years*, pp. 131–38; Bernard and Dubief, pp. 225–28; Gordon Wright, *France in Modern Times: From the Enlightenment to the Present*, 3rd ed. (New York, 1981), pp. 380–82; Larmour, pp. 140–49; Borne and Dubief, pp. 104–13.

2. Norman Bentwich, to James G. McDonald, Feb. 22, 1934. See also Bentwich, to McDonald, Feb. 15 and 26, 1934, all in MP:H 10; Weber, *Hollow Years*, p. 107.

3. "The Refugee Committee Meeting Called by McDonald," Feb. 25, 1934, JDC no. 404.

4. Cited in Omnès, p. 71. On the Stavisky Affair as a turning point, see "L'Activité juridique de la Ligue en 1933–1934," Apr. 20–30, 1934, *CDH*, p. 276, and Comité pour la Défense, pp. 1–2; Fabian and Coulmas, p. 31.

5. Norman Bentwich, to James G. McDonald, Feb. 22, 1934, MP: H 10; "Report on the Activities of the AJDC, with Special Attention to the Last Five Months," Apr. 16, 1934, JDC no. 249, p. 16. See also Bernhard Kahn, European director, JDC, to Mr. Stephany, Allocations Committee, Central British Fund for German Jewry, London, Mar. 8, 1934, JDC no. 617.

6. Cited in N. Bentwich, to James G. McDonald, Feb. 22, 1934, MP: H 10. On this radical shift in French policy, see also Hellmut von Gerlach, "Frankreich u. die Fremden," *PT*, no. 213 (July 13, 1934): 1–2; Gilbert Badia, "L'Emigration," p. 37; Peterson, p. 74.

7. Kahn, to Max Warburg, Oct. 16, 1934, JDC no. 617.

8. M. Troper, to J. C. Hyman, JDC, Nov. 6, 1934, JDC no. 617.

9. Minister of the interior, circular, Oct. 31, 1934, AN F^7 14662; "Le Séjour des étrangers en France: Une Note du Ministère de l'Intérieur," *L'Aube*, Oct. 27, 1934, p. 3; "Quels étrangers monsieur Marchandeau?," *L'Humanité*, Oct. 27, 1934, p. 2. See also Albert Ch.-Morice, "Les Etrangers chez nous: Manque de crédits, manque d'effectifs, manque de textes légaux," *Le Journal*, Nov. 5, 1934, clipped in APP BA 66 Provisoire.

10. Minister of the interior, Sûreté Nationale, 8ème Bureau, A.12, circulaire no. 257, Nov. 6, 1934, APP BA 64 Provisoire 51343-5. See also M. Régnier, minister of the interior, to the prefect of police, the prefects, etc., Dec. 4, 1934, APP BA 64 Provisoire 51343-5 (also in AN F^7 14662); J.-Ch. Bonnet, p. 302; Cahen-Molina, p. 35.

11. "Paris Police Seize Hundreds in Café Raids in Drive to Rid City of Undesirable Aliens," *NYT*, Nov. 26, 1934, p. 46. See also "Paris Raids Continue," *NYT*, Nov. 27, 1934, p. 10; "Les Rafles monstres de ces dernières nuits sont le résultat des campagnes xénophobes de la presse fasciste," Nov. 26, 1934, pp. 1, 3, and "Et les rafles xénophobes continuent," Nov. 27, 1934, pp. 1, 2, both in *Le Populaire*.

12. "Paris Raids Continue," *NYT*, Nov. 27, 1934, p. 10. See also "La Chasse aux travailleurs étrangers continue," *Le Populaire*, Nov. 28, 1934, p. 3. On the increased rate of expulsions, see Secours Rouge International, "Rapport sur la question du droit d'asile," [1935], in BDIC, Dos. Duchêne, FΔ Rés. 329/1; Badia, "L'Emigration," p. 37; Schramm and Vormeier, pp. 220–21.
   On the xenophobic reaction following the Marseilles assassination, see also Troper, "Summary Report of Trip (Oct. 24, 1934, to Dec. 13, 1934)," JDC no. 160, p. 14; *Le Matin*, editorial, Oct. 15, 1934, p. 1; "Gardons nos frontières!" *L'Ordre*, Oct. 18, 1934; Récouly: "Raymond Poincaré," pp. 153–70; Albert Ch.-Morice, "Les Etrangers chez nous: Manque de crédits, manque d'effectifs, manque de textes légaux," *Le Journal*, Nov. 5, 1934, clipped in APP BA 66 Provisoire; Luigi Campolonghi, "La Grande pitié des émigrés et des proscrits," *CDH*, Nov. 30, 1934, pp. 747–57; Emil Lengyel, "Saar Vote Swells Number of Exiles," *NYT*, Jan. 20, 1935, sec. IX, p. 2; Sperber, p. 60; Schor, *L'Opinion française et les étrangers*, pp. 552–54; Peterson, p. 76; Uhlman, pp. 163–64; Comité pour la Défense, p. 2.

13. "L'Activité juridique de la Ligue en 1933–1934," *CDH*, Apr. 20–30, 1934, pp. 276–77; Albert Ch.-Morice, "Les Etrangers chez nous: Manque de crédits, manque d'effectifs, manque de textes légaux," *Le Journal*, Nov. 5, 1934, clipped in APP BA 66 Provisoire.

14. On the creation of the Herriot Commission and its goals, see Foreign Ministry, "Note, a/s afflux de réfugiés sarrois en France après le plébiscite," Nov. 15, 1934, MAE Z 313, p. 18; "La Lutte contre le chômage," *Le Matin*, Nov. 21, 1934, pp. 1–2; "La Protection de la main-d'oeuvre française," *Le Temps*, Nov. 21, 1934, p. 8; "La Protection de la main-d'oeuvre nationale," *Le Temps*, Dec. 29, 1934, p. 3; "La

Protection de la main-d'oeuvre française," *L'Oeuvre*, Nov. 21, 1934, p. 4; "Droit ouvrier: La Limitation de l'emploi des étrangers," *Le Populaire*, Nov. 27, 1934, p. 6; Luigi Campolonghi, "La Grande pitié des émigrés et des proscrits," *CDH*, Nov. 30, 1934, pp. 747–57; Gaëtan Sanvoisin, "Près de 40 000 réfugiés sarrois vont franchir notre frontière," *Le Figaro*, Jan. 16, 1935, p. 1; Cross, pp. 198–200; Livian, *Le Parti socialiste*, pp. 49, 62–63; Schor, *L'Opinion française et les étrangers*, p. 578.

15. Luigi Campolonghi, "La Grande pitié des émigrés et des proscrits," *CDH*, Nov. 30, 1934, pp. 747–57; "Justice et humanité pour les travailleurs étrangers," *Le Populaire*, Dec. 2, 1934, p. 8; Livian, *Le Parti socialiste*, pp. 62–63.

16. M. Troper, to J. C. Hyman, Nov. 6, 1934, JDC no. 617; Morris Troper, "Summary Report of Trip (Oct. 24, 1934, to Dec. 13, 1934)," JDC no. 160, p. 14; "Les Rafles monstres de ces dernières nuits sont le résultat des campagnes xénophobes de la presse fasciste," *Le Populaire*, Nov. 26, 1934, p. 1, 3; "Paris Police Seize Hundreds in Café Raids in Drive to Rid City of Undesirable Aliens," *NYT*, Nov. 26, 1934, p. 46; "Paris Raids Continue," *NYT*, Nov. 27, 1934, p. 10; "La Question des étrangers devant la Chambre: Séances des 30 novembre et 1er décembre, 1934," *CDH*, Dec. 10, 1934, pp. 771–75; J.-Ch. Bonnet, p. 299; Cahen-Molina, pp. 35–36; Schramm and Vormeier, p. 203.

17. *JO, Lois et Décrets*, Feb. 8, 1935; "Travailleurs immigrés renouvelez vos cartes d'identité!" *L'Humanité*, Feb. 25, 1935, p. 5; Un juriste, "Le Décret sur les cartes d'identité," Feb. 6, 1935, in "La Question des étrangers," *CDH*, Mar. 10, 1935, pp. 154–56; "France Puts New Ban on Foreign Workers: Limits Freedom of Aliens in Drive on Idle," *NYT*, Feb. 9, 1935, p. 1; Schramm and Vormeier, pp. 202–4; Livian, *Le Parti socialiste*, p. 53; Livian, *Le Régime juridique*, pp. 69–75; Feblowicz and Lamour, pp. 65–66. On Feb. 28, 1935 another decree law was passed mandating that foreigners could reside only in the department in which they had obtained their identity card. Livian, *Le Parti socialiste*, p. 53.

18. Cited in Roblot, prefect, Bas-Rhin, to the minister of posts, Feb. 15, 1936, ADBR AL 98 393 (cartes d'identité).

19. This bill was the Project de loi no. 4144. See "Le Statut des étrangers," *CDH*, Dec. 10, 1934, pp. 789–90; "La Proposition de loi Moutet sur le statut des étrangers: La Question des étrangers," *CDH*, Mar. 10, 1935, pp. 157–66.

20. *JO, Lois et Décrets*, Oct. 31, 1935, pp. 11489–90. See also Comité pour la Défense, p. 221; Schor, *L'Opinion française et les étrangers*, p. 316; Livian, *Le Parti socialiste*, p. 56; Livian, *Le Régime juridique*, pp. 213–14. For criticisms of this law, see *CDH*, Nov. 10, 1935, pp. 702–3; "Le Comité de la CGT dénonce l'iniquité d'un décret-loi concernant les expulsions de proscrits politiques," *Le Populaire*, Nov. 17, 1935, p. 2; Magdeleine Paz, "Les décrets-lois et les étrangers," *Le Populaire*, Nov. 26, 1935, pp. 1–2; Paz, "La France aussi a ses parias," *Vendredi*, Nov. 22, 1935, p. 4, cited in Badia, "L'Emigration," pp. 37–38.

21. Bernhard Kahn, to Paul Baerwald, JDC, Nov. 6, 1934, JDC no. 250 (also in JDC no. 601).

22. Morris Troper, "Summary Report of Trip (Oct. 24, 1934, to Dec. 13, 1934)," JDC no. 160, p. 14; Morris Troper, to J. C. Hyman, JDC, New York, Nov. 6, 1934, JDC no. 617. For other Jewish organizations expressing similar fears of a mass ex-

pulsion, see Comité pour la Défense, pp. 2,15; *Pariser Haynt*, Nov. 25, 1934, trans. of article in ACIP B 129 (sociétés, organisations, groupements, *Pariser Haynt*, 1934).

23. Minister of the interior, to the foreign minister, Mar. 19, 1935, MAE Z 703, p. 32; minister of the interior, Sûreté Nationale, to the prefect of police, Paris, Nov. 14, 1935, APP BA 1815 241.155-2; M. de Bourdeille, managing vice-consul, Munich, to the Foreign Ministry, no. 137, June 4, 1935, MAE Z 703, pp. 90–91; "Les Conditions du retour des émigrés allemands," *Le Matin*, Jan. 17, 1934, p. 3; "Les Emigrés allemands rentreront difficilement en Allemagne hitlérienne," *La République*, Jan. 19, 1934, p. 2; Schramm and Vormeier, pp. 221–22.

24. For the use of this phrase, see Karl Retzlaw, cited in Vormeier, "La Situation administrative," p. 188. On the treatment of foreigners at the Prefecture, see Paul-Jean Lucas, "Les Hommes traqués," part IV, July 29, 1935, pp. 1–3; Sahl, pp. 162–70; Remarque, pp. 289–93; Sperber, *Ces Temps là*, pp. 104–5; Sauer, p. 119; Badia, "La France découverte," pp. 176–77; Schor, *L'Opinion française et les étrangers*, p. 584; Olievenstein, p. 18; Badia, "L'Emigration," pp. 72–73.

25. Un juriste, "Le Décret sur les cartes d'identité," Feb. 6, 1935, in "La Question des étrangers," *CDH*, Mar. 10, 1935, pp. 154–56.

26. On the protests of the League for the Rights of Man, see "Nos Interventions: Contre les refoulements en masse," Oct. 30, 1934, pp. 685–86; "Le Statut des étrangers: Une démarche de la Ligue," Nov. 10, 1934, p. 703; "Le Statut des étrangers," Dec. 10, 1934, pp. 789–90; "La Proposition de loi Moutet sur le statut des étrangers," in "La Question des étrangers," Mar. 10, 1935, pp. 157–66; Victor Basch, "Lettre ouverte au Président du Conseil," Feb. 20, 1935, pp. 102–3, all in *CDH*.

On the protests of the Gourevitch Committee, see W. Kotschnig, to James G. McDonald, "Record of Interview with Baron de Gunzburg," Dec. 17, 1934, MP: H 20, sent with report of Jan. 9, 1935; Comité pour la Défense, pp. 22–28; "M. Flandin et les juifs étrangers," *AI*, Jan. 10, 1935, p. 4.

On the petitions of the Comité National, see Foreign Ministry, "Note pour M. le Secrétaire Général: Séance du Comité Herriot, du 7 février 1935," Feb. 8, 1935, MAE Z 314, pp. 109–10. See also Serge Weill-Goudchaux, "Chronique juridique: Lois et modalités de l'expulsion," *AI*, Apr. 11, 1935, pp. 33–34.

On the protests of the HCR, see secretary-general, HCR, to D. Tétreau, Foreign Ministry (Unions Internationales), Nov. 15, 1934, MP: H 12; Dr. Walter Kotschnig, to James G. McDonald, Nov. 28, 1934, MP: H 19; Foreign Ministry (SDN), "Note," Feb. 1, 1935, MAE SDN I E 448, pp. 246–47; Statement by McDonald made at Session of the Permanent Committee of the Governing Body at London, Feb. 12, 1935, in MP: H 28. On these protests, see also Chapter 4, nn. 122–31, and Chapter 5, n. 91.

27. Basch, "Lettre ouverte au Président du Conseil," *CDH*, Feb. 20, 1935, pp. 102–3. See also Livian, *Le Parti socialiste*, pp. 53–54. On Mar. 21, 1935, a socialist delegation led by Raoul Evrard intervened with Charles Magny, director of the Sûreté Nationale, on behalf of the refugees. See *Le Populaire*, Mar. 22, 1935.

28. *JO, Débats Parlementaires, Chambre des Députés*, 2ème séance, Feb. 19, 1935, pp. 563–66; "La Question des étrangers," *CDH*, Mar. 10, 1935, pp. 148–66.

29. Léon Blum used this term in the parliamentary debates of both Nov. 30–Dec. 1, 1934, and Jan. 29, 1935. See "La Question des étrangers devant la Chambre: Séances des 30 novembre et 1er décembre, 1934," *CDH*, Dec. 10, 1934, pp. 773; *JO, Débats Parlementaires, Chambre des Députés*, Jan. 29, 1935, p. 258. See also Livian, *Le Parti socialiste*, pp. 52, 299; Schramm and Vormeier, pp. 203, 219.

30. "La Question des étrangers devant la Chambre: Séances des 30 novembre et 1er décembre, 1934," *CDH*, Dec. 10, 1934, pp. 771–75. See also J.-Ch. Bonnet, p. 299; Cahen-Molina, pp. 35–36; Schramm and Vormeier, p. 203.

31. *JO, Débats Parlementaires, Chambre des Députés*, Jan. 29, 1935, pp. 256–60; *JO, Débats Parlementaires, Chambre des Députés*, 2ème séance, Feb. 19, 1935, pp. 563–66; "La Question des étrangers," *CDH*, Mar. 10, 1935, pp. 148–66; "Déclaration de M. Pierre Laval, Ministre des Affaires étrangères," *Le Temps*, Jan. 31, 1935, p. 3; "A la Chambre: Séance du mardi 19 février," *Le Temps*, Feb. 21, 1935, p. 3. See also Livian, *Le Parti socialiste*, p. 52, 299; Schramm and Vormeier, pp. 203, 219.

32. "La Question des étrangers devant la Chambre: Séances des 30 novembre et 1er décembre, 1934," *CDH*, Dec. 10, 1934, pp. 771–75; *JO, Débats Parlementaires, Chambre des Députés*, 2ème séance, Feb. 19, 1935, pp. 563–66; "La Question des étrangers," *CDH*, Mar. 10, 1935, pp. 148–66; "A la chambre: Séance du mardi 19 février," *Le Temps*, Feb. 21, 1935, p. 3.

33. *JO, Débats Parlementaires, Chambre des Députés*, 2ème séance, Feb. 19, 1935, pp. 563–66; "La Question des étrangers," *CDH*, Mar. 10, 1935, pp. 148–66; "A la chambre: Séance du mardi 19 février," *Le Temps*, Feb. 21, 1935, p. 3. The League for the Rights of Man and Citizen sharply protested Régnier's remarks, declaring:

La Ligue proteste avec force contre la volonté exprimée par le Ministre de l'Intérieur de n'accorder le droit de résidence qu'aux réfugiés politiques "ayant des moyens d'existence."...

La Ligue trouve indigne des traditions d'hospitalité de la France de ne faire jouer le droit d'asile que pour les réfugiés riches ou aisés et de condamner à la faim, à la prison ou à une sorte de déportation, les réfugiés pour lesquels aux douleurs de l'exil s'ajoute celle de la pauvreté.

"Point d'asile pour les pauvres!" *CDH*, Feb. 18, 1935, p. 131.

34. For the text of this resolution, see MAE SDN I M 1819, p. 27. See also "Die Ausländerfrage in Frankreich," *PT*, no. 431, Feb. 10, 1935, p. 1. For de Jouvenel's address to the Senate on Feb. 15, see MAE SDN I M 1819, pp. 54–67; Henry de Jouvenel, "Situation des étrangers en France, exposé fait à la Commission senatoriale des Affaires Etrangères," Feb. 15, 1935, in Comité pour la Défense, pp. 31–39; "Exposé fait à la Commission Senatoriale des Affaires Etrangères par M. Henry de Jouvenel à la séance du vendredi 15 février 1935," MAE SDN I M (Questions Sociales) 1819 (Réfugiés en France), p. 62; "La Situation des étrangers en France: Un important rapport de M. Henry de Jouvenel...," *Le Matin*, Feb. 16, 1935, p. 2; "Le Sénat," *Le Temps*, Feb. 17, 1935, p. 4; "Das Asylrecht für politische Flüchtlinge," *PT*, no. 466, Mar. 23, 1935, p. 3; "Le Statut des étrangers et des réfugiés," *UI*, Feb. 15, 1935, p. 355; "Les Etrangers en France," *Le Temps*, Mar. 22, 1935.

In Mar. 1935, de Jouvenel was elected president of the newly created Centre d'Etudes du Problème des Etrangers en France. This committee's goal was to collect documentation to create a more humane and rational immigration policy for France. The other members of this committee were: William Oualid (vice president), Adolphe Landry (vice president), René Martial (vice president), Georges Mauco (secretary-general), Georges Duhamel (treasurer). See "Une Centre d'études du problème de étrangers en France est créee à Paris," Mar. 22, 1935, *L'Aube*, p. 2.

35. In Apr. 1933, the Radical Party, under the presidency of Herriot, passed the following resolution denouncing Nazi racism:

Le parti radical et radical-socialiste, fidèle à une doctrine essentielle de la France et de la République, rappelle que la Révolution, par le décret de la Constituante du 27 septembre 1791, a définitivement abolit toutes les lois d'exception relatives aux israélites.

Proteste avec energie contre les traitements injustifiables dont sont l'objet les israélites allemands, les assure de sa sympathie et demande que soient prises, avec l'accord de toutes les nations demeurées fidèles à l'esprit liberal, les mesures nécessaires à leur sauvegarde materielle, intellectuelle et morale.

"Nouvelles du jour: Au comité executif du parti radical et radical socialiste," *Le Temps*, Apr. 7, 1933; "Herriot et Delbos exposent au comité du parti radical la portée du pacte franco soviétique," *L'Ere nouvelle*, Apr. 6, 1933, p. 1; Herriot, "Peregrini sine civitate," *L'Ere nouvelle*, Apr. 6, 1933, p. 1. In May 1933, Herriot made another speech in which he declared that "la France républicaine, fidèle aux enseignements de Montesquieu, de l'abbé Grégoire et de tant d'autres, accueillerait avec la sympathie et le respect dus à des exilés, les infortunés qui ont du quitter leurs demeures dans des circonstances souvent tragiques." "A 'La Nouvelle Ecole de la Paix,'" *L'Europe nouvelle*, May 27, 1933, p. 513. According to the *UI*, Herriot was a member of the Committee of Honor of the Comité Lyonnais de Secours aux Réfugiés. Bernard Schönberg, "Une conférence du Président Herriot sur 'La Révolution et le racisme,'" *UI*, no. 30 (Apr. 14, 1939): 527.

36. Cross, pp. 198–99. For the attitude of the Radical Party on this question, see Chapter 4, nn. 77–80.

37. *JO, Débats Parlementaires, Chambre des Députés*, Jan. 29, 1935, pp. 256–60.

38. "La Question des étrangers devant la Chambre: Séances des 30 novembre et 1er décembre, 1934," *CDH*, Dec. 10, 1934, pp. 771–75; *JO, Débats Parlementaires, Chambre des Députés*, 2ème séance, Feb. 19, 1935, pp. 563–66; "La Question des étrangers," *CDH*, Mar. 10, 1935, pp. 148–66. On the position of the Radical Party leadership toward immigrant labor, see Chapter 4, nn. 42–48.

39. *JO, Débats Parlementaires, Chambre de Députés*, Jan. 29, 1935, p. 260.

40. Duroselle, pp. 125–30; Werth, *Twilight*; Kupferman, *Pierre Laval*, p. 39; Jeanneney, *François de Wendel*, pp. 544–45; Robert J. Young, *In Command of France: French Foreign Policy and Military Planning, 1933–1940* (Cambridge, Mass., 1978), p. 79. On Dec. 2, Laval inaugurated the first diplomatic contacts with the Nazi gov-

ernment by receiving the German foreign minister, Joachim von Ribbentrop, in Paris. See "Laval Bids Hitler to Show by Acts That He Favors Peace," Dec. 1, 1934, p. 1; "Paris Renews Efforts for Eastern Locarno," Dec. 2, 1934, sec. IV, p. 1; "Laval Receives Envoy of Hitler," Dec. 3, 1934, p. 8, all in *NYT*. For other press reports on this meeting and its relationship to the Sarre plebiscite, see also Sûreté Nationale reports, Nov. 30, 1934 and Dec. 1, 1934, P. 15.558, AN F^7 13433; Associated Press, Paris, to Associated Press, N.Y., Nov. 26, 1934, AN F^7 13472. In his remarks before the League of Nations just after the Sarre plebiscite, Laval declared that "en saluant le retour de la Sarre à l'Allemagne, le chancelier Hitler à, une fois de plus, affirmé sa volonté de paix," and he reiterated his view that Germany had no territorial ambitions with respect to France. "Déclaration de M. P. Laval devant le Conseil de la SDN," League of Nations, Procès verbal, 5ème séance, Jan. 17, 1935, c. 84ème session, P.LV. 5 (I), MAE SDN I G (Plébiscite, Sarre) 697, pp. 225–26.

Not all historians agree with the view that Laval's policy toward the Saar constituted the first step toward appeasement. See, for example, J. Neré, *The Foreign Policy of France from 1914 to 1945* (London, 1975), p. 169, and Jean-Paul Cointet, *Pierre Laval* (Paris, 1993), pp. 147–50. Given the fact that France did nothing to work for a pro status quo vote—a policy that marked a break with the strategy of Barthou—and that a significant portion of the contemporary press at home and abroad depicted Laval's rapprochement with the Nazis as a major shift in French foreign policy, it seems that Duroselle's interpretation is accurate.

41. HCR, "Aide-Mémoire concerning the care for possible refugees from the Saar Territory," in MP: H 20.

42. Marrus, *Unwanted*, p. 133.

43. The Herriot Commission had in fact been created in part to arrange for the reception of the Saar refugees in the event of a German victory in the plebiscite. See Gaëtan Sanvoisin, "Près de 40 000 réfugiés sarrois vont franchir nôtre frontière," *Le Figaro*, Jan. 16, 1935, p. 1; Foreign Ministry, "Note, a/s afflux de réfugiés sarrois en France après le plébiscite," Nov. 15, 1934, MAE Z 313, p. 18.

44. Foreign Ministry (Europe), "Admission de sarrois en France," Dec. 20, 1934, MAE Z 313, pp. 115–18; "Déclaration de M. P. Laval devant le Conseil de la SDN," League of Nations, Procès verbal, 5ème séance, Jan. 17, 1935, c. 84ème session, P.LV. 5 (I), MAE SDN I G 697, pp. 225–26; "Reich to Get Saar," *NYT*, Jan. 18, 1935, p. 1; "La Sarre est rattachée à l'Allemagne," *Le Temps*, Jan. 19, 1935, p. 1.

45. On the exclusion of East Europeans, see Foreign Ministry (Europe), "Note pour le Directeur Politique," Nov. 23, 1934, MAE Z 313, pp. 30–34; Foreign Ministry (Europe), "Admission en France des réfugiés sarrois," Nov. 25, 1934, MAE Z 313, pp. 32–34; F. Carles, prefect, Moselle, to minister of the interior, Sûreté Nationale, 4ème bureau, "Secret," "Report a/s Immigration sarroise en France à la veille ou au lendemain du plébiscite de la Sarre," Dec. 12, 1934, MAE Z 313, pp. 90–97; Foreign Ministry (Europe), "Note pour Massigli," Jan. 26, 1935, "a/s réfugiés de la Sarre," MAE Z 314, p. 33. On the debate over whether to include Nansen refugees, see J. Morize, to the Foreign Ministry, "Projet d'adaptation du Plan de Sécurité H à l'éventualité d'une immigration sarroise en France dans la période précédant ou suivant le Plébiscite du 13 janvier 1935," Dec. 11, 1934, pp. 67–84; Foreign Min-

istry, "Admission de sarrois en France," Dec. 20, 1934, pp. 115–18; Foreign Ministry (Contrôle des étrangers), to Guy Brun, Vice-consul, Sarrebruck, "a/s Admission en France des réfugiés sarrois," Jan. 10, 1935, pp. 166–67, all in MAE Z 313.

46. On the camp at Lizé-Nord, see M. Régnier, minister of the interior, Sûreté Nationale, Cabinet du Directeur-Général, to the Foreign Ministry (Secrétariat-Général), "a/s réfugiés de la Sarre," Jan. 21, 1935, MAE SDN I M 1810, pp. 35–36 (also in MAE Z 314); "Report on Visit of WMK to Strasbourg," Jan. 24, 1935, MP: H 20; minister of the interior, Sûreté Nationale, 4ème Bureau, to Foreign Ministry (Europe), Jan. 31, 1935, MAE Z 314, p. 60; president of the council, Direction Générale des Services d'Alsace et de Lorraine, to the Foreign Ministry, Feb. 5, 1935, MAE Z 314, p. 87; "Statistique du mouvement des réfugiés de la Sarre," Feb. 15, 1935, MAE Z 314, p. 150; Bernhard Kahn, to J. C. Hyman, JDC, New York, Feb. 15, 1935, JDC no. 617; Sarraz-Bournet, Inspecteur Général des Services administratives, to the Ministry of the [Interior], [Feb. 1935], ADBR D 460, paq. 6 (42); JDC, Confidential memorandum, Feb. 21, 1935, JDC no. 251; "Refugees Continue Flight from Saar," *NYT*, Feb. 21, 1935, p. 9; Commissaire de Police Mobile, Oswald, to the Commissaire Divisionaire de Police Spéciale, Strasbourg, Mar. 9, 1935, AN F[7] 13434; Fouques-Duparc, Foreign Ministry (SDN), "Note: a/s Problème des réfugiés sarrois," Mar. 9, 1935, MAE Z 314, pp. 231–33; Herriot, Ministry of the Interior, to the Foreign Ministry (Europe), no. 621, Mar. 15, 1935, ADBR D 460, paq. 6 (42); "Séance du Matin: Coordination des secours aux réfugiés politiques," *CDH*, Mar. 30–Apr. 5, 1935, pp. 206–7.

For left-wing protests against conditions at this camp, see Comité Mondial Contre la Guerre et le Fascisme, Report, "La Situation des émigrés sarrois," [1935], BDIC Dos. Duchêne, FΔ Rés. 329/1; "A Strasbourg la bourgeoisie française fait aux réfugiés de la Sarre une situation digne des camps hitlériens," *L'Humanité*, Feb. 19, 1935, p. 2; "Réfugiés allemands et sarrois," *CDH*, June 10, 1935, p. 405.

The Ministry of War did not want these refugees to stay in Alsace for security reasons. See Magny, Ministry of the Interior, Sûreté Nationale, 4ème bureau, Direction de la Police du Territoire et des étrangers, to the prefects of the Bas-Rhin, the Haut-Rhin, and the Moselle, no. 52, Jan. 14, 1936, ADBR D 460, paq. 6 (42).

47. On the influx of Saar Jews in particular, which began well before the plebiscite, see Norman Bentwich, Addendum to "Work of the Non-Jewish Organisations for Refugees in Paris: The Position in the Saar Region," Jan. 4, 1934, MP: H 10; Nahum Goldmann, to Jacques Fouques-Duparc, "Report of Comité des Délégations Juives," Feb. 6, 1934, MAE SDN I G 696 (Plébiscite, Sarre), pp. 83–98; *Bulletin du Comité des Délégations juives*, Paris, no. 26, May 1934, in ACIP B 129 (sociétés divers); Francus, "Plébiscite et Juifs de la Sarre," *Cahiers Juifs*, no. 10 (June–July 1934): 21; James G. McDonald, to J. C. Hyman, JDC, Jan. 22, 1935, JDC no. 251; "Geneva Publishes Hungary's Charge," *NYT*, May 15, 1934, p. 12; "Flight from Saar Doubles Refugees," *NYT*, Jan. 20, 1935, p. 31; "Refugees Continue Flight from Saar," *NYT*, Feb. 21, 1935, p. 9; "Anti-Nazis Start No Exodus from Saar," *NYT*, Jan. 16, 1935, p. 13.

On the decision to accord a liberal reception to Sarre Jews, see Foreign Ministry (Europe), "Note pour le Directeur Politique," Nov. 23, 1934, pp. 30–34; Foreign

Ministry (Europe), "Admission en France des réfugiés sarrois," Nov. 25, 1934, pp. 32–34; "Procès verbal: Conférence relative à l'immigration sarroise," Dec. 18, 1934, pp. 109–13; Foreign Ministry, "Admission de sarrois en France," Dec. 20, 1934, pp. 115–18, all in MAE Z 313. In the instructions issued in Nov. 1934, even German Jewish refugees who had taken refuge in the Saar after Hitler's seizure of power were to be accorded asylum. This provision was subsequently dropped.

48. On the provisions of the Treaty of Rome, see Procès-Verbal, 83ème Session du Conseil du SDN, Dec. 5, 1934, SDN I G 696, p. 303; "France and Reich Sign Saar Accord," Dec. 4, 1934, p. 12; "Exiled Jews in Saar Relieved at Accord," *NYT*, Dec. 7, 1934, p. 19; "Reich's Rule in Saar Disillusions People," Aug. 11, 1935, sec. IV, p. 5; "Saar Is Suffering for Shift in Rule," Dec. 25, 1935, p. 6; "Saar Now Shares Reich Hardships," Aug. 16, 1936, p. 5, all in *NYT*; Bernhard Kahn, "Report of Dr. Bernhard Kahn," Jan. 3, 1935, JDC no. 161; Laval, to Baron Aloisi, Feb. 19, 1935, MAE SDN I G 698 (Plébiscite, réfugiés sarrois en France), pp. 221–25; Président du Conseil, Foreign Ministry (Europe), to M. de Chambrun, French ambassador, Rome, no. 1859, "a/s des réfugiés sarrois," Nov. 30, 1935, MAE Z 315 (Réfugiés sarrois en France), pp. 259–60; M. S., "La Situation des israélites dans la Sarre," *UI*, June 28, 1935, p. 658; "Le Rattachement de la Sarre," *Le Temps*, Jan. 24, 1935, p. 1.

49. "France Chagrined by the Plebiscite," *NYT*, Jan. 16, 1935, p. 13.

50. Foreign Ministry (Europe), "Note a/s triage des réfugiés sarrois à l'entrée en France," Jan. 18, 1935, MAE Z 313, pp. 207–8. On the deluge at the consulate, see "L'Emigration sarroise semble se ralentir," *Le Matin*, Jan. 24, 1935, p. 3; "Refugees Shot at from Saar Side," *NYT*, Jan. 17, 1934, p. 15.

51. For the estimate of 40,000, see statements made by Jacques Helbronner at the Meeting of Advisory Council, HCR, Oct. 29, 1934, sent to the JDC, NYC, JDC no. 250; HCR, "Compte rendu de la session du Comité Consultatif," London, Oct. 29 and 30, 1934, in both LBI, AR 7162, box 5 (Collection: High Commissioner for Refugees), and JDC no. 250; James G. McDonald, HCR, to J. C. Hymans, JDC, Jan. 22, 1935, JDC no. 251; "Saar Goes German as Nazis Win 90%," Jan. 15, 1935, p. 8; "Refugees Shot at from Saar Side," Jan. 17, 1935, p. 15; Emil Lengyel, "Saar Vote Swells Number of Exiles," Jan. 20, 1935, sec. IX, p. 2, all in *NYT*.

For Guy Brun's estimate, see Brun, vice-consul, Sarrebruck, to the Foreign Ministry, "a/s de l'émigration massive des ressortissants sarrois," no. 4, Nov. 22, 1934, MAE Z 315 pp. 28–29. See also Brun, to the Foreign Ministry (Contrôle des étrangers), no. 6, Nov. 8, 1934, MAE Z 313, pp. 24–25.

52. For the text of this memorandum, see "Aide-Mémoire from the French Government to the League of Nations Relating to the Question of Refugees from the Saar," trans., Jan. 18, 1935, attached to "Statement of James G. McDonald, High Commissioner for Refugees . . . , made at the Session of the Permanent Committee of the Governing Body at London, Feb. 12, 1935, Confidential," document no. A/117, JDC no. 251; Aide-mémoire, "Territoire de la Sarre: Communication du Gouvernement français, Note du Secrétaire général, à la SDN," Jan. 18, 1935, MAE SDN I M 1810, p. 19; "Un Aide-mémoire français sur la situation des réfugiés est déposé à Genève," *L'Aube*, Jan. 19, 1935, p. 3; "Les Antihitlériens continuent à quitter en masse le territoire sarrois où les incidents se multiplient," Jan. 19, 1935, pp. 1, 3, "La

Situation en Sarre et le problème des réfugiés," Jan. 22, 1935, p. 3, both in *Le Quoti-dien*; "Saar and League Face Tense Period," *NYT*, Jan. 20, 1935, sec. IV, p. 2; "Suisse: La Question des réfugiés sarrois," *Havas*, Jan. 21, 1935, MAE Z 313, p. 229; "Le Texte de l'aide-mémoire français sur les réfugiés sarrois," *La République*, Jan. 22, 1935, p. 2; "Le Rattachement de la Sarre à l'Allemagne," *Le Temps*, Jan. 23, 1935, p. 1. See also Herriot's earlier threat that the border would be closed if the League of Nations did not send assistance. Havas clipping "France: Une Déclaration de M. Herriot, Lyon," Jan. 15, 1935, MAE Z 313, p. 186.

53. On the League's rejection, see "League Aid Asked for Saar Refugees," *NYT*, Jan. 22, 1935, p. 6; JDC, confidential memorandum, Feb. 21, 1935, JDC no. 251. On the decision to close the border, see Foreign Ministry, "Note," Jan. 20, 1935, p. 220; Foreign Ministry (Europe), "Note de M. Japy," Jan. 23, 1935, pp. 246–47, both in MAE Z 313; Foreign Ministry (Europe), "Note a/s réfugiés de Sarre," Jan. 24, 1935, p. 8; minister of the interior, to the prefect, Moselle (relayed to the prefects, Bas-Rhin and Haut-Rhin), no. 184, IV -S-2, Jan. 24, 1935, p. 15; Foreign Ministry (Europe), "Note pour le Ministre (en vue de la séance de la Commission des Affaires Etrangères)," Jan. 25, 1935, pp. 23–24; Foreign Ministry, "Note de M. Boissard a/s émigration sarroise vers la France," Jan. 25, 1935, pp. 28–29; Guy Brun, to Foreign Ministry (Europe), no. 17, Jan. 25, 1935, p. 32; Foreign Ministry (Europe), "Note pour le Ministre a/s réfugiés sarrois," Jan. 28, 1935, p. 39, all in MAE Z 314; [Massigli], Foreign Ministry (SDN), to Baron Aloisi, Feb. 6, 1935, MAE SDN I M 1810, p. 57; "Le Rattachement de la Sarre à l'Allemagne," *Le Temps*, Jan. 26, 1935, p. 1; "La France ferme ses frontières aux réfugiés sarrois," *L'Aube*, Jan. 25, 1935, p. 1.

54. Foreign Ministry (Europe), "Note pour Massigli a/s réfugiés de la Sarre," Jan. 26, 1935, MAE Z 314, p. 33; Foreign Ministry, "Note pour M. Charvériat," Jan. 28, 1935, MAE Z 314, p. 40; [minister of the interior, Sûreté Nationale], 4ème bureau, to the prefect, Bas-Rhin, Feb. 5, 1935, ADBR D 460, paq. 6 (dos. 42); president of the council, Direction Générale des Services d'Alsace et de Lorraine, to the Foreign Ministry, Feb. 5, 1935, MAE Z 314, p. 87.

55. "League Aid Asked for Saar Refugees," *NYT*, Jan. 22, 1935, p. 6. On Magny's fears, see Foreign Ministry (Europe), "Note de M. Japy," Jan. 23, 1935, MAE Z 313, pp. 246–47. According to Foreign Ministry estimates, only about 30% of all the refugees were leftists. See Foreign Ministry (SDN), "Note," July 22, 1935, MAE SDN I M 1810, pp. 210–11.

56. Foreign Ministry (Europe), "Note, a/s refoulement de nombreux réfugiés sarrois munis du visa du Consulat de France à Sarrebruck," Jan. 17, 1935, MAE Z 313, pp. 193–94. See also Foreign Ministry (Europe), "Note a/s réfugiés de Sarre," Jan. 24, 1935, MAE Z 314, p. 8; Foreign Ministry (Europe), "Note: Réfugiés de Sarre," Jan. 24, 1935, MAE Z 314, p. 8 (also in MAE SDN I M 1810, p. 31); Foreign Ministry (Europe), "Note pour le Ministre a/s réfugiés sarrois," Jan. 28, 1935, MAE Z 314, p. 39; Guy Brun, vice-consul, Sarrebruck, to Foreign Ministry (Europe), no. 17, Jan. 25, 1935, MAE Z 314, p. 32.

57. Foreign Ministry (Europe), "Note pour le Ministre (en vue de la séance de la Commission des Affaires Etrangères)," Jan. 25, 1935, MAE Z 314, pp. 23–24. See

also Foreign Ministry, "Note de M. Boissard a/s émigration sarroise vers la France," Jan. 25, 1935, MAE Z 314, pp. 28–29.

58. Knox, "Lettre adressée au nom de la Commission du Gouvernement à M. Pierre Laval," Jan. 24, 1935, telephoned by G. Brun, MAE Z 314, pp. 18–19 (also in MAE SDN I M 1810, p. 40). See also Foreign Ministry (Europe), "Note," Jan. 24, 1935, MAE Z 314, p. 10. On Knox's subsequent protests, see Foreign Ministry (Europe), Jan. 28, 1935, MAE Z 314, p. 41; Brun, to Foreign Ministry (Europe), MAE Z 314, p. 49.

59. Guy Brun, vice-consul, Sarrebruck, to Foreign Ministry (Europe), no. 17, Jan. 25, 1935, MAE Z 314, p. 32; "Les Fêtes de la Sarre s'achèveront-elles par une 'Saint-Barthelemy'?" *L'Aube*, Jan. 17, 1935, pp. 1, 3; *JO, Débats Parlementaires, Chambre des Députés*, Jan. 29, 1935, pp. 256–60.

60. Foreign Ministry (Europe), "Note pour le Ministre (en vue de la séance de la Commission des Affaires Etrangères)," Jan. 25, 1935, pp. 23–24; Foreign Ministry, "Note de M. Boissard a/s émigration sarroise vers la France," Jan. 25, 1935, pp. 28–29; Foreign Ministry (Europe), "Note pour le Ministre a/s réfugiés sarrois," Jan. 28, 1935, p. 39; Foreign Ministry (Europe), to Knox, Jan. 30, 1935, pp. 51–52; Foreign Ministry, French delegate to the Committee of Three, "Aide-Mémoire," Feb. 7, 1935, pp. 105–6, all in MAE Z 314; Laval, foreign minister, to Chambrun, French ambassador, Rome, teleg. nos. 182–86, Feb. 7, 1935, doc. 171, DDF, 1er série, vol. 9.

61. Foreign Ministry (Europe), "Note pour le Ministre a/s réfugiés sarrois," Jan. 28, 1935, MAE Z 314, p. 39.

62. Ibid. See also Guy Brun, vice-consul, Sarrebruck, to Foreign Ministry (Europe), Jan. 29, 1935, no. 25, MAE Z 314, p. 49.

63. Prefect, Moselle, to the Foreign Ministry, Cabinet, Mar. 13, 1935, MAE Z 314, pp. 241–44; Foreign Ministry (SDN), "Note a/s des réfugiés sarrois," July 28, 1936, MAE SDN I M 1811 (Réfugiés sarrois), pp. 185–97; minister of the interior, Sûreté Nationale, "Report on Sarre Refugees from Jan. 13, 1935, to Sept. 20, 1935," [late 1935–late 1936], MAE SDN I M 1811, pp. 8–31.

64. Foreign Ministry (SDN), "Note a/s des réfugiés sarrois," July 28, 1936, MAE SDN I M 1811, pp. 185–97. The League of Nations set the figure somewhat lower; it claimed there were 3,200–3,300 Saar refugees without financial means, and 800 Germans. Rapport du Représentant du Mexique (Rapporteur), "Réfugiés venant de la Sarre," Apr. 1, 1935, MAE SDN I M 1810, pp. 116–17. The government claimed it had spent nine million francs on refugee-related expenses between Jan. and Sept. 21, 1935, when the reception camps for the refugees were liquidated. See Fouques-Duparc, "Aide-Mémoire," Nov. 15, 1935, MAE SDN I M 1806, pp. 124–33; Foreign Ministry (SDN), "Rapport a/s réunion interministérielle du 21 juin 19[35] a/s des réfugiés sarrois," MAE SDN I M 1810, pp. 191–93; Foreign Ministry (SDN), "Note a/s des réfugiés sarrois," July 28, 1936, MAE SDN I M 1811, pp. 185–97.

65. Report, "Chief Points of Interviews A.W. [André Wurfbain] Had in Paris on May 15, 1935," May 16, 1935, MP: HP 4.

66. "Procès verbal: Conférence relative à l'immigration sarroise," Dec. 18, 1934,

MAE Z 313, pp. 109–13. On this conference, see also minister of the interior, Sûreté Nationale, to the Foreign Ministry (Europe), Dec. 24, 1934, MAE Z 313, p. 130.

67. On the decision to send the refugees to the southwestern departments, see Foreign Ministry (Europe), "Note pour M. Massigli," Dec. 1, 1934, MAE SDN I M 1810; M. Régnier, minister of the interior, Sûreté Nationale, Cabinet du Directeur-Général, to the Foreign Ministry (Secrétariat-Général), "a/s réfugiés de la Sarre," Jan. 21, 1935, MAE SDN I M 1810, pp. 35–36 (also in MAE Z 314); Magny (minister of the interior, Sûreté Nationale), to the prefect, Moselle, Feb. 5, 1935, MAE Z 314, p. 88; minister of the interior, Sûreté Nationale, "Report on Sarre refugees from Jan. 13, 1935, to Sept. 20, 1935," [late 1935 or early 1936], MAE SDN I M 1811, pp. 8–31; "Après le plébiscite de la Sarre," *UI*, Jan. 18, 1935, p. 290; "Les Anti-hitlériens continuent à quitter en masse le territoire sarrois où les incidents se multiplient," *Le Quotidien*, Jan. 19, 1935, pp. 1, 3; "Plus de mille réfugiés sont attendus à Bordeaux," *L'Aube*, Jan. 25, 1935, p. 1; Badia et al., "Bref aperçu," p. 173.

On the generally favorable reception of these refugees in the south see minister of the interior, Sûreté Nationale, to the Foreign Ministry and to the prefect of the Moselle, "Les Emigrés sarrois dans le Sud de la France: Les premiers rapports," Jan. 27, 1935, MAE Z 314, pp. 211–13; Maurice Icart, "Les premiers réfugiés sarrois sont installés à Toulouse," *Paris-Soir*, Jan. 20, 1935, p. 7; "Tarbes," *Le Temps*, Feb. 6, 1935, p. 8.

On the decision to allow them to stay only temporarily, see "Admission au travail des réfugiés Sarrois accueillis en France à la suite du plébiscite du 13 janvier 1935," Sept. 4, 1936, MAE SDN I M 1811, pp. 231–33. According to this memorandum, the Herriot Committee was firmly opposed to their being granted work permits, even in the south. According to this report, "Les décisions adoptées jusqu'à présent en ce qui concerne les réfugiés sarrois, répondaient au souci du gouvernement français d'éviter toute mesure qui pourrait faire croire à la stabilisation des sarrois sur notre territoire."

68. On the desire to send them to Latin America, especially Paraguay and Brazil, see Foreign Ministry (Chancelleries et du Contentieux), 2ème bureau, Office International, "Note pour la sous-direction de la SDN," Apr. [22], 1935, MAE SDN I M 1810, pp. 130–33; SDN c/86e session, P.V. 4 (1), Procès Verbal, 4ème séance, May 24, 1935, MAE SDN I M 1810, pp. 165–66; Massigli, to the Foreign Ministry (and communicated to Herriot), no. 85, May 24, 1935, MAE Z 315, pp. 115–16; Vaysset, Foreign Ministry, "Note pour le sous-direction d'Europe," July 28, 1935, MAE Z 315, p. 163; president of the council, foreign minister (Europe), to the minister of the interior, Sûreté Nationale, no. 644, Aug. 5, 1935, MAE Z 315, p. 170; Foreign Ministry (SDN), "Note," Oct. 13, 1936, MAE SDN I M 1811, p. 244; "Germany to Create Labor in the Saar," *NYT*, Apr. 27, 1935, p. 17; Millet, p. 46; Livian, *Le Parti socialiste*, p. 86–88; Marrus, *Unwanted*, p. 133. On efforts to send them to Brazil, see MAE SDN I M 1810. Saar refugees were still being sent to Paraguay in the spring of 1937. See Cranborne, Western Office, SDN, "Note," Apr. 7, 1937, PRO FO 371/21234 .W6688.

On efforts to send them to the Soviet Union, see Laval, foreign minister, to Moscow and to the Foreign Ministry (Contrôle des étrangers), SDN, Unions Internationales), Feb. 13, 1935, MAE Z 314, p. 137; Foreign Ministry (Europe), to the president of the council (Direction Générale des Services d'Alsace et de Lorraine), no. 96, Mar. 11, 1935, MAE Z 314, p. 233. Ultimately, the Soviet Union agreed to take some Saar refugees but insisted on reviewing their dossiers on a case-by-case basis.

On efforts to send them to Palestine, see Foreign Ministry (SDN), to the Ministry of the Interior, Sûreté Nationale, no. 293, Mar. 31, 1935, MAE Z 315, p. 9; Corbin, to the Foreign Ministry, no. 47, May 21, 1935, MAE Z 315, pp. 109–10.

69. On the reluctance of the refugees to go to Latin America, see minister of the interior, Sûreté Nationale, "Report on Sarre refugees from Jan. 13, 1935, to Sept. 20, 1935," [late 1935 to early 1936], MAE SDN I M 1811, pp. 8–31. See also Vaysset, Foreign Ministry, "Note pour la sous-direction d'Europe," July 28, 1935, MAE Z 315, p. 163; president of the council, Foreign Ministry (Europe), to the minister of the interior, Sûreté Nationale, no. 644, Aug. 5, 1935, MAE Z 315, p. 170. On the British position, see Corbin, to the foreign minister, no. 47, May 21, 1935, MAE Z 315, pp. 109–10.

70. Foreign minister (Ministre Plénipotentiaire), Directeur des Affaires politiques et commerciales, to the minister of the interior, Sûreté Nationale, Feb. 13, 1936, MAE SDN I M 1811, pp. 63–64. By the summer of 1935, Massigli also argued that it was a pipe dream to believe that the majority of these refugees would eventually leave and that it was time to absorb them in France. See Massigli, Foreign Ministry (SDN), "Note a/s réfugiés venant de la Sarre," July 2, 1935, MAE Z 315, pp. 152–56.

71. Ibid.; "Admission au travail des réfugiés sarrois accueillis en France à la suite du plébiscite du 13 janvier 1935," Sept. 4, 1936, MAE SDN I M 1811, pp. 231–33. On the distribution of work permits to Sarre refugees, see Badia et al., "Bref aperçu," p. 174, although the chronology here is incorrect. In Mar., the head of the Sûreté Nationale, on his own initiative, had ordered the prefects not to grant work permits at all to Saar refugees, but this order was subsequently rescinded—even the minister of the interior considered it too harsh. See Ch. Magny, Ministry of the Interior, Sûreté Nationale, to the minister of labor, Service Central de la Main d'Oeuvre, Mar. 12, 1935, MAE Z 314, p. 247.

72. Minister of labor, L.-O. Frossard, to the prefects, Sept. 13, 1935, no. 79, MAE SDN I M 1811, pp. 234–35. On the liquidation of the centers, see Ch. Magny, Ministry of the Interior, Direction Police du territoire et des étrangers, 4ème Bureau, Sûreté Nationale, to the prefects, Dec. 18, 1935, MAE SDN I M 1811, pp. 160–61; Foreign Ministry (SDN), "Note a/s des réfugiés sarrois," July 28, 1936, MAE SDN I M 1811, pp. 185–97.

In late Feb. 1935, the Jewish refugee organization Agriculture et Artisanat, which sponsored vocational retraining programs to train refugees to be farmers and artisans, asked the Foreign Ministry whether it might help resettle Sarre refugees in agricultural centers in southwestern France. The government refused, claiming that "besides, the League of Nations has been made aware of the problem regarding the definitive placement of the Saar refugees, and it would be premature to envision solutions according to an internal plan before the [League of Nations] Council has concluded its study of this question." Foreign Ministry (Unions internationales),

"Note pour la Direction Politique," Feb. 26, 1935, MAE Z 314, p. 205; M. de Menthon, Foreign Ministry (Europe), "Note pour la sous-direction des Unions," Mar. 5, 1935, MAE Z 314, p. 224.

73. About 200 Saar refugee families were ultimately sent to Paraguay. See Foreign Ministry, Directeur des Affaires Politiques et Commerciales, to the minister of the interior, Sûreté Nationale, Feb. 13, 1936, MAE SDN I M 1811, pp. 63–64; Foreign Ministry (SDN), to French diplomatic and consular agents abroad, circular no. 171, Nov. 2, 1936, MAE SDN I M 1819, pp. 191–92; Foreign Ministry (SDN) "Note a/s des réfugiés sarrois," July 28, 1936, MAE SDN I M 1811, pp. 185–97; Cranborne, Western Office [British Foreign Office], League of Nations, "Note," Apr. 7, 1937, PRO FO 371/21234.W6688; Comité pour la Défense, p. 3; Livian, *Le Parti socialiste*, p. 88. On the refugees sent to Brazil, see Foreign Ministry (SDN), "Note," Oct. 13, 1936, MAE SDN I M 1811, p. 244 and MAE SDN I M 1810. See also n. 68 above.

74. The decision had been made in Feb. 1935 but was not implemented until Sept., Fouques-Duparc, Foreign Ministry (SDN), "Note: a/s problème des réfugiés sarrois," Mar. 9, 1935, MAE Z 314, pp. 231–33; Rapport du représentant du Mexique (Rapporteur), League of Nations, "Réfugiés venant de la Sarre," Apr. 1, 1935, MAE SDN I M 1810, pp. 116–17; Foreign Ministry (Chancelleries et du Contentieux), 2ème bureau, Apr. [22], 1935, MAE SDN I M 1810, p. 130–33; League of Nations, c/86e session, P.V. 4(1), Procès Verbal, 4ème séance, May 24, 1935, MAE SDN I M 1810, pp. 165–66; Massigli, to the Foreign Ministry (and to Herriot), no. 85, May 24, 1935, MAE Z 315, pp. 115–16; minister of the interior, to the foreign minister, Aug. 12, 1935, no. 1917, MAE Z 315, p. 184 (also in MAE SDN I M 1810, p. 278); M. de Menthon, Foreign Ministry (Europe), "Note pour la sous-direction des Chancelleries et du Contentieux," Aug. 19, 1935, MAE Z 315, p. 183 (also in MAE SDN I M 1810, p. 276); president of the council, foreign minister, to the minister of the interior, Sûreté Nationale, Sept. 2, 1935, MAE Z 315, p. 211; "Germany to Create Labor in the Saar," *NYT*, Apr. 27, 1935, p. 17; Millet, p. 46; Livian, *Le Parti socialiste*, p. 86; Livian, *Le Régime juridique*, pp. 186–87; Feblowicz and Lamour, pp. 29–30.

As of this date, all Saar refugees who met the three-year residence requirement became eligible for Nansen passports. The German refugees from the Saar remained under the supervision of the HCR and were eligible to obtain only special *titres d'identité de voyage* instead of Nansen passports.

75. Livian, *Le Parti socialiste*, p. 88.

76. Livian, *Le Régime juridique*, p. 141; Foreign Ministry, "Exposé," [1935], MAE SDN I M 1810, pp. 207–8. See also Charles Levy, to the president of the council, foreign minister, Dec. 11, 1935, MAE Z 315, pp. 266–70.

77. See Chapter 4, pp. 80–86, 89–93.

78. According to the Secours Rouge International, the proportion of refugees expelled from France far exceeded that in other European countries. Secours Rouge International, "Rapport sur la question du droit d'asile," [1935], BDIC Dos. Duchêne, FΔ Rés 329/1.

79. Minister of the interior, to the president of the Foreign Affairs Commission

of the Chamber of Deputies, Nov. 1935, MAE SDN I M 1806, pp. 181–206. On growing fears among Nansen refugees, see Foreign Ministry (SDN), to the foreign minister, Apr. 2, 1935, MAE Z 315, pp. 14–15.

80. Depoid, p. 45, table. On the 1927 naturalization law, see Cross, p. 177.

81. "League Is Urged to Aid Refugees," *NYT*, July 18, 1935, pp. 1, 8. On the sense of profound despair that had gripped the refugee community by the fall of 1935, see Chapter 5, nn. 95–100.

82. André Wurfbain, HCR, to Walter Kotschnig, HCR, Aug. 27, 1935, MP: H 20.

83. M. de Bourdeille, managing vice-consul, Munich, to the Foreign Ministry (Europe), June 4, 1935, no. 137, MAE Z 703, pp. 90–91.

84. Italics in text. Minister of the interior, Sûreté Nationale, 6ème Bureau (R-5-C), to the prefect, Bas-Rhin, May 13, 1935, ADBR D 460, paq. 5 (36).

85. Corbin, French ambassador, Great Britain, to Laval, foreign minister, Jan. 7, 1936, no. 13, MAE SDN I E 449, p. 88–92.

86. M. de Bourdeille, managing vice-consul, Munich, to the Foreign Ministry (Europe), June 4, 1935, no. 137, MAE Z 703, pp. 90–91; M. de Bourdeille, to the Foreign Ministry, Oct. 8, 1935, no. 238, MAE Z 704, p. 89. On Jews being sent to concentration camps after the Nuremberg Laws, see also Inspecteur de Police Spéciale, Commissariat Spécial d'Erstein-Sélèstat, Poste de Gerstheim, no. 791, Dec. 22, 1935, AN F[7] 13434.

87. De Vaux Saint-Cyr, French consulate, Munich, to the Foreign Ministry (Europe), Sept. 7, 1935, no. 214, MAE Z 704, pp. 24–25.

88. Ministry of Foreign Affairs, circular no. 17, (Very Confidential), Oct. 10, 1935, MAE Z 704, pp. 90–91. On this hard-line policy in the wake of the Nuremberg Laws, see also Livian, *Le Parti socialiste*, p. 56; Schramm and Vormeier, p. 205; and with regard to German refugees seeking to enter France via the Saar, M. de Menthon, for the president of the council, foreign minister (Europe), to the minister of the interior, Sûreté Nationale, Direction de la police du territoire et des étrangers, Nov. 30, 1935, MAE Z 315, pp. 261–63; Foreign Ministry (Europe), "Note pour le Contrôle des étrangers: a/s des réfugiés sarrois," Dec. 4, 1935, MAE Z 315, pp. 260–61.

89. Minister of the interior, Sûreté Nationale, 6ème bureau, to Justin Godart, president, Comité pour la Défense, Nov. 26, 1935, cited in Comité pour la Défense, pp. 62–63. Despite these policies, the JDC noted an increase in Jewish immigration to France following the Nuremberg Laws. News from the AJDC, "French Legal Service to German Refugees Subsidized by JDC Reports Increase in Numbers Crossing Border; Engaged Couples Among Refugees," Dec. 13, 1935, JDC no. 602. In order to stem this continued influx of German Jews, the Ministry of the Interior, on the advice of Jean Dobler, the French consul in Cologne, instructed the police and prefects in early 1936 not to extend the short-term visas of German Jews who had recently come to France. Perrier de Feral, Directeur adjoint, minister of the interior, Sûreté Nationale, to the prefects and police, Paris, Jan. 7, 1936, APP BA 1814 241.155-1-A. In the spring, the Ministry of the Interior again instructed the police and prefects to expel immediately all Germans whose papers were not in order. Al-

though political refugees were to be exempted, Jews were not included in this category. See Ministry of the Interior, Sûreté Nationale, circular no. 70, Mar. 30, 1936, APP DA 783 (Textes); Ministry of the Interior, Sûreté Nationale, circular no. 306, May 28, 1936, APP BA 64 Provisoire 51-343-5.

90. François-Poncet, to the foreign minister, teleg. no. 2421, Sept. 22, 1935, MAE SDN I M 1806, p. 84; "M. Bérenger parle à Genève de l'assistance aux réfugiés," *Le Petit Parisien*, Sept. 22, 1935, p. 5; "Le Sénateur Bérenger sur la question des réfugiés," *UI*, Sept. 27, 1935, p. 6.

91. Foreign Ministry, *Bulletin périodique de la presse allemande*, no. 452, Oct. 5, 1935 [for period Aug. 12, 1935–Sept. 29, 1935], AN F^7 13434.

92. Corbin, to Laval, foreign minister, no. 13, Jan. 7, 1936, MAE SDN I E 449, p. 88–92.

93. Levin, "Le Droit d'asile en danger," *DdV*, Mar. 31, 1935, p. 1.

94. "Need of Refugees Told by Bentwich," *NYT*, Apr. 10, 1935, p. 18. Walter Friedländer, the director of the Service Social pour les Réfugiés Allemands, also reported that there were 10,000 to 11,000 German refugees in France by the beginning of 1936. See Friedländer, "Report of the Condition of the German Refugees in France, as of the Early Part of 1936," Mar. 31, 1936, JDC no. 602 (France: Organisations). The Foreign Ministry also estimated that there were between 8,000 and 12,000 refugees in France in Nov. 1935. Fouques-Duparc, "Aide-Mémoire," Nov. 15, 1935, MAE SDN I M 1806 pp. 124–33.

95. "Des réfugiés allemands partent de France en Palestine," *La Terre retrouvée*, no. 5 (Jan. 25, 1935): 18. On the liquidation of the relief effort, see Chapter 5, nn. 70–79.

96. "Excerpt of letter from Melvin M. Fagen to Mr. Waldman, London, Nov. 16, 1935," JDC no. 617. On the kidnapping of Berthold Jacob, see Peterson, pp. 124–27.

97. *CDH*, Nov. 10, 1935, pp. 702–3.

98. On France's repeated refusals to make financial contributions to the HCR, see Foreign Ministry (Europe), "Note pour le Directeur politique," Sept. 20, 1934, MAE Z 711, pp. 231–32; Corbin, to the foreign minister, no. 1052, Oct. 16, 1934, MAE SDN I E 448, p. 235 (also in MAE Z 711, pp. 238–39); Corbin, to the foreign minister, Nov. 2, 1934, teleg. no. 1042, MAE SDN I E 448, p. 239; Foreign Ministry (Europe), "Copie de la lettre le 27 octobre à M. Helbronner, Conseiller d'Etat...," Oct. 27, 1934, MAE Z 711, pp. 241–49; HCR, "Compte rendu de la session du Comité Consultatif, London," Oct. 29 and 30, 1934, LBI, AR 7162, box 5 (Collection: HCR, Minutes, Dec. 1933–Dec. 1935) (also in JDC no. 250); Jacques Helbronner, to the foreign minister, Nov. 5, 1934, MAE Z 313, p. 2; Bentwich, "Problem of the Refugees," p. 39.

On French fears that the HCR might seek to prevent the government from expelling unwanted refugees, see Report, "Chief Points of Interviews A. W. [André Wurfbain] had in Paris on May 15, 1935," May 16, 1935, MP: HP 4; "Note on an interview which N. B. had on June 12, 1935, with Monsieur Jacques Helbronner," MP: H 4; Foreign Ministry (SDN), "Note: L'Assemblée et le problème des réfugiés," Aug. 22, 1935, MAE SDN I M 1806, pp. 63–64. According to Bernhard Kahn of the

JDC, the French delegation to the HCR treated McDonald with utter disdain. In Oct. 1935, just after an advisory meeting of the HCR in London, he reported:

I must say that I have attended many meetings in the thirty-five years of my service but never such a depressing one as that one in London. Our French friends treated Mr. McDonald like a small office boy whose services are no longer needed and who should be dismissed on the spot. I tried my best even by using Mr. Nahum Goldman as an ally, to correct the situation, but against French verbosity we could not do much. Even Mr. McDonald lost his temper and made some bitter remarks which he later withdrew.

Kahn, to J. C. Hyman, JDC, Oct. 30, 1935, JDC no. 251 (cited also in Bauer, *My Brother's Keeper*, p. 149). See also Helbronner's disparaging comments toward McDonald in "Réunion du 25 novembre 1935 au Ministre des Affaires Etrangères," Nov. 29, 1935, MAE SDN I M 1806 pp. 147–52.

99. On Helbronner's role, see Chapter 5.

100. On Massigli's disillusionment with the international solutions, see Foreign Ministry (SDN), "Note a/s réfugiés venant de la Sarre," July 2, 1935, MAE Z 315, pp. 152–56. On Paganon's more liberal attitude, see "La Situation des réfugiés sarrois," *Le Populaire*, June 29, 1935, p. 2.

101. Minister of the interior, to the President of the Foreign Affairs Commission of the Chamber of Deputies, Nov., 1935, MAE SDN I M 1806, pp. 181–206.

102. On Paganon's support for these efforts, see "Note transmise par M. le Général Brissaud-Desmaillet à M. Paganon, Ministre de l'Intérieur," Oct. 16, 1935, in Comité pour la Défense, pp. 56–59.

103. Minister of the interior, Sûreté Nationale, circular no. 213, Nov. 19, 1935, AN F^7 14662. See also minister of the interior, Sûreté Nationale, circular no. 219, Nov. 23, 1935, AN F^7 14662.

104. On the exclusion of East European Jews from the provisions of these circulars, see A. Sarraut, president of the council, minister of the interior, Sûreté Nationale, to the prefects, no. 27, Feb. 6, 1936, ADBR D 460, paq. 4 (23). Until the election of the Popular Front, the Gourevitch Committee complained that these circulars had not been properly implemented. See Justin Godart, to the minister of the interior, May 25, 1936, in Comité pour la Défense, pp. 81–82.

In Sept. 1935, the Foreign Ministry (SDN) claimed that it would be willing to consider German refugees under the same regime as Nansen refugees but that it would not be willing to extend this status to other stateless refugees, including those expelled from Germany. Foreign Ministry (SDN), "Note pour M. Le Sénateur H. Bérenger," Sept. 12, 1935, MAE SDN I M 1806, pp. 67–69; Foreign Ministry (SDN), "Note pour la sous-direction des Chancelleries et du Contentieux," Sept. 25, 1935, MAE SDN I M 1806, p. 87.

105. See Chapter 6.

106. Foreign Ministry (Contrôle des étrangers), "Note pour la sous-direction de la Société des Nations," Jan. 14, 1936, MAE SDN I M 1806; Foreign Ministry (SDN), "Note pour le représentant de la France," Jan. 17, 1936, MAE SDN I M 1806, pp. 177–78; Foreign Ministry (SDN), "Note: Réfugiés allemands," Feb. 1936,

MAE SDN I E 449, pp. 197–99; Foreign Ministry, to Corbin, "a/s statut des réfugiés d'Allemagne," no. 385, Feb. 22, 1936, MAE SDN I E 449, pp. 193–95.

107. On the course of this discussion throughout 1934 and 1935, see especially Laval, foreign minister, to the French ambassador, London, Apr. 30, 1934, MAE Z 711, pp. 198–202; Fouques-Duparc, "Note: Réfugiés allemands," Feb. 18, 1935, MAE SDN I E 448, pp. 253–54; Fouques-Duparc, "Note pour le Secrétaire Général," Feb. 19, 1935, MAE SDN I M 1812 (Statut international des réfugiés), pp. 148–49; "Note de M. Avenol, Confidentiel," Mar. 4, 1935, pp. 4–6, Foreign Ministry (Chancelleries et Contentieux), "Note pour le Service de la SDN," Mar. 8, 1935, p. 11; [Fouques-Duparc], Foreign Ministry (SDN), confidential report, "La Question des étrangers et des réfugiés et la SDN," Apr. 2, 1935, pp. 19–23; Fouques-Duparc and J. Helbronner, Foreign Ministry (SDN), "Note pour le représentant de la France," no. 27, Sept. 1935 [no day given], pp. 91–95; Foreign Ministry (SDN), "Note: L'Assemblée et le problème des réfugiés," Aug. 22, 1935, pp. 63–64; "Réunion du 25 novembre au Ministre des Affaires étrangères," Nov. 29, 1935, pp. 147–52, all in MAE SDN I M 1806; Foreign Ministry (Europe), "Note pour le Directeur Politique," Mar. 13, 1935, MAE SDN I M 1819, pp. 76–81; Report, "Chief Points of Interviews AW Had in Paris on May 15, 1935," May 16, 1935, MP: H 4.

Other countries, and especially Great Britain, shared France's position on this issue. See Fox, "Great Britain," p. 44.

108. [Fouques-Duparc], Foreign Ministry (SDN), Apr. 2, 1935, confidential report, "La Question des étrangers et des réfugiés et la SDN," MAE SDN I M 1806, pp. 19–23; Fouques-Duparc and J. Helbronner, Foreign Ministry (SDN), "Note pour le représentant de la France," Sept. 1935 [no day given], no. 27, MAE SDN I M 1806, pp. 91–95.

On efforts of the HCR to persuade European governments to assimilate the German refugees to the Nansen refugees, see André Wurfbain, HCR, to J. C. Hyman, JDC, "Summary of Answers Received from Governments to the Recommendations of the High Commissioner Concerning Passports," doc. A/102, July 27, 1934, JDC no. 250.

109. Minister of the interior, to the president of the Foreign Affairs Commission of the Chamber of Deputies, Nov. 1935, MAE SDN I M 1806, pp. 181–206, esp. p. 205.

110. For a discussion of these issues, see Chapters 6 and 7.

111. Cited in Albert Ch.-Morice, "Les Etrangers chez nous: Comment fonctionnent les services du contrôle," *Le Journal*, Nov. 1, 1934, clipped in APP BA 66 Provisoire.

112. On these plans in the spring, see minister of the interior, to the Foreign Ministry (Contrôle des étrangers), Dec. 22, 1934, pp. 25–26; minister of the interior, to the Foreign Ministry (Chancelleries et du Contentieux), Mar. 12, 1935, pp. 86–87; Foreign Ministry (SDN), "Note pour le Bureau du Contrôle des étrangers: a/s immigration clandestine en France, (Urgent)," Jan. 26, 1935, pp. 32–34, all in MAE SDN I M 1819. On Paganon's opposition, see minister of the interior, to the president of the Foreign Affairs Commission of the Chamber of Deputies, Nov. 1935, MAE SDN I M 1806, p. 206.

Chapter Four

1. The moderate right did, however, use Nazi antisemitism as a bludgeon against Germany. The prominent publicist Pertinax (André Géraud), for example, wrote in 1933: "La guerre faite aux juifs d'Allemagne par la dictature hitlérienne mérite d'être signalée. Non seulement, parce qu'elle éclaire la brutalité fondamentale du nouveau régime mais aussi parce qu'elle a annihilé, en quelques jours, les concours, les complicités d'opinion publique dont le germanisme a si grandement profité depuis dix ans en Angleterre et aux Etats-Unis." Pertinax, "La Guerre aux juifs en Allemagne," *L'Echo de Paris*, Mar. 29, 1933, p. 3.

2. Police report, Aug. 20, 1932, APP BA 1813 241.155-B.

3. Morand, "Réfugiés politiques," *Le Temps*, Mar. 31, 1933, cited in Maurice Noël, "Revue de la presse," *Le Figaro*, Mar. 31, 1933, p. 3; Thalmann, "L'Immigration allemande," pp. 158–59; Thalmann, "L'Emigration du IIIe Reich," p. 134. On Morand's antisemitic and anti-refugee sentiments, see also Morand; Weber, *Hollow Years*, pp. 105–6, 232.

4. Le Provost de Launay, "L'Emigration israélite allemande doit être surveillée de très près dans l'intérêt même des émigrés," *L'Ordre*, June 29, 1933, pp. 1, 3, also cited in Schor, *L'Opinion française et les étrangers*, p. 623, and Schor, *L'Antisémitisme en France*, p. 162.

5. *AF*, Apr. 28, 1933, cited in Schor, *L'Opinion française et les étrangers*, p. 623. See also Daudet, "L'Invasion judéo-maçonnique," *AF*, June 18, 1933, clipped in APP BA 1814 241.155-1-C; Daudet, "La Rançon de l'affaire Dreyfus," *AF*, Apr. 11, 1933, clipped in APP BA 1814 241.155-1-C; F. Coty, "En face d'une invasion allemande," *Le Figaro*, Apr. 2, 1933, p. 1; N. P. [Nicolas Paillot], "L'Hitlérisme français," *La Lumière*, May 6, 1933, p. 4; N. P. [Nicolas Paillot], "Hitler est approuvé par les racistes français," *La Lumière*," Apr. 15, 1933, p. 8.

6. "Les réfugiés allemands de confession israélite," *Le Figaro*, June 6, 1933 and *L'Ami du peuple*, June 8, 1933, clipped in APP BA 1814 241.155-1-C.

7. Prefect, Haut-Rhin, to the minister of the interior, Sûreté Nationale, 6ème bureau, Jan. 30, 1936, ADBR AL 98 393 (16).

8. Letter to the prefect of police, Oct. 19, 1933, forwarded by the Commissaire de Police (Renseignements Généraux), to the prefect of police, Jan. 27, 1934, APP BA 1814 241.155-1-C.

9. "Que font les singuliers émigrés du centre allemand de Neuilly?" *Le Jour*, Mar. 31, 1935, clipped in AIU ms. 650 boîte 13 (45).

10. E. Berl, "Hitler et nous," *Marianne*, Nov. 22, 1933, p. 1.

11. "Méfiez-vous des socialistes allemands...," *Le Matin*, Mar. 24, 1935, p. 1.

12. On Coty, see Bernard and Dubief, p. 211; Millman, pp. 171–88; Weber, *Hollow Years*, pp. 87–88, 105–6; Ralph Schor, "Xénophobie et extrême droite: L'Exemple de l'*Ami du Peuple* (1928–1937)," *Revue d'histoire moderne et contemporaine*, Jan.–Mar. 1976, pp. 116–44; Kupferman, "François Coty," pp. 77–92.

13. Coty, "Camps de déconcentration?" *Le Figaro*, Mar. 8, 1933, p. 1. See also Coty, "Masses communistes sur la France," *Le Figaro*, Mar. 7, 1933, p. 1.

14. Coty, "Camps de déconcentration?" *Le Figaro*, Mar. 8, 1933, p. 1.

15. Coty, "Silence aux allemands réfugiés," *Le Figaro*, May 30, 1933, p. 1 (also in *L'Ami du peuple*, May 30, 1933). See also Coty, "Le Communisme au Collège de France," *Le Figaro*, May 18, 1933, p. 1; Schramm and Vormeier, p. 196; N. P. [Nicolas Paillot], "Nous avons aussi nos racistes," *La Lumière*, Apr. 8, 1933, p. 13; N. P. [Nicolas Paillot], "Hitlérisme français," *La Lumière*, Aug. 12, 1933, p. 5.

16. "A propos de l'immigration allemande," *AF*, June 9, 1933, clipped in APP BA 1814 241.155-1-C (also in APP BA 407^P 13.112-1); "Une Question sera posée au Conseil Municipal sur l'immigration à Paris des juifs chassés d'Allemagne," *Le Matin*, June 9, 1933, clipped in APP BA 1844 241.155-1-G (also in APP BA 1814 241.155-1-A). See also Clement Vautel, "Mon film," *Le Journal*, Mar. 30, 1933, clipped in APP BA 1815 241.155.2; Maurice Noël, "Revue de la presse," *Le Figaro*, Apr. 16, 1933, p. 3.

17. Gaëtan Sanvoisin, "L'Ordre public sera troublé si des mesures ne sont pas prises," *Le Figaro*, Apr. 3, 1934, pp. 1–2. See also Recouly, "Raymond Poincaré," pp. 162–63; Nicolas Lerouge, "Pas de xénophobie," *La République*, Oct. 10, 1934, p. 2; Louis de Chauvigny, "Mulhouse, ville française ou forteresse rouge?" *L'Echo de Paris*, Apr. 3, 1934, p. 1.

18. Dr. Toulouse, "Les Persécutions juives," *L'Oeuvre*, Sept. 1, 1935, p. 4.

19. J. Lassere, "France, Terre d'asile," *Le Matin*, Aug. 28, 1935, p. 6.

20. Jérôme and Jean Tharaud, pp. 141–42, 199. On this theme more generally, see Weber, *Hollow Years*, pp. 102–10 in general, 107, n. 57, 304–5.

21. Fabre-Luce, "Les Querelles de races," *Pamphlet*, no. 39, Dec. 25, 1933, pp. 9–10. See also P. Dominique, "La Question juive," *Pamphlet* 1, no. 40 (Dec. 22, 1933): 13–14; and remarks by the French municipal councilor, M. de Puymaigre, in *Bulletin Municipal officiel de la Ville de Paris*, no. 118, May 20, 1933, question of June 16, 1933, Conseil Muncipal de Paris, Questions écrites, no. 270, May 20, 1933, APP BA 407^P 13.112-1 (also in APP BA 1814 241.155-1-A); Schramm and Vormeier, p. 196.

22. Géo London, "Des Réfugiés allemands se livrent en plein Paris au trafic des stupéfiants," *Le Journal*, Sept. 3, 1933, p. 2; G. London, "Un Gamin récidiviste du vol...," *Le Journal*, July 25, 1934; J. M. Aimot, "Six pour cent...fournissent quinze pour cent de condamnés pour crimes et attentats," *Le Quotidien*, May 14, 1933, p. 2; Gascoin, pp. 289–91.

23. Mauclair, *L'Ami du peuple*, Sept. 10, 1933, cited in Schor, *L'Opinion française et les étrangers*, p. 357. On Mauclair's antisemitism, see also Weber, *Hollow Years*, p. 88.

24. Gaëtan Sanvoisin, "Préserver Paris," *Le Figaro*, Oct. 8, 1933, p. 1.

25. Gascoin, p. 289. See also Nigel, "En Marge: En l'île Saint-Louis," [1933 or 1934], clipped in ACIP B 127 (divers).

26. Robert Redslob, "Les Langues en Alsace," *Le Temps*, Feb. 5, 1934, p. 3.

27. J. Biélinky, "Paris hospitalier: Ce qu'on y fait pour les réfugiés," *UI*, Oct. 6, 1933, pp. 90–91; "Travailleurs français et immigrés," *L'Humanité*, Apr. 2, 1934, p. 5.

28. Jacques Dolor, "Tandis que des milliers de français chôment...," *L'Ami du peuple*, Nov. 6, 1933, and Nov. [8], 1933, clipped in APP BA 1814 241.155-1-G. See also L. Bailby, "Lettre d'un 'héros' désabusé," *Le Jour*, June 12, 1934, clipped in AN 72 AJ 600.

29. Gérard Noiriel, *Le Creuset français*, pp. 337–38; Millman, pp. 27, 145, 177; Letter by István Deák, in "Who Saved Jews? An Exchange," *New York Review of Books* 38, no. 8 (Apr. 25, 1991): 60–62.

30. *AF*, Nov. 5, 1933, clipped in APP BA 1814 241.155-1-C.

31. Police report, June 13, 1933, APP BA 1844 241.155-1-C; Férenzy, pp. 199–200.

32. "Intolérable concurrence des réfugiés juifs," *AF*, Jan. 28, 1934, clipped in APP BA 1814 241.155-1-A.

33. "A propos de l'immigration allemande," *AF*, June 9, 1933, clipped in APP BA 1814 241.155-1-C (also in APP BA 407^P 13.112-1); "Une Question sera posée au Conseil Municipal sur l'immigration à Paris des juifs chassés d'Allemagne," *Le Matin*, June 9, 1933, clipped in APP BA 1844 241.155-1-G (also in APP BA 1814 241.155-1-A).

34. Fernand Peter, president, Chambre des Métiers d'Alsace, to Edouard Herriot, Ministre d'Etat, Nov. 13, 1934, ADBR D 460, paq. 5 (33); Annexe No. 4148, *JO, Documents Parlementaires*, sect. 3, Chambre 1934, 2ème session extraordinaire, Nov. 22, 1934, pp. 131–32.

35. "Etrangers et chômage," *Le Temps*, Nov. 22, 1934, p. 1. This argument was found to be compelling by the Commission of Civil and Criminal Legislation of the Chamber of Deputies, which cited it in its report against the antiforeign decree laws in Dec. of 1936. See Annexe No. 1417, *JO, Documents Parlementaires*, sect. 3, chambre 1936, 2ème session extraordinaire, Dec. 8, 1936, pp. 940–41.

36. "L'Intérêt des commerçants," *Le Temps*, Mar. 17, 1936, p. 1; "Genèse des corporations," *Le Temps*, Apr. 9, 1936, p. 1.

37. [Buré], "Les Maladies de notre temps: Le Malthusianisme économique causera-t-il la chute du régime?" *L'Ordre*, July 10, 1938, p. 4.

38. D'Ormesson, "Tribune Libre: Un problème complexe," *Le Temps*, Dec. 1, 1934, p. 1.

39. Gascoin, p. 283, *passim*.

40. Bonsirven, "Chronique," pp. 107–9. See also extracts from this article in "La France et l'antisémitisme," *UI*, Feb. 1, 1935, pp. 323–24; "Revue de la Presse: Vitalité du judaisme français," *UI*, May 22, 1936, pp. 548–49; Bonsirven, *Juifs*, pp. 272–73. For Bernard Lecache's rebuttal, see Lecache, "Petit manuel rédigé à l'usage des catholiques amis des juifs," *DdV*, no. 24 (Feb. 2, 1935): 1–2. On Bonsirven, see also Schor, *L'Antisémitisme en France*, pp. 226–27; Landau, p. 255.

41. Bonsirven, "Chronique," pp. 110–11, 227–31, 236–37. See also Bonsirven, "Comment fraterniser?" *UI*, June 5, 1936, pp. 577–79. Oscar de Férenzy, another prominent philosemite, harbored similar views. See Férenzy, pp. 200–201; "Paroles d'Alsace, paroles de bons sens," *UI*, June 8, 1934, pp. 314–15.

42. E. Roche, "La Jeunesse française chôme," *La République*, Oct. 19, 1934, p. 1. On Roche's position toward immigrant workers in general, see the following articles by Roche in *La République*: "Sur l'immigration des travailleurs étrangers," Feb. 25, 1934, p. 4; "Les Travailleurs étrangers en France," Apr. 6, 1934, p. 4; "Le Chômage et la main-d'oeuvre étrangère," June 30, 1934, p. 1; "La Relève de la main-d'oeuvre étrangère," Aug. 31, 1934, p. 1; "La Main-d'oeuvre étrangère," Nov. 20, 1934, p. 1; "Toujours le chômage," Dec. 2, 1934, p. 1; "Contre la plaie du chômage," Feb. 14, 1935, p. 1. On the Radical Party's adoption of Roche's plan, see "Le Congrès de la

Fédération républicain," *Le Temps*, June 4, 1934, p. 2; Larmour, p. 67. On *La République*'s pro-refugee stance, see text below.

43. Elbel, "Indésirables," *L'Oeuvre*, Dec. 1, 1934, p. 1.

44. On the generally pro-immigrant and pro-refugee line of *Le Quotidien* see "Le Rôle de la main-d'oeuvre étrangère en France," *Le Quotidien*, Sept. 24, 1933, pp. 1–2; "L'Importance et l'avenir de la population étrangère en France," *Le Quotidien*, Sept. 26, 1933, p. 4; Paul-Jean Lucas, "Les Hommes traqués," parts 1 and 5, July 26 and July 30, 1935, *Le Quotidien*, pp. 1, 3.

45. Roussel, "Les Causes du mécontentement des étudiants en médecine," *Le Quotidien*, Apr. 10, 1935, pp. 1–2; Apr. 11, 1935, pp. 1–2.

46. Roussel, "Les Travailleurs étrangers en France," *Le Quotidien*, Oct. 19, 1934, p. 2.

47. Roussel, "Les Travailleurs étrangers en France," *Le Quotidien*, Oct. 20, 1934, p. 2. See also the article by Roussel with the same title on Oct. 14, 1934, p. 4; Jean Couvreur, "L'Angoissant problème des réfugiés allemands," *Le Quotidien*, Oct. 1 and 2, 1933, p. 2.

48. Carmen Ennesch, "La Naissance de l'antisémitisme et ses raisons," *L'Ere nouvelle*, Sept. 18, 1934, clipped in ACIP B 130 (Divers).

49. Schor, *L'Opinion française et les étrangers*, p. 28; Weber, *Hollow Years*, pp. 12–13; Larkin, pp. 6–8, 382.

50. In July 1933, Jean Fabry, president of the Army Commission in the Chamber of Deputies, had already appealed to the administration to speed up the naturalization of the German refugees in particular, since these youths were especially eager to fight for France "à la suite des persécutions hitlériennes." Fabry, to Paul-Boncour, July 12, 1933, MAE Z 710, p. 191. On subsequent pressure from the army to speed up the rate of naturalization, see Chapter 10.

51. Mauco, *Les Etrangers*; Mauco, *Mémoire*; Martial, pp. 83–92. For a discussion of Mauco's views in the late 1930's, when his anti-Jewish attitudes became even more pronounced, see Chapter 12.

52. Mauco, *Les Etrangers*, pp. 311–12. On Mauco's support for the protectionist claims of liberal professionals and merchants, see ibid., pp. 87, 301–2; Mauco, *Mémoire*, pp. 75–76.

53. Mauco, *Les Etrangers*, p. 467.

54. Mauco, "Le Problème démographique," *Esprit*, July 1, 1939, p. 541; Mauco, "Quelques conséquences du mouvement de la population en Europe," *L'Europe nouvelle*, Apr. 8, 1939, pp. 380–81.

55. Mauco, *Mémoire*, p. 76. For Mauco's comments about East European Jewish students, see ibid., p. 96.

56. Mauco, "Le Problème démographique," *Esprit*, July 1, 1939, p. 544.

57. Mauco, *Les Etrangers*, pp. 145–46, 269–70, 555, 558; Mauco, *Mémoire*, pp. 2, 42. On this notion of a hierarchy of races and ethnic groups, see W. Schneider, *Quality*, pp. 208–29, and Schor, "L'Image," pp. 89–90; Schor, *L'Opinion française et les étrangers*, pp. 263, 502. Although in his early writings Mauco tended to classify Christian Poles as unassimilable, by the end of the decade he assessed them in a more

positive light, due to their religious affinities with the French and to the fact that they were manual laborers. See Mauco, "Le Problème démographique," p. 540.

58. Georges Mauco, "Une politique de la population," *L'Europe nouvelle*, Apr. 15, 1939, p. 409.

59. Mauco, *Mémoire*, pp. 76–77; 113–15.

60. Martial, pp. 84, 89. See also ibid., pp. 86, 91–92.

61. Raymond Millet, "Visites aux étrangers de France," *Le Temps*, May 28, 1938, p. 8.

62. Cited in Jean Lefranc, "En Marge," [*Le Temps*], June 9, 1938, clipped in AIU ms. 650 boîte 13 (46). These ideas were based primarily on Martial's *Traité de l'immigration et de la greffe inter-raciale* (Paris, 1931); *La Race française; Race, hérédité, folie: Etude d'anthropo-sociologie appliquée à l'immigration* (Paris, 1934). Martial was immensely successful at popularizing his work, and he was frequently cited and interviewed by the mainstream press. For popular discussions of his work, in addition to the articles already cited, see also Gascoin; "Les Enquêtes des 'Nouvelles Littéraires': Le Problème des races," Jan. 30, 1937, clipped in AN 72 AJ 600; CDV, bull. no. 20, Apr. 21, 1937, p. 7; Dr. Edouard Toulouse, "Race, hérédité, folie," *La Dépêche de Toulouse*, May 16, 1938, p. 1; Maurice Ajam, "Le Mélange des races," *La Dépêche de Toulouse*, Aug. 29, 1938, p. 1; J.-H. Rosny ainé, "Le Sang français," *La Dépêche de Toulouse*, Dec. 14, 1938, p. 1; Millet, "Trois millions d'étrangers en France," *L'Ordre*, July 25, 1938; Millet, pp. 125–26.

63. W. Schneider, *Quality*, pp. 251–52; Dr. J. Brutzkus, "A Propos d'une enquête," *La Juste parole*, no. 40 (Sept. 5, 1938): 13–14, also in "Tolérance: A propos d'une enquête sur les étrangers en France," *UI*, Aug. 12–19, 1938, pp. 801–2; Schor, *L'Opinion française et les étrangers*, p. 502–4.

64. Dr. L. Filderman, "Tribune des Lecteurs: La 'Stérilisation philosémite' du Dr. Martial," *UI*, Feb. 23, 1934, pp. 731–32.

65. Martial, p. 85.

66. W. Schneider, *Quality*, pp. 245–46; on Martial's career in the 1930's, see ibid., pp. 228, 230–55; Schneider, "France for the French: Reactions to Immigration Between the Wars and the Growth of French Racial Thought," unpublished paper presented to the Society for French Historical Studies, Iowa City, Iowa, Apr. 8, 1983. See also Schor, *L'Opinion française et les étrangers*, p. 502. For an overview of the French eugenics movement, see W. Schneider, *Quality*, and W. Schneider, "Toward the Improvement," pp. 268–91. For a discussion of French ethnography in the 1930's and during Vichy, including a brief discussion of Martial's thought, see Lebovics, pp. 41–51. On the contemporary perception that Martial's theory was antisemitic, see Maurice Ajam, "Le Mélange des races," *La Dépêche de Toulouse*, Aug. 29, 1938, p. 1.

67. Morand, "Billet à Marianne," *Le Figaro*, Feb. 19, 1935, p. 1.

68. Daudet, "La Question juive," *AF*, Dec. 11, 1933, clipped in APP BA 1813 241.155-B.

69. After the celebrated essay of Maurice Barrès, *Les Diverses familles spirituelles de la France* (Paris, 1917). For an overview of the attitude of the right-wing leagues

toward Jews in the 1930's, see Millman; Soucy. On the attitude of the Croix de Feu in particular, see Chapter 12, n. 34.

70. Giraudoux, "Chômage et peuplement," *Le Figaro*, Mar. 22, 1935, pp. 1, 3, and "France et étrangers," *Le Figaro*, Feb. 21, 1935, pp. 1, 3.

71. H. Lémery, "La Question des étrangers," *La République*, Feb. 9, 1935, p. 2.

72. Maga, *America*, p. 137.

73. Marrus and Paxton, pp. 48–49.

74. Schor, *L'Opinion française et les étrangers*, pp. 555–96; Schor, "Les Partis politiques," pp. 445–59; Schor, "Le Parti communiste," pp. 84–86.

75. Arendt, p. 93.

76. "La Séance de nuit," *L'Ere nouvelle*, Apr. 6, 1933, p. 3. See also Ch. 3, pp. 48–50.

77. "La Persécution des juifs en Allemagne," *L'Ere nouvelle*, Apr. 5, 1933, p. 1; Gaëtan Sanvoisin, "Préserver Paris," *Le Figaro*, Oct. 8, 1933, p. 1.

78. "Nouvelles du jour: Au Comité exécutif du parti radical et radical socialiste," *Le Temps*, Apr. 7, 1933, p. 3; "Herriot et Delbos exposent au Comité du Parti Radical la portée du pacte franco-soviétique," *L'Ere nouvelle*, Apr. 6, 1933, p. 1.

79. Herriot's speech, as paraphrased in "A 'La Nouvelle Ecole de la Paix,'" *L'Europe nouvelle*, May 27, 1933, p. 513.

80. "Après le suicide de Sonia Rosenzweig," *L'Oeuvre*, Nov. 2, 1933, p. 4. On the background to the case, see Schor, *L'Antisémitisme en France*, p. 68; "D'une semaine à l'autre: Hitlérisme français," *La Lumière*, Oct. 14, 1933, p. 4; Charles Ancel, "Sonia Roszencwaig [sic] à 13 ans s'est suicidée," *DdV*, Sept.–Oct. 1933, pp. 1, 6; "Le Suicide de la petite Sonia Rozensweig," *L'Oeuvre*, Oct. 13, 1933, p. 2.

81. "Les Protestations contre l'antisémitisme hitlérien," *Le Petit Parisien*, Apr. 3, 1933, p. 2; "En France," *Le Temps*, Apr. 6, 1933, p. 2; "Les Protestations contre l'antisémitisme hitlérien: Un appel aux protestants et aux catholiques," *La Victoire*, Apr. 3, 1933, clipped in APP BA 1814 241.155-1-G.

82. "Christians of France Pray for the Jews of Germany," *NYT*, Apr. 9, 1933, sect. IV, p. 1; "French Catholics Pledge Aid to Jews in Anti-Hitler Protest," *NYT*, Apr. 3, 1933, p. 9; "La Protestation des israélites de Paris," *Le Figaro*, Apr. 5, 1933, p. 2; "En France," *Le Temps*, Apr. 9, 1933, p. 2; "Une Protestation du Cardinal Archevèque de Paris," *Le Temps*, Apr. 4, 1933, p. 8; CDV to R. P. Devaux, Sept. 22, 1937, in AIU ms. 650 boîte 7 (25); HCR, "Compte rendu de la session du Comité Consultatif," London, Oct. 29–30, 1934, in LBI, AR 7162, box 5 (also in JDC no. 250).

83. "Informations Religieuses," *L'Aube*, Apr. 20, 1933, p. 4. On the hostility between Rémond, who was a former militant of the left-wing Catholic movement, Sillon, and the Action Française, see Schor, *L'Antisémitisme en France*, p. 225.

84. Daudet, "L'Invasion judéo-maçonnique," *AF*, June 18, 1933, clipped in APP BA 1814 241.155-1-C.

85. Gaston Tessier, "A Propos d'antisémitisme," *L'Aube*, Apr. 14, 1933, p. 1; "Le Meeting de Wagram contre l'antisémitisme," *L'Ere nouvelle*, May 6, 1933, clipped in APP BA 1814 241.155-1-C; "Les Protestations dans le monde," *AI*, May 4, 1933, p. 70; "La Protestation de la France contre les persécutions antisémites," *TJ*, no. 49 (Dec. 8, 1933): 843–44.

86. "Souscription en faveur des Allemands réfugiés," *Le Temps*, Apr. 21, 1933, p. 3.

87. "En France: Une Lettre de la Fédération Protestante au grand rabbin de France," *Le Temps*, Apr. 7, 1933, p. 2; "Christians of France Pray for the Jews of Germany," *NYT*, Apr. 9, 1933, sect. IV, p. 1. See also "Une Protestation du Cardinal Archevèque de Paris," *Le Temps*, Apr. 4, 1933, p. 8; "En France," *Le Temps*, Apr. 9, 1933, p. 2. Boegner, who did much to protest antisemitism during the Vichy regime, offered his services on behalf of the refugees, especially those among them who were "Christian Hebrews"—that is, converts or their descendants. See Norman Bentwich, to M. Henriod and Dr. Keller, Geneva, Jan. 10, 1934, MP: H 10.

88. On the Matteotti Committee, see "Des Secours pour la classe ouvrière allemande," *Le Populaire*, May 3, 1933, p. 6; "Au Appel de la CGT en faveur des victimes du nazisme," *Le Populaire*, July 3, 1933, p. 6. On the left-wing committees, see Palmier, 1: 282–83, 365, 401–2; Omnès, pp. 65–101; Schiller et al., pp. 52–53.

89. L. Pappo, "L'Allemagne hitlérienne jugée par M. Edmund von Gerlach," *L'Oeuvre*, June 6, 1933, pp. 1–3; "La Protection internationale des réfugiés," *CDH*, Nov. 10–15, 1933, p. 668; Victor Basch, "Le Droit d'asile," *CDH*, Apr. 20, 1933, pp. 246–47.

90. "Hommage à Israël," *AI*, May 18, 1933, p. 78. On the campaign to secure a chair for Einstein in France, see Chapter 2, n. 22.

91. "Pour les universitaires allemands réfugiés en France," *Le Populaire*, May 9, 1933, p. 4.

92. Ibid.

93. Marcel Jans, president of LAURS, Fédération Nationale des Etudiants de la Ligue des Droits de l'Homme, "Appel aux étudiants français," *CDH*, Aug. 30– Sept. 10, 1933, p. 524.

94. Paraf, "L'Accueil aux réfugiés," *La République*, Apr. 23, 1933, p. 4; Paraf, "Lorsque Hitler est roi," *DdV*, no. 12 (May 1933): 1, 4. See also Chevreuse, pp. 126–40; Roland de Marès, "Revue de presse," *Le Temps*, May 1, 1933, clipped in ACIP B (not classified); Meyer Carasso, "L'Emigration peut-elle être employée?" *DdV*, no. 13 (June 1933): 2; "Les Réfugiés allemands en France: Problèmes nouveaux," *DdV*, Sept.–Oct., 1933, p. 2.

95. P. Dominique, "Le Meilleur de l'Allemagne," *La République*, Apr. 28, 1933, p. 3. See also Jean Couvreur, "Les Israélites allemands en France, Part II. Eux et nous," *Le Quotidien*, Aug. 6, 1933, pp. 1, 2; Jean-Baptiste Lebas, "...Ah! l'exil est impie!...," *La République*, Mar. 29, 1935, p. 1.

96. P. Dominique, "Nationalisme et xénophobie," *L'Europe nouvelle*, Feb. 23, 1935, p. 173.

97. M. Paz, "Terre d'asile," *Vendredi*, Nov. 22, 1935, p. 4; Paz, pp. 26, 30–31. See also Livian, *Le Régime juridique*, pp. 29–30. The argument that France had no choice but to incorporate its foreign population in general for both economic and military reasons had considerable popularity in certain quarters. See, for example: André Bossin, "Paris, capitale du monde: Les Peuples à Paris," *L'Aube*, Mar. 22, 1934, pp. 1–2; A. Bossin, "Les Etrangers en France," *L'Aube*, Apr. 4, 1935, pp. 1–2;

"Le Renvoi des salariés étrangers," *L'Aube*, July 6, 1935, p. 2; Probus, "Les Travailleurs étrangers en France," *L'Aube*, Dec. 14, 1934, pp. 1–2; Louis Martin-Chauffier, "Xénophobie antifrançaise," *La République*, Feb. 17, 1935, p. 1; Denise Moran, "Le Droit d'asile est un droit sacré," *La Lumière*, June 1, 1935, p. 4; "La Grande pitié des travailleurs étrangers," *Le Peuple*, Nov. 27, 1934, p. 4; P. Vaillant-Couturier, "Calvaire des jeunes immigrés," *L'Humanité*, Feb. 23, 1935, pp. 1, 4; "Le Rôle de la main-d'oeuvre étrangère en France," *Le Quotidien*, Sept. 24, 1933, pp. 1–2; "L'Importance et l'avenir de la population étrangère en France," *Le Quotidien*, Sept. 26, 1933, p. 4; Jean Guyon-Cesbron, "Près de trois millions d'étrangers vivent sur notre sol," *Le Petit Journal*, Nov. 1, 1936, clipped in AIU ms. 650 boîte 13 (45).

98. P. Paraf, "Les Etrangers," *La République*, Feb. 11, 1935, pp. 1–2.

99. Jean d'Alsace, "Veut-on réglementer ou veut-on prohiber l'exercice de la médecine par les étrangers?" *La Lumière*, June 29, 1935, p. 4. See also Jean d'Alsace, "Les Promesses de la France doivent être tenues," *DdV*, Dec. 12, 1936, pp. 1, 5.

100. Dr. Leblond, "La Communauté interraciale," *Esprit*, Apr. 1, 1935, pp. 148–50; Dr. A. Vincent, "Il n'y a pas pléthore médicale," *Esprit*, Apr. 1, 1935, pp. 52–53. See also "Ceux qu'on appelle métèques," *Esprit*, May 2, 1935, pp. 325–26; "Les Xénophobes contre la France," *La Lumière*, May 11, 1935, p. 3; Nicolas Lerouge, "Les Médecins contre la médecine," *La République*, Feb. 18, 1935; Lerouge, "Propos Ingenus: Xénophagie," *La République*, Mar. 27, 1935, p. 1; Nicolas Lerouge, "Des places de médecin? En voici!," *La République*, Apr. 6, 1935, p. 1; B. de B., "La France n'a pas assez de médecins," *La République*, Dec. 25, 1935; Delcourt-Haillot, "La Pléthore médicale," *L'Aube*, Aug. 3, 1935, pp. 1–2; B. de B., "Les Campagnes réclament des médecins suppléants," *L'Oeuvre*, Sept. 16, 1935, p. 2; Georges Limoux, "Futurs pionniers...ou chômeurs de demain: VIII. Le 'Péril métèque,'" *Le Populaire*, Dec. 25, 1935, pp. 1, 2.

101. Noiriel (p. 285) claims that the socialists had supported the Law of July 19, 1934, but this does not seem to have been the case, since there were numerous articles in *Le Populaire* opposing this law and the socialists sought to overturn it in Parliament. For the various protests in the press by the socialists, the League for the Rights of Man, and LICA, see "Contre les naturalisés," *Le Populaire*, Oct. 25, 1934, p. 4; Georges Limoux, "Futurs pionniers...ou chômeurs de demain: VIII. Le 'Péril métèque,'" *Le Populaire*, Dec. 25, 1935, pp. 1, 2. For the protests of the League for the Rights of Man and Citizen and other left-wing groups, see "Bulletin de la Ligue des Droits de l'Homme: Nos Interventions," Feb. 20, 1935, pp. 111–12; "L'Activité juridique de la Ligue en 1934–1935," *CDH*, May 20, 1935, pp. 336–38; "L'Activité juridique de la Ligue: médecins naturalisés," *CDH*, Aug. 20, 1935, p. 569; Ch.-Aug. Bontemps, "Etudiants, méfiez-vous de toute xénophobie," *DdV*, no. 24, Feb. 1935, pp. 1–2; André Féry, "L'Etranglement des naturalisés," *DdV*, Feb. 15, 1935, pp. 1, 5.

102. "L'Activité juridique de la Ligue en 1934–1935," *CDH*, May 20, 1935, pp. 336–38.

103. Georges Limoux, "Futurs pionniers...ou chômeurs de demain: VIII. Le 'Péril métèque,'" *Le Populaire*, Dec. 25, 1935, pp. 1, 2.

104. "La Situation des naturalisés," *Le Populaire*, Oct. 28, 19[34], clipped in BDIC Dos. Duchêne GFΔ Rés. 86; Annexe no. 1603, 2e session extraordinaire de

1936 (Chambre des Députés), "Annexe au procès-verbal de la séance du 31 décembre 1936," in Chambre des Députés, *Impressions: Projets de lois, Propositions, Rapports*, etc., tome 16 (nos. 1601–1800), Session 1936–1937 (Paris, 1946); "L'Oeuvre du gouvernement de Front Populaire en faveur des travailleurs immigrés," *Le Populaire*, Feb. 17, 1937, clipped in APP BA 67 Provisoire.

105. Cross, pp. 191–92, 207–8; Schor, *L'Opinion française et les étrangers*, pp. 260–71, 555–76; and Schor, "Le Parti communiste," pp. 84–86. For the position of the left-wing parties toward immigrant workers during the 1930's, see also J.-Ch. Bonnet, pp. 205–9, 215–16; Milza, "La Gauche," pp. 128–31.

106. Police report, Nov. 29, 1931, APP BA 67 Provisoire 331.500-1. See also Police report, teleg., Aug. 24, 1932, APP BA 67 Provisoire 331.500-1.

107. Eugène Hénaff, "Pour empirer les conditions de la classe ouvrière, le patronat tente de se servir des travailleurs immigrés," *L'Humanité*, Nov. 10, 1933, cited in Thalmann, "L'Emigration du IIIe Reich," p. 134; Thalmann, "L'Immigration allemande," p. 158.

108. *Le Populaire*, Aug. 3, 1933, cited in Thalmann, "L'Emigration du IIIᵉ Reich," p. 134; Thalmann, "L'Immigration allemande," p. 158.

109. Comité d'Aide et d'Accueil, "Compte rendu no. 2, Activité 20–30 mai 1933," AIU X D 56.

110. Jouhaux, "Pour l'installation des réfugiés allemands," *La République*, June 13, 1933, p. 4.

111. Schor, *L'Opinion française et les étrangers*, p. 615; Schor, "Les Partis politiques," p. 454; Schor, *L'Antisémitisme en France*, pp. 230–31.

112. J. Koepplin, "Le Fléau sur Israël," *L'Humanité*, Apr. 2, 1933, pp. 1, 3. In May of 1933, Emile Bureau, the secretary of the Paris branch of the Secours Rouge International, declared: "La campagne des journaux bourgeois contre l'antisémitisme a pour but de masquer que cette terreur est principalement dirigée contre le prolétariat et qu'elle a un caractère de classe." Cited in Omnès, p. 90. On this theme, see also "Les Banquiers israélites sont ménagés tandis que sont traqués les travailleurs juifs," *L'Humanité*, Apr. 6, 1933, clipped in APP BA 1815 241.155-2; "L'Excitation antisémite d'Hitler, diversion fasciste," *L'Humanité*, Apr. 9, 1933, p. 1; "Les Nazis assassinent les juifs pauvres et les juifs riches plaident pour Hitler," *L'Humanité*, Apr. 20, 1933, pp. 1, 3; Pierre Bost, "Où en sont les Juifs d'Allemagne," *Marianne*, May 3, 1933, p. 3; Pierre Mualdes, "A Propos...d'antisémitisme," *Le Libertaire*, May 19, 1933, clipped in APP BA 1814 241.155-1-C; Shamir, pp. 24–26.

113. "L'Antisémitisme en Allemagne," [*La Patrie humaine*], Apr. 8, 1933, clipped in APP BA 1815 241.155-2. See also Emil Ludwig, "Les Juifs et l'Allemagne," *Marianne*, Apr. 12, 1933, p. 1; Theodor Lessing, "Economie et antisémitisme," *La Dépêche de Toulouse*, Sept. 8, 1933, in *Propos d'exil: Articles publiés dans "La Dépêche" par les émigrés du IIIe Reich* (Toulouse, 1983), pp. 119–21; statement by a German communist refugee at a Communist Party meeting in Illzach, Haut-Rhin, Report, Sûreté Nationale, Mulhouse, Dec. 20, 1933, AN F⁷ 13432. On the friction between political refugees and Jewish refugees, notwithstanding the fact that many of the political refugees were Jews as well, see Palmier, 1: 153, 157–59; Schiller et al., pp. 144–47, 239.

114. "Dans le quartier des banques où nazis et israélites ont realisé le front commun," *L'Humanité*, Apr. 18, 1933, cited in Millman, p. 283.

115. "Un Grand meeting de protestation contre la terreur hitlérienne," *Le Populaire*, Apr. 9, 1933, clipped in APP BA 1814 241.155-1-C. Netter was president of the mutual aid society, the *Union des Dames Israélites de Paris* as well as of the *Union des Femmes Juives pour la Palestine*.

116. "Des familles israélites allemandes se sont réfugiées à Paris," *Le Populaire*, Mar. 16, 1933, p. 2 (also clipped in APP BA 1814 241.155-1-G). See also Claude Pierrey, "On opprime Israël: On ne le détruit pas," *La République*, May 29, 1933, pp. 1, 3.

117. P.-L. Darnar, "Einstein," *L'Humanité*, Sept. 11, 1933, p. 1.

118. Jeanne Ancelet-Hustache, "Malgré Hitler...," *L'Aube*, May 2, 1933, pp. 1, 2. See also Georges Hoog, "Devant l'Allemagne hitlérienne," *L'Aube*, May 14–15, 1933, p. 1.

119. Bayet, "L'Antisémitisme hitlérien déshonore l'Allemagne," *La Lumière*, Mar. 25, 1933, p. 4; Bayet, "Le Devoir du monde," *La République*, Apr. 3, 1933, p. 1; Bayet, "Contre l'antisémitisme; Contre le nationalisme!" *La République*, Mar. 30, 1933, p. 1; Bayet, "Les Fourriers de l'hitlérisme," *La République*, Dec. 12, 1933, p. 1. On this theme, see also Jacques Kayser, "Contre l'antisémitisme et le nationalisme," *La République*, Apr. 6, 1933, p. 1; Claude Pierrey, "On opprime Israël: On ne le détruit pas," *La République*, May 29, 1933, pp. 1, 3; Louis Masson, "La Sarre ne doit pas mettre le feu à l'Europe," *L'Aube*, Oct. 30, 1934, pp. 1–3.

120. Bertrand de Jouvenel, "C'est d'abord une rumeur légère...," *La République*, May 7, 1933, pp. 1–2.

121. "Daladier est-il devenu antisémite?" *DdV*, no. 15 (Sept.–Oct. 1933): 1. The Vatican's hesitation to make a clear-cut commitment to refugee relief, a hesitation that, according to the HCR, by 1934 had significantly cooled the enthusiasm of French Catholic leaders to participate in the relief effort, also probably stemmed from a reluctance to strain already tense relations with the Nazi state. Walter Kotschnig, to James G. McDonald, HCR, Nov. 28, 1934, in MP: H 19.

122. On the response of the League for the Rights of Man and Citizen, see "Une Résolution de la Ligue des Droits de l'Homme," *L'Aube*, Oct. 13, 1934, p. 2; "L'Activité juridique de la Ligue en 1934–1935," *CDH*, May 20, 1935, pp. 336–38; J.-Ch. Bonnet, pp. 236–37; "Les Résolutions du Congrès (17–19 Juillet 1936)," *CDH*, Aug. 10, 1936, p. 590. On the response of the CGT and the Socialist Party, see "Odieuse et hypocrite manoeuvre du gouvernement contre les travailleurs étrangers," *Le Populaire*, Mar. 2, 1935, clipped in APP BA 67 Provisoire; H. L., "Ne laissez pas en prison les sans-patrie," *Le Populaire*, Oct. 1, 1935, p. 2; "Le Comité de la CGT dénonce l'iniquité d'un décret-loi concernant les expulsions de proscrits politiques," *Le Populaire*, Nov. 17, 1935, p. 2; P. Perrin, "Tous les étrangers au bagne," *DdV*, Nov. 16, 1935, p. 1; "De Nombreux étrangers immigrés se voient refuser la carte d'identité," *L'Humanité*, Apr. 3, 1935, APP BA 66 Provisoire; "Mêmes salaires et mêmes droits pour les ouvriers immigrés," *L'Humanité*, Sept. 15, 1934, p. 5; Schramm and Vormeier, pp. 204, 233; Vormeier, "La Situation administrative des exilés allemands en France (1933–1945)," *Revue d'Allemagne*, vol. XVIII, no. 2

(Apr.–June 1986), p. 191; "La Confédération Générale du Travail et le droit d'asile" (Résolution du Congrès de Toulouse, 1936), pp. 52–53, and Mario Angeloni, "Pour un statut juridique des réfugiés étrangers," p. 63, both in *L'Homme réel*, special issue, "Droit d'asile," nos. 26–27 (Feb.–Mar., 1936). *L'Humanité* consistently defended the rights of foreign workers.

123. "Pour le droit d'asile," *CDH*, Dec. 20, 1931, p. 750. On the attempt to separate political refugees from other immigrants, see also "La Protection internationale des réfugiés," *CDH*, Nov. 10–15, 1933, p. 668.

124. See Chapter 3, nn. 31–32.

125. "Le Problème des émigrés politiques," *L'Oeuvre*, Mar. 19, 1935, p. 4; "Hilfe für politische Emigranten: Ein Vorschlag Ernst Tollers," *PT*, no. 462, Mar. 19, 1935, p. 1; "Un Statut pour les émigrés politiques," *Le Populaire*, Mar. 20, 1935, clipped in APP BA 67 Provisoire.

126. See especially, H. L., "Ne laissez pas en prison les sans-patrie," *Le Populaire*, Oct. 1, 1935, p. 2; Magdeleine Paz, "Terre d'asile," *Vendredi*, Nov. 22, 1935, p. 4 ; Paul-Jean Lucas, "Les Hommes traqués," *Le Quotidien*, July 26 and July 30, 1935, pp. 1, 3.

127. "La Défense des travailleurs étrangers," *L'Oeuvre*, Oct. 5, 1935, p. 2; "L'Association des 'Amis des Travailleurs Etrangers' est constituée," *Le Populaire*, Aug. 9, 1935, p. 1; Palmier, 1: 299. On Paz's denunciations of the 1935 antiforeign decree laws, see Chapter 3, n. 20.

128. On the creation of the Centre de Liaison, see *Fraternité*, no. 3 (Jan. 1936): 2; *Fraternité*, no. 20 (June, 1937): 3; Daniel Mayer, "Pour le droit d'asile," Jan. 6, 1936, p. 6, "Une Réunion d'information organisée par le Centre de Liaison des Organisations d'Immigrés en France a eu lieu hier," Jan. 7, 1936, p. 3; M. Paz, "Un Conférence internationale pour le droit d'asile," May 26, 1936, pp. 1, 2, all in *Le Populaire*; "Die Lage der Einwanderer: Eine Versammlung des 'Centre de liaison des Comités pour le statut des immigrés,'" *PT*, no. 757 (Jan. 8, 1936): 2; "Frankreich und die Auslander, *PT*, no. 548 (Dec. 13, 1937): 3; "Etrangers," *CDH*, June 20, 1936, p. 471; Omnès, pp. 91–96; Palmier, 1: 300. Among the organizations included in the Centre were: the LICA, the Italian, Spanish, and German branches of League for the Rights of Man; the CGT's Comité d'asile; the Secours Rouge International, the Amis des Travailleurs Etrangers; the American Friends Service Committee (Quakers); Assistance Médicale, Fédération des Immigrés d'Allemagne; Club Allemagne; the Comité National; Secours Populaire de France; Mouvement Populaire Juif; Office Général des Réfugiés Turcs.

Among the individuals that lent support to the Centre de Liaison were: M. Paz, Maria Veroné, Emile Borel, Joseph Caillaux, Eugène Frot, Raoul Evrard, Dumenil de Graumont, Georges Brugnier, Justin Godart, Léon Jouhaux, Lapierre, Bernard Lecache, Rabbi Louis-Germain Lévy, R. P. Mangold, Edmond Milhaud, Morizet, M. Moutet, Paul Perrin, Pourriau, G. Rodrigues, Romain Rolland, Jules Romains, Marc Sangnier.

129. On the aims of the Amis des Travailleurs Etrangers, see "La Défense des travailleurs étrangers," *L'Oeuvre*, Oct. 5, 1935, p. 2; "L'Association des 'Amis des travailleurs étrangers' est constituée," *Le Populaire*, Aug. 9, 1935, p. 1. On the aims of the Centre, see Daniel Mayer, "Pour le droit d'asile," *Le Populaire*, Jan. 6, 1936, p. 6;

"Pour le statut des immigrés," *Fraternité*, no. 3 (Jan. 1936), p. 2; "Une conférence de M. Henri Levin à Strasbourg sur le statut des immigrés," *UI*, Jan. 21, 1938, p. 334; Henri Levin, "Le Statut juridique des étrangers," *Fraternité*, no. 3 (Jan. 1936): 1.

130. "La Conférence Internationale du Droit d'Asile a terminée ses travaux hier," *Le Populaire*, June 22, 1936, pp. 1, 2; "Conférence internationale pour le droit d'asile," *UI*, June 26, 1936, p. 637.

131. J.-Ch. Bonnet, p. 316; *JO, Documents Parlementaires*, Chambre, Annexe no. 2632, July 9, 1936, p. 1265. The Chamber adopted this resolution with some minor changes on Jan. 27, 1937; see Annexe no. 1417, 2e session extraordinaire, 2e séance, Dec. 8, 1936, *JO, Documents Parlementaires*, sect. 3, Chambre 1936, pp. 940–41; *JO, Débats Parlementaires, Chambre des Députés*, Jan. 21, 1937, p. 100.

132. A German Refugee [author], "Le Problème angoissant des réfugiés allemands," *L'Oeuvre*, Sept. 2, 1935, p. 3. For a further discussion of the situation of the refugees in 1935, see Chapter 5, nn. 80–100.

133. Marguerite d'Escola, "Aubades: Colons sans colonies et colonies sans colons," *L'Aube*, Aug. 30, 1935, p. 2.

134. "Main-d'oeuvre étrangère et droit d'asile: Une lettre de la CGT au Président du Conseil," *Le Peuple*, Mar. 8, 1935, pp. 1, 2. On CGT support for agricultural schemes, see also "En faveur des réfugiés allemands: Une note de la CGT," *Le Peuple*, Aug. 10, 1933, clipped in APP BA 1814 241.155.1-G; Cross, p. 208. The League for the Rights of Man also began to look more favorably on agricultural and colonial solutions. See "Comité Central, Ligue des Droits de l'Homme, Extraits, Séance du 7 novembre 1935," *CDH*, June 20, 1936, p. 456.

135. "Les Juifs expulsés d'Allemagne," *AF*, Sept. 21, 1933, clipped in APP BA 1814 241.155-1-G.

136. Annexe no. 4148, *JO, Documents Parlementaires*, sect. 3, Chambre 1934, 2ème session extraordinaire, Nov. 22, 1934, pp. 131–32.

137. "Les Etrangers," *CDH*, Apr. 10, 1931, pp. 227–28.

Chapter Five

1. Rajsfus, *Sois Juif*, and Joly et al., pp. 37–64. Among the most prominent French Jews critical of the attitudes of the native establishment's refugee committees were the Zionist poet André Spire, the left-wing Zionist activist Wladimir Rabinovitch (Rabi), and Léon Blum, prime minister of France during the Popular Front. On Spire, see Hyman, p. 221; Spire, "Face à Hitler," *RJG*, 2ème année, no. 1 (Oct. 1933): 5. On Rabi, see Weinberg, p. 90; Rajsfus, *Sois Juif*, pp. 149, 151–52; Rabinovitch, "Charles Péguy: Témoinage d'un Juif," *Esprit* (June 1, 1939): 321–32; Rabi, "Le Scandale des comités," *Samedi*, Feb. 4, 1939, p. 4. On Blum, see "M. Léon Blum et la question juive," *L'Ordre*, Nov. 27, 1938, p. 3; "Le Discours de Léon Blum," *DdV*, Dec. 3, 1938, p. 6; Rabi, p. 384.

2. See Weinberg; Hyman, esp. pp. 199–232; Nicault, "L'Accueil." Although a much abbreviated version of this essay with the same title has been published in Bartosek et al., pp. 53–59, all citations below refer to the longer version. For a recent summary of these views, see also Grynberg, "L'Accueil," pp. 131–48.

To be sure, these three historians vary considerably in the degree to which they are critical of the native French Jewish establishment. Weinberg is decidedly the most critical, whereas Nicault is the most sympathetic. Nevertheless, even Weinberg takes into account the external limitations imposed by French government policy.

3. For biographical sketches of Lambert, see Richard I. Cohen, "Introduction," in Lambert, *Carnet*, pp. 13–62; Cohen, "A Jewish Leader in Vichy France, 1940–1943: The Diary of Raymond-Raoul Lambert," *Jewish Social Studies* XLIII (summer–fall 1981): 291–310.

4. Prague, "Une Histoire qui recommence!" *AI*, Mar. 16, 1933, p. 41. See also Prague, "Le Réveil," June 22, 1933, p. 93; "Les Leçons de l'histoire," July 6, 1933, pp. 101–2; "Un Autre foyer," Nov. 3, 1932, p. 173, all in *AI*.

5. Hyman, pp. 217–18; Rajsfus, *Sois Juif*, p. 106; Weinberg, pp. 107–8, 110–13, 123–26; Thalmann, "L'Immigration allemande," p. 157; Thalmann, "L'Emigration du IIIe Reich," p. 133; "Un Grand Meeting de protestation contre l'antisémitisme hitlérien," *L'Oeuvre*, Apr. 4, 1933, p. 2; "Les Protestations contre l'antisémitisme hitlérien," *Le Figaro*, Apr. 6, 1933, p. 4; "L'Antisémitisme," Apr. 13, 1933, p. 2, and "Contre les persécutions des juifs en Allemagne," Apr. 29, 1933, p. 3, both in *Le Temps*; "Le Meeting de la Ligue Internationale contre l'Antisémitisme," *L'Oeuvre*, Apr. 9, 1933, p. 2; "Les Protestations dans le monde," *AI*, May 4, 1933, p. 70; J. B. [Jacques Biélinky], "Un Meeting de la 'Lica' à la salle Wagram," *UI*, Sept. 15–22, 1933, p. 31; "La Protestation de la France contre les persécutions antisémites," *TJ*, Dec. 6, 1933, pp. 843–44; "Nazis Menace World Say Paris Speakers," *NYT*, May 11, 1933, p. 13; "A Lyon, M. Herriot s'élève contre la persécution des Juifs," *L'Aube*, Apr. 9–10, 1933, p. 3; and the numerous police reports and press clippings in APP BA 1814 241.155-1-C; APP BA 1815 241.155-1-B; APP BA 1813 241.155-C; AN F^7 13430; AN F^7 13432; AN F^7 13433.

6. Police report, Apr. 14, 1933, APP BA 1815 241.155-1-B; "Le Mouvement de protestation contre les menées antisémites d'Allemagne," *L'Oeuvre*, Apr. 2, 1933, p. 2; "Contre l'antisémitisme," Apr. 22, 1933, p. 3; Apr. 27, 1933, p. 3; May 4, 1933, p. 3, all in *Le Temps*.

7. Consistoire Israélite de Paris, Report, Apr.–Sept. 1933, ACIP B 135 bis; ACIP, Report, Aug. and Sept. 1933, ACIP B 128; "Les Réfuges parisiens s'attendent à voir affluer prochainement les victimes d'Hitler," *L'Oeuvre*, Mar. 15, 1933, p. 1; "La Protestation des israélites de Paris," *Le Figaro*, Apr. 5, 1933, p. 2; "Un Appel de M. Israël Lévi," *UI*, Apr. 21, 1933, p. 52; Resolution of the French Rabbinical Association of May 1, 1933, cited in Rajsfus, *Sois Juif*, p. 106; "Une Protestation des rabbins français contre les persécutions dont sont victimes les juifs allemands," clipped in *Le Journal d'Alsace et de Lorraine*, May 3, 1933, in ADBR D 460, paq. 5/36; "L'Assemblée Consistorial," *AI*, June 8, 1933, p. 86; "Appel aux Juifs de France en faveur des victimes de l'antisémitisme allemand," June 9, 1933, LBI, AR-C 1698/ 4099; Rothschild.

8. Joseph L. Cohen, "Report on HICEM and on the French National Committee for German Refugees," Aug. 8, 1933, JDC no. 617. According to a report of the Service Juridique pour les Réfugiés Allemands of Nov. 13, 1935, there were as many as 20 committees (JDC no. 602). For a description of major Jewish committees see

Nicault, "L'Accueil." The two most important left-wing refugee committees were the Matteoti Committee, affiliated with the Socialist Party, and the Secours Rouge International, affiliated with the Communist Party. On the work of the other committees, see "Quelques jours avec les proscrits allemands," *DdV*, no. 13 (July–Aug. 1933): 1, 4; Omnès, pp. 65–104; Joly, "L'Assistance des Quakers," in Badia et al., *Les Bannis*, pp. 105–16; Peterson, pp. 69–71; Fabian and Coulmas, pp. 38–45; Palmier, 1: 278–83, 364–65, 401–8; Schor, *L'Opinion française et les étrangers*, p. 614.

9. The Comité National was actually a federation of preexisting refugee relief committees. It was created primarily to avoid needless duplication of services and interventions with government authorities, but another goal of its founders was to concentrate authority in the hands of native Jews associated with consistorial circles. Among its sponsors were many prominent non-Jews. Its first honorary president was former prime minister Paul Painlevé, who was succeeded after his death in late 1933 by Senator Henry Bérenger. Other sponsors included Senator Justin Godart; Edouard Herriot, Radical Party deputy; Senator André Honnorat; Deputy François Piétri; Georges Risler, president of the Musée Social; Baron Edmond de Rothschild, president of the Consistoire Central; Israël Lévi, chief rabbi of France; and Sylvain Lévi, professor at the Collège de France and president of the Alliance Israélite Universelle. The Committee's executive committee in 1933 consisted of: Robert de Rothschild, acting president; Albert Cahen; Jaques Helbronner; Sylvain Lévi; Jacques Sée; Pierre Dreyfus; Maurice Stern; Maurice Rueff; Albert Manuel; Bernard Melamède; and Raymond-Raoul Lambert.

On the creation of the Comité d'Aide et d'Accueil and later the Comité National, see Nicault, "L'Accueil," pp. 4–5; Joly et al., pp. 37–64; Joseph C. Hyman, to Henry Wineman, Oct. 16, 1933, JDC no. 601; "The Activity of the HICEM for the Jewish Emigrants from Germany," reports for Mar., 1933 through Oct. 1934 and July through Aug., 1934, JDC no. 674; Joseph L. Cohen, "Report on HICEM and on the French National Committee for German Refugees," Aug. 8, 1933, JDC no. 617; "Aide Mémoire concernant la Réunion du Comité de Liaison du 28 mai," June 2, 1933, AIU France X D 56; "Minutes of meeting regarding the creation of the Comité National," June [22 or 23], 1933, LBI, AR-C 1698/4099; Raymond-Raoul Lambert, "L'Accueil de la France," RJG, no. 8 (May 1933), pp. 348–51; *AI*, June 22, 1933, p. 99; Bernard Schönberg, "L'Aide aux réfugiés allemands," *RJG*, 2ème année, no. 5 (Feb., 1934), pp. 180–85.

On official recognition of the Comité National as the sole spokesman on refugee matters, see Chautemps, to [Robert de Rothschild], president of the Comité National, July 19, 1933, attached to Comité National circular no. 1, Aug. 13, 1933, MAE SDN I E 451, pp. 47–55 (also in LBI, AR-C 1698/4099); "Création du 'Comité Nationale Français de Secours aux Emigrés Allemands Victimes de l'Antisémitisme,'" *UI*, June 30, 1933, pp. 349–52.

The Comité National also had provincial branches, the principal one being the Fédération des Comités de Secours de l'Est de la France headquartered in Strasbourg. See "Conférence régionale à Metz des Comités de Secours pour les réfugiés," *TJ*, Nov. 17, 1933, p. 793; "La Fédération des comités de secours de l'Est," *TJ*, Nov. 24, 1933, p. 809; "Metz: Pour les fugitifs d'Allemagne," *UI*, Nov. 17, 1933, p. 293.

10. Police report, Apr. 5, 1933, APP BA 1814 241.155-1-C. See also Foreign Ministry (Contrôle des étrangers), to the British ambassador in Paris, Apr. 12, 1933, MAE Z 710, pp. 51–52.

11. Comité d'Aide et d'Accueil, "Compte rendu, no. 2, Activité du Secrétariat Général du 20 au 30 mai 1933," "Compte rendu, no. 3, Activité du Secrétariat Général du 1er au 10 juin, 1933," both in AIU France X D 56; "Compte rendu, no. 4, Activité du Secrétariat Général du 10 juin–30 juin, 1933," MAE SDN I E 451, pp. 38–45; "L'Organisation des secours pour les réfugiés allemands," *AI*, July 6, 1933, p. 105; "Quelques jours avec les proscrits allemands," *DdV*, no. 14, July–Aug., 1933, pp. 1, 4.

12. Israël Lévi, the chief rabbi of France, and Sylvain Lévi, president of the Alliance Israélite Universelle, sent a desperate telegram to Cyrus Adler on June 2, 1933: "Need instant help. Five thousand Jewish refugees. Number constantly growing. Daily expense thirty thousand francs. Funds threaten exhaustion." JDC no. 617. See also Comité d'Aide et d'Accueil, "Compte rendu, no. 2, Activité du Secrétariat Général du 20 au 30 mai 1933," AIU France X D 56; "L'Organisation des secours pour les réfugiés allemands," *AI*, July 6, 1933, p. 105; "Paris and the German Emigrants," Report from Elizabeth T. Shipley, American Friends Service Committee (AFSC) representative in Europe, Innsbruck, Austria, to AFSC, Philadelphia, Oct. 1934, in Friedlander and Milton, 2, doc. no. 32: 94–95.

13. Joseph L. Cohen, "Report on HICEM and on the French National Committee for German Refugees," Aug. 8, 1933, JDC no. 617; Mr. Harvey, British Embassy, Paris, to J. V. Perowne, Jan. 10, 1934, PRO FO 371/17698.C308.

14. On the size of the French Jewish population in the mid-1930's, see J. Adler, p. 5. The FSJF was actually the first Jewish organization to establish a relief committee for the refugees, but it had to abandon these efforts due to lack of funds. See Weinberg, p. 111; Hyman, p. 208; Jacques Biélinky, "FSJF," *UI*, Dec. 15, 1933, p. 421; Joseph L. Cohen, "Report on HICEM and on the French National Committee for German Refugees," Aug. 8, 1933, JDC no. 617.

15. At Lévi's behest, Edward Mamelsdorf, Bernard J. Shoninger, Karl Hirschland, and Ludwig Lewisohn formed a committee in the United States to raise money for the French relief campaign. See their appeals to Justice Irving Lehman, June 22, 1933, and Mamelsdorf to Lehman, June 2, 1933, both in JDC no. 617. Robert de Rothschild also appealed to Stephen Wise, Felix Warburg, and Lewis Strauss for financial assistance over the summer and early fall. See J. Biélinky, "Deux manifestations du Comité français pour le Congrès Mondial Juif," *UI*, July 28, 1933, pp. 487–88; Anthony Rothschild, to Felix Warburg, Cable, Aug. 4, 1933, JDC no. 617; J. C. Hyman to McDonald, Nov. 16, 1933, MP: H 1.

16. Rothschild, to Chautemps, July 26, 1933, APP BA 407[P] 13.112-1. See also [Comité National], "Note pour M. le Président du Conseil," July 20, 1933, LBI, AR-C 1698/4099; "Procès verbal de la 2ème séance tenue par la Commission Interministérielle des Réfugiés Israélites Allemands," Oct. 16, 1933, MAE Z 711, pp. 39–40. The 3,500 refugees mentioned by Rothschild were only those receiving assistance. According to police estimates from late 1933, there were close to 10,000 refugees from Germany in the Department of the Seine alone, 7,304 of whom had

actually registered with the Préfecture de Police in Paris. Police report, Nov. 28, 1933 [attached to Police report "Renseignements concernant les réfugiés d'Allemagne," Nov. 10, 1933], APP BA 407^P 13.112-1.

17. In 1933, the JDC covered 20% of the Comité National's budget. Bauer, *My Brother's Keeper*, p. 141. On the JDC's fears that the borders would be closed, Kahn, cable to JDC, N.Y., Oct. 12, 1933, JDC no. 617; Bauer, *My Brother's Keeper*, p. 143. France regularly received the largest allotment of JDC funds of all refugee-receiving countries.

18. Police reports, Oct. 10, 1933, and "Les Réfugiés allemands dans la région parisienne," Nov., 1933, both in APP BA 1814 241.155-1-A; "Renseignements concernant les réfugiés d'Allemagne," Nov. 28, 1933, APP BA 407^P 13.112-1. See also Comité National, "Compte rendu, Activité du Secrétariat Général jusqu'au 16 octobre 1933," and "Compte rendu, Activité du Secrétariat Général du 16 octobre au 31 décembre 1933," both in AIU France X D 56; "Procès verbal de la 2ème séance tenue par la Commission Interministérielle des Réfugiés Israélites Allemands," Oct. 16, 1933, MAE Z 711, p. 40; "Procès verbal de la 4ème séance tenue par la Commission Interministérielle des Réfugiés Israélites Allemands," Nov. 11, 1933, MAE Z 711, pp. 99–100; "Report on the Activities of the AJDC for the Year 1933 and Early Months of 1934," p. 46, JDC no. 154; Jacques Fouques-Duparc, "Aide Mémoire," Nov. 22, 1933, MAE SDN I E 448, pp. 76–84; "Création du Comité National Français de Secours aux Emigrés Allemands Victimes de l'Antisémitisme," *UI*, June 30, 1933, p. 350; "In einer Pariser Emigrantenkaserne," *TJ*, no. 50 [mid-Dec. 1933]: 865–66; André Bossin, "Paris capitale du monde: Part III, Les Allemands," *L'Aube*, Mar. 30, 1934, pp. 1–2; Joly et al., pp. 53–54; Schramm and Vormeier, p. 197; Badia, "L'Emigration," pp. 32–33. Similar facilities had been made available in Mulhouse. See "L'Assemblée Consistoriale," *AI*, June 8, 1933, p. 87.

On the government's refusal to offer further assistance, see "Les Réfugiés allemands en France," *Le Matin*, Aug. 5, 1933, clipped in AN F^7 13431; secretary-general, League for the Rights of Man and Citizen, to the director of public assistance, Aug. 22, 1933, APP BA 1815 241.155-1-D; Police report, "Réunion à la Présidence du Conseil des répresentants des diverses départements et services intéressés [aux réfugiés allemands]," Sept. 23, 1933, APP BA 407^P 13.112-1.

19. Janine Auscher, "L'Oeuvre du Comité d'Aide et d'Accueil aux Réfugiés allemands," *UI*, July 28, 1933, p. 481. Jacques Helbronner also explained the delay in the organization of the French Jewish relief effort by saying: "C'est que les français de religion israélite sont français avant d'être juifs et que nous avons eu du mal à oublier ce que les juifs allemands ont été pendant la guerre." "Minutes, Meeting to Discuss the Creation of the Comité National," June [22 or 23], 1933, p. 11, LBI, AR-C 1698/4099. See also McDonald, to Miss Ogden, Nov. 27, 1933, MP: H 1; "Création du 'Comité National Français...,'" *UI*, June 30, 1933, p. 351; Biélinky, "Paris hospitalier," *UI*, Dec. 22, 1933, p. 440; F. W., "France: La question de l'immigration allemande," *UI*, May 3, 1935, p. 526.

20. Biélinky, "Deux réunions en faveur des réfugiés," *UI*, Jan. 26, 1934, p. 606; "Baron Robert de Rothschild über die Flüchtingsfrage," *PT*, no. 38 (Jan. 18, 1934): 2; Biélinky, "Les Victimes de Hitler en France," *Kadimah*, 5ème année, no. 11

(Sept. 28, 1934): 14; Robert de Rothschild, to James G. McDonald, confidential report, "Present Situation in France of the German Refugees," Dec. 16, 1933, MP: H 1.

21. "Minutes of Meeting Regarding the Creation of the Comité National," June [22 or 23], 1933, in LBI, AR-C 1698/4099. Rothschild obviously complained to his friend Felix Warburg about this problem since at a meeting of the HCR, Warburg proclaimed:

Then there is a small number of Jews who foresaw what was coming and who got some of their funds out of Germany, and they are rather noisy and objectionable in the cafés, in the public places in Paris. And they make the life of the Jews in Paris difficult and have a tendency to spread antisemitism. They have not contributed to any great extent to the relief funds. And they will be made to do so even if they are unwilling, but the process is painful and slow. . . . The refugees in France are slow and disagreeable, and the effect has been that antisemitism is growing in France by leaps and bounds.

"Refugee Committee Meeting Called by James G. McDonald," Feb. 25, 1934, JDC no. 404. For other examples of this resentment, see Ernest Ginsburger, "Tribune des lecteurs," *UI*, Nov. 3, 1933, p. 218; Pierre Lévy, letter to the editor, *UI*, Sept. 1, 1933, p. 654; "Nos Echos: Ouvert le samedi," *UI*, Feb. 16, 1934, p. 692.

22. "La Disparition de Comité de Secours aux Réfugiés," *TJ*, no. 10 (Mar. 9, 1934): 185.

23. L. D., "Que faut-il penser de l'immigration d'éléments indésirables?" *TJ*, July 9, 1937, p. 1.

24. Martin, "Ce qui se passe chez nous: Les Emigrés d'Allemagne en France et la question juive," *La Terre retrouvée*, Mar. 25, 1936, p. 10 (also reprinted as "Les Emigrés d'Allemagne en France et la question juive," *UI*, Apr. 24, 1936, pp. 485–86). See also "Billet Strasbourgeois," *TJ*, Mar. 25, 1933, p. 262; L. D., "Ce que nous apprennent les nouveaux immigrés," *TJ*, Mar. 6, 1936, pp. 145–46.

25. Hyman, p. 218; "Contre l'antisémitisme hitlérien," *L'Oeuvre*, Apr. 7, 1933, clipped in APP BA 1814 241.155-1-G; "Rabbi Asks French Not to Annoy Nazis," *NYT*, Apr. 7, 1933, p. 12. See also Lambert, "Tendons la main aux savants allemands juifs persécutés!" *UI*, Dec. 15, 1933, p. 406; William Oualid, "L'Antisémitisme allemand et le droit," *UI*, Apr. 7 and 14, 1933, p. 13.

26. In June 1933, Helbronner, for example, declared:

Ces groupements [left-wing refugee committees] sont en train de causer à ces réfugiés allemands d'un part et aux français israélites d'autre part, des dangers que l'on ne soupçonne pas; que des gens qui ont des préoccupations politiques prennent pour continuer leur politique l'arme de l'antisémitisme, c'est leur affaire, mais il est indispensable que les français israélites et que les autres personnalités de religion non israélite...n'aient pas l'impression qu'on veut se servir d'eux dans un but politique. Or il a été mis sous nos yeux des tracts et des journaux de ces groupements qui sont en train d'exciter les passions pour reprendre plus tôt des sentiments d'antisémitisme.

"Minutes, Meeting to Discuss the Creation of the Comité National," June [22 or 23], 1933, p. 10, LBI, AR-C 1698/4099. See also Assemblée Générale, Meeting of the Central Consistory, May 27, 1934, ACIP B 132 (affaires administratives); Dr. Jean Sterne, "Judaïsme et opinions politiques," *UI*, Apr. 24, 1936, pp. 483–84; Rabi, p. 382. On the political activities of the émigré community, see Fabian and Coulmas, pp. 50–61; Peterson; Palmier, 1; Langkau-Alex, 1.

27. Ernest Ginsburger, "Tribune des lecteurs," *UI*, Nov. 3, 1933, pp. 218–19.

28. Comité d'Aide et d'Accueil, "Compte rendu, no. 2, Activité du Secrétariat Général du 20 au 30 mai 1933," AIU France X D 56; [Lambert], Comité National, "Note pour M. le Préfecture de Police," July 25, 1933, APP BA 407^P 13.112-1.

29. Comité d'Aide et d'Accueil, "Compte rendu, no. 2, Activité du Secrétariat Général du 20 au 30 mai 1933," AIU France X D 56. One German refugee who worked for the Comité National described the tense conditions there as follows:

La plupart de ceux qui travaillaient n'avaient pas la formation professionnelle requise, ce qui explique qu'il y ait eu tant d'incapables au comité. Les émigrés s'en plaignaient et reprochaient aux employés, bien souvent réfugiés eux-mêmes, leur attitude de fonctionnaires bornés. L'ambiance était inimaginable: nous étions sans cesse débordés par des montagnes de courrier par le monde qui se pressait dans la salle d'attente et qui faisait parfois la queue dans la rue depuis la veille au soir. Il faut avoir l'esprit bien trempé ou le coeur insensible pour arriver à vivre et travailler au milieu de tant de misères.

R. C., "A Vichy," p. 124. See also Peterson, p. 73; Joly et al., pp. 50–51.

30. Police report, "a/s le distribution de tracts dans les bastions des réfugiés allemands," Nov. 21, 1933, APP BA 1814 241.155-1-A. On these disturbances, see Police report, Oct. 4, 1933, BA 1815 241.155-1-D; "Camps de concentration à Paris," *L'Humanité*, Sept. 20, 1933, clipped in APP BA 1814 241.155-1-A; Omnès, p. 90; Thalmann, "L'Immigration allemande," n. 8, p. 152.

Aside from this agitation, which, according to the police, ended in failure, the police and the committee reported that conditions in the camps were relatively good and that the refugees were well behaved. See G. Oudara, director, Commissaire spécial de police (Renseignments généraux), Oct. 9, 1933, BA 1814 241.155-1-A; Police report, Oct. 1933, BA 1813 241.155-B; "Les Réfugiés allemands dans la région parisienne," Nov. 1933, BA 1814 241.155-1-A, all in APP; "In einer Pariser Emigrantenkaserne," *TJ*, no. 50 [mid-Dec. 1933]: 865–66.

For less sanguine descriptions of conditions in these barracks, see Schramm and Vormeier, p. 197; Madeleine Misard, "Comment la France absorbe-t-elle l'immigration judéo-allemand?" *L'Excelsior*, Jan. 22, 1934, clipped in APP BA 1815 241.155-1-G; Margaret Hess, "Little Germany in Paris Gives a Haven to Exiles," *NYT*, Apr. 15, 1934, sec. IX, p. 11; Georges Imann, "Chanaan-sur Seine," *Je suis partout*, Jan. 25, 1934, clipped in AIU, ms. 650, boîte 15(50); and "Texte du discours de Sir James G. McDonald, Ht. Commissaire pour les réfugiés (juifs et autres) radiodiffusé par les stations de TSF de la National Broadcasting Co.," Jan. 14, 1934, LBI, AR-C 1638/4099.

31. Ernest Ginsburger, "Tribune des lecteurs," *UI*, Nov. 3, 1933, p. 219.

32. Lambert, "L'Avenir de l'émigration allemande et l'opinion française," *UI*, Oct. 12, 1934, p. 65. William Oualid, a professor at the Faculty of Law at the University of Paris; a member of the Paris Consistory, the AIU, and the Comité National's Executive Committee; and president of the Comité Central d'Assistance aux Emigrants Juifs, the French branch of the international Jewish emigration agency HICEM, similarly warned the refugees to abstain from all political activities in the wake of the massive street demonstrations of Feb. 1934, during which five communist refugees from Germany were arrested. Oualid, "Une Tendance à laquelle il faut savoir résister," *UI*, Mar. 9, 1934, p. 93. See also Peterson, p. 76.

33. Original draft of Rothschild's speech to the General Assembly of the Consistory of Paris held on May 26, 1935. According to Weinberg, this statement was deleted from the subsequent printed versions of the speech. Weinberg, p. 76; Hyman, p. 204.

34. On the impact of the Depression, see Chapter 2.

35. See the pessimistic outlook expressed already in Comité d'Aide et d'Accueil, "Compte rendu, no. 2, Activité du Secrétariat Général du 20 au 30 mai, 1933," AIU France X D 56.

36. "Création du *Comité National Français de Secours aux Emigrés Allemands Victimes de l'Antisémitisme*," *UI*, June 30, 1933, p. 351.

37. Corcos, "L'Inéluctable devoir," *UI*, Oct. 27, 1933, p. 179. See also "Une Lettre de M. Henry Bernstein," *UI*, Nov. 24, 1933, pp. 308–9; Julien Weill, "Servir Dieu," *UI*, Apr. 13, 1934, p. 54.

38. "Minutes, Meeting to Discuss the Creation of the Comité National," June [22 or 23], 1933, p. 20, LBI, AR-C 1698/4099. See also Police report, Oct. 24, 1933, APP BA 1814 241.155-1-A. The Comité des Savants was essentially a branch of the Comité National and was heavily subsidized by the AIU and the Rothschilds. For a further discussion of the Comité des Savants, see Mathieu, "Sur l'émigration," pp. 148–62.

39. Helbronner's closest ally was Louis Oungre, president of the Jewish Colonization Association (JCA). During this period, Helbronner was also frequently supported by William Oualid (see n. 32 above), although later in the decade Oualid became a supporter of Lambert's more moderate position.

40. "Minutes of the Meeting Regarding the Creation of Comité National," June [22 or 23], 1933, p. 12, LBI, AR-C 1698/4099.

41. "Réunion commune du bureau et des représentants du Comité Exécutif du Comité pour la Défense...avec le bureau et la Commission des Affaires Extérieures de l'Alliance Israélite Universelle," Mar. 24, 1936, LBI, AR-C 1698/4099. Also cited in Comité pour la Défense, p. 71. Norman Bentwich of the HCR similarly reported that the prominent right-wing banker Louis Dreyfus, refused to give money to the relief effort in France since "he was strongly opposed to encouraging refugees to come France, both because it tended to arouse antisemitism in France and because it reflected on the patriotism of those Jews who remain in Germany." Dreyfus, however, had no objection to giving money to help Jews who remained in Germany. Norman Bentwich, to McDonald, Feb. 22, 1934, MP: H 10. For similar views, see also Jean Lasserre, "France, terre d'asile," *Le Matin*, Aug. 28, 1935, p. 6.

42. "Procès verbal de la 3ème séance tenue par la Commission Interministérielle des Réfugiés Allemands," Oct. 23, 1933, MAE Z 711, pp. 70–74. With regard to Helbronner's efforts to close the borders, Maurice Moch, a member of the Consistory, wrote in 1971:

Devant l'accroissemement des entrées, l'impossibilité de vérifier aux frontières l'identité des réfugiés et le motif de leur exode, les membres du Comité Central de secours [that is, the Comité National] insisterent à plusieurs reprises pour demander la fermeture des frontières, et l'examen des passeports des réfugiés. Une premier mesure de restriction fut apportée par le Ministère Doumergue, et les frontières ne furent fermées, tout au moins "théoriquement" que sous le Ministère Laval. Nous disons "théoriquement" car par l'insuffisance du personnel, pratiquement, un grand nombre de réfugiés continua à pénétrer sur notre territoire, par les forêts bordant le Palatinat, la Sarre et le Luxembourg.

According to Moch, Helbronner was merely doing his patriotic duty. As he concludes, "On a peut, par les rapports fournis de 1934 à 1936 par Mr. Helbronner, voir quels efforts il a tenté pour écarter de son pays un danger qui allait en s'accroissant." M. Moch, "Note sur les réfugiés d'Allemagne," July 2, 1971, AIU, CDV ms. 650, boîte 12 (44).

43. "Note Confidentielle de M. Helbronner: Quelques considérations concernant l'établissement agricole en France de réfugiés allemands," July 1934, LBI, AR-C 1698/4099. See also "Réunion commune du bureau et des représentants du Comité Exécutif du Comité pour la Défense...avec le bureau et la Commission des Affaires Extérieures de l'Alliance Israélite Universelle," Mar. 24, 1936, LBI, AR-C 1698/4099; Comité d'Aide et d'Accueil, "Compte rendu, no. 3," June 1–10, 1933, AIU France X D 56; "Summary of the Meeting of the Advisory Council of the High Commission [for Refugees] Held in Paris," June 18, 1934, JDC no. 250.

44. Report of Dr. Bernhard Kahn, Jan. 3, 1935, JDC no. 161, pp. 7–8. On Jan. 7, 1935, Kahn again noted the "insurmountable opposition" of French Jewry to these agricultural settlements, and he cited their fear of antisemitism as the major reason for this opposition. Bauer, *My Brother's Keeper*, pp. 151–52. Lambert too attributed the failure to investigate the possibility of agricultural settlements to "des arguments d'ordre psychologique et politique." Comité d'Aide et d'Accueil, "Compte rendu, no. 2, Activité du Secrétariat Général du 20 au 30 mai 1933," AIU France X D 56. For the views of Rothschild and Oungre, see Rothschild, to Charles Liebman, vice-chairman, Refugee Rehabilitation Committee, N.Y., June 5, 1934, JDC no. 617; Bernhard Kahn, to Charles Liebman, Sept. 24, 1935, JDC no. 617; Comité d'Aide et d'Accueil, "Compte rendu, no. 3," June 1–10, 1933, AIU X D 56. On JDC plans for agricultural settlements, see Kahn, to Major Frank Goldsmith, Oct. 25, 1933, JDC no. 617.

45. For Helbronner's hard-line policy at the League of Nations, see Helbronner, to the foreign minister, Report "a/s de la IIIe session du conseil d'administration pour les réfugiés provenant d'Allemagne," Nov. 5, 1934, MAE Z 313, pp. 13–17; Minutes, HCR, "Summary report of the Meeting of the Advisory Council of the High Commission, London," July 15, 1935, p. 8, JDC no. 251; "Notes on Discussions of

Advisory Council of the High Commission," June 18, 1934, JDC no. 260; B. Kahn, to Paul Baerwald, Nov. 6, 1934, JDC no. 601; HCR, "Compte rendu de la session du Comité Consultatif du Haut-Commissariat tenue à Londres, 29–30 Octobre, 1934," JDC no. 250; Helbronner, to the foreign minister, Nov. 5, 1934, pp. 241–45, and Feb. 15, 1935, pp. 248–52, both in MAE SDN I E 448.

46. Kahn, to Robert de Rothschild, Nov. 28, 1933, MP: H 1; Kahn, "Report on the Activities of the AJDC with Special Attention to the Last Five Months," Apr. 16, 1934, pp. 13, 16, JDC no. 160; "Report on the Activities of the AJDC for the Year 1933 and Early Months of 1934," pp. 50–51, JDC no. 154. See also Kahn, to Paul Baerwald, Nov. 6, 1934, JDC no. 601; HCR, "Compte rendu de la session du Comité Consultatif du Haut-Commissariat tenue à Londres, 29–30 Octobre, 1934," JDC no. 250. On the credit banks, see "Statuts de la caisse israélite de prêts, société anonyme...," 1935, ACIP B 131, 1935 (divers); "Verbatim Notes of Meeting of the American Members of the A[merican] J[ewish] Reconstruction Foundation," Oct. 29, 1934, JDC no. 601; "La Caisse israélite de prêtes," *UI*, Aug. 2–9, 1935, p. 730; Emile Grant, "Konstructive Emigranten-Hilfe," *PT*, no. 277, Mar. 15, 1937, p. 3.

47. Kahn, to Max Warburg, Oct. 16, 1934, JDC no. 617. See also Bauer, *My Brother's Keeper*, pp. 150–53.

48. Cited in Comité pour la Défense, p. 3. This committee, also known as the Comité pour la Défense des Droits des Israélites en Europe Centrale et Orientale, was founded in Aug. 1933 and had as its directors Boris Gourevitch, a former Menshevik refugee in Paris, and Pierre Dreyfus, the son of Captain Alfred Dreyfus—hence, it was also known as the Gourevitch-Dreyfus Committee. After 1936, Pierre Dreyfus no longer played an active role on this committee. The Gourevitch Committee did not provide relief. Rather, it was essentially political in nature and lobbied the government on a wide range of issues dealing with refugees and antisemitism in Central and Eastern Europe as well as in France itself. Among its sponsors were many prominent non-Jews, including Anatole de Monzie, Pierre-Etienne Flandin, Justin Godart, Paul Reynaud, and Edouard Daladier, who became its honorary president in the late 1930's. See Nicault, "L'Accueil," p. 5; Hyman, pp. 222–23; "Paris Committee Formed to Aid Jews in Europe," *NYT*, Aug. 13, 1933, p. 24; Report on the "Comité pour la Défense des Droits des Israélites en Europe Centrale," [1933], ACIP B 127; and Comité pour la Défense.

49. See Rajsfus, *Sois Juif*, as well as Rajsfus, *Des Juifs*.

50. In his brief biographical sketch of Lambert, Richard I. Cohen makes no mention of Lambert's growing sympathies for Zionism in the 1920's (Cohen, "Introduction," in Lambert, *Carnet*, pp. 13–62). Nevertheless, Lambert was an active member of the Union Universelle de la Jeunesse Juive, which put forth a pro-Zionist program in the 1920's and promoted a definition of Jewishness that stressed that Jews were a people with their own culture and history and not merely a religious group. This broader definition of Judaism was central to Lambert's subsequent involvement in refugee work. On Lambert's Zionist sympathies in the 1920's, see Hyman, p. 187; Abitbol, *Les Deux terres*, pp. 119, 151. On Lambert's endorsement of Zionism in the late 1930's, see Chapter 13, n. 112.

51. "Raymond-Raoul Lambert fera la première conférence de la Tribune Juive," *TJ*, no. 4 (Jan. 26, 1934): 71; Cohen, "Introduction," in Lambert, *Carnet*, p. 18.

52. Lambert, "L'Accueil de la France," *RJG*, 1ère année, no. 8 (May 1933): 349–50. On the similarities between Lambert's views and those of the LICA, see Pierre Paraf, "Lorsque Hitler est roi," *DdV*, no. 12 (May 1933): 1, 4; Meyer Carasso, "L'Emigration peut-elle être employée?" *DdV*, no. 13 (June 1933): 2; "Les Réfugiés allemands en France: Problèmes nouveaux," *DdV*, Sept.–Oct. 1933, p. 2.

53. On Lambert's efforts to secure jobs for the refugees in general, see Comité d'Aide et d'Accueil, "Compte rendu, no. 2, Activité du Secrétariat Général du 20–30 mai, 1933," AIU France X D 56; Biélinky, "Les Victimes de Hitler en France," *Kadimah*, Sept. 28, 1934, pp. 12–15; [Lambert], "Note pour M. le Président du Conseil," July 20, 1933, LBI, AR-C 1698/4099; Joly et al., p. 55. For Lambert's request regarding the East European refugees, which was denied, see minister of labor, to the Foreign Ministry (Europe), Sept. 2, 1933, MAE Z 433, pp. 186–87. The Jewish refugee committee in Strasbourg was similarly opposed to making distinctions between refugees of German and East European origin. See prefect of the Bas-Rhin, Note, "Réfugiés," [spring 1933], ADBR D 460, paq. 5/36.

Other members of the Comité National had no desire to include these East European Jews, however. According to Felix Warburg, Robert de Rothschild had complained that the refugees:

are all not of an even class. There are in Paris, to the great difficulty of Rothschild, those people who have been homeless for a good many years, who had never any real right to be in Germany, who traded along in their small way and had no real homes, and because they had no rights and were afraid they would be kicked out soon anyhow, were the first ones to run. They are very hard to dispose of because they are unskilled, and some of them are not very easily employable.

"Refugee Committee Meeting Called by James G. McDonald," Feb. 25, 1934, JDC no. 404. On the generally negative attitude of the Comité National's Executive Committee toward East Europeans, see also R. C., "A Vichy," p. 124; Maurice Moch, "Projet d'organisation pour l'accueil et l'établissement des juifs allemands en France," May 26, 1933, AIU, ms. 650, boîte 14 (44).

54. "Conférence régionale à Metz des Comités de secours pour les réfugiés," *TJ*, Nov. 17, 1933, p. 793; Lambert, "L'Emigration allemande et la Société des Nations," *UI*, Nov. 3, 1933, p. 210.

55. Lambert, "L'Emigration allemande et la Société des Nations," *UI*, Nov. 3, 1933, pp. 210–11; Lambert, "De l'orientation morale," *Les Cahiers du Renouveau*, no. 1 (Dec. 1934): 25; Lambert, to Jacques Fouques-Duparc, Foreign Ministry (SDN), Mar. 21, 1934, MAE SDN I E 448, p. 164.

56. For a description of these early agricultural initiatives, see "Minutes of Meeting on Retraining," Feb. 14, 1934, included in Norman Bentwich's report to McDonald, Feb. 22, 1934, MP: H 10. For the Comité National's support of individual agricultural placement, see Comité National, "Rapport financier, Exercice, 1933–1934," LBI, AR-C 1698 4099.

57. Compiled from figures in Germany Emergency Relief, "Summary of Income and Expenditures of Organizations Occupied in Refugee Work Subsidized by the AJDC during 1933 and Jan.–June, 1934," JDC no. 181; "Rapport sur l'Activité du Comité National du 1er janvier au 31 décembre, 1934"; Comité National, "Activité du Secrétariat Général du Comité National pendant le mois de janvier 1935," both in AIU France X D 56. See also "Report on the Activities of the AJDC for the Year 1933 and early months of 1934," p. 48, JDC no. 154; J. Biélinky, "Paris hospitalier," *UI*, Dec. 22, 1933, pp. 438–40; Bernard Schönberg, "L'Aide aux réfugiés allemands," *RJG*, no. 5 (Feb. 1934): 183. According to Robert de Rothschild, the Committee had acquired only 1,200 work permits as of mid-1935; the other job placements were in artisanry or small-scale commerce. "Assemblée générale du Comité National de Secours," *UI*, Aug. 2–9, 1935, pp. 729–31. On the problem of work permits, see also "Le Problème des réfugiés allemands," *L'Europe nouvelle*, Feb. 17, 1934, pp. 171–72; Schramm and Vormeier, pp. 209–16.

58. Mr. Harvey, British Embassy, Paris, to J. V. Perowne, Jan. 10, 1934, PRO FO 371/17698.C308.

59. Comité National, "Note sur la situation légale des réfugiés d'Allemagne en France," [early 1934], LBI, AR-C 1698/4099.

60. "Les Pauvres réfugiés: Accusation au lieu d'aide," translation of "Die armen Flüchtlinge," in *PT*, no. 225 (July 25, 1934): 3, LBI, AR-C 1698/4099.

61. See Comité pour la Défense. On the Gourevitch Committee, see note 48 above.

62. As early as May 1933, the Committee instituted a rigorous selection process, whereby the refugees were divided into three categories: "A. les véritables proscrits politiques et confessionnels; B. les proscrits politiques douteux; C. les émigrants qui profitent dans circonstances pour chercher dans un autre pays la fortune qui ne leur saurait plus depuis longtemps en Allemagne." In late May 1933, 50% of category "A" consisted of Germans and the other half of Poles, stateless individuals, and others; 59% of category "B" consisted of Poles, stateless individuals, and others; and 68% of category "C" consisted of these groups. Comité d'Aide et d'Accueil, "Compte Rendu, no. 2, Activité du Secrétariat Général du 20 au 30 mai 1933," AIU France X D 56. See also Joly et al., p. 47; Nicault, "L'Accueil," p. 7; R. C., "A Vichy," p. 124. As Lambert made clear in a later report, however, the exclusion of the Poles was done at the request of the government. See "Rapport sur l'activité du Comité National du 1er janvier au 31 décembre, 1934," AIU France X D 56. On Lambert's intervention, see n. 53 above.

63. As of the summer of 1933, the three main policies of the Comité National were: (1) repatriation of refugees who could be sent back to their country of origin (that is, East Europeans); (2) overseas emigration with the assistance of international Jewish emigration associations; and (3) the settlement of "productive" elements in France, without harming unemployed French workers. See Comité National, "Compte rendu de l'Activité du Secrétariat Général du 1er juillet jusqu'au 1er octobre, 1933," MAE SDN I E 451, pp. 111–12; Comité National, "Compte rendu de l'Activité du Secrétariat Général du 11 mai 1933 jusqu'au 16 octobre, 1933," AIU France X D 56.

64. Lambert, "De l'orientation morale," *Les Cahiers du Renouveau*, no. 1 (Dec. 1934): 25. This article also appeared as "Die moralische Anpassung der Emigration," *PT*, Dec. 12, 1934, p. 5, cited in Peterson, p. 73.

65. Comité National, "Rapport financier, Exercice 1933–1934," LBI, AR-C 1698/4099.

66. R. C., "A Vichy," p. 124. The JDC also reported a sharp upswing in emigration during this period, including repatriation to Germany. JDC, "Report of Activities for the Months of Apr. to Sept. 1934," Oct. 23, 1934, JDC no. 250.

67. As paraphrased by Biélinky in "Deux réunions en faveur des réfugiés," *UI*, Jan. 26, 1934, p. 606. See also "Baron Robert de Rothschild über die Flüchtingsfrage," *PT*, no. 38 (Jan. 18, 1934): 2.

68. "Rapport sur l'Activité du Comité National du 1er janvier au 31 Décembre, 1934," AIU France X D 56.

69. Robert de Rothschild's speech of July 23, 1935, reported in "Assemblée générale du Comité National de Secours," *UI*, Aug. 2–9, 1935, p. 729.

70. Police report, Oct. 9, 1934, MAE Z 711, p. 237. In his announcement of the liquidation plans in Feb., Robert de Rothschild specifically mentioned the fear that a constant stream of new arrivals would inspire antisemitism. See Norman Bentwich, to McDonald, Feb. 15, 1934, MP: H 10. On the liquidation plans, see also Lambert's speech, in "Assemblée générale du Comité National de Secours," *UI*, Aug. 2–9, 1935, pp. 730–31; "Rapport sur l'Activité du Comité National du 1er janvier au 31 décembre, 1934," AIU France X D 56; "Des réfugiés allemands partent de France en Palestine," *La Terre retrouvée*, no. 5 (Jan. 25, 1935): 18; "Paris and the German Emigrants," Report from Elizabeth T. Shipley, AFSC representative in Europe, Innsbruck, Austria, to AFSC, Philadelphia, Oct. 1934, in Friedlander and Milton, 2, doc. no. 32, pp. 95–96; "Flüchtlinge in Not," *PT*, no. 63 (Feb. 13, 1934): 3; "Das Comité National liquidiert," *PT*, no. 76 (Feb. 26, 1934): 3.

71. In late July and early Aug. of 1934, the *PT* carried a series of articles sharply critical of the policies of the Comité National: "Die armen Flüchtlinge," *PT*, no. 225 (July 25, 1934): 3; "Doch Schliessung des Comité National?" *PT*, no. 230 (July 30, 1934): 3; "Die Not der Emigranten," *PT*, no. 232 (Aug. 1, 1934): 3; "Emigranten-Versammlung," *PT*, no. 235 (Aug. 4, 1935): 3; "Noch einmal: die Not der Emigranten!" *PT*, no. 240 (Aug. 9, 1934): 3. These articles infuriated Helbronner and may have determined the timing of the closure of the committee. According to one report, "Après un échange de vues avec M. Louis Oungre et après lecture des articles parus dans le *Pariser Tageblatt*, M. Helbronner décide d'accord avec M. Louis Oungre de fermer la rue de la Durance le 1er août et de liquider immédiatement." Comité National, "Executive Committee Meeting of July 25, 1934," LBI, AR-C 1698/4099.

72. *PH*, June 3, 1934, translated in ACIP B 129 (sociétés, organisations, groupements, PH).

73. "Conférence de M. Georg Bernhard," Oct. 11, 1934, AN F⁷ 13433. In July 1934, Bernhard had written, "Attitude of French Jews will probably not change before a scandal has occurred. They had no understanding of the problem and do not realize that they are creating in the long run, just what they want to avoid: anti-

semitism. France, which has a long liberal tradition in dealing with refugees, cannot afford to let these people starve or to expel them actually from the country." Translation of an article from the *PT* of July 24, 1934, in packet sent by Otto Nathan to McDonald, July 28, 1934, MP: H 3. See also "Flüchtlingselend!" *PT*, no. 203 (July 3, 1934): 3. For a list of the organizations belonging to the Federation of German Emigrés in France, see Schiller et al., p. 46–47. For a history of Bernhard and the *PT*, see Peterson.

74. Police report, "a/s des émigrés juifs," July 30, 1934, APP BA 1815, 241.155-1-B; "Emigranten-Versammlung," *PT*, no. 235 (Aug. 4, 1935): 3. See also Heinz Liepmann, "The Refugee People," *The Jewish Forum* (Feb. 1935): 19–20, clipped in JDC no. 617.

75. On Oct. 20, 1933, Kahn cabled Paul Baerwald of the JDC in New York: "Our negotiations with French Committee rather successful. While French government cannot give any financial aid to refugees they will do everything to absorb many hundreds more by giving Carte Travaille. Government also favors our settlement plan [to create agricultural settlements]. Under these circumstances am ready to assist French Committee with three hundred thousand francs. Told government and French Committee assistance dependent on not closing borders." Confidential cablegram, JDC no. 617. On the JDC's persistent efforts to persuade the Comité National to adopt a more constructive approach, see B. Kahn to Robert de Rothschild, Nov. 28, 1933, MP: H 1; J. C. Hyman, "Draft Statement of Observations on Conditions of the Refugees in France and on Organizational Problems of the Jewish Communities in Germany," Dec., 1933, JDC no. 617; B. Kahn, "Report on the Activities of the AJDC with Special Attention to the Last Five Months," Apr. 16, 1934, JDC no. 160; "Brief Report on the Work in Germany and on the Situation of the Refugees," Aug. 22, 1934, JDC no. 404; Morris Troper, "Summary Report of Trip (Oct. 24, 1934, to Dec. 13, 1934)," JDC no. 160, pp. 14–16.

76. Kahn, to Baerwald, July 25, 1934; Kahn, to Baerwald, Aug. 1, 1934, both in JDC no. 617. See also Bauer, *My Brother's Keeper*, pp. 149–52.

77. "Le Commissaire pour les réfugiés MacDonald à Paris," translation of "Flüchtlingskommissar MacDonald in Paris," *PT*, no. 226, July 26, 1934, p. 3, LBI, AR-C 1698/4099; "Doch Schliessung des Comite National?" *PT*, no. 230 (July 30, 1934): 3; "Emigranten-Versammlung," *PT*, no. 235 (Aug. 4, 1935): 3. See also Joly et al., p. 62.

78. "Minutes of Meeting with the High Commissioner for Refugees," Jan. 29, 1935, enclosure 3, p. 10, JDC no. 161. McDonald similarly complained that the premature liquidation of the Comité National's relief activities constituted a "threat of starvation to hundreds of Jewish refugees, including many children, [and] is an indictment of Jewish leadership and of the High Commission." McDonald, to Paul Baerwald, July 28, 1934, JDC no. 617. On Oungre's hard-line position, see High Commissioner for Refugees, "Minutes, Meeting of Advisory Council," Jan. 29, 1934, LBI, AR 7162, box 5; "Minutes of Meeting with the High Commissioner for Refugees, held at JDC offices, Paris," Jan. 29, 1935, p. 5, JDC no. 161.

79. A. Manuel, to Robert de Rothschild, June 4, 1934, ACIP B 129 (Emigrants).

80. Minister of the interior, Sûreté Nationale, circular no. 257, Nov. 6, 1934, and Dec. 4, 1934, APP BA 64 Provisoire 51343-5. On the crackdown beginning in late 1934, see Chapter 3.

81. On the laws regulating foreign artisans and peddlers, see Chapter 2, nn. 77, 85.

82. On B. Kahn's fear of a "wholesale expulsion" in late 1934, see Chapter 3, n. 21. The Yiddish press in Paris expressed similar concern; see "Exil en masse des juifs de France," *PH*, Nov. 25, 1935, translated into French in ACIP B 129 (sociétés, organisations, groupements, PH).

83. "Réunion Biennale des Associations Juives," July 7, 1935, LBI, AR-C 1627/ 4078.

84. Minutes, HCR, "Summary report of the Meeting of the Advisory Council of the High Commission," London, July 15, 1935, p. 8, JDC no. 251. At this same meeting, William Oualid, who here represented the Consistory, reiterated Helbronner's view that the refugees could not be treated as a privileged category. As he stated, although "the French government had shown its sympathy to the refugees, [it] could not give them a right to work which was not enjoyed even by its nationals. One million Frenchmen were wholly or partially unemployed." The Yiddish language press was extremely critical of Helbronner's lack of response to this crackdown. See "Exil en masse des Juifs de France," *PH*, Nov. 25, 1935, French translation in ACIP B 129 (sociétés, organisations, groupements, PH).

85. On McDonald's protests, see McDonald, to D. Tétreau, Ministry of Foreign Affairs, Nov. 15, 1934, MP: H 2; "McDonald Reports on Refugee Plight," *NYT*, Nov. 29, 1934, p. 31; McDonald, to the Foreign Ministry, "Note," Feb. 1, 1935, pp. 246–47, MAE SDN I E 448.

86. Kahn, to Baerwald, Nov. 6, 1934, JDC no. 601.

87. Lambert, "Le Statut des étrangers," *UI*, Dec. 14, 1934, pp. 209–10; Lambert, "L'Emigration juive d'Allemagne," *RJG*, 3ème année, no. 4 (Jan. 1935): 143. All quotes in the following two paragraphs are from "Le Statut" except when otherwise indicated. On the favorable reception of these articles by the Yiddish press, see *PH*, Dec. 16, 1934, translated in ACIP B 129 (sociétés, organisations, groupements, PH, 1934); *PH*, Feb. 1–3, 1935, translated in ACIP B 131 (1935). For Rajsfus's very different interpretations of these passages, see Rajsfus, *Sois Juif*, pp. 124–25.

88. Lambert, "L'Emigration juive d'Allemagne," *RJG*, 3ème année, no. 4 (Jan. 1935): 143. For similar condemnations of the government crackdown by native Jewish leaders, see Comité d'Entente des Associations d'Anciens Combattants et Volontaires Juifs de France, "Procès verbaux," Nov. 30, 1934, and Dec. 5, 1934, AN 72 AJ 590; Oualid, "Rapport du Comité Central d'Assistance aux Emigrants Juifs," *Les Cahiers du Renouveau*, no. 5 (Apr., 1935): 156–58; Oualid, "Les Etrangers en France," *UI*, Feb. 8, 1935, p. 314; Nicault, "L'Accueil," p. 25, n. 36. For criticisms of the government leveled by other sectors of the French Jewish community, see Maxime Piha, "Reprends ton bâton...et marche," *Cahiers Juifs*, no. 13 (Jan.–Feb. 1935): 3–5; "Heures d'angoisse," *Le Journal Juif*, no. 49 (Dec. 6, 1935): 1; Abraham Bezalel, president of the Foreign Workers' Textile Syndicate, "Memorandum to the Minister of Labor," late Nov. 1935, AIU, ms. 650, boîte 13:45.

89. Lambert, Confidential report, "La Situation des juifs en Allemand, Jan.

1936," to Flandin, Feb. 15, 1936, MAE Z 705, p. 50. Indeed, Lambert repeatedly chastised the French press for not paying adequate attention to antisemitism in Germany. See, for example, his articles: "L'Agonie du judaisme allemand," Aug. 1, 1933, pp. 541–42; "L'Avenir du judaisme allemand," Dec. 29, 1933, pp. 465–66; "Le IIIème Reich et les Juifs," Apr. 26, 1935, all in *UI*.

90. On the Saar refugee crisis, see Chapter 3.

91. On the Comité National's protest, see Oualid, "Rapport du Comité Central d'assistance aux Emigrants Juifs," *Les Cahiers du Renouveau*, no. 5 (Apr. 1935): 157; A. Wurfbain, to McDonald, Dec. 8, 1934, MP: H 12; "Minutes of Meeting with the High Commissioner for Refugees," Jan. 29, 1935, enclosure 3, JDC no. 161. On the protests of the FSJF and the Gourevitch-Dreyfus Committee, see "M. Flandin et les juifs étrangers," *AI*, Jan. 10, 1935, p. 4; Comité pour la Défense, pp. 22–28; "Ministerpräsident Flandin zur Emigrantenfrage," *PT*, no. 377 (Dec. 24, 1934): 3; "Une Mémoire de la Fédération des Sociétés Juives," *UI*, Jan. 25, 1935, p. 310; "Le Mémoire de la Fédération des Sociétés Juives de France," *UI*, Feb. 1, 1935, p. 326; Memorandum, "Extraits de lettres en réponse à l'envoi du mémoire concernant la situation particulière des juifs établis en France et faisant l'objet de mesures prises contre les étrangers," 1935, ACIP B 131 (FSJF); FSJF, "Rapport de l'Activité pour l'année 1934," (Paris, 1935), esp. pp. 6–9, ACIP B 131; Hyman, p. 209.

92. Foreign Ministry, "Note pour M. le Secrétaire Général," Feb. 8, 1935, MAE Z 314, pp. 109–10. According to a member of McDonald's staff, André Wurfbain, it appears that the Committee, almost certainly as a result of Lambert's entreaties, initially demanded the right to work as well, but ultimately backed down in the face of administrative opposition. A. Wurfbain, to McDonald, Dec. 8, 1934, MP: H 12.

93. "Assemblée générale du Comité National de Secours," *UI*, Aug. 2–9, 1935, p. 730. See also Comité National, "Rapport sur l'Activité du Comité National du 1er janvier 1934 jusqu'au 31 décembre 1934," AIU France X D 56.

94. Lambert, "Appel aux Grand-Rabbins d'Europe," *UI*, Oct. 18, 1935, p. 49.

95. On the figure of 15,000–17,000, see Kahn, to Baerwald, Nov. 6, 1934, JDC no. 601. The consequences were especially severe since all the other refugee committees were collapsing as well. See Bauer, *My Brother's Keeper*, p. 153.

96. Italics in original text. "Report of the German Commission of the National Committee," June 27, 1934, JDC no. 601. This report was signed by Hugo Simon, the president of the German Commission, and by Georg Bernhard, Dr. Sammy Gronemann, Dr. Oscar Cohn, Dr. W. Friedländer, L. Aron, Dr. M. Strauss, and Fritz Wolff. On the dire conditions, see also Walter Friedländer, director, Service Social pour les Réfugiés Allemands, and representative of the Comité Allemand, "Report of the Condition of the German Refugees in France, as of the Early Part of 1936," Mar. 31, 1936, JDC no. 602; "Paris and the German Emigrants," Report from Elizabeth T. Shipley, AFSC representative in Europe, Innsbruck, Austria, to AFSC, Philadelphia, Oct. 1934, and J. Mahlon Harvey, Service International de la Société des Amis (Quakers), to Elizabeth Shipley, Jan. 22, 1935, both in Friedlander and Milton, 2, doc. no. 32, pp. 90–102, and doc. no. 44, pp. 140–41. On the split between the Comité National and the German Commission, see Lambert to Hugo Simon, June 29, 1934, JDC no. 601.

97. Paula Kurgass, Germany Emergency Committee Report, "Extracts from a Study of the Situation of the German Refugees in Paris by Paula Kurgass," Oct. 1934, JDC no. 617.

98. Cited in "Pour le Pessah des réfugiés," *Le Journal juif*, no. 14 (Apr. 5, 1935): 8.

99. Police report, "Situation actuelle de l'immigration juive allemande dans le département de la Seine," Feb. 1934, APP BA 1814 241.155-1-A. Some refugees had already requested to be repatriated to Germany as early as June 1933. See Comité d'Aide et d'Accueil, "Compte rendu, no. 3," June 1–10, 1933, AIU France X D 56.

100. Morris C. Troper, "Summary Report of Trip (Oct. 24, 1934, to Dec. 13, 1934)," p. 18, JDC no. 160. On the desperate conditions, see also "Deutsche Emigranten in Frankreich," *PT*, no. 468 (Mar. 25, 1935): 3; "3000 brauchen noch Hilfe!" *PT*, no. 469 (Mar. 26, 1935): 3; Paul-Jean Lucas, "Les Hommes traqués," *Le Quotidien*, part II, July 27, 1935, pp. 1–2; part IV, July 29, 1935, pp. 1, 3; part VI, July 31, 1935, pp. 1–2; part VII, Aug. 1, 1935, pp. 1–3; "Excerpt of letter from Melvin M. Fagen to Mr. Waldman," London, Nov. 16, 1935, JDC no. 617; Sperber, *Ces Temps là*, pp. 77, 104–5; Comité pour la Défense, pp. 16, 20; Bauer, *My Brother's Keeper*, p. 151; Badia, "La France découverte," p. 174.

101. Wyman, *Abandonment*, esp. pp. 143–77.

102. On Lambert, see his article, "Nos Griefs," *UI*, Oct. 26, 1934, p. 98.

Chapter Six

1. In the early months of 1936, Sarraut's administration attempted to ease up on the expulsion of foreigners who had lost their work permits and to rationalize the system of allocating identity cards so that foreigners would not be expelled merely because of bureaucratic slipups. See minister of the interior, Sûreté Nationale, to the prefects and prefect of police, circular no. 22, Feb. 3, 1936, APP BA 64 Provisoire 51-343-5; minister of the interior, Sûreté Nationale, circular no. 64, Mar. 25, 1936, APP BA 65 Provisoire 51-343-4; Ch. Magny, Sûreté Nationale, minister of the interior, circular no. 303, Apr. 28, 1936, APP BA 64 Provisoire 51-343-5. On the liberalization of policy under Sarraut, see also Schramm and Vormeier, pp. 222–23; Livian, *Le Régime juridique*, p. 74, n. 1.

2. Sperber, *Ces Temps là*, p. 108. Similarly, the refugee newspaper *La Défense* proclaimed: "La France retrouve son généreux visage." Cited in Omnès, p. 98. In Aug. 1936, Rudolf Breitscheid wrote his friend Wilhelm Hoegner, a refugee in Switzerland: "Réjouissez-vous que nous puissions respirer un peu plus librement ici et réservez votre juste colère non à Blum et son équipe, mais à la politique suisse." Cited in Badia et al., *Les Barbelés*, p. 58.

3. J.-Ch. Bonnet, pp. 314–28. See also Schor, *L'Opinion française et les étrangers*, pp. 584, 641–42; Schor, "L'Opinion française et les réfugiés," pp. 33–35.

4. *JO, Débats Parlementaires, Chambre des Députés*, June 8, 1939, p. 1526, cited in Schramm and Vormeier, p. 233; Editorial board, "Carence de l'administration," *Esprit*, July 1, 1939, p. 569; Livian, *Le Parti socialiste*, pp. 132–33; Milza, "La Gauche," pp. 117–25.

5. Thalmann, "L'Immigration allemande," pp. 171–72; Thalmann, "L'Emigration allemande," pp. 48–49.

For similar criticisms, see also Marrus, *Unwanted*, p. 148; Schramm and Vormeier, p. 210; Cross, pp. 207–10.

6. Livian, *Le Parti socialiste*, pp. 3, 106–7, 114, 130–33, 181–92, *passim*. For a positive assessment of the Popular Front's efforts, see also Badia et al., *Les Barbelés*, pp. 55–59.

7. Comité pour l'Assistance Internationale aux Réfugiés, "Rapport du Comité soumis au conseil de la Société des Nations (SDN), Nov. 28, 1935," Jan. 3, 1936, MAE SDN I M 1806, pp. 158–65. The members of this committee included Stefan Osusky, the Czech ambassador in Paris (president); Pierre Roland-Marcel, a member of the Conseil d'Etat and former prefect of the Bas-Rhin (rapporteur); Sir Horace Rumbold, the former British ambassador in Berlin; Judge Michael Hansson of Norway; and Giusseppi de Michelis of Italy.
See also "Two Reports Made on Refugee Work," *NYT*, Dec. 8, 1935, p. 41; "League Aid Asked by McDonald to End Nazi Persecution," *NYT*, Dec. 30, 1935, pp. 1, 12; "League Body Asks Joint Refugee Aid," *NYT*, Jan. 10, 1936, p. 8; Zoltan Berkovits, "Lettre de Genève: Le Problème des réfugiés devant la SDN; Le rapport de M. Roland Marcel," *UI*, Jan. 3, 1936, p. 231; Simpson, *Refugees: Preliminary Report*, pp. 88–89; Simpson, *Refugee Problem*, pp. 211–12, 216–17.

8. See "Text of Resignation of League Commissioner for German Refugees," *NYT*, Dec. 30, 1935, p. 12.

9. League of Nations, "Refugees Coming from Germany, Report Submitted to the 17th Ordinary Session of the Assembly of the League of Nations by the High Commissioner, Sir Neill Malcolm," A.19. 1936, XII, Sept. 1, 1936, p. 2, JDC no. 252. With Malcolm's appointment, the office of the high commissioner was restructured so as to make it more closely integrated into the League itself. In contrast to the situation under McDonald, the high commissioner for the first time became a League official; he received fees and grants directly from the League. The high commissioner also reported to the League and had a secretary from the League who arranged intergovernmental conferences. Like McDonald's, Malcolm's office was in London. See Simpson, *Refugees: Preliminary Report*, pp. 87–88.

10. "Un Emigré d'Allemagne se suicide pendant une séance de la S.D.N.," *UI*, July 10, 1936, p. 663; "L'Emouvant testament de Stephen Lux," *UI*, July 10, 1936, p. 668.

11. League of Nations, "Refugees Coming from Germany, Report Submitted to the 17th Ordinary Session of the Assembly of the League of Nations by the High Commissioner, Sir Neill Malcolm," A.19. 1936, XII, Sept. 1, 1936, JDC no. 252; League of Nations, "Inter-Governmental Conference for the Adoption of a Statute for Refugees Coming from Germany (Geneva, July 2nd–4th, 1936): Final Act," Sept. 14, 1936, C.362 9(a).M.237 (a).1936.XII, MAE SDN I E 450. See also Livian, *Le Parti socialiste*, pp. 92–93; Vormeier, "La Situation administrative," pp. 188–89; CDV, "Bulletin," no. 1, Aug. 27, 1936, AIU, ms. 650, boîte 1.
The seven signatory countries consisted of Belgium, Czechoslovakia, Denmark, France, the Netherlands, Norway, and Switzerland.

12. Perrin, "Assistance internationale aux réfugiés," *DdV*, Dec. 19, 1936, p. 3. See also Kahn, to J. C. Hyman, July 15, 1936, JDC no. 252; Livian, *Le Parti socialiste*, p. 93; Schramm and Vormeier, p. 228; Vormeier, "La Situation administrative,"

pp. 188–89; Gourevitch, pp. 63–72. On the creation of the Centre de Liaison, see Chapter 4, n. 128.

13. Georg Bernhard, "Das Flüchtlingsabkommen," *PT*, no. 27 (July 8, 1936): 1–2; J. Rubinstein, "Le Statut des réfugiés politiques," *CDH*, Apr. 15, 1937, p. 230; Bureau International pour le Respect du Droit d'Asile et l'Aide aux Réfugiés Politiques, Paris, "Avant projet de Convention International relative aux réfugiés provenant d'Allemagne, SDN," Mar. 23, 1937, "Proposition de modification: Exposé des motifs," MAE Z 705, pp. 187–89.

14. On the Conférence Internationale pour le Droit d'Asile, held in Paris on June 20–21, 1936, see "Conférence Internationale contre le racisme et l'antisémitisme: Résolutions présentée au nom de la 3ème commission," BDIC Dos. Duchêne, FΔ Rés. 329/2; Livian, *Le Parti socialiste*, pp. 65, 90–91; Albert Grzesinski, "Zentralvereinigung der deutschen Emigration," *PT*, no. 33 (July 14, 1936): 2; Thalmann, "L'Emigration allemande," p. 48; Omnès, pp. 97–98; Schiller et al., pp. 47–48. On the HICEM/HIAS Conference held in Paris, see Jacques Biélinky, "La Conférence d'émigration juive, 29 juin au 1er juillet, 1936," *UI*, July 19, 1936, pp. 665–66.

According to Thalmann, the French branch of the Communist Secours Rouge International had also made similar demands; see Thalmann, "L'Emigration allemande," p. 48; Thalmann, "L'Immigration allemande," pp. 171–72.

15. League of Nations, "Refugees Coming from Germany, Report Submitted to the 17th Ordinary Session of the Assembly of the League of Nations by the High Commissioner, Sir Neill Malcolm," A.19. 1936, XII, Sept. 1, 1936, p. 2, JDC no. 252. See also League of Nations, "Intergovernmental Conference for the Adoption of a Statute for Refugees Coming from Germany, July 2nd–4th, 1936: Provisional Arrangement Concerning the Status of Refugees Coming from Germany, Signed at Geneva on July 4, 1936," Sept. 14, 1936, MAE SDN I E 450, p. 12.

16. League of Nations, "Refugees Coming from Germany, Report Submitted to the 17th Ordinary Session of the Assembly of the League of Nations by the High Commissioner, Sir Neill Malcolm," A.19. 1936, XII, Sept. 1, 1936, app. 2, p. 12, JDC no. 252. An earlier draft of Longuet's declaration drawn up by an interministerial conference in June 1936 read: "Enfin le Gouvernement français compte aller plus loin que le projet présent en faisant une déclaration sur l'octroi aux réfugiés des permis de travail, déclaration qui naturellement ne vise et ne peut viser que les réfugiés actuellement établis en France et non pas ceux qui pourraient y amener dans l'avenir de nouvelles persécutions hitlériens." Foreign Ministry (SDN), "Note," June 30, 1936, MAE I E 452, pp. 12–15. On Longuet's attitude toward the refugees, see also Livian, "Témoignage," pp. 93–102.

17. Kahn, to Otto Schiff, July 17, 1936, JDC no. 252. See also Kahn's criticisms in his letter to J. C. Hyman, July 15, 1936, JDC, no. 252, and in "League to Discuss German Refugees," *NYT*, Dec. 2, 1936, p. 31.

18. *JO, Lois et Décrets*, Sept. 23, 1936, pp. 10058–59, reprinted in "Création d'un certificat d'identité," *UI*, Oct. 9, 1936, p. 66. On the general provisions of the certificate and its implications, see Dr. S. Feblowicz, "Wer erhalt den neuen Flüchtlingspass?" *PT*, no. 109 (Sept. 28, 1936): 3; Feblowicz, "Wie man den neuen

Flüchtlingspass erhalt?" *PT*, no. 110 (Sept. 29, 1936): 3; Schramm and Vormeier, p. 223; Livian, *Le Parti socialiste*, p. 118; Feblowicz and Lamour, p. 31.

19. On the extensions of the deadline, see minister of the interior (Sûreté Nationale) to the prefects, circular no. 320, Dec. 30, 1936, APP BA 1814 241.155-1-A; "Le Statut des réfugiés allemands en France," *UI*, Dec. 25, 1936, p. 249; Paul Perrin, "Assistance internationale aux réfugiés," *DdV*, Dec. 19, 1936, pp. 1, 3; Grzesinski, "Neues zum deutschen Flüchtlingstatut in Frankreich," *PT*, no. 215 (Jan. 12, 1937): 3.

20. Italics in original text. Minister of the interior, circular no. 312, Aug. 14, 1936, APP BA 1814 241.155-1-A.

21. Minister of the interior, circular no. 314, Sept. 23, 1936, APP BA 1814 241.155-1-A. Two days after the convention was signed, a Foreign Ministry spokesman reported: "La liberté du gouvernement français demeure entière en ce qui concerne le droit de refuser l'accès du territoire à de nouveaux réfugiés." Foreign Ministry (SDN), "Note, remise à M. [Pierre] Viénot," July 6, 1936, MAE SDN I E 452, pp. 17–20. On Salengro's circulars, see also Schramm and Vormeier, pp. 228–29; Livian, *Le Parti socialiste*, pp. 56, 95–96, 108–9, 184–92; and Thalmann, "L'Immigration allemande," pp. 171–72.

22. At the end of 1936, Siegfried Rädel replaced Münzenberg on the Commission, and in 1937, Frederick Wagner replaced Grzesinski, who emigrated to South America, as president. On the Consultative Commission, see "Le Statut des réfugiés allemands en France," *UI*, Aug. 7–14, 1936, p. 749; Livian, *Le Parti socialiste*, pp. 100–105; Thalmann, "L'Emigration allemande," p. 49; Badia et al., *Les Barbelés*, pp. 56–57; Langkau-Alex, p. 38; Schiller et al., pp. 45–46; "Note sur le Comité Consultatif des réfugiés provenant d'Allemagne," Apr. 8, 1938, APP BA 1814 241.155-1-A; "Pour doter d'un statut les réfugiés allemands," *Le Populaire*, Aug. 25, 1936, clipped in APP BA 241.155-1-G; "Das neue Statut für die deutschen Flüchtlinge," *PT*, Aug. 24, 1936, p. 3; Foreign Ministry (SDN), "Note," June 30, 1936, MAE I E 452, pp. 12–15; Viénot, Sous-Secrétaire d'Etat, Foreign Ministry, "Memo," Aug. 1, 1936, MAE SDN I E 452, pp. 32–35; Viénot, Address to the League for the Rights of Man and Citizen on July 27, 1936, *CDH*, Mar. 1, 1937, p. 150; Omnès, pp. 98–99; Tartakower and Grossman, pp. 141–42. The first meeting of the Consultative Commission was held on Aug. 3, 1936.

23. Paul Perrin, "Assistance internationale aux réfugiés," *DdV*, Dec. 19, 1936, pp. 1, 3.

24. "Régularisation de la situation des émigrés allemands prévue par le gouvernement français," *TJ*, no. 44 (Oct. 30, 1936): 667–68. See also "Kongress für ein neues Auslanderstatut," *PT*, no. 582 (Jan. 16, 1938): 5; "L'Activité juridique de la Ligue en 1936–1937," June 15, 1937 to July 1, 1937, pp. 384–86.

25. Minutes, Meeting of Consultative Commission held at the Ministry of the Interior, Oct. 26, 1936, MAE SDN I E 452, pp. 36–47. See also Grzesinski, cited in Livian, *Le Parti socialiste*, pp. 187–88. When Grzesinski submitted his letter of resignation to Viénot in June 1937, he reiterated these concerns, stating:

Il est à remarquer que ces réfugiés [those arriving after the prescribed dates] sont surtout des réfugiés politiques qui viennent d'être libérés ou qui ont pu s'enfuir des prisons ou des camps de concentration allemands ou encore des réfugiés qui se sont trouvés en grave danger par suite d'autres circonstances. Je vous prie d'examiner si le Comité Consultatif ne pourrait être conservé—seulement consultativement—pour faciliter les enquêtes et permettre aux autorités françaises d'utiliser cet organisme à leur avantage.

Grzesinski, to Viénot, June 14, 1937, MAE SDN I E 452, p. 65. See also Livian, *Le Parti socialiste*, pp. 187–88.

26. Grzesinski, to Viénot, June 14, 1937, MAE SDN I E 452, p. 65.

27. On complaints of German Jews who had been denied visas, see Berthold Levi, Strasbourg, to Georges Weill, deputy, Bas-Rhin, May 15, 1936; Georges Weill, to Paul Valot, Sept. 24, 1936; Paul Valot, to Georges Weill, Sept. 24, 1936; and President of the Council, to the Foreign Ministry (Chancelleries et du Contentieux), Sept. 24, 1936, all in ADBR AL 98 396 (passeports, Sally Wolf).

Whether this policy reflected official policy or whether it reflected overzealousness on the part of certain French consuls is not entirely clear. There is no doubt that a generally harsh visa policy remained in effect during the Popular Front. An internal Foreign Ministry note of June 1936 remarked that with respect to the current strict visa regulations "la situation actuelle du marché du travail... nous fait un devoir d'autant plus strict de s'en tenir à cette règle." Foreign Ministry (Service Politique), to the Foreign Ministry (SDN), "Note," June 1936, MAE SDN I E 452, pp. 7–11. By the same token, Foreign Ministry officials noted with satisfaction in July 1936 that despite the Geneva Accord, "la liberté du Gouvernement français demeure entière en ce qui concerne le droit de refuser l'accès du territoire à de nouveaux réfugiés." Foreign Ministry (SDN), "Note, remise à M. Viénot," July 6, 1936, MAE, SDN I E 452, pp. 17–20.

On the harsh visa policy, see also Ch. Magny, Directeur Général, Sûreté Nationale, to the prefects, départements frontières, circular no. 151, Sept. 28, 1936, ADBR D 391/19 (181). According to Magny, many individuals in Germany were circumventing French consulates altogether by claiming that they were former French citizens of Alsace and Lorraine and requesting the *certificats de réintégration* [to French citizenship] that had been created by the Treaty of Versailles and that could be obtained through the offices of mayors in Alsace and Lorraine. This system, Magny claimed, was being abused by individuals "qui demeurent bons allemands durant plus de 15 ans [et] se sont soudainement découverts, à la suite du changement de régime survenu en Allemagne, une ascendance alsacienne." As a result, "M. le Ministre des Affaires étrangères à cru devoir prier nos consuls de ne plus attribuer aux certificats de réintegration de date récente une force probante absolue, et de n'accorder en pareils cas de passeport français qu'avec la plus grande circonspection." See also Maga, *America*, p. 86.

That the Popular Front strove to be more generous in the allocation of visas than its predecessors is illustrated by the fact that Dobler was again reprimanded for his harsh visa policies in 1937, although the Ministry of the Interior had actually stiffened these policies in response to Dobler's suggestions in early 1936. See M. Theodore Dan, president, Délégation à l'étranger au parti-social démocratic ouvrier de Russie, to M. Combes, Directeur adjoint de la Sûreté Nationale, May 1, 1937, AN F^7 14759 (Correspondence, 1933–1940). On Dobler's influence on visa policy in early 1936, see Chapter 3, n. 89.

28. Livian, *Le Parti socialiste*, pp. 56, 109.

29. Foreign Ministry, Direction Politique et administrative, to the Foreign Ministry (SDN), June 1936, MAE SDN I E 452, pp. 7–11.

30. Foreign Ministry (SDN), to M. Alphand, French ambassador to the Soviet Union, June 26, 1936, MAE SDN I E 449, pp. 254–55.

31. Foreign Ministry (SDN), to diplomatic agents and French consulates abroad, lettre circulaire no. 171, Nov. 2, 1936, MAE SDN I M 1819, pp. 191–92.

32. Minister of the interior, to the prefects, July 4, 1936, APP BA 64 Provisoire 51-343-5.

33. Minister of the interior, circular no. 320, Dec. 30, 1936, APP BA 1814 241.155-1-A.

34. Ibid.; Paul Perrin, "Assistance internationale aux réfugiés," *DdV*, Dec. 19, 1936, p. 3; Grzesinski, "Neues zum deutschen Flüchtlingstatut in Frankreich," *PT*, no. 215 (Jan. 12, 1937): 3.

35. Ministry of the Interior, "Conditions du séjour des étrangers en France, Rapport au Président de la République," Oct. 14, 1936," *JO, Lois et décrets*, no. 250, Oct. 24, 1936, p. 11107, clipped in APP BA 64 Provisoire 51-343-5; J.-Ch. Bonnet, p. 314; Simpson, *Refugees: Preliminary Report*, pp. 117–18; Feblowicz and Lamour, p. 55; Livian, *Le Parti socialiste*, pp. 76–78; "L'Oeuvre du gouvernement du Front Populaire en faveur des travailleurs immigrés," *Le Populaire*, Feb. 17, 1937, clipped in APP BA 67 Provisoire.

36. "L'Activité juridique de la Ligue en 1936–1937," *CDH*, June 15, 1937–July 1, 1937, p. 384.

37. "Nos échos: La reconnaissance des réfugiés d'Allemagne," *UI*, Nov. 27, 1936, p. 179. Salengro was driven to suicide by an extreme-right-wing campaign, led by the journal *Gringoire*, charging that he had been an army deserter during the First World War.

38. Foreign Ministry (SDN), "Note," June 30, 1936, MAE I E 452, pp. 12–15.

39. League of Nations, "Refugees Coming from Germany, Report Submitted to the 17th Ordinary Session of the Assembly of the League of Nations by the High Commissioner, Sir Neill Malcolm," A.19. 1936, XII, Sept. 1, 1936, app. 2, p. 12, JDC no. 252. Pierre Viénot, undersecretary of state of the Foreign Ministry, reiterated this pledge to the president of the CAR in July 1936; see Viénot, to the president of the CAR, July 28, 1936, English translation, JDC no. 617.

40. Kahn, to J. C. Hyman, July 15, 1936, JDC no. 252.

41. Kahn, to Otto Schiff, July 17, 1936, JDC no. 252.

42. Cited in R. S., "Le Problème international des réfugiés," *UI*, Oct. 2, 1936, p. 53.

43. Foreign Ministry, to the Foreign Ministry (SDN), "Note (Service Politique)," June 1936, MAE SDN I E 452, p. 11. On the desire for American financial contributions, see also Foreign Ministry, "Note: Avant-projet de Convention relative au statut des réfugiés venant d'Allemagne," MAE SDN I E 452, pp. 62–64.

44. Kahn, to J. C. Hyman, July 15, 1936, JDC no. 252.

45. Minutes, "Réunion préparatoire pour l'organisation de l'assistance aux réfugiés," held at JDC Paris bureau, July 7, 1936, JDC no. 617.

46. J.-Ch. Bonnet, pp. 317–19.

47. Livian, *Le Parti socialiste*, pp. 109, 123.

48. "L'Activité juridique de la Ligue en 1935–36," *CDH*, June 30–July 10, 1936, p. 490.

49. "L'Activité juridique de la Ligue en 1936–1937," *CDH*, June 15, 1937–July 1, 1937, p. 384. See also Livian, *Le Parti socialiste*, pp. 109, 123–25.

50. Simpson, *Refugee Problem*, p. 324. The 1935 figures are calculated from the monthly reports of the Comité National, "Activité du Secrétariat Général du Comité National...," for the year 1935, in AIU France X D 56.

51. League of Nations Report, "Refugees Coming from Germany, Submitted to the 18th Ordinary Session of the Assembly of the League of Nations by the High Commissioner, Sir Neill Malcolm, Geneva," A. 17. 1937, XII, p. 1, Sept. 1, 1937, JDC no. 252. (For the French version of this document, see MAE SDN I M 1813, pp. 7–8.) For similar high praise from the Nansen Office, see Nansen International Office for Refugees, "Report of the Governing Body for the Year Ending June 30, 1937, Geneva, Aug. 20, 1937," *League of Nations Publications*, XII A. 21, 1937, p. 2.

52. HICEM/HIAS report, 1936, in "Notes on JDC Activities during the Months of Jan.–Mar., 1938," Appendix VI, JDC no. 188.

53. Ibid. See also CDV, bulletin no. 9, Oct. 29, 1936, AIU, ms. 650, boîte 1. According to a Ministry of Labor report of June 1938, 1,200 Germans, primarily Jews, had been granted work permits that allowed them to work as salaried employees or artisans. See minister of labor, 3ème bureau, to the Foreign Ministry (Europe), June 30, 1938, MAE SDN I M 1815, pp. 282–85. For the 1935 figures, see monthly reports, "Activité du Secrétariat Général du Comité National," Jan.–June 1935, AIU France X D 56.

54. Minister of labor, circular no. 141, Jan. 4, 1937, APP BA 64 Provisoire 51-343-5.

55. "New Jobs Are Seen for Jewish Refugees," *NYT*, Mar. 28, 1937, p. 28. See also "Memo on Interview with Mr. Chantal, General Secretary of the *Centre de Reclassement Professionnel*," Mar. 5, 1937, JDC no. 601.

56. "Memo on Interview with Mr. Chantal, General Secretary of the *Centre de Reclassement Professionnel*," Mar. 5, 1937, JDC no. 601.

57. *JO, Documents Parlementaires, Chambre des Députés*, Mar. 14, 1937, p. 3033, cited in J.-Ch. Bonnet, p. 320.

58. Marcel Bernard, Ministry of Labor (3ème bureau), to the Prefecture de Police (étrangers et passeports), May 26, 1937, APP DA 783 (Textes).

59. Ibid. In 1938, even one of the foremost contemporary experts on the refugee problem, Sir John Hope Simpson, noted the lax enforcement of the Aug. 8, 1935 decree: the artisan identity cards mandated by the law were not available until Sept. 1937; no quota system was ever introduced, as originally intended; and, as the complaints alluded to suggest, there were numerous "privileged" categories. Simpson,

Refugee Problem, p. 276. See also Livian, *Le Parti socialiste*, p. 118; J.-Ch. Bonnet, p. 320.

60. CDV, bulletin no. 11, Nov. 12, 1936, p. 3, AIU, ms. 650, boîte 1; "Les Médecins étrangers en France," *Le Temps*, Aug. 17, 1936, p. 6.

61. CDV, bulletin no. 5, Sept. 30, 1936, AIU, ms. 650, boîte 1.

62. "Proposition de loi tendant à renforcer la répression de l'exercice illégal de la médecine dans l'intérèt des malades, et à revaloriser les titres professionels," presented by Georges Cousin, no. 1711, Chambre des Députés, *Impressions: Projets de lois, Propositions, Rapports, etc.*, tome 16, Session 1936–37 (Paris, 1946).

63. "Nos Interventions: L'Exercice de la médecine vétérinaire par les naturalisés," *CDH*, July 15, 1937, p. 457.

64. J.-Ch. Bonnet, p. 327; Vormeier, "La Situation administrative," p. 189; Schramm and Vormeier, pp. 201, 215.

65. "L'Activité juridique de la Ligue en 1936–1937," *CDH*, June 15, 1937–July 1, 1937, p. 385.

66. *JO, Documents Parlementaires, Chambre des Députés*, "Rapport fait au nom de la Commission des finances chargée d'examiner le projet de loi portant fixation du budget général de l'exercice 1937 (Justice-Services judiciaires,) par M. Bonevay," annexe no. 1277, sect. 3, 2ème session extraordinaire, Nov. 12, 1936, p. 257. See also "L'Oeuvre du gouvernement du Front Populaire en faveur des travailleurs immigrés," *Le Populaire*, Feb. 17, 1937, clipped in APP BA 67 Provisoire.

67. *Le Temps*, Apr. 5, 1937, cited in J.-Ch. Bonnet, p. 326.

68. "L'Activité juridique de la Ligue en 1936–1937," *CDH*, June 15, 1937–July 1, 1937, p. 385.

69. Depoid, p. 45. These figures include adults and children together. Although some of the naturalizations for 1938 occurred after the Popular Front, it is highly likely that the dossiers of these individuals were processed during the Popular Front. See also Schramm and Vormeier, p. 215. On the reaction of the right, see Edmond Jaloux, "Les Indésirables," *Le Petit Journal*, Oct. 16, 1937; CDV, bulletin no. 45, Oct. 21, 1937, p. 5, AIU, ms. 650, boîte 2; Livian, *Le Parti socialiste*, p. 127.

70. Schramm and Vormeier, p. 215.

71. Calculated from tables in Depoid, pp. 45, 52. According to Depoid, "L'immigration de réfugiés politiques et religieux à partir de 1933 a entraîné une augmentation des naturalisations de 1937 à 1939" (p. 53). Schramm and Vormeier, p. 215.

72. "L'Oeuvre du gouvernement du Front Populaire en faveur des travailleurs immigrés," *Le Populaire*, Feb. 17, 1937, clipped in APP BA 67 Provisoire. On these modifications, see also Annexe no. 1603, 2ème session extraordinaire de 1936 (Chambre des Députés), Annexe au procès-verbal de la séance du 31 décembre 1936, Chambre des Députés, *Impressions: Projets de lois, Propositions, Rapports*, etc., tome 16 (nos. 1601–1800), Session 1936–37 (Paris, 1946); Millet, p. 75.

73. On the power of the medical syndicates over naturalizations, see Dr. Jean d'Alsace, "Les Promesses de la France doivent être tenues," *DdV*, Dec. 12, 1936, pp. 1, 5.

74. Rucart, keeper of the seals, Ministry of Justice, to the prefects, Aug. 17, 1936, APP BA 407^P 200.263.

75. "L'Activité juridique de la Ligue en 1936–1937," *CDH*, June 15, 1937–July 1, 1937, p. 385.

76. For the full text of this accord, see Simpson, *Refugee Problem*, pp. 566–95; Feblowicz and Lamour, pp. 433–41. See also Simpson, *Refugee Problem*, pp. 285–86; Simpson, *Refugees: Preliminary Report*, pp. 106–7, 115; J. Rubinstein, "Le Statut des réfugiés politiques," *CDH*, Apr. 15, 1937, pp. 229–34; Solomon, pp. 29–32. On the earlier efforts of pro-refugee groups to get this convention ratified, see Moutet, Rubinstein, and Maklakof, "Note remise le 12 février 1935 au Président Laval," MAE SDN I M 1812, pp. 145–46. On the ratification of this convention, see *JO, Lois et Décrets*, Oct. 21, 1936, clipped in MAE SDN I M 1812, p. 182; Livian, *Le Parti socialiste*, p. 81; Leven, p. 25 (pamphlet in ACIP B 134^D).

77. Simpson, *Refugee Problem*, p. 578; J.-Ch. Bonnet, p. 314; Livian, *Le Régime juridique*, pp. 174–78, 184–87.

78. On Malcolm's text, see Foreign Ministry (SDN), "Conférence Internationale pour l'adoption d'une convention relative aux réfugiés provenant d'Allemagne," Mar. 23, 1937, MAE SDN I E 452, pp. 49–61; "Law Covering the Emigrants as Outlined by the Commissioner of the League of Nations," translated from *Jüdische Rundschau*, Apr. 6, 1937, JDC no. 252.

79. Foreign Ministry, Cabinet of the Undersecretary of State, "Questions à traiter par une prochaine conférence interministérielle relative au statut des réfugiés politiques," [Apr. 17, 1937], MAE SDN I M 1812, pp. 215–17.

80. Ibid. See also Foreign Ministry, "Note a/s Convention de Genève de 1933 relative au statut des réfugiés," February 27, 1937, MAE SDN I M 1812, pp. 194–201; "Interministériel Meeting du 20 avril 1937 a/s de l'application de la Convention de 1933 sur les réfugiés Nansen," Apr. 20, 1937, MAE SDN I M 1812, pp. 220–34, esp. p. 224.

81. Comments of M. Laugier, director of the Cabinet of the Minister of Foreign Affairs, in "Interministériel Meeting du 20 avril 1937 a/s de l'application de la Convention de 1933 sur les réfugiés Nansen," Apr. 20, 1937, MAE SDN I M 1812, p. 224.

82. Army chief of staff, "Projet de communiqué à soumettre à la réunion Interministérielle sur l'application de la Convention de 1933 sur les réfugiés," Apr. 26, 1937, MAE SDN I M 1812, pp. 233–36. As of 1937, Nansen refugees were drafted into the French army and accorded considerable privileges: they were allowed to serve in regular army units instead of the Foreign Legion, they were eligible for promotion to noncommissioned rank and a permanent career in the military, and their families were entitled to the same social benefits as were available to French nationals. Tartakower and Grossman, p. 143; Simpson, *Refugee Problem*, p. 289. Nevertheless, as long as refugees remained unnaturalized, they continued to be subject to the 1932 quotas governing the number of foreign laborers permitted to work in certain industries, although the minister of labor agreed to make a special effort to facilitate their acquisition of work permits. Minister of labor (3ème bureau, Main-d'Oeuvre Etranger), to the Foreign Ministry (Chancelleries et du Contentieux), 2ème bureau, Nov. 12, 1936, MAE SDN I M 1819, p. 201.

83. Foreign Ministry, "Réunion Interministérielle du 20 avril 1937 a/s de l'appli-

cation de la Convention de 1933 sur les réfugiés Nansen," Apr. 20, 1937, SDN I M 1812, pp. 220–32, esp. pp. 224–26.

84. As a result of pressure exerted by the French delegation, the wording of the clause regarding *refoulement* was changed in accordance with the wishes of the high commissioner. According to de Reffye, one of the French delegates to the Conference, the French delegation "a obtenu que la rédaction du projet 'Les parties contractantes d'engagent à ne refouler les réfugiés sur le Reich qu'après avertissement et s'ils ont refusé...' soit remplacée par l'affirmation que: 'Les Hautes Parties Contractantes s'engagent à ne pas refouler les réfugiés sur le territoire allemand sauf après avertissement et s'ils ont, de mauvaise foi, refusé....'" M. de Reffye, Ministre Plenipotentiaire en retraite, délégué suppléant à la Conférence de Genève pour les réfugiés allemands, to Yvon Delbos, foreign minister, Feb. 25, 1938, MAE SDN I E 450, pp. 65–77, esp. pp. 71–72. The liberal attitude of the French government was also manifest in its pressure to extend to a full year the period during which any signatory nation could denounce the treaty. See League of Nations, provisional minutes, "International Conference for the Adoption of a Convention Concerning the Status of Refugees Coming from Germany," second meeting, Feb. 7, 1938, JDC no. 253.

85. The only difference between the Feb. 1938 Convention and the Oct. 28, 1933 Convention on the right to work was that veterans of the First World War were no longer among the privileged categories automatically exempted from the regulations and quotas governing the right of foreigners to work. For a full text of the Feb. 10, 1938 Convention, see Simpson, *Refugee Problem*, pp. 566–95; Feblowicz and Lamour, pp. 441–54; League of Nations, "Convention Concerning the Status of Refugees Coming from Germany, (Geneva, Feb. 10, 1938)," C.75 (1).M.30 (1).1938, XIII, MAE SDN I E 450, pp. 46–54. See also Schramm and Vormeier, pp. 229–31.

86. Vormeier, "La République française," p. 14; Vormeier, "La Situation des réfugiés," p. 88.

87. The question of whether to ratify the accord was still being debated as late as Apr. 1940. Foreign Ministry (Affaires Administratives et des Unions Internationales), to the Foreign Ministry (SDN), Apr. 27, 1940, MAE SDN I E 451, p. 133.

88. Foreign Ministry (SDN), "Note," June 30, 1936, MAE I E 452, pp. 12–15.

89. "L'Activité juridique de la Ligue en 1936–1937," *CDH*, June 15, 1937–July 1, 1937, pp. 384–86. See also Minutes, "Réunion Interministérielle du 20 avril 1937 a/s de l'application de la Convention de 1933 relative au statut des réfugiés," MAE SDN I M 1812, p. 266; Badia et al., *Les Barbelés*, p. 59. In Jan. 1938, the Ministry of the Interior informed the Senate that 6,522 identity certificates had been given to German refugees. *JO, Débats Parlementaires, Sénat*, Jan. 25, 1938, p. 32, cited in J.-Ch. Bonnet, p. 325. See also Tartakower and Grossmann, p. 142; Schramm and Vormeier, pp. 228–29; Fabian and Coulmas, p. 35. According to Raymond-Raoul Lambert, the Consultative Commission decided on 6,300 cases between 1936 and 1938. Lambert, "L'Emigration juive d'Allemagne et le problème des étrangers en France," *UI*, no. 14 (Dec. 23, 1938): 222.

90. Perrin, "Cessons la décevante politique envers les immigrés!" *DdV*, June 12, 1937, pp. 1, 4. See also Perrin, "L'Assistance internationale aux réfugiés," *DdV*, Dec. 19, 1936, pp. 1, 3; Omnès, p. 99. For similar criticisms, see also "Le Statut juridique des réfugiés," *CDH*, Jan. 15, 1937, pp. 60–62; Foreign Ministry, "Note a/s de Convention de Genève de 1933 relative au statut des réfugiés," Feb. 27, 1937, MAE SDN I M 1812, pp. 194–201; Livian, *Le Parti socialiste*, p. 116. For several concrete examples of such abuses on the part of the prefect of Bas-Rhin, see Roblot, prefect, Bas-Rhin, to the sous-secrétaire d'état à la Présidence du Consul chargé des Affaires d'Alsace et de Lorraine, Feb. 9, 1937, in ADBR D 460, paq. 5(36); Roblot, prefect, Bas-Rhin, to the minister of the interior, Sûreté Nationale, 6ème bureau, Apr. 1, 1937, Apr. 13, 1937, and May 20, 1937, all in ADBR AL 98 387 B.

For an excellent analysis of the way in which the civil service, and the prefectoral corps in particular, often blocked the reform efforts of the Popular Front ministers, see Wall.

91. Bentwich, "Growing Refugee Problem," p. 194.

Chapter Seven

1. "Procès verbal de la Ier séance tenue par la Commission interministérielle des réfugiés allemands," May 27, 1933, MAE Z 711, pp. 93–96.

2. "La Détresse des réfugiés allemands," *UI*, Dec. 14, 1934, p. 210. The AIU, however, blamed the expulsion of these refugee doctors on their behavior. See AIU Secretary, to M. Max Bloch, Colmar, Apr. 23, 1936, AIU France V D 18.

3. Foreign Ministry (Europe), to the French Ambassador, London, dossier V. 49, Apr. 30, 1934, MAE Z 711, pp. 198–202; Foreign Ministry (Europe), to Jacques Helbronner, Oct. 27, 1934, MAE Z 711, pp. 242–49. See also Police report, Nov. 10, 1933, APP BA 1814 241.155-1-A.

4. *JO*, *Débats Parlementaires, Chambre des Députés*, 2ème séance, Feb. 19, 1935, p. 565.

5. Minister of the interior, Sûreté Nationale, to the minister of colonies, Feb. 27, 1935, MAE SDN I M 1819, pp. 84–85. For the conservative position on this issue, see also Géo London, "L'Acquittement d'un recidiviste de l'infraction à un arrêté d'expulsion," clipped in *Le Journal*, Nov. 25, 1936, in BDIC, Dos. Duchêne, G FΔ Rés. 86; Henry Leméry, "Réfugiés politiques," *La République*, Feb. 14, 1935, p. 2.

6. Minister of the interior, to the president of the Foreign Affairs Commission of the Chamber of Deputies, Nov. 1935, MAE SDN I M 1806, p. 206; minister of colonies, to Paul Reynaud, President of the Gourevitch-Dreyfus Committee, Apr. 9, 1936, Comité pour la Défense, p. 76.

7. "Allocution de M. Boris Gourevitch...prononcée lors de la réception par M. P-E. Flandin," Dec. 17, 1934, p. 25, and "Extrait du discours du Général Brissaud-Desmaillet, prononcé le 13 juin 1935," pp. 46–50, both in Comité pour la Défense; "Immigration israélite dans les états du Levant sous mandat français," Feb., 1935, MAE K Afrique 91 (1936–1939), pp. 56–61; "Siedlung in Syrien," *PT*, no. 153, May 14, 1934, p. 1; Abitbol, *Les Deux terres*, p. 166.

8. Foreign Ministry (Levant), to Laroche, French Ambassador, Poland, Nov. 29, 1930, MAE Z 330, pp. 24–27; Foreign Ministry (Europe), "Note a/s israélites allemands," July 20, 1933, MAE Z 720, pp. 206–7.

9. "La France et ses intérêts en Syrie et en Palestine," *TJ*, no. 44 (Nov. 3, 1933): 743–44.

10. Martel, to the Foreign Ministry (Levant), no. 134, Apr. 6, 1934, MAE SDN I F 571, pp. 3–5; D'Aumale, French Consul, Jerusalem, to Foreign Ministry (Levant), no. 73, Apr. 7, 1934, MAE SDN I F 571, pp. 7–10; Foreign Ministry, "Note pour le Cabinet," Apr. 28, 1933, MAE Z 710, pp. 85–88; D'Aumale, to the Foreign Ministry (Levant), June 6, 1933, MAE SDN I E 447, pp. 14–15; Martel, to Justin Godart, Apr. 4, 1935, and Martel, to Godart, June 27, 1935, both in Comité pour la Défense, p. 73 bis, 73 ter; "Palestine," *Le Temps*, Oct. 13, 1933, p. 2; Abitbol, *Les Deux terres*, pp. 164–65.

11. Martel, to the Foreign Ministry (Levant), May 14, 1934, MAE SDN I E 448, pp. 183–85; Foreign Ministry (Levant), "Note pour le Service Français de la SDN," June 28, 1934, MAE SDN I E 448, pp. 197–98; Foreign Ministry (SDN), "Note pour la sous-direction d'Afrique-Levant," July 4, 1934, MAE SDN I E 448, pp. 199–200; Martel, to Foreign Ministry (Levant), no. 688, Sept. 7, 1934, MAE SDN I E 448, pp. 202–203; Bernhard Kahn, to Charles J. Liebman, Sept. 24, 1935, JDC no. 617.

12. A.-M., "L'Immigration juive en Syrie," *RJG*, 3ème année (Jan. 1935): 145–48; André Wurfbain, HCR, to James G. McDonald, HCR, Dec. 8, 1934, MP: H 12; "La Détresse des réfugiés allemands," *UI*, Dec. 14, 1934, pp. 210–11; W. Kotschnig, HCR, to J. G. McDonald, HCR, Confidential, "Record of Interview with Baron de Gunzburg," Dec. 17, 1934, MP: H 20; W. Kotschnig, "Record of Interview with Mr. Justin Godart," Dec. 27, 1934, MP: H 20; "L'Emigration juive vers la Syrie et le Liban," *TJ*, no. 51, Dec. 21, 1934; HCR, "Memorandum on Emigration Possibilities," doc. A/119, Feb. 12, 1935, JDC no. 251.

13. B. Kahn, to Charles J. Liebman, Sept. 24, 1935, JDC no. 617.

14. [Lambert], "La Détresse des réfugiés allemands," *UI*, Dec. 14, 1934, pp. 210–11; Lambert, "Le Danger des mirages," *UI*, Sept. 6, 1935, p. 811; "Les Emigrés juifs aux colonies françaises," *UI*, Jan. 29, 1937, p. 321; "Madagascar où la fin d'un mirage," *UI*, Jan. 14, 1938, p. 310.

15. Comité pour la Défense..., to the Foreign Ministry and the High Commissioner of Syria and Lebanon, Mar. 1, 1935, LBI, AR-C 1698/4099; B. Kahn to Charles J. Liebman, Sept. 24, 1935, JDC no. 617.

16. Sûreté Nationale, Report, "a/s l'activité de l'association des émigrés israélites allemands en France," P.3.285, Feb. 28, 1935, AN F⁷ 13434.

17. *JO, Débats Parlementaires, Chambre des Députés*, 2ème séance, Feb. 19, 1935, pp. 563–66; "La Question des étrangers," *CDH*, Mar. 10, 1935, pp. 148–66.

18. Minister of the interior, to the Foreign Ministry (Europe), "Note (a/s M. Moutet)," Jan. 24, 1936, MAE SDN I M 1819, p. 134.

19. "Comité Central [League for the Rights of Man and Citizen] Extraits," Minutes of Meeting on Nov. 7, 1935, *CDH*, June 20, 1936, p. 456.

20. JDC, Euroexco Committee, Paris, "Possibilities of Land Settlement in the

French Colonies," Sept. 1938, AN AJ[43] 43 (86/90); Moutet, to the Foreign Ministry (Afrique-Levant), Feb. 16, 1937, MAE Z 330, p. 187; CDV, bulletin no. 37, June 17, 1937, pp. 3–4, AIU, ms. 650, boîte 1; "Perspectives de l'établissement d'immigrés juifs dans les possessions françaises," *TJ*, no. 5 (Jan. 29, 1937): 67.

21. Comité pour la Défense…, "Note sur les possibilités d'installation à Madagascar et en Nouvelle-Caledonie d'immigrants israélites provenant des pays d'Europe Orientale et Centrale," Nov. 4, 1936, MAE K Afrique 91 (1936–39), pp. 65–73.

22. Francis Mury, Délégué des Comores-Madagascar au Conseil Supérieur des Colonies, "La Métamorphose de Madagascar," *L'Europe nouvelle*, Nov. 2, 1935, p. 1067.

23. "Des Possibilités d'immigration juive dans les colonies françaises," *La Terre retrouvée*, no. 9 (Feb. 1, 1937): 7; Abitbol, *Les Deux terres*, p. 163.

24. Maurice Dormann (senator, former minister, for the Gourevitch Committee), to Cayla, Nov. 30, 1936, MAE K Afrique 91 (1936–39), p. 64; Jacques Fouques-Duparc, to the minister of colonies, "Note," Jan. 18, 1937, MAE K Afrique 91 (1936–39), p. 63. On Cayla's favorable response to proposals from the Gourevitch Committee, see also Cayla, to Henri Guernut, former minister and director of the Commission of Enquiry on Overseas Territories, Jan. 4, 1938, MAE SDN I E 453, pp. 56–58.

25. "A Propos d'un project d'établissement d'israélites dans les colonies françaises," *Le Petit Parisien*, Jan. 16, 1937, clipped in MAE Z 330, p. 171. See also "French Study Haven for Jewish Refugees," *NYT*, Jan. 20, 1937, p. 15; "A Propos d'un projet d'établissement d'israélites dans les colonies: Déclarations de M. Marius Moutet," *UI*, Jan. 22, 1937, p. 312; "Frankreich plant Ansiedlung verfolgter Juden in den Kolonien," *TJ*, no. 4 (Jan. 22, 1937): 57; "M. Marius Moutet, Ministre des Colonies, se déclare favorable à la colonisation agricole juive dans les possessions françaises," *Samedi*, no. 4 (Jan. 23, 1937): 3; "Les Emigrés juifs aux colonies françaises," *UI*, Jan. 29, 1937, p. 321; "La Colonisation agricole juive dans les possessions françaises," *La Juste parole*, Feb. 20, 1937, p. 7.

26. Figures given by the Jewish statistician Jacob Lestschinski in "The Jews in Poland: Problems of Emigration," *Times* of London, Feb. 2, 1937, p. 11. See also Mendelsohn, p. 23. Although Mendelsohn cites the 1931 census, according to which the Jewish population numbered 3,113,933, Lestschinski claimed that the number of Jews living in Poland increased by 100,000 between 1926 and 1935.

27. This was also Bernhard Kahn's estimate. Bauer, *My Brother's Keeper*, p. 187.

28. Ibid., pp. 183–84.

29. Ibid., pp. 187–88. On Polish Jewry during the interwar period, see ibid., pp. 19–56, 180–209; Mendelsohn, pp. 11–83; Israel Gutman and Shmuel Krakowski, *Poles and Jews Between the Wars* (New York, 1987); "Poland," *Encyclopedia Judaica*. For the French diplomatic reports on this worsening situation, see MAE Z 330, pp. 110 ff, and MAE Z 332.

30. French Ambassador, Poland, to the Foreign Ministry (Europe), "Annexe à la dépêche," no. 380–81, Aug. 5, 1936, MAE Z 330, pp. 153–55.

31. Léon Noël, to the Foreign Ministry, Sept. 30, 1936, MAE K Afrique 91 (1936–39), pp. 10–14.

32. Ibid., pp. 10–14.

33. Bauer, *My Brother's Keeper*, p. 192; Lahaque, p. 7.

34. Pierre Bressy, French Chargé d'Affaires, Warsaw, to the Foreign Minister, Delbos, Jan. 21, 1937, in MAE K Afrique 91 (1936–39), pp. 85–88. It should be pointed out that Polish demands for colonies were not exclusively linked to the Jewish issue. According to Léon Noël, Poland had other considerations in mind as well: the desire to become a great power and the attempt to deal with its general overpopulation problem. Thus, according to Noël, "si quelque bonne fée demandait à la Pologne de lui révéler ses désirs en matière coloniale, la Pologne répondrait qu'elle a envie de deux colonies: l'une pour y mettre ses juifs; l'autre pour y installer ses propres enfants." Noël, to Delbos, foreign minister, Sept. 30, 1936, MAE K Afrique 91 (1936–39), pp. 10–14.

35. Noël, to the Foreign Ministry (Europe), telegram no. 43–47, Jan. 17, 1937, MAE Z 330, pp. 172–76. See also Léger, to Moutet, minister of colonies, Jan. 22, 1937, MAE Z 330, pp. 184–86.

36. Léger, to Moutet, minister of colonies, Jan. 22, 1937, MAE Z 330, pp. 184–86.

37. "Project d'établissement d'israélites dans les colonies françaises," CDV, bulletin no. 19, Jan. 28, 1937, pp. 4–5; CDV, bulletin no. 26, Mar. 18, 1937, pp. 6–7, both in AIU, ms. 650, boîte 1.

38. "Statement of Mr. Paul Bouteille, Chef de Cabinet of Mr. Marius Moutet, re: Project for Jewish Colonization in the French Colonies" (n.d.), attached to JDC, Euroexco Committee, Paris, "Possibilities of Land Settlement in the French Colonies," Sept. 9, 1938, AN AJ[43] 43 (86/90); "Projet d'établissement d'israélites dans les colonies françaises," CDV, bulletin, Jan. 28, 1937, pp. 4–5; Henri Levin, "Nos colonies seront ouvertes aux juifs proscrits," *DdV*, Jan. 30, 1937, pp. 1, 5; "Des Possibilités d'immigration juive dans les colonies françaises," *La Terre retrouvée*, no. 9 (Feb. 1, 1937): 7 (also appeared in German as "Die jüdische Einwanderung in die französischen Kolonien: Ausnutzung lediglich für bereits in Frankreich lebende Juden gedachts—Aufnahme von Juden aus Polen kommt noch nicht in Frage," *TJ*, no. 5 [Jan. 29, 1937]: 488).

At another point, Moutet claimed that it might cost Jewish organizations up to 300,000 francs per settler, and he repeatedly appealed to Jewish organizations to pool their resources. Moutet, to the Foreign Ministry, Feb. 16, 1937, MAE Z 330, p. 187.

39. "Des Possibilités d'immigration juive dans les colonies françaises," *La Terre retrouvée*, no. 9 (Feb. 1, 1937): 7. Moutet declared on Feb. 10, 1938, that only Palestine was capable of absorbing a large-scale Jewish immigration. Cited in Lahaque, p. 7.

40. CDV, bulletin no. 19, Jan. 28, 1937, pp. 4–5; CDV, bulletin no. 26, Mar. 18, 1937, pp. 6–7, AIU, ms. 650, boîte 1.

41. Bauer, *My Brother's Keeper*, p. 193.

42. Excerpt from *Le Petit Parisien*, May 12, 1937, cited in Robert Gauthier, "A Propos d'un projet d'installation d'israélites polonais à Madagascar," *La Juste parole*, no. 14 (June 5, 1937): 16–17. Moutet's remarks were also recorded in "Colonisation

à Madagascar," *Samedi*, no. 21 (May 22, 1937): 6. Although these articles were supposed to be quoting Moutet directly, their wording is slightly different.

43. Raymond-Raoul Lambert, "Les Emigrés juifs aux colonies françaises," *UI*, Jan. 29, 1937, p. 321. See also "Encore Madagascar," *UI*, Jan. 8, 1937, p. 275; Lambert, "Madagascar ou la fin d'un mirage," *UI*, Jan. 14, 1938, p. 310.

44. Jacques Fouques-Duparc (Foreign Ministry, Cabinet), "Note pour la Direction Politique," Apr. 16, 1937, MAE K Afrique 91(1936–39), p. 101.

45. "Emigration Meeting to Discuss World Possibilities," Jan. 13, 1938, JDC no. 658. On Oungre's opposition, see also Council for German Jewry, "Settlement of Refugees in French Colonies," Apr. 24, 1936, AN AJ⁴³ 43 (86/90); "Emigration Meeting to Discuss World Possibilities," Jan. 13, 1938, JDC, Germany, no. 658; minister of colonies, Steeg, to minister of foreign affairs, no. 230, Feb. 9, 1938, MAE Z 332 (Cologne, 1937–40), pp. 82–83; "Pas d'émigration sans colonisation," *TJ*, no. 31 (Aug. 5, 1938): 483.

46. Leni Yahil claims that it was Moutet who first approached the JDC, but it seems the opposite was the case. Yahil, p. 317. On Liebman's approach to Bonnet, see Bonnet, to Delbos, foreign minister, no. 114, May 21, 1937, MAE K Afrique 91 (1936–39), pp. 105–6. On Liebman's interest in the scheme, see also B. Kahn and J. Rosen, to Charles J. Liebman, June 12, 1937, JDC Euroexco, "Possibilities of Land Settlement in the French Colonies," Sept., 1938, Paris, AN AJ⁴³ 43 (86/90).

47. B. Kahn and J. Rosen, to Charles J. Liebman, June 12, 1937, Euroexco, "Possibilities of Land Settlement in the French Colonies," Sept. 1938, Paris, AN AJ⁴³ 43 (86/90).

48. Ibid.; Yahil, p. 317; Christophe Delabroye, "Enquête sur un projet de colonisation juive à Madagascar, 1936–1942," Mini-mémoire, p. 12, located at the Archives of the minister of colonies, Aix-en-Provence. I would like to thank Juliette Nunez for bringing this essay to my attention.

49. Cited in "L'Etablissement de colons juifs dans les possessions françaises," *L'Union marocaine*, no. 93 (June 30, 1937): 1, clipped in AIU, ms. 650, boîte 14 (47).

50. Noël, to the Foreign Ministry (Europe), Oct. 9, 1937, MAE K Afrique 91 (1936–39), p. 123. Noël warned, however, that such reports should be taken with a healthy dose of skepticism. Always distrustful of the Polish government's intentions when it came to the Jews, Noël reported in Oct. 1937 that "quelles que puissent être les conclusions de la mission polonaise, il est permis de penser que, en présence du développement de l'agitation antisémitique et mu par le désir de donner des apaisements à l'opinion publique, le gouvernement de Varsovie pourrait être amené à se montrer favorable à un envoi de colons à Madagascar, sans prendre outre mesure en considération les conséquences plus ou moins lointaines de l'entreprise." Noël, to Foreign Ministry (Europe), no. 503, Oct. 26, 1937, MAE Z 330, pp. 247–48.

51. Noël, to the Foreign Ministry (Questions Commerciales), no. 572, Dec. 30, 1937, MAE SDN I E 453, p. 45. See also Foreign Ministry (Questions Commerciales), to Noël, Dec. 30, 1937, MAE Z 332, pp. 41–42; minister of colonies, to Foreign Ministry (Afrique-Levant), Dec. 23, 1937, MAE Z 332, p. 49.

52. Foreign Ministry, to the Ministry of Colonies, Nov. 5, 1937, MAE Z 330,

pp. 256–57; Foreign Ministry (Relations Commerciales), to Noël, Dec. 30, 1937, MAE K Afrique 91 (1936–19), pp. 136–37.

53. Minister of colonies, to the Foreign Ministry (Afrique-Levant), Dec. 23, 1937, MAE Z 332, p. 49.

54. Cited in "Statement of Dr. B. Kahn at Meeting of Council of Jewish Federations and Welfare Funds," Cincinnati, Ohio, Jan. 10, 1938, JDC no. 163. During this trip, Delbos, under pressure from Jewish groups in France and elsewhere in the West, cautioned the Romanians as well as the Poles to cease their antisemitic agitation. See Foreign Ministry (SDN), to the French Ambassador in Great Britain, [early Jan. 1938], MAE SDN I E 522, pp. 39–45. On Jewish efforts to persuade the Foreign Ministry to apply pressure to Poland and Romania to cease their antisemitic agitation, see foreign minister, Cabinet, "Note," Dec. 31, 1937, pp. 28–29; Jarblum, to Delbos, foreign minister, Dec. 31, 1937, pp. 30–32; Levin, Vice-President, AIU, to Delbos, foreign minister, Jan. 2, 1938, pp. 33–36, all in SDN I E 522; Fédération des Juifs Polonais en France, Resolution, July 6, 1936, pp. 149–51; "Un Groupe de juifs polonais," to Léon Blum, May 27, 1937, pp. 217–32, both in MAE Z 330; Paul Py, French Consul, Cologne, to the Foreign Ministry (Europe), no. 93, Dec. 1, 1937, pp. 1–2; World Jewish Congress, Aide-Mémoire: "La Situation des Juifs en Pologne," Dec. 2, 1937, sent by Jarblum to J. Fouques-Duparc, Chef de Cabinet, Foreign Ministry, Dec. 6, 1937, pp. 6–31; Léon Noël, to the Foreign Ministry, no. 43, Jan. 15, 1938, p. 65, all in MAE Z 332.

55. Noël, to Delbos, foreign minister, Jan. 18, 1938, MAE K Afrique 91 (1936–39), pp. 141–42. On the Polish press reactions, see also Lahaque, p. 8.

56. Jean de Seguin, French chargé d'affaires in Poland, to Delbos, foreign minister, Feb. 14, 1938, MAE Z 332, p. 80. The figures cited by de Seguin came from one Polish paper. According to Lahaque, p. 8, Lepecki recommended that only 5,000 to 7,000 families (that is, 25,000–30,000 persons) be settled at a cost of 30,000 francs per family.

57. General Marcel Olivier, "Madagascar—Terre d'asile?" in "Extrait de *L'Illustration*, du 19 février 1938, 96ème année," AIU, ms. 650, boîte 14 (47). See also Yahil, pp. 317–18.

58. Harry Rabinowitz, "The Madagascar Project," *Jewish Chronicle*, n.d., clipped in AIU, ms. 650, boîte 14 (47). On the views of Alter and Dyk, see also General Marcel Olivier, "Madagascar—Terre d'asile?" in "Extrait de *L'Illustration*, du 19 février 1938, 96ème année," AIU, ms. 650, boîte 14 (47); Yahil, pp. 317–18.

59. Cited in "L'Etablissement de colons juifs dans les possessions françaises," *L'Union Marocaine*, no. 93 (June 30, 1937): 1, clipped in AIU, ms. 650, boîte 14 (47).

60. Ibid.

61. Reported in Pierre Bressy, chargé d'affaires de France, Warsaw, to Delbos, foreign minister, Jan. 21, 1937, MAE K Afrique 91 (1936–39), pp. 85–88.

62. Léon Noël, to the Foreign Ministry (Afrique-Levant), Mar. 8, 1938, MAE Z 332, pp. 90–93. See also Pierre Bressy, French chargé d'affaires, Warsaw, to Delbos, foreign minister, Jan. 21, 1937, MAE K Afrique 91 (1936–39), pp. 85–88.

63. Noël, to Delbos, foreign minister, Jan. 15, 1938, MAE Z 332, pp. 61–63. See

also Noël, to the Foreign Ministry (Europe), no. 45, Jan. 18, 1938, MAE Z 332, pp. 68–69.

64. Cited in "L'Emigration juive dans les colonies françaises," *TJ*, May 21, 1937, p. 488.

65. Delabroye, p. 7.

66. Camille Margal, "Les Juifs [en] Madagascar," *AF*, Sept. 20, 1937, clipped in AN 72 AJ 600. See also "L'Invasion juive aux colonies," *AF*, Sept. 1, 1937; Schor, *L'Antisémitisme en France*, p. 191.

67. Delabroye, p. 7. See also *AF*, Jan. 3, 1938, cited in Lahaque, p. 6.

68. Georges Roux, "L'Emancipation nationale," Apr. 8, 1937, CDV, bulletin no. 28, Apr. 8, 1937, pp. 4–5, AIU, ms. 650, boîte 1.

69. Jacques Perret, "Une Option juive sur les colonies françaises," *Je suis partout*, Jan. 28, 1938. See also "Courrier colonial," extract, CDV, bulletin no. 45, Oct. 21, 1937, pp. 4–5, AIU, ms. 650, boîte 2; Alfred Silbert, in *L'Ordre*, Jan. 20, 1938, cited in CDV, bulletin no. 55, Jan. 27, 1938, p. 3, AIU, ms. 650, boîte 2; C. Cambiffard, "Des Emigrants pour Madagascar?" *L'Oeuvre*, Apr. 5, 1938; M. Wright, British embassy, Paris, to the Central Department of the British Foreign Office, Apr. 13, 1938, PRO FO 371/21634.C 3034; Lahaque, p. 8.

70. Marcel Olivier, "Madagascar—Terre d'asile?" in "Extrait de *L'Illustration* du 19 février 1938," AIU, ms. 650, boîte 14 (47). On Olivier's views, see also "Projet d'établissement d'israélites à Madagascar," CDV, bulletin no. 59, Feb. 24, 1938, p. 6, AIU, ms. 650, boîte 2; "Projet d'établissement d'israélites dans les colonies françaises," CDV, bulletin, no. 63, Apr. 14, 1938, AIU, ms. 650, boîte 2; *JDC Fortnightly Digest*, no. 11 (Mar. 15, 1938), JDC no. 150. On the Romanian government's attempt to jump on the bandwagon, see also Lahaque, p. 10; Delabroye, p. 9.

71. Henri Guernut, "Israélites aux colonies," *La Tribune des nations*, Mar. 17, 1938, clipped in AIU, ms. 650, boîte 11 (40).

72. Steeg, minister of colonies, to the Foreign Ministry (Contrôle des étrangers), no. 230, Feb. 9, 1938, MAE Z 332, pp. 82–83.

73. Yahil, pp. 321–22.

74. Ormsby-Gore, to Halifax, Apr. 26, 1938, PRO FO 371/21876.E2570. Cited also in Yahil, pp. 321–22. Ironically, French colonial circles wanted the British to do more to open their colonies to Jewish immigration. See especially Lahaque, pp. 9–10.

75. PRO FO 371/21876.E2570, p. 100.

76. On the influence of Mandel's Jewish background on his political behavior and his reactions to Nazism and the rise of antisemitism, see Sherwood, *Georges Mandel*, pp. 3, 213–14.

77. Mandel was especially close friends with Georges Wormser, a banker and a member of the Paris Consistory in the 1930's. Wormser wrote a biography of Mandel: *Georges Mandel: L'Homme politique* (Paris, 1967).

78. On the desire of the Romanians to jump on the bandwagon, see note 70 above. See also Foreign Ministry (Afrique-Levant), to the minister of colonies, Feb. 2, 1938, pp. 143–44, and Thierry, French minister, Romania, to Delbos, foreign minister, Feb. 7, 1938, pp. 145–47, both in MAE K Afrique 91(1936–39).

79. Mandel, minister of colonies, to Bonnet, foreign minister, May 25, 1938, MAE Z 332, pp. 115–18.

80. Noël, to Bonnet, no. 354, June 28, 1938, pp. 201–2, and Foreign Ministry (Afrique-Levant), "Note pour le Service d'Information et de Presse," Aug. 3, 1938, p. 206, both in MAE K Afrique 91 (1936–39).

81. "Procès verbal, Ier séance tenue par la Commission Interministérielle des Réfugiés Allemands," May 27, 1933, pp. 93–96; "Procès-verbal, 2ème séance tenue par la Commission Interministérielle des Réfugiés Israélites Allemands," Oct. 16, 1933, pp. 37–42; "Procès verbal, 3ème séance tenue par la Commission Interministérielle des réfugiés israélites allemands," Oct. 23, 1933, pp. 70–73, all in MAE Z 711. See also B. Kahn, to Paul Baerwald, confidential cablegram, Oct. 20, 1933, JDC no. 617.

82. On the origins of the Corsica scheme, see "Procès verbal, 3ème séance tenue par la Commission Interministérielle des Réfugiés Allemands," Oct. 23, 1933, and "Procès verbal, 4ème séance tenue par la Commission Interministérielle des Réfugiés Allemands," Nov. 13, 1933, both in MAE Z 711, pp. 72–73, 88–104; B. Kahn, to Paul Baerwald, confidential cablegram, Oct. 20, 1933, JDC no. 617; "Notes for the High Commissioner from N. Bentwich," Mar. 24, 1934, MP: H 11; André Spire, "J'Accuse le CNSR [Comité National]," *Pariser Haint*, Mar. 16, 1934, translated in ACIP B 129 (Sociétés, organisations, groupements, PH).

83. André Spire, "J'Accuse le CNSR [Comité National]," *Pariser Haint*, Mar. 16, 1934, translated in ACIP B 129 (Sociétés, organisations, groupements, PH); Emile Sari, Senator, Corsica, to the President of the French Republic, May 9, 1934, MAE Z 711, p. 218; Mauco, *Mémoire*, p. 77.

84. Police report, July 11, 1934, APP BA 1813 241.155-B; "Notes for the High Commissioner from N. Bentwich," Mar. 24, 1934, MP: H 11.

85. Police report, July 11, 1934, APP BA 1813 241.155-B; M. de Menthon, Foreign Ministry, (Affaires politiques, Europe), to the Foreign Ministry (Contrôle des étrangers), July 12, 1934, MAE Z 711, p. 224.

86. On the attempt to create agricultural settlements for Russian immigrants in the southwest after the First World War, see Simpson, *Refugee Problem*, pp. 310–11. On efforts to create agricultural settlements for Poles in the late 1920's, including several hundred Polish Jews, see Ponty, pp. 266–68. For a general discussion of the use of immigrant labor in French agriculture, see Demangeon and Mauco.

87. M. Chavin, Subprefect [Bethune], "Memo: Sur le reclassement social des Juifs, 1934," ACIP B129 (sociétés, LICA, etc.). See also A. Bonneaud, representative of the departmental agronomical laboratory station, Limoges, to M. J. R. Bloch, AIU France V D 18. For a description of the economic conditions in the departments of the southwest and the growing dependence on outside labor, see F. Vallatte, "Terres de soleil et de misère," *L'Humanité*, Oct. 22, 1934, p. 4.

88. On the support of the Gourevitch Committee, see Comité pour la Défense, pp. 48–82. On the LICA's support, see Marcel Feder, "Que faire des persécutés?" *DdV*, no. 13 (June 1933): 3; Feder, "La Cité du refuge," *DdV*, no. 14 (July–Aug., 1933): 2; Charles Ancel, "Quelques jours avec les proscrits allemands," *DdV*, no. 14 (July–Aug., 1933): 4. On JDC support and expenditures, see B. Kahn, to the Allocations Committee, Central British Fund for German Jewry, June 2, 1934, JDC

no. 617; B. Kahn, to J. C. Hyman, Feb. 14, 1935, JDC no. 602; B. Kahn, to Charles J. Liebman, Sept. 24, 1935, JDC no. 617; minister of the interior, Sûreté Nationale, 6ème Bureau, to Justin Godart, Nov. 26, 1935, LBI, AR-C 1698/4099; D. Klementinowski, "Des paysans juifs dans le Midi de la France," [1938], LBI AR-C 1648/4121 (William Graetz Collection). On the support of the HCR, see James G. McDonald, Press Communiqué, Jan. 31, 1934, LBI, AR-C 1638/4099 (file a); N. Bentwich, to Charles Liebmann, "For Prospectus," Mar. 17, 1934, MP: H 11; N. Bentwich, to J. G. McDonald, Jan. 8, 1935, MP: H 12.

89. Norman Bentwich, "Report, Council for Germany," Apr. 24, 1936, p. 6, MP: H 25; Mme. Pascale Saisset, Paris (Président du Comité féminin de l'Agriculture et Artisanat), 1936, cited in "Enquête sur le problème des réfugiés juifs," *RJG*, no. 40 (July 1936): 471. On the difficulties of the Renouveau, see B. Kahn, to J. C. Hyman, May 11, 1935, JDC no. 602; B. Kahn, to J. C. Hyman, Sept. 15, 1936, JDC no. 602; Appeal of Dr. Ernst Krotoschin, Temporary Chair, Comité pour la conservation de la ferme-école juive du château du Born, to B. Kahn, Sept. 23, 1936, JDC no. 602; "Excerpt from JTA Dispatch: Mizrachi to Operate Refugee Farm in France," Sept. 30, 1935, JDC no. 602.

90. See Bernhard Kahn's cricitisms of the Renouveau. B. Kahn, to J. C. Hyman, May 11, 1935 and Sept. 15, 1936, JDC no. 602.

91. "Procès verbal, 4ème séance tenue par la Commission Interministérielle des Réfugiés Allemands," Nov. 13, 1933, MAE Z 711, pp. 88–104.

92. Paul Bargeton, Foreign Ministry (Europe), "Note pour le Bureau du Contrôle des Etrangers," Dec. 11, 1933, MAE Z 711, p. 133. The Foreign Ministry also rejected petitions by Jewish leaders to arrange some sort of Ha'avara, or transfer arrangement, like that worked out between the Jewish Agency and the Nazis, to allow Jewish refugees coming to France to take some of their capital with them in return for a commitment to buy German products. The Foreign Ministry argued that such deals would have rewarded Germany for expelling Jews and would have given the Nazis a green light to continue to do so since France would seem ready to absorb the refugees permanently. See Foreign Ministry, "Note pour la direction des affaires politiques et commerciales," July 6, 1933, and Filderman, President of the Palestine Office in Paris, to the minister of agriculture, June 9, 1933, both in MAE Z 710, pp. 165, 166–69; B. Kahn, to the JDC, N.Y., Feb. 14, 1935, JDC no. 602.

93. Foreign Ministry, (Unions internationales), "Note pour la Direction Politique," Feb. 26, 1935, MAE Z 314, p. 205; Foreign Ministry (Europe), M. de Menthon, "Note pour la sous-direction des Unions," Mar. 5, 1935, MAE Z 314, p. 224. On the administration's determination not to allow Saar refugees to remain, see Chapter 3.

94. Foreign Ministry (Contrôle des étrangers), "Note pour la sous-direction d'Europe," June 12, 1934, MAE Z 711, pp. 220–21; Norman Bentwich, to James G. McDonald, Feb. 22, 1934, MP: H 10; B. Kahn, to J. C. Hyman, May 11, 1935, JDC no. 602; "Ce que 'A et A' [Agriculture et Artisanat] fait pour la jeunesse juive," *La Terre retrouvée*, no. 8 (Apr. 25, 1934): 9; "Berufsumschichtung in Frankreich," *PT*, no. 298 (Oct. 6, 1934): 3; J. B. [J. Biélinky], "Pour la ferme-école du 'Renouveau,'" *UI*, June 8, 1934, p. 321; "L'Oeuvre du 'Renouveau,'" *UI*, Dec. 7, 1934, p. 199; "Re-

nouveau: An Association to Foster Jewish Interests in Agriculture" [pamphlet], JDC no. 602.

95. B. Kahn, to J. C. Hyman, Mar. 8, 1935, JDC no. 602. On the ORT colony at Villeneuve, see also "Le Problème de l'adaptation professionelle des réfugiés: Mémoire présenté à la Conférence Intergouvernemental des réfugiés à Evian-les-Bains par le Comité Exécutif Central de l'ORT" [pamphlet], (Paris, July 2, 1938), p. 6, LBI, AR-C 1648/4121 (William Graetz Collection); D. Klementinowski, "Des Paysans juifs dans le Midi de la France," [1938], LBI, AR-C 1648/4121 (William Graetz Collection); Dr. A. Syngalowski, Executive of the Zentralverwaltung of the ORT, to B. Kahn, Sept. 17, 1934, JDC no. 602; "A Cross Section," *B'nai B'rith Magazine*, Jan. 1935, JDC no. 602.

96. Joseph Walden, "Hehalouts en France en 1936," *La Terre retrouvée* 6, no. 13 (Apr. 1, 1937): 8.

97. Comité National, circulaire no. 1, Aug. 13, 1933, p. 4, AIU France X D 56; Comité National, Rapport Financier, Exercice 1933–1934, annexe no. 3, LBI, AR-C 1698/4099; Norman Bentwich, to James G. McDonald, Feb. 22, 1934, MP: H 10; "Ce que 'A et A' fait pour la jeunesse juive," *La Terre retrouvée*, no. 8 (Apr. 25, 1934): 9.

98. André Spire, "J'Accuse le CNSR [Comité National]," *Pariser Haint*, Mar. 16, 1934, translated in ACIP B 129 (sociétés, organisations, groupements, PH).

99. Dobler, French Consul, Cologne, to the Foreign Ministry (Europe), May 17, 1934, and July 31, 1934, MAE Z 711, pp. 210–16, 228–30. On the reaction of the Comité National, see Lambert, to B. Kahn, June 4, 1934, JDC no. 601; Robert de Rothschild, to M. Saltiel, June 4, 1934, JDC no. 601; Robert de Rothschild, to Charles J. Liebman, June 5, 1934, JDC no. 617.

100. Nathan Netter, "Retour à la terre," *UI*, May 19, 1933, pp. 184–85; "Les Centres agricoles juifs en Alsace," *AI*, Apr. 26, 1934, p. 55; Henri Lévy, President, Comité d'Informations et d'Aide aux Réfugiés Allemands, Strasbourg, to the President, AIU, Aug. 9, 1933, and the AIU's response on Oct. 27, 1933, both in AIU IX D 54; "L'Agriculture juive en France," *Samedi*, no. 15 (Apr. 1, 1936): 12; "Die deutsch-jüdische Siedlung in der Gironde," *TJ*, no. 9 (Mar. 2, 1934): 165–66; Raphaël and Weyl, pp. 271–72. In 1933, the Sûreté Nationale reported on a group called the Amis de la Tradition Juive en Alsace, whose aim was to place refugees in agricultural jobs. The president of this organization was the chief rabbi of Colmar, Ernest Nathan Weill, and the general secretary was Emile Schnurmann, the well-known demographer of Alsatian Jews. Mallet, Sûreté Nationale, to the Prefect of the Bas-Rhin, no. 3265, June 15, 1933, ADBR AL 98 392 A.

The hostility of the native establishment to these schemes deeply embittered relations between French Jews and the refugees. In early 1935, the Villeneuve settlers denounced the lack of support for their endeavor, stating: "It is with regret that we German-Jewish refugees must note that we have been deserted by all the organizations whose object it should be to support our work. This has happened in spite of the fact that our settlement would seem to offer a sure future for us and our children, if we were to receive reasonable assistance." "'Resolution' of the settlers from Villeneuve," Feb. 23, 1935, JDC no. 602.

101. See Chapter 5, n. 43. See also N. Bentwich, to Charles Liebman, "For Prospectus," Mar. 17, 1934, MP: H 11.

102. "Note transmise par M. le Général Brissaud-Desmaillet à M. Paganon, Ministre de l'Intérieur, le 16 Octobre 1935, lors de la réception de la délégation du Comité pour la Défense...", in Comité pour la Défense, p. 58. For a recent discussion of the Société de Géographie Commerciale, see Lebovics, pp. 16, 43–46, 99, 115. The influential conservative deputy Louis Marin was president of this association.

103. Italics in original text. Minister of the interior, Sûreté Nationale, 6ème bureau, to Justin Godart, President of the Comité pour la Défense, Nov. 26, 1935, in Comité pour la Défense, pp. 62–63 (also in LBI, AR-C 1698/4099).

104. Maga, *America*, pp. 86–87; Simpson, *Refugee Problem*, pp. 328–29; L. Stein, p. 6. Many of those who initially fled to France from Spain were eventually repatriated.

105. Tamburini was eventually cleared of responsibility for this particular bombing. The police came to suspect the secret extreme-right-wing paramilitary organization the Cagoule. On the Cagoule's involvement in these bombings, see Pol, pp. 6–7; Lazareff, pp. 162–63; Werth, *Twilight*, pp. 129, 343. I also wish to thank Joel Blatt for this information.

106. On these right-wing charges, see "Un peu de pudeur, Monsieur Régnier," Sept. 26, 1937, p. 1, and "Mauvaise foi," Sept. 27, 1937, p. 2, both in *Le Populaire*.

107. For Chautemps's declaration, see "Tamburini fasciste notoire qui se prétend anarchiste est retrouvé," *Le Populaire*, Sept. 16, 1937, pp. 1–2; "A Propos des indésirables," *Le Peuple*, Apr. 30, 1938, p. 6; "Les Investigations en Catalogne française ne semblent pas avoir donné de résultat," *L'Aube*, Sept. 16, 1937, pp. 1, 3; Leo Lambert, "Zum Kommenden Fremdenstatut in Frankreich," *PT*, no. 462 (Sept. 18, 1937): 1; Schor, *L'Opinion française et les étrangers*, pp. 665–66. The Interministerial Commission appointed by Dormoy met only once, on Oct. 18. See "Note pour M. Bressy, Sous-Directeur des Unions Internationales," MAE SDN I M 1819, pp. 299–301.

108. Moitessier, minister of the interior, Sûreté Nationale, 6ème bureau (Service des étrangers), no. C-21, circular no. 328, Mar. 24, 1937, APP BA 64 Provisoire 51-343-5.

109. Bardot, Inspecteur de police spécial, Forbach, to the Commissaire spécial, Chef de Service, Forbach, (confidential), no. 6022, Oct. 7, 1937, ADBR AL 98 392 A. See also *Journal d'Alsace*, extract, Dec. 10, 1936, ADBR D 460, paq. 5 (36).

110. Jean Bourdeillette, French Consul, Nuremberg, to the Foreign Ministry, Dec. 27, 1937, MAE Z 705, p. 278; J. Telle, French Consul, Frankfurt a/M, to the Foreign Ministry (Contrôle des étrangers), no. 225, Dec. 22, 1937, MAE Z 706, pp. 3–4.

111. "Notes on JDC Activities During the Months of Jan.–Mar., 1938," Appendix VIIa, JDC no. 188; Police report, Mar. 31, 1939, APP BA^P 407.

112. Dormoy, circular no. 338 (confidential), July 9, 1937, APP DA 783 (Textes). As proof that Dormoy was not overly lenient toward undesirable foreigners, *Le*

Populaire pointed out that he had expelled more foreigners than his chief right-wing critic, Marcel Régnier, during his stint as minister of the interior in early 1935. "Mauvaise foi," *Le Populaire*, Sept. 27, 1937, p. 2.

113. Prefect of Police, to the minister of the interior, July 23, 1937, APP BA 65 Provisoire 51343-4.

114. Omnès, pp. 99–100. See also "400 000 étrangers à Paris et dans sa banlieue," *Le Matin*, Apr. 25, 1938, pp. 1–2.

115. CDV, bulletin no. 52, Dec. 23, 1937, pp. 5–6, AIU, ms. 650, boîte 2.

116. Chautemps had already declared his intention to create this post in late Dec., 1937. CDV, bulletin no. 52, Dec. 23, 1937, pp. 5–6, AIU, ms. 650, boîte 2. Serre had been serving as an undersecretary of state under the auspices of the Ministry of Labor since June 22, 1937. One of his main projects in this post was to curtail *travail noir*, or illegal work. On Jan. 18, 1938, Serre's office was brought directly under the aegis of the Président du Conseil, and he became responsible for immigration matters. From Mar. 13 until Apr. 10, 1938, the office was returned to the Ministry of Labor, but Serre continued to serve as undersecretary of state for immigration until Daladier assumed the premiership on Apr. 10, 1938. Herriot claimed that the idea of a special undersecretary of state for immigration was his own, which is certainly possible in view of his own role as head of the Interministerial Commission on Immigration. See *Le Progrès de Lyon*, Feb. 16, 1938, cited in CDV, bulletin no. 59, Feb. 24, 1938, AIU, ms. 650, boîte 2.

117. Racine, p. 614; A. Ulmann, "Une Interview avec M. Philippe Serre," *Vendredi*, May 6, 1938, p. 6. Serre already had specific individuals in mind for the consultative commission, including: Justin Godart; Jean Perrin; Léon Jouhaux, the head of the CGT; W. Oualid, a member of the Paris Jewish Consistory and the AIU and a well-known demographer; Paul Langevin, the famous physician; Jacques Maritain, the philosopher; Albert Demangeon, professor of geography at the Sorbonne; and the Rector Roussy. Serre also hoped to include other members of the Consistory in addition to Oualid. See "Entrevue de MM. Manuel et Schumann avec M. Philippe Serre," Feb. 11, 1938, AIU, ms. 650, boîte 7 (28); J.-Ch. Bonnet, p. 337.

118. Bauer's account suggests that Serre's plan was intended for German refugees (*My Brother's Keeper*, p. 237). This plan, however, was directed primarily at recently arrived East European Jews.

119. "Notes on JDC Activities During the Months of Jan.–Mar., 1938," Mar. 28, 1938, Appendix VII c, JDC no. 188; J. C. Hyman, to the Officers of the JDC, Apr. 25, 1938, JDC no. 617. See also "Entrevue de MM. Manuel et Schumann avec M. Philippe Serre," Feb. 11, 1938, AIU, ms. 650, boîte 7 (28). On the Serre Plan, see also Marc Jarblum, to Philippe Serre, Feb. 17, 1938, AIU, ms. 650, boîte 7(28); Oualid, "Les Juifs et l'agriculture," *RJG*, no. 58 (May 1938): 339–40; Marrus and Paxton, p. 57; Schor, *L'Opinion française et les étrangers*, pp. 645–46; J.-Ch. Bonnet, pp. 32–33, 328–39; Bauer, *My Brother's Keeper*, pp. 237–38; Marrus, "Vichy before Vichy," p. 17; Cross, pp. 209–10.

120. "La Situation des travailleurs immigrés," Sept. 29, 1937, p. 8; "L'Union des

Syndicats et les travailleurs immigrés," Dec. 29, 1937, p. 2; "Le Travail à domicile dans la fourrure," Mar. 14, 1938, p. 7; "La Grande misère des ouvriers chapeliers," Mar. 14, 1938, p. 7, all in *Le Populaire*; Szajkowski, *Analytical Franco-Jewish Gazetteer*, pp. 34–35, n. 145. See also Schor, *L'Opinion française et les étrangers*, p. 598.

121. "Entrevue de MM. Manuel et Schumann avec M. Philippe Serre," Feb. 11, 1938, AIU, ms. 650, boîte 7 (28); R. Schumann, Assistant Secretary, Central Consistory, to Philippe Serre, Feb. 17, 1938, AIU, ms. 650, boîte 7 (28).

122. "Notes on JDC Activities During the Months of Jan.–Mar., 1938," Mar. 28, 1938, Appendices VII b and c, JDC no. 188.

123. "Entrevue de MM. Manuel et Schumann avec M. Philippe Serre," Feb. 11, 1938, AIU, ms. 650, boîte 7 (28).

124. JTA Bulletin, Mar. 24, 1938, AIU, ms. 650, boîte 13 (46).

125. "Meeting sur la situation des étrangers," CDV, bulletin no. 68, June 16, 1938, AIU, ms. 650, boîte 2.

126. A. Ulmann, "Une Interview avec M. Philippe Serre," *Vendredi*, May 6, 1938, p. 6. See also Serre's speech to the LICA in the summer of 1938, reported in "Meeting sur la situation des étrangers," CDV, bulletin no. 68, June 16, 1938, AIU, ms. 650, boîte 2; "Entrevue de MM. Manuel et Schumann avec M. Philippe Serre," Feb. 11, 1938, AIU, ms. 650, boîte 7 (28). According to P. Racine, the distinction between "une immigration utile"—that is, one that "donne à la France les travailleurs agricoles ou industriels qui lui font défaut dans certaines régions ou professions" and "une immigration néfaste, ... qui se dirige vers les activités déjà encombrées: artisanat, commerce, professions libérales," was the principal criterion by which the new *statut des immigrés* was to determine which immigrants should be allowed to enter. Racine, pp. 610–11.

127. Italics in original text. Lambert, to Schumann, Feb. 21, 1938, AIU, ms. 650, boîte 7 (28). Robert Schumann, the assistant secretary of the Central Consistory, had initially been willing to include the Gourevitch Committee. See Schumann, to Oualid, Feb. 17, 1938, AIU, ms. 650, boîte 7 (28).

128. "Notes on JDC Activities During the Months of Jan.–Mar. 1938," Mar. 28, 1938, Appendix VII d, JDC no. 188. Already in Feb., Robert Schumann had notified Rabbi Schonberg of Lyon that Serre was planning to repatriate 85 Moroccan Jewish families from that region. Schumann wanted to know what Lyon Jews would think of this expulsion, and he asked Schonberg: "Approuvez-vous ce rapatriement des familles juives marocaines ou seriez-vous prêt à les aider à rester dans votre région?" Schumann, to Rabbi Schonberg, Feb. 10, 1938, AIU, ms. 650, boîte 7 (28).

129. "Notes on JDC Activities During the Months of Jan.–Mar. 1938," Mar. 28, 1938, Appendix VII a, JDC no. 188; Oualid, "Les Juifs et l'agriculture," *RJG*, no. 58 (May 1938): 340–41.

130. "Notes on JDC Activities During the Months of Jan.–Mar. 1938," Mar. 28, 1938, Appendix VII a, JDC no. 188.

131. Jarblum, to Serre, Feb. 17, 1938, AIU, ms. 650, boîte 7 (28); "Notes on JDC Activities During the Months of Jan.–Mar. 1938," Mar. 28, 1938, Appendix VII a, JDC no. 188. See also J.-Ch. Bonnet, pp. 338–39; "Revue de la Presse: Les Juifs immigrés: Une enquête du *Temps*," *UI*, May 27, 1938, p. 626.

132. "Notes on JDC Activities During the Months of Jan.–Mar. 1938," Mar. 28, 1938, Appendix VII c, JDC no. 188.

133. Ibid., Appendix VII a.

134. Ibid., Appendix VII d; JDC, Euroexco Meeting, Mar. 5, 1939, JDC no. 174.

135. "Notes on JDC Activities During the Months of Jan.–Mar. 1938," Mar. 28, 1938, Appendix VII a, JDC no. 188. Bauer is in error regarding the amount of money committed to this project. He suggests that the JDC initially proposed spending 3 million francs and ended up committing 20 million francs to this project. In reality, the JDC never promised more than 3 million francs. Bauer, *My Brother's Keeper*, p. 237.

136. The decree creating the three new administrative councils to implement the new immigration statute was already drawn up—with the signatures of both the president of the republic, Lebrun, and the president of the council, Chautemps— and scheduled to appear on Mar. 2, 1938. But due to the fall of Chautemps's and subsequently Blum's governments, the decree was never published. See "Le Décret du 2 mars 1938," in Racine, pp. 616–19.

137. Most accounts of the Serre Plan (Racine, p. 610; J.-Ch. Bonnet, pp. 331–32) claim that the plan was dropped in Mar., when Chautemps's ministry fell, and Serre's office was transferred back to the Ministry of Labor. However, the fact that Jewish leaders continued to negotiate over the Serre Plan throughout late Mar. and early Apr. indicates that the proposal was still on the table during Blum's second cabinet. When Daladier assumed power, Jewish leaders fully expected his government to enact the plan. See especially "Notes on JDC Activities During the Months of Jan.–Mar. 1938," Mar. 28, 1938, Appendix VII d, JDC no. 188.

138. Pierre Bressy, Foreign Ministry (Unions), to Serre, Mar. 5, 1938, MAE SDN I M 1819, pp. 305–13. Bressy excoriated the fraudulent methods East European immigrants often used to gain illegal entry to France. He also objected to the establishment of a consultative commission on refugees, claiming that "on donnerait aux manifestations émanant des milieux de réfugiés une importance et une portée exagérées." On the role of the Foreign Ministry in killing the plan, see also Racine, p. 614; J.-Ch. Bonnet, p. 339; Schramm and Vormeier, p. 234 n.3.

139. *Cahiers du Renouveau*, no. 5 (Apr. 1935), cited in Mauco, *Mémoire*, pp. 76–77.

140. "Asyl-und Arbeitsrecht für die Flüchtlinge!" *PT*, no. 44 (July 25, 1936): 2. André Maurois similarly supported such schemes. See "Enquête sur le problème des réfugiés juifs," *RJG*, no. 40 (July 1936): 463. On the support of the CGT for agricultural settlements for immigrants and refugees, see Chapters 2 and 4.

Chapter Eight

1. Remarque, p. 286.

2. Police report, "Information: La Situation des juifs à Vienne," Apr. 13, 1938, APP BA 269[P] 163.300-C.

3. Police report, "Information: Plan d'expulsion des juifs autrichiens," June 2, 1938, APP BA 269[P] 163.300-C; Bauer, *My Brother's Keeper*, p. 223.

4. On the situation of Austrian Jewry in general after the Anschluss, see Bauer, *My Brother's Keeper*, pp. 223–30; G. Schneider, pp. 11–23.

5. Schleunes, p. 145; Pierre Saintes, Acting Vice-Consul, Munich, to the Foreign Ministry (Europe), no. 1, Jan. 8, 1938, MAE Z 706, pp. 5–9. On Nazi aryanization policies in general, see Schleunes, pp. 133–68; Barkai, pp. 69–77, 125–38.

6. François-Poncet, to the Foreign Ministry, no. 651, June 23, 1938, MAE Z 706, pp. 162–75. See also François-Poncet, to the Foreign Ministry, teleg. no. 2523, June 18, 1938, teleg. no. 2525–27, June 18, 1938, and teleg. no. 2689, June 30, 1938, all in MAE Z 706, pp. 134, 136–38, 177; Wyman, *Paper Walls*, p. 29; Dawidowicz, pp. 128–29; Ben Elissar, p. 233.

7. J. Telle, French consul, Frankfurt a/M, to the Foreign Ministry (Contrôle des étrangers), no. 225, Dec. 22, 1937, MAE Z 706, pp. 3–4.

8. François-Poncet, to the Foreign Ministry, no. 651, June 23, 1938, MAE Z 706, pp. 162–75.

9. Gourevitch, pp. 12, 83–84; Bauer, *My Brother's Keeper*, pp. 243–44; Dawidowicz, pp. 133–34; Marrus, *Unwanted*, pp. 172–73; Sybil Milton, "The Expulsion of Polish Jews from Germany, Oct. 1938 to July 1939," *LBIYB* 29 (1984), pp. 169–74; Schleunes, pp. 236–39; Cahen-Molina, pp. 8–9. On antisemitism in Poland in the late 1930's, see Mendelsohn, pp. 68–83.

10. Cited in Adrien Thierry, French Minister, Romania, to the Foreign Ministry, no. 46, Dec. 31, 1938, MAE SDN I M 1818, pp. 111–12. On antisemitism in Romania, see also Bauer, *My Brother's Keeper*, pp. 209–18; Marrus, *Unwanted*, pp. 173–74; Dawidowicz, p. 519; Mendelsohn, pp. 202–11.

11. Minister of the interior, Sûreté Nationale, to the prefect de police, July 11, 1938, APP BA 407[P]; MAE, Sous-direction, Société des Nations (SDN), "Note pour M. Massigli," Jan. 21, 1938, MAE SDN I E 478, pp. 27–29. On antisemitism in Hungary, see also Bauer, *My Brother's Keeper*, pp. 219–20; Marrus, *Unwanted*, p. 174; Mendelsohn, pp. 112–28; Dawidowicz, pp. 512–15.

12. André Cochinal, "Simples réflexions à propos des étrangers," *L'Aube*, Apr. 28, 1938, p. 1; Werth, p. 167.

13. Depoid, p. 77; Direction de la Statistique Générale, pp. 91–95, 101, 103.

14. For the text of the May 2, 1938, decree law, see *Le Temps*, May 5, 1938, p. 4; Emile Kahn, "La Police et les étrangers," *CDH*, May 15, 1938, pp. 294–300; Gourevitch, pp. 17, 97–101; Feblowicz and Lamour, pp. 428–432, 461–65. See also Schramm and Vormeier, pp. 206–7, 223–24. On May 14, another decree law was declared that elaborated the legal mechanisms according to which foreigners could acquire and renew identity cards. Most of the provisions of the Feb. 6, 1935, law remained in place. For the text of this law, see Feblowicz and Lamour, pp. 465–85.

15. Leven, pp. 12–13, 16–24; Emile Kahn, "D'une semaine à l'autre," *La Lumière*, May 6, 1938, p. 2; E. Kahn, "La Police et les étrangers," *CDH*, May 15, 1938, pp. 297–300; Gourevitch, pp. 16–17; Henri Sinder, in Tartakower and Grossman, pp. 138–40; Thalmann, "L'Emigration allemande," p. 62; J.-Ch. Bonnet, pp. 341–48; Gilbert Badia, "L'Emigration en France," pp. 82–83; Vormeier, "Législation répressive," pp. 162–63; B. Pierlouis, "Les Etrangers en France," part 3, "Le Régime juridique," *Le Peuple*, June 17, 1939, pp. 1–2; J. N. Mégret, "A Quand le code de

l'étranger?: Une étape: Le décret du 2 mai," *L'Aube*, June 30, 1938, pp. 1–2; Cahen-Molina, pp. 1–7. Finally, Parliament accorded the minister of the interior five million francs to cover the costs of sheltering and repatriating "undesirable" foreigners, as well as an additional 3,229,578 francs to the Sûreté and the special mobile police forces. *JO, Lois et Décrets*, May 15, 1938, pp. 5530, cited in Schramm and Vormeier, pp. 206–7.

16. Ministry of the interior, circular no. 72, May 28, 1938, AN F^7 14662.

17. Maga, "Closing," pp. 424–42.

18. Minister of the interior, circular, Apr. 14, 1938, AN 72 AJ 590 (also in AN 72 AJ 590). See also Badia, "L'Emigration en France," p. 81.

19. Minister of the interior, circular, May 4, 1938, AN 72 AJ 590.

20. Marise Querlin, "Rendre 'humains' les décrets-lois sur les étrangers," *Marianne*, May 18, 1938, p. 3.

21. Sauvy, pp. 269–70, 554; Bernard and Dubief, p. 179; Jackson, p. 1; Berstein, *La France*, pp. 25–33.

22. Minister of the interior, to the Ministry of Finance, Direction Générale des douanes [A-17], [late spring or early summer 1938], AN F^7 14776.

23. Ministry of the interior, circular no. 356, C-2-11, May 16, 1938, AN 72 AJ 590. According to the Gourevitch Committee, some 500,000 foreigners faced the threat of losing their jobs as a result of this decree. Gourevitch, p. 17.

24. Léon Noël, to the Foreign Ministry (Unions), no. 56, June 8, 1938, MAE SDN I M 1806, pp. 239–42.

25. Cahen-Molina, p. 8; "Les Commerçants étrangers en France seront traités comme les commerçants français à l'étranger," *Le Petit Journal*, June 27, 1938, clipped in AIU, ms. 650, CDV, boîte 13 (46); minister of the interior, circular no. 373, Sept. 28, 1938, AN AJ 590.

On the protectionist campaign waged in Alsace and Lorraine as well as in Paris by the local Chambers of Commerce, see "La Chambre de Commerce de Metz réclame un statut pour les commerçants étrangers en France," newspaper clipping [n. title], Aug. 12, 1938, clipped in AIU, ms. 650, boîte 13 (46); CDV, bulletin no. 69, June 30, 1938, pp. 4–5, in AIU, ms. 650, boîte 2; "Les Demandes de naturalisation: Voeux des chambres de commerce de Paris et de Metz," *Le Matin*, July 9, 1938, clipped in AIU, ms. 650, boîte 13 (46); "La Confédération générale des classes moyennes," in CDV, bulletin no. 72, Oct. 20, 1938, pp. 7–8, in Documents of French Jewish History, JTS, box 12, folder 1; Prefect, Bas-Rhin, to the President du Conseil, Direction Générale des Services d'Alsace et de Lorraine [Paul Valot], no. 36988, Apr. 8, 1938, ADBR AL 98 397 A (dos. 68, case of Natan Dziewiecki); Prefect, Haut-Rhin, to the minister of the interior, Sûreté Nationale, 7th bureau, Oct. 7, 1938, ADBR AL 98 393 (D 57); CDV, bulletin no. 69, June 30, 1938, pp. 4–5, in AIU, ms. 650, boîte 2.

26. "Décret relatif à la carte d'identité de commerçant pour les étrangers," Nov. 12, 1938, *JO, Lois et Décrets*, Nov. 13, 1938, pp. 12923–24; Maurice Leven, p. 14, n. 1; Cahen-Molina, p. 9; Gourevitch, p. 43; "Handelsbeschrankungen für Auslander," *PT*, no. 723 (June 28, 1938): 2; Dr. Ch. Rosenberg and Dr. Herzfelder, "Zu den Niederlassungsbestimmungen für Kaufleute u. Handwerker," *PT*, no. 744

(July 23, 1938): 3; CDV, bulletin no. 69, June 30, 1938, pp. 4–5, in AIU, ms. 650, boîte 2.

27. Jean Berthoin, Secretary-General, ministry of the interior, circular no. 382, Dec. 26, 1938, AN F[7] 14662. See also Thalmann, "L'Emigration allemande," p. 63, n. 54.

28. Prefect of Police, Note pour M. le Directeur, [summer 1938], in APP DA 783; minister of the interior, circular no. 373, Sept. 28, 1938, AN 72 AJ 590. Restrictions on the validity of merchants' and artisans' cards to one department only became law in early 1939. See *JO*, *Lois et Décrets*, Feb. 4, 1939, p. 1645, cited in Schramm and Vormeier, p. 215, "Le Cas des forains et commerçants étrangers," *DdV*, Feb. 4, 1939, p. 3.

29. Minister of the interior, circular, Apr. 14, 1938, AN 72 AJ 590.

30. Minister of the interior, circular, May 18, 1938, AN 72 AJ 590.

31. Emile Kahn, "La Police et les étrangers," part 2: "Interprétation et application," *CDH*, May 15, 1938, pp. 297–300. This article originally appeared in two parts in *La Lumière* as "D'une semaine à l'autre," May 6, 1938, p. 2, and May 13, 1938. On Kahn's protests, see also J.-Ch. Bonnet, p. 348. The lawyer Cahen-Molina similarly praised articles 10 and 11 despite his otherwise critical view of the decree laws. See Cahen-Molina, pp. 3–4.

32. Henri Guernut, "Le Décret sur les étrangers," *La Tribune des nations*, May 19, 1938, clipped in AIU, ms. 650, boîte 13.

33. "220 étrangers sont expulsés," *Le Petit Parisien*, Apr. 23, 1938.

34. Emile Kahn, "La Police et les étrangers," part 2: "Interprétation et application," *CDH*, May 15, 1938, p. 299. For other depictions of scenes enacted at the police headquarters in Paris, see Vernier, *Tendre exil*, pp. 103–5; Vernier, "Les Tribulations," pp. 35–37; Olievenstein, p. 18.

35. Procès verbal, Bas-Rhin Consistory, Séance, May 17, 1938, CBR, Procès verbaux, 1938–42, p. 17.

36. Lambert, Commissioner of the Mobile Police, to the Division Commissioner, Chief of the 18th Regional Brigade, Nice, no. 105, Jan. 20, 1939, AN F[7] 14776; Ary Delman, "La Situation des étrangers en France," *RJG*, no. 67 (Apr., 1939): 329; René Rousseau, "Une Politique de l'immigration: L'exemple instructif des réfugiés autrichiens," *L'Epoque*, Feb. 10, 1939, p. 4.

37. Minister of the interior, circular no. 72, May 28, 1938, AN F[7] 14662 (also in AN 72 AJ 590); minister of the interior, circular no. 114, Aug. 25, 1938, ADBR D 460, paq. 7 (48). For an English translation of circular no. 114, see JDC report, "Material on the Position of Refugees in France," n.d., file of Bernhard Kahn, in JDC no. 617. Kahn referred to this circular as "Instructions of the Minister of the Interior virtually canceling the benefits of section 11, Decree-law of May 2, 1938, providing the replacement of imprisonment by obligatory residency in an assigned locality for those foreigners who are unable to leave French territory."

38. Berthoin, Secretary-General, minister of the interior, "Confidential Circular," Nov. 9, 1938, ADBR D 460 paq. 7 (48) (also in AN 72 AJ 590).

39. For examples of pro-refugee groups calling for the creation of camps, see Cahen-Molina, pp. 6, 13–15; "Les Réfugiés autrichiens en France," *Fraternité*,

no. 30, Dec. 1938, in AIU, ms. 650, boîte 14 (48); Franz Gravereau, "Les Emigrés autrichiens cherchent des rémèdes à une situation devenue sans issue," *Le Petit Parisien*, Mar. 5, 1939, p. 7; "Les Problèmes des réfugiés," *UI*, Dec. 2, 1938, p. 169; Gourevitch, pp. 17, 19, 85–93; *Bulletin de l'ATJ*, Nov. 25, 1938, p. 2, clipped in AIU, ms. 650, boîte 11 (41); Union for the Protection of the Human Person, Paris, to the Oecumencial Council of Christian Churches, Jan. 24, 1939, in Myron Taylor Papers, box 9, FDR Library; "Déclarations," *RJG*, no. 69 (June 1939): 414.

40. Prefect, Haut-Rhin, to the minister of the interior, Sûreté Nationale, Aug. 2, 1938, ADBR AL 98 397 B.

41. Reports of Prefect, Haut-Rhin, to the minister of the interior, Aug. 1938, ADBR AL 98 397 B (Réfugiés politiques).

42. C. Moitessier, ministry of the interior, Sûreté Nationale, to the prefect of police, Mar. 25, 1938; prefect of the police, to the minister of the interior, Mar. 31, 1938, both in APP BA 269[P] 163.300-0.

43. C. Moitessier, minister of the interior, Sûreté Nationale, to the prefect of police, Mar. 25, 1938, APP BA 269[P] 163.300-0. The bill introduced in the Chamber was sponsored by Victor Constant, Louis Foures, et Lionel Nastorg. "La Réglementation de l'immigration étrangère dans le département de la Seine," *Le Matin*, Apr. 1, 1938.

44. Police report, "Information: relative aux réfugiés autrichiens et à l'activité des comités d'assistance," Apr. 19, 1938, APP BA 269[P] 163-300-0.

45. Minister of the interior, Sûreté Nationale, Renseignements généraux, to the Prefect of Police, no. 2.374, Apr. 15, 1938, APP BA 269[P] 163.300-0.

46. Minister of the interior, Circular no. 354, Apr. 30, 1938, AN F[7] 14662 (also cited in Thalmann, "L'Emigration allemande," pp. 59–62).

47. Foreign Ministry (SDN), report no. 22, "Problème des réfugiés autrichiens, Conférence d'Evian," June 4, 1938, MAE I M 1815, pp. 108–13. This figure probably refers to the total number of Austrians who had fled to Germany by that summer.

48. Prefect, Gironde, to the Prefect, Bas-Rhin, June 21, 1938, ADBR D 391/19 (dos. 182).

49. HICEM report, "Note sur l'état actuel de l'émigration d'Allemagne et d'Autriche," sent from Oungre to George Rublee, Sept. 7, 1938, p. 3, AN AJ[43] 14 (13/56); 19th Ordinary Session of the League of Nations Assembly, 6th Committee, Sub-Committee, International Assistance to Refugees, Refugees from Germany, Note by the Secretary of the Sub-Committee Geneva, Sept. 17, 1938, A.VI./SCI/l. 1938, (Confidential), JDC no. 253; Foreign Ministry (Europe), to the minister of the interior, Direction de la Sûreté Nationale, June 13, 1938, MAE SDN I M 1815, pp. 135–35 bis.

50. Foreign Ministry (Europe), to minister of the interior, Sûreté Nationale, June 13, 1938, MAE SDN I M 1815, pp. 135–35 bis.

51. Prefect, Bas-Rhin, to MM. les Commissaires spéciaux de frontière, Bas-Rhin, no. 2618, July 28, 1938, ADBR D 460, paq. 5(36). On the *refoulement* of refugees to Germany beginning in May, see Commissaire spécial, Thionville, to the subprefect, Thionville, no. 5242, May 30, 1938, ADBR AL 98 392 (passports); controller general, Sûreté Nationale, to the director of the Sûreté Nationale, no. 8618, June 1, 1938,

ADBR, AL 98 392 (passports); "Die Flüchtlingstragödie an der deutsch-französischen Grenze," *PT*, no. 698 (May 29–30, 1938): 2; *L'Oeuvre*, May 25, 1938; Ben Elissar, p. 245; M. Milhaud, "La Question des réfugiés politiques," *CDH*, Aug. 15, 1938, pp. 510–16.

52. "M. Albert Sarraut réorganise et renforce les services des étrangers et la surveillance aux frontières," *La Dépêche de Toulouse*, Aug. 13, 1938, pp. 1–2; "M. Albert Sarraut annonce la création d'une puissante organisation policière contre les étrangers indésirables," *L'Epoque*, Aug. 13, 1938, pp. 1, 6; "Contrôle des étrangers et surveillance frontalière sont renforcés," *L'Ordre*, Aug. 13, 1938, p. 4. The Parliament had voted in favor of special credits to finance this police force in June. See *JO, Documents Parlementaires, Chambre des Députés*, annexes no. 4267, June 16, 1938, p. 930.

53. "La Suisse et la France ferment leurs frontières aux juifs autrichiens," *Le Progrès de Lyon*, Aug. 20, 1938; Prefect, Haut-Rhin, to minister of the interior, Sûreté Nationale, 6ème Bureau, Sept. 5, 1938, ADBR AL 98 397 B; HICEM report, "Note sur l'état actuel de l'émigration d'Allemagne et d'Autriche," sent from Oungre to George Rublee on Sept. 7, 1938, p. 3, AN AJ^{43} 14 (13/56).

54. HICEM Report, "Note sur l'état actuel de l'émigration d'Allemagne et d'Autriche," sent from Oungre to George Rublee on Sept. 7, 1938, p. 3, AN AJ^{43} 14 (13/56).

55. See Pfoser-Schewig.

56. Police report, "Information relative à l'émigration autrichienne en France," Apr. 13, 1938, APP BA 269^{P} 163.300-C.

57. French consul, Bratislava, to the foreign minister, May 10, 1938, MAE SDN I M 1814, pp. 144–45.

58. CDV, Bulletin no. 56, Feb. 3, 1938, p. 2, in AIU, ms. 650, boîte 2; "Le Nombre des réfugiés d'Allemagne," [1938], AIU, ms. 650, boîte 11 (41).

59. Léon Noël, to the Foreign Ministry (Unions), no. 56, June 8, 1938, MAE SDN I M 1806, pp. 239–42.

60. Moitessier, minister of the interior, Sûreté Nationale, circular no. 355, May 3, 1938, APP DA 783. Janine Ponty estimates that there were as many as 50,000–55,000 illegal Polish Jews in France in 1935 and about 80,000–90,000 in 1939. Ponty, p. 319. These figures are significantly higher than the JDC estimate of 42,000, however. See Chapter 10, n. 17.

61. Léon Noël to the Foreign Ministry (Unions), no. 56, June 8, 1938, MAE SDN I M 1806, pp. 239–42.

62. Foreign Ministry (SDN), "Note pour M. Massigli," Jan. 21, 1938, MAE SDN I E 478, pp. 27–29.

63. On Roosevelt's willingness to raise the East European Jewish refugee question at Evian, see "Les Réfugiés politiques: L'utile monnaie d'échange!" *Journal des nations*, July 11, 1938, clipped in BDIC, Dos. Duchêne, GFΔ Rés. 86; Kennedy, U.S. Ambassador, London, "Confidential Telegram to Myron Taylor," Jan. 14, 1939, National Archives, Washington, D.C., 840.48 Refugees/1290 B; Nicault, "L'Abandon," p. 107.

On Roosevelt's motives for convening the Evian Conference, see Wyman, *Paper*

Walls, pp. 43–51; Feingold, pp. 22–24. For the British position, see Sherman, pp. 112–36. On the Evian Conference in general, see Adler-Rudel; Ben Elissar, pp. 240–42; Marrus, *Unwanted*, pp. 170–72.

64. Police report, "Information: Résultats des travaux de la délégation des réfugiés autrichiens admise au sein de la Société des Nations," May 20, 1938, APP BA 269ᴾ 163-300-0; Foreign Ministry report, "Programme de la réunion du Comité Intergouvernemental d'Evian," June 24, 1938, MAE SDN I M 1815, pp. 211–18; Foreign Ministry, to the Ministry of the Interior, Sûreté Nationale, June 16, 1938, MAE SDN I M 1814, pp. 158–59.

65. Marrus, *Unwanted*, p. 170; Ben Elissar, p. 243.

66. Nicault, "L'Abandon," p. 102.

67. Foreign Ministry, "Note a/s réfugiés autrichiens. Réunion du Comité d'Evian," June 13, 1938, MAE SDN I M 1815, pp. 156–61; Foreign Ministry, "Programme de la réunion du Comité Intergouvernemental d'Evian," June 24, 1938, MAE SDN I M 1815, pp. 211–18; Foreign Ministry (Europe), "Note pour la sous-direction de la Société des Nations," (Très urgent), June 24, 1938, MAE SDN I M 1815, p. 210.

68. Minister of labor to the Foreign Ministry (Europe), June 30, 1938, MAE SDN I M 1815, pp. 282–85.

69. Foreign Ministry (Europe), to the Ministry of Colonies (Direction politique), June 17, 1938, MAE SDN I M 1815, pp. 153–54.

70. Minister of colonies, to the Foreign Ministry (Europe), June 21, 1938, MAE SDN I M 1815, pp. 220–21.

71. Minister of the interior (Direction du contrôle de la comptabilité des affaires algériennes), 4ème bureau, to the Foreign Ministry (Europe), July 2, 1938, MAE SDN I M 1816, pp. 25–26.

72. Charvériat, Foreign Ministry (Europe), to the Foreign Ministry, collective letter to the embassies and legations [stamped July 31, 1938], MAE SDN I M 1817, pp. 173–80.

73. Berthoin, Chef de Cabinet, minister of the interior, to the Foreign Ministry, July 1, 1938, MAE SDN I M 1815, pp. 286–91. All quotes in the paragraph below are from this document unless otherwise indicated.

74. Foreign Ministry, "Note a/s réfugiés autrichiens. Réunion du Comité d'Evian," June 13, 1938, MAE SDN I M 1815, pp. 156–61. A Foreign Ministry spokesman suggested in this report that a special "Sifting Commission" be established on German soil to sift out the undesirables prior to their departure to make sure only "desirables" would be allowed into France. For other statements at these meetings urging that France serve solely as a transit country, see Foreign Ministry (Europe), to the minister of colonies (Direction Politique), June 17, 1938, MAE SDN I M 1815, pp. 153–54; Foreign Ministry, "Note a/s réfugiés autrichiens. Réunion du Comité d'Evian," June 13, 1938, MAE SDN I M 1815, pp. 156–61; Charvériat, Foreign Ministry (Europe), to Foreign Ministry, collective letter to the embassies and legations [stamped July 31, 1938], MAE SDN I M 1817, pp. 173–180.

75. See also foreign minister, "Note: a/s réfugiés autrichiens. Réunion du Comité d'Evian," June 13, 1938, MAE SDN I M 1815, pp. 156–61. On original reser-

vations regarding the extension of these benefits to Austrian refugees, see Foreign Ministry (SDN), "Note pour la sous-direction des Union Internationales," May 30, 1938, MAE SDN I M 1815, pp. 82–84; Foreign Ministry (SDN), report no. 22, "Problème des réfugiés autrichiens, Conférence d'Evian," June 4, 1938, MAE I M 1815, pp. 108–13 (also in MAE SDN I M 1814, pp. 149–54).

76. On the request for these statistics, see Foreign Ministry, "Note a/s réfugiés autrichiens. Réunion du Comité d'Evian," June 13, 1938, MAE SDN I M 1815, pp. 156–61; Foreign Ministry (Europe), to Ministry of Public Health, Cabinet, June 18, 1938, MAE SDN I M 1815, pp. 179–80; Foreign Ministry (Europe), to minister of the interior, Sûreté Nationale, June 18, 1938, MAE SDN I M 1815, pp. 181–82; Ministry of Labor, to the Foreign Ministry (Europe), June 30, 1938, MAE SDN I M 1815, pp. 282–85.

77. For Bérenger's speech at Evian, see "Verbatim Record of the Plenary Meetings of the Committee: Resolutions and Reports, July 1938, Proceedings of the Intergovernmental Committee, Evian, July 6th–15th, 1938," AN AJ^{43} 5 (20G/329/80840); "Proceedings of the Intergovernmental Committee, Evian, July 6–15, 1938, Verbatim Record [in English]," Myron Taylor Papers, box 2, FDR Library; "Discours de M. Henry Bérenger," [July 11, 1938], MAE SDN I M 1816, pp. 98–100; "La Conférence d'Evian pour les réfugiés politiques," *Le Temps*, July 8, 1938, p. 2; Havas, "Evian, La Conférence d'Evian," July 6, 1938, no. 99 (94), clipped in MAE I M 1816, pp. 21–22; "La Conférence d'Evian sur les réfugiés politiques," *L'Oeuvre*, July 7, 1938; Adler-Rudel, pp. 246–47; Nicault, "L'Abandon," pp. 107–8; Maga, "Closing," pp. 436–38.

78. Wyman, *Paper Walls*, pp. 43–51; Bauer, *My Brother's Keeper*, pp. 230–31; Marrus, *Unwanted*, pp. 170–72.

79. Police report, "Information: Résultats des travaux de la délégation des réfugiés autrichiens admise au sein de la Société des Nations," May 20, 1938, APP BA 269^P 163-300-0; "Dr. Bernhard Kahn's Conversation with the London-Evian Committee," Sept. 1938, JDC Memo, JDC no. 255; Foreign Ministry (Contrôle des étrangers), "Note pour la sous-direction de la Société des Nations," Dec. 24, 1938, MAE SDN I M 1813, p. 39.

80. On the IGCR, see Ben Elissar, pp. 252–66; Marrus, *Unwanted*, pp. 171, 216–18; Wyman, *Paper Walls*, pp. 51–63; Tartakower and Grossmann, pp. 415–20; Sjöberg.

81. Foreign Ministry, "Note de la sous-direction des Affaires Administratives et des Unions Internationales: Le comité d'Evian et la question des réfugiés israélites allemands," Nov. 21, 1938, *DDF*, 2ème séries, tome XIII, doc. no. 348, pp. 680–88 (also in MAE SDN I M 1818, pp. 77–98).

82. On Roosevelt's willingness to consider the East European Jewish Question, see Roosevelt's message to Myron Taylor, sent by telegram from Kennedy, U.S. Ambassador in London, to Taylor, Jan. 14, 1939, National Archives, Washington, D.C., 840.48 Refugees/1290B, Confidential. On Romanian, U.S., and Jewish pressure to include the East European Jewish refugee question at Evian, see also [Bressy], Foreign Ministry (SDN), to the Foreign Ministry (Direction des Affaires Politiques et Commerciales), "Note pour la direction politique a/s l'émigration des

juifs roumains et le Comité Intergouvernemental de Londres," July 25, 1938, MAE SDN I E 523, pp. 54–58; vice-president, Alliance Israélite Universelle, to the Foreign Ministry, Jan. 2, 1938, MAE SDN I E 522, pp. 33–36; Foreign Ministry (SDN), to Corbin, French ambassador to Great Britain, [early Jan. 1938], MAE SDN I E 522, pp. 39–45; "Les Réfugiés politiques: l'utile monnaie d'échange!" *Journal des nations*, July 11, 1938, clipped in BDIC, Dos. Duchêne, GFΔ Rés. 86; Bauer, *My Brother's Keeper*, p. 235; Marrus, *Unwanted*, pp. 173–74.

83. Foreign Ministry, Report, "Programme de la réunion du Comité Inter-gouvernemental d'Evian," June 24, 1938, MAE SDN I M 1815, pp. 211–18; Foreign Ministry, "Note pour le Ministre," June 29, 1938, MAE, SDN I M 1815, pp. 253–58; "Les Réfugiés politiques: l'utile monnaie d'échange!" *Journal des nations*, July 11, 1938, clipped in BDIC, Dos. Duchêne, GFΔ Rés. 86; Foreign Ministry, "Note de la sous-direction des Affaires Administratives et des Unions Internationales: Le comité d'Evian et la question des réfugiés israélites allemands," Nov. 21, 1938, *DDF*, 2ème series, tome XIII, doc. no. 348, pp. 680–88; Nicault, "L'Abandon," pp. 108–9.

Bauer claims that Great Britain and France were not eager to create a new committee since their influence in League of Nations was paramount (*My Brother's Keeper*, p. 234). In reality, however, there were more specific reasons for their opposition. Both Britain and France believed that a primary task of the high commissioner was to remove refugees from countries of asylum as well as from Germany, whereas the IGCR's mission was solely to get refugees out of Germany. This exclusive focus on Germany, they feared, would only bring more refugees to Western Europe without alleviating conditions in the countries of asylum. See Rublee, telegram, transmitted from Johnson, the U.S. chargé in the U.K., to the U.S. State Dept., Aug. 25, 1938, *FRUS* 1, 1938, pp. 772–73.

84. Foreign Ministry, "Note pour le Ministre," June 29, 1938, MAE SDN I M 1815, pp. 253–58. See also Nicault, "L'Abandon," p. 109.

85. "Au Comité Intergouvernemental des réfugiés," *Le Temps*, Aug. 4, 1938, p. 5; "Intergovernmental Committee to Continue and Develop the work of the Evian Meeting, London 1938," Myron Taylor Papers, box 3, folder "Proceedings of the Intergovernmental Committee, Evian, July 6–15, 1938, Verbatim Record of the Plenary Meetings of the Committee, Resolutions and Reports," Aug. 3, 1938, pp. 3–4, FDR Library. See also "Reich Aid Sought on Refugee Issue," *NYT*, Aug. 4, 1933, clipped in JDC no. 255; "Va-t-on discuter avec l'Allemagne de l'émigration juive," *L'Ordre*, Aug. 4, 1933, p. 3.

Chapter Nine

1. Koestler, *Invisible Writing*, p. 189. See also Mann, pp. 266, 270.

2. Marrus, *Unwanted*, pp. 156–58; Ben Elissar, pp. 270–79; Adler-Rudel, pp. 250–51.

3. François-Poncet, to Foreign Ministry (Europe), Oct. 8, 1938, no. 3769, MAE Z 707, p. 3; Sûreté Nationale, Commissaire spécial, Forbach, to the subprefect of Forbach, no. 8218/38, Oct. 28, 1938, ADBR AL 98 392A.

4. Jean Chauvel, French General Consul, Vienna, to the Foreign Ministry (Europe), no. 255, Oct. 12, 1938, MAE SDN I E 450, pp. 122–26.

5. Gourevitch, p. 14. According to a contemporary estimate of the World Jewish Congress, the number of potential Jewish refugees from Czechoslovakia was as follows: 5,000 former Austrian and German refugees and 23,000 Jews from the annexed Sudeten territories. "Note" on the meeting between Stephane Barber, delegate of the Czech Committee of the World Jewish Congress and Georges Coulon, French representative to the IGCR, Oct. 11, 1938, AN AJ[43] 43 (86/90). See also Foreign Ministry (Europe), "Situation des Juifs des régions sudètes: droit d'option—Exportation de capitaux," Oct. 10, 1938, MAE Z 707, pp. 5–6. According to Yehuda Bauer, 15,000 of a total of 180,000–200,000 Sudeten refugees were Jews. *My Brother's Keeper*, p. 261. See also Marrus, *Unwanted*, pp. 174–75.

6. On the Italian antisemitic legislation, see Bauer, *My Brother's Keeper*, pp. 243, 269; Susan Zuccotti, *The Italians and the Holocaust: Persecution, Rescue, Survival* (New York, 1987), pp. 36–37; Meir Michaelis, "On the Jewish Question in Fascist Italy," *Yad Vashem Studies*, 4 (1960): 7–41; Meir Michaelis, *Mussolini and the Jews: German-Italian Relations and the Jewish Question in Italy, 1922–1945* (Oxford, 1978); Raul Hilberg, *The Destruction of the European Jews* (New York, 1973), pp. 423–24; Dawidowicz, pp. 500–501.

7. Adrien Thierry, French Minister, Romania, to the Foreign Ministry (Europe), no. 46, Dec. 31, 1938, MAE SDN I M 1818, pp. 111–12.

8. On the Polish passport law, see Chapter 8, n. 9, as well as Paul Lenglois, "La Chasse à l'homme sans défense," *La Justice*, May 31, 1939, clipped in AIU, ms. 650, boîte 14 (48); Ben Elissar, pp. 301–21; Schleunes, pp. 236–39; Sherman, pp. 164–65.

9. On attacks against Jews as warmongers at time of Munich, see Schor, *L'Antisémitisme en France*, pp. 166–67; "Faut-il se taire parce que les persécutés ne sont que des immigrés," *TJ*, Oct. 21, 1938, pp. 637–38; Groupement d'Etude et d'Information: Race et Racisme, 47, Service de Documentation, report, [after Nov. 1938], clipped in AIU, ms. 650, boîte 15 (50); [LICA], "Un Mutilé de guerre israélite est sauvagement attaqué à Lille par 4 fascistes," *L'Humanité*, Sept. 30, 1938, p. 2; "La Campagne antisémite en Allemagne et ses répercussions en France," mimeog. report, [after Kristallnacht], BDIC Dos. Duchêne, GΔ Rés. 82/1. A portion of this report was published as "La Campagne antisémite en France," *RJG*, no. 64 (Jan. 1939): 188–91.

10. Groupement d'Etude et d'Information: Race et Racisme, 47, Service de Documentation, report, [after Nov. 1938], clipped in AIU, ms. 650, boîte 15 (50).

11. Police report, Apr. 20, 1939, APP BA 1812, 79.501-882-C; "Auslander sollen dienen," *PT*, Mar. 11, 1939, p. 3; "Les Etrangers et nous: Réponse à Pierre Dominique," *DdV*, Oct. 29, 1938, clipped in AIU, ms. 650, boîte 12; J. Biélenky [*sic*], "L'Immigration juive en France," *La Juste parole*, no. 62 (Sept. 15, 1939): 10–14.

12. [LICA], "La Campagne antisémite en Allemagne et ses répercussions en France," mimeog. report, [after Kristallnacht], BDIC Dos. Duchêne, G Rés. 82/1.

13. G. de la Fouchardière, "'Vive la Guerre!': Est-il aujourd'hui un cri séditieux?" *L'Oeuvre*, Oct. 4, 1938, clipped in AIU, ms. 650, boîte 15 (51). On the charge of Jew-

ish warmongering, see also Lazareff, pp. 183–85, 200, 202–4; Weber, *Hollow Years*, pp. 106–109; Norman Ingram, pp. 189–91, 211, 233; Irvine, "Politics," pp. 18–19, 22–23.

14. François-Poncet, to the Foreign Ministry, no. 3810, Oct. 11, 1938, MAE Z 707, p. 7. On Nazi efforts to deny the assertion that these Jews could not return, see Ben Elissar, p. 279.

15. Chauvel, to the Foreign Ministry (Europe), no. 1171, Oct. 8, 1938, MAE Z 707, p. 4; Chauvel, to the Foreign Ministry, no. 255, Oct. 12, 1938, MAE SDN I E 450, pp. 122–26.

16. "L'Assistance à la persécution," *La Lumière*, Oct. 14, 1938, p. 4. On the virtual impossibility of obtaining a visa from the French consulate in Vienna beginning in the fall of 1938, see also René Rousseau, "Une Politique de l'immigration: L'exemple instructif des réfugiés autrichiens," *L'Epoque*, Feb. 10, 1939, p. 4. On the Swiss reaction to the new passport regulations, see Ben Elissar, pp. 278–79; Manès Sperber, *Until My Eyes Are Closed with Shards*, translated by Harry Zohn (New York, 1994), pp. 136–37.

17. Reports of prefect, Haut-Rhin, to the minister of the interior, Aug. 1938, ADBR AL 98 397 B (Réfugiés politiques). On the protectionist campaign in Alsace and Lorraine, see Chapter 8, n. 25.

18. Prefect, Haut-Rhin, to the minister of the interior, Sûreté Nationale, 6ème bureau, Oct. 18, 1938. See also prefect, Haut-Rhin, to the minister of the interior, Sûreté Nationale, 6th bureau, Sept. 20, 1938; Prefect, Haut-Rhin, to minister of the interior, Sûreté Nationale, 6th bureau, Oct. 10, 1938, all in ADBR AL 98 397 B (Réfugiés Politiques).

19. The French provided £4,000,000 and the British provided £10,000,000. Vago, pp. 102–3, and esp. British Foreign Office Minutes by Sir Orme G. Sargent, Jan. 5, 1939, PRO C 95/3/12, document no. 138, p. 377, and Meeting Between Sir Frederick Leith-Ross (Treasury) and Dr. Pospisil, PRO C 545/3/12, document no. 141, in Vago, p. 380; Simpson, *Refugees: A Review*, p. 40. Immediately after the Munich Agreement, the Czech government had requested a £30,000 loan. Sherman, pp. 145–46.

20. Foreign Ministry, to the French Consul, United States, teleg. no. 734, Oct. 19, 1938, MAE Z *156, p. 1.

21. French minister in Prague, to the Foreign Ministry, Oct. 18, 1938, MAE SDN I M 1814, pp. 247–48; "Note" on the meeting between Stephane Barber, delegate of the Czech Committee of the World Jewish Congress, and Georges Coulon, French representative to the IGCR, Oct. 11, 1938, AN AJ[43] 43 (86/90); Bureau International pour le Respect du Droit d'Asile et l'Aide aux Réfugiés Politiques, "Conférence pour l'aide aux réfugiés en Tchécoslovaquie," Oct. 22, 1938, stenog. of minutes, in AIU, ms. 650, boîte 11 (dos. Réfugiés italiens) (also in AN AJ[43] 13 [65/66]).

22. On the spread of antisemitism in Czechoslovakia after the Munich crisis, see French minister in Prague, to the Foreign Ministry, Oct. 18, 1938, MAE SDN I M 1814, pp. 247–48; "Note" on the meeting between Stephane Barber, delegate of the Czech Committee of the World Jewish Congress, and Georges Coulon, French representative to the IGCR, Oct. 11, 1938, AN AJ[43] 43 (86/90); Victor de Lacroix,

French minister in Prague, to the Foreign Ministry, no. 276, Oct. 26, 1938, MAE SDN I M 1814, pp. 256–60; Dr. Klumpar, Czech Ministry of Health and Social Administration, Prague, to Herbert Emerson, Feb. 20, 1939, MAE SDN I M 1914, pp. 359–60; Sherman, pp. 139, 153; Mendelsohn, pp. 166–67; Ben Elissar, pp. 285–86, 291–92; Vago, p. 101.

23. "Laissera-t-on livrer au Reich des réfugiés allemands en Tchécoslovaquie?" *L'Ordre*, Jan. 11, 1939, p. 1; "Le Sort tragique des réfugiés politiques en Tchécoslovaquie," *L'Aube*, Jan. 11, 1939, p. 3. On the attitude of the new Slovak government, see Mendelsohn, pp. 164–67; Vago, pp. 89–97, 109–13.

24. Bureau International pour le Respect du Droit d'Asile et l'Aide aux Réfugiés Politiques, "Conférence pour l'aide aux réfugiés en Tchécoslovaquie," Oct. 22, 1938, stenog. of minutes, AIU, ms. 650, boîte 11 (dos. Réfugiés italiens) (also in AN AJ[43] 13 [65/66]); "Conference on the German Jewish Situation, the Situation in the Refugee Countries and Emigration Possibilities, Held Dec. 14–15, 1938," JDC no. 363; Sherman, p. 116.

25. "Conference on the German Jewish Situation, the Situation in the Refugee Countries and Emigration Possibilities, Held Dec. 14–15, 1938," JDC no. 363. According to Emile Buré, only twenty visas had actually been delivered as of early January. See "Laissera-t-on livrer au Reich des réfugiés allemands en Tchécoslovaquie?" *L'Ordre*, Jan. 11, 1939, p. 1. See also "5000 réfugiés allemands en Tchécoslovaquie sont menacés d'être livrés à Hitler," *L'Humanité*, Dec. 28, 1938, clipped in AIU, ms. 650, boîte 11 (42).

26. R. M. Makins, British Foreign Office, "Draft Memo to M. Strang re: German and Czech refugees for use if these subjects are raised in conversations with France," Nov. 23, 1938, PRO FO 371/22537.W15402. The Czech Consul in France similarly reported, "En principe, il n'y a pas d'émigration massive qui se dirige vers la France. La masse des réfugiés a été dirigées sur l'Angleterre: 3275 Sudètes." "Report of Czech Consul, M. Trenka," [Oct.–Nov. 1938], from the Czech embassy in Paris, AIU, ms. 650, boîte 11 (42). For similar criticisms, see Léon Jouhaux, "Lettre ouverte au Ministre des Affaires Etrangères," *Le Peuple*, Jan. 5, 1939, p. 1.

On British policy toward Czech refugees after Munich, see Sherman, pp. 137–65. On Czechoslovakia in general after Munich, see Ben Elissar, pp. 291–301; Simpson, *Refugee Problem*, pp. 395–96; Vago, pp. 89–113.

27. "Note" on the meeting between Stephane Barber, delegate of the Czech Committee of the World Jewish Congress, with Georges Coulon, French representative to the IGCR, Oct. 11, 1938, AN AJ[43] 43 (86/90); Tartakower and Grossmann, p. 38; P. Pares, British consul, Bratislava, "Memorandum on Political Situation in Slovakia," document no. 145, in Vago, pp. 385–86.

28. "Réunion interministérielle du 25 octobre tenue à l'Hôtel Matignon, sous la présidence de M. Chautemps, Vice-Président du Conseil," MAE SDN I M 1814, pp. 239–43; Lamarle, Foreign Ministry, to the Foreign Ministry (SDN), Oct. 27, 1938, p. 245. On the petition of the Bureau International pour le Droit d'Asile to the Radical Party Congress in Lille, see "L'Aide aux réfugiés de Tchécoslovaquie," newspaper clipping, [Dec.] 28, 1938, clipped in AIU, ms. 650, boîte 11 (42); Bureau International pour le Respect du Droit d'Asile et l'Aide aux Réfugiés Politiques,

"Conférence pour l'aide aux réfugiés en Tchécoslovaquie," stenog. of minutes, Oct. 22, 1938, AIU, ms. 650, boîte 11 (dos. Réfugiés italiens) (also in AN AJ^{43} 13 [65/66]); Paul Perrin, "Pour l'aide aux réfugiés sudètes," *Le Peuple*, Oct. 17, 1938, p. 3. On the petition of the SFIO to Chautemps, see "Le Sort des prisonniers tchécoslovaques en Allemagne," *Le Populaire*, Oct. 21, 1938, clipped in AIU, ms. 650, boîte 12 (43). On the Communist Party petition, see "5000 réfugiés allemands en Tchécoslovaquie sont menacés d'être livrés à Hitler," *L'Humanité*, Dec. 28, 1938, clipped in AIU, ms. 650, boîte 11 (42), p. 62.

29. "Réunion interministérielle du 25 octobre tenue à l'Hôtel Matignon, sous la présidence de M. Chautemps, vice-Président du Conseil," MAE SDN I M 1814, pp. 239–43. On British efforts to distinguish between Jewish and non-Jewish refugees from Czechoslovakia, see Ben Elissar, pp. 287–88.

30. Report of M. Trenka, Czech Consul, Paris, [Oct. or Nov. 1938], AIU, ms. 650, boîte 11(42); Report of N. Aronivici for the JDC, Nov. 1938, p. 32, JDC no. 163.

31. Police report, "Information: relative à l'attitude de certains éléments étrangers," Sept. 15, 1938, APP BA 269^P 163-300-0.

32. [LICA], "La Campagne antisémite en Allemagne et ses répercussions en France," [after Kristallnacht], BDIC Dos. Duchêne, GΔ Rés. 82/1 (mimeog. report); "La Campagne antisémite en France," *RJG*, no. 64 (Jan., 1939): 188–91.

33. Berthoin, Secretary-General, Ministry of the Interior, Circular no. 376, Oct. 12, 1938, AN F^7 14662. According to various refugee organizations, this decree affected no less than nine-tenths of all Austrian refugees in France and resulted in a large number of suicides. Gourevitch, p. 23; "Les Réfugiés autrichiens en France," *Fraternité*, Dec. 1938, no. 30, AIU, ms. 650, boîte 14 (48).

34. "Brief Review of the Situation of Jewry in Eastern Europe and Central Europe (including Germany, Austria, and Italy), and JDC Activities in Connection Therewith," transcript of speech by Bernhard Kahn, Sept. 18, 1938, p. 8, JDC no. 163; "Conference on the German Jewish Situation, the Situation in the Refugee Countries and Emigration Possibilities, Held Dec. 14–15, 1938," JDC no. 363; "France Moves Refugees," *NYT*, Nov. 25, 1938, p. 12; H. S., "Les Réfugiés autrichiens en France," *Fraternité*, May 20, 1939, p. 4, clipped in AIU, ms. 650 boîte 11 (42); Berthoin, minister of the interior, circular no. 379, Nov. 25, 1938, AN F^7 14662; JDC, Euroexco Report, Jan. 1939, "Report on the Situation of German and Austrian Refugees in France in Jan. 1939," p. 6, JDC no. 189; "La Région parisienne désormais interdite aux nouveaux immigrants étrangers," *Le Matin*, Oct. 20, 1938, p. 1; "Le Contrôle des étrangers est renforcé aux frontières," *L'Aube*, Oct. 28, 1938, p. 1.

35. "Le Grand Paris en a assez de servir de dépotoir à la pègre cosmopolite," *AF*, Oct. 15, 1938, clipped in AN 72 AJ 601; Thalmann, "L'Emigration allemande," p. 63.

36. "France Moves Refugees," *NYT*, Nov. 25, 1938, p. 12.

37. Intercomité des Oeuvres Françaises des Réfugiés," Minutes, Meeting of Nov. 23, 1938, AN 72 AJ 590.

38. H. S., "Les Réfugies autrichiens en France," *Fraternité*, May 20, 1939, p. 4, clipped in AIU, ms. 650 boîte 11 (42); "Conference on the German Jewish Situation, the Situation in the Refugee Countries and Emigration Possibilities, Held Dec. 14–

15, 1938," JDC no. 363; "Ceux qu'il faut aider: 700 réfugiés d'Autriche vivent à Chelles," *DdV*, Jan. 14, 1939; Jacques Grosbois, "Quittant l'enfer hitlérien ils sont au purgatoire," *DdV*, Feb. 25, 1939, pp. 1, 3.

39. For the text of the decree law of Nov. 12, 1938, see *JO*, *Lois et Décrets*, Nov. 13, 1938, pp. 12920–24; "La Surveillance et le contrôle des étrangers," *Le Matin*, Nov. 13, 1938, p. 6; "Surveillance et contrôle des étrangers," *Le Temps*, Nov. 14, 1938, p. 2; *Le Petit Parisien*, Nov. 13, 1938; Gourevitch, pp. 102–7. See also *NYT*, Nov. 13, 1938, p. 34; Schramm and Vormeier, pp. 236–38; Vormeier, "Législation répressive," pp. 163–64; Thalmann, "L'Emigration allemande," p. 65; Badia "L'Emigration en France," pp. 87–88; Marrus and Paxton, p. 56.

40. On Moïse Lévy's calls for further restrictions on naturalization, see *JO*, *Documents Parlementaires, Sénat*, annexe no. 288, Apr. 13, 1938, p. 169; J.-Ch. Bonnet, p. 232; CDV, bulletin no. 70, July 21, 1938, p. 5, AIU, ms. 650, boîte 2. In Dec., Louis Marin and Fernand Laurent again pressed for a revision of the 1927 naturalization law. See Annexe no. 4422, in *JO, Documents Parlementaires, Chambre de Députés*, Dec. 8, 1938, p. 58; J.-Ch. Bonnet, p. 233. On Robert Schuman's campaign, see "Une Proposition de loi de M. Schuman," *L'Excelsior*, Oct. 30, 1938; CDV, bulletin no. 73, Nov. 3, 1938, pp. 10–11, clipped in AN 72 AJ 601; Marrus and Paxton, p. 50; Marrus, "Vichy before Vichy," p. 18.

41. *Le Temps*, Oct. 28, 1938, p. 6; Georges Gombault, "La Liberté," *CDH*, Nov. 15, 1938, p. 658.

42. Marrus and Paxton, p. 26; "La Persécution nazie," *L'Europe nouvelle*, Nov. 26, 1938, pp. 1283–84. On Kristallnacht and the events leading up to it, see Thalmann and Feinermann; Read and Fisher; Bauer, *My Brother's Keeper*, pp. 252–59; Dawidowicz, pp. 127–42, 506; and Schleunes, pp. 234–54.

43. Chauvel, French Consul, Vienna, to the Foreign Ministry, no. 305, Dec. 7, 1938, MAE Z 709, pp. 186–87.

44. "La Persécution nazie," *L'Europe nouvelle*, Nov. 26, 1938, pp. 1283–84; Coulondre, to the Foreign Minister, Dec. 15, 1938, MAE SDN I E 451, pp. 94–100; Schleunes, pp. 245–54; Dawidowicz, *The War Against the Jews*, pp. 136–42; Bauer, *My Brother's Keeper*, pp. 252–59.

45. Coulondre, to the Foreign Ministry, Dec. 15, 1938, MAE SDN I E 451, pp. 94–100, esp. 99–100.

46. *Le Temps*, Nov. 18, 1938, p. 8; "Tous est mis en oeuvre à Berlin pour éviter que cette affaire ait quelque répercussion sur le plan politique," Nov. 11, 1938, and "Interdictions au Juifs...," Nov. 15, 1938, p. 3, both in *Le Journal*; Schwab, pp. 10–12. Vom Rath's remains were ultimately transferred back to Dusseldorf, Germany, where a state funeral service was held. On Grynszpan's fate, see Schwab; Marrus, "The Strange Story," pp. 69–77; Thalmann and Feinermann, pp. 164–72; Read and Fisher, pp. 254–81.

47. "Tout est mis en oeuvre à Berlin pour éviter que cette affaire ait quelque répercussion sur le plan politique," *Le Journal*, Nov. 11, 1938. See also "Berlin reconnait que la police française a fait son devoir," *Le Journal*, Nov. 8, 1938, clipped in APP BA 269 Provisoire 25-341-H; "Recrudescence des mesures anti-juives en Allemagne," *Le Journal*, Nov. 9, 1938; "On ne songe nullement à imputer la moindre

responsabilité à la France," Nov. 8, 1938, p. 3, "Interdiction aux Juifs," Nov. 15, 1938, p. 3, both in *Le Figaro*; "Les Obsèques de M. Vom Rath," *Le Temps*, Nov. 16, 1938, p. 2; Ogilvie-Forbes, British Ambassador to Germany, to Halifax, Nov. 15, 1938, in *DBFP*, series 3, vol. 3, no. 311, pp. 272–73.

48. Montbas, to the Foreign Ministry, teleg. no. 4110, Nov. 8, 1938, *DDF*, 2ème séries, vol. XII, no. 279, p. 483 (also in MAE Z 707, pp. 19–20). See also Montbas, to the Foreign Ministry, teleg., Nov. 8, 1938, MAE SDN I E 450, pp. 142–44; Montbas, to the Foreign Ministry, teleg. no. 4132, Nov. 11, 1938; teleg. no. 4152, Nov. 12, 1938; teleg. no. 4138, Nov. 13, 1938, all in MAE Z 707, pp. 85–86, 58–59, 48; Montbas, to Bonnet, no. 303, Nov. 15, 1938, p. 552, and no. 300, Nov. 19, 1938, p. 561, both in *DDF*, 2ème séries, vol. XII; "Recrudescence des mesures antijuives en Allemagne," *Le Journal*, Nov. 9, 1938; *Le Petit Parisien*, Nov. 9, 1938; "L'Attentat contre un secrétaire à l'ambassade d'Allemagne," *Le Temps*, Nov. 9, 1938, p. 2; "L'Attentat contre un attaché de l'ambassade d'Allemagne," *Le Populaire*, Nov. 9, 1938, clipped in APP BA 269 Provisoire 163.300-0; "Hamburger Fremdenblatt, Nov. 15," news bulletin, cited in *La Dépêche de Toulouse*, Nov. 16, 1938, p. 1; "Reich and France Sign Treaty Today," *NYT*, Dec. 6, 1938, p. 101; Göbbels, "L'Affaire Grünspan," *Völkischer Beobachter*, Nov. 12, 1938, translated into French in Foreign Ministry, *Bulletin quotidien de la presse étrangère*, no. 6992, Nov. 15, 1938, MAE Z 706, pp. 74–75.

The Italian press, for its own purposes, joined in this condemnation of the émigré community in France, blaming it collectively for vom Rath's assassination. See François-Poncet, to the Foreign Ministry, teleg. no. 1873, Nov. 9, 1938, MAE SDN I E 450, pp. 149–51; *Le Populaire*, Nov. 9, 1938, p. 2; "Rome: Il y a une autre responsabilité: La France," *L'Epoque*, Nov. 9, 1938, clipped in AN 72 AJ 600; "L'Attentat contre vom Rath," *AF*, Nov. 9, 1938, clipped in APP BA 269 Provisoire 25-341-H; "La Mort de M. vom Rath: La Presse italienne demande que le contrôle des étrangers en France soit renforcé," *Le Matin*, Nov. 10, 1938, clipped in AN 72 AJ 600; "De Violentes manifestations antisémitiques ont éclaté en Allemagne," *AF*, Nov. 11, 1938, clipped in AN 72 AJ 600; "Terreur sur l'Allemagne," *L'Ordre*, Nov. 11, 1938, clipped in AN 72 AJ 600.

49. Montbas, to Bonnet, teleg. no. 4162, Nov. 14, 1938; Montbas, to Bonnet, teleg. no. 4179, Nov. 16, 1938, both in MAE Z 707, pp. 110, 193–98.

50. "A New Phase in Germany," *NYT*, Nov. 15, 1938, p. 22.

51. "U.S. Newspapers Assail Nazi Raids," *NYT*, Nov. 13, 1938, p. 41. On U.S. public opinion, see also CDV, bulletin, no. 74, n.d., in Documents of French Jewish History, JTS, box 12, folder 1; "American Press Comment on Nazi Riots," *NYT*, Nov. 12, 1938, p. 4; "Thousands in U.S. Offer to Help Assassin," *NYT*, Nov. 16, 1938, p. 9; "L'Indignation aux Etats-Unis," *Le Temps*, Nov. 14, 1938, p. 4; "L'Action antisémitique en Allemagne," *Le Temps*, Nov. 15, 1938, p. 1; "L'Amérique tout entière s'indigne des persécutions Nazies," *Le Figaro*, Nov. 16, 1938, p. 3. For a further discussion of British, French, and American responses to Kristallnacht, see Thalmann and Feinermann, pp. 146–63.

52. Cited in "British Indignant at Nazi Terror," *NYT*, Nov. 12, 1938, p. 5. The London *Times* similarly declared: "No foreign propagandists bent upon blackening Germany before the world, could outdo the tale of burning and beatings, of black-

guardly assaults upon defenceless innocent people, which disgraced that country." Cited in "Nazis Complicate Chamberlain's Task," *NYT*, Nov. 11, 1938, p. 2. According to the French ambassador in London, a large segment of the British press considered appeasement seriously impaired in the wake of Kristallnacht. See Corbin, to the Foreign Ministry, teleg. no. 2900, Nov. 11, 1938, pp. 50–54; teleg. no. 2934, Nov. 13, pp. 87–90; teleg. 1021, Nov. 16, 1938, pp. 214–20; teleg. no. 2962, Nov. 17, 1938, pp. 225–29, all in MAE Z 707; Corbin, to the Foreign Ministry, teleg. no. 2927, Nov. 12, 1938, MAE SDN I E 450, pp. 178–81; Corbin, to the Foreign Ministry, teleg. no. 3019, Nov. 22, 1938, MAE SDN I E 451, pp. 56–64; Corbin, to the Foreign Ministry, teleg. no. 3025, Nov. 23, 1938, MAE Z 292, pp. 45–46. For an excellent account of British press reactions to Kristallnacht in the context of Chamberlain's appeasement policies, see Sharf, pp. 58–69.

53. Von Dirksen, German ambassador to Great Britain, to Ribbentrop, German Foreign Minister, Nov. 17, 1938, *DGFP*, 1918–45, series D, vol. 4, no. 269, p. 334. George Rublee expressed similar sentiments in a memorandum to the U.S. Secretary of State in which he stated, "For the first time since my arrival in London, I feel that recognition is finding its way in high political quarters that the mistreatment by Germany of a half million oppressed people is a definite obstacle to general appeasement in Europe." Sent via Kennedy, U.S. ambassador to the U.K., to the U.S. secretary of state, Nov. 14, 1938, *FRUS* 1 (1938): 820–22. On the negative impact of German antisemitism on British plans for appeasement, see also Corbin, French ambassador to the United Kingdom, to Bonnet, Nov. 16, 1938, *DDF*, 2ème series, vol. XII, no. 312, p. 557; Corbin, to Bonnet, Dec. 9, 1938, *DDF*, 2ème series, vol. XIII, no. 74, pp. 146–48; "Nazis Complicate Chamberlain's Task," *NYT*, Nov. 11, 1938, p. 2, "Germany Forgets History" (editorial), *NYT*, Nov. 12, 1938, p. 14; "British Faith Hit by Reich Terror," *NYT*, Nov. 13, 1938, p. 4; "Nazis Now Drive to Complete Their Program," *NYT*, Nov. 20, 1938, sec. E, p. 3; "Chamberlain's Policies Again Upset by Nazis," *NYT*, Nov. 20, 1938, sec. E, p. 4; "L'Action anti-juive en Allemagne," *Le Temps*, Nov. 20, 1938, p. 1; "Avant la visite à Paris des ministres anglais," *Le Temps*, Nov. 22, 1938, p. 1; "Un Grand débat aux Communes," *Le Temps*, Nov. 23, 1938; "L'Angleterre proteste à Berlin...," Nov. 13, 1938, p. 3; "La Politique de rapprochement...," Nov. 21, 1938, p. 3, both in *Le Figaro*.

54. Halifax, British foreign minister, to Ogilvie-Forbes, British ambassador in Berlin, Nov. 11, 1938, *DBFP* (London, 1950), series 3, vol. III, no. 302, p. 268; Corbin, to the Foreign Ministry, teleg. no. 2964, Nov. 17, 1938, MAE Z 707, p. 236; "M. Chamberlain condamne les persécutions des Juifs," *Le Journal*, Nov. 15, 1938; "British Indignant at Nazi Terrorism," *NYT*, Nov. 12, 1938, pp. 1, 5; "Les Mesures antisémitiques en Allemagne sont évoquées aux Communes," *Le Matin*, Nov. 15, 1938, p. 3; "L'Angleterre proteste à Berlin contre les attaques de la presse Nazie," *Le Figaro*, Nov. 13, 1938, p. 3; "M. Chamberlain annonce que l'Angleterre a protesté à Berlin," *Le Figaro*, Nov. 15, 1938, p. 3; "Le Reich antisémite," *La Dépêche de Toulouse*, Nov. 22, 1938, p. 2.

55. "Roosevelt Condemns Nazi Outbreak," *NYT*, Nov. 16, 1938, p. 1; "Hitler's Silence a Sign of Nazi Second Thought," *NYT*, Nov. 20, 1938, sec. E, p. 3.

56. Montbas, to Bonnet, Nov. 16, 1938, *DDF*, 2ème séries, vol. XII, no. 313, p. 578;

"Washington Calls Envoy from Berlin," *NYT*, Nov. 15, 1938, p. 1; "Wilson to Depart from Reich Today," *NYT*, Nov. 16, 1938, p. 8; "Les Mesures contre les juifs en Allemagne," *Le Temps*, Nov. 17, 1938, p. 3. In retaliation, Germany also recalled its ambassador from the United States. Diplomatic relations between the two countries were not resumed. "Le Troisième Reich contre les Juifs," *Le Temps*, Nov. 21, 1938, p. 1; Adamthwaite, p. 289.

57. "Large Scale Move by Two Nations to Resettle Jews Held Urgent," *NYT*, Nov. 15, 1938, pp. 1, 6; "Washington Calls Envoy from Berlin," *NYT*, Nov. 15, 1938, p. 1; "The Refugees" (editorial), *NYT*, Nov. 16, 1938, p. 22; "World Searched for Havens," *NYT*, Nov. 20, 1938, sec. E, p. 4; "Excerpts from Commons Debate on Refugees," *NYT*, Nov. 22, 1938, pp. 1, 9; "Refugee Problem Arouses Britain to Action," *NYT*, Nov. 27, 1938, sec. E, p. 3; "Lundi aux Communes exposé de M. Chamberlain sur le problème israélite," *Le Matin*, Nov. 19, 1938, p. 3. Of course, Kristallnacht ultimately brought about neither a radical reversal of Chamberlain's appeasement policy nor any major alterations in American and British refugee policies. Nevertheless, the fact that it ignited even this temporary flourish of doubts regarding appeasement in the Anglo-Saxon world stands in marked contrast to the French response. On British and American reactions to the refugee crisis in the wake of Kristallnacht, see Sherman, pp. 166–222; Feingold, pp. 42–44; Wyman, *Paper Walls*, pp. 72–75.

58. Ferdinand Kuhn Jr., "Refugee Problem Arouses Britain to Action," *NYT*, Nov. 27, 1938, sec. E, p. 3.

59. Montbas, to Bonnet, Nov. 15, 1938, *DDF*, vol. XII, no. 309, pp. 572–73.

60. Tournès, to Bonnet, Nov. 14, 1938, no. 51, MAE Z 707, p. 132.

61. Coulondre, to Bonnet, Dec. 22, 1938, *DDF*, 2ème séries, vol. XIII, no. 203, p. 379.

62. Coulondre, to Bonnet, *DDF*, 2ème séries, vol. XII, no. 346, Nov. 21, 1938, p. 670.

63. Coulondre, to Bonnet, Nov. 19, 1938, *DDF*, 2ème séries, vol. XII, no. 332, p. 644; Adamthwaite, *France*, pp. 286–88. See also Welczeck, German Ambassador in France, to Ribbentrop, Nov. 19, 1938, *DGFP*, series D, vol. 4, no. 355, p. 455. In the end, the Germans rather than the French requested a postponement in the signing of the pact so that the furor over Kristallnacht could die down. The French ultimately agreed, less because of Kristallnacht than because of the massive strike movement that gripped the nation at the end of Nov. In addition to the above, see also Coulondre, to Bonnet, Nov. 19, 1938, *DDF*, 2ème séries, vol. XII, no. 332, p. 644; G. Bonnet, pp. 212–13; Wilson, U.S. chargé d'affaires in Paris, to U.S. secretary of state, teleg., 741.51/312, Nov. 25, 1938, *FRUS*, I, 1938, pp. 101–4; Kennedy, U.S. ambassador in the United Kingdom, to the U.S. secretary of state, 740.00/516, Nov. 22, 1938, *FRUS*, I, 1938, pp. 99–100; "Paris Defers Signing Accord with Berlin," *NYT*, Nov. 22, 1938, p. 6.

64. *Le Populaire*, Nov. 24, 1938, cited in CDV, bulletin no. 75, Dec. 11, 1938, p. 14, in Documents of French Jewish History, JTS, box 12, folder 1. See also Maurice Harmel, "Lord Halifax et M. Neville Chamberlain arrivent à Paris," *Le Peuple*, Nov. 23, 1938, p. 3.

65. Henri de Kérillis, "L'Antisémitisme, ciment des dictatures," Nov. 12, 1938. See also de Kérillis, "Chiffon de papier?" Nov. 24, 1938; "Vide mais dangereuse," Dec. 7, 1938, all in *L'Epoque*.

66. "A la Commission des Affaires Etrangères," *Le Populaire*, Nov. 23, 1938, p. 5. See also "Un Prochain Accord Franco-Allemand?" Nov. 16, 1938, p. 3; Nov. 25, 1938, p. 7, both in *Le Populaire*.

67. "Le Parlement français contre l'antisémitisme," *Samedi*, Dec. 24, 1938, pp. 1, 3; "Paris Receives Hitler Bid for 'Good-Neighbor' Ties," *NYT*, Nov. 23, 1938, p. 10; Le Guet d'Orsay, "Autour de la déclaration franco-hitlérienne," *L'Europe nouvelle*, Nov. 26, 1938, p. 1279.

68. Adamthwaite, pp. 286–88; G. Bonnet, p. 37; Lazareff, p. 207; Le Guet d'Orsay, "Autour de la déclaration franco-hitlérienne," *L'Europe nouvelle*, Nov. 26, 1938, p. 1279; "French Conclude Pact with Reich: Greet Chamberlain," *NYT*, Nov. 24, 1938, p. 1. According to Heinz Pol, relations between Mandel and Bonnet had so deteriorated in the aftermath of Munich that Mandel refused to acknowledge Bonnet, and "when Bonnet's name came up in Mandel's intimate circle, Mandel called him *Herr* Bonnet, lifting his arm in the Hitler salute." Pol, p. 167.

69. On Chamberlain's support, see "Five Hour Discussion," *NYT*, Nov. 25, 1938, p. 1; "L'Angleterre et la France," *La Dépêche de Toulouse*, Dec. 17, 1938, pp. 1–2; "La Déclaration commune Franco-Allemande," *Le Temps*, Nov. 25, 1938, p. 1; *Le Temps*, Nov. 26, 1938, p. 1; *L'Oeuvre*, Nov. 23, 1938, p. 3; Corbin, to Bonnet, Dec. 15, 1938, *DDF*, 2ème séries, vol. XIII, no. 144, pp. 284–85; Wilson, U.S. chargé d'affaires in France, to the U.S. secretary of state, Nov. 25, 1938, *FRUS*, vol. 1, 1938, p. 102; Kennedy, U.S. ambassador in the U.K., to the U.S. secretary of state, Nov. 22, 1938, *FRUS*, vol. 1, 1938, pp. 99–100.

70. Wilson, U.S. chargé d'affaires in France, to U.S. secretary of state, teleg. 740.00/520, Nov. 26, 1938, *FRUS*, vol. 1, 1938, p. 105. On Chamberlain's support for the Franco-German pact, see also *NYT*, Nov. 25, 1938, p. 1; *Le Temps*, Nov. 26, 1938, p. 1.

71. "Britain and France," London *Times*, Nov. 24, 1938, p. 14. On the hostility of British public opinion, see Corbin, to Bonnet, Dec. 15, 1938, *DDF*, 2ème séries, vol. XIII, no. 144, pp. 284–85.

72. Saint-Quentin, to Bonnet, teleg. 1329–34, Nov. 28, 1938, MAE Z 743, pp. 16–20; Sumner Welles, acting secretary of state, to Wilson, U.S. chargé d'affaires in France, 751.62/435, Dec. 5, 1938, *FRUS*, vol. 1, 1938, p. 107; Welczeck, to the German Foreign Ministry, no. 366, Nov. 30, 1938, *DGFP*, series D, vol. 4, pp. 465–66; Adamthwaite, *France*, p. 289. On American hostility, see also Coulondre, to Bonnet, Dec. 3, 1938, *DDF*, 2ème séries, vol. XIV, no. 18, p. 33; CDV, bulletin, no. 75, Dec. 1, 1938, p. 14, in Documents of French Jewish History, JTS, box 12, folder 1; "La Situation politique en France," *Le Temps*, Nov. 27, 1938, p. 6.

73. According to François-Poncet, now serving as French ambassador to Italy, the Italians "s'en sont consolés vite en exprimant l'idée que les Anglais seraient probablement furieux que la France songeât à se rapprocher de l'Allemagne à l'heure où la persécution antisémitique révoltait l'opinion britannique et tendait de nouveau

les rapports anglo-allemands." François-Poncet, to Bonnet, Dec. 7, 1938, *DDF*, 2ème séries, vol. XII, no. 54, p. 101.

74. Phipps, to the British Foreign Office, Nov. 11, 1938, in PRO FO 371/21637 C13793. Phipps subsequently reported that Bonnet, in response to rumors that Mandel, Herriot, and Reynaud favored war, had replied that "M. Mandel, though not M. Reynaud, was bellicose, but he alone in the cabinet could not do much. His feelings were doubtless prompted by his Jewish origins." Cited in Sherwood, *Georges Mandel*, p. 206. According to Pierre Lazareff, Bonnet's wife, upon seeing Raymond Philippe, the Jewish financial backer of the journal *L'Europe nouvelle* had remarked in the spring of 1939: "What's he doing here, that dirty Jew who criticizes my husband because he won't declare war?" Lazareff, p. 214. See also Bernier, p. 290. Finally, Nazi officials claimed that Bonnet was prepared to testify at the trial of Herschel Grynszpan, which was to be held in Germany in 1942, to prove that "the French government was put under such heavy pressure by the Jews that it could not avoid declaring war." Bonnet later denied these allegations, but the evidence presented in Gerald Schwab's recent book suggests the Nazi claims were probably justified. See Schwab, pp. 136, 138–40, 144–46, 155, 162–63, 182–83; Marrus, "Strange Story," p. 76.

Bonnet was certainly not alone in harboring these views. In Sept. 1938, one of his close friends, the industrialist Marcel Boussac, prevailed upon Lucien Lamoureux, the Radical-Socialist deputy from the Allier and a former minister, to return to Paris to help Bonnet against the "war party," which was "inspired by the Jews." Adamthwaite, "France and the Coming of War," p. 245, n. 19. At the same time, Lamoureux warned the Jews against "de terribles et légitimes règlements de comptes" if war were to break out. Cited in CDV, bulletin no. 71, Oct. 6, 1938, p. 7, in Documents of French Jewish History, JTS, box 12, folder 1; Marrus and Paxton, p. 52; and Marrus, "Vichy avant Vichy," p. 89. Joseph Caillaux leveled similar accusations. In late Oct. 1938, Sir Eric Phipps, the British ambassador in Paris, reported that he had been told over the phone by Caillaux

that the policy of the Prime Minister [Chamberlain] had been the only one to follow: it would have been an act of criminal folly to have gone to war "unprepared and for a bad cause...." M. Caillaux remarked that the anti-Jewish feeling that had begun to show itself during M. Blum's "lamentable" terms of office was now increasing because the French public realized that the chief warmongers in the recent crisis were Jews (including the Paris Rothschilds) and Communists. Certain members of the Socialist Party were in fact anxious to substitute some other leader for M. Blum whom they considered to be rather compromising for the party in consequence of the growth of antisemitism.

Eric Phipps, to British Foreign Office, teleg., Oct. 25, 1938, PRO FO 371/21600.C 12965. Finally, Pierre-Etienne Flandin made similar remarks following the assassination of vom Rath. In mid-Nov., he told a Congress of the Alliance Démocratique: "The most important problem of all is that of race.... It is no longer tolerable . . . that foreigners impose upon us their customs or their hatreds for such and such an ideology, itself foreign; that they take over the levers of command of opinion and the state, that they corrupt consciences and terrorize our cities and countryside, that they organize unrest and that they pave the way for war." *Le Matin*, Nov. 15, 1938, cited in Marrus, "Vichy before Vichy," p. 16, and in "Vichy avant Vichy," p. 84.

75. Welczeck, to the German Foreign Ministry, no. 366, Nov. 30, 1938, *DGFP*, series D, vol. 4, pp. 465–66. See also Welczeck, to the German Foreign Ministry, Jan. 1, 1939, *DGFP*, series D, vol. 4, p. 486.

76. *Le Matin*, Nov. 19, 1938, p. 1; *L'Europe nouvelle*, Nov. 26, 1938, p. 1298. Weill repeated these sentiments in Jan. 1939. See "M. Julien Weill," *La Tribune des nations*, Jan. 5, 1939, clipped in AN 72 602.

77. The principal clauses of the Franco-German pact were: (1) "the conviction that peaceful and good neighborly relations between France and Germany" constitute "one of the essential elements" for general peace; (2) recognition of that the existing frontiers between the two countries are fixed and final; (3) a stipulation that both governments were resolved with "due account being taken of their relations with other powers," to keep in contact and to consult on questions affecting them. Adamthwaite, *France*, p. 290.

78. Ibid., pp. 147–48; Corbin, to Bonnet, teleg. no. 3001, Nov. 21, 1938, MAE Z 291 (Great Britain), pp. 28–29. On Bonnet's efforts to muzzle the press, see also Werth, *Twilight*, pp. 299–300, 344.

79. "Protestation unanime" (Letter of Kérillis, deputy of the Seine and General Councilor, to the Director of the LICA), *DdV*, Dec. 17, 1938, p. 1; Thalmann, "L'Emigration allemande," p. 64, n. 61.

80. Palmier, 2: 113–14, n. 4; Markscheffel, p. 74.

81. "Reich and France Sign Treaty Today," *NYT*, Dec. 6, 1938, p. 10. Bonnet was so obsessed with public opinion surrounding the Franco-German pact that he had placed observers in all Parisian cinemas that showed films of the signing of the pact. According to the German ambassador in Paris, Welczeck, "with the insignificant exception of a case where émigrés were concerned, quite exceptional approval had been registered. In his rural constituency he had received ovations the like of which he had never known before." Welczeck, to the German Foreign Ministry, Jan. 1, 1939, no. 375-1580/382132-34, *DGFP*, series D, vol. 4, p. 486.

82. "Une Honte!" *Le Populaire*, Dec. 6, 1938, p. 1. See also "Du dîner de M. Bonnet à celui de l'ambassade du Reich," *Le Populaire*, Dec. 7, 1938. On Dec. 7, 1938, the *NYT* reported: "'Non-Aryans' were conspicuously absent from a brilliant dinner offered tonight by Foreign Minister Georges Bonnet to . . . Ribbentrop." "No Jewish Ministers at Dinner to Germans," *NYT*, Dec. 7, 1938, p. 15.

83. Bonnet, *De Munich à la Guerre*, p. 218, n. 1.

84. Abetz, p. 91. In *Carnets*, Jean Zay stated that even Daladier had opposed Ribbentrop's visit at this time, a charge Bonnet refuted in his memoirs. See Zay, p. 37; G. Bonnet, p. 216. It was, however, widely rumored that Daladier was unhappy with Bonnet's policies. See Werth, *Twilight*, pp. 239–40; Berstein, *Histoire*, pp. 546, 549; Bernier, p. 290. On the so-called Aryan dinner, see Corbin, to the Foreign Ministry, teleg. 3145, Dec. 7, 1938, MAE Z 743, p. 44; "France and Germany Adopt a 'Good Neighbor' Policy," *NYT*, Dec. 7, 1938, p. 1; "No Jewish Ministers at

Dinner to Germans," *NYT*, Dec. 7, 1938, p. 15; "Tour d'Horizon: Ribbentrop à Paris," *L'Aube*, Dec. 8, 1938, p. 2; Pol, pp. 137–38; Adamthwaite, *France*, pp. 290–91; Lazareff, p. 208; Berstein, "Le Parti radical-socialiste," p. 300; Berstein, *Histoire*, pp. 559–60; Ben Elissar, p. 370; Gallo, p. 262; Joll, pp. 102–3; Bloch, pp. 210–11; Werth, *Twilight*, p. 303; Weber, pp. 177, n. 67, p. 314. Adamthwaite accepts Bonnet's explanation, but it is unclear why.

85. Maurice Adriet, to Foreign Ministry, no. 75, Nov. 14, 1938, MAE Z 707, p. 135. For other sympathetic consular reports, see MAE Z 707, pp. 78, 103.

86. G. Bonnet, pp. 281–82. See also Bonnet's testimony before the post-war parliamentary commission set up to investigate the events leading up to the war. Assemblée Nationale, Commission d'Enquête Parlementaire, pp. 2663–64.

87. Phipps, to the British Foreign Office, Nov. 11, 1938, PRO FO 371/21637.C13793.

88. "Record of Anglo-French Conversation Held at the Quai d'Orsay," Nov. 24, 1938, *DBFP*, series 3, vol. 3, no. 325, pp. 294–96.

89. "Grand'mère au consulat," *Samedi*, Mar. 4, 1939, in AIU, ms. 650, boîte 13.

90. Cited in Police report, "Information a/s d'un article du journal autrichien *Der Socialistische Kampf*, sur l'attentat de l'ambassade d'Allemagne," Nov. 22, 1938, APP BA 269 Provisoire 25.341-H.

91. "Autour de la politique," *L'Oeuvre*, Oct. [1, 7, or 9] 1938, clipped in BDIC, Dos. Duchêne, GFΔ Rés. 86.

92. Ibid.; Pell (Assistant Director, IGCR), to Edwin Wilson, U.S. Embassy, Paris, Nov. 2, 1938, AN AJ[43] 29 (22/66); "Basic Principles which have governed my conduct in respect of the organization and the Procedures taken by the Evian Intergovernmental Committee for Political Refugees for the Year July 1, 1938, to June 30, 1939," Myron Taylor, speech in New York, July 8, 1939, in Myron Taylor Papers, box 6, FDR Library; "Conversations betw. Mr. R. T. Pell and Dr. Wohlthat: Memo of visit to Paris and Berlin," Apr. 17, 1939, PRO FO 371/24083.W 6856; A. W. G. Randall, British Foreign Office, to W. H. B. Mack in Paris, British embassy, June 21, 1939, PRO FO 371/24076.W8939; Philippe Perier, French Consul, London, "Note, a/s IGCR meeting of July 18–20, 1939," July 28, 1939, MAE SDN I M 1818, p. 251.

93. "Note de la sous-direction des Affaires Administratives et des Unions Internationales: Le Comité d'Evian et la question des réfugiés israélites allemands," doc. no. 348, Nov. 21, 1938, *DDF*, 2ème series, vol. XIII, pp. 680–88; Adler-Rudel, pp. 247–48.

94. Rublee, teleg., transmitted through the U.S. chargé in the U.K. (Johnson) to the U.S. secretary of state, Aug. 25, 1938, *FRUS*, vol. 1, 1938, pp. 772–73; Ben Elissar, p. 255.

95. Corbin, French ambassador, London, to the Foreign Ministry (SDN), teleg. 8108, Dec. 2, 1938, MAE SDN I M 1818, pp. 99–102; Kennedy, U.S. ambassador in the U.K., to U.S. secretary of state (message from G. Rublee), teleg., Dec. 3, 1938, 840.48 Refugees/1037, *FRUS*, vol. 1, 1938, p. 851; Ben Elissar, pp. 409–10.

96. Kennedy, U.S. ambassador to the U.K., to the U.S. secretary of state (message from Rublee), Nov. 14, 1938, teleg., 840.48 Refugees/896, *FRUS*, vol. 1, 1938, pp. 820–22.

97. Bussières, minister of the interior, Sûreté Nationale, to the prefect of police, no. A-11, B 3-20, Dec. 26, 1938, APP BA 407ᴾ; "Les Juifs immigrés clandestinement en Lorraine sont refoulés en Allemagne," *La Croix*, Nov. 25, 1938, clipped in AN 72 AJ 601; "Qui a donné cet ordre?" *DdV*, Nov. 19, 1938, clipped in AIU, ms. 650, boîte 13; "Des Réfugiés juifs allemands étaient transportés clandestinement de Suisse en France: La Police met fin à ce trafic," *La Nouvelliste de Lyon*, Dec. 16, 1938, clipped in AIU, ms. 650, boîte 11 (40); *Presse Alsacienne, La Dépêche*, Jan. 18, 1939, clipped in AN 72 AJ 601.

98. Intercomité des Oeuvres Françaises des Réfugiés, "Procès verbal de la séance de Comité du novembre 23, 1938," AN 72 AJ 590.

99. Bussières, minister of the interior, Sûreté Nationale, to the prefect of police, Dec. 14, 1938, no. 182.582, C-2-3, C-14-10, APP BA 66 Provisoire 51.343.12.

100. See, for example, Frances Henry, *Victims and Neighbors: A Small Town in Nazi Germany Remembered* (So. Hadley, Mass., 1984), p. 74. On occasion, French consulates in Germany even sold fraudulent visas to Jews. See for example "Report on the Situation in France, May 1939," Euroexco Report, JDC no. 191, pp. 80–83.

101. Minister of the interior, Sûreté Nationale, to the prefect of the Bas-Rhin, n.d., transmitted by the prefect of the Bas-Rhin to the subprefects on Dec. 16, 1938, teleg., "Urgent," ADBR D 460, paq. 5(36).

102. For Daladier's proclamation, see *Le Temps*, Dec. 16, 1938, cited in Marrus and Paxton, p. 63. On the efforts of other Western European nations to assist refugee children, see Ferdinand Kuhn Jr., "Refugee Problem Arouses Britain to Action," *NYT*, Nov. 21, 1938, sec. E, p. 3; Bauer, *My Brother's Keeper*, p. 273; Sauer, p. 138; Sherman, pp. 171, 183–184, 265.

103. "Conference on the German Jewish Situation in the Refugee Countries and Emigration Possibilities," Dec. 14–15, 1938, JDC no. 363.

104. Kennedy, U.S. ambassador to the United Kingdom, to the U.S. secretary of state, 840.48 Refugees/1037, teleg. 1391, [transmission of message from Rublee], Dec. 3, 1938, *FRUS*, vol. 1, 1938, p. 851. See also Ben Elissar, p. 410; "Le Problème des réfugiés," *UI*, Dec. 2, 1938, p. 169; Corbin, to the Foreign Ministry (SDN), teleg. 8108, Dec. 2, 1938, MAE SDN I M 1818, pp. 99–102; Adamthwaite, *France*, p. 293; "La France accueillera 10 000 réfugiés juifs dans ses colonies," *L'Ordre*, Nov. 26, 1938, p. 1; "La France recevra 10 000 réfugiés juifs si les autres puissances font de même," *Le Figaro*, Dec. 3, 1938, clipped in MAE SDN I M 1818, p. 104; "Nations Will Open Lands to Refugees," *NYT*, Dec. 3, 1938, p. 8; "M. Bonnet est entendu par la Commission des affaires étrangères," *Le Peuple*, Dec. 15, 1938, pp. 1, 3.

On U.S. pressure on France in the fall of 1938 to reconsider the colonial solution and especially the Madagascar scheme, see Foreign Ministry (Afrique-Levant), "Note pour M. Massigli," June 22, 1938, MAE K Afrique 91, p. 196; Saint-Quentin, to Ernest Lagarde, French Foreign Ministry (Afrique-Levant), Nov. 11, 1938, MAE K Afrique 91, p. 217; Saint-Quentin, to the Foreign Ministry, teleg. no. 1280, Nov. 18, 1938, MAE SDN I M 1818, pp. 66–69. The IGCR also pressured France to reconsider colonial options. See George L. Warren, to Joseph P. Cotton Jr., Sept. 14, 1938, AN AJ⁴³ 12 (18/56:1); "Note de la sous-direction des Affaires Administratives et des Unions Internationales: Le Comité d'Evian et la question des réfugiés israélites allemands," doc. no. 348, Nov. 21, 1938, *DDF*, 2ème séries, vol. XIII, p. 687; "Communication from the Director to the Chairman and Vice-Chairmen of the Intergovernmental Committee" [Sept. 1938], in "Proceedings of the Intergovernmental Committee, Evian, July 6th–15th, 1938, Verbatim Record of the Plenary Meetings," Myron Taylor Papers, box 3, folder "Proceedings of the Intergovernmental Committee, Evian, July 6th–15th, 1938," FDR Library. The United States exerted similar pressure on Great Britain. See Sherman, pp. 162–63.

105. "Note de la sous-direction des Affaires Administratives et des Unions Internationales: Le Comité d'Evian et la question des réfugiés israélites allemands," doc. no. 348, Nov. 21, 1938, *DDF*, 2ème séries, vol. XIII, p. 687.

106. Adamthwaite (p. 293) claims that the Americans were disappointed with Bérenger's proposal since the French refused to offer any financial assistance to help settle the refugees, but I have found no evidence for this. Ben Elissar states that Bonnet never had any serious intention of opening Madagascar to Jewish refugee settlement, but again there is no evidence for this claim (Ben Elissar, pp. 409–10).

107. U.S. chargé d'affaires in France (Wilson), to U.S. secretary of state, Nov. 26, 1938, teleg. 740.00/520, *FRUS*, vol. 1, 1938, p. 105. See also Bauer, *My Brother's Keeper*, pp. 273–78; Marrus, *Unwanted*, pp. 216–17; Sherman, pp. 159–64.

108. G. Bonnet, pp. 222–23; Adamthwaite, *France*, p. 293.

109. Wilson, U.S. chargé d'affaires in France, to the secretary of state, 840.48 Refugees/1116 teleg., Dec. 15, 1938, *FRUS*, vol. 1, 1938, pp. 871–72.

110. Adamthwaite, *France*, p. 293.

111. "Memorandum by the Foreign Minister," to Hitler, RM 266, Paris, doc. 372, Dec. 9, 1938, *DGFP*, series D, vol. 4, pp. 481–82; Welczeck, German Ambassador to France, to the Foreign Ministry, Dec. 9, 1938, *DGFP*, series D, vol. 4, doc. no. 351, pp. 451–52. See also Marrus and Paxton, pp. 60–61; Ben Elissar, pp. 369–71. J. Kennedy, U.S. ambassador to the United Kingdom, assessed Bonnet's effort to persuade the Germans to allow the Jews to leave with part of their property intact a failure. See Kennedy, to the U.S. secretary of state, 840.48 Refugees/1072, teleg., Dec. 8, 1938, *FRUS*, vol. 1, 1938, pp. 862–63.

112. Cited in Wilson, U.S. chargé d'affaires in France, to the secretary of state, 840.48 Refugees/1116, teleg., Dec. 15, 1938, *FRUS*, vol. 1, 1938, pp. 872–73.

113. Phipps, to Halifax, doc. no. 407, teleg. C 15195/85/18, Dec. 8, 1938, *DBFP*, 3rd series, vol. III, p. 397. See also Marrus and Paxton, pp. 60–61; Ben Elissar, pp. 370–71; Adamthwaite, *France*, p. 293.

The French were reluctant to endorse the Schacht/Rublee plan not only because of fears that the plan would result in another deluge of refugees on French soil. They also claimed that the plan sanctioned the expropriation by Germany of Jewish property, thus encouraging the expulsion of the Jews. See Corbin, to the Foreign Ministry, no. 1162, Dec. 22, 1938, MAE Z 712, p. 102; Foreign Ministry, "Réunion du Bureau du Comité Intergouvernemental pour continuer et développer les travaux du Comité d'Evian," held at the Foreign Ministry, Paris, Jan. 23, 1939, MAE SDN I M 1818, pp. 121–45; Corbin, to the Foreign Ministry, Feb. 13, 1939, MAE Z 712, pp. 140–41; Foreign Ministry (Unions internationales), "Note sur l'origine et les travaux des Comités Intergouvernmentaux...," Mar. 9, 1939, MAE SDN I M 1818,

p. 174; "Conversations between Mr. R. T. Pell and Dr. Wohlthat: Memo of visit to Paris and Berlin," Apr. 17, 1939, PRO FO 371/24083.W 6856; A. W. G. Randall, British Foreign Office, to W. H. B. Mack, British embassy in Paris, June 21, 1939, PRO FO 371/24076.W8939; Intergovernmental Committee to Continue and Develop the Work of the Evian Meeting 1938 (London Intergovernmental Committee), Draft stenographic notes of the 7th meeting of the Committee, held in the Locarno Rm. at the Foreign Office, July 19, 1939, pp. 26–27, AN AJ^{43} 37 (48/88).

Chapter Ten

1. On the Spanish refugee crisis, see L. Stein, pp. 5–106; Pike; Marrus, *Unwanted*, pp. 190–94.
2. [Corbin], to the foreign minister, teleg. no. 416, Feb. 14, 1939, MAE SDN I M 1881, pp. 148–49; "Stenographic Notes of the 3rd, 4th, 5th, and 6th Meetings of the Committee, Held at Lancaster House, St. James, SW (the London Museum), on 13th & 14th February, 1939," p. 19, AJ^{43} 5 (20 G/329/80840); "4th Meeting, IGCR to Continue and Develop the Work of the Evian Committee, 1938, London, Feb. 13–14, 1939," Myron Taylor Papers, box 4, folder "1939: Proceedings, Speeches, etc., IGCR," FDR Library; JDC, Euroexco Report for Feb. 1939, "Review of the Month of February 1939," JDC no. 189.
3. JDC, Euroexco Report for Jan. 1939, "The Political Scene," Feb. 2, 1939; JDC, "Report on the Situation of German and Austrian Refugees in France in January 1939," both in JDC no. 189. See also Sarraut's speech to the Police Benevolent Association on illegal refugees in Feb. "Le Problème des étrangers," *Le Petit Parisien*, Feb. 6, 1939, pp. 1, 5; "M. Albert Sarraut pose avec autorité et justice le problème des étrangers," *L'Ordre*, Feb. 6, 1939, p. 4; "M. Albert Sarraut sur le problème des étrangers," *Samedi*, no. 6, Feb. 11, 1939, p. 3; CDV, bulletin no. 78, Feb. 10, 1939, pp. 4–5, in Documents of French Jewish History, JTS, box 12, folder 1 (26); "M. A. Sarraut parle du problème des étrangers," *Affirmation*, Feb. 10, 1939, p. 3; René Rousseau, "Une Politique de l'immigration: Dans la foule des réfugiés," *L'Epoque*, Feb. 13, 1939, p. 5.
4. CAR, Séance, Conseil d'administration, May 30, 1939, JDC no. 604.
5. Amedée Bussières, Ministry of the Interior, Sûreté Nationale, circular to prefects, No. A-8, No. 391, Apr. 22, 1939, AN F^7 14662 (also in APP BA 72 Provisoire). See also Schramm and Vormeier, p. 241.
6. "Les Fugitifs aux Antilles," *Journal des débats*, Jan. 11, 1939, clipped in AN 72 AJ 602.
7. JDC, Euroexco Report for Jan. 1939, "The Political Scene," Feb. 2, 1939, JDC no. 189.
8. Prefect, Bas-Rhin, to the subprefect, Sélestat, no. 3309, May 8, 1939, ADBR D 319/19, dos. 184.
9. Chief Rabbi Isaïe Schwartz, President, Caisse Centrale pour l'Est, Comité Central d'Assistance aux Emigrants Juifs, to the prefect, Bas-Rhin, Feb. 20, 1939; Prefect, Bas-Rhin, to the vice president of the Council, Direction Général des Services d'Alsace et de Lorraine, Service Central, 2ème bureau, no. 2905, Feb. 8, 1939;

Chief Rabbi Isaïe Schwartz, to the prefect, Bas-Rhin, Mar. 6, 1939; general secretary, prefect, Bas-Rhin, to the president of the Comité Central des Réfugiés, July 27, 1939; minister of the interior, to the vice president of the Council, Mar. 30, 1939, all in ADBR D 460, paq. 5 (36).

10. JDC, "Emigration from Germany and Austria," July 5, 1939, JDC no. 658; René Rousseau, "Une Politique de l'immigration: L'Exemple instructif des réfugiés autrichiens," *L'Epoque*, Feb. 10, 1939, p. 4; Bouqueret, "Des Israélites italiens cherchent asile en France: Ils sont cinq mille," *Le Jour: Echo de Paris*, Mar. 12, 1939, clipped in AIU, ms. 650, boîte 11 (Italie).

11. "Nice," *NYT*, Aug. 20, 1939, p. 15; "Un Inspecteur de la Sûreté Nationale, chargé de l'examen des papiers de réfugiés venant d'Italie, s'est rendu coupable de faits graves," *L'Intransigeant*, Aug. 20, 1939; "L'Inspecteur taré Francal est inculpé de vol et d'octroi de facilités pour l'entrée irrégulière des étrangers en France," *L'Intransigeant*, Aug. 21, 1939; "Comment l'inspecteur Francal 'arrangeait' beaucoup d'affaires," *Le Matin*, Aug. 21, 1939; "Un Policier reçevait des 'cadeaux' des réfugiés juifs," *AF*, Aug. 20, 1939, all clipped in AIU, ms. 650, boîte 13 (46).

12. JDC, "Emigration from Germany and Austria," July 5, 1939, JDC no. 658. See also Le Commissaire de police mobile, Lambert, to M. le Commissaire Divisionnaire, Chef de la 18ème Brigade régionale, Nice, no. 105, Jan. 20, 1939, AN F^7 14776; JDC, Euroexco, "Introduction and Review of Events in the Month of March 1939: A Day-by-Day Record of the Jewish Situation Taken from News Stories in the International Press, March 1939," entry for Mar. 16, 1939, JDC no. 190, p. 141; René Rousseau, "Une Politique de l'immigration: L'Exemple instructif des réfugiés autrichiens," *L'Epoque*, Feb. 10, 1939, p. 4. On the ambivalent attitude of the police, see also Miller, pp. 148–50; Voigt, "Les Naufragés," pp. 93–117. For an attempt to quantify clandestine immigration from Italy to France see Philippon et al., pp. 17–51.

13. "Minutes of Conference of Various Committees Held on Thursday, Mar. 23, 1939, at the AJDC Paris," JDC no. 405, p. 20. See also "De Nombreux juifs italiens commencent à se réfugier en France," *Le Matin*, Mar. 12, 1939, clipped in AIU, ms. 650, boîte 11 (Italie); Noth, *Mémoires*, p. 451.

14. Pierre Lahaspe, "Les Réfugiés au service de l'agriculture; L'agriculture au secours des réfugiés," *La Lumière*, May 19, 1939, p. 2, clipped in AIU, ms. 650, boîte 14 (48).

15. See Chapter 8, n. 38.

16. S. M. Levy, to Morris Troper, "Memorandum," Mar. 21, 1939, JDC no. 617; JDC, Euroexco report for Apr. 1939, "Day-by-Day Record," Apr. 1939, JDC no. 190, p. 194; Société religieuse des Amis, pp. 5–6

17. "Intercommittee for the Work of Asssistance for Refugees in France, The Situation of the Refugees in France," [Aug./Sept. 1939], JDC no. 617; "Le Sort des réfugiés autrichiens," *La Juste parole*, no. 54 (Apr. 20, 1939): 29; "Conference on the German Jewish Situation: The Situation in the Refugee Countries and Emigration Possibilities, Held 14–15 Dec. 1938," JDC no. 363; Morris C. Troper, "War Relief Activities of the JDC," JDC pamphlet, p. 9, JDC no. 165.

It was Pastor Marc Boegner who gave the figure of 42,000 as the number of illegal Jewish refugees in France in early 1939. See Pierre Dominique, "Les Etrangers peuvent nous donner une armée," *La République*, Feb. 1, 1939, pp. 1, 3.

18. Y. Grosrichard, "Un An après... Les réfugiés autrichiens veulent 'servir' la France," *L'Oeuvre*, Mar. 4, 1939, clipped in APP BA 269 Provisoire, dossier: "Réfugiés autrichiens, 1938–1939"; René Rousseau, "Une Politique de l'immigration: L'Exemple instructif des réfugiés autrichiens," *L'Epoque*, Feb. 10, 1939, p. 4.

19. *JO, Débats Parlementaires, Sénat*, Mar. 28, 1939, no. 5127, p. 337. See also Gourevitch, p. 18; Cross, p. 211.

20. "Cache-cache et salles d'attente, ou de l'utilisation rationnelle des forces humaines," *Esprit*, July 1, 1939, p. 509.

21. Gourevitch, p. 17; "Un Aspect particulier du problème des étrangers," *Le Petit Parisien*, June 14, 1939, p. 5.

22. Cahen-Molina, p. 4.

23. Schapiro, p. 137; René Rousseau, "Une Politique de l'immigration: L'Exemple instructif des réfugiés autrichiens," *L'Epoque*, Feb. 10, 1939, p. 4.

24. Franz Gravereau, "Les Emigrés autrichiens cherchent des remèdes à une situation devenue sans issue," *Le Petit Parisien*, Mar. 5, 1939, p. 7; M. Milhaud, "La Question des réfugiés politiques," *CDH*, Aug. 15, 1938, pp. 510–16; J. Biélinky, "Oui, nous voulons empêcher les progrès du barbare!...," *Affirmation*, Jan. 20, 1939, p. 5; "Un Mémoire de M. Louis Rollin sur le problème des réfugiés en France," *UI*, no. 20, Feb. 3, 1939, p. 349; "Pour les victimes de la barbarie raciste," *La Juste parole*, no. 50 (Feb. 20, 1939): 19–20; "Emigranten-Noete in Frankreich: Ein Memorandum des Deputierten Louis Rollin," *PT*, no. 907 (Jan. 31, 1939): 3; "Les Polices jouent au ping-poing," *Esprit*, 7ème année, no. 82 (July 1, 1939): 508–9.

25. "La Situation actuelle des réfugiés autrichiens," *L'Accueil français aux autrichiens*, no. 2 (Jan. 1939): 2.

26. René Rousseau, "Une Politique de l'immigration: Dans la foule des réfugiés sachons distinguer les éléments utiles des éléments dangereux," *L'Epoque*, Feb. 13, 1939, p. 5; "Communiqué de Service Social d'Entraide aux Emigrants," *Esprit*, 7ème année, no. 82 (July 1, 1939): 500–501.

27. Gourevitch, p. 19.

28. René Rousseau, "Une Politique de l'immigration," *L'Epoque*, Feb. 13, 1939, p. 5. See also Rousseau, "Devant le problème des réfugiés les pouvoirs publics oscillent entre l'inertie et l'arbitraire," *L'Epoque*, Feb. 19, 1939, p. 4.

29. On the rising number of suicides, see Gourevitch, pp. 20–21, 28–30; "Les Réfugiés autrichiens en France," *Fraternité*, Dec. 1938, AIU, ms. 650, boîte 14 (48); Franz Gravereau, "Les Emigrés autrichiens cherche net des remèdes à une situation devenue sans issue," *Le Petit Parisien*, Mar. 5, 1939, p. 7; Paul Lenglois, "Les Sans-papiers," *La Justice*, May 28, 1939, part I, clipped in AIU, ms. 650, boîte 11 (42); "Un Israélite allemand condamné après appel tente de se suicider," *L'Oeuvre*, Nov. 3, 1938, clipped in AN 72 AJ 602; Miller, pp. 146–47.

30. On these schemes, see Miller, pp. 159–66; 19th Ordinary Session of the [League of Nations] Assembly, 6th Committee, Sub-Committee, International Assistance to Refugees, Refugees from Germany, Confidential Note by the Secretary

of the Sub-Committee Geneva, Sept. 17, 1938, A.VI./SCI/l. 1938, in JDC no. 253; L'Inspecteur Général, chargé des services de police criminelle, to M. le Directeur de la Police du territoire et des étrangers (6ème bureau—expulsions), Apr. 2, 1938, AN F^7 14775; Dossier "juifs allemands" (Adler-Strauss; Robert Reich), in AN F^7 14776; prefect of police, Paris, Police report, Mar. 31, 1939, APP BA^P 407; Foreign Ministry, to the Ministry of the Interior, "a/s Agences d'émigration israélite," no. 1748, July 28, 1939, AN BB 3211, dos. 1888 (A.39); "Note," British ambassador in France to the Foreign Ministry, Aug. 2, 1939, AN BB 3211, dos. 1888 (A.39); Procureur de la République, to the Procureur Général, Feb. 27, 1940, AN BB 18 3211, dos. 1888 (A. 39); "Dix-sept étrangers qui favorisaient l'entrée massive des indésirables en France sont arretés," *L'Epoque*, May 26, 1938, p. 6; "Dix étrangers indésirables seront jugés ou extradés," *L'Epoque*, Aug. 3, 1938, p. 7; René Rousseau, "Une Politique de l'immigration: L'Exemple instructif des réfugiés autrichiens," *L'Epoque*, Feb. 10, 1939, p. 4; "Winterton Praises Refugee Progress," *NYT*, Aug. 5, 1939, p. 6; "Passeports et faux papiers pour tous pays," *Le Matin*, Feb. 14, 1939, pp. 1–2; "Un Trafiquant d'émigrants," *Le Matin*, June 18, 1939, p. 1; "Un Réfugié allemand escroque," *Le Matin*, Aug. 1, 1939, pp. 1–2; "Les Parasites de la France," *Le Petit Parisien*, Nov. 20, 1938; "Naturalisation, permis de sejour, cartes d'identité...," *Le Petit Parisien*, Feb. 1, 1939, p. 4; "Un Proscrit allemand pour l'Amérique," *Le Populaire*, Jan. 8, 1939, p. 6; "Une Officine vendait de faux passeports et mariait des étrangers, *Le Populaire*, Feb. 14, 1939, p. 6; "Deux aigrefins escroquaient des étrangers en situation irrégulière," *Le Populaire*, Mar. 18, 1939, p. 8; "Une Affaire de faux passeports en correctionnelle," *Le Populaire*, Aug. 4, 1939, p. 6; "Voulez-vous un époux et devenir français?" *Le Journal*, Feb. 14, 1939, p. 1; "'Le Conseiller' Ury et ses collaborateurs mariaient les gens et leur fournissaient de faux passeports," *L'Oeuvre*, Feb. 14, 1939, p. 5; "Un Trafiquant de devises et sa maitresse avaient escroqué un réfugié allemand de 125 000 frs.," *L'Oeuvre*, Aug. 1, 1939, p. 5. For schemes run by East European Jewish refugees, see dossiers in AN F^7 14775 and APP BA 407^P 131.12-4.

31. "On découvre dans un sac le cadavre d'un israélite allemand étranglé avec une cravate," *L'Oeuvre*, Apr. 8, 1939, p. 1; "L'Assassin du réfugié allemand est identifié," *L'Oeuvre*, Apr. 9, 1939, p. 5; "Joseph Wolfrum l'assassin d'Arthur Lewy se cache-t-il à Anvers," *L'Oeuvre*, Apr. 10, 1939, p. 5; "L'Assassin d'Arthur Levy est arrêté à Anver," Apr. 13, 1939, *L'Oeuvre*, pp. 1, 5; "Des Cantonniers découvrent un cadavre ficelé dans un sac," *Le Petit Parisien*, Apr. 8, 1939, pp. 1, 5; "L'Arrestation de Wolfrum," *Le Petit Parisien*, Apr. 13, 1939, p. 5; "Dans un sac le cadavre d'un homme étranglé," *Le Populaire*, Apr. 8, 1939, p. 8; "Wolfrum déambulait à minuit dans les rues," *Le Populaire*, Apr. 9, 1939, pp. 1, 4; "L'Arrestation de Wolfrum l'assassin de Levy," *Le Populaire*, Apr. 13, 1939, p. 2; "L'Assassin du réfugié allemand...," *Le Peuple*, Apr. 13, 1939, p. 1; "L'Assassin du réfugié allemand est identifié," *Le Peuple*, Apr. 19, 1939, p. 3.

32. Paul Lenglois, "On serait volontiers antisémite dans notre administration policière," *La Justice*, May 25, 1939, clipped in AIU, ms. 650, boîte 14 (48).

33. Mulhouse refugee committee report, in "Report of the CAR, Paris, Apr. 1939," JDC, Euroexco report for Apr. 1939, JDC no. 190, p. 129.

34. Paris prefect of police, "Report," Mar. 31, 1939, APP BA^P 407.

35. Pierre Scize, "Ce qui se passe à la frontière italienne," *Messidor*, no. 58 (Apr. 21, 1939): 4–5.

36. Gourevitch, p. 17; Maga, "Closing," p. 438; Maga, *America*, p. 134.

37. "Pour une mesure de clémence en faveur des réfugiés politiques," *UI*, no. 41 (June 30, 1939): 738.

38. "Le Dr. Erich Frey sera-t-il condamné pour n'avoir pu quitter la France?" *Le Populaire*, Jan. 24, 1939, p. 6; "Six mois de prison pour le défenseur de Calmette," *Samedi*, no. 5 (Feb. 4, 1939); "German Exile Punished," *NYT*, Jan. 31, 1939, p. 5. For other instances of judges feeling uneasy with the decree laws, see Paul Lenglois, "Conclusions faites pour servir aux philosophes cyniques," *La Justice*, June 1, 1939, clipped in AIU, ms. 650, boîte 14 (48); "Report on the Situation in France, May 1939," Euroexco Report, JDC no. 191, pp. 80–83. Frey subsequently emigrated from France to Shanghai, and later to Chile.

39. Bouqueret, "Des israélites italiens cherchent asile en France: Ils sont cinq mille," *Le Jour: Echo de Paris*, Mar. 12, 1939, clipped in AIU, ms. 650, boîte 11 (Italie). See also "De nombreux juifs italiens commencent à se réfugier en France," *Le Matin*, clipped in AIU, ms. 650, boîte 11 (Italie); "Les Réfugiés politiques chassés d'Italie passent la frontière chaque jour plus nombreux," *L'Eclaireur de Nice*, Mar. 11, 1939, clipped in AIU, ms. 650, boîte 11 (Italie); "Les Juifs expulsés d'Italie se présentent en masse à la frontière française," *Le Petit Parisien*, Mar. 12, 1939, p. 2; CAR, "Assemblée Générale du 7 janvier 1940 de l'Exercice 1939, Nice," Jan. 31, 1940, JDC no. 604; Report of the CAR, Paris, Apr. 1939, JDC, Euroexco Report for Apr. 1939, JDC no. 190, p. 126; "Des juifs fuyant l'Italie arrivant à la frontière française," *UI*, Mar. 17, 1939, clipped in AIU, ms. 650, boîte 11 (42); Le Procureur Général près la Cour d'Appel d'Aix, to the keeper of the seals, Ministry of Justice, May 4, 1940, AN F^7 14776.

40. For a further discussion of this point, see Chapter 12.

41. R. Cahen-Molina, "Pour une mesure de clémence en faveur des réfugiés politiques," *UI*, no. 41 (June 30, 1939): 738. See also Leven, p. 24 and *passim*; J. Biélinky, "Israel... au Conseil Municipal," *Samedi*, no. 39 (Dec. 31, 1938): 7.

42. Gourevitch, p. 23.

43. Paul Lenglois, "La Chasse à l'homme sans défense," *La Justice*, May 31, 1939, clipped in AIU, ms. 650, boîte 14 (48).

44. "Le Discours de Léon Blum," *DdV*, Dec. 3, 1938, p. 6 (also in *UI*, Dec. 2, 1938, p. 173).

45. "Réfugié en France: Un Industriel de Prague se jette sous une rame de métro," *Le Populaire*, May 13, 1939, pp. 1, 2. See also Pierre Scize, "Ce qui se passe à la frontière italienne," *Messidor*, no. 58 (Apr. 21, 1939): 4–5. In June 1939, a British refugee organization appealed to the French Foreign Ministry to alleviate the plight of the refugees in French jails. See Foreign Ministry, to Corbin, French ambassador, London, [summer 1939], no. 1068, MAE Z 712, pp. 148–50.

46. Members of Amis de la République Française included: Jean Painlevé, general secretary; former ministers Jean-Paul Boncour, Léo Lagrange, and Yvon Delbos; deputies Gabriel Cudenet, Gabriel Delattre, and Louis Jacquinot; P.-O. Lapie,

Ernest Pezet, and Louis Rollin; the lawyers Henry Torrès and Moro Giafferi; Louise Weiss; Robert Lange; General Alphonse Weiller; Jean Perrin; Henri Pichot; G. Lechevallier-Chevignard; Mme. Maleterre-Sellier; General Armengaud; Paul Perrin; Reverend Père Riquet; and F. de Clermont-Tonnere. See "Les Amis de la République Française et les juifs immigrés," *Samedi*, no. 18 (May 27, 1939): 6.

47. "Un Manifeste de la Ligue: Pour les réfugiés politiques," *CDH*, June 1, 1938, pp. 331–32; J. Biélinky, "La Situation légale des immigrés juifs en France," *La Terre retrouvée*, no. 18 (June 15, 1938): 6; M. Milhaud, "La Question des réfugiés politiques," *CDH*, Aug. 15, 1938, pp. 510–16; minister of the interior, Sûreté Nationale, to the Foreign Ministry, Cabinet, c/s no. 3.927, "a/s Meeting en faveur des immigrés," May 24, 1938, MAE SDN I M 1819, pp. 334–36; Livian, *Le Parti socialiste*, p. 153; "Le Parti socialiste et les immigrés: Une délégation socialiste au Ministère de l'Intérieur," *Le Populaire*, May 25, 1938; Marcel Brenot, Secrétaire de l'Union des Syndicats ouvriers de la région parisienne, "Les Immigrés honnêtes ne doivent pas être menacés de décisions arbitraires," *Le Populaire*, May 19, 1938; Brenot, "Pour les travailleurs immigrés: Une délégation de l'Union des syndicats et de la CGT au Ministre de l'Intérieur," *Le Populaire*, May 26, 1938, p. 7; "Les Réfugiés autrichiens en France," *Fraternité*, no. 30, Dec. 1938, AIU, ms. 650, boîte 14 (48); H. S., "Les Réfugiés autrichiens en France," *Fraternité*, May 20, 1939, p. 4, clipped in AIU, ms. 650, boîte 11 (42); Pierre-Bloch, "La Détresse des réfugiés," *UI*, no. 25, Mar. 10, 1939, p. 444; Pierre-Bloch, "Le Statut des réfugiés," *L'Ordre*, May 16, 1939, p. 1 (also in *UI*, no. 34 [May 12, 1939]: 605); R. Cahen-Molina, "Pour une mesure de clémence en faveur des réfugiés politiques," *UI*, no. 41 (June 30, 1939): 738; "Le Décret loi sur les étrangers," *Le Peuple*, Nov. 26, 1938, p. 2; "Les Décrets-lois et les immigrés," *Le Peuple*, Nov. 29, 1938, p. 2.

48. J. Biélinky, "Oui, nous voulons empêcher le progrès du barbare!...," *Affirmation*, Jan. 20, 1939, p. 5; "Un Mémoire de M. Louis Rollin sur le problème des réfugiés en France," *UI*, no. 20 (Feb. 3, 1939) p. 349; "Pour les victimes de la barbarie raciste," *La Juste parole*, no. 50 (Feb. 20, 1939): 19–20; "Emigranten-Noete in Frankreich: Ein Memorandum des Deputierten Louis Rollin," *PT*, no. 907 (Jan. 31, 1939): 3; *JO, Débats Parlementaires, Sénat*, Mar. 28, 1939, no. 5127 (Question of Dec. 31, 1938), p. 337; Franz Gravereau, "Les Emigrés autrichiens cherchent des remèdes à une situation devenue sans issue," *Le Petit Parisien*, Mar. 5, 1939, p. 7.

49. "Note remise par M. Pierre Dreyfus (pour le Comité Central [AIU] à la Présidence du Conseil," Dec. 12, 1938, AIU France V D 18; *ATJ Bulletin*, Dec. 28, 1938, clipped in AIU, ms. 650, boîte 13 (46); "L'Oeuvre du comité israélite pour les enfants venant d'Allemagne," *UI*, no. 31 (Apr. 21, 1939), p. 545; JDC, Euroexco, Jan. 1939, "Report on the Situation of German and Austrian Refugees in France in January 1939," JDC no. 189; JDC, Euroexco, Report for Feb. 1939, "France," JDC no. 189, p. 84; "France: OSE Work on Behalf of Refugee Children from Central Europe," Mar. 1939," JDC, Euroexco, "Introduction and Review of Events in the Month of March 1939," JDC no. 190, p. 75; "Report of the OSE, April, 1939," in JDC, Euroexco report for Apr. 1939, JDC no. 190, p. 184; "Report of OSE, May 1939," in JDC, Euroexco, "Report on the Situation, France," JDC no. 191, p. 144; "200 jeunes réfugiés juifs trouvent un foyer en France" *L'Ordre*, June 13,

1939, p. 2; "Besuch bei Emigrantenkindern," *PT*, no. 953 (Mar. 25, 1939): 3; "200 enfants réfugiés seront accueillis en France avant la fin du mois," *Samedi*, no. 11 (Mar. 18, 1939): 5; Simpson, *Refugees: A Review*, p. 53.

50. Weiss had served as the director of the prestigious journal, *L'Europe nouvelle*. For a contemporary biographical note, see "Un Entretien avec Mme. Louise Weiss: Un effort français pour l'assistance aux réfugiés," *UI*, Jan. 27, 1939, pp. 321–22. See also "Weiss, Louise," in Bell et al., p. 435; Weiss, 3: 435–36.

51. "Report on the Activity of the Comité Central des Réfugiés, from January 14th to March 1st, 1939," JDC Euroexco, "Introduction and Review of Events in the Month of March 1939," JDC no. 190, p. 75.

52. On the creation of the Bonnet Committee, see *JO, Lois et Décrets*, Dec. 30, 1938, p. 14806; Weiss, 3: 233; G. Bonnet, pp. 281–82; Nathan Katz, JDC, to JDC, NYC, Dec. 29, 1938, JDC no. 617. In addition to Weiss, the other members of the Bonnet Committee were: Henry Bérenger, Jean Mistler, Cardinal Jean Verdier, Pastor Marc Boegner, Chief Rabbi of Paris Israël Lévi, François Mauriac, Georges Risler, Professor Robert Debré, de Nalèche, Marquis de Lillers, and Jacques Helbronner.

53. G. Bonnet, pp. 281–82.

54. For Bonnet's speech on the occasion of the inauguration of the Comité Central, see "La Première réunion du Comité pour les réfugiés," *Le Temps*, Jan. 15, 1939, clipped in BDIC, Dos. Duchêne GFΔ Rés. 86; "Texte, discours prononcé le 14 janvier 1939 par le Ministre des Affaires Etrangères à l'occasion de la première réunion du Comité récemment institué près du département," MAE Z 712, pp. 127–32; "L'Assistance aux réfugiés," *UI*, Jan. 20, 1939, p. 304; "Aucun pays n'a reçu autant de réfugiés que la France," *L'Epoque*, Jan. 15, 1939, clipped in AN 72 AJ 602; "La Première réunion du Comité pour les réfugiés," *L'Aube*, Jan. 15, 1939, p. 3; "Le Comité pour les réfugiés," *L'Ordre*, Jan. 15, 1939, p. 4; "France to Limit Immigrants," *NYT*, Jan. 15, 1939, p. 30; René Rousseau, "Devant le problème des réfugiés les pouvoirs publics oscillent entre l'inertie et l'arbitraire," *L'Epoque*, Feb. 19, 1939, p. 4; J.-Ch. Bonnet, pp. 348–49.

55. That Bonnet's goal was to convince France's allies that France had already done more than its share is illustrated by the memo the Foreign Ministry sent the French ambassador in the U.S., Saint-Quentin, on Jan. 17, which asked Saint-Quentin whether he thought Bonnet's remarks of Jan. 14 might be useful for propaganda purposes

auprès des milieux américains compétents et des principaux journalistes en relations avec l'Ambassade. Elles soulignent, en effet, l'importance de la contribution apportée par la France à cette oeuvre humanitaire et sont de nature à prouver que, si notre état ne peut aujourd'hui comme d'autres états paraissent disposés à le faire reçevoir sur son territoire, à titre définitif, un nouveau contingent appréciable d'immigrants, il faut en chercher la raison essentielle dans l'effort exceptionnel qu'il a déjà accompli.

Hoppenot, Ministre plénipotentiaire, Foreign Ministry (Europe), to Saint Quentin, no. 41, Jan. 17, 1939, MAE Z 712, pp. 125–26.

56. "Un Entretien avec Mme. Louise Weiss: Un effort français pour l'assistance aux réfugiés," *UI*, Jan. 27, 1939, pp. 321–22. On the work of the Bonnet committee see also Weiss, 3: 233–68; Auffray, pp. 76–77.

57. Pierre Dominique, "Les Quatre millions d'étrangers qui sont en France au service du pays," *La République*, May 28, 1939, clipped in AIU, ms. 650, boîte 14 (48); Paul Perrin, "Où est l'intérêt français?" *DdV*, Nov. 19, 1938, p. 2. Dominique had already supported the agricultural option at the time the Serre Plan was being debated. See Dominique, "Trois millions d'étrangers chez nous...," *La République*, Apr. 22, 1938, pp. 1, 3, and "Immigrants et réfugiés politiques," *La République*, Aug. 13, 1938, pp. 1–2.

58. On the Serre Plan, see Chapter 7.

59. Demangeon and Mauco. See also Georges Mauco, "Les Etrangers dans l'agriculture française," *Fraternité*, May 20, 1939, p. 2, clipped in AIU, ms. 650, boîte 11 (42); "L'Opinion des autres...," *Samedi*, no. 19 (June 3, 1939): 2–3.

For other commentators sympathetic to this argument, see Emile Buré, "Nos Etrangers! La façon de donner vaut mieux que ce qu'on donne: Pour une saine politique de l'immigration," [Dec. 1938], *L'Ordre*, clipped in BDIC, Dos. Duchêne, GBΔ Rés. 86; Is. Pasquier, "Puisqu'il n'y a plus de bras français pour cultiver la terre de France," *L'Aube*, Mar. 26, 1938, pp. 1–2; Claude Mauriac, "Réfugiés politiques, émigrés clandestins: Un grave problème qu'il faut résoudre," *La Flèche*, Aug. 11, 1939, p. 7, clipped in AIU, ms. 650, boîte 12 (43); "L'Attitude de la France vis-à-vis des étrangers," *TJ*, no. 1 (Jan. 6, 1939): 1–2; Jeanne Ancelet-Hustache, "Contre quelques arguments spécieux," *L'Aube*, Nov. 22, 1938, pp. 1, 2.

60. Jacques Saint-Germain, "Alerte, paysan! Ton sol change de mains...," *L'Emancipation nationale*, Jan. 20, 1939, clipped in AIU, ms. 650, boîte 13 (46), dossier "La France et les réfugiés"; Saint-Germain, p. 95.

61. "Pas eux, pas là!", *Choc*, Jan. 26, 1939, clipped in AIU, ms. 650, boîte 13 (46). According to Pierre Lazareff, this paper was actually owned by a Jew and was therefore denounced by the antisemite Darquier de Pellepoix as a fraud. Lazareff, pp. 183–84. See also "Israel en Bourgogne," *AF*, Jan. 20, 1939, clipped in AIU, ms. 650, boîte 13 (46); Firmin Bacconnier, "Un Projet d'occupation juive dans nos terres desertées," *AF*, Feb. 20, 1938, cited in "Un Projet d'occupation juive dans nos terres desertées," CDV, bulletin no. 59, Feb. 24, 1938, p. 7, AIU, ms. 650, boîte 2.

62. Jeanne Ancelet-Hustache, "Contre quelques arguments spécieux," *L'Aube*, Nov. 22, 1938, pp. 1, 2; Ancelet-Hustache, "La Grande pitié des réfugiés: Ce que nous attendons," *L'Aube*, June 14, 1939, p. 3. Ancelet-Hustache had already called for agricultural solutions at the time of the Serre Plan. See the fifth article in her series, "France: Terre hospitalière: Des solutions humaines," *L'Aube*, Feb. 15, 1938, pp. 1–2 (reprinted as "La France hospitalière," *La Juste parole*, no. 29 [Mar. 15, 1938]: 19–20).

63. "L'Opinion des autres...," *Samedi*, no. 19 (June 3, 1939): 2–3. See also Emile Buré, "Nos Etrangers! La façon de donner vaut mieux que ce qu'on donne: Pour une saine politique de l'immigration," *L'Ordre* [Dec. 1938], clipped in BDIC, Dos. Duchêne, GBΔ Rés. 86; "L'Attitude de la France vis-à-vis des étrangers," *TJ*, no. 1 (Jan. 6, 1939): 1–2.

64. Jouhaux, "Main-d'oeuvre étrangère et droit d'asile," *Le Peuple*, Mar. 8, 1939, clipped in APP BA 67 Provisoire.

65. "L'Antisémitisme jugé par le Comte de Paris," *Le Figaro*, Dec. 30, 1938, clipped in AIU, ms. 650, boîte 15 (51); "Le Comte de Paris contre le racisme," *UI*, Jan. 6, 1939, p. 265; [Letter to the editor], "Pour une politique de l'immigration," *L'Ordre*, Jan. 2, 1939, p. 4; "L'Immigration étrangère," *Le Matin*, Jan. 1, 1939, clipped in AIU, ms. 650, boîte 13 (46).

66. On Paon's support, see Comité de Coordination, "Tournée de prospection dans le Lot-et-Garonne, le Gers, et la Hte. Garonne et le Tarn et Garonne, 5–9 février 1939," AN 72 AJ 590 (for the English version of this report, see "Trips of Inspection in the Departments of Lot-et-Garonne, Gers, Haute Garonne and Tarn and Garonne," JDC Euroexco report, "Introduction and Review of Events in the Month of March 1939," JDC no. 190, pp. 80–83). On the support of local officials in southwestern France, in addition to the above, see also [Letter to the editor], "Pour une politique de l'immigration," *L'Ordre*, Jan. 2, 1939, pp. 1, 4 (reprinted as "Deutsche Emigranten als Landwirte in Frankreich," *PT*, no. 883 [Jan. 3, 1939]: 3). Although this letter was signed "a friend of *L'Ordre*," a subsequent report identified the author as the subprefect of Villeneuve.

67. Denis Decais, "Les Enracinés," *L'Ordre*, May 25, 1939, pp. 1, 4.

68. Martin Deschamps, "Des Réfugiés s'offrent à l'agriculture," *L'Aube*, May 14, 1939, p. 3; Pierre Lahaspe, "Les Réfugiés au service de l'agriculture; l'agriculture au secours des réfugiés," *La Lumière*, May 19, 1939, p. 2, clipped in AIU, ms. 650, boîte 14 (48).

69. Pierre Dominique, "La France n'est pas un 'tir aux ambassadeurs,'" *La République*, Nov. 9, 1938, pp. 1, 3. See also J. Biélinky, "La Drame douloureux des réfugiés," *La Juste parole*, no. 47 (Jan. 5, 1939): 20.

70. Intercomité des Oeuvres Françaises des Réfugiés, Minutes, Nov. 23, 1938, AN 72 AJ 590. See also René Rousseau, "Une Politique de l'immigration: Dans la foule des réfugiés sachons distinguer les éléments utiles des éléments dangereux," *L'Epoque*, Feb. 13, 1939, p. 5.

71. "Le Comité de la Population," *Le Temps*, Mar. 3, 1939, p. 1.

72. Joseph Bonsirven, "Le Judaisme européen et l'antisémitisme," in "La Question d'Israel," [pamphlet], *Bulletin catholique* (publié par les prêtres missionnaires de Notre Dame de Sion), no. 68 (May 1, 1939): 495. See also Robert de Beauplan, "Un Problème de l'heure: Le Drame juif," extract from *La Petite Illustration*, Feb. 4, 1939, p. 31, in AIU, ms. 650, boîte 14 (48).

73. Pierre Dominique, "La France n'est pas un 'tir aux ambassadeurs,'" *La République*, Nov. 9, 1938, p. 1.

74. JDC, Euroexco Report, "Report on the Situation of German and Austrian Refugees in France in Jan. 1939," p. 7, JDC no. 189; [CDV] Report, "Le Problème des réfugiés," [late 1938], AIU, ms. 650, boîte 12 (44), p. 8; "Migration Conference, AJDC-HICEM," Paris, Aug. 22–23, 1939, JDC no. 367, pp. 150–51.

75. Comité de Coordination, "Tournée de prospection dans le Lot-et-Garonne, le Gers, et la Hte. Garonne et le Tarn et Garonne, 5–9 février, 1939," AN 72 AJ 590. See also JDC, "Report on the Situation in France, May 1939," JDC no. 191, pp. 80-

83; J. Biélinky, "L'Immigration juive en France," *La Juste Parole*, no. 62 (Sept. 15, 1939): 10–14; Centre Industriel de Rééducation Professionnelle (CRIP), Report, [n.d.], clipped in AIU, ms. 650, boîte 13 (46); Auffray, pp. 73–74.

76. Intercomité des Oeuvres Françaises des Réfugiés, Minutes, Nov. 23, 1938, AN 72 AJ 590.

77. Eleven departments were completely open to refugee settlement: le Lot, la Dordogne, le Finistère, la Mayenne, la Creuse, l'Orne, le Morbihan, le Cantal, les Deux-Sèvres, la Lozère, and l'Ile-et-Vilaine. Intercomité des Oeuvres Françaises de Réfugiés, Minutes, May 25, 1939, AN 72 AJ 590.

78. Intercommittee for the Work of Assistance for Refugees in France, "The Situation of the Refugees in France," [Aug.–Sept. 1939] in JDC no. 617; Nathan Katz, JDC, to JDC, NYC, Dec. 29, 1938, JDC no. 617; "Migration Conference, AJDC-HICEM," Paris, Aug. 22–23, 1939, JDC no. 367, pp. 150–51; "Comité Central d'Assistance aux Emigrants Juifs," *TJ*, no. 20 (May 19, 1939): 307.

79. On the EIF center, see Treasurer, EIF, to the Consistory of Paris, "Brief Account of Activities for the Academic Year, May 31, 1939," ACIP B 134^E (1939: EIF). On the Château de Bures, see "Programme d'action au Château de Bures (S & O), Centre d'hébergement temporaire et de réadaptation sociale des réfugiés Tchécoslovaques, service civil international (section française), and Comité Central d'Accueil aux Réfugiés Tchécoslovaques," Paris, n.d., in AIU, ms. 650, boîte 11, dossier "Réfugiés italiens." On the planning for this and other centers for Czech refugees, see JDC, Euroexco Report for Apr. 1939, "Situation of the Jews in Slovakia," Apr. 28, 1939, JDC no. 190, p. 89; Arnal, Foreign Ministry (SDN), to Sir Herbert Emerson, the High Commissioner for Refugees, Feb. 10, 1939, MAE SDN I M 1814, pp. 347–48; Emerson to Dr. Klumpar, Minister for Health and Social Administration, Prague, Feb. 6, 1939, MAE SDN I M 1814, pp. 350–51.

On the centers in Nice, see Felix Stössinger, "Emigranten an der Côte d'Azur," *PT*, July 6, 1939, p. 3; H. Séméria, "Errants à travers le monde," *Le Petit Niçois*, July 25, 1939, clipped in AIU, ms. 650, boîte 13 (45); CAR [Nice], "Assemblée Générale du 7 Janvier 1940 de l'Exercice, 1939," brochure, Nice, Jan. 31, 1940, JDC no. 604. On the Gumbel Center, see "Emigranten lernen und wollen arbeiten," *PT*, no. 940 (Mar. 10, 1939): 2. On Martigny, see "Un Centre de réfugiés à Martigny-les-Bains," *UI*, no. 23 (Feb. 24, 1939): 414; "Le Centre de réfugiés de Martigny-les-Bains," extrait de *L'UI*, Aug. 4, 1939, pp. 827–30, in AIU, ms. 650, boîte 11 (41); Centre d'accueil de Martigny, "*TJ*, no. 13–14 (Mar. 31, 1939): 205; Troper, JDC, Paris, to JDC, N.Y., Aug. 21, 1939, JDC no. 617; Letter from refugees at Martigny "au Foyer de Chelles à nos amis," Feb. 26, 1939, AN 72 AJ 590.

80. C.I.R.P. (Centre Industriel de Rééducation professionnelle), Report, [n.d.] in AIU, ms. 650, boîte 13 (46).

81. Intercommittee for the Work of Assistance for Refugees in France, "The Situation of the Refugees in France," [Aug.–Sept. 1939], JDC no. 617; "Migration Conference, AJDC-HICEM," Paris, Aug. 22–23, 1939, JDC no. 367, pp. 150–51.

82. "Conference on the German Jewish Situation, the Situation in the Refugee Countries and Emigration Possibilities, Held December 14–15, 1938," JDC no. 363; JDC, Euroexco report for Feb. 1939, JDC no. 189, pp. 83–84; "Report of the CAR,"

Paris, Apr. 1939, in JDC, Euroexco Report for Apr. 1939, JDC no. 190, pp. 122–23; "700 réfugiés d'Autriche vivent à Chelles," *DdV*, Jan. 14, 1939; Jacques Grosbois, "Quittant l'enfer hitlérien ils sont au purgatoire," *DdV*, Feb. 25, 1939, pp. 1,3, clipped in AIU, ms. 650, boîte 13 (45); "Was geschieht für die osterreishischen Flüchtlinge?" *PT*, Sept. 18–19, 1938, p. 5; Peter Kaufmann, "Der Emigrant lernt um Kurse der ORT in Chelles," *PT*, no. 1046 (July 12, 1939): 3; Stefan Fingal, "Die oesterreichische Emigrantenkolonie Chelles," *PT*, no. 1070 (Aug. 10, 1939): 3; "Dans les communautés: Au foyer de Chelles," *Samedi*, no. 11 (Mar. 18, 1939): 4.

83. Intercomité des Oeuvres Françaises des Réfugiés, Minutes, Nov. 23, 1938, AN 72 AJ 590.

84. CAR, "Séance du Conseil d'Administration, 30 mai 1939," JDC no. 604; "Report of the CAR, Paris, avril 1939," JDC, Euroexco Report for Apr. 1939, JDC no. 190, pp. 115–17, 119.

85. CIRP report, [n.d.], AIU, ms. 650, boîte 13 (46); Intercomité des Oeuvres Françaises des Réfugiés, Minutes, Meeting of Nov. 23, 1938, AN 72 AJ 590; JDC, Euroexco Report, Feb. 1939, JDC no. 189, pp. 82–83; Intercommittee for the Work of Assistance for Refugees in France, "The Situation of the Refugees in France," [Aug.–Sept. 1939], JDC no. 617.

86. "Migration Conference, AJDC-HICEM, Paris, Aug. 22–23, 1939," JDC no. 367; "Memorandum on International Conference of Youth Organizations for Increased Relief to Refugees and Civil War Victims," Mar. 17, 1939, JDC no. 405; "Migration Conference, JDC-Hicem," Aug. 22–23, 1939, JDC no. 367.

87. Comité de Coordination, "Tournée de prospection dans le Lot-et-Garonne, le Gers, et la Hte. Garonne et le Tarn et Garonne, 5–9 février 1939," AN 72 AJ 590.

88. "Report of the Dijon refugee committee," in "Report of the CAR, Paris, April 1939," JDC, Euroexco, Report for Apr. 1939, JDC no. 190, p. 130.

89. CAR [Nice], "Assemblée Générale du 7 Janvier 1940 de l'Exercice, 1939," [brochure], Nice, Jan. 31, 1940, JDC no. 604.

90. Intercomité des Oeuvres Françaises de Réfugiés, Minutes, Feb. 23, 1939, AN 72 AJ 590. See also Léon Groc, "Les Etrangers chez nous," *Le Petit Parisien*, Apr. 7, 1939, pp. 1–2; JDC, "Report on the Situation in France, May 1939," JDC no. 191, pp. 80–83.

91. "Migration Conference, AJDC-HICEM," Paris, Aug. 22–23, 1939, JDC no. 367, pp. 150–51.

92. "Report of the CAR," Paris, Apr. 1939, in JDC, Euroexco Report for Apr. 1939, JDC no. 190, pp. 122–23.

93. "Le Centre de Réfugiés de Martigny-les-Bains," extract from the *UI*, Aug. 4, 1939, p. 829, AIU, ms. 650, boîte 11 (41).

94. Roche, "Pour une négociation," *La République*, Aug. 3, 1938, p. 1.

95. "La France doit faire un geste de solidarité en faveur des juifs chassés d'Allemagne," *L'Ordre*, Nov. 19, 1938, clipped in AIU, ms. 650, boîte 12 (43).

96. Y. Grosrichard, "Un An après... Les réfugiés autrichiens veulent 'servir' la France," *L'Oeuvre*, clipped in APP BA 269 Provisoire, dossier: "Réfugiés autrichiens, 1938–1939." See also Stéphane Lausanne, "Pour que la tragédie du

'Saint-Louis' ne se reproduise pas: La France ne pourrait-elle installer les juifs réfugiés dans certains de ses territoires d'outre mer?" *Le Matin*, June 11, 1939, p. 1.

97. "Va-t-on ressusciter le projet d'émigration juive aux colonies françaises?" *AF*, Nov. 27, 1938, AIU, ms. 650, boîte 14 (47).

98. Foreign Ministry (Afrique-Levant), "Note pour M. Massigli," June 22, 1938, MAE K Afrique 91 (1936–39), p. 196 (also in MAE SDN I E 453, p. 125).

99. Roosevelt, cited in Kennedy, U.S. ambassador to Great Britain, to Myron Taylor, confidential teleg., 840.48 Refugees/1290B, Jan. 14, 1939, National Archives, Washington, D.C.

100. "Communication from the Director to the Chairman and Vice-Chairmen of the Intergovernmental Committee" [Sept. 1938], and "Communication from the Director to the Chairman of the Intergovernmental Committee" [Sept. 1938], both in Myron Taylor Papers, box 3, folder "Proceedings of the Intergovernmental Committee, Evian, July 6th–15th, 1938, Verbatim Record of the Plenary Meetings," FDR Library; "Excerpt from Mr. Cotton's letter to Mr. Warren," Sept. 30, 1938, Myron Taylor Papers, box 8, folder "PAC," FDR Library; George L. Warren, to Joseph P. Cotton Jr., Sept. 14, 1938, AN AJ^{43} 12 (18/56:1).

101. Saint-Quentin to the Foreign Ministry, no. 1144, Oct. 15, 1938, MAE K Afrique 91 (1936–39), pp. 211–14 (also in MAE SDN I E 450, pp. 129–32); Saint-Quentin, to Ernest Lagarde, Foreign Ministry (Afrique-Levant) Nov. 11, 1938, MAE K Afrique 91, p. 217; Saint-Quentin, to the Foreign Ministry, teleg. no. 1280, Nov. 18, 1938, MAE SDN I M 1818, pp. 66–69.

102. "Large Scale Move by 2 Nations to Resettle Jews Held Urgent," *NYT*, Nov. 15, 1938, pp. 1, 6; "Roosevelt Condemns Nazi Outbreak . . . London Studies Jewish Colonization," *NYT*, Nov. 16, 1938, pp. 1, 9; Ferdinand Kuhn Jr., "World Searched for Havens," *NYT*, Nov. 20, 1938, sec. E, p. 4; "Excerpts from Commons Debate on Refugees: Text of the Statement by Chamberlain," *NYT*, Nov. 22, 1938, p. 8; "Britain Offers Reich Jews Land in Africa and Guiana," *NYT*, Nov. 22, 1938, pp. 1, 9; Ferdinand Kuhn Jr., "Refugee Problem Arouses Britain to Action," *NYT*, Nov. 27, 1938, sec. E, p. 3; Saint-Quentin to the Foreign Ministry, nos. 842–43, Nov. 19, 1938, MAE Z 712, pp. 11–12; Sherman, pp. 187–93.

103. Saint-Quentin, to Foreign Ministry, teleg. no. 1280, Nov. 18, 1938, MAE SDN I M 1818, pp. 66–69; Foreign Ministry, "Note de la sous-direction des Affaires Administratives et des Unions Internationales: Le Comité d'Evian et la question des réfugiés israélites allemands," Nov. 21, 1938, *DDF*, 2ème séries, vol. XIII, doc. no. 348, p. 687 (also in SDN I M 1818, pp. 77–79); "Paris Receives Hitler's Bid, for 'Good-Neighbor' Ties," *NYT*, Nov. 23, 1938, p. 10.

104. Saint-Quentin, to Ernest Lagarde, Foreign Ministry (Afrique-Levant), Nov. 11, 1938, MAE K 91, p. 217.

105. Makins, British Foreign Office, "Draft Memo to M. Strang re: German and Czech refugees for use if these subjects are raised in the conversations with the French," Nov. 23, 1938, PRO FO 371/22537.W15402; "Record of Anglo-French Conversation held at the Quai d'Orsay," Nov. 24, 1938, *DBFP*, series 3, vol. 3, no. 325, p. 295; Ben Elissar, p. 369.

106. Cited in Ben Elissar, p. 400.

107. Cited in ibid., p. 409.

108. Léon Noël, to the Foreign Ministry, Jan. 2, 1939, MAE Z 332, p. 181.

109. Léon Noël, to the Foreign Ministry (Contrôle des étrangers), no. 92, Feb. 6, 1939, MAE Z 332, pp. 191–94. As late as Oct. 1938, Noël and his colleagues were advising the Foreign Ministry that Polish Jews were not being persecuted and that they had no right to claim refugee status. Noël, to the Foreign Ministry (Chancelleries et du Contentieux), no. 121, Oct. 1, 1938; A. Ronflard, French Consul, Warsaw, to the Foreign Ministry (Contrôle des étrangers), Oct. 12, 1938, both in APP BA 407[P] 13.112-4.

110. Léon Noël, to the Foreign Ministry (Afrique-Levant), no. 84, Feb. 7, 1939, MAE K Afrique 91, pp. 243–52. See also Paul Py, Vice Consul, Cracow, to M. Pinoteau, French Consul, Katowicze and Cracow, no. 21, Feb. 24, 1939, MAE Z 332, pp. 199–200.

111. See Chapter 9, n. 103. Although Ben Elissar has dismissed Bonnet's reference to Madagascar as a "gaffe," these prior developments suggest that Bonnet was entirely serious when he told Ribbentrop on Dec. 7 that France was planning to send 10,000 Jews to Madagascar. Ben Elissar, p. 409.

112. George L. Warren (PAC), to Joseph Cotton (ICGR), Oct. 5, 1938, p. 2, AN AJ[43] 12 (18/56:1); Emile C. Bataille, to George L. Warren (PAC), Oct. 10, 1938, AN AJ[43] 12 (18/56:1) (also in Papers of Myron C. Taylor, box 8, file "President's Advisory Committee," FDR Library); George L. Warren, to Th. Achilles, Nov. 1, 1938, AN AJ[43] 12 (18/56:1); George L. Warren, to Myron Taylor, Dec. 25, 1938, AN AJ[43] 12 (18/56:1).

113. George L. Warren (PAC), to Joseph Cotton, ICGR, Oct. 5, 1938, p. 2, AN AJ[43] 12 (18/56:1).

114. George L. Warren, to Myron Taylor, Dec. 25, 1938, AN AJ[43] 12 (18/56:1).

115. Intercomité des Oeuvres Françaises de Réfugiés, Minutes, Jan. 6, 1939, AN 72 AJ 590; JDC, Euroexco Report for Jan. 1939, JDC no. 189; "Notes on Status of Jewish Refugees from Germany and Former Austria in Various Countries of Europe . . . ," July 5, 1939, JDC no. 666; H. Katzki, "Status of Jewish Refugees from Germany in Various European Countries," July 5, 1939, JDC no. 617; Alexis Danan, "Dix juifs allemands vont partir pour la Guyane," *Paris-Soir*, Jan. 20, 1939, clipped in AIU, ms. 650, boîte 13 (46); "En route pour la Guyane française," *Samedi*, Jan. 28, 1939, clipped in AIU, ms. 650, boîte 13 (46); "Pour la Guyane," n. d., clipped in AIU, ms. 650, boîte 13 (45); "Des colons juifs pour la Guyane," *L'Oeuvre*, Feb. 4, 1939, clipped in AIU, ms. 650, boîte 13 (45); J. Biélinky, "Des colons pour la Guyane," *UI*, Feb. 10, 1939, p. 368; J. Biélinky, "La Guyane comme centre de colonisation juive," *La Juste parole*, no. 54 (Apr. 20, 1939): 12–16. On French Jewish responses to these proposals, see Chapter 13.

116. JDC, Euroexco Minutes, Feb. 1, 1939, JDC no. 174, pp. 18–19; [Pell], to George Warren (PAC), Feb. 10, 1939, pp. 2–3, in AN AJ[43] 12 (18/56:2).

117. Kohen, "Entreprise pratique pour l'installation des victimes du racisme dans les colonies," Paris [1937 or 1938], [pamphlet], AIU, ms. 650, boîte 14 (47). For a

biographical note on Kadmi Kohen (sometimes spelled Cohen), see R. I. Cohen, *Burden*, pp. 20–21.

118. Police reports, Paris, "a/s Réunion sur le sujet 'l'installation des israélites dans les colonies françaises,'" Jan. 31, 1939, and Feb. 1, 1939, both in APP BA 1813 241.155-B.

119. Alexis Danan, "Dix juifs allemands vont partir pour la Guyane," *Paris-Soir*, Jan. 20, 1939, clipped in AIU, ms. 650, boîte 13 (46); "En route pour la Guyane française," *Samedi*, Jan. 28, 1939, clipped in AIU, ms. 650, boîte 13 (46); JDC, Euroexco, Report for Jan. 1939, JDC no. 189. On the refugees who left from Chelles, see Jacques Grosbois, "Quittant l'enfer hitlérien ils sont au purgatoire," *DdV*, Feb. 25, 1939, pp. 1, 3.

120. French Minister, Romania, to Foreign Ministry (Contrôle des étrangers), no. 5, Jan. 23, 1939, pp. 262–63; Foreign Ministry (Contrôle des étrangers), to the Minister of Colonies (Direction des Affaires politiques), Feb. 8, 1939, p. 264; Minister of Colonies to Foreign Ministry (Contrôle des étrangers), no. 242, Feb. 1939, p. 265, all in MAE K Afrique 91.

121. JDC, Euroexco, "Introduction and Review of Events in the Month of Mar. 1939," JDC no. 190, p. 85. See also "Memorandum on International Conference of Youth Organizations for Increased Relief to Refugees and Civil War Victims," Mar. 17, 1939, JDC no. 405.

122. Robert J. Stopford, British Legation, Prague, to Herbert Emerson, High Commissioner for Refugees, Feb. 16, 1939, MAE SDN I M 1814, p. 354; Emerson, to P. Arnal, Foreign Ministry, Feb. 23, 1939, MAE SDN I M 1814, p. 353.

123. Herbert Katzki, Confidential, "Notes on Status of Jewish Refugees from Germany and Former Austria in Various Countries of Europe . . . ," July 5, 1939, JDC no. 666; JDC, Euroexco, "Report for June 1939, Day-by-Day Press Record," June 20, 1939, JDC no. 191, p. 99.

124. Intercommittee for the Work of Assistance for Refugees in France, "The Situation of the Refugees in France," [Aug.–Sept. 1939], JDC no. 617.

125. "France Plans Refugee Settlements in Africa," *The Sentinel*, July 18, 1939, clipped in AIU, ms. 650, boîte 14 (47). In yet another move, the press reported in Aug. that U.S. Congressman Hamilton Fish had come to France to discuss with Bonnet and Mandel the possibility of creating an autonomous Jewish state in Africa, and that Mandel had agreed to appoint a commission to study this proposal. This project was to be financed with private American funds and was to encompass the area south of Lake Chad, part of British Nigeria, and part of the former German Cameroun. *NYT*, Aug. 11, 1939, p. 4; "Le Projet de la création en Afrique d'un état pour les réfugiés," *Journal des débats*, Aug. 12, 1939, clipped in AIU, ms. 650, boîte 14 (47).

126. "Traite de blancs en 1939," *Je suis partout*, Aug. 18, 1939, clipped in AIU, ms. 650, boîte 13 (46). See also M. A. L., "Un de nos correspondents guyanais de Paris nous écrit," *Le Petit Guyannais*, July 8, 1939, clipped in AIU, Ms. 650, boîte 11 (40).

127. Pierre Dominique, "Les Etrangers peuvent nous donner une armée," *La République*, Feb. 1, 1939, pp. 1, 3. See also Dominique, "Les Prendra-t-on ces

étrangers qui veulent être français?" Feb. 5, 1939, pp. 1, 3, and "Est-il vrai que 750000 étrangers veulent devenir français?" Feb. 18, 1939, p. 1, all in *La République*.

128. Dominique, "La Mystique de la grandeur par la puissance du nombre," *La République*, May 3, 1939, clipped in AIU, ms. 650, boîte 14 (48). See also Pierre La-haspe, "Les Réfugiés au service de l'agriculture; l'agriculture au secours des réfugiés," *La Lumière*, May 19, 1939, p. 2, clipped in AIU, ms. 650, boîte 14 (48); Maurice Violette, "Le Problème des réfugiés espagnols et celui des étrangers," *Ce Soir*, Apr. 4, 1939, clipped in AIU, ms. 650 boîte 13(45); Raymond Millet, "La Situation nouvelle des étrangers en France," *L'Europe nouvelle*, May 13, 1939, pp. 514–15.

129. Pierre Dominique, "Les Etrangers peuvent nous donner une armée," *La République*, Feb. 1, 1939, pp. 1, 3.

130. "Impressions de la Chambre des députés," no. 5317, session de 1939, cited in Schramm and Vormeier, pp. 238–39. See also Szajkowski, *Jews*, p. 57. In May of 1939, however, the Union Nationale des Officiers Anciens Combattants voted in favor of a resolution denouncing the presence of "une foule d'étrangers indésirables est dangereuse" and claiming that "le devoir d'asile ne peut incomber à la France seule, sous peine de la voir devenir le dépotoir de l'Europe." They therefore requested the government to send back the Spanish republicans as quickly as possible. Crémieux-Brilhac, 1: 479.

131. See Chapter 1, n. 12.

132. *JO, Lois et Décrets*, Apr. 16, 1938, pp. 4910–11; "Conférence interministérielle relative au régime des étrangers," *Le Matin*, Apr. 14, 1939, p. 2; "Le Statut des étrangers résident en France," *Le Matin*, Apr. 16, 1939, p. 1; "Le Statut des étrangers," *Le Temps*, Apr. 18, 1939, p. 1; "Une Conférence ministérielle a fixé le statut des étrangers," *Le Figaro*, Apr. 14, 1939, p. 1; Tartakower and Grossmann, pp. 142–44; "Les Décrets-lois sur les étrangers," *Le Populaire*, Apr. 17, 1939, p. 5; Bothereau, "Les Devoirs et les droits des étrangers en France," *Le Peuple*, Apr. 22, 1939, pp. 1, 3; Schramm and Vormeier, pp. 239–40. For an official explanation of who was considered to have the right of asylum, see minister of the interior, to the prefects, circulaire no. 423, Feb. 7, 1940, AN F[7] 14662.

133. *JO, Lois et Décrets*, July 22, 1939; Gourevitch, pp. 2–5; Schramm and Vormeier, p. 241; Vormeier, "La Situation des émigrés," p. 158; "Migration Conference, AJDC-HICEM, Paris," Aug. 22–23, 1939, JDC no. 367; Tartakower and Grossmann, p. 144; "Le Statut des réfugiés," *UI*, no. 46 (Aug. 4, 1939): 822; Sarraut, minister of the interior, "Instructions concernant le dénombrement des étrangers sans nationalité et autres étrangers bénéficiaires du droit d'asile—application du décret du 20 juillet 1939," Aug. 4, 1939, AN F[7] 14662; "La Situation des étrangers en France," *L'Oeuvre*, Aug. 25, 1939, p. 2; "Les Etrangers et les événements actuels," *Le Peuple*, Sept. 1, 1939, p. 2.

134. Cited in "Anti-juif et anti-français," *Affirmation*, Apr. 14, 1939, p. 5. See also "L'Interprétation de la presse fasciste sur l'utilisation militaire des étrangers résidant en France," *La Dépêche de Toulouse*, July 24, 1939, cited in Schramm and Vormeier, p. 240, n. 16.

135. "Pour utiliser les réfugiés étrangers," *AF*, May 17, 1939, clipped in AIU, ms. 650, boîte 13.

136. "Le Statut des étrangers résidant en France," *Le Matin*, Apr. 16, 1939, p. 1. See also "Le Statut des étrangers" (editorial), *Le Temps*, Apr. 18, 1939, p. 1.

137. M. Sande, "Un Peu de logique et d'humanité!" *Le Populaire*, Apr. 17, 1939, p. 5. See also Jacques Martel, "Il faut réviser le régime actuel," *Fraternité*, no. 35 (May 20, 1939): 1, clipped in AIU, ms. 650, boîte 11 (42); Andrée Jack, "Enfin, un statut pour les étrangers!" *DdV*, Apr. 22, 1939, pp. 1, 3; Paul Perrin, "Le Droit d'asile," *Le Peuple*, July 3, 1939, p. 5.

138. CDV, bulletin no. 78, Feb. 10, 1939, pp. 5–6, Documents of French Jewry, JTS, box 12, folder 1. For the figure of 15,000, see "Auslander sollen dienen," *PT*, Mar. 11, 1939, p. 3; Police report, Paris, Apr. 20, 1939, APP BA 1812 79.501-882-C.

139. "Le Statut des réfugiés," *UI*, no. 46 (Aug. 4, 1939): 822. See also Lambert, "Dépopulation et xénophobie," *UI*, Apr. 14, 1939, p. 521.

140. "Une Solution," *Samedi*, Mar. 11, 1939, pp. 1–2.

141. R. de Saint-Pourçain, "Les Solutions industrielles," *Esprit*, July 1, 1939, pp. 638–39; "Les Réfugiés, main-d'oeuvre de complément," *La Juste parole*," no. 60 (July 20, 1939): 20–21. See also "General Review of Events During the Month of April," May 16, 1939, in JDC, Euroexco Report for Apr. 1939, JDC no. 190; "Comité des réfugiés et son oeuvre (janvier–septembre 1939)," [pamphlet], (Paris [1939]), p. 13. For a recent discussion of Britain's efforts to attract refugee industrialists, see Carsten, pp. 17–18; and especially Loebl, pp. 219–49.

142. "Décret tendant à favoriser l'établissement en France d'industries d'intérêt national," *JO, Lois et Décrets*, Apr. 22, 1939, p. 5237, mimeograph extract in APP DA 783 (Règlements); Gourevitch, pp. 110–11.

143. "Emigranten, die Frankreich sucht," *PT*, no. 986 (May 3, 1939): 2.

144. Saint-Pourçain, p. 639.

145. Ibid., p. 638.

146. "Erwünschte Emigranten," *PT*, no. 979 (Apr. 25, 1939): 1.

147. *JO, Lois et Décrets*, Feb. 24, 1939, p. 2550; J.-Ch. Bonnet, p. 240; Simpson, *Refugees: A Review*, p. 50; "Le Comité de la Population," *Le Temps*, Mar. 3, 1939, p. 1; "L'Immigration et la naturalisation des étrangers vont être sévèrement réglementées," *L'Epoque*, Mar. 3, 1939, p. 7; "Le Projet de loi sur le régime des naturalisations," *Le Matin*, Mar. 3, 1939, p. 6; "Le Plan de M. Marchandeau sur la naturalisation," *L'Oeuvre*, Mar. 3, 1939, p. 4; "Le Règlement de l'immigration et de la naturalisation des étrangers," *Excelsior*, Mar. 3, 1939, clipped in BDIC, Dos. Duchêne, GF△ Rés. 86.

148. The other refugees from the Saint-Louis were distributed among Belgium, Holland, and England. Of the 224 refugees who came to France, 162 were scheduled to depart for the United States and the rest were to go to various provincial centers. See J. C. Harsch (London IGCR), to Pierrepont Moffat, U.S. State Dept., June 26, 1939, AN AJ^{43} 36 (40/84); "L'Accueil des réfugiés en France," *UI*, July 6, 1939, pp. 753–55; Bauer, *My Brother's Keeper*, pp. 278–81, 288–89; Weiss, pp. 242–48; Ben Elissar, pp. 447–52; Moch, p. 28; H.-F. Potecher, "Cinquante juifs du 'Saint-Louis' sont arrivés à Paris ce matin," *Paris-Soir*, June 27, 1939, clipped in BDIC, Dos. Duchêne, F△ Rés. 329/2; R. du Chastaignt, "Ils se rendent à Poitiers...," *Ce Soir*, June 17, 1939, clipped in BDIC, Dos. Duchêne, F△ Rés. 329/2; "224 réfugiés allemands israélites ont débarqué à Boulogne," *Le Matin*, June 21, 1939, pp. 1–2; J. C.

Hyman, "Dumped Emigration," JDC bulletin, July 1939, clipped in JDC no. 666; *CDH*, July 15, 1939, p. 442; "Refuge Is Assured for All on Liner," *NYT*, June 14, 1939, p. 11; "St. Louis Emigrés Head for Antwerp," *NYT*, June 15, 1939, p. 14; "Refugees Reach France," *NYT*, June 29, 1939, p. 11; "Un Accord international en faveur des réfugiés juifs du 'St. Louis,'" *Le Populaire*, June 14, 1939, clipped in APP BA 1814 241.155-1-A; "Paris," *Le Populaire*, June 27, 1939, p. 14.

149. J. C. Harsch (London IGCR), to Pierrepont Moffat, U.S. State Dept., June 26, 1939, AN AJ^{43} 36 (40/84); D. P. Reilly, British Foreign Office, to J. C. Harsch, June 16, 1939, AN AJ^{43} 36 (40/84).

150. "Refugees to Bolivia Set at 250 Monthly," *NYT*, June 27, 1939, p. 14; JDC, Euroexco, "June Report, 1939," June 20, 1939, JDC no. 191, pp. 41–44; "Cinquante juifs du 'Saint-Louis' sont arrivés à Paris ce matin," *Paris-Soir*, June 27, 1939, clipped in BDIC, Dos. Duchêne, FΔ Rés. 329/2; "Ils se rendent à Poitiers où ils séjourneront en attendant de reçevoir l'autorisation d'aller s'établir aux Etats-Unis," *Ce Soir*, June 17, 1939, clipped in BDIC, Dos. Duchêne, FΔ Rés. 329/2; "224 réfugiés du St.-Louis débarquent à Boulogne sur-mer," *Le Peuple*, June 21, 1939, p. 1; "Dans un petit hôtel de la gare du Nord avec huit réfugiés du 'St.-Louis,'" *L'Oeuvre*, June 27, 1939, p. 5.

151. On the S.S. *Flandre*, see [Raymond-Raoul Lambert], "L'Accueil des réfugiés en France," *UI*, no. 42 (July 6, 1939): 753–55; "500 Refugees on Way to Temporary Homes," *NYT*, June 20, 1939, p. 6; "Activité de la HIAS-JCA Emigration Association (HICEM) du 1 janvier au 30 mai, 1939," p. 5, AN AJ^{43} 14 (13/56); JDC, Euroexco, "June Report, 1939," June 20, 1939, JDC no. 191, pp. 41–44; "Les Réfugiés du 'Flandre,'" *L'Oeuvre*, June 17, 1939, p. 1.

In addition to the *Saint-Louis* and the *Flandre*, there were several less sensational incidents in which France also accepted some stranded refugees temporarily. See George Warren (PAC), to Robert T. Pell, Vice Director of the IGCR, Mar. 30, 1939, AN AJ^{43} 12 (18/56:2); "Quinze émigrés débarquent du 'Cap Norte,'" *L'Oeuvre*, June 27, 1939, p. 5.

152. Weiss, pp. 242–43; [Raymond-Raoul Lambert], "L'Accueil des réfugiés en France," *UI*, no. 42, July 6, 1939, p. 753.

153. *JO, Lois et Décrets*, Apr. 16, 1939, p. 4911, and Apr. 25, 1939, p. 5296; "Le Nouveau statut des étrangers en France," *Le Temps*, Apr. 18, 1939, p. 2; "Les Décrets-lois sur les étrangers," *Le Populaire*, Apr. 17, 1939, p. 5; Andrée Jack, "Enfin, un statut pour les étrangers!" *DdV*, Apr. 22, 1939, pp. 1, 3; "Le Statut des étrangers," *Le Temps*, Apr. 18, 1939, p. 1; Schramm and Vormeier, pp. 241–42. A Ministry of the Interior list of July 3, 1939, shows that this law was aimed exclusively at far-right-wing organizations. Berthoin, Secretary, minister of the interior, to the prefects, circular, July 3, 1939, AN F^{E} 14711.

154. *JO, Lois et Décrets*, Apr. 25, 1939, p. 5295; JDC, "General Review of Events During the Month of April," May 16, 1939, JDC no. 164; "Le Décret sur la propagande raciste est signé," *L'Oeuvre*, Apr. 25, 1939, p. 1. It appears that this law was due, at least in part, to the lobbying of the CDV and the LICA. On the role of the CDV, see unsigned letter to President of the Central Consistory, Oct. 9, 1938, AIU France V D 18; Georges Schmoll, President, Consistory, Bas-Rhin, and Chief Rabbi Isaïe

Schwartz, Bas-Rhin, to the Central Consistory, Sept. 22, 1938, AIU, ms. 650, boîte 6, dossier 14 (Alsace-Lorraine); Henri Bender, "Vice President pour le Comité de Direction" [of the CDV], to General Alphonse Weiller, President of the USI [or USJ] (Union et Sauvegarde israélites [or juives]), Oct. 8, 1938, AIU, ms. 650, boîte 7 (31); Robert Schumann, to Jacques Helbronner, Oct. 6, 1938, AIU, ms. 650, boîte 7 (31); [CDV], to M. Edmond Israel, Nov. 4, 1938, AIU, ms. 650, boîte 6 (15). According to a 1981 report on the CDV drawn up by Georges Weill and Blandine Busson based on documentation in the AIU Archives: "Le Comité de Vigilance confia à un groupe de juristes composé de Me. Dorville, Edgar Sée et Paul David, le soin de préparer la base des motifs du décret-loi du 21 avril 1939 (*JO* du 25 avril)." Georges Weill and Blandine Busson, "Notes sur le CDV: Les Comités de Vigilance et de Coordination," Dec. 23, 1981, AIU, ms. 650, boîte 1, chemise "CDV." On the role of the LICA, see Landau, pp. 197, 279.

155. On the Gourevitch Committee's petitions to the French government protesting the decree laws, see *JTA Bulletin*, May 29, 1938, AIU, ms. 650, boîte 13 (49); Comité pour la Défense des Droits, to Daladier, May 15, 1938, MAE SDN I E 453, pp. 102–15; Gourevitch, pp. 20–41; "M. Edouard Daladier reçoit une délégation du Comité de Défense des droits des israélites...," *JTA Bulletin*, Nov. 25, 1938, pp. 2–3, AIU, ms. 650, boîte 11 (41); "Le Problème des réfugiés," *UI*, Dec. 2, 1938, p. 169; "Le Problème des réfugiés: M. Daladier reçoit une délégation du Comité de Défense des droits des juifs," *Samedi*, no. 35 (Dec. 3, 1938): 1; J. Biélinky, "Oui, nous voulons empêcher les progrès du barbare!...," *Affirmation*, Jan. 20, 1939, p. 5; "Eine Demarche," *PT*, no. 874 (Dec. 23, 1938): 2.

On the protests of the LICA, see Henri Levin, "Droit d'Asile," *DdV*, Apr. 30, 1938, p. 4; M. Salembier, "Droit d'Asile," *DdV*, June 11, 1938, p. 1; Police report, Paris, "a/s IXème Congrès National de la Lica, 27 novembre 1938," Nov. 28, 1938, APP BA 1812 79.501-882-C; "Conseil extraordinaire de la LICA," *DdV*, Apr. 8, 1939, p. 4; Thalmann, "L'Emigration allemande," p. 65.

156. See Chapter 13 for a detailed discussion of the French Jewish response.

157. On the protests of the Centre de Liaison des Immigrés, see [Henri Levin], General Secretary, Centre de Liaison, "Lettre à M. le Président Sarraut," "Notre délégation," "Memorandum remis à M. le Ministre de l'Intérieur," all in *Fraternité*, May 20, 1939, p. 3, clipped in AIU, ms. 650, boîte 11 (42); "Une Délégation du Centre de Liaison des Immigrés reçue par M. Albert Sarraut," *L'Humanité*, May 18, 1939, clipped in AIU, ms. 650, boîte 13 (45); Philippe Lamour [Centre de Liaison], "Pour un statut des étrangers," *Messidor*, May 19, 1939, clipped in AIU, ms. 650, boite 13 (45); "Pour un statut des étrangers," *Messidor*, no. 64 (June 2, 1939): 8; Levin.

158. Pierre-Bloch, "Le Statut des étrangers et la défense nationale," *Fraternité*, May 20, 1939, p. 1, AIU, ms. 650, boîte 11 (42).

159. J. Biélinky, "Un Meeting à la Mutalité," *UI*, no. 35 (May 19, 1939): 627. See also "Ce soir, meeting à la Mutalité sur les étrangers et la France," *L'Oeuvre*, May 9, 1939, p. 4; "Les Etrangers et la France," *Le Peuple*, May 9, 1939, p. 5; Report, "Meeting tenu sous la Présidence de M. Paul-Boncour sur les étrangers et la France," May 9, 1939, clipped in AIU, ms. 650, boîte 13 (45); Stefan Fingal, "Frankreich und

die Fremden," *PT*, no. 993 (May 11, 1939): 2; "Les Amis de la République Française," *Samedi*, no. 18 (May 27, 1939): 6.

Participants at this rally included: Jean Painlevé, the general secretary of the association; Jean-Paul Boncour; Henry Torrès; Léo Lagrange; Gabriel Cudenet of the League for the Rights of Man and Citizen; Louis Jacquinot, a deputy and president of the executive committee of the Amis; Louis Rollin, a deputy; Robert Lange; General Alphonse Weiller; Jean Perrin; Henri Pichot; P.-O. Lapie, a deputy; G. Lechevallier-Chevignard; Mme. Maleterre-Sellier; General Armengaud; Gabriel Delattre, a deputy; Paul Perrin; Reverend Père Riquet, a delegate of Cardinal Verdier; Louise Weiss; Ernest Pezet, rapporteur of the Foreign Affairs Commission of the Chamber of Deputies; Yvon Delbos, former minister; Moro Giafferi; and F. de Clermont-Tonnere.

160. "L'Action de M. Louis Rollin en faveur des réfugiés," *La Juste parole*, no. 51 (Mar. 5, 1939): 31; J. Biélinky, "L'Action de M. Louis Rollin en faveur des réfugiés," *Affirmation*, no. 6 (Feb. 17, 1939): 1; Lambert, introduction to Pierre-Bloch, "La Détresse des réfugiés," *UI*, no. 25 (Mar. 10, 1939): 444; "Au Comité central des réfugiés présidé par M. Georges Bonnet," *UI*, May 5, 1939, p. 584.

161. "Amnistie pour les réfugiés," *UI*, May 19, 1939, p. 627; translation of "Police des réfugiés," *Pariser Haynt*, May 16, 1939, AIU, ms. 650, boîte 18 (60); Report of the Comité d'Entente des Oeuvres de Réfugiés en France [Intercommittee], June 23, 1939, AN 72 AJ 590.

162. Comité d'Entente des Oeuvres de Réfugiés en France [Intercommittee], Report of June 23, 1939, AN 72 AJ 590.

163. Lambert, introduction to Pierre-Bloch, "La Détresse des réfugiés," *UI*, no. 25 (Mar. 10, 1939): 444.

164. J. Biélinky, "L'Action de M. Louis Rollin en faveur des réfugiés," *Affirmation*, no. 6 (Feb. 17, 1939): 1; "L'Action de M. Louis Rollin en faveur des réfugiés," *La Juste parole*, no. 51 (Mar. 5, 1939): 31. For Rollin's petition, see n. 48 above.

165. "Au Comité central des réfugiés présidé par M. Georges Bonnet," *UI*, May 5, 1939, p. 584.

166. For the text of this debate, see *JO, Débats Parlementaires, Chambre de Députés*, June 8, 1939, pp. 1524–27; Gourevitch, pp. 85–93; J.-Ch. Bonnet, p. 346; Maga, *America*, p. 134; Maga, "Closing," pp. 438–39; Y. Grosrichard, "L'Amnistie devant la Chambre," *L'Oeuvre*, June 9, 1939, p. 4.

167. *JO, Débats Parlementaires, Chambre des Députés*, June 8, 1939, p. 1526. See also Gourevitch, p. 85; R. Cahen-Molina, "Pour une mesure de clémence en faveur des réfugiés politiques," *UI*, no. 41, June 30, 1939, p. 738.

168. Gourevitch, pp. 112–13; "Review of M. R. Cahen-Molina's, 'Le Monstrueux statut des étrangers...,'" *Affirmation*, Aug. 18, 1939, p. 9; Rémy Sicard, "Les Etrangers en France," *Le Populaire*, July 12, 1939, pp. 1–2; Maga, "Closing," p. 439; R. Schor, "L'Opinion française et les réfugiés," in Institut d'Histoire 1: 17, n. 41. The decision to grant suspended sentences was left to the individual judge.

169. In 1939, the JDC did allocate this money for agricultural settlements. See JDC, Euroexco Minutes, Mar. 5, 1939, JDC no. 174; JDC, "Estimated Budget— May 1939," Apr. 28, 1939, JDC no. 111.

170. Italics in original text. Sarraut, to Rothschild, President de Groupement de Coordination, July 16, 1939 (transcribed by M. Moch, Oct. 2, 1964), AIU, ms. 650, boîte 14 (49) (also in AN 72 AJ 590).

171. On this point, see also "Deux projets constructifs," *L'Accueil français aux autrichiens*, 1er année, no. 2, (Jan. 1939): 3, clipped in AIU, ms. 650, boîte 11 (42); CIRP, memo, [n.d.], AIU, ms. 650, boîte 13 (46).

172. Intercommittee for the Work of Assistance for Refugees in France, "The Situation of the Refugees in France," [Aug.–Sept. 1939], JDC no. 617.

173. Minutes, JDC, "Migration Conference, AJDC-HICEM, Paris, Aug. 22–23, 1939," JDC no. 367, pp. 151–53. See also Intercommittee for the Work of Assistance for Refugees in France, "The Situation of the Refugees in France," [Aug.–Sept. 1939], JDC no. 617.

174. JDC, Euroexco, "June Report 1939," June 20, 1939, JDC no. 191, pp. 41–44.

175. CAR, Séance, Conseil d'administration, May 30, 1939, JDC no. 604.

176. JDC, Euroexco, "Report on the Situation in France, June, 1939," June 20, 1939, JDC no. 191, pp. 41–44.

177. JDC, Euroexco, "Report on the Situation in France, June, 1939," June 20, 1939, JDC no. 191, pp. 41–44.

178. Lambert, "Special Note on the Subject of Polish Immigrants," in Lambert, "Note on the situation of strangers set at liberty after being condemned for administrative infringements," Mar. 10, 1939, attached to Morris Troper's report to JDC, Feb. 28, 1939, JDC no. 617.

179. Weiss, p. 237.

180. "Emigranten-Betriebe, die in Frankreich erwunscht sind," *PT*, no. 1083 (Aug. 25, 1939): 3.

181. See Chapter 9, n. 29. See also Madeleine Jacob, "Grandeur et misère des déracinés," *Messidor*, no. 60 (May 5, 1939): 8–9.

182. Foreign Ministry (SDN), to the minister of colonies, no. 1586, Dec. 24, 1938; minister of colonies, to the Foreign Ministry (SDN), Dec. 29, 1938, both in MAE SDN I G (Danzig) 644, pp. 143–47, 150.

183. M. Sande, "Un Peu de logique et d'humanité!" *Le Populaire*, Apr. 17, 1939, p. 5. On the denial of gas masks to foreigners, see also Koestler, *Scum*, p. 156.

184. "Autour des enrôlements d'étrangers," *Le Petit Parisien*, Apr. 19, 1939, p. 5. See also "Les Etrangers et la France: Une délégation des Amis de la République Française chez M. Albert Sarraut," *Le Petit Parisien*, May 11, 1939, p. 2; Paul Delon, "Si la démocratie française était en danger, les immigrés repondraient à son appel," *L'Humanité*, Apr. 16, 1939; Tartakower and Grossmann, pp. 144–45.

185. B. Pierlouis, "Les Etrangers en France," *Le Peuple*, June 21, 1939, pp. 1–2. See also Jacques Martel, "Il faut réviser le régime actuel," *Fraternité*, no. 35 (May 20, 1939): 1, clipped in AIU, ms. 650, boîte 11 (42); "Les Etrangers et les événements actuels," *Le Peuple*, Sept. 1, 1939, pp. 1–2.

186. Gourevitch, pp. 43–44.

187. Firmin Bacconnier, "Union des corporations françaises: Les étrangers dans notre vie professionnelle," *AF*, Jan. 8, 1939, clipped in AN 72 AJ 603.

188. "Extrait des déliberations du Conseil Général [du Bas-Rhin]," Session d'automne, Séance du 14 novembre 1938, ADBR D 460, paq. 5 (34).

189. It was also recommended that the fees for registering a name change be raised from 3,000 frs. to 20,000 frs. "Les Naturalisations hâtives de commerçants immigrés," *Le Temps*, Feb. 3, 1939, clipped in BDIC, Dos. Duchêne GFΔ Rés. 86. On the xenophobia of the Metz Chamber of Commerce in 1938–39, see also "Les Démandes de naturalisation: Voeux des chambres de commerce de Paris et de Metz," *Le Matin*, July 9, 1938, clipped in AIU, ms. 650, boîte 13 (46); "Une Attaque réactionnaire du Conseil général de Metz," *Fraternité*, Dec. 1938, in AIU, ms. 650, boîte 14 (1939).

190. This measure was ultimately passed in the Senate, but defeated in the Chamber. "La Commission de législation civile de la Chambre a adopté hier le rapport de M. Mallarmé concernant les changements de nom," *Excelsior*, Dec. 30, 1938, BDIC, Dos. Duchêne GFΔ Rés. 86.

191. "A Propos du régime des naturalisations," *Le Nouvelliste de Lyon*, June 23, 1939, clipped in AIU, ms. 650, boîte 14 (48). See also "La Naturalisation des étrangers et le Conseil municipal," *Le Nouvelliste de Lyon*, Feb. 23, 1939, clipped in AIU, ms. 650, boîte 13.

192. Charles Maurras, "L'Intérieur à défendre: Ni Juifs, ni Allemands," *AF*, Jan. 8, 1939, clipped in AN 72 AJ 602. See also "Discours prononcé par le Dr. Choyau, …au banquet du 17 décembre 1938, présidé par M. le Ministre du Travail," Mar. 15, 1939, in *Le Médecin de France* 49 (Jan.–May 1939): 286.

193. "Les Médecins de la Seine et l'invasion dans leur profession des médecins de nationalité étrangère," *Le Petit Parisien*, July 6, 1939, p. 2; "Les Etrangers agrégés de médecine ne pourront professer en France," *L'Epoque*, July 8, 1939, p. 4; "L'Admission des étrangers aux épreuves du concours d'agrégations des Facultés de Médecine," *L'Oeuvre*, July 8, 1939, p. 4; "Les Etrangers et le concours d'agrégation de médecine," *Le Temps*, July 8, 1939, p. 8.

194. The journalist, Paul Lenglois, for example wrote: "Ici, les Chambres de Commerce ont agi comme si elles étaient vraiment dans des pays totalitaires.… Pour les Chambres de Commerce et pour les auteurs du décret-lois …un commerçant d'un autre pays que le nôtre est une crapule! C'est simple." "La Chasse à l'homme sans défense," *La Justice*, May 31, 1939, clipped in AIU, ms. 650, boîte 14 (48).

195. Minister of the interior, Sûreté Nationale, to the prefect, Bas-Rhin, no. 9364, Aug. 8, 1938, ADBR D 460, paq. 5 (36); prefect, Bas-Rhin, to the minister of the interior, Sûreté Nationale, 7ème Bureau, no. 2646, Oct. 21, 1938, ADBR D 460, paq. 5/36.

196. "Une Proposition de loi de M. Schuman," *Excelsior*, Oct. 30, 1938, clipped in AN 72 AJ 601 (also in CDV, bulletin no. 73, Nov. 3, 1938, pp. 10–11, Documents of French Jewish History, JTS, box 12, folder 1). These proposals had the support of many representatives from the frontier provinces, such as the deputies from the Moselle, Jean-Arthur Heid and Emile Béron, and the deputy of the Vosges, Paul Elbel. See *JO, Débats Parlementaires, Chambre de Députés*, Dec. 18, 1938, pp. 1890–91; Elbel, "Mise au point," *L'Oeuvre*, Nov. 8, 1938, pp. 1, 4. See also Marrus and Paxton, p. 50, Marrus, "Vichy before Vichy," p. 18.

197. Italics in original text. Prefect of the Moselle, to the keeper of the seals, minister of justice [and to the Ministry of the Interior), confidential report, Jan. 12, 1939, ADBR AL 98 392 A.

198. *JO, Documents Parlementaires, Chambre de Députés*, annexe no. 4422, Dec. 8, 1938, p. 58. See also J.-Ch. Bonnet, p. 233.

199. "Pour que les commerçants étrangers ne puissent pas changer leur nom," *Le Journal*, Mar. 14, 1939, clipped in BDIC, Dos. Duchêne, GFΔ Rés. 86. For other examples of politicians supporting middle-class protection, see François Delcos's speech in Parliament on Mar. 14, 1939. Although this debate was initially sparked by the Spanish refugee problem, it soon focused on Central and East European refugees and the "ruinous competition" they posed to the French middle classes. *JO, Débats Parlementaires, Chambre des Députés*, 2ème séance, Mar. 14, 1939, pp. 943–59.

200. While serving as minister of commerce in 1935, Marchandeau had reiterated the 1933 restrictions imposed on the creation of refugee-owned businesses. Despite the fact that "les autorités locales sont souvent enclinées à donner des avis favorables à l'établissement d'entreprises nouvelles, même étrangères, espérant ainsi diminuer le chômage dans leur région et y susciter de nouvelles transactions," he believed that such activity was harmful in the long run. As he declared, "les cas seront, en effet, très rares ou il s'agira d'introduire sur le sol français une industrie entièrement nouvelle et qui serait de nature à procurer un gain au pays sans contrepartie désavantageuse." Marchandeau, to the prefects, Jan., 14, 1935, APP DA 783 (Textes). See also Albert Ch.-Morice, "Les Etrangers chez nous: Manque de crédits, manque d'effectifs, manque de textes légaux," *Le Journal*, Nov. 5, 1934, clipped in APP BA 66 Provisoire; "Une Solution," *Samedi*, Mar. 11, 1939, pp. 1–2.

201. Cited in Secretary-General of the Confédération des Syndicats Médicaux Français, speech of Feb. 15, 1939, in *Le Médecin de France* 49 (Jan.–May 1939): 209. See also Evleth, p. 99.

202. "Réunion Interministérielle du 25 octobre 1938, tenue à l'Hôtel Matignon, sous la présidence de M. Chautemps, Vice Président du Conseil," MAE SDN I M 1814, p. 241.

203. Charvériat, Direction des affaires politiques et commerciales et des affaires concernant la Société des Nations, Foreign Ministry, "Observations sur le problème des naturalisations," Apr. 3, 1939, MAE SDN I M 1819, p. 358.

Chapter Eleven

1. Cited in Michael R. Marrus, "Introduction," in Anna C. Bramwell, ed., *Refugees in the Age of Total War* (London, 1988), p. 6.

2. As early as Dec. 29, 1937, Rudolf Breitscheid expressed the fear that "tous les réfugiés allemands seront, en cas de conflit, envoyés dans des camps de concentration." Cited in Thalmann, "L'Emigration allemande," p. 57.

3. Police report, "L'Emigration en face de la perspective d'une guerre européenne," Feb., 1939, APP BA Provisoire 407, dos. 13.112-4.

4. Police report, Apr. 20, 1939, APP BA 1812, 79.501-882-C; "Autour des enrôlements d'étrangers," *Le Petit Parisien*, Apr. 19, 1939, p. 5. See also "Les Etrangers et la

France: Une délégation des Amis de la République française chez M. Albert Sarraut," *Le Petit Parisien*, May 11, 1939, p. 2; Paul Delon, "Si la démocratie française était en danger, les immigrés repondraient à son appel," *L'Humanité*, Apr. 16, 1939; Tartakower and Grossmann, pp. 144–45.

5. "Pour les étrangers amis de la France," *L'Oeuvre*, Sept. 6, 1939, p. 4.

6. "L'Enrôlement des volontaires étrangers est entré dans sa phase de réalisation," *L'Epoque*, Sept. 11, 1939, p. 4; "Des Etrangers appartenant à 55 nationalités offrent leurs services à la France," *L'Epoque*, Sept. 17, 1939, p. 3; "Pour les étrangers amis de la France," *L'Oeuvre*, Sept. 6, 1939, p. 4; "L'Enrôlement des étrangers," *L'Oeuvre*, Sept. 11, 1939, p. 5; "Les Etrangers résidant en France se mettent au service du pays," *Le Populaire*, Sept. 2, 1939, p. 2; "30,000 Aliens Aid France: Foreigners from 55 Nations Ask for War Duties," *NYT*, Mar. 5, 1940, p. 5; Fabian and Coulmas, p. 67; Szajkowski, *Jews*, p. 60; Lania, p. 10; Lazareff, p. 249.

7. "Appel des étrangers vivant sur le sol français," *Le Populaire*, Aug. 30, 1939, p. 4. For statements of other émigré organizations, see "Un Vibrant appel des organisations des étrangers vivant en France," *L'Epoque*, Aug. 30, 1939, pp. 1, 5; "Le Loyalisme des émigrés," *L'Oeuvre*, Aug. 30, 1939, p. 5; "Les Etrangers et les événements actuels," *Le Peuple*, Sept. 1, 1939, pp. 1–2. For statements of Jewish immigrant organizations, see "France: Les Juifs immigrés au service de la France," *UI*, May 5, 1939, p. 595, clipped in AIU, ms. 650, boîte 13 (46); "Les Immigrés aux côtés de la France," *Le Populaire*, Aug. 29, 1939, p. 3; "Le Loyalisme des immigrés," *L'Oeuvre*, Aug. 29, 1939, p. 7; J. Biélinky, "L'Immigration juive en France," *La Juste parole*, no. 63 (Dec. 1, 1939): 7–9.

8. Lania, p. 9.

9. President of the Council, Ministry of National Defense and War, circular no. 464, Sept. 8, 1939, SHAT 7N 2475, dos. 3.

10. This decree was issued on Sept. 1, 1939, and appeared in the *JO* on Sept. 4. See *JO, Lois et Décrets*, 1939, pp. 11091–94; Schramm and Vormeier, pp. 244–47; Vormeier, "La Situation des émigrés," pp. 155, 159; Vormeier, "La Situation des réfugiés," pp. 88–89; "Le Premier camp de concentration pour les ressortissants allemands est crée," *L'Oeuvre*, Sept. 7, 1939, p. 6; "L'Internement des sujets allemands," *L'Oeuvre*, Sept. 18, 1939, p. 4; Hans Escher, "Avec les réfugiés ex-autrichiens dans les camps: Du Stade de Colombes à Meslay-du-Maine (septembre 1939–mai 1940)," *Archives juives*, no. 1 (1982): 9–18; Walter, "Internierung," p. 285; Peterson, p. 241; Schapiro, p. 137; Kempner, pp. 449–50; Fabian and Coulmas, p. 67; Pfoser-Schewig, pp. 5–6; Schiller et al., p. 382; "Appendix no. 20," Sept. 3, 1939, JDC no. 617.

11. Cable, Morris Troper (Amsterdam), to JDC, N.Y., Oct. 9, 1939, JDC no. 617; Lania, pp. 93–96, 99; Schapiro, p. 137; Feuchtwanger, p. 77.

12. Edith Peters, "German Exiles Interned," *NYT*, Dec. 3, 1939, sec. IV, p. 9.

13. On conditions at the Colombes Stadium, see Magdeleine Paz, "Aux portes du camp de rassemblement des sujets allemands et autrichiens," *Le Populaire*, Sept. 12, 1939, pp. 1, 3; Schramm and Vormeier, pp. 248–49; Palmier, 2: pp. 119–20; Joly et al., pp. 175–78; Pol, pp. 24–25; Lania, pp. 36–45; Escher, "Avec les réfugiés ex-autrichiens," pp. 10–14.

14. Schramm and Vormeier, pp. 7, 246–47; Vormeier, "La Situation des réfugiés," pp. 88–89.

15. Minister of the interior, "Circulaire ayant pour objet de déterminer la situation en temps de guerre des étrangers suspects ou dangereux," Sept. 17, 1939, APP DA 783 (Règlements). See also Schramm and Vormeier, pp. 248–49; Vormeier, "Législation répressive," p. 165; Gilbert Badia, "Réfugiés et immigrés d'Europe Centrale dans le mouvement antifasciste et la résistance en France (1933–1945)," in Institut d'Histoire, 1: 2.

16. For Arthur Koestler's account of his arrest during these roundups, see Koestler, *Scum*, pp. 57–69.

17. Berthoin, General Secretary, Ministry of the Interior, circular, Oct. 9, 1939, AN F^7 14662; Ministry of the Interior, Sûreté Nationale, to the Prefects, teleg. received on Oct. 8, 1939, ADBR D 391/24, dos. 240; General Louis Colson, Ministry of National Defense and War, president of the Council, to the military governor general of Paris and the commanding generals of the Paris regions, Oct. 17, 1939, ADBR D 391/24, dos. 240 (also in SHAT 7N 2475, dos. 1$_2$); E. Ricard, Ministry of National Defense and War, president of the Council, circular no. 6139, 1/EMA, to the military governor general of Paris and the commanding generals of the Paris regions, Oct. 30, 1939, SHAT 7N 2462, dos. 3; Escher, p. 10.

18. General Louis Colson, chief of staff for the Army of the Interior, to the military governor general of Paris and the commanding generals of the Paris regions, Sept. 17, 1939, no. 1270, 1/EMA, SHAT 7N 2475, dos. 1$_2$.

19. Morris Troper, "War Relief Activities of the JDC," pamphlet, spring 1940, JDC no. 165, pp. 10–11; "Jewish Life in Paris Today: The Situation of the French Jews and the Situation of the Refugees—What is Being Done for Them?" Special correspondence to the "Day" by Clipper B. Smollar, *The Day*, Oct. 3, 1939, JDC no. 617.

20. "Nos Lecteurs nous écrivent: Les réfugiés allemands," *L'Ordre*, Sept. 10, 1939, p. 4. See also Pol, pp. 229–32.

21. According to Schramm and Vormeier, by the end of Sept. only 532 internees who had served in the International Brigades in Spain had enlisted in Foreign Legion. According to *Le Populaire*, however, significant numbers of Austrian Jews enlisted in Sept. Schramm and Vormeier, p. 263; "Des israélites autrichiens s'engagent dans la Légion étrangère," *Le Populaire*, Sept. 8, 1939, clipped in AIU, ms. 650, boîte 11 (41).

22. Although government sources claimed that 15,000 "enemy aliens" had been interned in Sept. and Oct., private organizations, such as the JDC, generally set the figure at around 18,000. Also, the number of camps fluctuated throughout the fall as some camps were consolidated and others eliminated altogether. Many sources set the number of camps in the fall at 60, the JDC claimed there were 80, and Joly et al. have recently estimated that there were over 100 camps. One problem in counting the camps is that many smaller camps were actually annexes of larger ones. For the JDC estimate see Troper, "JDC Activities During Early Months of the War," Mar. 14, 1940, JDC no. 165. For sources setting the number at 60, see "French Speed Aid for Enemy Aliens," *NYT*, Dec. 17, 1939, p. 37; Edith Peters, "German Exiles In-

terned," *NYT*, Dec. 3, 1939, sec. IV, p. 9; Pfoser-Schewig, pp. 5–6; Schapiro, p. 138; Kempner, p. 450; "Review of the Year 5700," p. 449. For Joly et al.'s estimate, see Joly et al., pp. 180–81.

23. L. Stein, pp. 27–28, 93; Grynberg, *Les Camps*, pp. 40–63; Marrus and Paxton, pp. 63–64; Marrus, "Vichy before Vichy," p. 19; Marrus, "Vichy avant Vichy," p. 91.

24. On the creation of Rieucros on Jan. 21, 1939, see "Un Premier camp de concentration vient d'être installé dans la Lozère près de Mende," *Le Matin*, Feb. 17, 1939, pp. 1–2; "Les Réfugiés et les indésirables qui ont inauguré le premier camp de concentration...," *Le Matin*, Feb. 18, 1939, pp. 1–2; *Le Temps*, Feb. 22, 1939; *L'Oeuvre*, Feb. 18, 1939; *Journal des débats*, Feb. 22, 1939, all cited in "Report on the decree laws," n. auth., n. title, n.d., AIU, ms. 650, boîte 14 (1939); Schramm and Vormeier, pp. 237–39; Vormeier, "Législation répressive," p. 163; Grynberg, *Les Camps*, pp. 19–20; *Esprit*, 7ème année, no. 82 (July 1, 1939): 504; JDC, European Executive Committee (Euroexco), Feb. report, 1939, "Excerpts from the Press, Feb. 1939," JDC no. 189, p. 143.

25. Morris Troper, "War Relief Activities of the JDC," pamphlet, spring 1940, JDC no. 165, pp. 10–11. For a map of the camp locations, see Grynberg, *Les Camps*.

26. "Rapport sur la visite de MM. Davis et Guillon, secrétaires des UCJG (Comité Universel des Unions Chrétiens de Jeunes Gens) aux Centres de Rassemblement d'Etrangers de France," Dec. 15–22, 1939, MAE Z 791 (Régime des sujets allemands en France), pp. 2–8.

27. Koestler, *Scum*, p. 98.

28. Koestler, *Scum*, pp. 98, 94, 123–24. "HICEM (Jewish Emigration Society) report on Marmagne camp, Nov. 17, 1939," sent from E. Oungre, HICEM, to JDC Paris, Nov. 29, 1939, JDC no. 617. On Le Vernet, see also L. Stein, pp. 73–74; Palmier, 2: 121–23; Schiller et al., pp. 444–53; Badia, "Camps répressifs," pp. 310–32; Grynberg, *Les Camps*, pp. 69–70; Magazine excerpt, "Germans in France: The War Against Hitler Finds Thousands of Anti-Nazi Fighters in French Concentration Camps," in *Friday* 1, no. 10 (May 17, 1940), clipped in JDC no. 617.

29. For Lania's description of conditions at Meslay-du-Maine, see Lania, pp. 46–83. See also Escher, pp. 11–18.

30. Cited in Kempner, p. 450; Tartakower and Grossmann, p. 147. See also Feuchtwanger, pp. 27–28; Lania, pp. 94–95; Hertha Kraus, American Friends Service Committee, to Clarence Pickett, Nov. 19, 1939, citing report of Dr. Otto Frey, in Friedlander and Milton, doc. no. 204, p. 594; W. Bein, "Digest of Letter dated Oct. 24, 1939, from a lady in Paris who visited a concentration camp for German aliens in France," Nov. 27, 1939, JDC no. 617.

31. W. Bein, "Digest of Letter dated Oct. 24, 1939, from a lady in Paris who visited a concentration camp for German aliens in France," Nov. 27, 1939, JDC no. 617; "Record of Telephone Conversation with Mr. Troper in Geneva on Nov. 6, 1939, 3:30 PM," JDC no. 175.

32. Feuchtwanger, pp. 34, 52, 55.

33. "Le Vrai visage du Camp de Gurs," *La Flèche*, Aug. 11, 1939, AIU, ms. 650, boîte 12 (43); L. Oungre, HICEM, to JDC, Paris, Nov. 7, 1939, JDC 617; Jewish

Telegraphic Agency report on camps of Orléans and Montargis, Nov. 22, 1939, JDC no. 617. For other HICEM reports on the camps, see "Report on Marmagne Camp," Nov. 17, 1939, sent from E. Oungre, HICEM, to JDC, Paris, Nov. 29, 1939, JDC no. 617; "Minutes of Plenary Meeting of Commission des Centres de Rassemblement de l'Intercomité des Oeuvres Françaises," Dec. 1, 1939, JDC no. 617; Dossier of Félix Chevrier at the CDJC, cited in Joly et al., pp. 173–74, and Grynberg, *Les Camps*, pp. 74–75; "Rapport sur la visite de MM. Davis et Guillon, secrétaires des UCJG (Comité Universel des Unions Chrétiens de Jeunes Gens) aux Centres de Rassemblement d'étrangers de France," Dec. 15–22, 1939, MAE Z 791, pp. 2–8; Tartakower and Grossmann, p. 147. Grynberg claims that the reports of Chevrier and the Commission des Centres de Rassemblements tended to whitewash camp conditions so as not to alienate government authorities (p. 75), but these reports were often quite critical.

34. Feuchtwanger, pp. 15, 21. For similar comments, see also Heinz Soffner, former Secretary of the Federation of Austrian Emigrants in Paris, "The Internment of refugees in France during the War: Legal situation, facts, conclusions," JDC no. 618; Dr. Hans Rott, President, 1939–1940, document of the Ligue Autrichienne, AN F^7 14717; Memorandum, Ligue Autrichienne, 1939, n.d., AN F^7 14717; Pol, pp. 229–237; Palmier, 2: 119; Lania, pp. 73–84.

35. Miss Rott, American Friends, "Memorandum on Conditions in the 'Camps de Rassemblement' of the Loire and Cher departments in France," Nov. 1, 1939, attached to JDC, Paris, to JDC, N.Y., Nov. 11, 1939, JDC no. 617; Feuchtwanger, pp. 3–4; Ernst Erich Noth, "15 Jours dans un centre de rassemblement," *Nouvelles Littéraires*, Oct. 7, 1939, clipped in AIU, ms. 650, boîte 13 (dos. 1939–1940).

36. Koestler, *Scum*, p. 187. See also Feuchtwanger, p. 4.

37. Noth, *L'Allemagne exilée*, p. 27 ff. See also Maurice Carité, "Ernst Erich Noth nous parle...," *L'Aube*, Dec. 18, 1939, p. 1.

38. On the British reaction in the fall, see Kempner, pp. 444–49; Koessler, pp. 98–127; "Review of the Year 5700," pp. 450–52; Wasserstein, *Britain*, pp. 82–86; Cesarani, p. 44; Fox, "German- and Austrian-Jewish Volunteers," pp. 24–26; Seyfert, pp. 163–67; Joly et al., p. 171; Sir Herbert Emerson, League of Nations, "Assistance Internationale aux Réfugiés," A.18(a) 1939, XII, Rapport supplémentaire, Sept. 23, 1939, MAE, Société des Nations (SDN) I M (Questions sociales, Réfugiés en France) 1814, p. 387; Bernhard Kahn, to Paul Baerwald, "Memorandum," Oct. 13, 1939, JDC no. 255; "Telephone Conversation with Mr. Troper in Amsterdam today at 2 PM," Oct. 9, 1939, JDC no. 175; "Meeting of the Officers of the IGC [Intergovernmental Committee] on Political Refugees, Department of State, Washington, D.C.," Oct. 17, 1939, in Myron Taylor Papers, box 7, FDR Library.

39. For several examples of how fifth-column hysteria seized the population, see Feuchtwanger, pp. 44, 47; Procureur Général, Nancy, to the keeper of the seals, Sept. 24, 1939, and Oct. 14, 1939, in AN F^7 14882 (propos défaitistes); Mahler-Werfel, p. 314.

40. French consul, Ventimiglia, Italy, to the General Inspector (Criminal Police), Sûreté Nationale, Oct. 20, 1939, AN F^7 14776 (divers).

41. A. Castaing, Contrôleur Général, Ministry of the Interior, circular no. S. O. /

G. 400, to the Commissaires spéciaux des portes et frontières, des ports aeriens, les Commissaires de la surveillance du Territoire, Dec. 23, 1939, AN F⁷ 14662; Grynberg, *Les Camps*, pp. 67–68.

42. Fabian and Coulmas, p. 69.

43. Weiss, p. 238; Lazareff, p. 109.

44. Schapiro, p. 140.

45. Miller, pp. 144–72; "Situation of the Refugees in France During the Year 1939," n.d., JDC no. 604.

46. Koessler, p. 115; Miller, pp. 152–53.

47. Cited in Grynberg, *Les Camps*, p. 67. See also Fittko, p. 11; Henry Pachter, *Weimar Etudes* (New York, 1982), p. 314, cited in Peterson, p. 76.

48. Berthoin, Ministry of the Interior, Sûreté Nationale, circular no. 405, Aug. 29, 1939, APP DA 783 (also in ADBR D 460, paq. 5 [36]).

49. This lack of preparation was noted in the report of the subcommittee of the Parliamentary Commission on Civil and Criminal Legislation headed by Marius Moutet. For the text of this report, which had been compiled with the cooperation of the Foreign Affairs Commission of the Chamber, see "Rapport présenté par MM. Marius Moutet, André Le Troquer et Gaston Moreau devant la délégation permanente de la Commission de la Législation Civile et Criminelle, et adopté le 16 novembre 1939," AN F⁶⁰ 391.

50. Kempner, pp. 443–58. On the British response, see also n. 38 above.

51. Schramm and Vormeier, p. 245, esp. n. 4, and p. 247, n. 11. On the decree law of Sept. 9, 1939, see *JO, Lois et Décrets*, Sept. 14, 1939, p. 11400; Ministry of the Interior, circular of Sept. 21, 1939 (a/s du décret-loi du 9 septembre 1939), AN F⁷ 14662.

52. Cobban, p. 174. See also Réau, pp. 374–77.

53. "Une déclaration des socialistes allemands," *Le Populaire*, Aug. 31, 1939, p. 6; "Les Etrangers résidant en France se mettent au service du pays," *Le Populaire*, Sept. 2, 1939, p. 2; "Les Protestations de l'opposition allemande contre le pacte Hitler-Staline se multiplient," *Le Populaire*, Sept. 2, 1939, p. 2; "Une Protestation des allemands de l'émigration," *Journal de débats*, Aug. 29, 1939, clipped in AIU, ms. 650, boîte 14 (48); Lania, pp. 9–10; Manès Sperber, *Until My Eyes Are Closed with Shards*, translated by Harry Zohn (New York, 1994), pp. 152–55, 159–60; Palmier, 2: 117; Thalmann, "L'Emigration allemande," p. 68.

54. Koestler, *Invisible Writing*, p. 419; Badia et al., *Les Barbelés*, pp. 92–93; Herbert Luethy, *France Against Herself*, translated by Eric Mosbacher (New York, 1955), pp. 82–88.

55. Kempner, p. 449. On the defeatist propaganda of the Communist Party, see Réau, pp. 374–77; Ory, *Les Collaborateurs*, pp. 33–34. Both claim the extent of this sabotage was extremely limited.

56. Curt Reiss, "Refugees in France: Their Treatment Unfortunate but Forced by Circumstances," *NYT*, Dec. 10, 1939, sec. IV, p. 9; Schapiro, p. 140; Kempner, p. 451.

57. "JDC Activities During Early Months of the War," Mar. 14, 1940, JDC no. 165. On the legal basis for these seizures, see Kempner, p. 453.

58. Bernhard Kahn, to Paul Baerwald, "Memorandum," Oct. 13, 1939, JDC

no. 255; Paul Baerwald, to George L. Warren, President's Advisory Committee on Refugees (PAC), teleg., Oct. 25, 1939, JDC no. 658; Dr. Feldmann and Dr. Speigel, from the Camp des Passagers du Pacific Line, Montguyon (Charente Inférieure), to the JDC, N.Y., Sept. 15, 1939, JDC no. 617; Robert Pilpel, Secretary, Subcommittee on Refugee Aid in Central and South America, to Erna Zweig, Santiago, Chile, Oct. 16, 1939, JDC no. 617; August Rothschild, Santiago, Chile, to Ike G. Cadden family, Nov. 18, 1939, JDC no. 617; Jeanette Robbins, Personal Inquiry Dept. of the JDC, to Mr. Paul Herzog, Dec. 22, 1939, JDC no. 617; JDC, N.Y., to Morris Troper, Amsterdam, Oct. 5, 1939, JDC no. 617; chargé d'affaires de France, to M. le ministre du blocus, Dec. 15, 1939, MAE Z 790 (Régime des sujets allemands en France), pp. 21–23; Hertha Kraus, AFSC, to Clarence Pickett, Nov. 19, 1939, in Friedlander and Milton, p. 594; Fontaine, "L'Internement," p. 119. For an excellent summary of this issue, see Kempner, pp. 453–54.

59. On JDC protests against seizures of refugees from neutral ships, see "JDC Activities During Early Months of the War," Mar. 14, 1940, JDC no. 165; "Budgetary Forecast of the HICEM for 1940," JDC no. 675; Cable, JDC, N.Y., to Troper, Amsterdam, Sept. 29, 1939, JDC no. 658; J. C. Hyman, to JDC officers, "Memorandum," Feb. 8, 1940, JDC no. 617; Joly et al., p. 191. For problems relating to military allowances, see "Situation of the Refugees in France During the Year 1939," n.d., JDC no. 604; Bernhard Kahn, to Paul Baerwald, "Memorandum," Oct. 13, 1939, JDC no. 255; Jacques Piskine, Treasurer, Workmen's Circle [and Medem Federation] Paris, to JDC, N.Y., Sept. 14, 1939, JDC no. 617; M. P., "Les Etrangers qui se sont engagés demandent à être fixés sur leur sort," *Le Populaire*, Oct. 3, 1939, p. 1; "Les Etrangers qui se sont engagés," *L'Oeuvre*, Oct. 17, 1939, p. 5; CAR, "Rapport de l'Exercice 1939," [Jan. 1940], pp. 16–17, JDC no. 605.

60. For several examples, see *Cyrano*, Sept. 29, 1939; *Cri de Paris*, Oct. 13, 1939, "Qui protesterait?" *Choc*, Jan. 8, 1940; "Les Commerçants étrangers," *Mutilés et Combattants*, Mar. 24, 1940; "Conseil Muncipal de Metz," *La Républicain Lorrain*, Jan. 1, 1940, all clipped in AIU, ms. 650, boîte 12 (43); "Pour utiliser les réfugiés étrangers," *AF*, May 17, 1939, clipped in AIU, ms. 650, boîte 13. On the protests of doctors specifically, see "Les Médecins étrangers," *AF*, Oct. 16, 1939, clipped in AIU, ms. 650, boîte 15 (50); André Billy, "Médecins français ...et autres," *L'Oeuvre*, Dec. 19, 1939, p. 2; Billy, "La Question des médecins étrangers," *L'Oeuvre*, Dec. 27, 1939, p. 2; "Encore des étrangers," *Le Cri de Paris*," Dec. 24, 1939; "Pour la protection des médecins français," *Le Temps*, Jan. 6, 1940, clipped in AIU, ms. 650, boîte 12 (43); "Profiteurs," *L'Ordre*, Jan. 11, 1940, clipped in AIU, ms. 650, boîte 12 (43).

61. "Prenez note: La situation des travailleurs étrangers," *Le Populaire*, Sept. 21, 1939, p. 4; "Mesures de sécurité," *L'Epoque*, Oct. 26, 1939, p. 2; "Un Décret règle depuis hier la situation des travailleurs de nationalité étrangère," *L'Oeuvre*, Sept. 21, 1939, p. 2; CAR, "Rapport de l'Exercice, 1939," [Jan. 1940], p. 18, JDC no. 605; "L'Action du C... A ...R de Paris," *La Juste parole*, May 20, 1940, p. 23; "France Cuts Alien Labor," *NYT*, Aug. 30, 1940, p. 5; Schramm and Vormeier, pp. 215–16.

62. "Situation of the Refugees in France During the Year 1939," n.d., JDC no. 604; CAR, "Rapport de l'Exercice, 1939," [Jan. 1940], p. 18, JDC no. 605.

63. Paul Baerwald, to George L. Warren, teleg., JDC, Oct. 25, 1939, JDC no. 658;

Saint-Quentin, to the Foreign Ministry, Paris, no. 1912–13, Oct. 26, 1939, MAE Z 790, pp. 13–14.

64. Saint-Quentin, to the Foreign Ministry, teleg. no. 2303–4, Dec. 22, 1939, MAE Z 790, pp. 81–82.

65. Foreign Ministry, to Saint-Quentin, teleg. no. 2103, Dec. 27, 1939, MAE Z 790, p. 88. The only reported case in which real spies may have been netted through such seizures was when the French authorities forced 10 of the 26 midgets who had been employed at the Lilliputian Village of the New York World's Fair to disembark from an Italian liner. These midgets were subsequently brought to an internment camp in southern France, where the camp commander reportedly stated: "Those little fellows would make ideal spies because of their small size. They could hide almost in a desk drawer." Although this incident would seem to reflect fifth-column hysteria, Feuchtwanger reported that these midgets were indeed pro-Nazi. Kempner, p. 453; "Midgets Interned in a French Camp," *NYT*, Dec. 19, 1939, p. 11; Feuchtwanger, p. 98.

66. Foreign Ministry, to the French ambassador in Madrid, teleg. no. 514, Oct. 22, 1939, MAE Z 790, p. 8.

67. "France Copies Hitler," *The New Republic*, Jan. 15, 1940, clipped in JDC no. 617. See also Edith Peters, "German Exiles Interned," *NYT*, Dec. 3, 1939, sec. IV, p. 9.

68. Saint-Quentin, to the Foreign Ministry, teleg. no. 2280–81, Dec. 9, 1939, MAE Z 790, pp. 24–25. On Foreign Ministry discussions regarding how to handle queries on the refugee question at the Washington Conference, see Foreign Ministry, to Saint-Quentin, Oct. 18, 1939, no. 1526, MAE Z 712 (Réfugiés israélites à l'étranger, supplément), pp. 162–63; "Meeting of the officers of the IGC [Intergovernmental Committee] on Political Refugees," Dept. of State, Washington, D.C., Oct. 17, 1939, in Myron Taylor Papers, box 7, FDR Library.

69. Moutet, "Quel sort réserver aux réfugiés politiques?" *La Lumière*, Nov. 17, 1939, pp. 1–2; Moutet, "La Chambre veut une prompte solution du problème des réfugiés politiques," *La Lumière*, Dec. 15, 1939, pp. 1–2. These criticisms were echoed in a report of the parliamentary subcommittee of the Commission on Civil and Criminal Legislation, headed by Moutet, that was adopted on Nov. 16. See "Rapport présenté par MM. Marius Moutet, André le Trocquer et Gaston Moreau devant la délégation permanent de la Commission de la Législation Civile et Criminelle, et adopté le 16 novembre 1939," AN F^{60} 391.

70. D'Ormesson, "Un Problème à résoudre," *Le Figaro*, Nov. 23, 1939, p. 1. D'Ormesson favored a liberalization of the camp regime for Austrians only. On d'Ormesson's protests, see also Goldner, pp. 20.

71. Honnorat to the President of the Council, n.d., but forwarded to the Ministry of Defense on Sept. 28, 1939, SHAT 7N 2475, dos. 1$_2$.

72. Jean-L. Prim, "Paris en guerre, toujours les étrangers," *L'Ordre*, Oct. 14, 1939, p. 1. See also "Jewish Life in Paris Today: The Situation of the French Jews and the Situation of the Refugees—What Is Being Done for Them?" Special correspondence to the "Day," by Clipper B. Smollar, *The Day*, Oct. 3, 1939, JDC no. 617; Crémieux-Brilhac, 1: 480.

73. Army chief of staff, 1èr Bureau, no. 8312, "Note pour le cabinet militaire du Ministre," Nov. 13, 1939, SHAT 7N 2475, dos. 1.

74. *JO, Débats Parlementaires, Chambre des Députés*, Dec. 8, 1939, pp. 2109–10, 2120–23. See also Schramm and Vormeier, pp. 254–55; J. Biélinky, "L'Immigration juive en France," *La Juste parole*, no. 63 (Dec. 1, 1939): 7; Koessler, p. 118; Kempner, pp. 450–51; Tartakower and Grossmann, p. 150. For the commission's earlier report on which Moutet's remarks were based, see "Rapport présenté par MM. Marius Moutet, André Le Troquer et Gaston Moreau devant la délégation permanent de la Commission de la Législation Civile et Criminelle, et adopté le 16 novembre 1939," AN F^{60} 391.

75. *JO, Débats Parlementaires, Chambre des Députés*, Dec. 8, 1939, p. 2121. See also Schramm and Vormeier, pp. 255–56.

76. "French Speed Aid for Enemy Aliens," *NYT*, Dec. 17, 1939, p. 37; JDC, *Aid to Jews Overseas: Report for 1939* (pamphlet), pp. 33–34, JDC no. 156.

77. Statement of Robert de Rothschild, in "Minutes of Plenary Meeting of Commission des Centres de Rassemblements de l'Intercomité des Oeuvres Françaises," Dec. 1, 1939, JDC no. 617.

78. On the Groupement and the reorganization of the Jewish refugee relief effort in late 1938, see Robert de Rothschild, "Le Consistoire de Paris et la coordination des oeuvres," *UI*, June 2, 1939, pp. 661–64; Franz Gravereau, "Le Problème des étrangers," *Le Petit Parisien*, Mar. 4, 1939, clipped in AIU, ms. 650, boîte 14 (48); Caron, "Politics," pp. 333–35.

79. On the creation of the commission, see "Minutes of Plenary Meeting of Commission des Centres de Rassemblements de l'Intercomité des Oeuvres Françaises," Dec. 1, 1939, JDC no. 617; J. C. Hyman, "Telephone Conversation with Mr. Troper, in Amsterdam," Oct. 9, 1939, JDC no. 175; "Group Formed to Aid Refugees in France," *NYT*, Nov. 15, 1939, p. 2; "Memorandum on Camps of German Refugees in France," [Nov. 1939], JDC no. 617; JDC, "Aid to Jews Overseas: Report for 1939," pp. 33–34, JDC no. 156; "Situation of the Refugees in France During the Year 1939," n.d., JDC no. 604; J. C. Hyman, "Memorandum to JDC Officers," Feb. 8, 1940, JDC no. 617; M. Troper, "JDC Activities During Early Months of the War," Mar. 14, 1940, JDC no. 165; Grynberg, *Les Camps*, pp. 72–76; Joly et al., pp. 216–17; Schapiro, p. 139.

80. "Situation of the Refugees in France During the Year 1939," n.d., JDC no. 604. On the commission's impact, see "Minutes of Plenary Meeting of Commission des Centres de Rassemblement de l'Intercomité des Oeuvres Françaises," Dec. 1, 1939, JDC no. 617. For reports on camp conditions, see n. 33 above.

81. "French Speed Aid for Enemy Aliens," *NYT*, Dec. 17, 1939, p. 37; Emerson, to George L. Warren, Mar. 19, 1940, AN AJ^{43} 12 (18/56:3); "Various reports of Dr. Junod and Minister F. Barbey and other Red Cross delegates on the occasion of their visits to internment camps for civil internees and POW's, Feb. 19, 1940–Feb. 24, 1940," SHAT 7N 2480, dos. 5; President of the Council, Foreign Ministry, to Ministry of National Defense and War, EMA, 1er Bureau, Mar. 19, 1940, SHAT 7N 2480, dos. 5.

82. Lania, p. 83.

83. Joly et al., p. 191; Schramm and Vormeier, p. 249; Schapiro, p. 139; "Review of the Year 5700," p. 450; Amédée Bussière, Director, Sûreté Nationale, Ministry of the Interior, circular no. 413, Oct. 27, 1939, AN F^7 14662; E. Ricard, secretary, Ministry of National Defense and War, president of the Council, 1/EMA, to the military governor general of Paris and the commanding generals of the Paris regions, teleg. no. 5.343, Oct. 26, 1939, SHAT 7N 2462, dos. 3; Ricard, to the military governor general of Paris and the commanding generals of the Paris regions, 1/EMA, circular no. 7458, Nov. 9, 1939, SHAT 7N 2475, dos. 1; JDC Paris, Cable to JDC, N.Y., Oct. 30, 1939, JDC no. 617; "Memorandum on Camps of German Refugees in France," [Nov. 1939], JDC no. 617; L. Oungre, HICEM, to JDC, Paris, "Expedition of Refugees Interned in Camps," Nov. 7, 1939, JDC no. 617; Jewish Telegraphic Agency, report on camps of Orléans and Montargis, Nov. 22, 1939, JDC no. 617; "Budgetary Forecast of the HICEM for 1940," JDC no. 675; "Report on the Activity of the HICEM," Jan. 3, 1940, JDC, no. 675; J. C. Hyman, to JDC Officers, "Memorandum," Feb. 8, 1940, JDC no. 617; Joseph J. Schwartz, JDC, N.Y., to Frances G. Marshall, Mar. 7, 1940, JDC no. 617.

84. "Les Allocations militaires seront accordées aux familles des étrangers combattants en France," *Le Populaire*, Nov. 2, 1939, p. 3.

85. Recruitment of the internees into the Foreign Legion began in Oct.. See E. Ricard, Ministry of Defense and War, president of the Council, 1/EMA, to the commanding generals, no. 4.910, (Urgent), Oct. 22, 1939, SHAT 7N 2475, dos. 1$_2$. On this regulation being the result of Foreign Ministry pressure, see Ministry of National Defense and War, president of the Council, to the commander in chief of the North African theater of operations, no. 13091, Dec. 16, 1939, SHAT 7N 2475, dos. 1$_2$.

86. Ministry of Interior, circular no. 416, Nov. 21, 1939, AN F^7 14662.

87. "Report on the Activity of the HICEM," Jan. 3, 1940, JDC no. 675; "JDC Activities During Early Months of the War," Mar. 14, 1940, JDC no. 165; Sir Herbert Emerson (Intergovernmental Committee on Refugees), to George Warren, Nov. 30, 1939, p. 4, AN AJ^{43} 12 (18/56:2). On the relative satisfaction of Jewish organizations with the direction of French policy, see also "Memorandum on Camps of German Refugees in France," [Nov. 1939], JDC no. 617.

88. Colson, army chief of staff for the interior, Ministry of National Defense and War, president of the Council, circular no. 5.008 1/E.M.A., (Secret and Very Urgent), Oct. 23, 1939, SHAT 7N 2462, dos. 3. See also Vormeier, "La Situation des réfugiés," pp. 89–90.

89. Colson, army chief of staff for the interior, Ministry of Defense and President of the Council, to the commanders and generals, no. 1270, 1/EMA, Sept. 17, 1939, SHAT 7N 2475, dos. 1$_2$.

90. Koestler, *Scum*, pp. 143–45, 163.

91. See various documents in MAE Z 790 and 791.

92. Lania, p. 78; Koestler, *Scum*, pp. 144–45.

93. J. Berthoin, Secretary-General, Ministry of the Interior, Sûreté Nationale, circular, Oct. 29, 1939, AN F^7 14662. On this decree and subsequent orders by the Ministry of the Interior to cut down on arbitrary arrests, see also A. Bussière, Di-

rector General, Sûreté Nationale, Ministry of Interior, 7ème Bureau, to the prefects, Mar. 23, 1940, APP DA 784 (Règlements); Badia, "Camps répressifs," p. 295; Badia, "Réfugiés et immigrés d'Europe Centrale dans le mouvement antifasciste," in Institut d'Histoire, 1: 3; Grynberg, *Les Camps*, p. 79.

94. Berthoin, Secretary-General, Ministry of the Interior, circular, Oct. 9, 1939, AN F⁷ 14662; Ministry of the Interior, Sûreté Nationale, to the prefects, teleg., received Oct. 8, 1939, ADBR D 391/24, dos. 240; Colson, army chief of staff for the Interior, Ministry of National Defence and War, president of the Council, to the commanding generals, Oct. 17, 1939, ADBR D 391/24, dos. 240 (also in SHAT 7N 2475, dos. 1₂); Lania, pp. 76–77.

95. J. C. Hyman, Memorandum to JDC Officers, Feb. 8, 1940, JDC no. 617. See also Joly et al., pp. 190–91; Koessler, pp. 116–18; Heinz Soffner, "The Internment of Refugees in France During the War: Legal Situation, Facts, Conclusions," JDC no. 618.

96. Lania, pp. 76–77.

97. Ministry of the Interior, Sûreté Nationale, 7ème bureau, to the prefects, Nov. 11, 1939, SHAT 7N 2475, dos. 1 (reproduced in Badia et al., *Les Barbelés*, photos). See also Badia, "Réfugiés et immigrés d'Europe Centrale dans le mouvement antifasciste," in Institut d'Histoire, 1: 4; Fabian and Coulmas, p. 70; Ministry of Defense, 1/EMA, and the Ministry of Interior, 2ème bureau, to the prefects, Dec. 21, 1939, APP DA 783 (Règlements) (for an English translation of this decree, see "France, Refugees, 1933–1940," JDC no. 617); Morris Troper, to M. Stephany, Central Council for Jewish Refugees, Jan. 12, 1940, JDC no. 617; president of the Council, Ministry of National Defense, 1/EMA, to the military governor general of Paris and the commanding generals of the regions of Paris, no. 1617, Jan. 23, 1940, SHAT 7N 2480; Schramm and Vormeier, p. 256. The age of those to be inducted into *prestataire* service was originally 40 but was subsequently raised to 48.

98. Heinz Soffner, "The Internment of Refugees in France During the War: Legal Situation, Facts, Conclusions," JDC no. 618.

99. "French Speed Aid for Enemy Aliens," *NYT*, Dec. 17, 1939, p. 37; Foreign Ministry to Saint-Quentin, teleg. no. 2013, Dec. 14, 1939, MAE Z 790; "Liste des camps d'internés prestataires et effectifs à réviser," Feb. 20, 1940, SHAT 7N 2480; "Situation of the Refugees in France During the Year 1939," n.d., JDC no. 604.

100. Joly et al., pp. 182–83. For those cases not yet settled by Apr., the government planned a second triage.

101. CAR, "Note on the Activity of the CAR from May 1, 1940," translated in JDC no. 604.

102. Ministry of the Interior, 2ème bureau, to the prefects, Dec. 21, 1939, APP DA 783 (Règlements) (for an English translation, see "France, Refugees, 1933–1940," JDC no. 617); Morris Troper, to M. Stephany, Central Council for Jewish Refugees, Jan. 12, 1940, JDC no. 617.

103. "Situation du recrutement et de l'utilisation des étrangers à la date du 12 novembre [1939]," SHAT 7N 2475, dos. 1.

104. On the decree of Jan. 13, 1940, see *JO, Lois et Décrets*, Jan. 18, 1940, pp. 515–16; Schramm and Vormeier, pp. 240, 256; Vormeier, "La Situation des émi-

grés," p. 159; Vormeier, "La Situation des réfugiés," p. 91; Fontaine, "L'Interne-ment," p. 120. On the overhaul of the *prestataire* service in Jan., see Heinz Soffner, "The Internment of Refugees in France During the War: Legal Situation, Facts, Conclusions," JDC no. 618; Grynberg, *Les Camps*, p. 77; Tartakower and Gross-mann, pp. 150–51; Kempner, pp. 451–52. On the salaries of the *prestataires*, see Kempner, pp. 451–452; Badia, "Camps répressifs," p. 297, n. 18.

105. "CAR Rapport de l'Exercice, 1940," Marseilles, Jan. 13, 1940, pp. 1, p. 5; J. Biélinky, "Le Réclassement professionnel des immigrés," *UI*, Mar. 29, 1940, p. 105.

106. Porch, p. 445; Koestler, *Scum*, p. 186, note. To ensure that these regiments of foreign volunteers not be confused with the "real" Legion, which wanted to dis-tance itself from them, they were assigned numbers over 20; hence they became the 21e, 22e, and 23e Régiments de Marche des Volontaires Etrangers (RMVE).

107. On the ethnic composition of the legion, see L'Adjudant-Chef Mazzoni, Chef de l'Annexe de Barcarès, Camp de Barcarès, to M. le Capitaine, Chef du S.I.L. at Sathonay, no. 118/AB, Jan. 25, 1940, SHAT 7N 2475, dos. 3. On antisemitism in the Polish Legion, see "Nos Lecteurs: nous écrivent: 'Des volontaires,'" *L'Ordre*, Sept. 25, 1939, p. 4; Szajkowski, *Jews*, pp. 66–67.

108. Amedée Bussière, Director, Sûreté Nationale, Ministry of the Interior, cir-cular no. 419, Jan. 4, 1940, AN F^7 14662.

109. Jean-L. Prim, "Paris en Guerre, Toujours les étrangers," *L'Ordre*, Oct. 14, 1939, p. 1; Lania, pp. 79–80; Pol, p. 260.

110. E. Ricard, Ministry of Defense and War, president of the Council, to the commanding generals [of the camps], no. 4.910, 1/EMA, (Urgent), Oct. 22, 1939, SHAT 7N 2475, dos. 1₂; army chief of staff, overseas section, "Note sur l'utilisation des allemands, engagés volontaires pour la durée de la guerre," 9/EMA, Dec. 2, 1939, SHAT 7N 2475, dos. 2.

111. Lania, pp. 79–80; Pol, pp. 237–50; W. Bein, "Digest of letter dated Oct. 24, 1939, from a lady in Paris who visited a concentration camp for German aliens in France," Nov. 27, 1939, JDC no. 617; Palmier, 2: 120–121, n. 6.

112. Pol, p. 246; Lania, p. 80; Szajkowski, *Jews*, pp. 64–65.

113. Police report on LICA meeting, Dec. 17, 1939, in APP BA 1812 79.501-882-C; "French Speed Aid for Enemy Aliens," *NYT*, Dec. 17, 1939, p. 37.

114. Schramm and Vormeier, p. 256; Vormeier, "La Situation des réfugiés," p. 91; Tartakower and Grossmann, p. 150; Pol estimated the number of German and Austrian refugees in Legion at 7,000 to 8,000 (pp. 249–50).

115. Georges Reyer, "Nieder mit Hitler: C'est à ce cri de 'A bas Hitler' que la pre-mière légion de volontaires allemands s'est embarquée pour Sidi-bel-Abbès...," *Paris-Soir*, Dec. 30, 1939, clipped in AIU, ms. 650, boîte 11 (41).

116. Bonnet, Ministry of Justice, keeper of the seals, to the prefects, [Oct. 22, 1939], APP BA 407^P 200.263; "On décrète, on recommande, on communique, on suggère...," *L'Oeuvre*, Oct. 27, 1939, p. 5; "La Naturalisation des étrangers qui veu-lent servir la France sera accélérée," *L'Epoque*, Oct. 29, 1939, p. 4; Crémieux-Brilhac, 1: 489.

117. Depoid, p. 45.

118. Colson, army chief of staff of the Interior, president of the Council, Min-

istry of National Defense and War, 1/EMA, to the keeper of the seals (Service des Naturalisations), Nov. 2, 1939, SHAT 7N 2475, dos. 1. On public disgruntlement that the refugees were sitting idle in the camps while French citizens were dying, see the comments by Camille Blaisot during the Chamber of Deputies' debate over naturalization on Dec. 8, 1939, *JO, Débats Parlementaires, Chambre des Députés*, p. 2112; "Rapport présenté par MM. Marius Moutet, André le Troquer et Gaston Moreau devant la délégation permanent de la Commission de la Législation Civile et Criminelle, et adopté le 16 novembre 1939," AN F^{60} 391; *La Petite Gironde*, Dec. 2, 1939, cited in Vormeier, "Les Internés," p. 242.

119. *JO, Débats Parlementaires, Sénat*, Dec. 7, 1939, pp. 699–700; "Le Problème des étrangers devant les Chambres," *Le Monde libre*, Dec. 16, 1939, clipped in AIU, ms. 650, boîte 13 (45). In a debate over naturalization in the Chamber of Deputies the next day, Laurent Bonnevay similarly declared that naturalizations had to be limited to those "qui appartiennent à des races assimilables, notamment aux races latines." *JO, Débats Parlementaires, Chambre des Députés*, Dec. 8, 1939, p. 2111.

120. Keeper of the seals, Ministry of Justice, circular, Dec. 26, 1939, APP DA 783 (Règlements).

121. Army chief of staff, overseas section, "Note sur l'utilisation des allemands, engagés volontaires pour la durée de la guerre," 9/EMA, Dec. 2, 1939, SHAT 7N 2475, dos. 2.

122. Gamelin, "Annotation du Général Commandant en Chef les Forces Terrestres," Dec. 3, 1939, SHAT 7N 2475, dos. 2; Ministry of National Defense and War, President of the Council, to the Commander in Chief of the North African Theater of Operations, no. 13091, Dec. 16, 1939, SHAT 7N 2475, dos 1$_2$.

123. Army chief of staff, overseas section, "Note sur l'utilisation des allemands, engagés volontaires pour la durée de la guerre," 9/EMA, Dec. 2, 1939, SHAT 7N 2475, dos. 2. According to Pol, however, the refugees had been promised they would be put into special units when they arrived in North Africa; they were instead put into regular Legion units (p. 247).

124. Army Chief of Staff, Overseas Section, "Note sur l'utilisation des allemands, engagés volontaires pour la durée de la guerre," 9/EMA, Dec. 2, 1939, SHAT 7N 2475, dos. 2. See also Crémieux-Brilhac, 1: 490.

125. Ministry of National Defence, EMA, [sometime after May 10, 1940], "Note pour M. le Général Ménard, chargé de l'utilisation des étrangers pour la Défense Nationale," SHAT 7N 2475, dos. 1$_2$. See also "Anti-Nazis Herded Back into Germany," *NYT*, Aug. 21, 1940, p. 3. Crémieux-Brilhac claims that this quota was never implemented, but this does not seem to be the case (vol. 1, p. 491).

126. Foreign Ministry (Contrôle des étrangers), to the French ambassador, Berne, no. 590, May 29, 1940, MAE Z 760, p. 5.

127. Szajkowski, *Jews*, pp. 61, 70–71. See also Szajkowski, *Analytical Franco-Jewish Gazetteer*, pp. 22–25.

128. Adjudant-Chef Mazzoni, Chef de l'Annexe de Barcarès, Camp de Barcarès, to M. le Capitaine, Chef du S.I.L. at Sathonay, Jan. 25, 1940, no. 118/AB, SHAT 7N 2475, dos. 3; Porch, pp. 452–53.

129. Porch, p. 451.

130. Szajkowski, *Jews*, p. 71.

131. Note verbale (Secret), "Israélites de la Légion," Jan. 10, 1940, SHAT 7N 2475, dos. 3.

132. Perisse, battalion chief, 1er Bureau, army chief of staff, to the army chief of staff, overseas section, "Note pour information," Feb. 13, 1940, SHAT 7N 2475, dos. 1₂.

133. Szajkowski, *Jews*, p. 70.

134. Porch, pp. 446–47.

135. Ibid., pp. 442–43; Koestler, *Scum*, p. 186, note.

136. Szajkowski, *Jews*, p. 83.

137. Porch, p. 454.

138. Moutet, "Le Sort des réfugiés politiques: Le régime imposé à de nombreux amis de notre pays a pu être amelioré: il n'est pas encore satisfaisant," *La Lumière*, Mar. 1, 1940, pp. 1, 2. As the title of this article suggests, Moutet believed that many problems persisted.

139. Feuchtwanger, p. 77.

140. "Note de la Sûreté Nationale: Mesures à prendre a/s des étrangers ressortissants allemands," May 15, 1940, MAE Z 791, pp. 90–91; Colson, Ministry of National Defense and War, 1/EMA, to the military governor general of Paris and the commanding generals of the Paris regions, no. 121. III (Very Urgent), May 15, 1940, APP DA 784 (Règlements) (also in MAE Z 791, pp. 93–94); Bussière and Colson, Ministry of National Defense, 2/EMA, 2ème bureau, no. 12.207-I/EMA, and Ministry of the Interior, Sûreté Nationale, 7ème bureau, to the prefects and commanding generals of the Paris regions, no. 46, May 17, 1940, APP DA 784 (Règlements) (also in SHAT 7N 2462, dos. 3); CAR, "Note on the Activity of the CAR from May 1, 1940," translated in JDC no. 604; "L'Internement des allemands," *Le Matin*, May 15, 1940, p. 2; "Contre la cinquième colonne," *Le Matin*, May 18, 1940, pp. 1–2; "Les Allemands au Vélodrome d'Hiv," *Le Matin*, May 24, 1940, p. 2; "Les Mesures de sécurité à l'égard des réfugiés étrangers sont renforcées," *Le Matin*, May 25, 1940, p. 2; "France Interns Germans," *NYT*, May 16, 1940; "Paris Will Check on Refugees," *NYT*, May 25, 1940, p. 3; Kempner, pp. 456–57; Koessler, p. 119; Schramm and Vormeier, pp. 271–72; Walter, "Internierung," pp. 300–302; Fabian and Coulmas, pp. 75–76; Grynberg, *Les Camps*, pp. 81–83; Tartakower and Grossmann, p. 152.

On the extension of the age limit, see Winter, Ministry of National Defense, I/EMA, 2ème Bureau, no. 12. III., and Ministry of the Interior, Sûreté Nationale, 7ème Bureau, to the prefects, no. 46, May 29, 1940, APP DA 784 (Règlements); Vormeier, "La Situation des émigrés," p. 155.

141. Grynberg, *Les Camps*, p. 83. As always, there were exemptions. These included men currently employed in defense-related industries, men currently mobilized in either the *prestataire* service or the Foreign Legion, men having at least one son serving in the army, and women related to someone in these categories or having children under 16 or French husbands. Prominent political personalities whose loyalty was attested to by the Foreign Ministry, the General Staff, and the Ministry of the Interior were also to be exempted. In the chaos of the times, however, these exemptions were often ignored. President of the Council, Ministry of National Defense and War, to the commanding general of the North African Theater of Op-

erations, no. 13091, Dec. 16, 1939, SHAT 7N 2475, dos. 12; Feuchtwanger, p. 45; Lania, pp. 120–21.

142. Although the French agreed to take German, Czech, and Austrian refugees from the Low Countries on condition that they register with the police and ultimately go to the camps, every effort was made to prevent the East European and stateless refugees among them, nearly all of whom were Jews, from entering the country. "Review of the Year 5700," p. 450; Belgian refugee committee member, "Report on the Events from May 10th to July 30, 1940," Sept. 26, 1940, JDC no. 618; Joseph J. Schwartz, "Memorandum on the Situation of Jewish Refugees from Belgium in France," Sept. 8, 1940, JDC no. 618. According to this last report, there were 15,000–20,000 Jewish refugees from the Low Countries in France by Sept. 1940.

143. Koessler, pp. 104–14; Kempner, pp. 455–57; "Review of the Year 5700," p. 452; Jong, pp. 87–88; Cesarani, p. 45; Wasserstein, *Britain*, p. 88; Fox, "German- and Austrian-Jewish Volunteers," p. 29; Seyfert, pp. 170–79.

144. Letter from St. Cyprien, Sept. 16, 1940, JDC no. 618; Fittko, pp. 11, 17, 32; Schramm and Vormeier, p. 10; Lania, pp. 129–30.

145. Lania, p. 131.

146. Letter from St. Cyprien, Sept. 16, 1940, JDC no. 618. On the odyssey of the Belgian refugees, see also Feuchtwanger, p. 96.

147. Koestler, *Scum*, p. 176. See also "L'Internement des allemands," *Le Matin*, May 15, 1940, p. 2; Jong, pp. 90–93; Felstiner, pp. 117–19.

148. Pol, pp. 171, 175; Sherwood, *Georges Mandel*, pp. 234–36; Kempner, pp. 454–55; Lazareff, p. 303; Ory, *Les Collaborateurs*, pp. 32–33. On these right-wing collaborators in the 1930's in general, see Ory, *Les Collaborateurs*, pp. 11–35.

149. Sherwood, *Georges Mandel*, pp. 234, 236.

150. "Communists' Wives Seized in France," *NYT*, May 26, 1940, p. 33. See also Jong, p. 93.

151. Ministry of the Interior, Sûreté Nationale, to the Prefects, P.A. 7.364/I, "Efforts allemands pour atteindre le moral français," May 14, 1940, AN F⁷ 14713.

152. Colson, Ministry of National Defense, to the military governor general of Paris and the commanding generals of the Paris regions, 1/EMA, May 7 and 13, 1940, SHAT 7N 2462, dos. 3; Fabian and Coulmas, pp. 68–69; Koessler, p. 120.

153. For descriptions of St. Cyprien from May through the fall of 1940, see Member of the Belgian refugee committee, "Report on the Events from May 10th to July 30, 1940," Sept. 26, 1940, JDC no. 618; Letter from St. Cyprien, Sept. 16, 1940, JDC no. 618; "The Plight of Jewish Refugees in French Camps," excerpt from *Jewish Daily Forward*, Oct. 31, 1940, JDC no. 618.

154. Letter from St. Cyprien, Sept. 16, 1940, JDC no. 618. See also "The Plight of Jewish Refugees in French Camps," excerpt from *Jewish Daily Forward*, Oct. 31, 1940, JDC no. 618.

155. Lazareff, diary entry, May 16, 1940, p. 288.

156. Grynberg, *Les Camps*, p. 81.

157. Foreign Ministry (Europe), "Note pour la sous-direction Unions," May 31, 1940, MAE Z 791, p. 277. See also Lania, pp. 120–21; Feuchtwanger, p. 41.

158. Feuchtwanger, p. 110. See also Lania, pp. 157–58.

159. Hans-Albert Walter, "Internierung," pp. 302–3, 305–7; Tartakower and Grossmann, pp. 153–54; Fittko, p. 51; Grynberg, *Les Camps*, p. 138; Feuchtwanger, pp. 100–126; A. Herenroth, to M. Troper, July [15], 1940, JDC no. 618, pp. 121–22; Herbert Zivi, I. Kampf, and Moise Torczyner, St. Cyprien Camp, to Morris Troper of the JDC, July 17, 1940, JDC no. 618. International organizations also appealed to the French government to release the refugees from the camps. See "Asks France to Free Refugees," *NYT*, June 21, 1940, p. 13.

160. Fry, pp. ix–x; Palmier, 2: 129–30; Fabian and Coulmas, p. 77; Schramm and Vormeier, p. 265; Tartakower and Grossmann, p. 154; Walter, "Internierung," p. 309; Koestler, *Scum*, p. 151.

161. Tartakower and Grossmann, pp. 156–57; Feuchtwanger, pp. 131, 171–74; Lania, p. 160; Koestler, *Scum*, pp. 205–6, 238, 260–61; A. Herenroth, to M. Troper, July [15], 1940, JDC no. 618, pp. 121–22. Benjamin tried to escape over the Pyrenees; when this failed, he committed suicide. Fittko, pp. 103–15. Koestler suggests that many of those who committed suicide might not have done so had they believed that Great Britain would fight on.

162. Feuchtwanger, p. 129.

163. Lazareff, p. 342; Koestler, *Scum*, pp. 206–7.

164. On problems obtaining exit visas in the summer of 1940, see Fry, pp. 6–7, 14–19; Fittko, p. 96.

165. Fry, p. 13. See also Tartakower and Grossmann, pp. 156–57; Kempner, pp. 449–50. For other descriptions of this period, see Koestler, *Scum*, pp. 155–264; Feuchtwanger, pp. 169–261; Döblin, pp. 150–210; Fittko, pp. 55–101; Jungk, pp. 179–92.

166. Lazareff, p. 342; Koestler, *Scum*, pp. 276–77.

167. Szajkowski, *Jews*, p. 72; Porch, pp. 454–55.

168. Habe, pp. 165, 137. According to Koestler, one army colonel maintained that his troops had been attacked not by the Germans, but by "a column of Jewish refugees" near Longwy, and his troops found this claim entirely credible. Koestler, *Scum*, p. 232.

169. Tartakower and Grossmann, pp. 145–46; Porch, pp. 458–61. According to Porch, losses in other regiments were similarly high. The 11th REI lost 75% of its men and the 12th REI lost over 90%.

170. Szajkowski, *Jews*, pp. 72–73; Habe, p. 199.

171. Porch, p. 457, see also p. 461.

172. Habe, pp. 46, 54–55, 130. According to Koestler, even left-wing soldiers, although they knew what they were fighting against, no longer knew what they were fighting for because they too had lost faith in democracy. See Koestler, *Scum*, pp. 48, 273. For another émigré account of the military experience in 1939–40, see Manès Sperber, *Until My Eyes Are Closed with Shards*, translated by Harry Zohn (New York, 1994), pp. 165–82.

173. "Extraits de fiches de renseignements établis après l'armistice de 1940 par le commandant Jacquot," n.d., SHAT 7N 2475, dos. 3.

174. Porch, p. 454. See also Crémieux-Brilhac, 1: 491.

175. Porch, p. 461, and pp. 458–62.

176. Crémieux-Brilhac also stresses the distinction between the treatment of for-

eigners during the "phony war" and their subsequent treatment under the Vichy regime (vol. 1, pp. 484–99).

177. Porch, pp. 444–46; "Report on the Visit to the Camp of St. Juste en Chaussée," Dec. 21, 1939, attached to "Minutes of Plenary Meeting of Commission des Centres de Rassemblement de l'Intercomité des Oeuvres Françaises," Dec. 1, 1939, JDC no. 617. See also Heinz Soffner, "The Internment of Refugees in France During the War: Legal Situation, Facts, Conclusions," JDC no. 618; Feuchtwanger, p. 4.

178. Feuchtwanger, pp. 40–42, 48–49, 85.

179. Koestler, *Scum*, pp. 67, 141–43, 159, 193. Koestler draws a sharp distinction between this slogan and the initial slogan of the troops at the outset of the war, "Il faut en finir" ("It's necessary to get the job done"). Pol, p. 273, claims the motto that summed up the mentality that led to debacle was "Tout s'arrangera."

180. Habe, pp. 151, 153.

181. Döblin, pp. 18, 115–16.

182. Member of the Belgian refugee committee, "Report on the Events from May 10th to July 30, 1940," Sept. 26, 1940, JDC no. 618.

Chapter Twelve

1. Phipps, to the Foreign Office, Apr. 13, 1938, PRO FO 371/21634.C3205, pp. 207–10.

2. According to Pierre-Bloch, this slogan was commonly heard in Parisian salons. Pierre-Bloch, pp. 88, 106. In 1938, Emmanuel Mounier also commented, "On ne comprendra rien au comportement de cette fraction de la bourgeoisie française, si on ne l'entend murmurer à mi-voix: 'Plutôt Hitler que Blum.'" Cited in Winock, *Histoire politique*, p. 176. See also Y. R. Simon, pp. 147–77.

3. Schor, "Les Partis politiques," p. 458.

4. R. Laffargue, "Les Cléricaux hitlériens d'Alsace sont de plus en plus menaçant," *La Lumière*, Sept. 16, 1936, pp. 1–2.

5. The full text of this debate is cited in Birnbaum, *Un Mythe politique*, pp. 327–29. See also Lacouture, p. 271; Schor, *L'Antisémitisme en France*, pp. 172–73; "Documents pour l'édification des braves gens," *DdV*, June 10, 1936, p. 3; "Blum Wins in a Test," *NYT*, June 7, 1936, pp. 1, 29.

6. Vallat, to Paul David, Feb. 17, 1934, in ACIP B (not classified).

7. Birnbaum, *Un Mythe politique*, p. 173; Lacouture, p. 390.

8. Phipps, to the Foreign Office, Apr. 13, 1938, PRO FO 371/21634.C3205, pp. 207–10; Schuker, p. 156–57.

9. "On sollicite des éclaircissements," *La Juste parole*, no. 7 (Feb. 20, 1937): 6; La Rocque, "Avertissements," *Le Petit journal*, Apr. 7, 1938, cited in CDV, bulletin no. 63, Apr. 14, 1938, in AIU, ms. 650, boîte 2.

10. Phipps, to the Foreign Office, Apr. 13, 1938, PRO FO 371/21634.C3205, pp. 207–10; Lacouture, p. 267.

11. "France, terre d'asile," *AF*, Aug. 25, 1936, clipped in APP BA 241.155-1-G. Also cited in Thalmann, "L'Emigration allemande," p. 49.

12. "Mise au Point," *Revue des deux mondes*, July 1, 1936, back cover.

13. "Les Informations parisiennes: Les machinations contre les lois sociales," Paris, Oct. 11, 1937, clipped in APP BA 67 Provisoire 331-500-1. On Herriot's restrictionist policies as head of the Interministerial Commission on Immigration in 1934–35, see Chapter 3.

14. Sir George Clerk, British embassy, Paris, to the Foreign Office, telegrams of Mar. 18–19, 1936, PRO FO 371/19855.C2049.

15. Italics in original text. Jaloux, "Les Indésirables," *L'Echo de Paris*, Oct. 5, 1936, pp. 1, 5; Jaloux, *Le Petit journal*, Oct. 16, 1937, cited in CDV, bulletin no. 45, Oct. 21, 1937, in AIU, ms. 650, boîte 2. See also Paul Perrin, "Divagations xénophobes d'un académicien," *Le Peuple*, Nov. 16, 1936. On Jaloux's antisemitism, see also Weber, p. 103, and for a general discussion of the theme of Jews as warmongers, see Weber, pp. 19, 22–24, 106–10.

16. *JO, Documents Parlementaires*, annexe no. 1319, "Proposition de lois, 2ème session extraordinaire, séance du 13 novembre, 1936," Nov. 13, 1936, pp. 850–51.

17. Phipps, to Foreign Office, Apr. 13, 1938, PRO FO 371/21634.C3205, pp. 207–10; Report, [CDV], "L'Antisémitisme en France," Jan. 1939, in AIU, ms. 650, boîte 15 (50).

18. Cited in "Bagatelles pour un massacre," *Je suis partout*, Mar. 4, 1938.

19. Céline, pp. 81–82. On Céline's antisemitism, see also Kingston, part II, pp. 75–129; Weinberg, p. 182; Millman, pp. 276–78; Betz, pp. 716–27; Carroll, pp. 171–72, 180–95; Soucy, pp. 299–305.

20. Report, Groupement d'Etude et d'Information, Race et Racisme [late Nov. or early Dec. 1938], in AIU, ms. 650, boîte 15 (50).

21. Cited in Rabi, p. 382, and in Azéma, pp. 9–10. See also Landau, p. 187.

22. "Un Juif polonais blesse grièvement un conseiller de l'ambassade d'Allemagne," *AF*, Nov. 8, 1938, clipped in APP BA 269 Provisoire (dossier: "L'Assassination de M. vom Rath"), also cited in Thalmann, "L'Emigration allemande," p. 63.

23. *AF*, Nov. 20, 1938, p. 1. Contrary to Maurras's assertion, 91 Jews were killed during Kristallnacht.

24. Cited in Pierrard, p. 261. Similarly, at the time of the Franco-German pact, *L'Action française* warned the nation not to allow German antisemitism to interfere with attempts at Franco-German reconciliation. As J. Delebecque wrote: "Laissons Washington et Berlin échanger des menaces ou des injures, laissons les Juifs et les Nazis se débrouiller entre eux. Ne nous mêlons pas de leurs affaires. Nous voulons bien nous faire tuer pour défendre notre terre et notre honneur. Pour les beaux yeux d'Israël, non, et mille fois non." "Campagne juive en Amérique," *AF*, Dec. 25, 1938, pp. 1–2. See also Charles Maurras, "La Politique," *AF*, Dec. 26, 1938, p. 1.

25. "'Bagatelles': Les Francs-tireurs d'Israël à l'oeuvre," *Je suis partout*, Sept. 16, 1938, clipped in AN 72 AJ 600.

26. L. Rebatet, "L'Attentat de l'ambassade d'Allemagne," *Je suis partout*, Nov. 11, 1938, clipped in AIU, ms. 650, boîte 11 (40). On Rebatet's antisemitism in the 1930's and 1940's, see Carroll, pp. 196–221.

27. Jeanneney, *François de Wendel*, p. 587; L'Huillier, pp. 418–19. Kérillis was indeed sensitive to this charge and sought to downplay the significance of Jewish sup-

port for his views. See "Une Lettre de Henri de Kérillis à M. Louis Dreyfus," *L'E-poque*, Dec. 1, 1938.

28. "La France aux français!" *Le Matin*, Dec. 21, 1938, clipped in AIU, ms. 650, boîte 14 (48). See also Jean Luchaire's statements in *Notre Temps*, which was heavily subsidized by the Nazis. Cited in Dumoulin, pp. 15, 96.

29. "Faisons le point," *Gringoire*, Oct. 13, 1938, clipped in AIU, ms. 650, boîte 15 (50).

30. "Des Centres spéciaux de concentration pour les étrangers indésirables," *Le Journal*, Nov. 21, 1938.

31. L. Rebatet, "Les Emigrés politiques en France: Peut-on éviter le pogrom?" *Je suis partout*, Mar. 4, 1938, clipped in AIU, ms. 650, boîte 13 (45).

32. "La Politique," *AF*, Oct. 7 1938, p. 1.

33. Report [Groupement d'Etude et d'Information, Race et Racisme], Paris, Service de Documentation, Nov. 1938, AN 72 AJ 601. See also Millman, p. 259.

34. For La Rocque's ambivalent position on the Jewish question, see Férenzy, "Le Parti Social Français et les juifs," *La Juste parole*, Apr. 20, 1939, pp. 3–7; Centre de Documentation et de Propagande [Henry Coston's antisemitic committee]; Confidential report [Groupement Race et Racisme], Nov. 7, 1938, in Vanikoff Collection, AN 72 AJ 601; CDV, bulletin no. 74 [n.d.], p. 6, in Documents of French Jewish History, JTS, box 12, folder 1; CDV, bulletin no. 75 [Nov. 1938], in AN 72 AJ 601; Marrus and Paxton, p. 47; Schor, *L'Antisémitisme en France*, pp. 44, 79, 220, 286; Millman; Irvine, "Fascism," pp. 290–93; Soucy, pp. 152–58; J.-Ch. Bonnet, p. 228.

35. L. Rebatet, "Les Emigrés politiques en France: Peut-on éviter le pogrom?" *Je suis partout*, Mar. 4, 1938, clipped in AIU, ms. 650, boîte 13 (45).

36. Rebatet, "Pour un statut des Juifs en France," *Je suis partout*, Feb. 17, 1939, cited in *UI*, Feb. 24, 1939, no. 23, p. 415. "Les Juifs et la France," *Je suis partout*, special no., cited in CDV, bulletin no. 79, Mar. 3, 1939, p. 1, in Documents of French Jewish History, JTS, box 12, folder 1; *Je suis partout*, Apr. 15, 1938, special issue on the Jewish question, cited in CDV, bulletin no. 64, Apr. 28, 1938, in AIU, ms. 650, boîte 15 (52). On extreme-right-wing demands for a Jewish statute, see Schor, *L'Anti-sémitisme en France*, pp. 183–97; Carroll, pp. 111–12.

37. CDV, bulletin no. 63, Apr. 14, 1938, p. 9, in AN 72 AJ 592 (also in AIU, ms. 650, boîte 2).

38. *Bulletin municipal officiel de la ville de Paris*, Mar. 21, 1939, pp. 44–45, clipped in AIU, ms. 650, boîte 6 (15). Robert de Rothschild personally thanked Le Provost de Launay for having suppressed Darquier's remarks. Rothschild, to Le Provost de Launay, Apr. 4, 1939, in AIU, ms. 650, boîte 6 (15). See also "Bagarre au sujet du grand Rabbin," *Samedi*, no. 12 (Mar. 25, 1939): 2; "Les Fantaisies de M. Darquier et l'avenant de la CPDE," *La Justice*, Mar. 30, 1939, in AN 72 AJ 592 (press clippings); "M. Darquier de Pellepoix est vertement remis à sa place par M. Le Provost de Launay," *La Juste parole*, no. 53 (Apr. 5, 1939): 19–20; Schor, *L'Antisémitisme en France*, pp. 221–22.

39. "Darquier sans Pellepoix rédacteur du 'Bulletin municipal officiel,'" *DdV*, n.s., no. 129 (Dec. 17, 1938): 2.

40. "Le Nombre des enfants étrangers dans les écoles atteint à peine 8%," [*La République*], Dec. 20, 1938, clipped in AIU, ms. 650, boîte 13 (46). For a biography of Darquier de Pellepoix that focuses primarily on his career after 1940, see Laloum. For additional information about antisemitism in the Paris Municipal Council, see various letters and clippings in AN 72 AJ 592 (Vanikoff Collection) (file: "L'Antisémitisme en France avant la Guerre: Darquier de Pellepoix, Muncipal Council, etc."); "Revue de la Presse," *UI*, July 17, 1936, pp. 681–83; "Revue de la Presse: Au Conseil Général de la Seine," *UI*, July 24, 1936, pp. 698–700; "Les Provocations antisémites des amis d'Hitler continuent," *Le Populaire*, May 28, 1936, p. 3; "Le Grand Paris en a assez de servir de dépotoire à la pègre cosmopolite," *AF*, Oct. 15, 1938, clipped in AN 72 AJ 601; "Un Juif polonais blesse grièvement un conseiller de l'ambassade d'Allemagne," *AF*, Nov. 8, 1938, clipped in APP BA 269 Provisoire; "Darquier de Pellepoix dénonce le péril juif," *AF*, Dec. 16, 1938, clipped in AN 72 AJ 592; J. B., "Israel ...au Conseil Municipal," *Samedi*, Dec. 31, 1938, pp. 2, 7; "Question relative aux étrangers: Compte rendu de la séance du Conseil Municipal du jeudi 15 décembre 1938," *Je suis partout*, Jan. 31, 1939, p. 59, clipped in AIU, ms. 650, boîte 13; Thalmann, "L'Emigration allemande," p. 63; Birnbaum, pp. 331–32.

41. "Les Etrangers en France," editorial, *Le Temps*, Nov. 2, 1938, p. 1.

42. "Le Problème des réfugiés," editorial, *Le Temps*, July 8, 1938, p. 1.

43. Ibid., p. 1.

44. "Les Etrangers en France," editorial, *Le Temps*, May 16, 1938, p. 1.

45. Ibid., p. 1. The point that immigration was dangerous precisely because of the low birthrate was also made by Henry Lémery, a conservative senator and former minister of justice; see "Pour la protection des réfugiés politiques," *Tribune des nations*, July 11, 1938, pp. 1, 3, clipped in AIU, ms. 650, boîte 13.

46. "Politique d'immigration," editorial, *Le Temps*, Mar. 13, 1939, clipped in AIU, ms. 650, boîte 14 (48).

47. "La Police des étrangers," *Le Temps*, Nov. 9, 1938, p. 1. See also Marrus and Paxton, p. 41.

48. "Hospitalité oblige," editorial, *Le Temps*, Feb. 7, 1939, p. 1.

49. "Nos Hôtes et nous," editorial, *Le Temps*, Mar. 9, 1939, p. 1.

50. "Les Etrangers en France," editorial, *Le Temps*, Mar. 26, 1939, clipped in AIU, ms. 650, boîte 14 (48).

51. "Politique d'immigration," editorial, *Le Temps*, Mar. 13, 1939, clipped in AIU, ms. 650, boîte 14 (48).

52. "Les Etrangers en France," editorial, *Le Temps*, Mar. 26, 1939, clipped in AIU, ms. 650, boîte 14 (48); J.-Ch. Bonnet, p. 368; Marrus and Paxton, p. 64.

53. "Herschel Grunszpan [*sic*] est interrogé cet après-midi," *L'Intransigeant*, Nov. 9, 1938, clipped in AN 72 AJ 600; Gallus, "Assez d'étrangers," *L'Intransigeant*, Nov. 20, 1938, clipped in AIU, ms. 650, boîte 13.

54. "La Leçon d'un crime," editorial, *Journal des débats*, Nov. 11, 1938, clipped in AN 72 AJ 600. See also "Après la Conférence d'Evian," editorial, *Journal des débats*, July 17, 1938, clipped in AIU, ms. 650, boîte 12 (44).

55. Lauzanne, "Le Problème juif," *Le Matin*, Feb. 2, 1939, pp. 1–2. See also "Le

Problème juif vu par Stéphane Lauzanne dans *Le Matin*," *La Juste parole*, no. 50 (Feb. 20, 1939): 32.

56. José Germain, "Francis Croisset oui! Les Natan non!" *L'Epoque*, Jan. 23, 1939, pp. 1–2.

57. "Was wir von den wahren Juden erwarten?" *Elsässer Kurier*, Oct. 2, 1938, clipped in ADBR AL 98 698.

58. "La Lettre de M. Rossé," *L'Aube*, Oct. 14, 1938, pp. 1, 3; E. Buré, "L'Alsace est française et elle veut le rester," *L'Ordre*, Oct. 15, 1938, pp. 1, 4; CDV, bulletin no. 72, Oct. 20, 1938, p. 9, in Documents of French Jewish History, JTS, box 12, folder 1. See also Millman, p. 292.

59. E. Buré, "L'Alsace est française et elle veut le rester," *L'Ordre*, Oct. 15, 1938, pp. 1, 4. For a general overview of the press reactions to Rossé's letters, see Lucidus, "Tour d'horizon, Non! Il n'y a pas d'affaire d'Alsace," *L'Aube*, Oct. 16–17, 1938, p. 2.

60. René Laffargue, "Que valent les protestations de M. Rossé?" *La Lumière*, Oct. 21, 1938, p. 3.

61. Erhard, "La Campagne d'excitation des députés cléricaux contre la France," *Le Populaire*, Oct. 8, 1938, clipped in AN 72 AJ 601. See also [CDV], Confidential, "Rapport sur l'agitation antisémitique en Alsace et en Lorraine," Oct. 9, 1938, in AIU, France V D 18. Rossé's antisemitism appears to have been more deeply rooted, however. Already in 1937, he had castigated the Popular Front as a Jewish government, and he warned Léon Blum that if anticlerical legislation was introduced into Alsace, there would be a fierce antisemitic backlash. "Un Mouvement antijuif menace les communautés de l'Est," *UI*, Feb. 19, 1937, p. 374.

62. Léon Merklen, "Le Problème juif et l'universalité de la rédemption," *La Croix*, Sept. 1, 1938.

63. Jean Guiraud, "Position de l'église en face de la xénophobie," *La Croix*, Sept. 27, 1938, pp. 1, 5.

64. S. Fumet, "L'Antisémitisme," *Le Temps présent*, Sept. 9, 1938. See also "A Travers la presse: L'Antisémitisme vu par M. Stanislas Fumet," *La Juste parole*, no. 43 (Nov. 5, 1938): 20–22; CDV, bulletin no. 71, Oct. 6, 1938, p. 8; Documents of French Jewish History, JTS, box 12, folder 1; Marrus and Paxton, p. 52; Schor, *L'Antisémitisme en France*, p. 233; Birnbaum, *Un Mythe politique*, p. 251. At the time of Kristallnacht, *Le Temps présent* again expressed this view. See Georges Hourdin, "L'Allemagne, les juifs et nous," editorial, *Le Temps présent*, Nov. 18, 1938, cited in *La Juste parole*, no. 45 (Dec. 5, 1938): 10, and in CDV, bulletin no. 75, Dec. 1, 1938, pp. 22–23, Documents of French Jewish History, JTS, box 12, folder 1. Another liberal Catholic paper, *Le Voltigeur*, also supported a *numerus clausus* for Jews. See P. Henri Simon, "De la qualité de citoyen," *Le Voltigeur*, no. 11 (Mar. 1, 1939): 3.

65. "M. François Mauriac, de l'Académie française...," *La Juste parole*, no. 9 (Mar. 20, 1937): 1; "Remerciements et réponse à M. Charles-François Mauriac," *La Juste parole*, no. 11 (Apr. 20, 1937): 2–3; "Le C...D...V remercie M. François Mauriac et lui répond," *UI*, Apr. 23, 1937, p. 508; Birnbaum, *Un Mythe politique*, pp. 245–46.

66. Mauriac, "Réponse à B. Lecache," *La Flèche*, Oct. 28, 1938, cited in Birnbaum, *Un Mythe politique*, p. 247.

67. D'Harcourt, "Le Douloureux problème des émigrés," *La Croix*, July 14, 1938, clipped in AIU, ms. 650, boîte 12. See also Schor, *L'Opinion française et les étrangers*, p. 329; and Katz, pp. 113–14. On the Mauriac Committee's financial dependence on the CAR, see Renée Bedarida, "Les Catholiques français face aux réfugiés allemands et autrichiens (1933–1939)," in Bartosek et al., pp. 70–71.

68. Férenzy, "Les Limites du refuge," no. 43 (Nov. 5, 1938): 3–8; Férenzy, "Le Parti Social Français et les juifs," Apr. 20, 1939, pp. 3–7; Férenzy, "Comment combattre l'antisémitisme?" no. 59 (July 5, 1939): 2–5, all in *La Juste parole*. See also Férenzy, "Imposantes manifestations de protestation contre la persécution juive en Roumanie," no. 27 (Feb. 5, 1938): 19–20; Férenzy, "Catholiques antisémites," no. 57 (June 5, 1939): 1–7, all in *La Juste parole*.

69. "Si on laissait d'abord rentrer les religieux," *La Liberté du Sud-Ouest*, Aug., 1938, clipped in AIU, ms. 650, boîte 11 (40). See also "Die Verfolgungen, die man verschweigt," *Elsässer Kurier*, Dec. 5, 1938, clipped in ADBR AL 98 698. On the anticlerical campaign after the Dreyfus Affair, see Cobban, pp. 58–65.

70. L. Donnas, "Justice et charité pour tout," *La Croix du Rhône*, July 18, 1939, clipped in AIU, ms. 650, boîte 12 (43).

71. L.-A. Gaboriaud, "La Primauté de la personne humaine," *L'Ere nouvelle*, Aug. 2, 1938, clipped in AN 72 AJ 601. See also "Revue de la presse: Le sort des israélites," *Le Temps*, Aug. 3, 1938, p. 3, clipped in BDIC Dos. Duchêne, GFΔ Rés. 86; Berstein, "Le Parti radical-socialiste," pp. 300–301; Berstein, *Histoire*, pp. 585–86.

72. "Frontgegen alle Verfolger!" Letter from Alsatian Catholic leaders to Pastor Debu, n.d., in ADBR AL 98 698.

73. Phipps, to Foreign Office, Apr. 13, 1938, PRO FO 371/21634.C3205, pp. 207–10.

74. "Le Congrès Radical des Fédérations du Sud-Est réclame un contrôle sévère des étrangers," *Le Matin*, Jan. 10, 1938, clipped in AIU, ms. 650, boîte 13 (46) (dossier: La France et les réfugiés).

75. "La Nouvelle loi sur les étrangers en France," *L'Oeuvre*, Apr. 22, 1938.

76. Paul Elbel, "L'Hitlérisme et l'Alsace," Oct. 20, 1938, pp. 1, 4, and "Mise au point," Nov. 8, 1938, pp. 1, 4, both in *L'Oeuvre*. After the assassination of vom Rath, *L'Oeuvre* reiterated Elbel's demand for a statute for foreigners and admonished the refugees not to treat France as "un foyer de complots." "Asile? Oui! Dépotoire? Non!" *L'Oeuvre*, Nov. 9, 1938.

77. Maurice Ajam, "Le Mélange des races," *La Dépêche de Toulouse*, Aug. 29, 1938, p. 1.

78. Cited in Férenzy, "Les Limites du refuge," *La Juste parole*, no. 43 (Nov. 5, 1938): 5. See also CDV, bulletin no. 71, Oct. 6, 1938, p. 7, in Documents of French Jewish History, JTS, box 12, folder 1.

79. Dominique, "Les Affaires de la France ne vous regardent pas," *La République*, Oct. 4, 1938, AIU, ms. 650, boîte 15 (50). For Fouchardière's views during the Munich crisis, see Chapter 9. On Dominique's views regarding foreigners and military service, see Chapter 10.

80. Dominique, "La France n'est pas un 'tir aux ambassadeurs,'" *La République*, Nov. 9, 1938, pp. 1, 3. See also Chapter 10.

81. Phipps, to the Foreign Office, Apr. 13, 1938, PRO FO 371/21634.C3205, pp. 207–10. On *L'Ere nouvelle*'s use of antisemitism to attack Blum, see also Birnbaum, *Un Mythe politique*, p. 295, and Millman, p. 88.

82. Henri Lebre, "La Conférence d'Evian," *L'Ere nouvelle*, July 16, 1938, clipped in AIU, ms. 650, boîte 12 (44).

83. Cited in Berstein, *Histoire*, p. 587, and Berstein and Becker, pp. 322–23.

84. *L'Ere nouvelle*, editorial, Nov. 8, 1938, clipped in AN 72 AJ 600 (also cited in CDV, bulletin no. 74, [Nov. 1938] p. 9, in Documents of French Jewish History, JTS, box 12, folder 1).

85. "Après les pogromes," *AF*, Nov. 14, 1938, clipped in AN 72 AJ 600.

86. Nicolas Paillot, "La Terreur nazie laisse nôtre grande presse indifférente," *La Lumière*, Nov. 18, 1938, p. 1. See also A. Bayet, "Une telle barbarie! ...Le monde s'indigne, la France se tait," *La Lumière*, Nov. 18, 1938, p. 1; Aragon, "Un Jour du monde, le 7 novembre 1938," *Ce Soir*, Nov. 9, 1938, clipped in AN 72 AJ 600.

87. "L'Attentat contre un attaché de l'ambassade d'Allemagne," *Le Populaire*, Nov. 9, 1938, p. 2, clipped in APP BA 269 Provisoire 163.300-0.

88. J. Ancelet-Hustache, "Attention chez nous aussi!" *L'Aube*, Nov. 19, 1938, p. 1.

89. All above quotes cited in Birnbaum, *Un Mythe politique*, pp. 290–91. According to Pierre-Bloch, Faure was taking subsidies from the Germans; see Pierre-Bloch, *Jusqu'au dernier jour*, p. 87.

90. "L'Antisémitisme renait: Pour le combattre enlevons lui ses prétextes," *La Flèche*, Nov. 11, 1938, pp. 1–2, clipped in AIU, ms. 650, boîte 17 (57). On the antisemitism of the pacifist left, see also Irvine, "Politics," pp. 18–19, 22–23; Philippe Burrin, *La Dérive fasciste: Doriot, Déat, Bergery, 1933–1945* (Paris, 1986); Lacouture, p. 201; Millman, pp. 280–83; Weber, pp. 22–24; Ingram, pp. 181, 189–91, 211, 233; Schor, "L'Antisémitisme dans la France," pp. 212–13.

91. Georges Mauco, "Quelques conséquences du mouvement de la population en Europe," *L'Europe nouvelle*, Apr. 8, 1939, pp. 390–91; Mauco, "Une Politique de la population," *L'Europe nouvelle*, Apr. 15, 1939, pp. 409–10; Mauco, "Le Problème démographique," pp. 538–44.

92. R. Millet, "Visites aux étrangers de France," part I, *Le Temps*, May 7, 1938, p. 8; Millet, p. 9. For Millet's discussion of competition in artisanry, petty commerce, and the liberal professions, see Millet, pp. 54–56, 73–101. For the series in *Le Temps*, see May 7, 10, 15, 19, 22, 24, and 28, 1938.

93. Millet, "Visites aux étrangers de France," part V, *Le Temps*, May 22, 1938, p. 6.

94. Millet, p. 11.

95. Millet, "Trois millions d'étrangers en France," *L'Ordre*, July 26, 1938, pp. 1, 4.

96. Millet, "Visites aux étrangers de France," part V, *Le Temps*, May 22, 1938, p. 6; Millet, "Visites aux étrangers de France," part VII (conclusion), *Le Temps*, May 28, 1938, p. 8.

97. Millet, "Visites aux étrangers de France," part III, *Le Temps*, May 15, 1938, p. 6; Millet, p. 48.

98. Millet, "Visites aux étrangers de France," part I, *Le Temps*, May 7, 1938, p. 8. On Millet, see also his articles, "La Grand pitié des parias," Mar. 19, 1938, p. 274;

"Trois millions d'étrangers en France," July 23, 1938, p. 794; "La Situation nouvelle des étrangers en France," May 13, 1939, pp. 514–15, all in *L'Europe nouvelle* and Millet's two articles titled "Trois millions d'étrangers en France," *L'Ordre*, July 25, 1938, pp. 1, 4, and July 26, 1938, pp. 1, 4.

99. Marrus and Paxton, p. 53; Marrus, "Vichy avant Vichy," pp. 89–90; Marrus, "Vichy before Vichy," p. 18.

100. Giraudoux, p. 62. For Giraudoux's discussion of the demographic problem, see ibid., pp. 35–77.

101. Ibid., pp. 65–66.

102. Ibid., pp. 75–76.

103. A. Bayet, "Une Telle barbarie!" *La Lumière*, Nov. 18, 1938, p. 1; Bayet, "Oui, mais notre peuple est antiraciste," *DdV*, Dec. 17, 1938, pp. 1–2. For Bayet's earlier views, see Chapter 4.

104. Bayet, "Tout peut encore être sauvé," *La Lumière*, Dec. 2, 1938, p. 3; Bayet, "Unissons-nous ou le fascisme passera," *La Lumière*, Dec. 9, 1938, pp. 1, 3.

105. Cot, "Réjoignons le camp des anti-racistes," *DdV*, Feb. 4, 1939.

106. E. Mounnier, "De la complicité de meurtre," *Esprit*, Dec. 1, 1938, pp. 469–70.

107. "On ne fondera pas la paix sur le pogrom," *L'Oeuvre*, Nov. 12, 1938, p. 1. Also cited in "Rites Set in Paris for Slain German," *NYT*, Nov. 12, 1938, p. 5, and "Les Journaux français, anglais et américains élèvent de vigoureuses protestations contre les terribles persécutions anti-juives en Allemagne," *UI*, Nov. 18, 1938, p. 127.

108. Léon Archimbaud, "L'Antisémitisme en France," *L'Oeuvre*, Jan. 2, 1939, pp. 1, 4 (reprinted in "Der Antisemitismus in Frankreich," *PT*, no. 884 [Jan. 4, 1939]: 2; *DdV*, Jan. 7, 1939, p. 4). See also "Une Lettre de Léon Archimbaud," *DdV*, Apr. 1, 1939, p. 1; Berstein, *Histoire*, p. 588.

109. E. Buré, "Une Déclaration commune franco-allemande...," *L'Ordre*, Nov. 24, 1938, p. 1 (also cited in "Tour d'Horizon: L'Accord Franco-Allemand," *L'Aube*, Nov. 25, 1938). On Buré's criticism of appeasement in the aftermath of Kristallnacht, see also E. Buré, "En Pleine barbarie," *L'Ordre*, Nov. 11, 1938, clipped in AN 72 AJ 600; Bernard Lavergne, "De Munich à Tunis," *L'Ordre*, Dec. 5, 1938, p. 4.

110. Pertinax, "La Conférence franco-britannique, La déclaration franco-allemande," *L'Europe nouvelle*, Nov. 26, 1938, p. 1276.

111. Kérillis, "L'Antisémitisme, ciment des dictatures," *L'Epoque*, Nov. 12, 1938 (also cited in "Les Journaux français, anglais et américains élèvent de vigoureuses protestations contre les terribles persécutions anti-juives en Allemagne," *UI*, Nov. 18, 1938, p. 127, and *La Juste parole*, no. 45 [Dec. 5, 1938]: 11). See also Kérillis, "Les Nationalistes devant le drame juif," *L'Epoque*, Nov. 20, 1938; Kérillis, "La Campagne antisémite, 1938–1939," *L'Epoque*, Jan. 5, 1940, clipped in AN 72 AJ 604; "Henri de Kérillis proteste," *Samedi*, no. 3 (Jan. 21, 1939): 2. The communist deputy Gabriel Péri agreed that the Franco-German pact was being used by the Nazis to split France from its democratic allies. See "Tour d'horizon: Pour les quatre," *L'Aube*, Nov. 24, 1938, and Marcel Brunelet, "La Presse française: La déclaration franco-allemande," *L'Ordre*, Nov. 25, 1938, p. 4.

112. On the activities of the Erfurt Center, see minister of the interior, Sûreté Nationale, to the Foreign Ministry, Feb. 9, 1937, and Apr. 19, 1937, MAE Z 705, pp. 181–82, 199–205; Groupement d'Etudes et d'Information, Race et Racisme, Service de Documentation, *Mémoire sur les partis anti-français en Alsace* (pamphlet [1939]), AN 72 AJ 601; Pol, pp. 127–37; Georges Oudard, "Hitler en Alsace," Apr. 26, 1939, p. 3; May 3, 1939, p. 3; May 10, 1939, p. 3, all in *Marianne*; René Laffargue, "Une Minorité pro-naziste s'évertue à troubler l'Alsace et la Lorraine," Apr. 1, 1938, pp. 1–2; "L'Appel du IIIe Reich," May 4, 1938, p. 3; "Laissera-t-on l'hitlérisme miner l'Alsace?" Apr. 15, 1938, pp. 1–2; "En Alsace, les ligues factieuses sont les auxiliaires de Hitler," May 20, 1938, pp. 1, 2; "La Lumière a demasqué l'hitlérisme en Alsace," June 3, 1938, pp. 1, 3; "Toléra-t-on des 'Sudètes' en France," Oct. 7, 1938, all in *La Lumière*; Laffargue, "La Propagande hitlérienne en Alsace," *Le Populaire*, Apr. 5, 1939, clipped in AN 72 AJ 601; "Les Causes de l'antisémitisme en Alsace," *UI*, May 20, 1938, p. 608; Schor, *L'Antisémitisme en France*, pp. 42–43, 45; Ory, *Les collaborateurs*, pp. 11–35; Kingston, p. 23; Pierre-Bloch, p. 87.

113. Claude Allain, "La 5e colonne," *Le Messidor*, no. 69 (July 7, 1939); Tribunal Correctionnel de la Seine, 12e Chambre, audience du 26 juillet 1939, Président M. Roux, in AN 72 AJ 592; "Jails Paris Antisemites: French Court Convicts Two under Decree Against Incitement," *NYT*, July 27, 1939, p. 7; press clippings in AN 72 AJ 592 (dossier: "L'Antisémitisme en France avant la Guerre"); Pol, p. 166.

114. "Paris Decrees Death for 2 Radio Traitors," *NYT*, Mar. 7, 1940, p. 11; Ory, *Les Collaborateurs*, pp. 16, 33. On the crackdown against the extreme right in general in the summer of 1939, see also Claude Allain, "La 5e colonne," *Le Messidor*, no. 69 (July 7, 1939); and the series of articles by Léon Groc titled "La Propagande hitlérienne dans le Nord," July 25, 1939, p. 2; July 26, 1939, p. 5; July 30, 1939, p. 8; Aug. 2, 1939, p. 3, all in *Le Petit Parisien*.

115. "La Carrière significative de Sturmel et Rossé," *Le Populaire*, Oct. 16, 1939, pp. 1, 3. On the general crackdown against extreme-right-wing leagues in Alsace, see [Madeleine Jacob], "La Croix gamée en Alsace et ailleurs," *Le Messidor*, May 5, 1939.

116. P. Dominique, "Est-il vrai que 750 000 étrangers veulent devenir français?" *La République*, Feb. 18, 1939, p. 1. See also Dominique, "Les prendra-t-on ces étrangers qui veulent être français?" *La République*, Feb. 5, 1939, pp. 1, 3. For Dominique's views on military service, see also Chapter 10, nn. 127–28.

117. "Politique d'immigration," editorial, *Le Temps*, Mar. 13, 1939, clipped in AIU, ms. 650, boîte 14 (48). See also "Les Etrangers en France," editorial, *Le Temps*, Mar. 26, 1939, clipped in AIU, ms. 650, boîte 14 (48); "Le Problème des étrangers," editorial, *Le Temps*, Apr. 15, 1939, p. 1.

118. D'Ormesson, "Naturalisations," *Le Figaro*, May 29, 1939, p. 1. See also Jean Schlumberger, "Etrangers et étrangers," *Le Figaro*, Apr. 20, 1939, p. 1.

119. The Count of Paris had disowned the Action Française in 1937. See Bernard and Dubief, p. 210. On this debate, see Henri Comte de Paris, "L'Antisémitisme devant la tradition française," *Le Courrier Royal*, [n.d.] clipped in AN 72 AJ 602; "Le Comte de Paris contre le racisme," *UI*, Jan. 6, 1939, p. 265; "L'Antisémitisme jugé par le Comte de Paris," extract from the *Courrier royale*, in *Le Figaro*, Dec. 30, 1938,

in AIU, ms. 650, boîte 15 (51); Kérillis, "Le Comte de Paris et les juifs," *L'Epoque*, Jan. 7, 1939, p. 1; "Vouloir exclure les juifs...," *La Juste parole*, no. 48 (Jan. 20, 1939): 25; "Réfutés par eux-mêmes," *La Lumière*, Jan. 6, 1939, clipped in AN 72 AJ 602; Schor, *L'Antisémitisme en France*, p. 221.

120. Stéphane Lauzanne, "Le Problème des réfugiés juifs," June 7, 1939, p. 1; S. Lauzanne, "Pour que la tragédie du St. Louis ne se reproduise pas," June 11, 1939, p. 1; "De nouveaux dons généreux sont adressés pour les réfugiés au *Matin*," June 14, 1939, p. 3; "Les Dons adressés au *Matin* pour les réfugiés du St. Louis," June 15, 1939, p. 1; "Des Industries nouvelles se créent," June 13, 1939, pp. 1–2, all in *Le Matin*.

Why *Le Matin* changed its position so abruptly is not known. It is possible that the paper, which had a tradition of taking subsidies from foreign governments, was taking subsidies from the native French Jewish community, with whom it had close contacts, as its interview with Chief Rabbi Julien Weill after Kristallnacht reveals. We do know that the community subsidized the press in certain circumstances. When the refugees from the S.S. *Saint-Louis* and *Flandres* were about to be resettled in the provinces, the JDC reported: "In Le Mans there was a rumour that the refugees coming there would be an added expense to the municipality and appropriate articles were thereupon published in the press [by the native Jewish community] to prove that this was not the case." JDC, Euroexco, "Report on the Situation in France, June 1939," June 20, 1939, JDC no. 191, pp. 41–44.

121. R. Millet, "La Situation nouvelle des étrangers en France," *L'Europe nouvelle*, May 13, 1939, pp. 514–15.

122. Italics in original text. "Les Etrangers en France," editorial, *Le Temps*, May 16, 1938, p. 1.

123. Robert Aron, "Les 'Sans-patrie,'" *Vendemiaire*, Oct. 12, 1938, clipped in AIU, ms. 650, boîte 13 (45).

124. Sherwood, *Georges Mandel*, p. 205.

125. Pertinax, "La Grande défiance," *L'Europe nouvelle*, Sept. 24, 1938, pp. 1024–25.

126. Kérillis, "Non, non, nous ne serions pas 'soviétisés' si nous sortions vainqueurs d'une guerre!" *L'Epoque*, Mar. 5, 1938. On the widespread belief that war would inevitably lead to social revolution at home, see Adamthwaite, *France*, pp. 26, 108–9, 220; Micaud; Irvine, *French Conservatism*; Johnson, p. 58; Y. R. Simon, pp. 147–77.

127. On these fears among the Radicals and Radical-Socialists in particular, see Berstein, *Histoire*, pp. 586–88; Berstein, "Le Parti radical-socialiste," pp. 276–306; Adamthwaite, France, 108–9, 220; Micaud, pp. 179, 203, n. 34, 203.

128. Léon Blum, "Je suis français," *Le Populaire*, Nov. 19, 1938, p. 1. Also cited in CDV, bulletin no. 75, Dec. 1, 1938, p. 6, Documents of French Jewish History, JTS, box 12, folder 1; "M. Léon Blum est français," *UI*, Dec. 2, 1938, clipped in AIU, ms. 650, boîte 11 (41), and in "Tour d'Horizon," *L'Aube*, Nov. 22, 1938, p. 2. Commenting on the depth of antisemitism directed against Blum, Sherwood states, "On the eve of the war, anti-semitism had risen to heights unequalled in France since the Dreyfus case. After Sumner Welles spoke to Léon Blum in March 1940, he received

more than three thousand letters from Frenchmen complaining of the honor he had bestowed on a Jew by his visit" (*Georges Mandel*, p. 244).

129. Sherwood, *Georges Mandel*, pp. 203–4, 213–14, 244–46.

Chapter Thirteen

1. Weinberg, p. 203 and pp. 171–211; Hyman, pp. 199–236, and esp. pp. 222–30; Nicault, "L'Accueil." For an abbreviated version of this article with the same title, see Bartosek et al., pp. 53–59. All citations of Nicault below are from the longer version. For a recent summary of these views, see also Grynberg, "L'Accueil," pp. 142–47.

2. Oualid served as director of the Comité Central d'Assistance aux Emigrants Juifs, a committee devoted to facilitating the emigration of East European Jews from France. He was also a prominent professor of demography at the Sorbonne and wrote extensively on the subject of immigration. On Oualid see Wormser, pp. 143–48.

3. On Weiss, see "Weiss, Louise," in Bell et al., pp. 435–36.

4. Emile Grant, "Konstructive Emigranten-Hilfe: Die Tätigkeit der Pariser 'Caisse israélite de prêts,'" *PT*, no. 277 (Mar. 15, 1937): 3. See also Chapter 5, n. 46. The officers of the loan bank included: Julius Hayem, president; Guy de Rothschild, treasurer; Albert Lévy, assistant treasurer; Raymond-Raoul Lambert, secretary; and Hugo Simon, who represented German Jewry.

5. Bauer, *My Brother's Keeper*, p. 153; E. M. Morissey, JDC Report, Mar. 1, 1936, JDC no. 162; JDC, "Aid to Jews Overseas, Report on the Activities of the American JDC for the Year 1936," New York, 1937, JDC no. 156, p. 43; "Refugees' Needs Urged," *NYT*, May 24, 1936, sec. II, p. 8; "Weitere Verschärfung der Emigranten-Not in Paris: Das Comité Allemand liquidiert," *PT*, no. 9 (June 20, 1936): 3.

6. B. Kahn, to Joseph C. Hyman, JDC Executive Director, May 11, 1936, JDC no. 617; JDC, Report and bulletin no. 2, Apr. 1936, JDC no. 162, p. 7; JDC, "Aid to Jews Overseas, Report on the Activities of the American JDC for the Year 1936," New York, 1937, JDC no. 156, p. 43; Minutes, "Réunion préparatoire pour l'organisation de l'assistance aux réfugiés," July 7, 1936 (attached to B. Kahn, to J. C. Hyman, July 15, 1936), JDC no. 617.

7. B. Kahn, to J. C. Hyman, July 15, 1936, JDC no. 617.

8. The members of the CAR's executive committee were: Albert Lévy, president; Maxime Lévy-Hermanos, treasurer; Lambert, secretary-general; Jacques Ullmann, deputy treasurer; Samuel Blum; J. Donald-Dreyfus; Israel Jefroykin; Robert Loewel; Hugo Simon; and André Weill.

9. M. Moch, "Note sur les réfugiés d'Allemagne," n.d., AIU, ms. 650, boîte 14 (48). Helbronner continued to play an important role in the Consistory, and he was instrumental in founding and directing the Centre de Documentation et de Vigilance (CDV), a self-defense organization created by the Central Consistory and the Paris Consistory in Sept. 1936 to monitor antisemitism in France and wage a campaign against it in the press. On the creation of the CDV, see Georges Weill and Blandine Busson, "Notes sur le CDV," Dec. 23, 1981, AIU, ms. 650, boîte 1; Moch,

p. 30; "Un Centre de Documentation et de Vigilance," *UI*, Sept. 11, 1936, p. 9; "Un 'Centre de Documentation et de Vigilance,'" *La Terre retrouvée*, no. 1 (Oct. 1, 1936): 7–8, clipped in AIU, ms. 650, boîte 6 (11); and various documents in AIU, ms. 650, boîtes 1, 6 (12), 6 (16), 6 (20), 7 (31), 14 (49).

10. On the Consultative Commission, see Chapter 6, n. 22.

11. R. S., "Le Problème international des réfugiés," *UI*, Oct. 2, 1936, p. 53; M. Moch, "Note sur les réfugiés d'Allemagne," n.d., AIU, ms. 650 boîte 14 (48).

12. "Le Statut des réfugiés allemands en France," *UI*, Aug. 7–14, 1936, p. 732. See also B. Kahn, to J. C. Hyman, July 15, 1936, JDC no. 617; "Appel du Comité d'Assistance aux Réfugiés," *UI*, Dec. 17, 1937, p. 250; "Konstruktive Emigrantenhilfe," *PT*, no. 532, Nov. 27, 1937, p. 3; Excerpt from the *Jüdische Rundschau*, July 14, 1936, JDC no. 617.

13. "Appel du Comité d'Assistance aux Réfugiés," *UI*, Dec. 17, 1937, p. 250.

14. B. Kahn, to J. C. Hyman, July 15, 1936, JDC no. 617.

15. "Memo on Interview with Mr. Chantal, General Secretary of the Centre de Reclassement Professionnel," Mar. 5, 1937, JDC no. 601; "New Jobs Are Seen for Jewish Refugees," *NYT*, Mar. 28, 1937, p. 28; Norman Bentwich, Report, Council for Germany, Apr. 24, 1936, p. 6, MP: H 25; "The State Railway Lines and Professional Retraining," Feb. 25, 1937, JDC no. 601. On the CIRP, see Chapter 7. After the outbreak of war in 1939, Dautry was appointed minister of armaments.

16. B. Kahn, to James G. McDonald, June 28, 1937, JDC no. 601.

17. On the rise of antisemitism in Eastern Europe in general in the 1930's, see Mendelsohn; Bauer, *My Brother's Keeper*, pp. 180–250. On the impact of these events, see Chapters 8 and 9.

18. Ninety percent of all refugees who arrived between July 1, 1938, and Dec. 31, 1938, entered the country illegally. "Intercommittee for the Work of Assistance for Refugees in France, The Situation of the Refugees in France," [Aug.–Sept. 1939], JDC no. 617. See also "Le Sort des réfugiés autrichiens," *La Juste parole*, no. 54 (Apr. 20, 1939): 29; "Conference on the German Jewish Situation: The Situation in the Refugee Countries and Emigration Possibilities, Held 14–15 December, 1938," JDC no. 363; Morris C. Troper, "War Relief Activities of the JDC," JDC pamphlet (spring 1940), JDC no. 165, p. 9.

19. Marrus and Paxton, pp. 39–41; Caron, "Prelude," pp. 157–76; and Chapters 8 and 9.

20. Quoted in Marise Querlin, "Rendre 'humains' les décrets–lois sur les étrangers," *Marianne*, May 18, 1938, p. 3.

21. *Le Matin*, Nov. 19, 1938, p. 1. See also *L'Europe nouvelle*, Nov. 26, 1938, p. 1298. Weill repeated these sentiments in Jan. 1939; see "M. Julien Weill," *Tribune de nations*, Jan. 5, 1939, clipped in AN 72 602. Weill's statement must be seen as a direct response to Bonnet's complaints about Jewish warmongering. For these complaints, see Chapter 9. Bonnet had met with Weill and Helbronner on Nov. 18, one day before Weill's interview with *Le Matin*, and he undoubtedly conveyed these sentiments to them. On this meeting, see "M. Bonnet s'entretient avec M. Heilbronner [*sic*]," *Le Matin*, Nov. 18, 1938, and "L'Aide aux réfugiés d'Allemagne," *UI*, Nov. 25, 1938, p. 142. On French official and popular responses to the assassination of vom

Rath and to Kristallnacht, see Caron, "Prelude,"; Marrus and Paxton, pp. 25, 41; and Chapters 9 and 12.

22. Hyman, pp. 229–32; Weinberg, pp. 186–87. On the youth movements more generally, see especially Hyman, pp. 179–98; Hyman, "Challenge to Assimilation: French Jewish Youth Movements Between the Wars," *Jewish Journal of Sociology* 18, no. 2 (Dec. 1976): 105–14.

23. Rabi, "Charles Péguy: Témoignage d'un juif," *Esprit*, June 1, 1939, pp. 326–27.

24. "Riposte des jeunesses juives de Strasbourg," *DdV*, Dec. 10, 1938, p. 2. See also "Les Juifs et la France," *Samedi*, no. 34 (Nov. 26, 1938): 1–2; "Lettre ouverte au Grand-Rabbin de Paris," *Samedi*, no. 37 (Dec. 17, 1938): 2; "D'Un Samedi," *Samedi*, Nov. 26, 1938, p. 2; Hyman, p. 231.

25. "Le Discours de Léon Blum," *DdV*, Dec. 3, 1938, p. 6.

26. The accounts of Weinberg, Hyman, Nicault, and Rajsfus all take Weill's statements to be emblematic of the dominant sentiment in the native Jewish community.

27. "Nécessité pénible," *UI*, Dec. 16, 1938, p. 206.

28. *UI*, Dec. 2, 1938, p. 173.

29. "Un Appel des israélites des départements frontières," *UI*, Nov. 18, 1938, p. 122. On the vigorous role of the Jewish community in Alsace and Lorraine, see also "'Appel!' of the Caisse Centrale pour l'Est," *TJ*, no. 38 (Sept. 23, 1938): 596.

30. "Texte de réprobation" condemning Kristallnacht, written by the Paris Consistory's treasurer, Georges Wormser, immediately after Kristallnacht and adopted on Nov. 29, 1938. Read by Robert de Rothschild at the 31st General Assembly of the Consistory of Paris, May 21, 1939, pp. 6–7, ACIP B 133[1].

31. Robert de Rothschild, "Le Consistoire de Paris et la Coordination des Oeuvres," *UI*, June 2, 1939, pp. 661–64; Franz Gravereau, "Le Problème des étrangers," *Le Petit Parisien*, Mar. 4, 1939, clipped in AIU, ms. 650, boîte 14 (48). Lambert served as secretary-general of both the Groupement and the Intercomité. The presidents of the Groupement and the Intercomité were Robert de Rothschild and Maurice Stern, respectively. The other members of the Intercomité were: W. Oualid (vice president), Maurice Leven, Gaston Kahn, Dr. Zadoc-Kahn, Marcel Bernard, Bertrand Goldschmidt, Bernard Melamède, Raymond Weyl, Rabbi René Hirschler, Mlle. de Penmarc'h, Louis Oungre, Edouard Oungre, Chantal, Robert Gamzon, and Robert Schumann.

32. On the activities of the Bonnet Committee, see "Report on the Activity of the Comité Central des réfugiés, from January 14th to March 1, 1939," in JDC, European Executive Committee (Euroexco), "Introduction and Review of Events in the Month of March 1939," JDC no. 190, pp. 77–79; *Comité des réfugiés*; "Un Entretien avec Mme. Louise Weiss: Un effort français pour l'assistance aux réfugiés," *UI*, Jan. 27, 1939, pp. 321–22; Weiss, pp. 233–68; Auffray, pp. 76–77; "Migration Conference, JDC-HICEM, Paris, 22–23 August, 1939," JDC no. 367. On the creation of the committee, its membership, and Bonnet's speech announcing its creation, see Chapter 10, nn. 52–54. On these committees in general, see also Nicault, "L'Accueil," pp. 12–13.

33. The AIU initiated efforts to coordinate the rescue of children immediately after Kristallnacht. Jewish Telegraphic Agency (JTA) Bulletin, Dec. 28, 1938, clipped in AIU, ms. 650, boîte 13 (46). The first formal appeal to save the children was made on Dec. 12, 1938. See "Note remise par M. Pierre Dreyfus (pour le Comité Central [AIU]) à la Présidence du Conseil," Dec. 12, 1938, AIU, France V D 18. Once again, the Jewish community of Alsace and Lorraine made an independent effort on behalf of refugee children. See Hammel, pp. 3–4, 10–11.

34. "L'Oeuvre du Comité Israélite pour les Enfants venant d'Allemagne," *UI*, Apr. 21, 1939, p. 545; "France: OSE Work on Behalf of Refugee Children from Central Europe, March 1939," in JDC, Euroexco, "Introduction and Review of Events in the Month of March 1939," JDC no. 190, p. 75; JDC, Euroexco, "February Report, 1939: France," JDC no. 189, p. 84; "Besuch bei Emigrantenkindern," *PT*, no. 953 (Mar. 25, 1939): 3; "200 enfants réfugiés seront accueillis en France avant la fin du mois," *Samedi*, no. 11 (Mar. 18, 1939) 5; "200 jeunes réfugiés juifs trouvent un foyer en France," *L'Ordre*, June 13, 1939, p. 2; Simpson, *Refugees: A Review*, p. 53, Myron Taylor Papers, box 7, FDR Library.

35. See Chapter 10, n. 9.

36. Lambert, to A. Lévy, Feb. 15, 1939, in Morris Troper, "Report to the JDC," Feb. 28, 1939, JDC no. 617; JDC, Euroexco, "Report on France, February 1939," JDC no. 189, p. 81. It is possible that these reforms were in part prompted by a series of scathing articles by Rabi on the deplorable reception of the refugees by the committees. See Rabi's three articles titled "Le Scandale des comités," in *Samedi*, no. 4 (Jan. 28, 1939): 4; *Samedi*, no. 5 (Feb. 4, 1939); and *Samedi*, no. 6 (Feb. 11, 1939): 2. See also letter to the editor, "Toujours les comités!" *Samedi*, no. 5 (Feb. 4, 1939): 2. On Rabi, see p. 306 above.

37. "Minutes of Conference of Various Committees Held on Thursday, March 23, 1939, at the Offices of the JDC, Paris," JDC no. 405, p. 17. See also "Appel en faveur des réfugiés," *UI*, Dec. 23, 1938, p. 223; Bernard Schönberg, "Les Réfugiés et nous," *RJG*, Mar. 1939, p. 257. In the spring of 1939, Rothschild sent a personal emissary to the United States to appeal to wealthy Jewish donors. J. C. Hyman, JDC Executive Director, Memorandum, May 27, 1939, JDC no. 617.

38. J. C. Hyman, JDC Executive Director, Highly Confidential Report, to the JDC Executive Committee, Mar. 17, 1939, JDC no. 164; Bauer, *My Brother's Keeper*, p. 264. See also JDC, Euroexco, "Report on France, February 1939," JDC no. 189, p. 81; "Conference on the German Jewish Situation, the Situation in the Refugee Countries and Emigration Possibilities, 14–15 December, 1938," JDC no. 363.

39. See especially Oualid, "Le Problème de l'émigration juive," *UI*, Mar. 10, 1939, p. 445; Oualid, "Pour une politique," pp. 547–61; Lambert, "Dépopulation et xénophobie," *UI*, Apr. 14, 1939, p. 521; "Bruno Walter à Paris," *UI*, Nov. 18, 1938, p. 12; "Deux projets constructifs," *L'Accueil français aux autrichiens*, no. 2 (Jan. 1939): 3, clipped in AIU, ms. 650, boîte 11 (42). At the Conférence Internationale de la Jeunesse pour l'Aide aux Réfugiés et Victimes de la Guerre, sponsored by the World Congress of Youth, Louise Weiss appealed to the youth of the world to dispose public opinion in their respective countries favorably toward the refugees. "La Jeunesse juive et le problème des réfugiés," *UI*, Apr. 21, 1939, p. 551. This propaganda

campaign was pursued vigorously in the philosemitic journal *La Juste parole*, directed by Oscar de Férenzy.

40. Weiss, p. 237.

41. Euroexco, "Report on the Situation in France, May 1939," JDC no. 191. See also CAR, "Séance du Conseil d'Administration, May 30, 1939," JDC no. 604. CAR statistical reports for 1939 did not even include figures on job placement, in contrast to reports of previous years. The CAR reports for 1939 and 1940 can be found in MAE SDN I M 1819, pp. 354–400, and JDC no. 605.

42. Report of the CAR, Paris, Apr. 1939, JDC, Euroexco, "Report for Apr. 1939, JDC no. 190.

43. Weiss, p. 237.

44. Oualid, "Le Problème de l'émigration juive," *UI*, Mar. 10, 1939, p. 445. See also Oualid, "Pour une politique," pp. 547–61. Lambert too believed that the major problem at this point was more psychological than economic. See Lambert, "L'Emigration juive d'Allemagne et le problème des étrangers en France," *UI*, Dec. 23, 1938, pp. 221–22. For other harsh criticisms of French Malthusianism by Jewish leaders and pro-refugee advocates, see Mémoire of the Jewish committees submitted to the Conférence Nationale des Comités pour le Statut des Immigrés, 22–23 July, 1938," JTA Bulletin, July 25, 1939, AIU, ms. 650, boîte 13 (45); Pierre Paraf, "Trois millions d'étrangers en France," *La République*, Aug. 24, 1938, p. 2; Pierre-Bloch, "Le Statut des réfugiés," *L'Ordre*, May 16, 1939, p. 1; and the following articles by J. Biélinky: "Victimes et indésirables...," Aug. 27–Sept. 3, 1938, p. 8; "Les *Amis de la République Française* et les juifs immigrés," no. 18 (May 27, 1939): 6, both in *Samedi*; "Les Juifs dans la vie économique," no. 21 (Nov. 5, 1937): 12–15; "Les Juifs persécutés et le droit d'asile," no. 25 (Jan. 5, 1938): 14–18; "Les Juifs dans la vie économique," no. 27 (Feb. 5, 1938): 9–12; "Le Drame douloureux des réfugiés," no. 47 (Jan. 5, 1939): 17–20; "L'Immigration juive en France," no. 62 (Sept. 15, 1939): 10–14, all in *La Juste parole*; "Deux projets constructifs," *L'Accueil français aux autrichiens*, 1st année, no. 2 (Jan. 1939): 3, clipped in AIU, Ms 650, boîte 11 (42).

45. See Chapter 7, esp. nn. 88, 100.

46. See Chapters 5 and 7.

47. Jacques-Fouques Duparc, French Foreign Ministry, Cabinet, "Note pour la Direction Politique," Apr. 16, 1937, MAE K Afrique (Emigration juive dans les colonies françaises) 91, p. 101. On the opposition of native Jewry, see Chapter 7.

48. On the growing support for agricultural schemes, see esp. Raoul Mourguès, "Une Paysannerie juive en France," *RJG*, no. 52 (Nov. 1937): 55–60; L. D., "Une Paysannerie juive en France," *TJ*, Nov. 19, 1937, pp. 709–10; "Plea for Agricultural Settlements in France," JDC *Fortnightly Digest*, no. 4 (Dec. 1, 1937): 2; Enrico Luzzatto, "Une Paysannerie juive en France," *TJ*, no. 51 (Dec. 17, 1937): 779; Luzzatto, "A Propos d'une paysannerie juive en France," *RJG*, no. 53 (Dec. 1937): 143–44; "Le Problème des immigrés," *UI*, May 20, 1938, p. 608; Biélinky, "Le Drame douloureux des réfugiés," *La Juste parole*, no. 47 (Jan. 5, 1939): 20; "Memorandum on International Conference of Youth organizations for increased relief to refugees and civil war victims," Mar. 17, 1939, JDC no. 405; Centre Industriel de Rééducation Professionnelle, "Report," n.d., AIU, ms. 650, boîte 13 (46); JDC, Euroexco

persistent attempts to downplay antisemitism and avoid behavior that might be construed as being motivated by Jewish rather than French national interests, see Sherwood, *Georges Mandel*, pp. 3, 213–14, 227.

53. See Chapter 9.

54. On Lambert's efforts especially, see Nathan Katz, JDC Paris, to JDC, New York office, Dec. 29, 1938, JDC no. 617; "Notes on JDC Activities During the Months of January–March, 1938," JDC no. 188, appendix VII c; Minutes, "Migration Conference, JDC-HICEM," Paris, August 22–23, 1939, JDC no. 367. The FSJF, under the presidency of Marc Jarblum, had always favored the Serre Plan and had petitioned the Ministry of Labor in May 1938 to resurrect it. "Le Problème des immigrés," *UI*, May 20, 1938, p. 608.

55. Intercommittee for the Work of Assistance for Refugees in France, "The Situation of the Refugees in France," [Aug.–Sept. 1939], JDC no. 617; "Migration Conference, AJDC-HICEM," Paris, Aug. 22–23, 1939, JDC no. 367, pp. 150–51; "Comité Central d'assistance aux émigrants juifs," *TJ*, no. 20 (May 19, 1939): 307. See also Chapter 10, nn. 78–79.

For descriptions of life at these centers, see "Le Centre de réfugiés de Martigny-les-Bains," *UI*, Aug. 4, 1939, pp. 827–30; JDC, Euroexco Report, Feb., 1939, JDC no. 189, pp. 82–83; "Minutes of Conference of Various Committees held on Thursday, Mar. 23, 1939, at the Offices of the AJDC, Paris," JDC no. 405, p. 18; Letter from refugees at Martigny to their Austrian compatriots in Chelles outside Paris, "Au foyer de Chelles à nos amis," Feb. 26, 1939, AN 72 AJ 590.

56. Minutes, Intercomité des Oeuvres, Jan. 6, 1939, AN 72 AJ 590; JDC, Euroexco Minutes, Feb. 1, 1939, JDC no. 174, pp. 18–19; Biélinky, "Des Colons pour la Guyane," *UI*, Feb. 10, 1939, p. 368; Biélinky, "La Guyane comme centre de colonisation juive," *La Juste parole*, no. 54 (Apr. 20, 1939): 12–16; Alexis Danan, "Dix juifs allemands vont partir pour la Guyane," *Paris-Soir*, Jan. 20, 1939, clipped in AIU, ms. 650, boîte 13 (46); "En route pour la guyane française," *Samedi*, Jan. 28, 1939, clipped in AIU, ms. 650, boîte 13 (46); "Pour la Guyane," newspaper clipping, n.d., clipped in AIU, ms. 650, boîte 13 (45); "Des Colons juifs pour la Guyane," *L'Oeuvre*, Feb. 4, 1939, clipped in AIU, ms. 650, boîte 13 (45).

The Guiana scheme apparently ended in disillusionment, and several of the refugees involved claimed they had been swindled. See "Un de nos correspondents guyannais de Paris nous écrit," *Le Petit Guyannais*, July 8, 1939, clipped in AIU, ms. 650, boîte 11 (40); "Traite de blancs," *Je suis partout*, Aug. 18, 1939, clipped in AIU, ms. 650, boîte 13 (46).

57. "France Plans Refugee Settlements in Africa," *The Sentinel* [Chicago], July 8, 1939, clipped in AIU, ms. 650, boîte 14 (47); JDC, Euroexco, "Introduction and Review of Events in the Month of March 1939," JDC no. 190, p. 85; JDC, Euroexco, "Report for June 1939, Day-by-Day Press Record," June 20, 1939, JDC no. 191, p. 99; Herbert Katzki, Confidential Report, "Notes on Status of Jewish Refugees from Germany and Former Austria in Various Countries of Europe...," July 5, 1939, JDC no. 666. See also Chapter 10, nn. 123–25.

58. The tremendous rise in the number of East European Jewish refugees was

due not only to the uprooting of Jews of East European origin from Austria and Czechoslovakia, but also to the implementation of antisemitic legislation in Eastern Europe and in Italy. On Mar. 25, 1938, the Polish government began to strip Poles living outside Poland for more than five years of their citizenship—a measure clearly intended to prevent the forcible repatriation of Jews of Polish origin from Nazi-controlled territories. As a result, thousands of Polish Jews in France and elsewhere suddenly became stateless. On this legislation, see Chapter 8, n. 9. By the same token, the Italian decree of Sept. 7, 1938, revoked the citizenship of all Jews naturalized after 1919 and ordered them to leave the country by Mar. 12, 1939. This decree affected 15,000 foreign Jews, of whom approximately 6,000 were German and Austrian refugees. On the Italian laws, see Chapter 9, n. 6. Finally, in 1938 Romania and Hungary also revoked the citizenship of all Jews naturalized after 1919. On Romania and Hungary, see Chapter 8, nn. 10–11.

59. There was considerable controversy over the number of refugees arrested and imprisoned. The Gourevitch Committee estimated that there were as many as 10,000 refugees in prison as of Sept. 1939. See Gourevitch, p. 18. At a JDC-sponsored meeting on the refugee situation in Mar. 1939, Dr. Baum estimated that approximately 9,000 prison sentences been handed down by the courts for various violations of the decree laws between May 1938 and Mar. 1939. Of these, he estimated that 3,000 involved German refugees, but he added that as of Mar. 1939, only 300–400 refugees were in jail. Lambert, at this same meeting, claimed that there were only 60 German refugees in Paris prisons. See "Minutes of Conference of Various Committees held on Thursday, March 23, 1939, at the JDC, Paris," JDC no. 405. So too the Jewish chaplain for the Paris prisons, Rabbi Joseph Sachs, refuted rumors that as many as 700 refugees (mostly East Europeans) were in the Paris prisons at the time of Passover in 1939. Rather, he claimed that there were approximately 100 refugees at the Santé prison and 164 at the Fresnes prison. Hence, Sachs commented: "Nous sommes bien loin des chiffres fantastiques qui ont été avancés." Of course, refugees were in prisons outside of Paris also. See Sachs, to the President of the Paris Consistory, Apr. 18, 1939, ACIP B 135 bis; and Lambert's statements at "Migration Conference, JDC-HICEM," Paris, Aug. 22–23, 1939, JDC no. 367. For the charge that 700 Jews were in French prisons, see Letter of Jarblum, to *L'Ordre*, cited in "Toujours le problème des réfugiés," *Samedi*, no. 12 (Mar. 25, 1939): 2. Finally, Marrus and Paxton claim that within nine months of the May 2, 1938, decree law, 8,405 refugees had been sent to prison (p. 56). It seems that these higher figures represent the total number of prison sentences handed down, while the lower figure of 300–400 represents the actual number of refugees in prison in all of France in the spring of 1939.

60. CAR, "Report, April 1939," in JDC, Euroexco Report for Apr. 1939, JDC no. 190, p. 126. See also Philippon et al., p. 40.

61. Marcel Lowenstein, to Robert Schumann, Apr. 6, 1939, AIU, ms. 650, boîte 7 (28); Pierre Scize, "Ce qui se passe à la frontière italienne," *Le Messidor*, no. 58 (Apr. 21, 1939): 4–5.

62. Cited in Pierre Scize, "Ce qui se passe à la frontière italienne," *Le Messidor*,

no. 58 (Apr. 21, 1939): 4–5. See also H. Séméria, "Errants travers le monde," *Le Petit Niçois*, July 24, 1939, clipped in AIU, ms. 650, boîte 13 (45).

63. On the situation in Nice, see CAR, "Assemblée Générale du 7 janvier 1940 de l'Exercice 1939, Nice," Jan. 31, 1940, JDC no. 604; CAR, "Report, April 1939," in JDC, Euroexco Report for Apr. 1939, JDC no. 190, p. 126; JDC, "Report on the Situation in France, June 1939," June 20, 1939, JDC no. 191, pp. 41–44; "Conseil extraordinaire de la LICA: Proceedings," Apr. 8, 1939, *DdV*, p. 4. Similarly, the Lyon Jewish community succeeded in regularizing the status of nearly all the illegal refugees, to the great chagrin of one police official who believed these "undesirables" should have been expelled. Police Mobile, Augustin Berard, to the Commissaire Divisionnaire, Chef de la 19e Brigade régionale de Police Mobile à Annecy (Sûreté Nationale), Nov. 28, 1938, and Jan. 7, 1939, AN F^7 14776 (divers). On successful attempts to regularize the status of refugees, see also Auffray, p. 74.

64. JDC, Euroexco, "Introduction and Review of Events in the Month of March 1939, France," JDC no. 190, p. 2. See also "Minutes of Conference of Various Committees Held on Thursday, March 23, 1939, at the JDC, Paris," JDC no. 405, esp. the comments of Lambert; CAR, "Séance du conseil d'administration, 30 mai 1939," JDC no. 604; "Report of CAR, April 1939," in JDC, Euroexco, "Report for April, 1939," JDC no. 190, p. 134. For several vivid case studies exemplifying this bureaucratic runaround and its disastrous consequences for the relief effort, see "Charity Case Histories," JDC no. 604, and "Sous 'la protection de la loi' communiqué par le CAR," *Esprit*, no. 82 (July 1, 1939): 502.

65. JDC, "Migration Conference, JDC-HICEM," Paris, 22–23 Aug., 1939, JDC no. 367, pp. 151–52. Sarraut, to Rothschild, July 16, 1939, in AIU, ms. 650, boîte 14 (49). See also Oualid, "Pour une politique," p. 547; Intercommittee for the Work of Assistance for Refugees in France, "The Situation of the Refugees in France," [Aug.–Sept. 1939], JDC no. 617. For a further discussion of Sarraut's amnesty proposal, see Chapter 10, nn. 169–73.

66. "Minutes of Conference of Various Committees Held on Thursday, March 23, 1939, at the JDC, Paris," pp. 19–20, JDC no. 405; CAR, "Séance du Conseil d'Administration," May 30, 1939, JDC no. 604.

67. "Intercommittee for the Work of Assistance for Refugees in France: The Situation of the Refugees in France," [Aug.–Sept. 1939], JDC no. 617, p. 5; Minutes, "Migration Conference, JDC-HICEM," Paris, 22–23 August, JDC no. 367, pp. 151–52. See also CAR, "Report, Situation des réfugiés en France," n.d., JDC no. 604; "Discours du Baron Robert de Rothschild, Président du Consistoire de Paris," May 21, 1939, ACIP B 133^1 (1935–39); "Le Consistoire de Paris et la Coordination des Oeuvres," *UI*, June 2, 1939, p. 664.

68. Intercomité des Oeuvres Françaises des Réfugiés, "Minutes, Meeting of November 23, 1938," AN 72 AJ 590. See also Intercomité des Oeuvres..., "Aide-Mémoire pour le Président," Nov. 23, 1938, AN 72 AJ 590.

69. Biélinky, "Le Problème des réfugiés," *La Juste parole*, no. 57 (June 5, 1939): 15. See also [Biélinky], "Le Sort des réfugiés autrichiens," *La Juste parole*, no. 54 (Apr. 20, 1939): 29.

70. Lambert, "Note on the subject of probation for those departing," Mar. 10,

1939, attached to Morris Troper, "Report to the JDC, New York," Feb. 28, 1939, JDC no. 617.

71. JDC, Euroexco Report, "France, February 1939," JDC no. 189, p. 83; CAR, "Report of the CAR, Paris, April 1939," JDC no. 190, p. 122.

72. Paraphrased in Biélinky, "Assemblée Générale de l'oeuvre philanthropique des asiles israélites," *UI*, Apr. 21, 1939, p. 552. See also Biélinky, "Victimes et indésirables...," *Samedi*, Aug. 27–Sept. 3, 1938, p. 8; Biélinky, "Les *Amis de la République française* et les juifs immigrés," *Samedi*, no. 18 (May 27, 1939): 6; Biélinky, "Le Problème des réfugiés," *La Juste parole*, no. 57 (June 5, 1939): 14–16; [Biélinky], "Le Sort des réfugiés autrichiens," *La Juste parole*, no. 54 (Apr. 20, 1939): 29; "Sus aux étrangers," *Samedi*, Nov. 12, 1938, pp. 1–2.

73. Lambert, "Dépopulation et xénophobie," *UI*, Apr. 14, 1939, p. 521. In another article, Lambert called the decree laws inhumane and claimed that the government was seeking to "résoudre par des mesures de police un problème d'ordre économique et humaine." Lambert, "L'Emigration juive d'Allemagne et le problème des étrangers en France," *UI*, Dec. 23, 1938, pp. 221–22. See also Lambert, "Bruno Walter à Paris," *UI*, Nov. 18, 1938, p. 121; Lambert, "La Détresse des réfugiés," *UI*, Mar. 10, 1939, p. 444; "Pour une mesure de clémence en faveur des réfugiés politiques," *UI*, no. 41, June 30, 1939, p. 738; "Note on the Subject of Probation for those departing," Mar. 10, 1939, attached to Morris Troper, "Report to the JDC, N.Y.," Feb. 28, 1939, JDC no. 617. For similar condemnations of government policy, see also Oualid, "Pour une politique," p. 547.

74. "Discours du Baron Robert de Rothschild, Président du Consistoire de Paris," in ACIP B 133[1] (1935–39) (also reprinted in Rothschild, "Le Consistoire de Paris et la coordination des oeuvres," *UI*, June 2, 1939, p. 662). On the general campaign by left-wing and liberal groups against the decree laws see Schor, *L'Opinion française et les étrangers*, pp. 670–72; Chapter 10, nn. 46–48.

75. Lambert, "Dépopulation et xénophobie," *UI*, Apr. 14, 1939, p. 521. For other calls to restore the Popular Front initiatives, see Henri Levin, "Droit d'Asile," *DdV*, Apr. 30, 1938, p. 4; Pierre-Bloch, "Le Statut des réfugiés," *L'Ordre*, May 16, 1939, p. 1; "Une Interview avec M. Philippe Serre: Statut des étrangers en France," *Vendredi*, May 6, 1938, p. 6.

76. On the Gourevitch Committee, see Chapter 5, n. 48.

77. On the petitions of the Gourevitch Committee and the LICA to the government protesting the decree laws, see Chapter 10, nn. 154–55. Bernard Lecache, director of the LICA, even intervened directly with Sarraut in Apr. 1939 to try to prevent those refugees fleeing Italian persecution from being thrown into jail. See "Conseil extraordinaire de la LICA," *DdV*, Apr. 8, 1939, p. 4.

78. JDC, "Report on the Meeting of the Liaison Committee of the High Commissioner of the League of Nations for Refugees Coming from Germany," (Strictly Confidential), Feb. 21, 1939, in JDC, Euroexco Report for Feb. 1939, JDC no. 189.

79. "Au Comité Central des Réfugiés présidé par M. Georges Bonnet," *UI*, May 5, 1939, p. 584.

Minutes, Mar. 5, 1939, JDC no. 174; "Discours du Baron Robert de Rothschild, Président du Consistoire de Paris," May 21, 1939, ACIP B 133[1] (1935–39); JDC, "Report on the Situation in France, May 1939," JDC no. 191.

On growing support for colonial settlements, see JDC, Paris, "Possibilities of Land Settlement in the French Colonies," Sept. 1938, p. 5, AN AJ[43] 43 (86/90); "Riposte des jeunesses juives de Strasbourg," *DdV*, Dec. 10, 1938, p. 2; Oualid, "Le Problème de l'émigration juive," *UI*, Mar. 10, 1939, p. 445; Biélinky, "Les Juifs et la France," *Samedi*, no. 34 (Nov. 26, 1938): 1–2; Biélinky, "Des colons pour la Guyane," *UI*, Feb. 10, 1939, p. 368; E. Schnurmann, "Cours de géographie coloniale," article in three parts: Dec. 16, 1938, pp. 765–66; Dec. 30, 1938, pp. 799–800; Jan. 20, 1939, p. 39, all in *TJ*.

Even the Zionists, previously among the most ardent opponents of colonial schemes, admitted in 1939: "Nous ne sommes pas ici des partisans de la solution territorialiste de la question juive. Cependant, vu les nécessités urgentes auxquelles les juifs ont à faire face, par suite de l'angoissante questions des réfugiés, les palliatifs eux-mêmes doivent être examinés avec sérieux." "La Nouvelle Calédonie?" *Affirmation*, May 5, 1939, p. 3, clipped in AIU, ms. 650, boîte 13 (46); Joseph Fisher, "La Palestine a une place unique," *La Terre retrouvée* 6, no. 9 (Feb. 1, 1937): 2.

To be sure, there were still lingering reservations, particularly over the colonial schemes. See for example Lambert, "Les Problèmes juifs et la politique internationale," *Politique*, no. 11 (Nov. 12, 1938): 926; Pierre-Bloch, "Le Racisme en action: arme essentielle de la diplomatie germano-italienne," *L'Ordre*, Jan. 20, 1939, pp. 1–2.

49. On the Serre Plan and these negotiations with Jewish leaders, see Chapter 7.

50. According to Ministry of the Interior, circular no. 354, Apr. 30, 1938, Austrian refugees were banned from settling in the departments of the Haut-Rhin, the Bas-Rhin, the Moselle, the Seine, and the Seine-et-Oise. This ban was subsequently extended to the Eure, the Eure-et-Loire, the Loire, the Oise, the Seine-et-Marne, the Seine-et-Cire, the Seine-Inférieure, the Haut-Rhin, the Bas-Rhin, and the Moselle. A text of this circular is located in AN F[7] 14662. See also Thalmann, "L'Emigration allemande," pp. 59–62; Bernhard Kahn, "Brief Review of the Situation of Jewry in Eastern Europe and Central Europe, and JDC Activities in Connection Therewith," JDC no. 163; "Conference on the German Jewish Situation, the Situation in the Refugee Countries and Emigration Possibilities, Held on 14–15 December, 1938," JDC no. 363; CAR, "Séance du Conseil d'Administration," May 30, 1939, JDC no. 604; "Compte rendu de l'activité du Comité," *L'Accueil français aux autrichiens*, 1ᵉ année, no. 2 (Jan. 1939): 2, clipped in AIU, ms. 650, boîte 11 (42); JDC, Euroexco Report, "Report on the Situation of German and Austrian Refugees in France in January 1939," JDC no. 189, p. 7.

51. "Migration Conference, JDC-HICEM," Paris, 22–23 Aug. 1939, JDC no. 367, pp. 151–52. (For the English version of these minutes, see "Intercommittee for the Work of Assistance for Refugees in France: The Situation of the Refugees in France," [Aug. 1939], JDC no. 617.) This resettlement project was enormously expensive. According to one estimate, it cost 5,000 francs to settle a single refugee in the countryside. See "Deux projets constructifs," *L'Accueil français aux autrichiens*, no. 2 (Jan. 1939): 3, clipped in AIU, ms. 650, boîte 11 (42).

52. On Mandel's extreme sensitivity regarding his Jewish background and his

80. "Amnistie pour les réfugiés," *UI*, May 19, 1939, p. 627; Excerpt from *Pariser Haynt*, May 16, 1939, in AIU ms. 650, boîte 14 (49).

81. Comité d'Entente des Oeuvres de Réfugiés en France [Intercommittee], Report of June 23, 1939, AN 72 AJ 590.

82. Simpson, *Refugees: A Review*, pp. 50–51; Gourevitch, pp. 108–9; "Le Statut des étrangers," *Le Temps*, Apr. 18, 1939, clipped in AIU, ms. 650, boîte 14 (48); Andrée Jack, "Enfin, un statut pour les étrangers!" *DdV*, Apr. 22, 1939; J.-C. Bonnet, pp. 370–71. On the reception of this decree in general, see Chapter 10, nn. 134–40. On its reception by Jewish refugees, see Weinberg, p. 201.

83. See Chapter 10, nn. 141–44.

84. See ibid., nn. 148–50.

85. Sarraut, to Rothschild, July 16, 1939, AIU, ms. 650, boîte 14 (49). Indeed, Sarraut also requested that Rothschild provide a census of all refugees, broken down by department of residence and nationality, so that the agricultural placement schemes for refugees with guarantees from the committees could be carried out on an even grander scale than before. This census was implemented on July 22, 1939. See "En France: Le Statut des réfugiés," *UI*, no. 46 (Aug. 4, 1939): 822. On the debate over amnesty for the refugees in the Chamber of Deputies, see Y. Grosrichard, "L'Amnistie devant la Chambre," *L'Oeuvre*, June 9, 1939, p. 4; Gourevitch, pp. 85–93. On the high rates of illegal immigration in the spring of 1939, see J. C. Hyman (Highly confidential), to Officers and Members of the Executive Committee, n. d. [received May 19, 1939], JDC no. 164; "1 476 réfugiés juifs nouvellement arrivés en France en 1939," *Affirmation*, June 16, 1939, p. 2.

86. On these subsidies, see JDC, Euroexco, "Report on the Situation in France, June 1939," June 20, 1939, JDC no. 191, pp. 41–44.

87. "Migration Conference, JDC-HICEM, Paris, 22–23 August, 1939," JDC no. 367, pp. 151–52. See also Intercomité des Oeuvres, "The Situation of the Refugees in France," [Aug.–Sept. 1939], JDC no. 617.

88. Lambert, "Dépopulation et xénophobie," *UI*, Apr. 14, 1939, p. 521.

89. "Le Statut des réfugiés," *UI*, no. 46 (Aug. 4, 1939): 822. See also Lambert, "Dépopulation et xénophobie," *UI*, Apr. 14, 1939, p. 521.

90. A JDC report vividly describes the impact of the internments on the relief effort:

Although the French Government provided food and shelter, other necessities such as clothing, blankets, medicines and soap were frequently lacking. Even worse than the plight of the interned men themselves was the status of their dependent women and children, who were left behind, helpless. Such little income as the refugee men had been able to earn in the past was immediately cut off. The rise in prices of all commodities made for additional distress. The number of new relief applicants at the refugee service agencies mounted rapidly.

This same report noted that many Eastern European refugees who had been in France since the 1920's and had previously been self-sufficient were now losing their jobs and becoming dependent on the committees as well. See JDC, "Aid to Jews Overseas: Report for 1939," JDC no. 156, pp. 33–34. On the impact of the internments on the relief effort, see CAR, "Rapport de l'Exercice, 1939," [Jan. 1940], JDC no. 605; CAR, "Rapport de l'Exercice, 1940," [Marseilles, Jan. 13, 1941], JDC no. 605; Gourevitch, pp. 5–7; Bernhard Kahn, to Paul Baerwald, "Memorandum," Oct. 13, 1939, JDC no. 255; JDC, "Report," Oct. 24, 1939, JDC no. 164; CAR, "Assemblée Générale du 7 janvier 1940 de l'Exercice 1939, Nice," Jan. 31, 1940, JDC no. 604; Morris Troper, to JDC, N.Y., Jan. 25, 1940; Troper, to Rothschild, Feb. 14, 1940, JDC no. 405; Troper, "JDC Activities During Early Months of the War," Mar. 14, 1940, JDC no. 165; Troper, "The Administration of Relief for Jews in Europe Today," Mar. 14, 1940, JDC no. 165; JDC, Euroexco, "Introduction and Review of Events in the Month of March 1939," JDC no. 190; "Situation of the Refugees in France During the Year 1939," n.d., JDC no. 604; "Review of the Year 5700," pp. 449–50.

91. Troper, "JDC Activities During Early Months of the War," Mar. 14, 1940, JDC no. 165. See also Troper, "A Relief Agency Faces the War," Apr. 30, 1940, JDC no. 165; J. C. Hyman, "Telephone Conversation with Mr. Troper, in Amsterdam today at 2 PM," Oct. 9, 1939, JDC no. 175.

92. On this committee, see Chapter 11, nn. 78–80. With JDC support, the Fédération des Sociétés Juives de France (FSJF), the major immigrant organization in France, also created a special committee to assist the internees—the Comité de Coordination pour l'Action de Secours.

93. "Memorandum on the Meeting Held at Mr. Moutet's Office on February 1, 1940," JDC no. 594; Morris C. Troper, "War Relief Activities of the JDC," pamphlet, JDC no. 165, p. 10; CAR, "Assemblée Générale du 7 Janvier 1940 de l'Exercice 1939, Nice," Jan. 31, 1940, JDC no. 604.

94. "L'Action du C... A... R de Paris," *La Juste parole*, May 20, 1940, p. 23; "Situation of the Refugees in France During the Year 1939," n.d., JDC no. 604; J. Biélinky, "Le Reclassement professionnel des immigrés," *UI*, Mar. 29, 1940, p. 105.

95. For assessments of this progress, see "Memorandum on Camps of German Refugees in France," [Nov. 1939], JDC no. 617 ; Morris Troper, "The Administration of Relief for Jews in Europe Today," Mar. 14, 1940, JDC no. 165. See Chapter 11.

96. J. C. Hyman, to Sydney Lansburgh (forwarded to Harry Greenstein, Executive Director Associated Charities), "Administrative One-Time Reports, 1940," May 22, 1940, JDC no. 165; CAR, "Note on the Activity of the CAR from May 1, 1940," translated in JDC no. 604; CAR, "Rapport de l'Exercice, 1940," Marseilles, Jan. 13, 1941, JDC no. 605, p. 6; "Aiding Jews Overseas, a JDC-published report for 1940 and first 5 months of 1941, N.Y.," pp. 20–22, JDC no. 157.

97. In early 1940, Troper wrote that French Jewish leaders "all feel that, figuratively speaking, they are 'sitting on the lid' and that at any moment a disturbance in the balance they are maintaining between their respective Governments, the refugees and the local populations, might set off an explosion, the results of which they do not care to contemplate." Troper, Paris, to JDC, N.Y., Jan. 25, 1940, JDC no. 405. The CAR's annual report for 1939 also stated that a renewed fund-raising drive for the refugees might appear unpatriotic at a time when everyone's first priority was supposed to be the war effort. See CAR, "Rapport de l'Exercice, 1939," [Jan.,

1940], JDC no. 605, p. 21; "Situation of the Refugees in France During the Year 1939," n.d., JDC no. 604. In early 1941, a CAR spokesman also claimed that with respect to the CAR's efforts in 1939–40 to secure military allocations for the wives of refugees serving in the armed forces: "Il importait, aussi en effet, qu'aux yeux de l'opinion publique, une femme de réfugiés mobilisés n'apparut pas trop privilégiée, en touchant d'avantage qu'une Française dans la même situation." CAR, "Rapport de l'Exercice 1940," Marseilles, Jan. 13, 1941, JDC no. 605, p. 4. It was largely because of these fears that French Jewish leaders stepped up fund-raising in the United States. See A. Lévy, to Felix Warburg, Feb. 7, 1940, JDC no. 604; N. Aronovici, "Memorandum to Mr. Troper," Feb. 27, 1940, JDC no. 604.

98. "L'Action du C... A... R de Paris," *La Juste parole*, May 20, 1940, p. 22. Catherine Nicault interprets an earlier statement made by Albert Lévy as an uncritical acceptance of government policy. In a CAR report of Jan. 1940, Lévy declared: "Il ne nous appartient pas de porter un jugement sur l'opportunité de la mesure de sûreté nationale devant aboutir à l'internement de quelque 13 à 14 000 réfugiés. Si notre gouvernement a cru devoir prendre cette mesure, c'est que sans doute il la jugeait nécessaire et indispensable." But Lévy then went on to describe the immense suffering and distress brought on by this measure, suggesting a veiled criticism of the government's policy. CAR, "Rapport de l'Exercice, 1939," [Jan. 1940], JDC no. 605, p. 5; Nicault, "L'Accueil," p. 16. The number of internees cited by Lévy is lower than that cited in the text because those individuals who volunteered either for the Foreign Legion or *prestataire* service were eventually liberated from the camps by the end of 1939. See JDC, "Aid to Jews Overseas: Report for 1939," pp. 33–34, JDC no. 156.

99. Roche, cited in "Tour d'Horizon," *L'Aube*, Nov. 22, 1938, p. 2.

100. All cited in "Minutes of Meeting Held at the Consistory," Feb. 1, 1938, AIU, ms. 650, boîte 6 (20). (Also cited in Schor, *L'Antisémitisme en France*, pp. 202–3).

101. Lambert, "Le Problème des étrangers," *RJG* 10, no. 70 (July 1939): 467. This article (pp. 465–67) is actually presented as a dialogue among four Jews in France, three of whom are native French and one of whom is of East European background. The four speakers represent different perspectives on the refugee issue and simultaneously reflect different aspects of Lambert's own views. Interestingly, only one of the speakers—the superpatriot Dufer, who perhaps represents Edmond Bloch, president of the Union Patriotique des Israélites Français—is firmly opposed to the right of asylum. The other three agree that the decree laws are unjust. As the moderate, Ducoeur, whose statements are remarkably similar to those of the socialist deputy Pierre-Bloch, states, "J'estime que mon pays fait offense à sa propre tradition en laissant à la police le pouvoir de traquer les étrangers de bonne foi pour de simples raisons administratives." Two of the spokesmen demand not only the right to asylum, but also the right to work, to prevent the refugees from becoming public charges.

102. Lambert, "Les Problèmes juifs et la politique internationale," *Politique*, no. 11 (Nov. 12, 1938): 927–28. See also the statements of the character Lévy-Fleur in Lambert, "Le Problème des étrangers," *RJG* 10, no. 70 (July 1939): 467.

103. Lambert, "Le Problème des étrangers," *RJG* 10, no. 70 (July 1939): 467.

104. Cited in Marrus, "Jewish Leadership," p. 387.
105. See Cahen-Molina.
106. Millet, pp. 104–5.
107. The manual appeared in a bilingual edition in *La Juste parole*, no. 38 (July 20, 1938) 17. See also CDV, bulletin, June 16, 1938, pp. 5–6, in AIU, ms. 650, boîte 2.
108. To be sure, such sentiments were often expressed in private, but they never again impeded the relief effort as they had in 1934–35. Robert Schumann, assistant secretary-general of the Paris Consistory, was particularly xenophobic and frequently blamed the refugees themselves for provoking antisemitism. In a letter to Paul Lang, he wrote: "Nous déplorons comme vous le manque de tact et l'ingratitude de beaucoup d'immigrés. Il s'agit, au fond, d'une éducation qui exige souvent plusieurs générations." Jan. 24, 1938, AIU, ms. 650, boîte 7 (28).
109. In early 1939, the Consistory appealed to the heads of the Catholic and Protestant Churches in France to join it in protesting this measure. See secretary-general, Consistory of Paris, to S. E. Beaussart, assistant bishop of Paris, and Pastor Marc Boegner, head of the Protestant Federation of France, Feb. 10, 1939, ACIP B 135 bis.
110. Rajsfus, *Sois Juif*, esp. p. 149. See also Nicault, "L'Accueil," p. 16.
111. "Le Discours de Léon Blum," *DdV*, Dec. 3, 1938, p. 6. On the same theme, see also Biélinky, "Le Problème des réfugiés," *La Juste parole*, no. 57 (June 5, 1939): 16; "L'Opinion des autres," *Samedi*, no. 12 (Mar. 25, 1939): 2.
112. On growing support for Zionism in the native Jewish establishment, see Jacob Kaplan, "Un Sermon sur le sionisme," *UI*, Apr. 16, 1937, pp. 489–90; "Le Judaïsme français et le sionisme," *La Juste parole*, no. 12 (May 5, 1937): 14; Hyman, p. 172; Weinberg, pp. 51–53; Abitbol, *Les Deux terres*, pp. 187–201. For Lambert's view that Zionism offered the only solution to the refugee problem, see Lambert, "Les Problèmes juifs," p. 929. On his earlier Zionist sympathies, see Chapter 5, n. 50.
113. Rajsfus, *Des Juifs*. For a more scholarly but equally critical assessment of the UGIF, see J. Adler.
114. R. I. Cohen, *Burden of Conscience*; R. I. Cohen, "Introduction," in Lambert, *Carnet*, pp. 13–62. On the UGIF, see also Szajkowski, *Analytical Franco-Jewish Gazetteer*; Szajkowski, "The General Union of the Jews in France," in *Imposed Jewish Governing Bodies Under Nazi Rule* (New York, 1972); Caron, "UGIF." For an excellent review essay on the role of native French Jewish leadership during the Vichy period, see Marrus "Jewish Leadership," pp. 380–96.
115. Lambert, "Rapport succinct sur l'activité du CAR pendant les six premiers mois de l'année 1941," p. 8, JDC no. 605.

Chapter Fourteen

1. Walter Baum, Report, "Jewish Refugees in France" [translated from German], Dec. 10, 1940, JDC no. 618.
2. Edwin L. James, "Are the French Fooling Hitler or Themselves?" *NYT*, July 14, 1940, sec. IV, p. 3.

3. For the precise terms of the armistice, see Zuccotti, p. 42.

4. For a list of those who sailed on the *Massilia*, see Christiane Rimbaud, *L'Affaire du Massilia: éte 1940* (Paris 1984), p. 99.

5. For the text of Pétain's speech of June 25, 1940, see Berl, p. 278.

6. The standard work on Vichy France remains Paxton, *Vichy France*.

7. Marrus, "Vichy Before Vichy," p. 13. See also Marrus, "Vichy avant Vichy," pp. 77–92; Marrus and Paxton, pp. 25–71.

8. Cited in Vallat, p. 238. See also Zuccotti, p. 56.

9. "French Spur Move for Seat in Paris," *NYT*, July 14, 1940, p. 27. For overviews of Vichy's antisemitic legislation, see [CAR] Report, "La Situation actuelle du Judaisme en France," July 1941, JDC no. 601; Zuccotti, pp. 53–57; Marrus and Paxton, pp. 3–4, 12–13, 92, 98–99; Paxton, *Vichy France*, 173–80.

10. H. Freeman Mathews, U.S. chargé d'affaires, Vichy, to the secretary of state, Sept. 11, 1940, 851.00/2081, National Archives, Washington, D.C. On Vichy's denaturalization legislation, see Laguerre, pp. 3–15.

11. Robert Murphy, U.S. attaché, Vichy, to U.S. secretary of state, teleg. 146, July 24, 1940, 851.012/114, National Archives, Washington, D.C.; "France to Seize Fortunes of Rothschild, Louis-Dreyfus and Other Noted Exiles," *NYT*, Aug. 1, 1940, p. 1; "Antisemitism Launched," *NYT*, Aug. 2, 1940, p. 8; "France Deprives 15 of Their Citizenship," *NYT*, Sept. 7, 1940, p. 5; "A Plea for Discrimination," letter to the editor, *NYT*, Sept. 10, 1940, p. 22; "Foreigners Face Seizure in France," *NYT*, Sept. 11, 1940, p. 8.

12. Cited in "Antisemitism Launched," *NYT*, Aug. 2, 1940, p. 8.

13. "France Frees Defamers," *NYT*, Aug. 30, 1940, p. 5.

14. "Foreigners Face Seizure in France," *NYT*, Sept. 11, 1940, p. 8.

15. On the severe application of this legislation, see Zuccotti, pp. 56–57; Marrus and Paxton, pp. 127, 141, 151; Ryan, *Holocaust*, pp. 23–51. On the fate of Jews in the universities, see especially Singer, *Vichy*. On the role of the lawyers, see Badinter and Weisberg.

16. Laguerre, p. 11. See also [CAR] Report, "La Situation actuelle du Judaisme en France," July 1941, JDC no. 601, pp. 28–29; Paxton, *Vichy France*, pp. 170–71; Marrus and Paxton, p. 323; Zuccotti, p. 53.

17. Evleth, pp. 95–116. I would like to thank Dolores Peters for bringing this article to my attention. See also Singer, "Les Etudes médicales," pp. 197–209, esp. pp. 204–8; Ryan, *Holocaust*, pp. 43–47.

18. "La Répartition des juifs en France," newspaper clipping, Apr. 13, 1941, clipped in MAE Guerre, 1939–45, Vichy C, Etat Français, vol. 139, bobine P 2854, p. 62.

19. In the spring of 1942, the government initiated court proceedings at Riom against several of these politicians, including Daladier and Blum. When the defendants turned the trial into a debate over the broader causes for the defeat, including the failures of the General Staff, however, the government stopped the trial, and the case was never brought to conclusion.

20. "Vichy to Penalize Jews for Defeat," *NYT*, Oct. 18, 1940, p. 5. For the French text of the statute, see "Le Statut des juifs français," *Le Temps*, Oct. 19, 1940, p. 3. On the scapegoating of Jews for the defeat, see also Herbert Katzki, "Draft Report on Situation of Jews in France," July 23, 1940, JDC no. 594; Zuccotti, p. 41.

21. "Manifeste soumis au gouvernement Pétain par le général Weygand, Ministre de la Défense nationale (July 1940)," in Berl, pp. 282–83. For an article that did make the direct link to Jews, see Raymond Millet, "Le Problème des étrangers et son aspect nouveau," *Le Temps*, Oct. 3, 1940, p. 2.

22. Inspection générale des services de police administrative, P.A. no. 2137/I, "Note, Réaction juive," Nov. 21, 1940, MAE Guerre, 1939–45, Vichy C, Etat Français, vol. 139, bobine P 2854, p. 45.

23. For the attacks of Pétain and Weygand on the financial plutocracy, see Pétain's speech of July 11, 1940, and "Manifeste soumis au gouvernement Pétain par le général Weygand, Ministre de la Défense nationale (July 1940)," both in Berl, pp. 280–81, 282–85, 291–93. The following discussion is based on Vallat, pp. 226–42.

24. On Vallat's programs as head of the Commissariat Général aux Questions Juives, see Marrus and Paxton, pp. 83–119; Marrus, "Coming to Terms," pp. 23–41, esp. 30–31. On the Vatican's failure to protest Vichy's antisemitic policies, see Marrus and Paxton, pp. 200–3, 262.

25. JDC, "Aiding Jews Overseas, Published Report for 1940 and First 5 Months of 1941," JDC no. 157; Zuccotti, p. 37; Bauer, *American Jewry*, p. 155.

26. Marrus and Paxton, pp. 6–7.

27. See Chapter 11, n. 142.

28. [CAR] Report, "La Situation actuelle du Judaisme en France," July 1941, JDC no. 601; Joseph C. Hyman, Report, "Terror and Affliction Occupy Unoccupied France," Dec. 13, 1940, JDC no. 618; Marrus and Paxton, p. 68.

29. Foreign Ministry, Note, Sept. 27, 1940, MAE Guerre, 1939–45, Vichy C, Etat Français, vol. 146, bobine P 2813, p. 20.

30. Schramm and Vormeier, pp. 268–69.

31. Schramm and Vormeier, pp. 265–66.

32. Cited in Bernhard Kahn, to Joseph C. Hyman, JDC, Sept. 23, 1940, JDC no. 618.

33. JDC, "One-Time Reports (July–Dec. 1940): Anecdotes used by Mr. Troper," Lisbon, Dec. 1940, JDC no. 166. On the Kundt Commission, see also "Anti-Nazis Herded Back into Germany," *NYT*, Aug. 21, 1940, p. 3; Christian Eggers, "Le Periple de la mission Kundt: Les camps du midi de la France d'après le journal de voyage de Jubitz juillet–août 1940," in Grandjonc and Grundtner, pp. 213–26; Vormeier, "La Situation des réfugiés," p. 94; Fontaine, "L'Internement," p. 124; Koessler, pp. 119–20; Marrus and Paxton, pp. 22–23, 70.

34. On both these expulsions, see JDC, "Rept. on the Situation in Free France," JDC no. 618; JDC, "Aiding Jews Overseas, Published Report for 1940 and First 5 Months of 1941," JDC no. 157; Joseph C. Hyman, Report, "Terror and Affliction Occupy Unoccupied France," Dec. 13, 1940, JDC no. 618; JDC, "Rept. on the Situation in the Camp de Gurs," translated into English, Jan. 8, 1941, JDC no. 618; Quaker Report on camps, Dec. 20, 1940, JDC no. 618; Walter Baum, Report, "Jewish Refugees in France," [translated from German], Dec. 10, 1940, JDC no. 618; Chavin, Secretary, Ministry of the Interior (Police du Territoire des étrangers, 7ème bureau), to the vice president of the Council, Foreign Ministry (Europe), Nov. 28,

1940, MAE Guerre, 1939–45, Vichy C, Etat Français, vol. 143, pp. 18–20; "Reich Jews Sent to South France, 10,000 Reported Put into Camps," *NYT*, Nov. 9, 1940, clipped in JDC no. 618; "Plain Language Press," *NYT*, Nov. 22, 1940, p. 3; Marrus and Paxton, pp. 10–11, Zuccotti, pp. 65–68; Bauer, *American Jewry*, p. 160; Schramm and Vormeier, p. 276; Vormeier, *Die Deportierung*, pp. 52–53. According to Zuccotti (p. 68), of the German Jews dumped into southern France, 60% were women, 39% were over 60 years of age, and 10% were over 75 years of age.

35. General Paul Doyen, to General Otto von Stülpnagel, no. 6566/AE (Affaires Etrangères), Oct. 27, 1940, MAE Guerre, 1939–45, Vichy C, Etat Français, vol. 143, p. 24.

36. Doyen, Foreign Ministry Representative, Wiesbaden, DSA, Hôtel Thermal, Vichy, no. 7958/AE, Nov. 18, 1940, and Nov. 20, 1940, both in MAE Guerre, 1939–45, Vichy C, Etat Français, vol. 143, pp. 13–14, 9–11.

37. Huntziger, telephone message, minister of war, DSA, to the French delegation at Wiesbaden, no. 5258/M/DSA, Oct. 26, 1940, p. 2; Foreign Ministry, "Note pour le Ministre (Direction Politique)," Oct. 25, 1940, p. 1; General Paul Doyen, to General Otto von Stülpnagel, President of the German Armistice Commission, no. 6566/AE, Oct. 27, 1940, p. 24; General Doyen, to General Stülpnagel, no. 7922/AN, Nov. 18, 1940, p. 23, all in MAE Guerre, 1939–45, Vichy C, Etat Français, vol. 143; Marrus and Paxton, pp. 11–12, 70.

38. Doyen, Foreign Ministry Representative, Wiesbaden, DSA, Hôtel Thermal, Vichy, Nos. 7958/AE, Nov. 18, 1940; no. 7922/AN, Nov. 18; and Nov. 20, 1940, all in MAE Guerre, 1939–45, Vichy C, Etat Français, vol. 143, pp. 9–11, 23, 13–14; Chavin, Secretary, Ministry of the Interior (Police du Territoire des étrangers, 7ème bureau), to the Vice President of the Council, Foreign Ministry (Europe), Nov. 28, 1940, MAE Guerre, 1939–45, Vichy C, Etat Français, vol. 143, pp. 18–20.

39. Koeltz, Minister of War (Armistice), to the French Delegation, Wiesbaden, Telephone message, Nov. 27, 1940, MAE Guerre, 1939–45, Vichy C, Etat Français, vol. 143, p. 17; Foreign Ministry, Bureau de M. Sarrien, "Note," no. R110, Feb. 4, 1941, and Foreign Ministry, Bureau de M. Sarrien, "Note," no. 219, Mar. 3, 1941, both in MAE Z Vichy 563 (Luxembourg), pp. 5, 6.

40. Doyen, to von Stülpnagel, no. 13199/AE, Feb. 10, 1941, MAE Guerre, 1939–45, Vichy C, Etat Français, vol. 143, pp. 54–59. See also Foreign Ministry (Direction Politique), to Ministry of War, Armistice Commission, Jan. 28, 1941, MAE Guerre, 1939–45, Vichy C, Etat Français, vol. 143, p. 24.

41. Zuccotti especially minimizes Vichy's efforts to facilitate emigration (p. 67). Marrus and Paxton see emigration as a serious policy, but at the same time they suggest that this policy was not pursued consistently, as evidenced by the numerous problems in attaining exit visas. While the top levels of the administration favored emigration, they claim that the midlevel bureaucrats in charge of the day-to-day handling of issues relating to emigration obstructed the policy. See Marrus and Paxton, pp. 112–15, 161–64. On difficulties with exit visas, see Grynberg, *Les Camps*, p. 275; Ryan, *Holocaust*, pp. 129–30.

42. Minister of the interior, Sûreté Nationale, Direction de la Police du Territoire et des étrangers, 6ème bureau, to the vice president of the Council, Foreign

Ministry (Direction Politique), Nov. 29, 1940, MAE Guerre, 1939–45, Vichy C, Etat Français, vol. 146, pp. 120–21.

43. Laval, to Henry-Haye, Nov. 21, 1940, MAE Guerre, 1939–45, Vichy C, Etat Français, vol. 146, pp. 109–10.

44. Foreign Ministry, Direction Politique, Dec. 5, 1940, pp. 129–30; minister of the interior, Sûreté Nationale, Direction de la Police du Territoire et des étrangers, 6ème bureau, Nov. 16, 1940, pp. 101–2, both in MAE Guerre, 1939–45, Vichy C, Etat Français, vol. 146.

45. Chavin, Secretary, Ministry of the Interior (Police du Territoire des étrangers, 7ème bureau) to the vice president of the Council, Foreign Ministry (Europe), Nov. 28, 1940, MAE Guerre, 1939–45, Vichy C, Etat Français, vol. 143, pp. 18–20.

46. Foreign Ministry (Europe), to the French ambassador, Portugal, Dec. 21, 1940, p. 146; French ambassador, Madrid, to the Foreign Ministry (Europe), Dec. 23 and 26, 1940, pp. 148, 151, all in MAE Guerre, 1939–45, Vichy C, Etat Français, vol. 146.

47. In addition to Les Milles, which was for men, two smaller camps were set up for women: Bompard and Terminus-des-Ports. Peyrouton, minister of the interior, Sûreté Nationale, to the foreign minister, Feb. 5, 1941, MAE Guerre, 1939–45, Vichy C, Etat Français, vol. 150, bobine P 2813, pp. 131–33; "Camps for Aliens Revised in France," *NYT*, Nov. 17, 1940, p. 34; "Report on HICEM's activities for the months of June and July 1941," MP: PAC Taylor; Fontaine, pp. 103–34; Ryan, *Holocaust*, pp. 92–95.

48. "Report on HICEM's Activities for the Months of June and July 1941" [translated into English], MP: PAC Taylor.

49. Joseph C. Hyman, to Robert Pell, U.S. State Dept., Aug. 15, 1940, p. 3, in JDC no. 594; Vormeier, "La Situation des réfugiés," pp. 94–95.

50. "Record of Telephone Conversation with Dr. Joseph J. Schwartz," Aug. 9, 1940, to JDC, N.Y., JDC no. 594. See also Herbert Katzki, "Draft Report on Situation of Jews in France," July 23, 1940, JDC no. 594; "Letter from St. Cyprien, dated Sept. 16, 1940," JDC no. 618.

51. Vallat, p. 253.

52. JDC, One-Time Reports (July–Dec. 1940), "Anecdotes Used by Mr. Troper," Lisbon, Dec., 1940, JDC no. 166. On these restrictions, see minister of the interior, Sûreté Nationale, Direction de la Police du Territoire et des étrangers, 7ème bureau, circular to Prefects, no. 49, Oct. 10, 1940, MAE Guerre, 1939–45, Vichy C, Etat Français, vol. 146, pp. 53–63; Doyen, to von Stülpnagel, no. 13199, Feb. 10, 1941, MAE Guerre, 1939–45, Vichy C, Etat Français, vol. 143, pp. 54–59; Joseph C. Hyman, Report, "Terror and Affliction Occupy Unoccupied France," Dec. 13, 1940, JDC no. 618.

53. Minister of the interior, Sûreté Nationale, 6ème bureau, no. 282 P, Jan. 22, 1942, p. 239; Darlan, admiral of the fleet, Foreign Ministry (Direction Politique), to M. de la Baume, French ambassador, Berne, teleg. 2256, Feb. 19, 1942, p. 208, both in MAE Guerre, 1939–45, Vichy C, Etat Français, vol. 146; Foreign Ministry (Eu-

rope), "Note," Feb. 9, 1942, MAE Guerre, 1939–45, Vichy C, Etat-Français, vol. 149, bobine P 2813, pp. 15–31.

54. Minister of finance, Direction des Finances extérieures et des changes, to the vice president of the Council, foreign minister, no. J/3.391, Nov. 4, 1940, and "Projet d'instructions pour M. Lacour-Gayet," Nov. 10, 1940, pp. 89–90; minister of finance, to the Foreign Ministry (Direction Politique), p. 179, all in MAE Guerre, 1939–45, Vichy C, Etat Français, vol. 146.

55. Tartakower and Grossmann, p. 157.

56. French ambassador, Madrid, to the Foreign Ministry (Europe), Dec. 23, 1940, p. 148; French ambassador, Lisbon, to the Foreign Ministry (Europe), teleg. 1034–36, Dec. 30, 1940, p. 155, both in MAE Guerre, 1939–45, Vichy C, Etat Français, vol. 146.

57. Foreign Ministry (Direction Politique), to the Ministry of the Interior, Sûreté Nationale (Direction de la Police du Territoire et des étrangers, 6ème bureau), Jan. 2, 1941, MAE Guerre, 1939–45, Vichy C, Etat Français, vol. 146, pp. 168–69. For an analysis of Brazil's refugee policy during the 1930's and 1940's, see Lesser.

58. Robert Pell, U.S. State Department, to Henry-Haye, Dec. 20, 1940, AN AJ^{43} 12 (125/54) ("Relations with individuals," Robert Pell); Pell, to Sir Herbert Emerson, Jan. 4, 1941, AN AJ^{43} 12 (18/56:2); Henry-Haye, to the Foreign Ministry, teleg. 2395–98, Dec. 30, 1940, MAE Guerre, 1939–45, Vichy C, Etat Français, vol. 146, p. 156. Pell was serving as U.S. ambassador to Portugal.

59. Marrus and Paxton, p. 114.

60. JDC, "Aiding Jews Overseas, Published Report for 1940 and First 5 months of 1941," JDC no. 157; minister of the interior, Sûreté Nationale, Direction de la Police du territoire et des étrangers, 7ème bureau, no. [4]038 P, Sept. 23, 1941, MAE Guerre, 1939–45, Vichy C, Etat Français, vol. 150, bobine P 2813, pp. 277–84.

61. Foreign Ministry (Europe), "Note," July 28, 1940, MAE Guerre, 1939–45, Vichy C, Etat Français, vol. 146, bobine P 2813, pp. 3–6; "Rapport du Chef du Service d'Information sur la 'liquidation' du Camp du Vernet," July 30, 1940, MAE Guerre, 1939–45, Vichy C, Etat Français, vol. 150, bobine P 2813, pp. 5–9; JDC, Report, "France," Oct. 1, 1941; JDC no. 625; Marrus and Paxton, p. 113.

62. Huntziger, to Darlan, no. 8680, Mar. 20, 1941, pp. 1–2; Koeltz, minister of war, Direction des Services de l'Armistice, "Note pour la Délégation française d'armistice à Wiesbaden, Vichy," Mar. 17, 1941, pp. 1–2; Chavin, to the general of the army, minister of war, Direction des Services de l'Armistice, no. 2826 P, July 10, 1941, pp. 16–29, all in MAE Guerre, 1939–45, Vichy C, Etat Français, vol. 159, bobine 2853; St. Hardouin, to the Foreign Ministry, telephone message, Mar. 19, 1941, MAE Guerre, 1939–45, Vichy C, Etat Français, vol. 143, p. 61; Rochat, Foreign Ministry (Europe), to the minister of the interior, Sûreté Nationale, no. 6092, May 1, 1942, p. 35; councilor of state, general secretary for the police, to the prefect of the Marseilles Region, Cabinet [Spring, 1942], pp. 26–29, both in MAE Guerre, 1939–45, Vichy C, Etat Français, vol. 142, bobine 2854.

63. Peyrouton, minister of the interior, Sûreté Nationale, to the Foreign Min-

istry, Feb. 5, 1941, MAE Guerre, 1939–45, Vichy C, Etat Français, vol. 150, bobine P 2813, pp. 131–33. According to Marrus and Paxton (p. 247), during the first six months of 1942, approximately 2,000 Jews emigrated legally (via HICEM) from the unoccupied zone, compared to just over 3,000 during all of 1941.

64. For the view that Laval had no prior history of antisemitism, see Kupferman, *Pierre Laval*, p. 127; Marrus and Paxton, pp. 18–19. On Laval's decision to collaborate with the Germans in the deportations, see Marrus and Paxton, pp. 228–34.

65. Robert Murphy, U.S. State Department attaché, Vichy, to the U.S. secretary of state, Aug. 15, 1940, National Archives, Washington, D.C., 851.4016/5 (cited also in Marrus and Paxton, p. 18).

66. Laval, to the French Minister, Lima, Peru (teleg. Nos. 107–10) and to the French Ambassador, Washington, D.C. (teleg. no. 1555–58), Aug. 9, 1942, pp. 75–76; Laval, teleg. to French diplomats abroad, Sept. 30, 1942, pp. 119–20, both in MAE Guerre, 1939–45, Vichy C, Etat-Français, vol. 140. On these memoranda, see also Grynberg, *Les Camps*, p. 319; Vormeier, *Die Deportierung*, pp. 58–59; Fontaine et al., pp. 348–49. All quotes in this paragraph, unless otherwise indicated, are from these two memoranda. On the eagerness of other Vichy officials, especially René Bousquet, the head of the police, to get rid of foreign Jews in the unoccupied zone, see also Zuccotti, p. 98; Marrus and Paxton, p. 232; Ryan, *Holocaust*, pp. 114–27.

67. The theme that the deportations were necessary because the Germans feared the opening up of a second front was reiterated by Fernand de Brinon, Vichy's representative in Paris. According to an Associated Press telegram from Berne, de Brinon explained to members of the French clergy who had protested the deportations that the deportations were necessary because:

Le programme antisémite était une partie bien définie de la politique du gouvernement et devrait être executé. Il aurait ajouté que les arrestations actuelles de Juifs à Paris et Lyon étaient liées aux préparatifs pour un second front qui constitueraient une des affaires les plus importantes auxquelles la France avait à faire face. Il aurait parlé des actes terroristes accomplis à Paris et de la necessité de combattre les [ ] terroristes servant le bolchevisme et ses alliés anglo-saxons.

Cited in Henry-Haye, to the foreign minister, teleg. 2948–50, Aug. 7, 1942, MAE Guerre, 1939–45, Vichy C, Etat-Français, vol. 140, p. 74.

68. "Hull Warns Vichy on Labor Draft; Condemns Deportation of Jews," *NYT*, Sept. 16, 1942, p. 1; Henry-Haye, to the foreign minister, Vichy, teleg. no. 3370–80, Sept. 16, 1942, MAE Guerre, 1939–45, Vichy C, Etat Français, vol. 140, pp. 107–9. On Laval and the "Final Solution," see Marrus and Paxton, pp. 261–62, 352.

69. Myron Taylor, to Herbert Emerson, Sept. 10, 1942, MP: PAC Taylor (also in AN AJ[43] 22 [123/60]); Marrus and Paxton, pp. 261–62; Wyman, *Abandonment*, p. 36; Bauer, *American Jewry*, p. 175.

70. Henry-Haye, to the Foreign Ministry, teleg. no. 3370–80, Sept. 16, 1942, pp. 107–9; Haye, to the Foreign Ministry (Europe), teleg. 3322–23, Sept. 11, 1942, p. 103, both in MAE Guerre, 1939–45, Vichy C, Etat Français, vol. 140. On the unwillingness of either the United States or Britain to take the refugees, see also Her-

bert Emerson, to Myron Taylor, Aug. 11, 1942, MP: PAC (Taylor) (also in AN AJ[43] 22 [123/60]).

71. Wyman, *Abandonment*, p. 37; Marrus and Paxton, pp. 265–68. Wyman claims that none of the children ever got to the United States, but according to Marrus and Paxton, 350 ultimately did arrive there as part of this arrangement.

72. "Note Concerning the Project to Expel or to 'Send Away' Foreign Jews," [spring 1941], JDC no. 618. As always, there were numerous exemptions, including: former legionnaires, men with French wives and/or children, men whose fathers or sons had been mobilized, Austrians, mothers of French children, mothers of sons who had been moblized, pregnant women, and women unable to physically withstand camp life.

73. On these measures, see "Note Concerning the Project to Expel or to 'Send Away' Foreign Jews," [spring 1941], JDC no. 618; Zuccotti, pp. 53, 57.

74. According to the decree law of Nov. 12, 1938, individual women were subject to internment, but the first mass internment of women took place in May 1940.

75. "Rept. of the Union for the Protection of the Human Person," Feb. 25, 1941, JDC no. 606.

76. Bauer, *American Jewry*, p. 164. See also Zuccotti, p. 37, p. 300 n. 17; Grynberg, *Les Camps*, p. 12. Grynberg gives a higher figure—40,000—for the number of Jews, but JDC reports suggest that Bauer's lower figure is probably correct. Discrepancies in the numbers of internees are due to the fact that the camp population was constantly fluctuating as a result of liberations as well as new internments.

77. Marrus and Paxton, p. 176; Zuccotti, p. 67. For general discussions of the internment camps under Vichy, see Marrus and Paxton, pp. 165–76; Zuccotti, pp. 65–80; Grynberg, *Les Camps*, pp. 91–346; Ryan, *Holocaust*, pp. 87–114.

78. American Jewish Congress, "Memorandum: On the Conditions Prevailing in the Internment Camps of France," forwarded by U.S. State Dept., Curtis T. Everett, first secretary of the embassy, to M. de Chambrun, Foreign Ministry, Vichy, Aug. 5, 1941, MAE Guerre, 1939–45, Vichy C, Etat Français, vol. 150, bobine P 2813, pp. 232–45.

79. "Europe as Letters Reveal It: France," *NYT*, Oct. 20, 1940, p. 36. See also "The Plight of Jewish Refugees in French Camps: A Letter from One of the Victims to his Relatives in America," *Jewish Daily Forward*, Oct. 31, 1940, JDC no. 618.

80. American Jewish Congress, "Memorandum: On the Conditions Prevailing in the Internment Camps of France," forwarded by U.S. State Dept., Curtis T. Everett, first secretary of the embassy, to M. de Chambrun, foreign minister, Vichy, Aug. 5, 1941, pp. 232–245; Robert de la Baume, French ambassador, Berne, to Flandin, Foreign Ministry (Europe), no. 80, Feb. 8, 1941, p. 134, both in MAE Guerre, 1939–45, Vichy C, Etat Français, vol. 150, bobine P 2813.

81. Letter from Henry-Haye, Feb. 7, 1941, cited in "Rept. of the Union for the Protection of the Human Person," Feb. 25, 1941, JDC no. 606.

82. "Annexe de la note R 283 du Bureau de M. Sarrien, "La Question des travailleurs étrangers en France et la solution du problème," July 28, 1942, MAE Guerre, 1939–45, Vichy C, Etat Français, vol. 161, bobine 2853, pp. 22–27. See also "Camps for Aliens Revised in France," *NYT*, Nov. 17, 1940, p. 34.

83. Chavin, Secretary, Ministry of the Interior (Police du Territoire des étrangers, 7ème bureau) to the foreign minister (Direction Politique), no. 1991, Apr. 22, 1941, p. 219; and minister of the interior, Sûreté Nationale, "Note, pour M. Ingrand, Réprésentant du Ministre de l'Intérieur auprès de la délégation du gouvernement français dans les territoires occupés," no. 1989, Apr. 22, 1941, p. 220, both in MAE Guerre, 1939–45, Vichy C, Etat Français, vol. 146.

84. On these revolts, see Foreign Ministry (Europe), "Note" (confidentiel), Feb. 9, 1942, MAE Guerre, 1939–45, Vichy C, Etat-Français, vol. 149, bobine P 2813, pp. 15–31; Palmier, 2: 131–32.

85. On the shift to civilian authority, see General Lacaille, to the commanding generals, "a/s internés civils," no. 693-2/EMA. 1C, Nov. 1, 1940, MAE Guerre, 1939–45, Vichy C, Etat Français, vol. 150, bobine P 2813, p. 51; "Camps for Aliens Revised in France," *NYT*, Nov. 17, 1940, p. 34; "France Puts Camps Under Civil Control," *NYT*, Nov. 22, 1940, p. 3; "Vichy Provides $500,000 to Aid Refugee Camps," *New York Herald Tribune*, Nov. 20, 1939, clipped in JDC no. 618; Grandjonc, "L'Emigration allemande," pp. 10–11. For the report of the critical relief worker, see Comité Americain de Secours, Report, "Le Camp d'Argelès," Nov. 10, 1940, MAE Guerre, 1939–45, Vichy C, Etat Français, vol. 150, bobine P 2813, pp. 78–79.

86. Chavin, Secretary, Ministry of the Interior (Police du Territoire des étrangers, 7ème bureau) to the vice president of the Council, Foreign Ministry (Direction Politique), Jan. 11, 1941, p. 118; Foreign Ministry, to Henry-Haye, no. 95, Jan. 24, 1941, pp. 125–26, both in MAE Guerre, 1939–45, Vichy C, Etat Français, vol. 150; Jacques Dumaine, councilor of the French embassy, Washington, D.C., to Henry Smith Leiper, President, and Boris Gourevitch, Vice President, Union for the Protection of the Human Person, Jan. 30, 1941; "Rept. of the Union for the Protection of the Human Person," Feb. 25, 1941; Henry Smith Leiper and Boris Gourevitch, Union for the Protection of the Human Person, to Alexander Kahn, Apr. 21, 1941, all in JDC no. 606; Bauer, *American Jewry*, p. 163; Grynberg, *Les Camps*, p. 282.

87. Foreign Ministry (Europe), "Note (confidentiel)," Feb. 9, 1942, MAE Guerre, 1939–5, Vichy C, Etat-Français, vol. 149, bobine P 2813, pp. 15–31; Grynberg, *Les Camps*, p. 151. On Jean-Faure's mission, see Marrus and Paxton, pp. 171–76; Grynberg, *Les Camps*, pp. 236–50.

88. Foreign Ministry (Europe), "Note," Jan. 7, 1941, in MAE Guerre, 1939–45, Vichy C, Etat-Français, vol. 149, bobine P 2813, p. 4; Grynberg, *Les Camps*, pp. 236–38; Marrus and Paxton, pp. 171–72.

89. Bauer, *American Jewry*, pp. 163–64. See also Marrus and Paxton, p. 256.

90. Marrus and Paxton, p. 19. See also Sweets, pp. 119–36.

91. Cited in "Il y a des étrangers parmis les responsables," *L'Oeuvre*, Sept. 3, 1940, clipped in AN 72 AJ 604.

92. J. Miguet, "Ecroulement," *La Croix*, Aug. 12, 1940, clipped in AN 72 AJ 604. On the Catholic reaction to Vichy, see Paxton, "France," pp. 67–91, esp. pp. 81–82.

93. La Rocque, "La Question juive," *Le Petit Journal*, Oct. 6, 1940, clipped in AIU, ms. 650, boîte 15 (51).

94. Lambert, *Carnet*, p. 110.

95. Evleth, p. 111; Singer, "Les Etudes médicales," pp. 205–7.

96. Evleth, pp. 102, 105. See also Singer, "Les Etudes médicales," p. 201. For the strong support of the Action Française for the quotas on Jews in the medical profession, see also "Plus de métèques dans la profession médicale!" *AF*, Aug. 21, 1940, clipped in AN 72 AJ 604.

97. Maurice Cammage, "Ou va le cinéma français?" *Emancipation*, Dec. 28, 1940, clipped in AN 72 AJ 604. See also "Le Cinéma et ses ombres: Plan," *Marianne*, Aug. 21, 1940, clipped in AN 72 AJ 604. On antisemitism in the film industry, see Bertin-Maghit, pp. 213–32.

98. Ronflard, Directeur du Bureau d'Administration des Polonais, Foreign Ministry, to Directeur du Bureau Central d'Administration des Polonais, Sept. 2, 1942, MAE Guerre, 1939–45, Vichy C, Etat Français, vol. 140, p. 90.

99. Ryan, "Commissariat Général," pp. 424–31; Ryan, *Holocaust*, pp. 65–78, 211, 214. On Vichy's aryanization policy, see Marrus and Paxton, pp. 152–60.

100. Herbert Katzki, Report, July 23, 1940, attached to Joseph J. Schwartz, vice-chairman, to JDC, Lisbon, Aug. 31, 1940, JDC no. 618. On the prewar discussions of antisemitism by Consistorial leaders, see Caron, "The Antisemitic Revival."

101. Lambert, *Carnet*, pp. 85, 104, 101.

102. Ibid., *Carnet*, p. 87.

103. See especially Rajsfus, *Des Juifs*; and J. Adler.

104. R. I. Cohen, *Burden*; Szajkowski, *Analytical Franco-Jewish Gazetteer*; Caron, "UGIF"; Ryan, *Holocaust*, pp. 156–63.

105. JDC, "Aiding Jews Overseas, Published Report for 1940 and First 5 Months of 1941," JDC no. 157.

106. On this xenophobia, see R. I. Cohen, *Burden*, esp. pp. 58, 177; J. Adler, pp. 84–85; Lambert, *Carnet*, p. 42; Szajkowski, "French Central Jewish Consistory," pp. 187–202, esp. pp. 190, 194. For a more sympathetic analysis of the Consistory's role, see Moch.

107. "Contribution à l'Histoire de l'UGIF," pp. 2, 15, Documents of French Jewish History, JTS, box 15; Herbert Katzki, "Report," July 23, 1940, attached to Joseph J. Schwartz, Vice-Chairman, to JDC, Lisbon, Aug. 31, 1940, JDC no. 618.

108. Jewish leaders worked hard to persuade Vallat to promise that the work of the UGIF would be limited "exclusively" to relief work, but they were unsuccessful. See Centre de Documentation Juive Contemporaine, p. 222; Caron, "UGIF," p. 12.

109. R. I. Cohen, *Burden*, p. 61. Cohen suggests that Lambert's break with Consistorial circles during Vichy was sudden (see Lambert, *Carnet*, p. 36). Throughout the 1930's, however, Lambert used his position at the *UI* to criticize the native Jewish establishment.

110. On Vallat's negotiations with Helbronner and Lambert, see J. Adler, pp. 81–106; R. I. Cohen, *Burden*, pp. 52–67; R. I. Cohen, "Jewish Community," pp. 190–94; Lambert, *Carnet*, pp. 33–41; Marrus and Paxton, pp. 108–10. Both Lambert and Helbronner were ultimately deported by the Germans in 1943. For an excellent review article on the role of French Jewish leadership during the Vichy period, see Marrus, "Jewish Leadership," pp. 380–96.

111. "Minutes of Meeting of UGIF Council in May 1942—Marseilles," Documents of French Jewish History, JTS, box 15.

112. See especially Rajsfus, *Des Juifs*; J. Adler; Joseph Weill, *Contribution à l'histoire des camps d'internement dans l'anti-France* (Paris, 1946), p. 178.

113. Latour, pp. 111–12.

114. On Vichy's failure to fulfill its corporate promises, see Paxton, *Vichy France*, pp. 196–220; Kuisel, *Capitalism*, pp. 128–86; Henry Rousso, "Les Paradoxes de Vichy et de l'Occupation," in Fridenson and Straus, pp. 67–82; Dolores Peters, "Vichy, the Order des Médecins, and French Medical Men's Return to Republicanism, 1940–1944," unpublished paper presented at the Society for French Historical Studies, 40th Annual Meeting, Wilmington, Del., Mar. 24–26, 1994; Zdatny, *Politics*, pp. 128–53.

115. Herriot and Jeanneney, to the Chief Rabbi, Aug. 30, 1942, Jewish Consistory, Bas-Rhin, Archives, Strasbourg (divers, 1937–42). On their opposition to the first Statut des Juifs, see Paxton and Marrus, pp. 149–50.

Conclusion

1. On the use of the term "twisted road," see Chapter 1, n. 7.

2. Noiriel, *Le Creuset français*; Millman. On the distinction between xenophobia and antisemitism in the 1930's, see Caron, "Antisemitic Revival."

3. *JO, Débats Parlementaires, Chambre des Députés*, 2ème séance, Mar. 14, 1939, pp. 943–59.

4. See Chapter 14, n. 113.

5. Another conservative who spoke out strongly against antisemitism was Henri de Kérillis. Kérillis, however, did not argue in favor of a more generous refugee policy; rather, he believed that the government had to encourage the majority of refugees to go to North or South America.

6. On November 24, 1941, Heinz Auerswald, the German Kommissar of the Warsaw ghetto, reported to Berlin that "the disappointment of the Jewish population [when confronted with food shortages] is directed against the Jewish ghetto apparatus rather than against the German authorities." See Yisrael Gutman, *The Jews of Warsaw, 1939–1943: Ghetto, Underground, Revolt* (Bloomington, Ind., 1989), p. 38. On the role of the Jewish councils in general, see Isaiah Trunk, *Judenrat: The Jewish Councils in Eastern Europe Under Nazi Occupation* (New York, 1972).

7. On Lambert's arrest and deportation see R. I. Cohen, *Burden*, pp. 129–30, 162, 181–82, 190; R. I. Cohen, "Introduction," in Lambert, *Carnet*, pp. 58–62; J. Adler, pp. 151–52. On Helbronner's arrest and deportation, see R. I. Cohen, *Burden*, p. 183; J. Adler, pp. 227–31.

8. Conan and Rousso, pp. 269–70.

9. Werth, *Twilight*, p. 356.

10. See Arendt. See also George Lichtheim, "Socialism and the Jews," *Dissent*, July–Aug. 1968, pp. 314–42.

11. For a detailed discussion of the number of deportees and the actual death rate among French Jews, see Zuccotti, pp. 206–8.

Bibliography

Archives

Archives, Alliance Israélite Universelle, Paris (AIU)
Archives, Consistoire Central, Paris (CC)
Archives, Consistoire Israélite de Paris (ACIP)
Archives, Consistoire Israélite du Bas-Rhin, Strasbourg (CBR)
Archives Départementales du Bas-Rhin, Strasbourg (ADBR)
Archives, Ministère des Affaires Etrangères, Paris (MAE)
Archives Nationales, Paris (AN)
Archives de Paris
Archives, Préfecture de Police, Paris (APP)
Bibliothèque de Documentation Internationale Contemporaine, Université Paris X, Nanterre, Fonds Duchêne (BDIC)
Documents of French Jewry, Jewish Theological Seminary, New York (JTS)
James G. McDonald Papers, Herbert H. Lehman Collection, School of International Affairs, Columbia University, New York (MP)
Joint Distribution Committee Archives, New York (JDC)
Leo Baeck Institute Archives, New York (LBI)
Myron C. Taylor Papers, Franklin Delano Roosevelt Library (FDR Library), Hyde Park, N.Y.
National Archives, Washington, D.C.
Public Records Office, London (PRO)
Service Historique de l'Armée de Terre, Vincennes, France (SHAT)

Newspapers and Periodicals

L'Action française (AF)
Affirmation
Die Aktion
Archives israélites (AI)
L'Aube
Les Cahiers des droits
    de l'homme (CDH)
Les Cahiers du Renouveau
Cahiers juifs
Choc
Le Crapouillot
La Croix
La Dépêche de Toulouse
Le Droit de vivre (DdV)
L'Epoque
L'Ere nouvelle
Esprit, revue internationale
L'Europe nouvelle
Fraternité
L'Humanité
Kadimah
Je suis partout
Le Journal
Le Journal juif
La Juste parole
La Lumière
Marianne
Le Matin

Messidor
New York Times (NYT)
L'Oeuvre
L'Ordre
Pamphlet (Aug. 4, 1933–Mar. 1934)
Paris-Soir
Pariser Tageblatt (*PT*; became the *Pariser*
    Tageszeitung after June 12, 1936)
Pavés de Paris
Le Petit Parisien
Le Peuple
Politique: Revue de doctrine et d'action
Le Populaire
Le Quotidien
Races et racisme: Bulletin du Groupement d'étude et
    d'information
La Revue juive de Genève (RJG)
La République
La Revue de France
La Revue des deux mondes
Samedi
Le Temps
La Terre retrouvée
Times of London
La Tribune juive (TJ)
L'Univers israélite (UI)
Vendredi
Le Voltigeur

Printed Documents

Assemblée Nationale, Commission d'Enquête Parlementaire. *Les Evénements survenus en France de 1933 à 1945. Rapport presenté par M. Charles Serre, Député, au nom de la Commission d'Enquête Parlementaire, Témoignages et documents recueillis par la Commission d'Enquête Parlementaire.* Vol. 9, no. 2344. Paris, 1951.

Chambre des Députés. *Impressions: Projets de lois, propositions, rapports, etc.* Vol. 16, nos. 1601–1800, session 1936–37. Paris, 1946.

Documents Diplomatiques Français, 1932–39 (DDF)

Documents on British Foreign Policy, 1931–39 (DBFP)

Documents on German Foreign Policy, 1918–45 (DGFP)

Foreign Relations of the United States (FRUS)

Journal Officiel (JO)

Books and Articles

Abella, Irving, and Harold Troper. "The Line Must Be Drawn Somewhere: Canada and Jewish Refugees, 1933–1939." *Canadian Historical Review* LX, no. 2 (1979): 178–209.

———. *None Is Too Many: Canada and the Jews of Europe, 1933–1948*. Toronto, 1982.

Abetz, Otto. *Histoire d'une politique franco-allemande, 1930–1950: Mémoires d'un ambassadeur*. Paris, 1953.

Abitbol, Michel. *Les Deux terres promises: Les Juifs de France et le sionisme, 1897–1945*. Paris, 1989.

Adamthwaite, Anthony. *France and the Coming of the Second World War, 1936–1939*. London, 1977.

———. "France and the Coming of War." In Wolfgang J. Mommsen and Lothar Kettenacker, eds., *The Fascist Challenge*, pp. 246–56. London, 1983.

Adler, Jacques. *The Jews of Paris and the Final Solution: Communal Response and Internal Conflicts, 1940–1944*. New York, 1987.

Adler, Raya Cohen. "Le Camp d'internement de Gurs (1940–1942)." In Institut d'Histoire du Temps Présent, Centre National de la Recherche Scientifique (CNRS), *Réfugiés et immigrés d'Europe Centrale dans le mouvement anti-fasciste et la résistance en France (1933–1945)*. Vol. 3, Mimeog. Proceedings, Colloquium, Paris, Université Paris VIII, Oct. 17–18, 1986.

Adler-Rudel, S. "The Evian Conference on the Refugee Question." *LBIYB* 13 (1968): 235–73.

Anchel, Robert. "L'Histoire des juifs en France." In W. Simon, ed., *La Question juive vue par vingt-six éminentes personalités*, pp. 19–34. Paris, 1934.

Angeloni, Mario. "Pour un statut juridique des réfugiés étrangers." In *L'Homme réel*, special issue, "Droit d'asile," nos. 26–27 (Feb.–Mar. 1936): 54–63.

Arendt, Hannah. *The Origins of Totalitarianism*. Part I: *Antisemitism*. New York, 1951.

Auffray, Bernard. *Sur mon chemin j'ai rencontré: Du service de l'opinion au service du bien public*. Paris, 1979.

Avni, Haim. "Latin America and the Jewish Refugees: Two Encounters, 1935 and 1938." In Judith Laikin Elkin and Gilbert W. Merkx, eds., *The Jewish Presence in Latin America*, pp. 45–68. Boston, 1987.

Azéma, Jean-Pierre. *From Munich to the Liberation, 1938–1944*. Translated by Janet Lloyd. Cambridge, Eng., 1984.

Azéma, Jean-Pierre, and François Bédarida, eds. *Le Régime de Vichy et les Français*. Paris, 1992.

Badia, Gilbert. "Les Camps d'internement (1939–1944)." In Institut d'Histoire du Temps Présent (CNRS), *Réfugiés et immigrés d'Europe Centrale dans le mouvement anti-fasciste et la résistance en France (1933–1945)*. Vol. 1, Mimeog. Proceedings, Colloquium, Paris, Université Paris VIII, Oct. 17–18, 1986.

———. "Camps répressifs ou camps de concentration?" In Gilbert Badia et al., *Les Barbelés de l'exil: Etudes sur l'émigration allemande et autrichienne (1938–1940)*, pp. 288–332. Grenoble, 1979.

———. "L'Emigration en France: Ses conditions et ses problèmes." In Badia et al., *Les Barbelés de l'exil: Etudes sur l'émigration allemande et autrichienne (1938–1940)*, pp. 11–95. Grenoble, 1979.

———. "La France découverte par les émigrés." *Revue d'Allemagne* 18, no. 2 (Apr.–June 1986): 171–84.

———. "Introduction." In Gilbert Badia, *Exilés en France: Souvenirs d'antifascistes allemands émigrés (1933–1945)*, pp. 5–22. Paris, 1982.

Badia, Gilbert, Jean-Baptiste Joly, and Jacques Omnès. "Bref aperçu sur d'autres aspects de l'accueil." In Gilbert Badia et al., *Les Bannis de Hitler: Accueil et luttes des exilés allemands en France (1933–1939)*, pp. 169–77. Paris, 1984.

Badia, Gilbert, et al. *Les Bannis de Hitler: Accueil et luttes des exilés allemands en France (1933–1939)*. Paris, 1984.

Badia, Gilbert, et al. *Les Barbelés de l'exil: Etudes sur l'émigration allemande et autrichienne (1938–1940)*. Grenoble, 1979.

Badia, Gilbert, et al. *Exilés en France: Souvenirs d'antifascistes allemands émigrés (1933–1945)*. Paris, 1982.

Badinter, Robert. *Un Antisémitisme ordinaire: Vichy et les avocats juifs (1940–1944)*. Paris, 1997.

Baker, Donald N. "The Surveillance of Subversion in Interwar France: The Carnet B in the Seine, 1922–1940." *French Historical Studies* 10, no. 3 (spring 1978): 486–516.

Banine. *La France étrangère*. Paris, 1968.

Bankwitz, Philip Charles Farwell. *Alsatian Autonomist Leaders, 1919–1947*. Lawrence, Kans., 1978.

Barkai, Abraham. *From Boycott to Annihilation: The Economic Struggle of German Jews, 1933–1943*. Hanover, N.H., 1989.

Bartosek, Karel, René Gallisot, and Denis Peschanski, eds. *De l'exil à la résistance: Réfugiés et immigrés d'Europe Centrale en France*. Saint-Denis, 1989.

Batault, Georges. *Israël contre les nations: Essai d'histoire contemporaine*. Paris, 1939.

Bauer, Yehuda. *American Jewry and the Holocaust: The American Jewish Joint Distribution Committee, 1939–1945*. Detroit, 1981.

———. *My Brother's Keeper: A History of the American Jewish Joint Distribution Committee, 1932–1939*. Philadelphia, Pa., 1974.

Beauplan, Robert de. *Un Problème de l'heure: Le Drame juif* [pamphlet], extract from *La Petite illustration*, no. 906, Feb. 4, 1939.

Bell, David, Douglas Johnson, and Peter Morris, eds. *A Biographical Dictionary of French Political Leaders Since 1870*. New York, 1990.

Bellanger, Claude, Jacques Godechot, Pierre Guiral, and Fernand Terrou. *Histoire générale de la presse française*. Vol. 3, 1871–1940. Paris, 1972.

Ben Elissar, Eliahu. *La Diplomatie du IIIe Reich et les juifs (1933–1939)*. Paris, 1969.

Bentwich, Norman. "The Growing Refugee Problem." *Contemporary Review*, 153 (Feb. 1938): 190–96.

———. "The Problem of the Refugees in Europe." *Contemporary Review* 150 (July 1936): 35–42.

Bérenger, Henry. "Conclusions générales." In W. Simon, ed., *La Question juive vue par vingt-six éminentes personalités*. Paris, 1934.

Berger, Klaus. "Bienvenue Monsieur Berger!" In Gilbert Badia et al., *Exilés en France: Souvenirs d'antifascistes allemands émigrés (1933–1945)*, pp. 103–20. Paris, 1982.

Berl, Emmanuel. *La Fin de la IIIe République*. Paris, 1968.

Bernard, Philippe, and Henri Dubief. *The Decline of the Third Republic, 1914–1938*, Translated by Anthony Forster. Cambridge, Eng., 1985.

Bernier, Olivier. *Fireworks at Dusk: Paris in the Thirties*. Boston, 1993.

Berstein, Serge. *La France des années 30*. 2d. ed. 1988. Reprint, Paris, 1993.

———. *Histoire du Parti radical*. Vol. 2, *Crise du radicalisme, 1926–1939*. Paris, 1982.

———. "Le Parti radical-socialiste, arbitre du jeu politique français." In René Rémond and Janine Bourdin, eds., *La France et les français en 1938–1939*, pp. 276–306. Paris, 1978.

Berstein, Serge, and Jean-Jacques Becker. *Histoire de l'anti-communisme en France*. Vol. 1. Paris, 1987.

Bertin-Maghit, Jean-Pierre. "Les Juifs dans l'économie du cinéma français (1940–1944)." In Chantal Banayoun, Alain Medam, and Pierre-Jacques Rojtman, eds., *Les Juifs et l'économique: Miroirs et mirages*, pp. 213–32. Toulouse, 1992.

Betz, Albrecht. "Céline im Dritten Reich." In Hans Manfred Bock, Reinhart Meyer-Kalkus, and Michel Trebitsch, eds., *Entre Locarno et Vichy: Les relations culturelles franco-allemandes dans les années 1930*. Vol. 2, pp. 716–27. Paris, 1993.

Birnbaum, Pierre. *Un Mythe politique: "La République juive" de Léon Blum à Pierre Mendès France*. Paris, 1988. [For the English translation, see Birnbaum, Pierre. *Anti-Semitism in France: A Political History from Léon Blum to the Present*, translated by Miriam Kochan. Oxford, 1992.]

Blakeney, Michael. *Australia and the Jewish Refugees, 1933–1948*. Sydney, Australia, 1985.

Bloch, Michael. *Ribbentrop*. New York, 1992.

Blumenfeld, Erwin. *Jadis et daguerre*. Paris, 1975.

Bock, Hans Manfred, Reinhart Meyer-Kalkus, and Michel Trebitsch, eds. *Entre Locarno et Vichy: Les relations culturelles franco-allemandes dans les années 1930*. 2 vols. Paris, 1993.

Bolle, Pierre. "Les Réfugiés et les protestants français." In Institut d'Histoire du Temps Présent, Centre National de la Recherche Scientifique (CNRS), *Réfugiés et immigrés d'Europe Centrale dans le mouvement anti-fasciste et la résistance en France (1933–1945)*. Vol. 3, Mimeog. Proceedings, Colloquium, Paris, Université Paris VIII, Oct. 17–18, 1986.

Bonnet, Georges. *De Munich à la guerre: Défense de la paix*. Paris, 1967.

Bonnet, Jean-Charles. *Les Pouvoirs publics français et l'immigration dans l'entre-deux-guerres*. Lyons, 1976.

Bonsirven, Joseph. "Chronique du Judaïsme français: Y a-t-il un réveil de l'antisémitisme?" *Etudes: Revue catholique d'intérêt général*, 222 (2 parts), Jan. 5, 1935: 97–116, and Jan. 20, 1935: 226–38.

———. "Le Judaïsme européen et l'antisémitisme." In *La Question d'Israel* [pamphlet], *Bulletin catholique*, no. 68 (May 1, 1939): 473–95.

———. *Juifs et chrétiens*. Paris, 1936.

Borne, Dominique, and Henri Dubief. *La Crise des années 30, 1929–1938*. 2d ed. Paris, 1989.

Bourdet-Pozzi, Claude. "Faux problèmes économiques: (II) Quelques contresens économiques." *Esprit*, no. 82 (July 1, 1939): 535–37.

Brubaker, Rogers. *Citizenship and Nationhood in France and Germany*. Cambridge, Mass., 1992.

C., R. "A Vichy, dans la gueule du loup." In Gilbert Badia et al., *Exilés en France: Souvenirs d'antifascistes allemands émigrés (1933–1945)*, pp. 121–32. Paris, 1982.

Cahen-Molina, R. *Le Monstrueux statut des étrangers en France* [pamphlet]. Paris, 1939. In AIU, ms. 650, boîte 13 (46) (dossier: La France et les réfugiés).

Camou, Philippe. "Détresses de l'émigré." *Esprit*, no. 82 (July 1, 1939): 475–80.

Caron, Vicki. "The Antisemitic Revival in France in the 1930's: The Socioeconomic Dimension Reconsidered," *Journal of Modern History* 70 (Mar. 1998): 22–73.

———. "Loyalties in Conflict: French Jewry and the Refugee Crisis, 1933–1935." *Leo Baeck Institute Year Book*, vol. 36 (1991): 305–37.

———. "The Missed Opportunity: French Refugee Policy in Wartime, 1939–1940." *Historical Reflections, The French Defeat of 1940: Reassessments*, edited by Joel Blatt, 22, no. 1 (winter 1996): 117–57. [Also in Joel Blatt, ed., *The French Defeat of 1940: Reassessments* [Providence, R.I., 1997], pp. 126–70.]

———. "The Politics of Frustration: French Jewry and the Refugee Crisis in the 1930's." *Journal of Modern History* 65, no. 2 (June, 1993): 311–56.

———. "Prelude to Vichy: France and the Jewish Refugees in the Era of Appeasement." *Journal of Contemporary History* 20, no. 1 (Jan., 1985): 157–76.

———. "The UGIF: The Failure of the Nazis to Establish a Judenrat on the Eastern European Model." Center for Israel and Jewish Studies, Working Papers I, Columbia University, spring 1977.

Carroll, David. *French Literary Fascism: Nationalism, Anti-Semitism, and the Ideology of Culture*. Princeton, N.J., 1995.

Carsten, Francis L. "German Refugees in Great Britain, 1933–1945." In Gerhard Hirschfeld, ed., *Exile in Great Britain: Refugees from Hitler's Germany*, pp. 11–28. Warwickshire, Eng., 1984.

Céline, Louis-Ferdinand. *Bagatelles pour un massacre*. Paris, 1937.

Centre de Documentation et de Propagande. *La Rocque et les juifs. Un nouveau scandale!!* Paris, n.d.

Centre de Documentation Juive Contemporaine. *L'Activité des organisations juives en France sous l'occupation*. Paris, 1947.

Cesarani, David. "An Alien Concept? The Continuity of Anti-Alienism in British Society before 1940." *Immigrants and Minorities* 11, no. 3 (Nov. 1992): 25–52.

Chevreuse, Irène. "Chez les émigrés allemands de Paris." *La Revue de France*, no. 9 (May 1, 1933): 126–40.

Claudel, Paul, et al. *Les Juifs*. Paris, 1937.

Cobban, Alfred. *A History of Modern France*. Vol. 3. Middlesex, Eng., 1965.

Cohen, Richard I. *The Burden of Conscience: French Jewry's Response to the Holocaust*. Bloomington, Ind., 1987.

———. "The Jewish Community of France in the Face of Vichy-German Prosecution: 1940–1944." In Frances Malino and Bernard Wasserstein, eds., *The Jews in Modern France*, pp. 181–204. Hanover, N.H., 1985.

Comité Central d'Assistance aux Emigrants Juifs. *Rapport Annuel du Comité Central d'Assistance aux Emigrants Juifs pour 1933*. Paris, 1934.

Comité des réfugiés et son oeuvre (janvier-septembre, 1939) [pamphlet]. Paris [1939].

Comité Français pour la Protection des Intellectuels Juifs Persécutés. *La Protestation de la France contre les persécutions antisémites*. Paris, 1933.

Comité pour la Défense des Droits des Israélites en Europe Centrale et Orientale. *La Défense des droits et de la dignité des réfugiés et apatrides, israélites et non-israélites en France, 1934, 1935, 1936*. Paris, n. d.

Conan, Eric, and Henry Rousso. *Vichy, un passé qui ne passe pas*. Paris, 1994.

"La Confédération Générale du Travail et le droit d'asile" (Résolution du Congrès de Toulouse, 1936), in *L'Homme réel*, special issue, "Droit d'asile," nos. 26–27 (Feb.–Mar. 1936): 52–53.

Crémieux-Brilhac, Jean-Louis. *Les Français de l'an 40*. 2 vols. Paris, 1990.

Cross, Gary S. *Immigrant Workers in Industrial France: The Making of a New Laboring Class*. Philadelphia, Pa., 1983.

D'Alsace, Jean. *Les Juifs en France mais surtout en Alsace* [pamphlet]. Strasbourg, 1937.

Dawidowicz, Lucy S. *The War Against the Jews, 1933–1945*. New York, 1976.

Delabroye, Christophe. *Enquête sur un projet de colonisation juive à Madagascar, 1936–1942*. Mini-mémoire pour la License, 1986–87, in Archives of the Ministry of Colonies, Aix-en-Provence.

Demangeon, Albert, and Georges Mauco. *Documents pour servir à l'étude des étrangers dans l'agriculture française*. Paris, 1939.

Depoid, P. *Les Naturalisations en France (1870–1940)*. In Direction de la Statistique Générale, *Etudes démographiques, no. 3*. Paris, 1942.

Dessare, Eve. *Mon Enfance avant le déluge*. Paris, 1976.

Dior, Raymond A. "Les Juifs." Special issue of *Le Crapouillot*, Sept. 1936.

Dioudonnat, Pierre-Marie. *L'Argent nazi à la conquête de la presse française, 1940–1944*. Paris, 1981.

Direction de la Statistique Générale. *Mouvements migratoires entre la France et l'étranger. Etudes démographiques*, no. 4, Paris, 1943.

Döblin, Alfred. *Destiny's Journey*. Translated by Edna Pässler. New York, 1992.

Droz, Jacques. "Le Parti socialiste français devant la montée du nazisme." In *La France et l'Allemagne, 1932–1936*, n. auth., pp. 173–89. Paris, 1980.

Dumoulin, Pierre. *L'Affaire Grynszpan: Un attentant contre la France*. Paris, 1942.

Duroselle, Jean-Baptiste. *Politique étrangère de la France: La Décadence, 1932–1939*. Paris, 1979.

Emigrés français en Allemagne; émigrés allemands en France, 1685–1945. Paris, 1983.

"Enquête sur le problème des réfugiés juifs." *La Revue juive de Genève*, no. 40 (July 1936): 433–77.

Epstein, Simon. *L'Antisémitisme français: Aujourd'hui et demain*. Paris, 1984.

Escher, Hans. "Avec les réfugiés ex-autrichiens dans les camps du stade de Colombes à Meslay-du-Maine (septembre 1939–mai 1940)." *Archives juives* 18, no. 1 (1982): 9–18.

Esprit, editorial board. "Carence de l'administration." *Esprit*, no. 82 (July 1, 1939): 562–78.

———. "La Main d'oeuvre étrangère en France." *Esprit*, no. 82 (July 1, 1939): 620–32.

———. "Pour un statut légal des étrangers." *Esprit*, no. 82 (July 1, 1939): 645–51.

Evleth, Donna. "Vichy France and the Continuity of Medical Nationalism." *Social History of Medecine* 8, no. 1 (Apr. 1995): 95–116.

Fabian, Ruth, and Corinna Coulmas. *Die Deutsche Emigration in Frankreich nach 1933*. Munich, 1978.

Feblowicz, S., and Philippe Lamour. *Le Statut juridique des étrangers en France: Traité pratique*. Paris, n.d.

Feingold, Henry L. *The Politics of Rescue: The Roosevelt Administration and the Holocaust, 1939–1945*. New Brunswick, N.J., 1970.

Felstiner, Mary Lowenthal. *To Paint Her Life: Charlotte Salomon in the Nazi Era*. New York, 1994.

Férenzy, Oscar de. *Les Juifs, et nous chrétiens*. Paris, 1935.

Feuchtwanger, Lion. *The Devil in France*. Translated by Elisabeth Abbott. New York, 1941.

Fittko, Lisa. *Escape Through the Pyrenees*. Translated by David Koblick. Evanston, Ill., 1991.

Fontaine, André. "Les Emigrés autrichiens au camp des Milles." *Austriaca* 19 (1984): 11–32.

———. "L'Internement au camp des Milles et dans ses annexes: septembre 1939–mars 1943." In Jacques Grandjonc, ed., *Les Camps en Provence: exil, internement, déportation, 1933–1944*, pp. 103–34. Aix-en-Provence, 1984. [Also in Jacques Grandjonc and Theresia Grundtner, eds., *Zone d'ombres, 1933–1944: Exil et internement d'Allemands et d'Autrichiens dans le sud-est de la France*, pp. 227–67. Aix-en-Provence, 1990.]

Fontaine, André, Jacques Grandjonc, and Barbara Vormeier. "Les Déportations à partir des Milles (août-septembre 1942)." In Jacques Grandjonc and Theresia Grundtner, eds., *Zone d'ombres, 1933–1944: Exil et internement d'Allemands et d'Autrichiens dans le sud-est de la France*, pp. 327–51. Aix-en-Provence, 1990.

Fouchardière, Georges de la. *Histoire d'un petit juif*. Paris, 1938.

Fox, John P. "German- and Austrian-Jewish Volunteers in Britain's Armed Forces, 1939–1945." *Leo Baeck Institute Year Book* 40 (1995): 21–50.

———. "Great Britain and the German Jews, 1933." *Wiener Library Bulletin* 26, nos. 1–2, n.s. nos. 26–27 (1972): 40–46.

François-Poncet, André. *The Fateful Years: Memoirs of a French Ambassador in Berlin, 1931–1938*. Translated by Jacques LeClercq. New York, 1949.

Fridenson, Patrick. "Le Patronat français." In René Rémond and Janine Bourdin, eds., *La France et les français en 1938–1939*, pp. 139–58. Paris, 1978.

Fridenson, Patrick, and André Straus, eds. *Le Capitalisme français, xix–xx siècle: Blocages et dynamismes d'une croissance*. Paris, 1987.

Friedlander, Henry, and Sybil Milton, coordinating eds. *Archives of the Holocaust*. Vol. 2., *American Friends Service Committee, Philadelphia, 1932–1939* (Jack Sutter, ed.). New York, 1990.

Friedman, Georges. *Journal de Guerre, 1939–1940*. Paris, 1987.

Fry, Varian. *Surrender on Demand*. New York, 1945.

Gallo, Max. *Cinquième Colonne, 1930–1940. Et ce fut la défaite*. Paris, 1970.

Gascoin, E. "Paris, capital étrangère?" *La Revue de France* 14, no. 22 (Nov. 15, 1934): 283–302.

Gastineaud, Pierre. "Réactions devant Israël." In Paul Claudel et al., *Les Juifs*, pp. 77–104. Paris, 1937.

Genizi, Haim. "James G. McDonald: High Commissioner for Refugees, 1933–1935." *Wiener Library Bulletin*, n.s. 30, 43/44 (1977): 40–52.

Gide, André. "Les Juifs, Céline et Maritain." *La Nouvelle revue française* (Apr. 1, 1938): 635.

Giraudoux, Jean. *Pleins Pouvoirs*. Paris, 1939.

Goldner, Franz. *Austrian Emigration, 1938–1945*. [Translation of German edition of *Die österreichische Emigration: 1938 bis 1945*, Vienna, 1972.] New York, 1979.

Gourevitch, Boris. "The Legal Position of the Refugees and Stateless Persons to Whom the Right of Residence is Refused in the West European Countries of Refuge" [mimeographed pamphlet]. New York, Sept. 25, 1939, in FDR Library, Myron Taylor Papers, Box 9.

Gourfinkel, Nina. *Aux Prises avec mon temps*. Vol. 2, *L'Autre patrie*. Paris, 1953.

Goyau, Georges. "La Vie courante, hier et aujourd'hui: Un devancier de l'antisémitisme hitlérien." *La Revue de France*, no. 5 (Mar. 1, 1934): 165–72.

Grandjonc, Jacques. "Aspects de la recherche sur l'exil allemand et autrichien dans le sud-est de la France." *Revue d'Allemagne* 18, no. 2 (Apr.–June 1986): 195–205.

———. "L'Emigration allemande (1933–1945) et les camps d'internement (1939–1944) dans le sud-est de la France." *Amiras*, no. 8 (1984): 5–17.

Grandjonc, Jacques, ed. *Les Camps en Provence: Exil, internement, déportation, 1933–1944*. Aix-en-Provence, 1984.

Grandjonc, Jacques, and Theresia Grundtner, eds. *Zone d'ombres, 1933–1944: Exil et internement d'Allemands et d'Autrichiens dans le sud-est de la France*. Aix-en-Provence, 1990.

Grunewald, Michel. "Das Neue Tage-Buch et la France." *Revue d'Allemagne* 18, no. 2 (Apr.–June 1986): 200–249.

Grynberg, Anne. "L'Accueil des réfugiés d'Europe Centrale en France (1933–1939)." In *Les Cahiers de la Shoah (1993–1994)*, pp. 131–48. Paris, 1994.

———. *Les Camps de la honte: Les Internés juifs des camps français, 1939–1944*. Paris, 1991.

Guériot, Paul. "Politique d'immigration." *Revue politique et parlementaire* CXVIV (June 10, 1924): 419–35.

Guillaume, Pierre. "Du Bon usage des immigrés en temps de crise et de guerre, 1932–1940." *Vingtième siècle: Revue d'histoire*, no. 7 (July–Sept. 1985): 117–25.

Habe, Hans. *A Thousand Shall Fall*. Translated by Norbert Guterman. New York, 1941.

Hagen, Friedrich. *Les Cuves de la colère*. [Translation of *Die Kelter des Zorns*.] Translated by Magda Michel. Paris, 1968.

Hammel, Frédéric Chimon. *Souviens-toi d'Amalek: Témoignages sur la lutte des juifs en France (1938 à 1944)*. Paris, 1982.

Heidelberger, Ernst. "Une Vie en tranches." In Gilbert Badia et al., *Exilés en France: Souvenirs d'antifascistes allemands émigrés (1933–1945)*, pp. 190–213. Paris, 1982.

Herzstein, Robert E. "Le Nazisme et la France (1939–1942): Population et racisme." *Revue d'histoire de la deuxième guerre mondiale* 115 (July 1979): 1–25.

Hildebrand, Klaus. "La Politique française de Hitler jusqu'en 1936." In *La France et l'Allemagne, 1932–1936*, n. auth., pp. 339–71. Paris, 1980.

Hutton, Patrick H., ed. *Historical Dictionary of the Third French Republic, 1870–1940*. New York, 1968.

Hyman, Paula E. *From Dreyfus to Vichy: The Remaking of French Jewry, 1906–1939*. New York, 1979.

Ingram, Norman. *The Politics of Dissent: Pacifism in France, 1919–1939*. Oxford, 1991.

Institut d'Histoire du Temps Présent, Centre National de la Recherche Scientifique (CNRS). *Réfugiés et immigrés d'Europe Centrale dans le mouvement anti-fasciste et la résistance en France (1933–1945)*. 3 vols. Mimeog. Proceedings, Colloquium, Paris, Université Paris VIII, Oct. 17–18, 1986.

Irvine, William D. "Fascism in France and the Strange Case of the Croix de Feu." *Journal of Modern History* 63, no. 2 (June 1991): 271–95.

———. *French Conservatism in Crisis: The Republican Federation of France in the 1930's*. Baton Rouge, La., 1979.

———. "Politics of Human Rights: A Dilemma for the Ligue des Droits de l'Homme." *Historical Reflections* 20, no. 1 (winter, 1994): 5–28.

Jackson, Julian. *The Politics of Depression in France, 1932–1936*. New York, 1985.

Jeanneney, Jean-Noël. "Concordances des Temps." *Le Monde*, July 24, 1987, 2.

———. *François de Wendel en République: L'Argent et le pouvoir, 1914–1940*. Paris, 1976.

Johnson, Douglas. "The French View." In Roy Douglas, ed., *1939: A Retrospect Forty Years After*, pp. 54–63. Hamden, Conn., 1983.

Joll, James, ed. *The Decline of the Third Republic*. London, 1959.

Joly, Françoise, Jean-Baptiste Joly, and Jean-Philippe Mathieu. "Les Camps d'internement en France de septembre 1939 à mai 1940." In Gilbert Badia et al., *Les Barbelés de l'exil: Etudes sur l'émigration allemande et autrichienne (1938–1940)*, pp. 168–220. Grenoble, 1979.

Joly, Jean-Baptiste. "L'Aide aux émigrés juifs: Le Comité National de Secours." In Gilbert Badia et al., *Les Bannis de Hitler: Accueil et luttes des exilés allemands en France (1933–1939)*, pp. 37–64. Paris, 1984.

Jong, Louis de. *The German Fifth Column in the Second World War*. Translated by C. M. Geyl. Chicago, 1956.

Josse, Prosper, and Pierre Rossillion. *L'Invasion étrangère en France en temps de paix*. Paris, 1938.

Jungk, Peter Stephan. *Franz Werfel: A Life in Prague, Vienna, and Hollywood*. Translated by Anselm Hollo. New York, 1987.

Kantorowicz, Alfred. *Exil in Frankreich: Merkwürdigkeiten und Denkwürdigkeiten*. Bremen, 1971.

Kaspi, André. *Les Juifs pendant l'occupation*. Paris, 1991.

Katz, Shlomo. "Public Opinion in Western Europe and the Evian Conference of July 1938." *Yad Vashem Studies* 9 (1973): 105–32.

Kempner, Robert M. W. "The Enemy Alien Problem in the Present War." *The American Journal of International Law* 34 (1940): 443–58.

Kingston, Paul J. *Anti-Semitism in France during the 1930's: Organisations, Personalities and Propaganda*. Hull, Eng., 1983.

Klarsfeld, Serge. *Vichy-Auschwitz: Le Rôle de Vichy dans la solution finale de la question juive en France, 1943–1944*. Paris, 1985.

Koessler, Maximilian. "Enemy Alien Internment: With Special Reference to Great Britain and France." *Political Science Quarterly* LVII (Mar. 1942): 98–127.

Koestler, Arthur. *The Invisible Writing*. New York, 1954.

———. *Scum of the Earth*. New York, 1941.

Kuisel, Richard F. "Businessmen." In Patrick H. Hutton, ed., *Historical Dictionary of the Third French Republic, 1870–1940*, vol. 1, pp. 148–54. New York, 1968.

———. *Capitalism and the State in Modern France: Renovation and Economic Management in the Twentieth Century*. Cambridge, Eng., 1981.

Kupferman, Fred. "François Coty." In Olivier Barrot and Pascal Ory, eds., *Entre Deux guerres: La Création française entre 1919 et 1939*, pp. 77–92. Paris, 1990.

———. *Pierre Laval*. Paris, 1976.

Kushner, Tony. *The Holocaust and the Liberal Imagination: A Social and Cultural History*. Oxford, 1994.

Lacouture, Jean. *Léon Blum*. Translated by George Holoch. New York, 1982.

Lafond, Gervais de. *De l'étude et de l'exercice de la médicine en France par les étrangers*. Tours, 1934.

Laguerre, Bernard. "Les Dénaturalisés de Vichy, 1940–1944." *Vingtième siècle: Revue d'histoire* (Oct.–Dec. 1986): 3–15.

Lahaque, A. "Colonisation juive et colonies françaises." *L'Afrique française*, Jan. 1938: 6–10.

Laloum, Jean. *La France antisémite de Darquier de Pellepoix*. Paris, 1979.

Lambert, Raymond-Raoul. *Carnet d'un témoin, 1940–1943*. Introduction and annotation by Richard I. Cohen. Paris, 1985.

———. "Les Problèmes juifs et la politique internationale." *Politique*, no. 11 (Nov. 12, 1938): 921–31.

Landau, Lazare. *De l'aversion à l'estime: Juifs et catholiques en France de 1919 à 1939*. Paris, 1980.

Langkau-Alex, Ursula. *Volksfront für Deutschland? Vorgeschichte und Gründung des "Ausschusses zur Vorbereitung einer deutschen Volksfront," 1933–1936*. Vol. 1. Frankfurt a/M, 1977.

Lania, Leo. *The Darkest Hour: Adventures and Escapes*. Boston, 1941.

Lapie, Pierre-Olivier. "Pour une politique de l'étranger en France." *Politique*, no. 12 (Dec. 12, 1938): 1003–13.

Larkin, Maurice. *France Since the Popular Front: Government and People, 1936–1986*. Oxford, 1988.

Larmour, Peter J. *The French Radical Party in the 1930's*. Stanford, Calif., 1964.

Latour, Anny. *La Résistance juive en France (1940–1944)*. Paris, 1970.

Lazareff, Pierre. *Deadline: The Behind-the-Scenes Story of the Last Decade in France*. Translated by David Partridge. New York, 1942.

Lebovics, Herman. *True France: The Wars over Cultural Identity, 1900–1945*. Ithaca, N.Y., 1992.

Lengyel, Emil. "Refugees from Hitlerism." *New York Herald Tribune, Magazine*, Nov. 19, 1933, 9–10.

Leonhard, Rudolf. "Les Emigrés allemands." *L'Homme réel*, special issue, "Droit d'asile," nos. 26–27 (Feb.–Mar. 1936): 41–43.

Léontin, L. "La France pays d'assimilation." *Esprit*, no. 82 (July 1, 1939): 545–46.

Leroux, P. de S. "L'Antisémitisme est inadmissible." in *La Question d'Israël* [pamphlet], *Bulletin catholique*, May 1, 1939, 496–502.

Lesser, Jeffrey. *Welcoming the Undesirables: Brazil and the Jewish Question*. Berkeley, Calif., 1995.

Leven, Maurice. *Le Statut juridique des étrangers* [pamphlet, extrait des Travaux du Comité Français de Droit International Privé (1937–38)]. Paris, 1938. In ACIP B 134 D.

Levin, Henri. *Pour un statut légal des étrangers en France*. Paris, 1939.

L'Huillier, Fernand. "Les Français et l'Accord du 6 décembre 1938." In F. G. Dreyfus, ed., *Les Relations Franco-Allemandes, 1933–1939*, pp. 411–24. Paris, 1976.

Lilienfeld, André de. "Le Problème international des réfugiés et apatrides." *Esprit*, no. 82 (July 1, 1939): 579–605.

Livian, Marcel. *Le Parti socialiste et l'immigration*. Paris, 1982.

———. *Le Régime juridique des étrangers en France*. Paris, 1936.

———. "Témoignage: Jean Longuet et les réfugiés." In Gilles Candar, ed., *Jean Longuet, la conscience et l'action*, pp. 93–102. Paris, 1988.

Loebl, Herbert. "Refugee Industries in the Special Areas of Britain." In Gerhard Hirschfeld, ed., *Exile in Great Britain: Refugees from Hitler's Germany*, pp. 219–49. Warwickshire, Eng., 1984.

Loffler, Paul-A. *Journal de Paris d'un exilé (1924–1939)*. Rodez, France, 1974.

London, Louise. "British Government Policy and Jewish Refugees, 1933–1945," *Patterns of Prejudice* 23, no. 4 (1989): 26–43.

———. "British Immigration Control Procedures and Jewish Refugees, 1933–1939." In Werner Mosse, coord. ed., and Julius Carlebach et al., eds., *Second Chance: Two Centuries of German-Speaking Jews in the United Kingdom*, pp. 485–517. Tübingen, Ger., 1991.

———. "Jewish Refugees, Anglo-Jewry and British Government Policy, 1930–1940." In David Cesarani, ed., *The Making of Modern Anglo-Jewry*, pp. 163–90. Oxford, 1990.

Lottman, Herbert R. *The Fall of Paris: June 1940*. New York, 1992.

Luethy, Herbert. *France Against Herself*. Translated by Eric Mosbacher. New York, 1955.

Machefer, Philippe. "Les Croix de Feu devant l'Allemagne." In *La France et l'Allemagne, 1932–1936*, n. auth., pp. 109–130. Paris, 1980.

Maga, Timothy. *America, France and the European Refugee Problem, 1933–1947*. New York, 1985.

———. "Closing the Door: The French Government and Refugee Policy, 1933–1939." *French Historical Studies* 12, no. 3 (spring, 1982): 424–42.

Mahler-Werfel, Alma. *Ma Vie*. Translated by Gilberte Marchegay Juilliard. Paris, 1961.

Malino, Frances, and Bernard Wasserstein, eds. *The Jews in Modern France*. Hanover, N.H., 1985.

Mann, Klaus. *The Turning Point: Thirty-Five Years in This Century*. New York, 1942.

Marbo, Camille. *Flammes juives: Ruth et Rachel*. Paris, 1936.

Marès, Antoine. "Les Tchèques et les Slovaques, 1933–1945." In Institut d'Histoire du Temps Présent, Centre National de la Recherche Scientifique (CNRS), *Réfugiés et immigrés d'Europe Centrale dans le mouvement anti-fasciste et la résistance en France (1933–1945)*. Vol. 2. Mimeog. Proceedings, Colloquium, Paris, Université Paris VIII, Oct. 17–18, 1986.

Maritain, Jacques. *A Christian Looks at the Jewish Question*. New York, 1939.

Markscheffel, Günter. "Comment un social-démocrate allemand devint tirailleur algérien et résistant français." In Gilbert Badia et al., *Exilés en France: Souvenirs d'antifascistes allemands émigrés (1933–1945)*, pp. 66–102. Paris, 1982.

Marrus, Michael R. "Coming to Terms with Vichy." *Holocaust and Genocide Studies* 9, no. 1 (spring, 1995): 23–41.

———. "Jewish Leadership and the Holocaust: The Case of France." In Jehuda Reinharz, ed., *Living with Antisemitism: Modern Jewish Responses*, pp. 380–96. Hanover, N.H., 1987.

———. "The Strange Story of Herschel Grynszpan." *The American Scholar* 57 (1987–88): 69–79.

———. *The Unwanted: European Refugees in the Twentieth Century*. New York, 1985.

———. "Vichy Before Vichy: Antisemitic Currents in France During the 1930's." *Wiener Library Bulletin*, n.s., 33, nos. 51/52 (1980): 13–19.

———. "Vichy avant Vichy." *H-Histoire*, no. 3 (Nov. 1979): 77–92.

Marrus, Michael R., and Robert O. Paxton. *Vichy France and the Jews*. 1981. Reprint, Stanford, Calif., 1995.

Martial, René. "Indésirables et refoulements." *Mercure de France* 46, no. 880 (Feb. 15, 1935): 83–92.

Mathieu, Jean-Philippe. "Einstein et le Collège de France." In Gilbert Badia et al., *Les Bannis de Hitler*, pp. 163–69. Paris, 1984.

———. "Sur l'émigration des universitaires." In Gilbert Badia et al., *Les Bannis de Hitler*, pp. 133–62. Paris, 1984.

Mauco, Georges. *Les Etrangers en France: Etude géographique sur leur rôle dans l'activité économique*. Paris, 1932.

———. *Mémoire sur l'assimilation des étrangers en France*. Paris, 1937.

———. "Le Problème démographique, français et les étrangers." *Esprit*, no. 82 (July 1, 1939): 538–44.

Maurras, Charles, and Benjamin Crémieux. "Un Juif, celui-là. . . ." *Nouvelle revue française* 22, no. 250 (July 1, 1934): 100–108.

Mayer, Hans. *Ein Deutscher au Widerruf: Erinnerungen*. Vol. 1. Frankfurt a/M, 1982.

Mendelsohn, Ezra. *The Jews of East Central Europe Between the World Wars*. Bloomington, Ind., 1983.

Micaud, Charles. *The French Right and Nazi Germany 1933–1939: A Study of Public Opinion*. Durham, N.C., 1943.

Michael, Robert. *The Radicals and Nazi Germany: The Revolution in French Attitudes Toward Foreign Policy, 1933–1939.* Washington, D.C., 1982.

Miller, Michael B. *Shanghai on the Métro: Spies, Intrigue, and the French Between the Wars.* Berkeley, Calif., 1994.

Millet, Raymond. *Trois Millions d'étrangers en France: Les Indésirables, les bienvenus.* Paris, 1938.

Millman, Richard. *La Question juive entre les deux guerres: Ligues de droite et antisémitisme en France.* Paris, 1992.

Milza, Olivier. *Les Français devant l'immigration.* Brussels, 1988.

———. "La Gauche, la crise et l'immigration (années 1930–années 1980)." *Vingtième siècle: Revue d'histoire,* no. 7 (July–Sept. 1985): 127–40.

Moch, Maurice. *L'Etoile et la Francisque: Les Institutions juives sous Vichy.* Edited by Alain Michel with the assistance of Claire Darmon. Paris, 1990.

Morand, Paul. *France la doulce.* Paris, 1934.

Mordagne, Maurice. "La Situation des étudiants en médecine et médecins juifs allemands dans les facultés de médecine." *Le Concours Médical,* Sept. 2, 1934, 2453–56.

Moore, Bob. *Refugees from Nazi Germany in the Netherlands, 1933–1940.* Dordrecht, 1986.

Mouskhéli, Michel. "Le Plébiscite de la Sarre." *Revue générale de droit international public* XLII (1935): 361–410.

Neilson, William Allan. *We Escaped: Twelve Personal Narratives of the Flight to America.* New York, 1941.

Nicault, Catherine. "L'Abandon des Juifs avant la Shoah: La France et la conférence d'Evian." In *Les Cahiers de la Shoah,* pp. 101–29. Paris, 1994.

———. "L'Accueil des juifs d'Europe Centrale par la communauté juive française (1933–1939)." In Institut d'Histoire du Temps Présent, Centre National de la Recherche Scientifique (CNRS), *Réfugiés et immigrés d'Europe Centrale dans le mouvement anti-fasciste et la résistance en France (1933–1945).* Vol. 3. Mimeog. Proceedings, Colloquium, Paris, Université Paris VIII, Oct. 17–18, 1986.

Noiriel, Gérard. *Le Creuset français: Histoire de l'immigration XIXe-XXe siècles.* Paris, 1988.

———. "Difficulties in French Historical Research on Immigration." In Donald L. Horowitz and Gérard Noiriel, eds., *Immigrants in Two Democracies: French and American Experience,* pp. 66–79. New York, 1992.

———. "Immigration: Amnesia and Memory." *French Historical Studies* 19, no. 2 (fall 1995): 367–70.

———. "Immigration: Le Fin mot de l'histoire." *Vingtième siècle: Revue d'histoire,* no. 5 (Jan.–Mar. 1985): 141–50.

———. *La Tyrannie du national: Le Droit d'asile en Europe, 1793–1993.* Paris, 1991.

Norek, Claude, and Frédérique Doumic-Doublet. *Le Droit d'asile en France.* Paris, 1989.

Noth, Ernst Erich. *L'Allemagne exilée en France: Témoignage d'un allemand proscrit.* Paris, [1940].

———. *Mémoires d'un allemand.* Translated by Paul Marie Flecher. Paris, 1970.

Olievenstein, Claude. *Il n'y a pas de drogués heureux.* Paris, 1977.

Olten, Harry. *Pour le droit d'asile: Rassemblement!* [pamphlet]. Paris, [1936 or 1937].

Omnès, Jacques. "L'Accueil aux émigrés politiques (1933–1938): L'Exemple du Secours Rouge de la Ligue des Droits de l'Homme, et du Parti socialiste." In Gilbert Badia et al., *Les Bannis de Hitler*, pp. 65–104. Paris, 1984.

Ory, Pascal. *Les Collaborateurs, 1940–1945.* Paris, 1976.

———. *La France allemande: Paroles du collaborationnisme français (1933–1945).* Paris, 1977.

Oualid, William. "Les Etrangers en Alsace." In *L'Alsace depuis son retour à la France.* Vol. 1, pp. 572–81. Strasbourg, 1932.

———. "Pour une politique de l'immigration." In *Esprit*, no. 82 (July 1, 1939): 547–61.

Palmier, Jean-Michel. *Weimar en exil: Le Destin de l'émigration intellectuelle allemande antinazie en Europe et aux Etats-Unis.* 2 vols. Paris, 1988.

Paul-Boncour, Joseph. *Entre deux guerres: Souvenirs sur la IIIe République, 1935–1940.* Vol. 3. Paris, 1946.

Paulien, André, and Andrien Paulien. "The Problem of Aliens in France." *The Nineteenth Century and After*, XCVII (June 1925): 823–34.

Paxton, Robert O. "France: The Church, the Republic, and the Fascist Temptation, 1922–1945." In Richard J. Wolff and Jörg K. Hoensch, eds., *Catholics, the State, and the European Right, 1919–1945*, pp. 67–91. New York, 1987.

———. "La Spécificité de la persécution des juifs en France." *Annales, ESC*, no. 3 (May–June 1993): 605–19.

———. *Vichy France: Old Guard and New Order, 1940–1944.* New York, 1972.

Paz, Magdeleine. "La Défense des étrangers." *L'Homme réel*, special issue, "Droit d'asile," nos. 26–27 (Feb.–Mar. 1936): 22–33.

Pécout, Jean. *L'Etude et l'exercice de la médecine par les étrangers.* Paris, 1939.

Pertinax [André Géraud]. *Les Fossoyeurs: Défaite militaire de la France, armistice, contre-révolution.* Vol. 2: *Pétain.* Paris, 1943.

Peschanski, Denis. "Exclusion, persécution, répression." In Jean-Pierre Azéma and François Bédarida, *Le Régime de Vichy et les Français*, pp. 209–34. Paris, 1992.

———. "La France, terre de camps?" In Institut d'Histoire du Temps Présent, (CNRS), *Réfugiés et immigrés d'Europe Centrale dans le mouvement anti-fasciste et la résistance en France (1933–1945).* Vol. 3. Mimeog. Proceedings, Colloquium, Université Paris VIII, Oct. 17–18, 1986.

Peterson, Walter F. *The Berlin Liberal Press in Exile: A History of the Pariser Tageblatt—Pariser Tageszeitung, 1933–1940.* Tübingen, Ger., 1987.

Pfanner, Helmut. "Trapped in France: A Case Study of Five German Jewish Intellectuals." *Simon Wiesenthal Center Annual* 3 (1986): 107–20.

Pfoser-Schewig, Kristina. "L'Exil autrichien—France (1934–1940)." In Institut d'Histoire du Temps Présent, (CNRS), *Réfugiés et immigrés d'Europe Centrale dans le mouvement anti-fasciste et la résistance en France (1933–1945).* Vol. 3. Mimeog. Proceedings, Colloquium, Paris, Université Paris VIII, Oct. 17–18, 1986.

Philippon, Jean, Jean-Louis Paniacci, and Michèle Robert. "L'Emigration autrichienne et la résistance dans les Alpes Maritimes." *Austriaca* 17 (1975): 17–51.

Pierrard, Pierre. *Juifs et catholiques français: De Drumont à Jules Isaac (1886–1945)*. Paris, 1970.

Pierre-Bloch, [Jean]. *Jusqu'au dernier jour: Mémoires*. Paris, 1983.

Pike, David Wingeate. *In the Service of Stalin: The Spanish Communists in Exile, 1939–1945*. Oxford, 1993.

Pol, Heinz. *Suicide of a Democracy*. Translated by Heinz and Ruth Norden. New York, 1940.

Politique, editorial board. "Les Premiers objectifs d'une action commune." *Politique: Revue de doctrine et d'action* 12, no. 11 (Nov. 1938): 901–10.

Ponty, Janine. *Polonais méconnus: Histoire des travailleurs immigrés en France dans l'entre-deux-guerres*. Paris, 1988.

Porch, Douglas. *The French Foreign Legion: A Complete History of the Legendary Fighting Force*. New York, 1991.

Poznanski, René. "Vichy et les juifs: Des marges de l'histoire au coeur de son écriture." In Jean-Pierre Azéma and François Bédarida, eds., *Le Régime de Vichy et les Français*, pp. 57–67. Paris, 1992.

Propos d'exile: Articles publiés dans la Dépêche par les émigrés du III Reich. Toulouse, 1983.

Rabi, Wladimir. "De 1906 à 1939." In Bernhard Blumenkranz, ed., *Histoire des Juifs en France*, pp. 363–88. Toulouse, 1972.

Racine, Pierre. "Une Expérience administrative à reprendre: Le Sous-secrétariat d'état à l'immigration et les projets Philippe Serre." *Esprit*, no. 82 (July 1, 1939): 609–19.

Rajsfus, Maurice. *Des Juifs dans la collaboration: L'U.G.I.F. (1941–1944)*. Paris, 1980.

———. *Sois Juif et tais-toi! 1930–1940: Les français "israélites" face au nazisme*. Paris, 1981.

Raphaël, Freddy, and Robert Weyl. "La Double demeure: Les Juifs d'Alsace et le sionisme." In Freddy Raphaël and Robert Weyl, *Regards nouveaux sur les juifs d'Alsace*, pp. 255–74. Strasbourg, 1980.

Read, Anthony, and David Fisher. *Kristallnacht: Unleashing the Holocaust*. London, 1989.

Réau, Elisabeth du. *Edouard Daladier: 1884–1970*. Paris, 1993.

Recouly, Raymond. "L'Allemagne hitlérienne et la paix de l'Europe." *La Revue de France*, no. 17 (Sept. 1, 1933): 160–73.

———. "Le Coup de poing allemand." *La Revue de France*, no. 21 (Nov. 1, 1933): 167–78.

———. "La France, Terre d'asile." *La Revue de France* 13, part 2, no. 8 (Apr. 15, 1933): 733–44.

———. "Raymond Poincaré: L'Attentat de Marseille." *La Revue de France*, no. 21 (Nov. 1, 1934): 153–70.

Remarque, Erich Maria. *Les Exilés*. Translated by Andrée R. Picard. Paris, 1962.

Rémond, René, and Janine Bourdin, eds. *La France et les français en 1938–1939*. Paris, 1978.

"Review of the Year 5700—Refugee Problem." *American Jewish Yearbook* 42 (Oct. 3, 1940–Sept. 21, 1941): 444–57.

Reynaud, Paul. "Discours de Monsieur Paul Reynaud, député, ancien ministre." Paris, 1935.

Rothschild, Baron Edmond. "Appel au judaïsme français: Discours prononcé à la réunion du 11 juillet 1933." Paris, 1933.

Roussel, Hélène. "Les Premières réactions aux autodafés de livres dans l'opinion publique française." *Revue d'Allemagne* 18, no. 2 (Apr.–June 1986): 206–20.

Ryan, Donna F. "The Commissariat Général aux Questions Juives and Economic Aryanization: The Case of Marseille." *Proceedings of the Annual Meeting of the Western Society for French History* 18 (1991): 424–31.

———. *The Holocaust and the Jews of Marseille: The Enforcement of Anti-Semitic Policies in Vichy France*. Urbana, Ill., 1996.

Sahl, Hans. *Le Troupeau perdu.* [Translation of *Die Wenigen und die Vielen.*] Translated by Maurice Muller-Strauss. Paris, 1964.

Saint-Germain, Jacques. *La Grande Invasion.* Paris, 1939.

Saint-Pourçain, R. de. "Les Solutions industrielles." *Esprit*, no. 82 (July 1, 1939): 638–44.

Sauer, Paul. *Die Schicksale der jüdischen Bürger Baden-Wurttembergs wärhrend der National-sozialistischen Verfolgungszeit, 1933–1945.* Stuttgart, 1969.

Sauvy, Alfred. *Histoire économique de la France entre les deux guerres (1931–1939).* 3 vols. Paris, 1965, 1967, 1972.

Schapiro, Michael. "German Refugees in France." *Contemporary Jewish Record* 3 (1940): 134–40.

Schiller, Dieter, Karlheinz Pech, Regine Herrmann, and Manfred Hahn, eds. *Exil in Frankreich: Kunst u. Literatur im anti-faschistischen Exil, 1933–1945.* Frankfurt a/M, 1981.

Schleunes, Karl. *The Twisted Road to Auschwitz: Nazi Policy Toward German Jews, 1933–1939.* 1970. Reprint, Urbana, Ill., 1990.

Schneider, Dieter Marc. "Saarpolitik u. Exil 1933–1955." *Vierteljahrshefte f. Zeitgeschichte* 25, no. 4 (Oct. 1977): 467–545.

Schneider, Gertrude. *Exile and Destruction: The Fate of Austrian Jews, 1938–1945.* Westport, Conn., 1995.

Schneider, William. *Quality and Quantity: The Quest for Biological Regeneration in Twentieth-Century France.* New York, 1990.

———. "Toward the Improvement of the Human Race: The History of Eugenics in France." *Journal of Modern History*, 54 (June 1982): 268–91.

Schor, Ralph. "L'Antisémitisme dans la France des années 1930: Essai d'approche sociologique." *Peuples méditérranéens*, no. 51 (Apr.–June 1990): 203–13.

———. *L'Antisémitisme en France pendant les années trente: Prélude à Vichy.* Paris, 1992.

———. "L'Image de l'italien dans la France de l'entre-deux-guerres." In Pierre Milza, ed., *Les Italiens en France de 1914 à 1940*, pp. 89–109. Rome, 1986.

———. *L'Opinion française et les étrangers, 1919–1939.* Paris, 1985.

———. "L'Opinion française et les réfugiés d'Europe Centrale, 1933–1939." In Karel Bartosek, René Gallissot, and Denis Peschanski, eds., *De l'exil à la résistance: Réfugiés et immigrés d'Europe Centrale en France*, pp. 27–51. Saint-Denis, 1989. [A longer version of this article appeared in Institut d'Histoire du Temps Présent (CNRS), *Réfugiés et immigrés d'Europe Centrale dans le mouvement anti-fasciste et la résistance en France (1933–1945)*. Vol. 1. Mimeog. Proceedings, Colloquium, Paris, Université Paris VIII, Oct. 17–18, 1986.]

———. "Le Parti communiste et les immigrés." *Histoire*, no. 35 (June 1981): 84–86.

———. "Les Partis politiques français et le droit d'asile (1919–1939)." *Revue Historique*, no. 540 (Oct.–Dec. 1981): 445–59.

Schramm, Hanna, and Barbara Vormeier. *Vivre à Gurs: Un camp de concentration français, 1940–1941*. Translated by Irène Petit. Paris, 1979.

Schuker, Stephen A. "Origins of the 'Jewish Problem' in the Later Third Republic." In Frances Malino and Bernard Wasserstein, eds., *The Jews in Modern France*, pp. 135–80. Hanover, N.H., 1985.

Schwab, Gerald. *The Day the Holocaust Began: The Odyssey of Herschel Grynszpan*. New York, 1990.

Sergent, Emile. "Etudiants et médecins étrangers en France." *Revue des deux mondes*, Apr. 15, 1935, 814–28.

———. "La Pléthore médicale: Ses causes, ses dangers, ses remèdes." *La Revue de France* 11, no. 2 (Jan. 15, 1935): 338–60.

Seyfert, Michael. "His Majesty's Most Loyal Internees." In Gerhard Hirschfeld, ed., *Exile in Great Britain*, pp. 163–93. London, 1984.

Shamir, Haim. "French Press Reaction in 1933 to Hitler's Anti-Jewish Policies." *Wiener Library Bulletin* 21, no. 2 (n.s. no. 7; spring 1967): 23–32.

Sharf, Andrew. *The British Press and Jews Under Nazi Rule*. London, 1964.

Sherman, A. J. *Island Refuge: Britain and Refugees from the Third Reich, 1933–1939*. London, 1973.

Sherwood, John M. *Georges Mandel and the Third Republic*. Stanford, Calif., 1970.

———. "The Tiger's Club: The Last Years of Georges Mandel." In James Joll, ed., *The Decline of the Third Republic*, pp. 86–125. London, 1959.

Simon, W. *La Question juive vue par vingt-six éminentes personalités*. Paris, 1934.

Simon, Yves R. *The Road to Vichy, 1918–1938*. Rev. ed. Translated by James A. Corbett and George J. McMorrow. Lanham, Md., 1988.

Simpson, John Hope. *The Refugee Problem: Report of a Survey*. London, 1939.

———. *Refugees: Preliminary Report of a Survey*. New York, 1938.

———. *Refugees: A Review of the Situation since Sept. 1938* [pamphlet]. London, Aug. 1939. In Myron Taylor Papers, box 7, FDR Library.

Singer, Claude. "Les Etudes médicales et la concurrence juive en France et en Algérie (1931–1941)." In Chantal Banayoun, Alain Medam, and Pierre-Jacques Rojtman, eds., *Les Juifs et l'économique: Miroirs et mirages*, pp. 197–209. Toulouse, 1992.

———. *Vichy, l'université et les juifs*. Paris, 1992.

Sjöberg, Tommie. *The Powers and the Persecuted: The Refugee Problem and the Intergovernmental Committee on Refugees (IGCR) 1938–1947*. Lund, Sweden, 1991.

Société Religieuse des Amis (Quakers). *Les Réfugiés austro-allemands en France* [pamphlet]. Paris, 1939.

Solomon, Robert. *Les Réfugiés*. Paris, 1963.

Soucy, Robert. *French Fascism: The Second Wave, 1933–1939*. New Haven, Conn., 1995.

Sperber, Manès. *Ces Temps là: Au delà de l'oubli.* Paris, 1979. [For the English translation from the German, see Manès Sperber, *Until My Eyes Are Closed with Shards,* translated by Harry Zohn. New York, 1994.]

Stein, Joshua B. "Great Britain and the Evian Conference of 1938." *Wiener Library Bulletin,* n.s. 29, nos. 37/38 (1976): 40–52.

Stein, Louis. *Beyond Death and Exile: The Spanish Republicans in France, 1939–1955.* Cambridge, Mass., 1979.

Steinberg, Lucien. "Documents allemands sur l'affaire Grynszpan," *Le Monde juif,* n.s. 37 (Apr.–June 1964): 17–24.

Sweets, John F. *Choices in Vichy France: The French Under Nazi Occupation.* New York, 1986.

Szajkowski, Zosa. *Analytical Franco-Jewish Gazetteer, 1939–1945.* New York, 1966.

———. "The French Central Jewish Consistory during the Second World War," *Yad Vashem Studies* 3 (1959), pp. 187–202.

———. *Jews and the French Foreign Legion.* New York, 1975.

Tartakower, Arieh, and Kurt R. Grossmann. *The Jewish Refugee.* New York, 1944.

Thalmann, Rita. "L'Accueil des émigrés allemands en France de 1933 à la déclaration de guerre." In *Emigrés français en allemagne; émigrés allemands en France, 1685–1945,* pp. 122–38. Paris, 1983.

———. "L'Emigration allemande et l'opinion française de 1936 à 1939." In *Deutschland u. Frankreich, 1936–1939,* Beihefte der *Francia,* vol. 10, pp. 47–70, 637–38. Munich, 1981.

———. "L'Emigration du IIIe Reich dans la France de 1933 à 1939." *Le Monde juif* 35, no. 96 (Oct.–Dec. 1979): 127–39.

———. "L'Immigration allemande et l'opinion publique en France de 1933 à 1936." In *La France et l'Allemagne, 1932–1936,* pp. 149–72. Paris, 1980.

———. "Jewish Women Exiled in France After 1933." In Sibylle Quack, ed., *Between Sorrow and Strength: Women Refugees of the Nazi Period,* pp. 51–62. Cambridge, Eng., 1995.

Thalmann, Rita, and Emmanuel Feinermann. *Crystal Night, 9–10 Nov. 1938.* Translated by Gilles Cremonesi. New York, 1974.

Tharaud, Jerôme, and Jean Tharaud. *Quand Israël n'est plus roi.* Paris, 1933.

Torrès, Henry. *Pierre Laval.* New York, 1941.

Uhlman, Fred. *Il fait beau à Paris aujourd'hui: Récit.* Translated from the English by Leo Lack. Paris, 1985.

Ulmann, André. "Les Parasites de l'émigré." *Esprit,* no. 82 (July 1, 1939): 513–20.

Union des Sociétés Juives de France, *Les Immigrés juifs dans les journées de septembre* [brochure]. Paris, Dec. 1939.

Union Suisse des communautés israélites (Documentation internationale). *La Persécution des juifs en Allemagne: Attitude des églises chrétiennes des Etats-Unis d'Amérique, du Canada, de France, de Grand Bretagne, des Pays Bas, de Roumanie, de Suisse, et de Syrie.* Geneva, Sept. 1933.

Vago, Bela. *The Shadow of the Swastika: The Rise of Fascism and Antisemitism in the Danube Basin, 1936–1939.* London, 1975.

Vaisse, Maurice. "Against Appeasement: French Advocates of Firmness, 1933–1938."

In Wolfgang J. Mommsen and Lothar Kettenacker, eds., *The Fascist Challenge*, pp. 227–35. London, 1983.

Vallat, Xavier. *Le Nez de Cléopâtre: Souvenirs d'un homme de droite (1919–1944)*. Paris, 1957.

Véricourt, Etienne de. "Le Problème des étrangers dans le cadre de la profession médicale." *Les Etudes: Revue catholique d'intérêt général*, no. 5 (May 5, 1935): 350–60.

Vernier, Claude. *Tendre exil: Souvenirs d'un réfugié antinazi en France*. Paris, 1983.

———. "Les Tribulations d'un comédien." In Gilbert Badia et al., *Exilés en France: Souvenirs d'antifascistes allemands émigrés (1933–1945)*, pp. 23–65. Paris, 1982.

Villard, Claude. "Feuchtwanger et la France: Mai 1940 ou la rencontre avec le 'Diable du je-m'en foutisme.'" *Revue d'Allemagne* 18, no. 2 (Apr.–June 1986): 337–52.

Voigt, Klaus. "Les Naufragés: L'arrivée dans les Alpes-Maritimes des réfugiés allemands et autrichiens d'Italie (septembre 1938–mai 1940)." In Jacques Grandjonc and Theresia Grundtner, eds., *Zone d'ombres, 1933–1944: Exil et internement d'Allemands et d'Autrichiens dans le sud-est de la France*, pp. 93–117. Aix-en-Provence, 1990.

———. "Refuge and Persecution in Italy, 1933–1945." *Simon Wiesenthal Center Annual* 4 (1987): 3–64.

Vormeier, Barbara. *Die Deportierung deutscher und österreichischer Juden aus Frankreich (1942–1944)*. Paris, 1980.

———. "Les Internés allemands et autrichiens en 1939–1940." In Gilbert Badia et al., *Les Barbelés de l'exil: Etudes sur l'émigration allemande et autrichienne (1938–1940)*, pp. 224–42. Grenoble, 1979.

———. "Législation répressive et émigration (1938–1939)." In Gilbert Badia et al., *Les Barbelés de l'exil: Etudes sur l'émigration allemande et autrichienne (1938–1940)*, pp. 159–67. Grenoble, 1979.

———. "La République française et les réfugiés et immigrés d'Europe Centrale: Accueil, séjour, droit d'asile (1919–1939)." In Institut d'Histoire du Temps Présent (CNRS), *Réfugiés et immigrés d'Europe Centrale dans le mouvement anti-fasciste et la résistance en France (1933–1945)*. Vol. 2. Mimeog. Proceedings, Colloquium, Paris, Université Paris VIII, Oct. 17–18, 1986.

———. "La Situation administrative des exilés allemands en France (1933–1945): Accueil-répression-internement-déportation." *Revue d'Allemagne* 18, no. 2, Apr.–June 1986): 185–94.

———. "La Situation des émigrés allemands en France pendant la guerre." In *Emigrés français en Allemagne; émigrés allemands en France, 1685–1945*, pp. 155–71. Paris, 1983.

———. "La Situation des réfugiés en provenance d'Allemagne, septembre 1939– juillet 1942." In Jacques Grandjonc, ed., *Les Camps en Provence: exil, internement, déportation, 1933–1944*, pp. 88–102. Aix-en-Provence, 1984 [Also in Jacques Grandjonc and Theresia Grundtner, eds., *Zone d'ombres, 1933–1944: Exil et internement d'Allemands et d'Autrichiens dans le sud-est de la France*, pp. 190–209. Aix-en-Provence, 1990.]

Waldeck, Countess. "The Great New Migration." *Foreign Affairs* 15, no. 3 (Apr. 1937): 537–46.

Wall, Irwin M. "Socialists and Bureaucrats: The Blum Government and the French Administration, 1936–1937." *International Review of Social History* 19, part 3: 325–46.

Walter, Hans-Albert. *Asylpraxis und Lebensbedingungen in Europa*. Darmstadt, 1972.

———. "Internierung in Frankreich zur Situation der exilierten deutschen Schrift-steller Politiker und Publizisten nach Beginn des Zweiten Weltkriegs." *Jahresrins*, 1970, pp. 281–310.

Wasserstein, Bernard. *Britain and the Jews of Europe, 1939–1945*. Oxford, 1979.

———. "The British Government and the German Immigration, 1933–1945." In Gerhard Hirschfeld, ed., *Exile in Great Britain*, pp. 63–81. London, 1984.

Weber, Eugen. *The Hollow Years: France in the 1930s*. New York, 1994.

Weinberg, David H. *A Community on Trial: The Jews of Paris in the 1930s*. Chicago, 1977.

Weisberg, Richard. *Vichy Law and the Holocaust in France*. New York, 1996.

Weiss, Louise. *Mémoires d'une européenne*. Vol. 3 (1934–39). Paris, 1970.

Werth, Alexander. "French Fascism." *Foreign Affairs* 15, no. 1 (Oct. 1936): 141–54.

———. *The Twilight of France, 1933–1940*. New York, 1942.

Winkler, Michael, ed. *Deutsche Literatur im Exil, 1933–1945: Texte und Dokumente*. Stuttgart, 1977.

Winock, Michel. *Histoire politique de la revue* Esprit, *1930–1950*. Paris, 1975.

———. "Une Parabole fasciste: Gilles de Drieu la Rochelle." *Le Mouvement social*, no. 80 (July–Sept. 1982): 29–42.

Wlocevski, Stéphane. "Y-a-t-il trop de travailleurs étrangers en France?" *Revue d'économie politique* 49 (Mar.–Apr. 1935): 324–59.

Wormser, Georges. *Français israélites: Une doctrine—une tradition—une époque*. Paris, 1963.

Wyman, David S. *The Abandonment of the Jews: America and the Holocaust, 1941–1945*. New York, 1984.

———. *Paper Walls: America and the Refugee Crisis, 1938–1941*. 1968. Reprint, New York, 1985.

Yahil, Leni. "Madagascar—Phantom of a Solution for the Jewish Question." In Bela Vago and George L. Mosse, eds., *Jews and Non-Jews in Eastern Europe, 1918–1945*, pp. 315–34. New York, 1974.

Zadkine, Ossip. *Le Maillet et le ciseau: Souvenirs de ma vie*. Paris, 1968.

[Zay, Jean.] *Carnets secrets de Jean Zay: De Munich à la guerre*. Paris, 1942.

Zdatny, Steven M. "The Class That Didn't Bark: French Artisans in an Age of Fas-cism." In Rudy Koshar, ed., *Splintered Classes: Politics and the Lower Middle Classes in Interwar Europe*, pp. 121–41. New York, 1990.

———. *The Politics of Survival: Artisans in 20th-Century France*. New York, 1990.

Zerapha, Georges. "Les Faux problèmes: 1) Hitler donne le ton." *Esprit*, no. 82 (July 1, 1939): 528–34.

Zuccotti, Susan. *The Holocaust, the French and the Jews*. New York, 1993.

Index

In this index an "f" after a number indicates a separate reference on the next page, and an "ff" indicates separate references on the next two pages. A continuous discussion over two or more pages is indicated by a span of page numbers, e.g., "57–59." *Passim* is used for a cluster of references in close but not consecutive sequence.

Library of Congress Cataloging-in-Publication Data

Caron, Vicki.
  Uneasy asylum : France and the Jewish refugee crisis,
1933–42 / Vicki Caron.
      p.   cm. — (Stanford studies in Jewish history
and culture)
  Includes bibliographical references and index.
  ISBN 0-8047-3312-0 (cloth : alk. paper)
    1. Jews—France—History—20th century.
  2. Refugees, Jewish—France—History—20th century.
  3. Refugees, Jewish—Government policy—France.
  4. France—Ethnic relations.   I. Title.   II. Series.
DS135.F83C366   1999
944′.004924—dc21   98-36350

⊗ This book is printed on acid-free, recycled paper.

Original printing 1999

Last figure below indicates year of this printing:

08 07 06 05 04 03 02 01 00 99